Charles J. Ellicott

Historical Lectures on the Life of our Lord Jesus Christ

being the Hulsean lectures for the year 1859. Sixth Edition

Charles J. Ellicott

Historical Lectures on the Life of our Lord Jesus Christ
being the Hulsean lectures for the year 1859. Sixth Edition

ISBN/EAN: 9783337260002

Printed in Europe, USA, Canada, Australia, Japan

Cover: Foto ©Lupo / pixelio.de

More available books at **www.hansebooks.com**

HISTORICAL LECTURES

ON

THE LIFE OF OUR LORD JESUS CHRIST.

Cambridge:
PRINTED BY C. J. CLAY, M.A.
AT THE UNIVERSITY PRESS.

HISTORICAL LECTURES

ON

THE LIFE OF OUR LORD JESUS CHRIST,

BEING THE HULSEAN LECTURES FOR THE YEAR 1859.

BY

C. J. ELLICOTT, D.D.
BISHOP OF GLOUCESTER AND BRISTOL.

SIXTH EDITION.

LONDON:
LONGMANS, GREEN, READER & DYER.
1876.

PREFACE.

The following work consists of eight Lectures, of which the first six were preached before the University of Cambridge in the year 1859. The two remaining Lectures, owing to recent changes, were not preached, but are added as giving a necessary completeness to the subject, and as in substantial accordance with the will of the munificent Founder.

It is scarcely necessary to make any preliminary remarks upon the text of the Lectures, as nearly all that seems required in the way of introduction to the subject will be found in the opening Lecture. It may, however, be desirable to remind the reader that he has before him no attempt at a complete Life of our Lord, but only Lectures upon it. These it has been my object to make as complete as I have been able in everything that relates to the *connexion* of the events, or that in any way illustrates their probable order and succession. The separate incidents, however, have not in every case been dwelt upon at equal length; some being related by a single Evangelist and requiring no explanatory comments, while others, from being related by two or more, and sometimes *appearing* to involve discordant statements, have called for somewhat lengthened considerations. Those portions in which, for every reason, it has seemed desirable that some regular continuity of narrative should be carefully preserved, viz. the Last Passover, and the Forty Days, were not required to be delivered from the pulpit, and have thus approached more nearly to regular history. I have, however, in both been most careful to preserve the same tone and character which marked the rest, and I have been thankful that the circumstances under which the others were written and delivered have prescribed for me in these last two Lectures, almost as a matter of course, that gravity and solemnity of tone which is so especially called for in the recital of events so blessed and so holy, yet withal so awful and so stupendous. To adopt the usual tone of mere historical writing when such subjects are before us seems to me little short of profanity, and I have been taught by the repulsiveness of some narratives of the closing scenes of our Lord's ministry, written in the conventional style of ordinary history, to be more than usually thankful that the nature of my present undertaking has at any rate prevented me from sharing in an error so great and so grievous.

A few remarks must be made on the notes. In these it has been my effort to combine two things which are not always found in union,—a popular mode of treating the question under consideration, and accuracy both in outline and detail. How far I may have succeeded it is for others to judge; all I will venture to ask the reader kindly to bear in mind is this,—that much time and very great care and thought have been expended on these notes (more perhaps than might have been needful if they had been longer or their language more technical), and that thus they are not always to be judged of by their brevity or the familiar list of authorities to which they refer. In my references I have aimed solely at being useful, not to the special, but to the general student, and thus have but rarely permitted myself to direct attention to any works or treatises that are not perfectly well known and accessible. I have not, by any means, attempted to exclude Greek from my notes, as this seems to me, in such works as the present, to savour somewhat of an affectation of simplicity, but I have still, in very many cases, either translated or quoted from the translations of others the longer passages from the great Greek commentators which form so considerable and so valuable a portion of these notes. A similar course has been pursued in reference to German expositors, though longer quotations from them are only occasional. These latter writers are, as it will be observed, often referred to; but care has been taken only to give prominence to the better class of them, and further to refer, where translations exist, to the work in its English rather than its German form. In a word, my humble aim throughout these notes has been to engage the interest of the general reader, and I pray God that herein I may have succeeded, for much that is here discussed, has of late years often been put forward in popular forms that neither are nor perhaps were intended to be conformable to the teaching of the Church. Of my own views it is perhaps not necessary for me to speak. This only will I say, that though I neither feel nor affect to feel the slightest sympathy with the so-called popular theology of the present day, I still trust that, in the many places in which it has been almost necessarily called forth in the present pages, no expression has been used towards sceptical writings stronger than may have been positively required by allegiance to Catholic truth. Towards the honest and serious thinker who may feel doubts or difficulties in some of the questions connected with our Lord's life all tenderness may justly be shown, but to those who enter upon this holy ground with the sinister intentions of the destructive critic or of the so-called unprejudiced historian, it is not necessary or desirable to suppress all indication of our repulsion.

Marginal references have been added as indicating the authority for the expressions and statements of the text. When these are not present, and guarded conjecture has been resorted to, particular care has been taken to make this most distinctly apparent.

It is not necessary to detain the reader with further comments, and it only remains for me with all lowliness and reverence to lay before Almighty God this attempt, this poor and feeble attempt, to set forth the outward connexion of those incidents that inspired pens have been moved to record of the life of His Eternal Son. May He pardon its many failings and defects, may He look with pity on efforts, many of which have been made while the shadow of His hand has rested darkly over him who strove to make them, and may He bless this partial first-fruits of a mercifully spared life, by permitting it to minister in its humble measure and degree to His honour and glory, and to the truth as it is in His blessed Son.

ΤΡΙΑΣ, ΜΟΝΑΣ, ἘΛΕΗΣΟΝ.

CAMBRIDGE,
Oc.o^ber, 1860.

ADVERTISEMENT TO THE FIFTH EDITION.

THE present Edition has been generally revised. The text has been left unaltered, but additions have been made in many places to the notes, and in a few instances corrections have been introduced. The whole volume has been read over in connexion with the recent work of Caspari, entitled, *Chronologisch-geographische Einleitung in das Leben Jesu Christi* (Hamburg 1869), and is now supplied with continuous references to this excellent treatise. The attentive reader will not fail to observe the clear coincidences in opinion in many important points between these Lectures and the treatise just alluded to. Attention may be particularly called to the similarity of opinion in reference to the difficult and much debated question of the date of the celebration of the Lord's Supper, and especially to the similar recognition of Wieseler's error in computation, owing to his having not distinguished with sufficient precision between the Jewish and ordinary or Julian day. Caspari here supplies a welcome and apparently independent confirmation of the opinion maintained in this volume. In other points of difficulty where there is not the same coincidence the opinion of Caspari deserves the most careful consideration. For example, in his arrangement of the events of the first year of our blessed Lord's ministerial life, greater chronological elasticity (so to speak) is obtained for the events in the second year by making the date of our Lord's first journey through Samaria coincide, not with the time of sowing, but with the time of the anterior harvest: and again, in Caspari's explanation of the "second-first" sabbath there is much that will be found greatly to commend itself to the consideration of the student. His objections also to the festival, noticed in John v. 1, being identified with the feast of Purim are fairly and forcibly urged. The student will do well to consider these points in connexion with the views still retained in this volume. A small amount of further evidence would appear sufficient to justify some slight changes of opinion on these points in the text of these Lectures. As yet, however, the chronological and exegetical arguments, fairly weighed, seem slightly to preponderate in favour of the opinions originally advanced. These opinions then are still maintained, but candid criticism requires that the student's full attention should be called to the few but not unimportant points in which the chronological arrangement of Caspari differs from that of the present work.

Thus generally revised and reconsidered it is anew submitted to the reader, with the humble and earnest prayer that in these days of unstable and precarious opinion, it may be permitted on the one hand to furnish some answer to current objections, and on the other to lead the earnest student to fuller measures of faith in our adorable and ever blessed Lord and Saviour, Jesus Christ.

GLOUCESTER,
September, 1869.

CLAUSES FROM THE WILL OF THE REV. JOHN HULSE[1], LATE OF ELWORTH IN THE COUNTY OF CHESTER.

By the will of this liberal supporter of Christian learning and truth, bearing date July 21, 1777, it is directed that four clauses of it are to be prefixed to every series of Lectures. Of these Clauses 1 specifies the proportions in which the proceeds of certain estates are to be divided between a Dissertator and a Lecturer; Clause 2 directs that a salary of £60 be paid to the latter; Clause 3 names a further augmentation. The most important is Clause 4, which relates to the office and duties of the Lecturer. The discourses are to be twenty in number (reduced by an order of the Court of Chancery, Dec. 21, 1830, to eight); ten to be preached in the Spring and ten in the Autumn of each year. The subject of the discourses is to be in conformity with the following sensible provisions:

> The subject of five sermons in the Spring and likewise of five sermons in the Autumn shall be to shew the evidence for Revealed Religion, and to demonstrate in the most convincing and persuasive manner the truth and excellence of Christianity, so as to include not only the prophecies and miracles general and particular, but also any other proper and useful arguments, whether the same be direct or collateral proofs of the Christian Religion, which he may think fittest to discourse upon, either in general or particular, especially the collateral arguments, or else any particular article or branch thereof, and chiefly against notorious infidels, whether Atheists or Deists, not descending to any particular sects or controversies (so much to be lamented) amongst Christians themselves, except some new or dangerous error, either of superstition or enthusiasm, as of Popery or Methodism or the like, either in opinion or practice shall prevail, in which case only it may be necessary for that time to write and preach against the same......And as to the ten sermons that remain the lecturer or preacher shall take for his subject some of the more difficult texts or obscure parts of the Holy Scriptures, such as may

---

[1] See *Trusts, Statutes, and Directions affecting the Endowments of the University of Cambridge*, p. 262 sq., Cambridge, 1857.

appear to be more generally useful or necessary to be explained, and which may best admit of such a comment or explanation, without presuming to pry too far into the profound secrets and awful mysteries of the Almighty. And in all the said twenty sermons such practical observations shall be made and such useful conclusions added, as may best instruct and edify mankind; and the said twenty sermons to be every year printed.

After the recital of the last clause Mr Hulse directs that the following invocation which occurs at the conclusion of the will is "to be printed by way of preface in each particular work."

And may the Divine blessing for ever go along with all my benefactions, and may the Greatest and the Best of Beings by His all-wise providence and gracious influence make the same effectual to His own glory and the good of my fellow-creatures!

After this pious invocation follow words which, in memory of this good and bountiful man, it does not seem unmeet to quote:

Thus earnestly praying that due honour and reverence may be ever paid to the Supreme Fountain of bliss and goodness, and sincerely wishing all increase of true religion and virtue and satisfaction to mankind, I desire, when the Divine Providence shall think fit, to exchange this frail and transitory state for one that is infinitely and eternally happy in Jesus Christ.

CONTENTS.

LECTURE I.

Introductory considerations on the characteristics of the four Gospels 1

PAGE

Statement of the subject, 1. Reasons for choosing it. Method adopted in the Lectures, 1 sq. Caution in applying the principles laid down, 9. Sources of the History, 10. Details mainly in reference to internal characteristics, 12 sq. Necessity of recognizing the individualities of the four Gospels, 15. Errors of earlier Harmonists, 17 sq. Individuality of St Matthew's Gospel, 20. St Matthew's portraiture of our Lord, 22. Individuality of St Mark's Gospel, 23. St Mark's portraiture of our Lord, 25. Individuality of St Luke's Gospel, 27. St Luke's portraiture of our Lord, 28. Individuality of St John's Gospel, 30 sq. St John's portraiture of our Lord, 33. Conclusion.

LECTURE II.

The Birth and Infancy of our Lord 37

General aspects of the present undertaking, 37. Arrangement of the subject, 39. The miraculous Conception of our Lord; its mystery and sublimity, 40 sq. The narrative of the Conception considered generally, 43. The narrative of the Conception considered in its details, 45 sq. Self-evident truth of the narrative, 48. Journey of the Virgin to Elisabeth, 50 sq. Internal truthfulness of the two inspired Canticles, 53. Return of the Virgin and the Revelation to Joseph, 55. Journey to Bethlehem, and taxing under Quirinus, 57 sq. The Nativity and its attendant circumstances, 61 sq. The Presentation in the Temple, 65 sq. The visit and adoration of the Magi, 70. The guiding star, 72 sq. The extreme naturalness of the sacred narrative, 75. Flight into Egypt and murder of the Innocents, 77. The silence of Josephus, 78. The return to Judæa, 79 sq. Conclusion.

LECTURE III.

The Early Judæan Ministry 84

The early years of our Lord's Life, 84. Reserve of the Evangelists, 84. The brief notice of our Lord's childhood, 85. Equally brief notice of our Lord's youth, 86. Visit to the Temple when twelve years old, 88. Search for, and discovery of the Holy Child, 90 sq. Frivolous nature of the objections urged against the narrative, 94. Silence of the Evangelists on the next eighteen years of our Lord's life, 96 sq. The mental and spiritual development of our Lord, 99. The ministry of the Baptist and its probable effects, 102 sq. Journey of our Lord to the Baptism of John, 104 sq. The nature of St John's recognition of our Lord, 107. The Temptation of our Lord: its true nature and circumstances, 109. The Temptation no vision or trance, 110. The Temptation an assault from without, 111. The Temptation addressed to the three parts of our nature, 112. The ministoring angels, and the return to Galilee, 114. The testimony of the Baptist, 115. The journey to, and miracle at, Cana in Galilee, 116. Remarks on the miracle, 117 sq. Brief stay at Capernaum, and journey to Jerusalem, 121. The expulsion of the traders from the Temple, 122. Impression made by this and other acts, 124. The discourse of our Lord with Nicodemus, 125. Our Lord leaves Jerusalem and retires to the N.E. parts of Judæa, 127. The final testimony of the Baptist, 128 sq. Our Lord's journey through Samaria, 130 sq. The further journey of our Lord to Galilee, 133. Our Lord's return to Jerusalem at the feast of Purim, 135 sq. Main objection to this opinion, 138 sq. The miracle at the pool of Bethesda, 139. Distinctive character of this epoch, 142. The termination of the early Judæan ministry, 143. Concluding remarks and Exhortation.

Lecture IV.

The Ministry in Eastern Galilee 148

Resumption of the subject, 148. Brief recapitulation of the events of the Judæan ministry, 148 sq. Two preliminary observations, 151. The exact period of time embraced in the present Lecture, 152. The variations of order in the three synoptical Gospels, 153. The order of St Mark and St Luke followed in this lecture, 154 sq. Appearance of our Lord in the synagogue at Nazareth, 159. Departure to, and abode at Capernaum, 161. Special call of the four disciples, 162. Healing of a demoniac in the synagogue at Capernaum, 163. Continued performance of miracles on the same day, 165. The nature of our Lord's ministerial labours as indicated by this one day, 167. Probable duration of this circuit, 169. The return to Capernaum, and healing of the faithful paralytic, 170. The call of St Matthew and the feast at his house, 172. Further charges; the plucking of the ears of corn, 174. The healing of a man with a withered hand on a Sabbath, 176. Choice of the Twelve Apostles, and Sermon on the Mount, 178. Probable form of the Sermon on the Mount, 179. The healing of the centurion's servant, and raising of the widow's son, 181 sq. Short circuit: fresh charges of the Pharisees, 185. The teaching by parables, 187. The passage across, and storm on the lake, 188. The Gergesene demoniacs, 189. The raising of Jairus' daughter, 191. The second visit to the synagogue at Nazareth, 192. The sending forth of the Twelve Apostles, 193 sq. The feeding of the Five thousand, 196. Concluding remarks.

Lecture V.

The Ministry in Northern Galilee 200

General features of this part of our Lord's history, 200. Special contrasts and characteristics, 201. Chronological limits of the present portion, 202. Progressive nature of our Lord's ministry, 203. Contrasts between this and preceding portions of the narrative, 204. Teaching and preaching rather than miracles characteristic of this period, 205. Such a difference probable from the nature of the case, 207. The return across the lake; our Lord walks on the water, 208 sq. Return to Capernaum; our Lord's discourse in the synagogue, 211 sq. Healings in Gennesareth, and return of the xiv *Contents.*

PAGE

Jewish emissaries, 214 sq. Journey to Tyre and Sidon, and the miracle performed there, 217. Return towards Decapolis and the eastern shore of the lake, 219. Journey to Decapolis; healing of a deaf and dumb man, 220. The feeding of the Four thousand, 221. Not identical with the feeding of the Five thousand, 222. Return to the western side of the lake, 223. Journey northward to Cæsarea Philippi, 225. The locality and significance of the Transfiguration, 227. The healing of a demoniac boy, 228. Return to, and probable temporary seclusion at Capernaum, 230 sq. Conclusion and recapitulation, 233 sq.

LECTURE VI.

The Journeyings toward Jerusalem 236

General character of the present portion of the inspired narrative, 236. Limits of the present section, 237. Harmonistic and chronological difficulties, 237 sq. Precise nature of these difficulties, 240. Comparison of this portion of St Luke's Gospel with that of St John, 242 sq. Results of the above considerations, 245. Brief stay at Capernaum; worldly request of our Lord's brethren, 245 sq. Journey to Jerusalem through Samaria, 248. Our Lord's arrival and preaching at Jerusalem 250. The woman taken in adultery: probable place of the incident in the Gospel history, 252. Further teaching and preaching at Jerusalem, 253 sq. Departure from Jerusalem, and mission of the Seventy, 256. Further incidents in Judæa recorded by St Luke, 257. Our Lord's visit to Jerusalem at the Feast of Dedication, 259 sq. The Lord's message to Herod, and preparation to leave Peræa, 262. Probable events during the last two days in Peræa, 264 sq. Apparently confirmatory notice in St John, 267. Effect produced by the raising of Lazarus, 268. Incidents in the last journey to Judæa, 270 sq. Onward progress toward Jerusalem, 273. Arrival at Jericho, 274. Conclusion.

LECTURE VII.

The Last Passover 278

Introductory comments, 278. Characteristics of the preceding portion of the narrative, 279. Characteristics of the present portion, 280. The journey to, and supper at, Bethany, 282.

Contents. XV

The Triumphal entry into Jerusalem, 284 sq. Reflections on the credibility of the narrative, 289. Our Lord's entry into Jerusalem, 291. The cursing of the barren fig-tree (Monday), 292 sq. The cleansing of the Temple, and works of mercy performed there, 295. Answers to the deputation from the Sanhedrin (Tuesday), 297 sq. Continued efforts on the part of the deputation, 301. The question about the duty of paying tribute to Cæsar, 301 sq. Exposure and frustration of the stratagem, 304. The question of the Sadducees touching the Resurrection, 306. The question of the lawyer about the greatest commandment, 308. The question relative to the woman taken in adultery, 310. Our Lord's question respecting the son of David, 312. The offering of the poor widow, 314. The request of the Greek proselytes, 315 sq. The departure from the temple, and the last prophecies, 318. Consultation of the Sanhedrin and treachery of Judas (Wednesday), 320. The celebration of the Last Supper (Thursday), 321 sq. The agony in Gethsemane (Thursday night), 327 sq. The betrayal of our Lord, 331. The preliminary examination before Annas, 332. The examination before the Sanhedrin, 335 sq. The brutal mockery of the attendants, 338. The fate of Judas Iscariot, 340. Our Lord's first appearance before Pilate, 341 sq. The dismissal of our Lord to Herod, 344. Second appearance before Pilate; his efforts to set our Lord free, 345 sq. Scourging of our Lord; renewed efforts of Pilate, 348 sq. The CRUCIFIXION, 352. Occurrences from the third to the sixth hour, 354. The darkness from the sixth to the ninth hour, 356 sq. The portents that followed our Lord's death, 359. The removal from the cross and burial of the Lord's body, 361 sq. Conclusion, 365.

LECTURE VIII.

The Forty Days 368

Introductory comments, 368. Doctrinal questions involved in this portion of the history, 369 sq. Characteristics of the present portion of the narrative: number of the accounts, 372. Their peculiarities and differences, 373 sq. Resumption of the narrative: visit of the women to the sepulchre, 377 sq. The appearance of the angels to the women at the sepulchre, 382. The two Apostles at the tomb, 384. The Lord's appearance to Mary Magdalene, 385 sq. Probable effect produced on the Apostles by Mary's tidings, 389. The Lord's appearance to the other ministering women, 390 sq. The appearance of our Lord to the two disciples journeying to Emmaus, 393 sq. Inability of the disciples to recognize our Lord, 396. Appearance to the *ten* Apostles, 398 sq. Disbelief of Thomas: our Lord's appearance to the *eleven* Apostles, 403. Appearance by the lake of Tiberias, 404 sq. Reverential awe of the Apostles, 408. Appearance to the brethren in Galilee, 410. The Lord's Ascension, 412 sq. Conclusion, 415 sq.

LECTURE I.

INTRODUCTORY CONSIDERATIONS ON THE CHARACTER-
ISTICS OF THE FOUR GOSPELS.

St John xx. 31.

These are written, that ye might believe that Jesus is the Christ, the Son of God; and that believing ye might have life through his name.

THESE words, brethren, which, in the context from which they are taken, allude more particularly to the miracles of Christ, but which I venture here to extend in application to the whole evangelical history, will in some degree prepare you for the subject that I purpose laying before you in this series of Lectures. After serious meditation on the various subjects which the will of the munificent founder of these Lectures leaves open to the preacher, it has appeared to me that none would be likely to prove more useful and more edifying than the history and connexion of the events in the earthly life of our Lord and Master, Jesus Christ.

Statement of Subject.

Two grave reasons have weighed with me in choosing this momentous subject, one more exclusively relating to the younger portion of my audience, the other relating to us all.

Reasons for choosing it.

The *first* reason has been suggested by the feeling, which I believe is not wholly mistaken, that these Lectures are too often liable, from the nature of the subjects to which they are restricted,

First reason.

to prove unattractive to the younger portion of those among us. It is but seldom that the young feel much interested in the debated questions of Christian evidence. Nay it is natural that they should not. With the freshness and warmth of springing life, with the generous impulses of yet unchilled hearts, they are ready for the most part to believe rather than to doubt, to accept rather than to question. The calm and impartial investigation, the poised judgment, the suspended assent, which must all characterize the sober disputant on Christian evidences, and which we of a maturer age may admire and appreciate, are, I truly believe, often so repulsive to our younger brethren, that after having sat out a sermon or two, they company with us no more. This applies with still greater force, as has been thoughtfully suggested to me, to the new comers in the October term, whose first entrance into the Church of this our mother University is commonly during the second part of the course of the Hulsean Lecturer. They have thus all the disadvantage of coming among us in the middle of a course; and when to that is added a consciousness of defective sympathy with the theme of the preacher, they are tempted, I fear, thus early to withdraw from what they deem unedifying, and so to lay the foundation of the evil habit of neglecting attendance at this Church, and of treating lightly the great Christian duty of assembling ourselves together in the house of God.

It has thus seemed desirable to choose a subject which, if properly treated, ought to interest and to edify the very youngest hearer among us, and which may admit of such natural divisions as may cause the later hearers to feel less sensibly the disadvantage of not having attended the earlier portion of the course.

My *second* reason, however, for the selection of this peculiar subject is one that applies to us all, and is still more grave and momentous. It is based on the deep conviction, that to the great questions connected with the life of our Redeemer, Jesus Christ, the Son of Adam, the Son of God[a], all the controversies of these latter days are tending noticeably to converge. Here it is that even the more abstract questions, that try the faith of our own times,—questions as abstract as the degree of inspiration of the Written Word[1], or

Second reason.

[a] Lk. iii. 38

---

[1] In every complete discussion on the Inspiration of the Scriptures, the nature of the more special references of our Lord to the Old Testament must be fully and fairly considered. To take an extreme case; when our Lord refers, distinctly and explicitly (Matth. xii. 39, 40), to 'the sign of the prophet Jonas,' have we any escape from one of two alternatives, either, (*a*) that in spite of all that has been urged to the contrary, and all the scarcely disguised contempt with which the history of Jonah has been treated by modern criticism (com. Hitzig, *Kleinen Propheten*, p. 361 sq.), the narrative is notwithstanding *true* and *typical*, and referred to by our Lord as such; or, (*b*) that it is *fabulous*, and that our Lord wittingly made use of a fabulous narrative to illustrate His Resurrection? Modern speculation does not hesitate to accept (*b*), and to urge that it was not a part of our Lord's mission to correct all the wrong opinions, more or less connected with religion, which might be prevalent in the minds of those with whom He was conversing (comp. Norton, *Genuineness of Gospel*, Vol. II. p. 477). If we rest contented with such unhappy statements, we must be prepared to remodel not only our views of our Lord's teaching, but of some of the highest attributes of His most holy life; consider and contrast Ullmann, *Un-sündlichkeit Jesu*, § 19 (Transl. p. 8, 75, Clark). The assertion that ' the sign of Jonah ' was *not* referred by our Lord to His resurrection, but to His whole earthly life, seems distinctly untenable (see esp. Meyer on *Matth*. xii. 40); but were it otherwise, it could scarcely affect the above considerations.

To contemplate a rejection of these words from the inspired narrative in the face of the most unquestioned

1—2

LECT. I.

the nature of the efficacies of the Atonement[1] which that Word declares to us,—must seek for their ultimate adjustment. Here is the battleground of the present, here perchance the mystic Armageddon of coming strife. Already forms of heresy more subtle than ever Ebionite propounded or Marcionite devised,—forms of heresy that have clad themselves in the trappings of modern historical philosophy[2], and have learned to accommodate themselves to the more distinctly earthly aspects of modern speculation, have appeared in other Christian lands, and are now silently producing their influence on thousands and tens of thousands who bear on their foreheads the baptismal cross of Christ. Already even in our own more favoured country, humanitarian views with regard to the Person of our Redeemer are thrusting themselves forward with a startling and repulsive activity,—intruding themselves into our popular literature as well as into our popu-

external evidence (Maurice, *Kings and Prophets*, p. 357) cannot be characterized as otherwise than as in the highest degree arbitrary and uncritical.

[1] Everything which tends to derogate from the Divinity of our Lord, tends, as Priestley long ago clearly perceived (*History of Corruptions*, Vol. I. p. 153), to do away with the idea of an atonement, in the proper sense of the word, for the sins of other men; comp. Magee, *Atonement*, Dissert. 3. So conversely, all limitations of the atonement, all tendencies to represent our Lord's sacrifice as merely an act of moral greatness (comp. Jowett, *Romans*,

Vol. II. p. 481), will be found inevitably to lead to indirect denials of the Catholic doctrine of the union of the two natures in our Lord, and to implied limitations of His divinity: compare, but with some reserve, Macdonell, *Lectures on the Atonement* (Donellan Lectures), p. 61 sq.

[2] For a clear statement of the two problems connected with the Gospel history (the criticism of the evangelical writings, and the criticism of the evangelical history), and the regular development of modern speculation, see the introduction to the useful work of Ebrard, *Wissenschaftliche Kritik der evangelischen Geschichte*, § 2—7, p. 3 sq. (ed. 2).

lar theology[1], yea, and winning assent by their seductive appeal to those purely human motions and feelings within us, which, while we are in the flesh, we can hardly deem separable from the nature of even sinless man. Already too a so-called love of truth, a bleak, barren, loveless love of truth which the wise Pascal[2] long since denounced,—a love of truth that like Agag claims to walk delicately, and to be respected and to be spared,—is gathering around itself its Epicurean audiences: already is it making its boast of fabled civilizations that rest on other bases than on Christ and His Church[3], daily and hourly labouring with that restless energy that belongs to 'the walkers in dry places,' to make us regard as imaginary or illusory those holy prepossessions in reference to the Evangelical history,

---

[1] See Preface to *Commentary on the Philippians, Coloss. and Philemon*, p. x.

[2] The following remark of this thoughtful writer deserves consideration: 'On se fait une idole de la vérité même: car la vérité hors de la charité n'est pas Dieu; elle est son image, et une idole qu'il ne faut point aimer, ni adorer; et encore moins faut-il aimer et adorer son contraire, qui est le mensonge.' *Pensées*, II. 17. 74, p. 297 (Didot, 1846).

[3] It does not seem unjust to say that the views advocated in the most recent history of civilization that has appeared in this country (Buckle, *History of Civilization*, Lond. 1858) cannot be regarded as otherwise than plainly hostile to Christianity. There is a special presupposition in viewing the history of Christ in its relation to the world, which such writers as Mr Buckle unhappily either scorn or reject,—a presupposition which an historian of a far higher strain has well defined as the root of all our modern civilization, and as that from which civilization can never separate itself, without assuming an entirely changed form; 'it is the presupposition that Jesus is the Son of God, in a sense which cannot be predicated of any human being,—the perfect image of the supreme personal God in the form of that humanity that was estranged from Him; the presupposition that in Him appeared the source of the divine life itself in humanity, and that by Him the idea of humanity was realized.' Neander, *Leben Jesu Chr.* p. 5 (Transl. § 2, p. 5, Bohn). Contrast with this the unhappy and self-contradictory comments of Hase, *Leben Jesu*, § 14, p. 16.

6   Introductory Considerations on the

LECT. I.

that ought, and were designed by God Himself to exercise their unquestioned influence and sovereignty over our whole inner life[1]. It is this feeling that has more especially led me to fix upon the Life of our Lord and Master as the subject of these Lectures. It is the deep feeling, that every effort, however humble and homely, to set forth the groupings, the harmonies, and the significancies of that Holy History, is a contribution to the spiritual necessities of our own times,—that has now moved me to enter upon this lofty theme. Here it is, and here only is it, that our highest ideal conceptions of perfection find only still higher practical realizations. Here it is that while we humbly strive to trace the lineaments of the outward, we cannot fail, if we be true to God and to our own souls, to feel the workings of the inward[2], and while the

---

[1] It has been well said by Ebrard, 'We do not enter on the Evangelical History, with spy-glass in hand, to seek our own credit by essaying to disclose ever fresh instances of what is contradictory, foolish, or ridiculous, but with the faithful, clear, and open eye of him, who joyfully recognizes the Good, the Beautiful, and the Noble wheresoever he finds it, and on that account finds it with joy, and never lays aside his favourable prepossession, till he is persuaded of the contrary. We give ourselves up to the plastic influence of the Gospels, live in them, and at the same time secure to ourselves, while we thus act in the spirit of making all our own, a deeper insight into the unity, beauty, and depth of the Evangelical History.' *Kritik der Evang. Geschichte,* § 8, p. 38.

[2] It is satisfactory to find in most of the higher class of German writers on the Life of our Lord a distinct recognition of this vital principle of the Gospel narrative: 'As man's limited intellect could never, without the aid of God's revelation of Himself to the spirit of man, have originated the idea of God, so the image of Christ could never have sprung from the consciousness of sinful humanity, but must be regarded as the reflection of the actual life of such a Christ. It is Christ's self-revelation, made through all generations in the fragments of His history that remain, and in the workings of His Spirit which inspires these fragments, and enables us to recognize in them one complete whole.' Neander, *Leben Jesu Chr.* p. 6 (Transl. § 3, p. 4, Bohn): see

eyes dwell lovingly on the inspired outlines of the history of Jesus and of Him crucified, to feel His image waxing clearer in the soul, His eternal sympathies mingling with our infirmities, and enlarging into more than mortal measures the whole spiritual stature of the inner man[1].

After this lengthened, but I believe not unnecessary introduction, let me, with fervent prayer for grace and assistance from the illuminating Spirit of God, at once address myself to my arduous and responsible task.

(I.) And *first*, as to the method which with the help of God I intend to pursue.

Method adopted in these Lectures.

My first object in these Lectures is to arrange, to comment upon, and, as far as possible, to illustrate the principal events in our Redeemer's earthly history; to show their coherence, their connexion[2], and their varied and suggestive meanings; to place, as far as may be safely attempted, the different divine discourses in their *apparently* true positions, estimated chronologically[3], and to indicate how

---

further the eloquent remarks of Dr Lange in the introduction to his valuable work, *Das Leben Jesu nach den Evangelien*, I. 1. 6, Vol. I. p. 71 sq. (Heidelb. 1844), and compare the introductory comments of Ewald, *Geschichte Christus'*, p. xi. xii.

[1] The admirable introductory exhortation of Bp Taylor, prefixed to his *Life of Christ*, deserves particular attention. The prayer with which it concludes is one of the most exalted of those rapt devotional outpourings which illustrate and adorn that great monument of learning and piety.

[2] On the two methods of relating the events of our Lord's life, whether by adhering strictly to chronological sequence, or by grouping together what seems historically similar, see Hase, *Leben Jesu*, § 16, p. 17. The latter method is always precarious, and in some cases, as for example in the *Leben Jesu Christi* of Neander, tends to leave the reader with a very vague idea of the real connexions of the history.

[3] It may perhaps be safely affirmed, and many parts of the succeeding lectures will serve to illustrate the truth of the remark, that the *exact* chronological position of all our Lord's discourses can never be satisfactorily ascertained. One of the most sharpsighted and trustworthy of modern

they both give to and receive illustration from the outward events, with which they stand in more immediate connexion.

But all this must be, and the very nature of the subject prescribes that it should be, subordinated to the desire to set forth in as much fulness and completeness as my limits may permit, not only the order and significance of the component features, but the transcendent picture of our Redeemer's life, viewed as one divine whole[1]. Without this ulterior object all such labour is worse than in vain. Without this higher aim, the divine harmonies of our Master's life become lost in mere annalistic detail; the spiritual epochs of His ministry forgotten in the dull, earthly study of the varied problematical arrangements of contested history. These last points the nature of my present office may compel me not to leave wholly untouched; nay, I trust that those who are acquainted with the nature of such investigations will here-

chronologers of our Lord's life prudently observes: 'I will not deny that the chronology of the discourses of our Lord, and especially of all the separate discourses, is very hard to be ascertained,—nay the problem viewed under its most rigorous aspects, owing to the nature of the evangelical accounts that have come down to us,—I refer particularly to the Gospel of St Matthew, in which especially so many of these portions of discourses occur,—is perhaps never to be solved.' Wieseler, *Chronologische Synopse*, p. 287; compare too Stier, *Reden Jesu*, Vol. I. p. xi. (Transl. Vol. I. p. 7, Clark).

[1] 'It is the problem of faith,' says Dr Lange, 'to introduce into the church's contemplation of the life of Jesus, viewed as a whole, more and more of the various features of the gospel narrative, regarded in their consistent relations with one another. On the contrary, it is the problem of theological science to endeavour to exhibit more and more, by successive approximations, the completed unity of the life of Jesus from the materials ready to its hand. *Leben Jesu*, I. 7. 2, Vol. I. p. 233. Some thoughtful remarks on the contrast between the ideal and the outward manifestation of the same (*Gegensatz zwischen der Idee und der Erscheinung*) in the lives of men, but the perfect harmony of this ideal and phenomenal in Christ, will be found in Neander, *Leben Jesu Chr.* p. 9.

after perceive that I have not shrunk from entering into this very difficult and debateable province of our subject, and that opinions are not put forth without some knowledge of what has been urged against them. Still the details will not appear in the text of the Lectures, or appear only in affirmative statements that are subordinated to the general current and spirit of the narrative.

Caution in applying the above.

Let us never forget, in all our investigations, that the history of the life of Christ is a history of *redemption*,—that all the records which the Eternal Spirit of truth has vouchsafed to us bear this indelible impress, and are only properly to be seen and understood from this point of contemplation[1]. It is the history of the *Redeemer* of our race that the Gospels present to us, the history, not of Jesus of Nazareth but of the Saviour of the world, the record, not of merely idealized perfections[2] but of redemptive workings,—'My Father worketh hitherto, and I work[a];' and he who would presume to trace out that blessed history, without being influenced by this remembrance in all his thoughts

[a] Joh. v. 17

---

[1] Some very valuable remarks on the true points of view from which the Evangelical History ought to be regarded by the Christian student, will be found in the eloquent introduction of Lange to his *Leben Jesu:* see esp. Book I. 4. 6, Vol. I. p. 141 sq.

[2] Compare Lange, *Leben Jesu*, I. 1. 5, 6, Vol. I. p. 41 sq. It has been well remarked by Neander, in answer to Strauss, that the picture of the Life of Christ does not exhibit the spirit of the age in which it appeared, nay that 'the image of human perfection thus concretely presented, stands in manifold contradiction to the tendencies of humanity in that period; no one of them, no combination of them, dead as they were, could account for it.' *Leben Jesu*, p. 6, note (Transl. p. 4, Bohn). The true conception of the mingled divine and human aspects of our Lord's life has been nowhere better hinted at than by Augustine, —'Ita inter Deum et homines mediator apparuit, ut in unitate personae copulans utramque naturam, et solita sublimaret insolitis et insolita solitis temperaret.' *Epist.* CXXXVII. 3. 9, Vol. II. p. 519 (ed. Migne).

and words, must be prepared to find himself adding one more unhonoured name to the melancholy list of those who have presumed to treat of these mysteries, with the eclectic and critical spirit of the so-called biographer—the biographer[1] (a strangely inappropriate and unbecoming word) of Him in whom dwelt bodily the whole fulness of the Godhead[a].

^a Col. ii. 9

Sources of our history.

(II.) In the next place a few words must on this occasion necessarily be said both on the sources of our history, and our estimate of their divinely-ordered differences and characteristics.

Our sources are the four Gospels, four inspired narratives, so mysteriously overruled in their interdependence, that regarded from the point of view in which the history of our Lord alone ought to be regarded,—viz. as a history of *redemption*,—they are all, and more than all, that our most elevated conceptions of our own spiritual needs could have sought for or devised. Such words perchance may sound strange in an age that has busied itself in noting down the seeming deficiencies of the Gospels rather than recognizing their divine fulness, that looks out for diversities rather than accordances[2];

---

[1] The essential character of biography is stated clearly and fairly enough by Hase (*Leben Jesu*, § 12, p. 15), but the proposed application of it to the life of Our Lord can scarcely be defined as otherwise than as in a high degree startling and repulsive. This cold, clear, but unsound writer seems to imagine that some height can be reached from which the modern historical critic can recognize the individualizing characteristics of the life of Christ as the Evangelists *desired* to portray them, and may sketch them out in their true (?) relations to the time and age in which they were manifested: compare the somewhat similar and equally objectionable remarks of Von Ammon, *Geschichte des Leben Jesu*, Vol. I. p. vii. (Preface).

[2] A popular but good article (by Prof. C. E. Stowe) on the nature of the modern assaults upon the four Gospels will be found in the *Biblio-*

and that never seems to regard its historical criticism with more complacency than when it presents to us the four inspired witnesses as involved in the discrepancies of a separate story[1]. Such words, I repeat, may sound strange, but they are the words of soberness and truth; and I will be bold to say that no patient and loving spirit will ever rise from a lengthened investigation of the four evangelical records without having arrived at this honest conviction,—that though here there may seem difficulty because faith has to be tried[2], there a seeming discrepancy because we know not all, yet that the histories themselves, no less in their arrangements and mutual relations than in the nature of their contents, exhibit vividly the pervading influence of that Spirit which it was declared[a] should guide, aye and infallibly has guided, their writers into all truth[3]. But let us carry out these observations somewhat in detail.

[a] John xvi. 13.

theca Sacra for 1851, Part. III. The details are well sketched out by Ebrard, *Kritik der Ev. Geschichte*, § 3—7, p. 5 sq.

[1] The early Church was fully aware of the discrepancies, not merely in detail, but even in general plan and outline, that were deemed to exist between the Gospels; but she well knew how they were to be estimated and regarded: οὐδὲ γὰρ τοὺς εὐαγγελιστὰς φαίημεν ἂν ὑπεναντία ποιεῖν ἀλλήλοις, ὅτι οἱ μὲν τῷ σαρκικῷ τοῦ Χριστοῦ πλέον ἐνησχολήθησαν, οἱ δὲ τῇ θεολογίᾳ προσέβησαν· καὶ οἱ μὲν ἐκ τῶν καθ' ἡμᾶς, οἱ δὲ ἐκ τοῦ ὑπὲρ ἡμᾶς ἐποιήσαντο τὴν ἀρχήν· οὕτω τὸ κήρυγμα διελόμενοι πρὸς τὸ χρήσιμον οἶμαι τοῖς δεχομένοις, καὶ οὕτω παρὰ τοῦ ἐν αὐτοῖς τυπούμενοι Πνεύματος. Greg. Naz. *Orat.* xx. Vol. I, p. 365 (Paris, 1609).

[2] 'Ipsa enim simplici et certa fide in illo permanere debemus, ut ipse aperiat fidelibus quod in se absconditum est: quia sicut idem dicit apostolus, *In illo sunt omnes thesauri sapientiæ et scientiæ absconditi*. Quos non propterea abscondit, ut neget, sed ut absconditis excitet desiderium.' Augustine, *Serm.* LI., Vol. v. p. 336 (ed. Migne).

[3] The language of Augustine on the subject of the plenary inspiration of the Gospels is clear and decided: 'Quidquid ille [Christus] de suis factis et dictis nos legere voluit, hoc scribendum illis tanquam suis manibus imperavit. Hoc unitatis

LECT. I.

Details,— mainly in reference to internal characteristics.

Omitting, on the present occasion, all investigations into the more distinctly external characteristics of the Gospels, whether in regard of the general aspect of these inspired documents, or the particular styles in which they are composed, let us turn our attention to the more interesting subject of their *internal* peculiarities and distinctions. And yet we may pause for a moment even on the outward; for verily the outward is such as can never be overlooked; the outward differences and distinctions are indeed such as may well claim the critical reader's most meditative consideration. We may note, for example, the pervading tinge of Hebrew thought and diction[1] that marks, what we may perhaps correctly term, the *narrative*[2] of St

consortium et in diversis officiis concordium membrorum sub uno capite ministerium quisquis intellexerit, nou aliter accipiet, quod narrantibus discipulis Christi, in Evangelio legerit, *quam si ipsam manum Domini, quam in proprio corpore gestabat, scribentem conspexerit.*' *De Consensu Evang.* I. 35, Vol. III. p. 1070 (ed. Migne); comp. *in Joann.* Tract. XXX. 1, Vol. III. p. 1632.

[1] Nearly all modern critics agree in recognizing not merely in isolated words and phrases, but in the general tone and diction of the first Gospel, the Hebraistic element. The 'physiognomy of this first of our Gospels,' to use the language of Da Costa, 'is eminently Oriental:' the language, though mainly simple and artless, not unfrequently rises to the rhythmical and even poetical, and is marked by a more frequently recurring parallelism of words or clauses (comp. Lowth, *Prelim. Dissert. to Isaiah*, p. viii. Lond. 1837)

than is to be found in the other Gospels; compare, for example, Matth. vii. 24—27, with Luke vi. 47—49, and see Da Costa, *The Four Witnesses*, p. 28 sq. (Transl. Lond. 1851).

[2] Perhaps the term *narrative* may be more correctly applied than any other to the Gospel of St Matthew: it neither presents to us so full a recital of details as we find in St Mark, nor the same sort of historical sequence which we observe in St Luke, nor yet again the same connexion in our Lord's discourses which we observe in St John, but to a certain extent combines some distinctive features of all. Antiquity well expressed this feeling in the comprehensive title τὰ λόγια (Papias, ap. Euseb. *Hist. Eccl.* III. 39), which we may perhaps suitably paraphrase, as Papias himself *seems* to suggest (by his subsequent use of the terms τῶν κυριακῶν λογίων,—but the reading is not certain), as τα

Matthew;—we may observe the more isolated though more unqualified Hebraistic expressions[1], and even the occasional Latinisms[2] that diversify the graphic but more detached *memoirs*[3] of the exponent of the preaching of St Peter[4];—we may trace the Hellenic colouring that gives such grace

---

ὑπὸ Χριστοῦ λεχθέντα ἢ πραχθέντα: see Lücke, in *Studien u. Kritiken* for 1833, p. 501 sq., Meyer, *Kommentar über Matth.* p. 4, note, and Lange, *Leben Jesu*, I. 5. 2, Vol. I. p. 161. The general structure of this Gospel has been well investigated in a programme by Harless, entitled *Lucubrationum Evangelia Canonica spectantium* Pars II. Erlang. 1842. As essays of this character are not always accessible, it may be worth noticing that the learned author finds in the Gospel five divisions,—the *first*, ch. i.—iv., ver. 23—25 forming the epilogue; the *second*, ch. iv.—ix., ver. 35—38 similarly forming the epilogue; the *third*, ch. x.—xiv.; the *fourth*, ch. xv.—xix. 1, 2; and the *fifth*, ch. xix. 3 to the end: see pp. 6, 7.

[1] We may especially notice the occasional introduction of Aramaic words, most probably the very words that fell from our Lord's lips; comp. ch. iii. 17, βοανεργές; ch. v. 41, ταλιθὰ κοῦμι; ch. vii. 34, ἐφφαθά; ch. xiv. 36, ἀββᾶ: see Da Costa, *Four Witnesses*, p. 89.

[2] These have been often specified; it may be enough to notice, σπεκουλάτωρ, ch. vi. 27; ξεστής, ch. vii. 4, 8; κεντυρίων, ch. xv. 39, 44, 45, and the use of χαλκός for money, ch. vi. 8. Some good remarks on other peculiarities of the style of St Mark, especially in reference to his adoption of less usual words and forms of expression, will be found in Credner, *Einleitung in das N. T.* § 49, p. 102 sq., and in the Introd. of Fritz. *Evang. Marci*, p. xlv. sq. The assertion that this Gospel was originally written in Latin, and the appeal to a so-called Latin original, have been long since disposed of: see Tregelles and Horne, *Introduction to the N. T.* Vol. IV. p. 438.

[3] This term may perhaps serve to characterize the general aspects of the Gospel of St Mark, and to distinguish it from the more distinctly *historic* Gospel of St Luke: it also seems well to accord with the spirit of the statements preserved by Eusebius, *Hist. Eccl.* III. 39. A few remarks by De Wette on the characteristics of this Gospel will be found in the *Studien u. Kritiken* for 1828, p. 789; see also Lange, *Leben Jesu*, I. 7. 2, Vol. I. p. 247; and for details, Da Costa, *Four Witnesses* p. 87 sq., Guerike, *Einleitung in das N. T.* § 39. 3, p. 258 (ed. 2).

[4] It is perhaps unnecessary to substantiate this assertion by special quotations, as the connexion between the second Evangelist and St Peter seems now distinctly admitted by all the best modern critics. The most important testimonies of antiquity to this effect are Papias, ap. Euseb. *Hist. Eccl.* III. 39, Irenæus, *Hær.* III. 1, Clem. Alex. ap. Euseb. *Hist. Eccl.* VI. 14, and Origen, ap. *Ib.* VI. 25.

and interest to the compiled *history* of St Luke[1]; we may recognize the marvellous and divine simplicity of the longer and more collective discourses[2] that form the bulk of the *spiritual*[3] and in some respects *supplemental*[4] Gospel of St John...All

[1] If in the first Gospel we recognize the Oriental tinge of thought and diction, and if in the second we detect some traces of the influence of Latin modes of thought, and of a primary destination for Roman converts, we can scarcely fail to acknowledge in the third Gospel the impress of Greek thought and culture (comp. Jerome, *Comment. in Esaiam*, vi. 9), and in its well-ordered and often flowing periods to discern the hand of the Greek proselyte: comp. Col. iv. 14, and notes *in loc.*; and see further, Da Costa, *The Four Witnesses*, p. 148, Lange, *Leben Jesu*, I. 7. 4. Vol. I. p. 253 sq., and for some details in reference to language, Credner, *Einleitung*, § 59, p. 132 sq., Guerike, *Einleitung*, § 40. 4, p. 278, Patritius, *de Evangeliis*, I. 3. 5, Vol. I. p. 83 sq. In those parts (*e. g.* ch. i.) where we find a clearly marked Hebraistic colouring, it seems natural to conclude that we have before us, in perhaps not greatly changed forms, trustworthy documents supplied either by the Blessed Virgin (in the chapter in question) or other privileged eye-witnesses (comp. ch. i. 2) and ministers of the word: compare Gersdorf, *Beiträge z. Sprachcharacteristik des N. T.* p. 160 sq., Patritius, *de Evangeliis*, I. 3. 4, Vol. I. p. 80; and for some general comments on St Luke, the good lecture of Dr Wordsworth, *New Test.* Vol. I. p. 130.

[2] The discourses of our Lord, as recorded by St John, have been defined by Schmidt (*Biblische Theologie*, § 3, p. 23) as 'central,' in contrast with those of the Synoptical Gospels, which he calls more 'peripherisch.' The observation is fanciful, but perhaps has some truth in it: in St John the Lord's discourses certainly seem to turn more on His own Divine person and His true relation to the Father, and the *ideas* and truths which flow therefrom, while those in the Synoptical Gospels relate more frequently to the general *facts*, features, and aspects of the kingdom of God; comp. Ebrard, *Kritik der Evang. Gesch.* § 35, p. 143.

[3] Compare Clem. Alex. ap. Euseb. *Hist. Eccl.* VI. 14. τὸν μέντοι Ἰωάννην ἔσχατον συνιδόντα ὅτι τὰ σωματικὰ ἐν τοῖς εὐαγγελίοις δεδήλωται, προτραπέντα ὑπὸ τῶν γνωρίμων, Πνεύματι θεοφορηθέντα, πνευματικὸν ποιῆσαι εὐαγγέλιον. The same distinction is preserved by Augustine:—'Tres isti Evangelistæ in his rebus maxime diversati sunt quas Christus per humanam carnem temporaliter gessit: porro autem Joannes ipsam maxime divinitatem Domini qua Patre est æqualis intendit.' *De Consensu Evang.* I. 4, Vol. III. p. 1045 (ed. Migne).

[4] This character of St John's Gospel has of late been denied, but as it would seem wholly unsuccessfully. That this was not the *special* object of that sublime Gospel may be fully conceded (see Luthardt, *das*

these things may well suggest to us meditations of the freshest interest; but as they belong to the critical essay rather than to the popular lecture, we shall be wise perhaps to confine ourselves now only to the more strictly *internal* peculiarities, more especially those which characterize the different pictures presented to us of our Blessed Lord and Redeemer.

The Individualities of the four Gospels must be felt and recognized.

Let us, however, never forget that in every effort to set forth the life of our Master, our whole superstructure not only rests upon the four Gospels, but has to be formed out of the elements which they supply, and that unsymmetrical will it be and incongruous, unless, like wise master-builders, we learn to appreciate the inner and essential distinctions between the precious materials which we are presuming to employ. Here has been the grave error of only too many of those who have taken in hand to draw up an account of those things that are fully believed among us^a. Here harmonies have failed to edify, here critical histories have often proved so lamentably deficient. Nay, I believe that there is no one thing which the long roll of harmonies and histories, extending from the days of Tatian down to our own[1], teach

^a Luke i. 1

Johan. Evang. IV. 1, Vol. I. p. 109 sq.), but that St John wrote with a full cognizance of what his three predecessors had related, that he presupposed it in his readers, and enlarged upon events not recorded elsewhere, seems almost indisputable. That this was distinctly the belief of antiquity is fully conceded by Lücke, *Comment. über Johann.* III. 13, Vol. I. p. 187 (ed. 3): see especially Euseb. *Hist. Eccl.* III. 24; Jerome, *de Viris Illustr.* cap. 9; and *compare* the expressions in the Muratorian fragment on the Canon, reprinted in Routh, *Reliq. Sacræ,* Vol. IV. p. 3 sq. (ed. 1).

[1] A full list of these will be found in the useful but unsound work of Hase, *Leben Jesu,* § 21, p. 21 sqq., and a shorter and selected list in the *Harmonia Evangelica* of Tischendorf, p. ix. sqq. Those which most deserve consideration seem to be,

us more distinctly than this—that no true picture of the earthly life of our Redeemer can ever be realized, unless by God's grace we learn both to feel and to appreciate the striking *individuality* of the four Gospels in their portraiture of the life of Christ, and are prepared to estimate duly their peculiar and fore-ordered characteristics[1].

That antiquity failed not to recognize these individualities, we are reminded by the admirable treatise of Augustine on the Consent of the Evangelists[2]—a treatise from which, though we may venture to differ in details, we can never safely depart in our general principles of combination and adjustment[3]. No writer has more ably main-

---

Gerson, *Concordia Evangelistarum* (about 1471), Chemnitz, *Harmonia Quatuor Evangelistarum* (Vol. I. published in 1593); Lightfoot, *Harmony, &c. of the N. T.* (Lond. 1655); Lamy, *Harmonia sive Concordia Quatuor Evangelistarum*, Paris, 1689; Bengel, *Richtige Harmonie der vier Evangelien*, Tubing. 1736; Newcome, *Harmony of Gospels*, Dubl. 1778; Clausen, *Tabulæ Synopticæ*, Havniæ, 1829; Greswell, *Harmonia Evangelica*, Oxon. 1840; Robinson, *Harmony of the Four Gospels*, Boston, 1845, and (with useful notes) Lond. (Relig. Tract Society): Anger, *Synopsis Evangeliorum*, Lips. 1851; Tischendorf, *Synopsis Evangelica*, Lips. 1851; and, lastly, the voluminous work of Patritius, *de Evangeliis*, Friburg. 1853.

[1] See some good remarks in the Introduction to Lange, *Leben Jesu*, especially I. 3. 1, Vol. I. p. 98 sq.

[2] We might also specify, as illustrative of this view of the individual character of the four Gospels, the ancient and well-known comparison of the four Gospels to the four living creatures mentioned in the Apocalypse (Irenæus, *Hær.* III. 1). Though later writers (Athanasius, Augustine, Jerome, al.) varied somewhat in their adaptations of the symbols (see Wordsworth, *Greek Test.* Vol. I. p. li.), this fourfold comparison may be considered as the practical manifestation of the belief of the ancient Church in the distinct individuality of the four Gospels. The more usual order and application of the symbols is stated by Sedulius in the following lines, which may bear quotation:—

Hoc Matthæus agens hominem generaliter implet,
Marcus ut alta fremit vox per deserta Leonis,
Jura sacerdotii Lucas tenet ore juvenci,
More volans aquilæ verbo petit astra Johannes.

[3] Augustine appears from his own statements to have taken especial pains with this treatise. He alludes to it twice in his commentary on 'St John (Tract. CXII. 1, Vol. III. p. 1929, and again Tract. CXVII. 2,

tained the fundamental position, that the four evangelical records in their delineation of the life of Christ have noticeably different characteristics— that they present our Redeemer to us under different aspects[1],—and that these four histories (to use the simile of another ancient writer[2]), though flowing from one paradise, go forth to water the earth with four currents of different volume and direction.

It was the neglect of these principles that made so many of the laborious Harmonies of the sixteenth and seventeenth centuries both valueless and unedifying, and not improbably served to call out that antagonistic criticism, which in these later days has acquired such an undue, and it must be said undesirable prominence[3]. These earlier efforts

Errors of earlier Harmonists.

Vol. III. p. 194.5), and in both cases speaks of it as composed with much labour: compare also his *Retractationes*, Book II. ch. 16.

[1] See especially Book I. 2, 3, 4 (Vol. III. p. 1044, ed. Migne), where the different aspects under which our Redeemer was viewed by the Evangelist are specially noticed. What we have to regret in this valuable treatise is the somewhat low position assigned to St Mark's Gospel, the author of which, according to Augustine, is but the 'pedissequus et breviator' of St Matthew (chap. 2). Modern criticism has strikingly reversed this judgment.

[2] Jerome, *Praef. in Matth.* cap. 4, Vol. VII. p. 18 (ed. Migne).

[3] I regret that I cannot agree with some of the expressions of my friend, Dean Alford, in the Introduction to his *New Testament*, Vol. I. § 7. Careful investigation seems to justify the opinion that between the forced harmonies, which found favour in older times, and the blank rejection of evangelical harmony, except in its broadest outlines, which has been so much advocated in our own times, there is a safe *via media*, which, if followed thoughtfully and patiently, will often be found to lead us to aspects of the sacred narrative, which are in the highest degree interesting and instructive. Variations are not 'consequently inaccuracies' (§ 7. 6): could we only transport ourselves to the *right point* of view we should see things in their true perspective; and that we can more often do so than is generally supposed, has, I venture to think, been far too generally denied. For some good remarks on Gospel harmony, see Wieseler, *Chron. Synops.* p. 5 sqq., Da Costa, *Four Witnesses*, p. 1 sqq. (Transl.).

we may have never seen, perhaps never heard of. We may smile perhaps at the luckless sedulity that deemed it necessary to assign to St Peter nine denials of our Lord[1], and we may perhaps scarcely believe that such abuses of Evangelistic harmony could have been originated by one who co-operated with Luther, and whose works were not without influence on his contemporaries, and on them that followed him. We may perhaps now smile at such efforts, but still if one only looks at some of the harmonies of the present century, it seems abundantly clear that these influences are even now not wholly inoperative[2], and that efforts to interweave portions of the sacred narrative, without a proper estimate of the different objects and characteristics of the Evangelists, still find among us some favour and reception. In our desire, however, to reject such palpably uncritical endeavours, let us at any rate respect the principle by which they appear to have been actuated—a reverence, mistaken it is true, but still a reverence for every jot and tittle of the written word; and let us beware too that we are not tempted into the other extreme,—

---

[1] Osiander, *Harmon. Evang.* p. 128 (Bas. 1561). This rigid and somewhat arrogant divine was born A.D. 1498: he was educated at Wittemberg and afterwards at Nuremberg, in which latter city he became a preacher at one of the churches. He warmly supported Luther in his attack on Papal indulgences, but afterwards fell into errors respecting the application of Christ's righteousness and the divine image, which he appears to have defended with undue confidence and pertinacity; see Mosheim, *Eccl. Hist.* IV. 3. 2. 1, Vol. III. p. 357 (ed. Soames); Tholuck, *Lit. Anzeiger* for 1833, No. 54; and for a short notice of his life, Schröckh, *Kirchengeschichte* (Reformation), Vol. IV. p. 572.

[2] I fear I must here specify the learned and laborious work of Dr Stroud (*New Greek Harmony of the Four Gospels*), in which in this same case of St Peter's denials, the event is recounted under different forms seven times; see the Introduction, p. clxxxix.

that equally exaggerated view of modern times, that the discordances of the sacred writers are such as defy reconciliation[1], and that all, save the great events in the history of our Redeemer, must ever remain to us a collection of confused and inconsequent details.

In one word, let us remember that though it is uncritical, unwise, and even presumptuous to fabricate a patchwork narrative, yet that it is not only possible, but our very duty to endeavour judiciously to *combine*[2]. Let us remember that we have four holy pictures, limned by four loving hands, of Him who 'was fairer than the children of men[a],'— and that these have been vouchsafed to us, that by varying our postures we may catch fresh beauties and fresh glories[3]. Let us then fear not to use

Judicious combination the true principle.

[a] Ps. xlv. 2

---

[1] For some useful observations on, and answers to the extreme views that have been maintained on the supposed discrepancies or divergences that have been found in the Gospel history, see Ebrard, *Kritik der Evang. Geschichte*, § 19, p. 71 sqq.

[2] Modern writers on harmonistic study commonly draw distinctions between Synopsis and Harmony, and again between Chronology and Order of Events (*Akoluthie*). Such distinctions are useful, and serve to assist us in keeping clearly in view the principles on which our combination is constructed. The problem, however, we have to solve can really be regarded under very simple aspects: it is merely this, (1) to determine, where possible, *by reference to chronological data*, the order and connexion of events; (2) to reconcile any striking divergences we may meet with in accounts of the same event; compare Chemnitz, *Harmon. Quatuor Evang.* Proem. cap. 5. In regard of (2) we must be guided by the results of a sound exegesis of each one of the supposed discordant passages combined with a just appreciation of the apparently leading aims, objects and characteristics of the inspired records to which they respectively belong. In regard of (1), where chronology fails us, we can only fall back on the principle of Chemnitz:—'Nos quærimus ordinem, cujus rationes, si non semper certæ et ubique manifestæ, probabiles tamen nec absurdæ nec vero absimiles reddi possunt.' *Harmonia Evang.* Vol. I. p. 18 (Hamb. 1704).

[3] Compare with this the judicious observations of Da Costa:—'To picture Christ to the eye in equal *fulness*, that is, as an actual *whole*, and that in all His aspects, one witness was very far from being sufficient; but Divine wisdom could

LECT. I.

one to see more in light what another has left more in shade; let us scruple not to trace the lineament that one has left unexpressed, but another has portrayed. Let us do all this, nothing doubting; but let us beware, let us specially beware, lest in seeking to work them up mechanically into what might seem to us a well-adjusted whole, instead of order we bring in confusion, distortion instead of symmetry, burning instead of beauty.

Illustrations of the internal characteristics above alluded to.

Let me conclude with a few illustrations of those internal characteristics and individualities of the four Gospels, especially in reference to the picture of our Lord's life, to which I have alluded, and so prepare ourselves for thoughtful recognitions, in future lectures, of divinely ordered differences, and for wise and sober principles of combination.

Individuality of St Matthew's Gospel.

How striking is the coincidence between the peculiar nature of the contents of the Gospel of St Matthew, and what Scripture relates to us of the position of him that wrote it. How naturally we might expect from him who sat at the receipt of custom on the busy shores of the lake of Gennesareth, and who had learnt to arrange and to methodize in the callings of daily life,—how naturally we might expect careful grouping and well-ordered combination[1]. And how truly

---

here accomplish its object by means of a *fourfold* testimony and a *four-sided* delineation. In order to this, it was meet that each of four Evangelists should represent to us not only the doings and sayings, but the very person of the Saviour from his own individual point of view and in harmony with his own personal character and disposition.' *The Four Witnesses*, p. 118 (Transl.).

[1] See the thoughtful comments of Lange, *Leben Jesu*, 1. 7. 2, Vol. I. p. 237 sq. It may perhaps be urged that we are here tacitly assuming that the details of the office of a τελώνης were more in harmony with modern practice than can actually

we find it! To leave unnoticed the vexed question of the exact nature of the Sermon on the Mount[1],—to whom save to St Matthew do we owe that effective grouping of parables which we find in the thirteenth chapter[2], wherein each one by its juxtaposition imparts additional force and clearness to those with which it stands in immediate contact? Whose hand was it save the wise publican's that wove into narrative that glorious garland of miracles of which the eighth and ninth chapters are nearly entirely composed[3]?

---

be demonstrated. That an ἀρχιτελώνης (*sub magistro*) was especially concerned with administrative details can be distinctly shown, but that the simple collector (*portitor*), such as St Matthew probably was, had any duties of an analogous nature, may be regarded as doubtful. The very necessities of the case, however, imply that the 'portitor' would have to render constant accounts to his superior officer,—and this seems quite enough to warrant the comments in the text; see Smith, *Dict. of Antiq.* s. v. 'Publicani;' Jahn, *Archæolog. Bibl.* § 241; Winer, *Realwörterb.* s. v. 'Zoll,' Vol. II. p. 739 sq.

[1] See the comments on its probable structure in Lecture IV.

[2] In this chapter we have the longer parables of the Sower (ver. 3—9) and of the Tares and the Wheat (ver. 24—30), and the shorter comparisons of the kingdom of heaven with the Grain of Mustard Seed (ver. 31, 32), Leaven (ver. 33), the Treasure in a field (ver. 44), the Merchantman and the Pearl (ver. 45, 46), and the Net cast into the sea (ver. 47, 48). The illustrative connexion that exists between these parables can hardly escape the notice of the observant reader. We have, as it were, seven varied aspects of the kingdom of God on earth. In the *first* parable we have placed before us the various classes in the visible Church; in the *second* we contemplate the origin and presence of evil therein, and its final removal and overthrow; in the *third* we see the kingdom of God in its aspects of growth and extension; in the *fourth* in its pervasive and regenerative character; in the *fifth* and *sixth* in reference to its preciousness, whether as discovered accidentally or after deliberate search; in the *seventh* in its present state of inclusiveness combined with its future state of selection and unsparing separation: see Wordsworth, *New Test.* Vol. I. p. 39; and compare Knox, *Remains*, Vol. I. pp. 407—425.

[3] In these two chapters we have the narrative of the cleansing of a leper (viii. 2—4); the healings of the centurion's servant (viii. 5—13), of St Peter's wife's mother (viii. 14, 15), and of numerous demoniacs (viii. 16); the stilling of the winds and sea (viii. 24—26); the healing of the demoniacs of Gadara (viii. 28—34);

who but he, who has brought together in such illustrative combinations the Lord's last prophecies, and the partially prophetic parables that usher in that most solemn revelation of our Redeemer to His Church, which concludes with the twenty-fifth chapter[1]?

Especially in his portraiture of our Lord.

But to narrow our observations to that with which we are more especially concerned,—with what force and effect are the contrasts, which such habits of combination naturally suggest[2], employed in presenting to us vivid and impressive aspects of our *Redeemer's history*. In what striking antithesis do the opening chapters set before us the new-born king of Peace and the savage Herod[a], the mysterious adoration of the Magi, and the hasty flight for life into a strange land[b], the baptism with the opened heavens and descending Spirit, and the temptation with all its circumstances of Satanic trial[c]. Observe too how thus heightened by contrast as well as heralded by prophecy, the Lord appears to us as the Son of David and the Son of Abraham[d], the spiritual King of spiritual Judaism, the Messiah of the Israel of God[3]. Yet withal observe how

[a] ii. 1, 3
[b] ii. 11, 13
[c] iii. 13 sq. and iv. 1 sq.
[d] i. 1

of the paralytic on his bed (ix. 2—8), and of the woman with an issue of blood (ix. 20—22); the raising of Jairus' daughter (ix. 23—25), the healing of two blind men (ix. 28—30), and the dispossession of a dumb demoniac (ix. 32—34).

[1] Especially the similitude of the Unready Servant (xxiv. 43—51), and the parables of the Ten Virgins (xxv. 1—12), and of the Talents (xxv. 14—30).

[2] Compare Lange, *Leben Jesu*, 1. 7. 2, Vol. I. p. 240. The outlines and general construction of St Matthew's Gospel are described by Ebrard, *Kritik der Evang. Geschichte*, § 22, p. 86 sq. but not under any very novel or suggestive aspects. For some remarks on the characteristic peculiarities of this Gospel, see Davidson, *Introduction to N. T.* Vol. I. p. 52 sq.

[3] Compare the fragments of Irenæus, taken from Possini, *Catena Patrum*, and cited in the various

the Theocratic King and the suffering Messiah pass and repass before our eyes in ever new and ever striking interchange, and how a strange and deep tone of prophetic sadness blends with all we read, and prepares us as it were for Gethsemane and Calvary; and yet again when the Lord has broken the bands of death, whose save St Matthew's is that inspired pen that records that outpouring of exalted majesty, 'All power is given me in heaven and in earth[a]'? To whom save to the first Evangelist owe we the record of that promise which forms the most consolatory heritage of the Church, 'Lo! I am with you alway, even unto the end of the world[b]'?

[a] Matt. xxviii. 18.
[b] Matt. xxviii. 20.

Individuality of St Mark's Gospel.

No less strongly marked is the individuality of St Mark's Gospel. No less clearly in this inspired record can we trace the impressible and fervid character which we almost instinctively ascribe to John Mark the son of Mary[c] (for I hold the identity of the Evangelist with the nephew of Barnabas)[1],—to him that seems to

[c] Act. xii. 12

---

editions of that ancient writer (Grabe, p. 471; Massuet, Vol. I. p. 347); it is as follows: Τὸ κατὰ Ματθαῖον εὐαγγέλιον πρὸς Ἰουδαίους ἐγράφη· οὗτοι γὰρ ἐπεθύμουν πάνυ σφόδρα ἐκ σπέρματος Δαβὶδ Χριστόν. Ὁ δὲ Ματθαῖος, καὶ ἔτι μᾶλλον σφοδροτέραν ἔχων τὴν τοιαύτην ἐπιθυμίαν, παντοίως ἔσπευδε πληροφορίαν παρέχειν αὐτοῖς, ὡς εἴη ἐκ σπέρματος Δαβὶδ ὁ Χριστός. Διὸ καὶ ἀπὸ γενέσεως αὐτοῦ ἤρξατο. Comp. Ebrard, *Kritik der Evang. Geschichte*, § 21, p. 85.

[1] This opinion has of late been considered doubtful (see Kienlen, *Stud. u. Krit.* for 1843, p. 423), but apparently on insufficient grounds. The silence of Papias as to the connexion with Barnabas, on which an argument has been based, cannot fairly be pressed, as in the passage in question (Euseb. *Hist. Eccl.* III. 39) Papias appears occupied not with the question who St Mark was, but simply with the nature of the testimony which he delivered and his dependence on St Peter. Ecclesiastical tradition seems to have recognized *three* bearing this name, the Evangelist, John Mark, and the nephew of Barnabas,—but for such a distinction still less can be said; comp. Coteler, *Constit. Apost.* II. 57, Vol. I. p. 265. The opinion of Da Costa (*Four Witnesses*, p. 114 sq.), that St Mark was the devout soldier

have been so forward in action, and yet on one occasion at least too ready to fall away. I say on one occasion *at least*, for there are many whose judgment demands our respect who also find in the young man with the hastily-caught up linen garment who followed but to flee[a], him who alone has handed down to us that isolated notice[1].

Time would fail me if I were to name all the many touches that stamp this impress of individuality on the work of the second Evangelist. Do we not recognize his *graphic* pen and his noticeable love of the objective and the circumstantial, in almost every event, and especially in every miracle which he has been moved to record? Is not this plainly apparent in the narrative of the healing of the paralytic[b], in that of the Gadarene demoniac[c], in the account of the gradual recovery of the blind man of Bethsaida[d], and in the striking description of the demoniac boy[e]? Is not this to be felt in the various touches that diversify almost every incident that finds a place in his inspired record[2]? Is it not St Mark that

*Mk.xiv.51
[b] ii. 3 sq.
[c] v. 2 sq.
[d] viii. 22 sq.
[e] ix. 20 sq.

who attended on Cornelius (Acts x. 7), is a mere fancy, wholly destitute of even traditional testimony.

[1] Such was the opinion of Chrysostom (*in loc.*), Gregory the Great (*Moral.* XIV. 23), and one or two other ancient writers. It may, however, justly be considered very precarious, as the common and not unnatural supposition that the young man was a disciple does not seem to accord with the comment of Papias, οὔτε γὰρ ἤκουσε τοῦ Κυρίου, οὔτε παρηκολούθησεν αὐτῷ, ap. Euseb. *Hist. Eccl.* III. 39.

[2] These touches are very numerous, but are perhaps more easily felt than specified. We may notice, however, the effective insertion on three occasions of the very Aramaic words that our Lord was pleased to use (ch. v. 41, vii. 34, xiv. 36), of the emphatic ἀκούετε prefixed to the parable of the Sower (ch. iv. 3), and of the words of power addressed to the winds and sea (ch. v. 39). Sometimes details are brought out by the introduction of a single word (ch. xv. 43, τολμήσας), sometimes by the simple use of a stronger expression than is found in the corresponding passage in the other

presents to us our Master amid all the loneliness and horrors of the wilderness, 'with the wild beasts^a'? Is it not he who brings up, as it were before our very eyes, our Redeemer on the storm-tost lake 'in the hinder part of the ship asleep on a pillow^b'? Is it not he who so frequently and precisely notes almost every distinctive gesture and look[1], and is it not to him that we owe the last touch, as it were, to that affecting picture of our Lord's tenderness and love^c, when He '*took up* the young children *in His arms*, and put His hands upon them, and blessed them'?

^a Mk. i. 13

^b iv. 38

^c x. 16

But still more does this individuality appear, and with this we are now most concerned, in the broad and *general* picture which this Evangelist presents to us of his heavenly Master. If in the first Gospel we recognize transitions from theocratic glories to meek submissions, in the

Especially in his portraiture of our Lord.

Gospels (compare for instances Mark i. 10, σχιζομένους τοὺς οὐρανούς, with Matth. iii. 16, Luke iii. 21; ch. i. 12, ἐκβάλλει, with Matth. iv. 1, Luke iv. 1; ch. ii. 12, ἐξίστασθαι, with Matth. ix. 8; ch. iv. 37, γεμίζεσθαι, with Matth. viii. 24, Luke viii. 23; ch. vi. 46, ἀποταξάμενος, with Matth. xiv. 23; ch. xiv. 33, ἐκθαμβεῖσθαι καὶ ἀδημονεῖν, with Matth. xxvi. 37), while at other times we seem made conscious, perhaps merely by a repetition of a word or phrase (ch. i. 14, 15, ii. 16, iv. 1, xi. 28, al.), perhaps merely by a strengthened form (*e.g.* cognate accus., ch. iii. 29, iv. 41, v. 42, vii. 13, xiii. 19), of that graphic vigour which so peculiarly characterizes the record of the second Evangelist. The single parable which is peculiar to this Gospel (ch. iv. 26 sq.) may be alluded to as bearing every impress of the style of St Mark.

[1] Many instances of this could be cited: we may pause to specify the all-embracing look (περιβλέπεσθαι) of our Lord which, with the exception of Luke vi. 10, is noticed only by this Evangelist (ch. iii. 5, 34, v. 32, x. 23, xi. 11); the expression of inward emotions on different occasions (ch. vii. 34, viii. 12, x. 14, 21); and the very interesting fact of our Lord's heading His band of disciples on the last journey to Jerusalem, mentioned in ch. x. 32: compare Da Costa, *Four Witnesses*, p. 121; Lange, *Leben Jesu*, I. 7. 2, Vol. I. p. 179 sq.; Guericke, *Einleitung*, § 39. 3, p. 258 note; and Davidson, *Introduction to N. T.* Vol. I. p. 150.

LECT. I.

second we see our Redeemer in one light only, of majesty and power. If in St Matthew's record we behold now the glorified and now the suffering Messiah, in St Mark's vivid pages we see only the all-powerful incarnate Son of God; the voice we hear is that of the Lion of the Tribe of Judah...With what peculiar variety of expression does this inspired writer notice the awe and amazement, no less of the familiar circle of the disciples[a] than of the more impressible multitude[b]. With what circumstantial touches does he put before us—Him on whose lips the multitude so hung that they had scarce room to stand[c], or time to eat[d],—Him that wrought such wondrous works that all men did marvel[e], yea, and unbelieving Nazareth was astonished[f],—Him whose fame was spread all the more that He sought to conceal it[g],—Him before whose feet 'whithersoever He entered, villages or cities[h],' the sick were laid out, and laid out only to be made whole.

These things can escape the observation of no attentive reader, nor will they perhaps fail almost to convince him, as they have almost convinced me, that he whose narrative like Stephen's glance penetrates beyond the clouds, and tells us how the Lord 'was received up into heaven and sat down at the right hand of God[i],' was John Mark the Evangelist[1].

[a] Mk. x. 32
[b] ix. 14; xi. 18
[c] iv. 1
[d] iii. 20; vi. 31
[e] v. 20
[f] vi. 2
[g] vii. 36
[h] vi. 56
[i] xvi. 19.

[1] It is right to speak with diffidence on a point on which modern critics and commentators (even Dr Wordsworth) have judged differently. It is not desirable here to enter upon a criticism of external evidence, which will be found clearly and ably stated elsewhere (see especially the critical notes to the new edition of Tischendorf's *Greek Testament;* Meyer, *Comment on St Mark*, p. 170 sqq.; and Tregelles, *Printed Text of the N. T.* pp. 246—261), except to remark that the only *clear* and *unqualified* external evidence against the passage is B, the newly found ℵ, the Latin

Characteristics of the four Gospels. 27

Still more clearly, if it be possible, can we recognize the individuality of the Gospel of St Luke. Here the coincidences between the nature of the history and what we know of him who wrote it,—the wise physician of Antioch[1],—the proselyte as it has been thought of the gate,— the only one of the four Evangelists who bore in his body the mark of belonging to the wide world that was not of the stock of Abraham[2],— meet us again and again, and press themselves

LECT. I.
Individuality of St Luke's Gospel.

Codex Bobbiensis, some MSS. of the Armenian Version, an Arabic Version in the Vatican, and perhaps we may add Severus of Antioch, and Hesychius of Jerusalem (see Tischendorf *l. c.*),—the testimonies of Eusebius and Jerome being not so certain (see Wordsworth, *Four Gospels*, p. 127). As a set-off against the arguments founded on differences in the use of a few words and expressions (see Norton, *Genuineness of the Gospels*, Vol. I. p. 219, ed. 2), we may certainly plead the circumstantial tone of ver. 10 (πενθοῦσιν καὶ κλαίουσιν), of ver. 12 (ἐν ἑτέρᾳ μορφῇ, πορευομένοις εἰς ἀγρόν), the specifications of ver. 17 sq.,—against which the objections commonly urged seem most noticeably weak,—and the conclusion of ver. 19. Why may not this portion have been written by St Mark at a later period when mere verbal peculiarities might have altered, but when general sentiment and style might, as we seem to observe is the case, remain wholly unchanged? To speculate on the causes which led to the interruption at the end of the 8th verse is perhaps idle. The terrible persecution under Nero, A.D. 64, is, however, somewhat plausibly urged as a possible period when the Evangelist might have suddenly sought safety by flight, leaving the record, which he had been so pressed to write (Euseb. *Hist. Eccl.* II. 15, VI. 14), unfinished, and to be concluded perhaps in another land, and under more peaceful circumstances: comp. Norton, *Genuineness of the Gospels*, Vol. I. p. 221.

[1] Compare Euseb. *Hist. Eccl.* III. 4,—Λουκᾶς τὸ μὲν γένος ὢν τῶν ἀπ' Ἀντιοχείας; see also Jerome, *Catal. Script.* cap. 16. This statement has been recently considered doubtful (Winer, *RWB.* Art. 'Lucas,' Vol. II. p. 35; Meyer, *Einleitung*, p. 182), and due merely to a mistaken identification of the Evangelist with Lucius (Acts xiii. 1), but apparently without sufficient reason. The recent attempt to identify St Luke with Silas has been noticed, but refuted by Dr Davidson, *Introduction*, Vol. II. p. 20.

[2] This has been usually and, as it would seem, correctly inferred from Col. iv. 14, where St Luke and Demas are named by themselves, and, with Epaphras, not included in the list which preceded (ver. 10, 11) of those who were of the circumcision; see notes *in loc.*

LECT. I.

upon our attention, in ever new and ever suggestive combinations. I may allude in passing to the frequent and characteristic statement of the circumstances or reasons that gave rise to the events or discourses recorded[1], which we find so strikingly in this Gospel. I may notice the peculiarly reflective, and, if I may use the term, *psychological* comments[2], which the thoughtful physician so often passes on the actors or the circumstances which he brings forward in his inspired narrative.

Portraiture of our Lord.

These things we can here only allude to in

[1] This may be observed especially in the way in which the parables, peculiar to this Evangelist, are commonly introduced into the sacred narrative : compare ch. vii. 39 sq., x. 30 sq., xii. 13 sq., xviii. 1, and very distinctly xix. 11. We may also here specify St Luke's account of the outward circumstances that led to our Lord's being born at Bethlehem, the valuable clue he gives us to one of the significances of the Transfiguration (ch. ix. 31), the notice how St Peter came to be armed with a sword (ch. xxii. 38), the mention of our Lord's being first blindfolded, and then bidden to prophesy who struck Him (ch. xxii. 63); compare Blunt, *Coincidences of the Gospels,* No. XII. p. 47); and to conclude a list, which might be made much longer, the allusion to the circumstances which led to our Lord's being taken before Herod (ch. xxiii. 6 sq.); compare also Lange, *Leben Jesu,* I. 7. 2, Vol. I. p. 256.

[2] We may specify a few instances ; *e.g.* the passing comment on the as yet imperfect perceptions of Joseph and Mary, ch. ii. 50, 51; the notice of the expectancy of the people, ch. iii. 15; the glimpse given us of the inward thoughts of the Pharisee, ch. vii. 39; the passing remark on their spiritual state generally, ver. 30; the brief specification of their prevailing characteristic, ch. xvi. 14; the sketch of the principles of action adopted by the spies sent forth by the chief priests and scribes, ch. xx. 20; the notice of the entry of Satan into Judas, ch. xxii. 3, and the significant comment on the altered relations between Pilate and Herod, ch. xxiii. 12. We may remark in passing that the difference between these comments and those which we meet with in St John's Gospel is clear and characteristic. In St John's Gospel such comments are nearly always specially introduced to *explain* or to *elucidate* (comp. ch. iii. 23, 24, iv. 8, 9, vi. 4, 10, 23, 71, vii. 39, xi. 2, 13, al.); in St Luke's Gospel they are rather *obiter dicta*, the passing remarks of a thoughtful and reflective writer, called up from time to time by the varied aspects of the events which he is engaged in recording; comp. Lange, *Leben Jesu,* I. 7. 2, Vol. I. p. 256 sq.

Characteristics of the four Gospels. 29

passing; we may, however, with profit to ourselves pause somewhat on the portraiture of our Redeemer as presented to us by this Evangelist. If, as I said, St Matthew presents to us our Redeemer more especially as the Messiah, the Son of Abraham and the Son of David; if St Mark more especially presents Him to us as the incarnate and wonder-working Son of God, assuredly St Luke presents Him to us in the most wide and universal aspects[1] as the God-man, the Friend and Redeemer of fallen humanity, yea even as his own genealogy declares it, not merely the Son of David and the Son of Abraham, but the Son of Adam and the Son of God[2]....With what affecting delineation does He who tenderly loved the race He came to save appear to us in the raising of the son of the widow of Nain[a],—in

LECT.
I.

[a] vii. 13

---

[1] The universality of St Luke's Gospel has been often commented on. Not only in this Gospel do we feel ourselves often, as it were, transported into the domain of general history (comp. Da Costa, *Four Witnesses*, p. 154),—not only can we recognize the constantly recurring relations or contrasts of Judaism and Gentilism (Ebrard, *Kritik der Evang. Gesch.* § 31, p. 120),—not only may we, with most modern critics, see this universality very distinctly brought out in the notice of the mission of the Seventy Disciples (Credner, *Einleitung*, § 60, p. 144), but we may trace the same characteristic in some of the recitals of leading events, in some of the miracles and parables, and in several of our Lord's isolated comments and observations: consider, for example, ch. ii. 31, 32; iv. 27; ix. 1—6 (especially when contrasted with Matth. x. 5—6), ix. 52 sq., x. 30 sq., xvi. 16, xvii. 11 sq., xix. 38 (as contrasted with Matth. xxi. 9, Mark xi. 9, 10, John xii. 13,—in all of which the reference is to the theocratic rather than to the universal King), xxiv. 47, and compare Patritius, *de Evangeliis*, I. 3. 5. 80, Vol. I. p. 92.

[2] This difference did not escape the notice of Chrysostom; 'Ο μὲν Ματθαῖος, ἅτε Ἑβραίοις γράφων, οὐδὲν πλέον ἐζήτησε δεῖξαι, ἢ ὅτι ἀπὸ Ἀβραὰμ καὶ Δαυὶδ ἦν· ὁ δὲ Λουκᾶς ἅτε κοινῇ πᾶσι διαλεγόμενος καὶ ἀνωτέρω τὸν λόγον ἀνάγει, μέχρι τοῦ Ἀδὰμ προϊών. *in Matth.* Hom. I. p. 7 (ed. Bened.); see also Origen, ap. Euseb. *Hist. Eccl.* VI. 25, and the comments on this Gospel of Ebrard, *Kritik der Ev. Geschichte*, § 31, p. 120 sq.

the narrative of her who was forgiven and who 'loved much[a],'—in the three parables of the lost sheep[b], the lost coin[c], and the prodigal son[d],—in the address to the daughters[1] of Jerusalem[e],—in the prayer for those who had crucified Him[f],—in the gracious promise to the penitent malefactor[g], vouchsafed even while the lips that spake it were quivering with agonies of accumulated suffering.

[a] Lk. vii. 37 sq.
[b] xv. 3 sq.; also in Mt. xviii. 12
[c] xv. 8 sq.
[d] xv. 11 sq. xxiii. 27 sq.
[f] xxiii. 34
[g] xxiii. 43

In all these things, and in how many more than these that could easily be adduced, see we not the living picture of Him who was at once the Son of Man in mercy and the Son of God in power, whose grace and redemptive blessings extended to both Jew and Gentile, and who, even as He is borne up into the clouds of heaven, passes from our view in the narrative of St Luke blessing those from whom He is parting[h];—'and it came to pass while He blessed them, He was parted from them and carried up into heaven, and they worshipped Him, and returned to Jerusalem with great joy'?

[h] xxiv. 50

Individuality of St John's Gospel.

On the internal characteristics of the Gospel of St John, and the picture that is there vouchsafed to us of our Lord, I need perhaps say but little, as that blessed Gospel is to so large an extent composed of the Redeemer's own words, and as modern thought no less than the meditations of antiquity

---

[1] It may be observed that consistently with the characteristic of universality above alluded to, St Luke brings before us, more frequently than the other Evangelists, notices of pious and ministering *women;* comp. ch. ii. 36, viii. 2, xxiii. 27, 55, and see also vii. 37 sq. The same feature is especially noticeable in the Acts; comp. ch. i. 14, viii. 12, ix. 2, ix. 36, xii. 12, xvi. 1, 14, al.; comp. Da Costa, *Four Witnesses,* p. 189 sq., Lange, *Leben Jesu,* Vol. I. p. 259.

seems rarely to have missed seizing the true aspects of the divine image of the Son of God that is there presented to us[1]. The very words which I have chosen as my text declare the general object of the Gospel,—even 'that we may believe that Jesus is the Christ, the Son of God[a];' the very opening words suggest the lofty sense in which that sonship is to be understood,—'the Word was with God, and the Word was God[b].' As in the synoptical Gospels the Incarnate Son is mainly displayed to us in the operative majesty of outwardly-exercised omnipotence, so in the fourth Gospel is He mainly revealed to us in the tranquil majesty of conscious unity with the eternal Father[2]. Here we are permitted to catch mysterious glimpses of the very inner life of our redeeming Lord; we behold the reader of the thoughts and intents of

[a] xx. 31
[b] i. 1

---

[1] The excellent work of Luthardt (das Johanneische Evangelium, Nürnberg, 1852) may here be especially noticed. In this the reader will find full and careful notices of all that is peculiar and distinctive in this Gospel, an exposition of the plan of development, and comments on the component parts of the narrative. The writer is perhaps too much carried away by his theory of the regular and dramatic structure of the Gospel, and sometimes too artificial in his analysis of details, still his work remains, and will probably long remain, as one of the best essays on St John's Gospel that has ever appeared. For a review, see Reuter, *Repertor.* Vol. LXXXV. p. 97.

A good essay on the life and character of the Apostle will be found in Lücke, *Comment. über Joh.* § 2, Vol. I. p. 6 sqq., and some useful remarks on the general plan and arrangement of the Gospel, in Ebrard, *Kritik der Ev. Geschichte,* § 35, p. 141 sq.; see also Davidson, *Introduction,* Vol. I. p. 334.

[2] Compare Augustine, *de Consensu Evang.* I. 5: 'Intelligi datur, si diligenter advertas, tres Evangelistas temporalia facta Domini et dicta quæ ad informandos mores vitæ presentis maxime valerent, copiosius persecutos, circa illam *aetiram* virtutem fuisse versatos: Joannem vero facta Domini multa pauciora narrantem, dicta vero ejus, ea præsertim quæ Trinitatis unitatem et vitæ æternæ felicitatem insinuarent, diligentius et uberius conscribentem, in virtute contemplativâ commendandâ, suam intentionem prædicationemque tenuisse.' Vol. III. p. 1046 (ed. Migne); compare Lange, *Leben Jesu,* I. 7. 2, Vol. I. p. 265 sq.

the human heart¹, we note the ever-present consciousness of truest and innermost union with the Father of Spirits². Yet we feel rather than see; we are made conscious rather than observe. Here, in the stillness of our hearts, as we read those heavenly discourses, we seem to feel the Son of God speaking³ to us 'as a man speaketh with his friendᵃ:' His image seems slowly to rise up before us; the ideal picture gathers shape; we seem to see, yea in exalted moments we do see, limned as it were in the void before our eyes, 'the King in His beautyᵇ;' heaven and earth melt away from our rapt gaze, we spiritually behold the very Re-

ᵃ Exodus xxxiii. 11

ᵇ Isai. xxxiii. 17

---

¹ This seems a decided and somewhat noticeable characteristic of this Gospel; see, for example, ch. i. 47, ii. 24, iv. 17, 18, v. 42, vi. 15, 61, 64, xiii. 11; compare xi. 4, 15. It may be observed that in some instances, c. g. our Lord's conversation with Nicodemus, a remembrance of this characteristic will greatly assist us in understanding the true force of our Lord's words. It would certainly seem, in a few cases, as if our Lord was not so much replying to the words of the speaker, as to the thoughts which He knew were rising up within; compare Meyer, on Joh. iii. 3; Stier, Reden Jesu, Vol. IV. p. 376 sq. (Clark).

² Compare ch. iii. 16, 35 sq., v. 17 sq., vi. 57, viii. 42, x. 15, 30, xi. 42, al. It may be further observed that it is in St John's Gospel alone that we find the title μονογενὴς applied to the Eternal Son; see ch. i. 14, 18, iii. 16, 18, and comp. 1 John iv. 9.

³ In this Gospel our Lord is truly to us what the significant appellation of the inspired writer declares Him to be,—the Word. In the other Gospels our attention is mainly centered on our Lord's acts, but in this last one He speaks; see Da Costa, Four Witnesses, p. 240. It may indeed be noticed as one of the striking features of this Gospel that it makes all its characters exhibit their individuality to us by what they *say* rather than by what they do. We may recognize this kind of self-portraiture partially in the case of Nathanael (ch. i. 47 sq.) and Nicodemus (ch. iii. 1 sq.), and very distinctly in that of the woman of Samaria (ch. iv. 7 sq.) and of the man born blind (ch. ix. 1, 39). The very enemies of our Lord appear similarly before us; all their doubts (ch. viii. 22), divisions (ch. x. 19), and machinations (ch. xi. 47) are disclosed to us as it were by themselves and in the words that fell from their own lips. For some good remarks on the individualizing traits and characteristics of those who appear on the pages of St John's Gospel, see Luthardt, Das Johann. Evang. III. 2, Part I. p. 98 sq.

deemer of the world, we hear the reassuring voice, and we say, with a conviction deep as that of him whom this Gospel tells us of, "My Lord and my God[a]."

LECT. I.

[a] Joh. xx. 28

On the picture of our Lord which this Gospel presents to us[1], I am sure then I need say no more. I will only in conclusion call your attention to the mystical completeness which this Gospel gives to the evangelical history. I will only ask you to spend a moment's thought on that everlasting wisdom by which it was foreordained that a Gospel should be vouchsafed to us in which the loftiest ideal purities and glories with which we might be able to invest the Son of David, the Son of God, and the Son of Man, might receive a yet loftier manifestation, and by which the more distinctly historical pictures disclosed to us by the synoptical Evangelists might be made instinct with a quickening life, which assuredly they lack not, but which we might never have completely realized if we had not been endowed with the blessed heritage of the Gospel of St John[2].

---

[1] For some further notices and illustrations, see especially Luthardt, *Das Johann. Evang.* III. 2, p. 92 sq., and for comparisons between the pictures of our Redeemer as displayed to us in this and the three other Gospels, Lange, *Leben Jesu*, I. 7. 2, Vol. I. p. 271 sq.; compare also Da Costa, *Four Witnesses*, p. 286 sq.

[2] We may perhaps profitably close this comparison of the characteristics of the four Gospels with a brief statement of some of the distinctions which have either been above alluded to, or may be further adduced as evincing the clear individuality of each one of the inspired records. In regard of (1) the *External features and characteristics*, we are perhaps warranted in saying that (a) the *point of view* of the first Gospel is mainly Israelitic; of the second, Gentile; of the third, universal; of the fourth, Christian;— that (b) the general aspect and, so to speak, *physiognomy* of the first is mainly Oriental; of the second, Roman; of the third, Greek; of the fourth, spiritual;—that (c) the *style* of the first is stately and rhythmical; of the second, terse and precise; of the third, calm and copious; of the

LECT. I.

Conclusion.

And now I must close these meditations. Fain would I dwell on some practical applications, but the remembrance that these are Lectures rather than Sermons, and that the time is far spent, warns me to say no more. Yet I cannot part from you, my younger brethren, without simply yet earnestly urging you, ere we again meet in this church, to spend a brief hour in reviving your remembrance of the events in our Redeemer's history which conclude with the return of the Holy family to Nazareth, and precede the isolated notice of our Lord's visit to the Temple when twelve years old; for thus far my next Lecture will extend. I venture to suggest this, for I feel that you will thus be enabled to enter with a fresher interest into the meditations, into which with the help of Almighty God

fourth, artless and colloquial;—that (*d*) the most striking *characteristic* of the first is symmetry; of the second, compression; of the third, order; of the fourth, system;—that (*e*) the *thought* and *language* of the first are both Hebraistic; of the third, both Hellenistic; while in the second the thought is often Occidental though the language is Hebraistic; and in the fourth the language Hellenistic, but the thought Hebraistic. Again, (2), in respect of *Subject-matter and contents* we may say perhaps, (*a*), that in the first Gospel we have narrative; in the second, memoirs; in the third, history; in the fourth, dramatic portraiture;—(*b*) that in the first we have often the record of events in their accomplishment; in the second, events in the detail; in the third, events in their connexion; in the fourth, events in relation to the teaching springing from them;—that thus, (*c*), in the first we more often meet with the notice of impressions; in the second, of facts; in the third, of motives; in the fourth, of words spoken;—and that lastly, (*d*), the record of the first is mainly collective and often antithetical; of the second, graphic and circumstantial; of the third, didactic and reflective; of the fourth, selective and supplemental. We may, (3), conclude by saying that in respect of the *Portraiture of our Lord*, the first Gospel presents Him to us mainly as the Messiah; the second, mainly as the God-man; the third, as the Redeemer; the fourth, as the only-begotten Son of God. For illustrations of this summary the reader may be referred to the *Four Witnesses* of Da Costa, to Davidson, *Introduction to the N. T.* Vol. I.; Lange, *Leben Jesu,* I. 7. 2, Vol. I. p. 234—281; Ebrard, *Kritik der Evang. Geschichte,* § 10—39.

I hope to lead you next Sunday afternoon. Yet withal remember, I beseech you, that this is no mere investigation of chronological difficulties, no dry matter of contested annals, but involves an effort to see and feel with more freshness and reality the significance of the recorded events in the earthly life of the Eternal Son[1]. Remember that it implies a humble endeavour by the grace of the inworking Spirit to gain a more vital and personal interest in the inspired history of Him who stooped to wear the garments of our mortality, who submitted for our sakes to all the conditioning circumstances of earthly life, was touched with a sense of our infirmities, yea, as an inspired writer has told us, was pleased to learn obedience 'by the things that He suffered[a],' though Himself the King of Kings and Lord of Lords, God blessed for ever; Amen.

[a] Heb. v. 8

Such a work, if regarded under such aspects, and with such remembrances, both is and must be blessed. Such contemplations, if engaged in with a humble and loving spirit, will add a strength to your faith, which, it may be, the storm and stress of coming life will never be able successfully to weaken, and against which those doubts and difficulties which at times try the hearts of the young and inexperienced, will be found both powerless and unprevailing.

---

[1] For some excellent remarks on the unity of the Gospel-history on the one hand, and its fourfold, yet organically connected revelation of our Redeemer's life and works on the other, see especially the eloquent and thoughtful work of Dr Lange, already several times referred to, *Das Leben Jesu*, I. 7. 1, 2, Vol. 1. p. 230 sq.—a work which, we are glad to observe, has recently been translated (Clark, Edinburgh).

LECT. I.

May the grace of our Redeemer be with you; may He quicken your young hearts, may He show unto you His glorious beauty, may His image grow in your souls, and both in you and in us all may His life-giving Spirit enlighten the eyes of our understanding^a, and fill us, heart and soul and spirit, with all the fulness of God.

^a Eph. i. 18

LECTURE II.

THE BIRTH AND INFANCY OF OUR LORD.

St Luke ii. 40.

And the child grew, and waxed strong in spirit, filled with wisdom: and the grace of God was upon Him.

THE text which I have just read, brethren, forms the concluding verse of that portion of the Evangelical history to which, with God's assisting grace, I purpose directing your attention this afternoon. We may now be said to have fairly entered upon the solemn subject which I propose treating in these lectures; and we shall do well at once to address ourselves to its discussion. And that too without any further preliminary matter, as I trust that my remarks last Sunday will have so far prepared us for the sound and reverential use of the four sources of our Redeemer's history, that we need no longer delay in applying the principles which were there alluded to.

I will pause only so far to gather up the results of our foregoing meditations, as to remind you that, if our observations on the general character and relations of the four inspired records were in any degree just and reasonable, it would certainly seem clear that our present endeavour to set forth a continuous and connected life of our Master, must involve a constant recognition of two seemingly opposite modes of proceeding. On the one hand, we must regard the four holy histories as to

LECT. II.

General aspects of the present undertaking.

a great degree independent in their aims, objects, and general construction,—as marked by certain fore-ordered and providentially marked characteristics; and yet, on the other hand, we must not fail to observe that they stand in such relations to each other as may both sanction and justify our combining them in a general delineation of the chief features of our Redeemer's earthly life. While we may shrink from mere cold and sometimes forced harmonizing on this side, we must not, on that, so exaggerate seeming differences[1] as to plead exemption from the edifying task of comparing Scripture with Scripture[2], and of supplying from one inspired writer what another might have thought it meet to leave unnoticed or unexplained. Nay more, we must not shrink from noting even seeming discrepancies[3], lest we fail to learn, by a more attentive consideration of them,

[1] This, which Augustine (*de Consensu Evang.* I. 7. 10) well calls 'palmare vanitatis,' has been far too much the tendency of modern commentators and essayists, especially in Germany. We may observe this not merely in the repulsive productions of men like Strauss and his followers, but even in the commentaries of more sober and thoughtful writers. I may specify, for instance, the otherwise valuable commentary of Dr Meyer. Here we have not only the fewest possible efforts to adjust or account for differences in the order of events in the Gospel history, but only too often a tendency to represent them greater than they really are found to be; compare, for example, this writer's objectionable remarks on Luke v. 1—11, *Kommentar*, p. 263.

The results of the modern destructive school are stated fairly and clearly by Ebrard, *Kritik der Evang. Gesch.* § 114—118, p. 608; see especially p. 641.

[2] Some judicious remarks on the true Christian method of estimating, comparing, and criticizing the inspired records of the four Evangelists, will be found in the introduction to Lange's *Leben Jesu*; see especially Book I. 4. 7, Vol. I. p. 141 sq.

[3] The duty of the critic in this respect is well stated by Dr Lange in the work above referred to: 'The Evangelist,' he says, 'may certainly, nay must *appear* to contradict himself; for the appearance of such contradiction is the mark of life, depth, and freshness. Nature appears a thousand times over to con-

how they commonly arise from our ignorance of some unrecorded relations,—and how the seeming discord is due only to the Selahs and silences in the mingled strains of Evangelical harmony[1].

But let us delay no longer, for the subject before us is so extended, that it will fully occupy all our time, and so varied that it will require some adjustment to adapt it to the prescribed limits of these lectures.

As the present course of the Hulsean Lectures is limited in its duration to one year, and consequently will, at the very utmost, only afford me eight opportunities of addressing you[2], it will perhaps be best to adopt the following divisions. In the present lecture we will consider the events of the Lord's infancy. Next Sunday we will meditate on the single recorded event of our Lord's boyhood, and that portion of the history of His manhood, which commences with His baptism, and concludes with the miracle at the pool of Bethesda,—in a word, what may be roughly though conveniently termed our Lord's early *Judæan* ministry. A

Arrangement of the subject.

tradict herself. If a critic finds a difficulty in such an *appearance* of contradiction, and demands from the Gospels the precision of notaries, he clearly enough evinces his own incapability of forming a just estimate of them.' *Leben Jesu*, I. 4. 7, Vol. I. p. 144. See also some brief but good remarks on seeming discrepancies in the introduction to Chrysostom's *Homilies on St Matth.* I. p. 5 (ed. Bened.).

[1] 'But if in recounting the wonders (of the Gospel history) all did not mention the same things, but one mentioned this set of incidents and another that, do not be disturbed thereby. For if one had related everything the rest would have been superfluous; or if all had written new and peculiar matter in reference to one another there would not have appeared the present evidence of agreement.' Chrysostom, *ib.* p. 6. See further some judicious remarks in the introduction to *The Four Witnesses* of Da Costa, p. 1 sq.

[2] Owing to recent regulations, this number of Lectures has been finally reduced to six. The last two Lectures were thus not *preached*, but are added both for the sake of still maintaining some conformity to the will of the founder, and also for the sake of giving a necessary completeness to the subject.

LECT. II.

fourth and a fifth lecture may be devoted to the ministry in Galilee and the neighbouring districts; a sixth may contain a brief account of the Lord's last three journeys to or towards Jerusalem; a seventh may well be given exclusively to the events of the last passover,—that period of such momentous interest, and so replete with difficulties of combination and arrangement;—and a concluding lecture may embrace the history of the last forty days.

The miraculous Conception of our Lord; its mystery and sublimity.

In the present portion, if we leave out the commencement of St John's Gospel and the early history of the Baptist[1], the first recorded event is of an importance that cannot be over-estimated, —that single event in the history of our race that bridges over the stupendous chasm between God and man. That first event is the miraculous conception of our Redeemer[2]. It is related to us both by the first and third Evangelists[3], and by

[1] These portions of the inspired narrative are not commented on. The former belongs more to the province of dogmatical theology, the latter to the general history of our Lord's times, into neither of which our present limits and the restricted nature of our subject will now permit us to enter. The student will find an elaborate and, in most respects, satisfactory article on the Baptist, in Winer, *Realwörterb.* Vol. I. p. 585—590; and some good comments on his ministry in Greswell, *Dissert.* XIX. Vol. II. p. 148 sq.

[2] Some good remarks on this profound subject will be found in Neander, *Life of Christ*, p. 13 sq. (Bohn). The student will there find an able exposure of the mythical view, as it is called, of this sublime mystery, and brief but satisfactory answers to current objections. The main position of Neander is, that the miraculous conception was demanded *à priori*, and confirmed *à posteriori*. As regards any explanation of the special circumstances of this holy miracle, all that can be said has been said by Bp Pearson, *Creed*, Art. III. Vol. I. p. 203 (ed. Burton); see also Andrewes, *Serm.* IX. Vol. I. p. 135 sq. (A.-C. Libr.). The dignity of the conception is well touched upon by Hilary, *de Trinitate*, Book II. p. 17 (Paris 1631).

[3] The objection founded on the assumed silence of St John is wholly futile. If our view of St John's Gospel be correct (see above, p. 14), it may be fairly urged that a formal notice of an event which had been so fully related by one Evangelist and so distinctly confirmed by ano-

the latter with such an accuracy of detail, that we may bless God for having vouchsafed to us a record, which if reverently and attentively considered will be found to suggest an answer to every question that might present itself to an honest though amazed spirit. Yea, and it *is* a subject for amazement[1]. Dull hearts there may be that have never cared to meditate deeply on these mysteries of our salvation, and to which the wonder and even perplexity of nobler spirits may have seemed unreasonable or inexplicable. Such there may be: but who of higher strain, as he sees and feels the infirmities with which he is encompassed, the weakness and frailty of that flesh with which he is clothed[2], the sinfulness that

---

ther would have seemed out of place in a Gospel so constructed as that of St John. What we might have expected we meet with,—the fullest and most unquestioned statement of this divine truth (ch. i. 14, comp. ver. 13), nay more, reasoning which depends upon it (ch. iii. 6), but no historical details; see Neander, *Life of Christ*, p. 17, note (Bohn); and compare Da Costa, *Four Witnesses*, p. 286. The similarly assumed silence of St Paul (Von Ammon, *Gesch. des Lebens Jesu*, I. 4, Vol. I. p. 186) is abundantly confuted by Lange, *Leben Jesu*, II. 2. 4, Part I. pp. 72, 73.

[1] Well may Augustine say: 'Quid mirabilius virginis partu! concipit et virgo est; parit et virgo est. Creatus est de eâ quam creavit: attulit ei fecunditatem, non corrupit ejus integritatem.' *Serm.* CLXXXIX. 2, Vol. v. p. 1605 (ed. Migne). So, too, Gregory of Nazianzus, in a fine sermon on the nativity: Προελθὼν δὲ Θεὸς μετὰ τῆς προσλήψεως ἓν ἐκ δύο τῶν ἐναντίων, σαρκὸς καὶ Πνεύματος· ὧν τὸ μὲν ἐθέωσε, τὸ δὲ ἐθεώθη. Ὢ τῆς καινῆς μίξεως, ὢ τῆς παραδόξου κράσεως, ὁ ὢν γίνεται, καὶ ὁ ἄκτιστος κτίζεται, καὶ ὁ ἀχώρητος χωρεῖται διὰ μέσης ψυχῆς νοερᾶς μεσιτευούσης θεότητι καὶ σαρκὸς παχύτητι. *Orat.* XXXVIII. p. 620 (ed. Morell).

[2] 'What say you to flesh? is it meet God be manifested therein? "Without controversy" it is not. Why what is flesh? it is no mystery to tell what it is; it is dust, saith the patriarch Abraham. It is grass, saith the prophet Esay; *fœnum*, "grass cut down, and withering." It is "corruption," not corruptible, but even corruption itself, saith the Apostle Paul....We cannot choose but hold this mystery for great, and say with Augustine, *Deus; quid gloriosius? caro; quid vilius? Deus in carne; quid mirabilius?*' Andrewes, *Serm.* III. Vol. I. p. 37 (A.-C. Libr.).

seems wound round every fibre, and knit up with every joint of his perishing body,—who has truly felt all this, and not found himself at times overwhelmed with the contemplation of the mystery of Emmanuel[1],—the everlasting God manifested in, yea tabernacling in this very mortal flesh? Wild heathenism we say may have dreamed such dreams. The pagan of the West may have vaunted of his deified mortality and his brother-men ascending to the gods; the pagan of the East may have fabled of his encarnalized divinities, and of his gods descending to men[2],—but this mystery of mysteries, that the Eternal Son of the Eternal Father, He whose outgoings had been from everlasting, whose hands had laid the bases of the hills, and spread out the floods, that *He* should become incarnate, should take upon Him our nature and our infirmities,—can it be? Can such a thought have found an expression in prophecy[3]? Can it have become realized in history? Say,—can it be? Can the world produce a narrative that can make such a conception imaginable? Is there a record that can make such an event seem credible, seem

---

[1] 'Oh! the height and depth of this super-celestial mystery,' says the eloquent Bishop Hall, 'that the infinite Deity and finite flesh should meet in one subject, yet so as the humanity should not be absorbed of the Godhead, nor the Godhead contracted by the humanity, but both inseparably united; that the Godhead is not humanized, the humanity not deified, both are indivisibly conjoined; conjoined so as without confusion distinguished.' *Great Mystery of Godliness*, § 2, Vol. VIII. p. 332 (Oxf. 1837). Chrysostom has expressed very similar sentiments and with equal eloquence: see *Hom. in Matth.* II. p. 21 (ed. Bened.).

[2] This thought is well expressed and expanded by Dr Dorner in his valuable work on *the Person of Christ*, Vol. I. p. 4 sq. (ed. 2, 1845).

[3] The prophecies of the Old Testament relating to the miraculous conception, so often and so recklessly explained away or denied, will be found calmly and critically, though not in all respects satisfactorily, discussed by Hofmann, *Schriftbeweis*, II. 1. 5. 3, Vol. II. p. 54—69.

possible, we will not say to a doubting but even to a receptive and to a trustful spirit? Yea verily, blessed be God, we have that narrative, and on that narrative not only in its general outlines, but its most special details, we may rely with a confidence which every meditative reading will be found to enhance and to corroborate.

The narrative of the Conception considered generally.

Let us pause a moment to consider a few of the more striking portions of the narrative, especially from the point of view in which we are for the moment regarding it,—that of supplying the fullest conviction to every honest but anxious, every longing but inquiring heart. Does the idealizing spirit that views the transcendent event in all the circumstances of its widest universality, —that seems to recognize the mysterious adaptations of earthly dominion[1], to read the tokens of

---

[1] The state of the world at the epoch when our Lord appeared was exactly that which, according to our mere human conceptions, might seem most fitted for the reception of Christianity. Judaism, on the one hand, had lost all those external glories and prerogatives which, at an earlier period, would have prevented any recognition of the Messiah save as a national ruler and king. There would have been no Israel of God with chastened hearts and more spiritualized expectancies waiting, as we know they now were, for a truer redemption of Israel. Heathenism, on the other hand, had now gained by its contact with Judaism truer conceptions of the unity of God; and many a proselyte of the gate was there, who like the centurion of Capernaum (Luke vii. 5) loved well the nation that had taught him to kneel to the one God, and could bear to receive from that despised people a knowledge of his own and the world's salvation: compare Jost, *Geschichte des Judenthums*, III. 1. 4, Vol. I. p. 330, and Milman, *Hist. of Christianity*, ch. I. Vol. I. p. 21 sq. When we add to this the remembrance of the recent consolidation of the power of Rome (see esp. Merivale, *Hist. of Romans*, ch. XXXIX. Vol. IV. p. 383 sq.) and recognize a political centralization which could not but aid, however unwittingly and unwillingly, the pervasive influences of the new faith, we may well feel that the very appearance of Christianity, at the time when it did appear, is in itself an indirect evidence of its divine nature and truth. See some good remarks on this subject in Lange, *Leben Jesu*, II. 1. 1, p. 15 sq.; and for a fairly

LECT. II.

the fulness of the times, and to discern the longings pervading not only the chosen people[1] but the whole wide realms of the Eastern world[2]— does such a spirit, meditating thus loftily and perchance blamelessly upon the mighty coincidences of time and place and history, seek in vain for some features in the record of the incarnation of the Son of God that shall respond to such feelings? Does not the direct message from Jehovah[a], the angelic ministration[b], the operative influence of the Eternal Spirit[c], all tend to work a conviction that to the receptive heart becomes of inexpressible strength[3]? Or again, to the more humble and meek spirit that seeks only by the holy leadings of simple narrative to gain for itself a saving knowledge of the history of its own salvation, is

[a] Lk. i. 26
[b] i. 28
[c] i. 35

candid statement of the relations of Judaism to Christianity, the learned work of Jost, *Geschichte des Judenthums*, III. 3. 11, Vol. I. p. 394 sq.

[1] The gradual development of this feeling, and the circumstances which helped to promote it are well noticed by Ewald, *Geschichte Christus*', pp. 55—96.

[2] It has been recently considered doubtful whether the well-known passages from Tacitus (*Hist.* v. 13) and Suetonius (*Vespas.* 4) relating to the feeling that pervaded the whole Eastern world, and the attention that was directed to Judæa, may not have been imitated from Josephus (*Bell. Jud.* VII. 5. 4): see Neander, *Life of Christ*, p. 28, note (Bohn); and compare Whiston, *Dissert.* III., appended to his translation of Josephus, esp. Vol. III. p. 612 (Oxford, 1839). Such an imitation does not seem clearly made out: still even if in part we concede it, we have only thus far weakened the testimony from without as to consider it an acceptance of a statement made from within, because that statement was felt to be correct.

[3] 'Our own idea of Christ compels us to admit that two factors, the one natural, the other supernatural, were coefficient in His entrance into human life; and this too, although we may be unable, *à priori*, to state how that entrance was accomplished. But at this point the historical accounts come to our aid, by testifying that what our theory of the case requires, did, in fact, occur.' Neander, *Life of Christ*, p. 13 (Bohn),—a loose, but substantially correct representation of the original (*Leben Jesu Christi*, p. 15): compare Bp Taylor, *Life of Christ*, I. *ad* sect. I. 4, Vol. I. p. 28 (Lond. 1836).

there not here disclosed, in the many notices of the purely human and outward relations of those whom the opening of the Gospel brings before us, those artless traits of historic truth that on some minds work such a fulness of conviction? Yes, let us take the very objections of adversaries or sceptics, and see in this portion of St Luke's Gospel the more direct agencies of the spiritual world, and in the short notice of St Matthew's Gospel their more mediate workings[1],—let us accept the statement, and see in it only one more proof, if proof be needed, of the diverse forms in which Evangelical Truth is presented to the receptive mind, let us recognize in it only one more example of the varied aspects of the manifold wisdom of God.

Let us now substantiate the foregoing remarks by a brief notice of the details of the inspired history.

The narrative of the Conception considered in its details.

What a vivid truth, speaking humanly, there is in the narrative of St Luke! With what a marvellous aptitude to human infirmity do things, divine and human, mingle with each other in ever illustrative and ever confirmatory combinations.

---

[1] See, for example, Von Ammon, *Gesch. des Lebens Jesu*, I. 5, Vol. I. p. 194. We do not in these lectures notice, nor do we consider it either useful or edifying to notice, the repulsive opinions of writers like Strauss (*Leben Jesu*), Weisse (*die Evang. Geschichte*), or Gfrörer (*Geschichte des Urchristenthums*): their general tendencies are so simply destructive, their unhappy criticisms so almost judicially infatuated, and their progressions in doubt and denials (see Ebrard, *Kritik der Ev. Gesch.* § 6, 7) such melancholy instances of a very μεθοδεία πλάνης (Ephes. iv. 14), that we may well leave them to themselves, and to their own mutual confutations. Writers of the character of the one above alluded to may however sometimes be profitably referred to, as evincing, as Von Ammon especially does in respect of this narrative (see pp. 190, 191), what an amount of unhappy *effort* it takes to resist the impression of its vital truth which the evangelical history makes upon doubting minds that will consent to be reasonable and candid.

LECT. II.

With what striking persuasiveness do mysteries seemingly beyond the grasp of thought blend lovingly with the simplest elements, and become realizable by the teachings of the homely relations of humble and sequestered life. With what a noble yet circumstantial simplicity,—a simplicity that in the language no less than in the facts related bewrays the record of her who saw and believed[1],—is the opening story told of man's redemption! The angel Gabriel, he who stood among the highest of the angelic hierarchy, and whose ministrations, if it be not too bold a thing to affirm, appear to have been specially *Messianic*, just as those of Raphael might have pertained to individual need, and those of Michael to judicial power[2],—that blessed Spirit, who a few months before had been sent to announce the future birth of the forerunner[a], is now sent from God to a rude

[a] Lk. i. 11

---

[1] See Lange, *Leben Jesu*, II. 2. 6, Part I. p. 93 sq. We can perhaps hardly go so far with this able writer as positively to find in the recital of the events a diction that belongs rather to a woman than to a man; but when we mark the specialities of the narrative, the preservation of the exact expressions of the sacred canticles, and above all the tone of artless reality, which pervades the whole, we seem perfectly justified in believing that we have here, partly perhaps in substance, partly in precise terms, a record that came to St Luke mediately or immediately, from the lips of the Virgin herself,—her Son's first evangelist. And with such a belief the peculiarities of the diction seem fully to coincide. While throughout we can trace the hand of St Luke (see esp. Gersdorf, *Beiträge*, p. 160 sq.), we can also see in the transition from the studied dedication to the simple structure of the ancient Scriptures just that change which a faithful incorporation of the recital of another would be certain to introduce: compare Mill, *on Pantheistic Principles*, Part II. p. 23 sq.

[2] This remark (valeat quantum) is due to Lange (*Leben Jesu*, II. 2. 2, Vol. II. p. 46), whose whole chapter on the subject of angelic ministrations deserves perusal. For further references on the nature of angels, see notes *on Eph.* i. 21; and for a most able confutation of the arguments against this portion of the sacred narrative founded on angelic appearances, Mill, *Obss. on Pantheistic Principles*, Part II. 4, p. 52 sq.

and lone village in the hills of Galilee, Nazareth the disesteemed[1], and to a betrothed virgin[2] whose name was Mary. Of the early history of that highly favoured one we know nothing. Yet without borrowing one thought from the legendary notices of apocryphal narrative[3], it does not seem a baseless fancy to recognize in her one of those pure spirits that in seclusion and loneliness were looking and longing for the theocratic King, and that deeply imbued, as we see the Virgin must have been, both with the letter and with the spirit of the Old Testament[a], were awaiting the evolution of the highest of all its transcendent prophecies. Rapt as such a one might well have been in devotion or in Messianic meditation[4], she sees before her, at no legendary spring-side[5], but

[a] Luke i. 46—55

---

[1] See Stanley, *Palestine*, chap. X. 1, p. 361 (ed. 2), and compare John i. 46, and the notes of Meyer *in loc.* The savage act recorded by St Luke (ch. iv. 29) is a good commentary on the meaning of Nathanael's question. For an interesting description of Nazareth, especially considered with reference to the Gospel history, see Robinson, *Palestine*, Vol. II. p. 333 sq. (ed. 2).

[2] 'So it was that the Virgin was betrothed, lest honourable marriage might be disreputed, and seem inglorious, by a positive rejection from any participation in the honour.' Taylor, *Life of Christ*, I. ad sect. I. 6, Vol. I. p. 29 (Lond. 1836). Other, and some of them singular reasons, are assigned by the older writers: see Spanheim, *Dub. Evang.* Part I. p. 116. The use of the word μεμνηστευμένην is investigated with much learning by Bynæus, *de Natali Jes. Chr.* X. p. 28 sq.

[3] The history of the Virgin is told at great length in the *Protevangelium* of James, and in the so-called Gospels *de Ortu* (Pseudo-Matth.) and *de Nativitate Mariæ*: see Tischendorf, *Evang. Apocrypha* (Lips. 1853); and for a connected history formed out of these apocryphal writings, the laborious work of Hofmann (R), *das Leben Jesu nach den Apocryphen* (Leipz. 1851).

[4] Bp Taylor censures any speculation of this kind; but it seems, to say the least, harmless, and not inconsistent with the meditative spirit which reveals itself in the Virgin's inspired canticle. Bengel hints at the time as *evening*, comparing Dan. ix. 21.

[5] Compare *Protevang.* cap. 11, *Hist. de Nat. Mariæ*, cap. 9, and compare Hofmann, *Leben Jesu*, p. 74. The expressions of inspired narrative (ver. 28) seem in this particular to justify the statement made in

LECT. II.

ᵃ Lk. i. 28

ᵇ i. 28.

as the words of the Evangelist seem rather to imply, in her own humble abodeᵃ, the divinely-sent messenger, and hears a salutation which expressed in the terms in which it was expressed,—" Hail highly-favoured one! the Lord is with theeᵇ,"— and coming as it did from an angel's lips, must well have troubled that meek spirit and cast it into awe and perplexity¹.

Self-evident truth of the narrative.

What persuasive truth there is in the nature of the terms in which the announcement is conveyed. To that highly favoured one that perchance had long communed in stillness on the prophecies of the Messianic kingdom, to her is Jesus the Son of the Highest portrayed in that form, which partially Israelitic in general outline, yet Christian in essence², must have begun to work in her the most lively conviction. Yet how characteristic is the question, "How shall this beᶜ?" the question not of outwardly expressed doubt like that of Zachariasᵈ, or of an inwardly felt sense of impossibility like that of Abrahamᵉ and Sarahᶠ in the old

ᶜ i. 34

ᵈ i. 18
ᵉ Gen. xvii. 17
ᶠ Gen. xviii. 12

Suidas s.v. 'Ιησοῦς, where the Virgin is related as specifying,—εἰσελθὼν ἐν ᾧ ἤμην οἰκήματι. The spring in question is alluded to and briefly described by Stanley, *Palestine*, p. 362 (ed. 2).

¹ The addition of the participle ἰδοῦσα in the received text, though not without great external support (see Tischendorf *in loc.*), must still be considered as somewhat doubtful. Even if retained we may perhaps more naturally refer the troubled feelings of the Virgin *simply* to the terms in which the salutation was couched; observe the specific ἐπὶ τῷ λόγῳ, and the concluding clause, καὶ διελογίζετο ποταπὸς εἴη ὁ ἀσπασμὸς οὗτος.

² We seem to recognize this distinction in the expressions of ver. 33.—If, on the one hand, the heavenly messenger declares, in continuation of the image at the concluding part of the former verse, that the Eternal Son 'shall reign over the house of Jacob for ever;' he, on the other hand, seems to *imply* by the very seeming repetition, 'And of His kingdom there shall be no end,' a reference to a still more universal dominion: comp. Dan. vii. 14, and see Bynæus, *de Natali Jes. Chr.* XXXVI. p. 117 sq.

and typical past, but of a child-like innocence, that sought to realize to itself, in the very face of seeming impossibilities the full assurance of its own blessedness. No, there was no lack of real faith in that question[1]. It was a question to which the heavenly messenger was permitted to return a most explicit answer, and to confirm by a most notable example, even that of her kinswoman Elisabeth[a], that with God no word was impossible[2], —no promise that was not to receive its completest and most literal fulfilment.

[a] Lk. i. 36

With these words of the angel all seems to have become clear to her in regard of the wonder-working power of God; much too must have already seemed clear to her on the side of man. With the rapid foreglance of thought she must have seen in the clouded future, scorn, dereliction, the pointed finger of a mocking and uncharitable

---

[1] The utmost that can be said is that the Virgin felt the seeming impossibility, and that in avowing the feeling she sought for that further assurance which she also felt would not be withheld, and would at once allay her doubts. Even the following excellent remarks of Jackson attribute to the Virgin somewhat more mistrust than the words and the case seem to imply: "It is far from my disposition at any time, or my purpose at this, to urge further to aggravate the infirmity of a vessel so sanctified, elect, and precious: and I am persuaded the Evangelist did not so much intend to disparage hers, as to confirm her belief, by relating her doubtful question, and the angel's reply; the one being but Sarah's mistrust refined with maidenly modesty, the other Sarah's check mitigated and qualified by the angel." *Creed*, Book VII. 1. 12, Vol. VI. p. 209 (Oxf. 1844). The earlier commentators, though perhaps they slightly overpress the πῶς in the Virgin's question (ἐπιζητοῦσα τὸν τρόπον τοῦ πράγματος, Theoph.), have in most cases rightly appreciated the true state of feeling which prompted the question: comp. Lange, *Leben Jesu*, II. 2. 3, Part I. p. 66.

[2] It is usual to consider ῥῆμα in this text as co-extensive in meaning with the Hebrew דָּבָר and as implying 'thing,' 'matter,' (Wordsworth *in loc.*). This is now rightly called in question by the most accurate interpreters; the meaning is simply as stated by Euthymius,—πᾶν ὃ λέγει, πᾶν ὃ ἐπαγγέλλεται: see Meyer, *Komment. über Luk.* p. 203.

LECT. II.

world, calumny, shame, death. But what was a world's scorn or a world's persecution to those words of promise? Faith sustains that possible shrinking from more than mortal trial, and turns it into meekest resignation. "Behold the handmaid of the Lord; be it unto me according to thy word." From that hour the blessed Virgin seems ever to appear before us in that character, which the notices of the Gospels so consistently adumbrate[1], meek and pensive, meditative and resigned, blessed with joys no tongue can tell, and yet even in the first hours of her blessedness beginning to feel one edge of the sword[a], that was to pierce through her loving and submissive heart.

[a] Lk. ii. 35

Journey of the Virgin to Elisabeth.

The last words of the miraculous message seem to prepare us for the next event recorded by the Evangelist,—the hasty journey of the Virgin to her aged relative Elisabeth[2] in the hill-country of Judæa: "and Mary arose and went into the hill-country, with haste, unto a city of Juda[b]." But why this haste? Why this lengthened, and, as

[b] Lk. i. 39

---

[1] The character of the blessed Virgin, as far as it can be inferred from the Scriptures, has been touched upon by Niemeyer, *Character*, Vol. I. p. 54 sq. Some thoughtful notices, as derived from St John's Gospel, will be found in Luthardt, *das Johann. Evang.* Vol. I. p. 114 sq.

[2] It seems impossible to state confidently the nature of this relationship. It has been thought possible that the Virgin may have been of the tribe of Levi, and thus connected with Elisabeth, who we know was of that tribe: so the apocryphal document called the *Testamentum xii. Patrum*, § 2, 7, and Faustus Manichæus, as referred to by Augustine, *contra Faust. Manich.* XXIII. 9, Vol. VIII. p. 471 (ed. Migne). The more probable opinion is, that the Virgin was of the tribe of Judah, and that the relationship with Elisabeth arose from some intermarriage. Such intermarriages between members of the tribe of Levi and members of other tribes can be shown to have occurred in earlier periods of sacred history (comp. 2 Chron. xxii. 11); and in these later periods might have been far from uncommon: see Bynæus, *de Natali Chr.* I. 1. 47, p. 141; and comp. *Mishna*, Tract, 'Kiddushin,' IV. 1 sq. Vol. III. p. 378 sq. (ed. Surenhus.).

far as we can infer from national custom[1], unusual journey in the case of a young and secluded maiden? Are we to believe, with a recent and eloquent writer of a life of our Lord, that it was in consequence of a communication on the part of the Virgin and a subsequent rejection on the part of Joseph[2]? Are we to do such wrong to both our Lord's earthly parents? Are we to make that righteous son of Jacob the first Ebionite? Are we to believe that the blessed Virgin thus strangely threw off that holy and pensive reserve, which, as I have remarked, seems her characteristic throughout the Gospel history? It cannot be. That visit was not to receive consolation for wrong and unkindness from man, but to confer with a wise heart on transcendent blessings from God, which the unaided spirit even of Mary of Nazareth might not at first be able completely to grasp and to realize. And to whom could she go so naturally as to one towards whom the wonder-working power of God had been so signally displayed? Nay, does not the allusion to her "kinswoman Elisabeth[a]," in the angel's concluding words, [a] Lk. i. 36

---

[1] Passages have been cited from Philo, *de Legg. Spec.* III. 31, Vol. I. p. 327 (ed. Mangey), and *Talm. Hieros.*, Tract, 'Chetuboth,' VII. 6, which would seem to imply that such journeys in the case of virgins were contrary to general custom. 'The journey,' says Lange, 'was not quite in accordance with Old Testament decorum: the deep realities of the cross, however, give a freedom in the spirit of the New.' *Leben Jesu*, Part I. p. 85.

[2] See Lange, *Leben Jesu*, I. 2. 5, Part I. p. 84 sq.,—fully and satisfactorily answered by Ebrard, *Kritik der Ev. Gesch.* § 45, p. 214 sq. There seems no sufficient reason for placing, with Alford and others, what is recorded in Matth. i. 18—25 before this journey. The discovery noticed in Matth. i. 18 (εὑρέθη δὲ εἶπε διὰ τὸ ἀπροσδόκητον. Euthym.) and the events which followed would seem much more naturally to have taken place after the Virgin's return: so rightly August. *de Consensu Evang.* II. 17, Vol. III. p. 1081 (ed. Migne); compare Tischendorf, *Synops. Evang.* p. xxi.

LECT. II.

suggest the very quarter to which she was to turn for further spiritual support, and for yet more accumulated verification? To her then the Virgin at once hastens. A few days[1] would bring the unlooked-for visitant to the 'city of Juda[a]'— whether the nearer village which tradition still points to as the home of Zacharias and Elisabeth[2], or the more remote town of Juta, or perhaps, more probably, ancient and priestly Hebron[3], which Jewish tradition has fixed upon as the birth-place of the last and greatest scion of the old dispensation[4]. There she finds, and

[a] Lk. i. 39

---

[1] If Hebron (see below) be considered the Virgin's destination, the distance could not have been much short of 100 English miles, and would probably have taken at least four days. We learn from Dr Robinson's *Itinerary* that the time from Hebron to Jerusalem, with camels, was in his case 8h. 15m., and from Jerusalem to Nazareth, with mules, 29h. 45m. The rate of travelling with the former is estimated at about two geographical miles an hour, and with the latter somewhat less than three; see Robinson's *Palestine*, Vol. II. pp. 568, 574 (ed. 2). A learned dissertation on the rate of a day's journey will be found in Creswell, *Dissertations*, Vol. IV. p. 525 sq. (ed. 2).

[2] Now called Ain Karim, and a short distance from Jerusalem. Its claims are strongly supported by Dr Thomson in his excellent work, *The Land and the Book* (Vol. II. p. 537), and seem to rest mainly on the concurrent traditions of the Greek and Latin Churches: see, however, below, note 4.

[3] This last supposition, which is that of Grotius, Lightfoot, and others, is perhaps slightly the most probable, as Hebron appears to have been preeminently one of the cities of the Priests: see Josh. xxi. 11; and comp. Lightfoot, *Hor. Hebr. in Luc.* i. 39, Vol. II. p. 386 (Lond. 1684). The second supposition is due to Reland (*Palæst.* p. 870), and is adopted by Robinson (*Palestine*, Vol. II. p. 206, ed. 2), who identifies it with the modern Yūtta. The supposition that 'Ιούδα is only a corrupted form, by a softer pronunciation, of 'Ιούτα (Reland), is highly questionable; no trace of such a reading occurs in any of the ancient manuscripts.

[4] See Otho, *Lex. Rabbin.* p. 324, and compare Joshua xxi. 11, where Hebron is specially defined as being 'in the hill-country of Judah.' This general definition of locality is perhaps slightly less suitable to the first-mentioned place, Ain Karim, which though in the uplands of Judæa is scarcely in that part which seems commonly to have been known as 'the hill-country.' Sepp (*Leben Chr.* Vol. II. p. 8) cites *Talm. Hieros.*

there, as St Luke especially notices, she *salutes*[a] the future mother of the Baptist. That salutation perchance was of a nature that served, under the inspiration of the Spirit, in a moment to convey all. Elisabeth, yea and the son of Elisabeth, felt the deep significance of that greeting[1]. The aged matron at once breaks forth into a mysterious welcome of holy joy, and with a loud voice[b], the voice of loftiest spiritual exaltation, she blesses[c] the chosen one who had come under the shadow of her roof, adding that reassurance which seems to supply us with the clue to the right understanding of the whole, 'and blessed is she that believed: for there shall be a performance of those things which were told her from the Lord[d].'

[a] Lk. i. 4
[b] ver. 42
[c] ver. 42
[d] ver. 45

We need not pause on this inspired greeting and on the exalted hymn of praise uttered in response by the Virgin, save to protest against the discreditable, and, to use the mildest term, the unreasonable attempts that have been made to throw doubt on the credibility of the sacred narrative, by appealing to the improbability of these so-called lyrical effusions[2] on the part of Mary and Elisabeth. Lyrical effusions! What! are we to say that this strange and unlooked-for meeting on the part of the mother of the

Internal truthfulness of the two inspired canticles.

'Schevith,' fol. 38, 4,—'Quodnam est montanum Judææ? mons regalis.'

[1] It has been well, though perhaps somewhat fancifully said by Euthymius: 'Ὁ μὲν Χριστὸς ἐφθέγξατο διὰ τοῦ στόματος τῆς ἰδίας μητρός· ὁ δὲ Ἰωάννης ἤκουσε διὰ τῶν ὤτων τῆς οἰκείας μητρός, καὶ ἐπιγνοὺς ὑπερφυῶς τὸν ἑαυτοῦ δεσπότην ἀνεκήρυξεν αὐτὸν τῷ σκιρτήματι. Comment. in Luc. I. 41.

[2] Compare Schleiermacher, *Essay on St Luke*, p. 24,—well and completely answered by Dr Mill in his admirable comments on these inspired hymns: see *Observations on Pantheistic Principles*, Part II. 3, p. 39 sq.

LECT. II.

Forerunner and the mother of the Redeemer was as common-place and prosaic as that of any two matrons of Israel that might have met unexpectedly under the terebinths[1] of Hebron? Are we so utterly to believe in all the modern Epicurean views of the history of our race as to conceive it possible that the greatest events connected with it were unmarked by all circumstances of higher spiritual exaltation? If there be only that grain of truth in the Evangelical history that our adversaries may be disposed to concede; if there be any truth in those ordinary psychological laws, to which, when it serves their purpose, they are not slow to appeal,—then beyond all doubt both Elisabeth and the Virgin could not be imagined to have met in any way less striking than that which is recorded; their words of greeting could have been none other than those we find assigned to them by the Evangelist[2]. Every accent in the salutation of the elder matron is true to the principles of our common nature when subjected to the highest influences; every cadence of the Virgin's hymn is in most life-like accordance with all we know of the speaker, and with all we can imagine of the circumstances of this momentous meeting. No

[1] Kitto, *Cycl.* s. v. 'Alah.'

[2] 'Such a vision of coming power and light and majesty as these hymns indicate,—a picture so vivid as to the blessedness of the approaching reign, so indistinct and void as to the means by which that blessedness was to be realized,—in which, while the view of faith is so concentrated on the Source of salvation then initially manifested, the whole detail of His acts and the particulars of His redemption continue closely wrapped up in the figure and symbol which represented them in the ancient dispensation,—such a vision could belong only to the particular position assigned to it, in the boundary of the old and new covenants.' Mill, *Observations*, Part II. 3, p. 51.

verily! let us not hesitate to express our full and hearty conviction that the words we have here are no collection of Scriptural phrases, no artful composition of an imaginative or credulous writer, but the very words that fell from the lips of Mary of Nazareth, words which the rapture of the moment and the inspiration of the Holy Ghost alike called forth and alike imprinted indelibly on the memory both of her that spake and her that listened[1]. All speaks truth, life and reality. On the one hand the diction of the Old Testament that pervades this sublime canticle, the reminiscences perchance of the hymn of Hannah, type of her who spake; on the other hand, the conscious allusions to mysterious blessings that Hannah never knew,—all place before us as in a portraiture of most living truth the rapt maiden of Nazareth pouring forth her stored-up memories of history and prophecy in one full stream of Messianic joyfulness and praise.

After a few months' sojourn with Elisabeth the Virgin returns[2], and then, or soon after it, came the trial of faith to the righteous Joseph.

Return of the Virgin, and the revelation to Joseph.

---

[1] Even without specially ascribing to the Virgin, as indeed we fairly might do, that spiritually strengthened power of recollection which was promised to the Apostles of her Son (John xiv. 26), we may justly remind our opponents that the rhythmical character of these canticles would infallibly impress them on the minds of both the speakers with all that peculiar force and vividness which, we must often observe, metre does in our own cases: comp. Mill, *Observations*, p. 42.

[2] It has been doubted whether the notices of time may not lead us to suppose that the Virgin staid with Elisabeth till the birth of the Baptist, and that St Luke has specified the return of the Virgin in the place he has done merely to connect closely the notices of her journey and her return: see Wieseler, *Chron. Synops.* I. 3, p. 151. There is some plausibility in the supposition; but on the whole it seems more natural to conceive that the events took place in the order in which they are described: comp. Greswell, *Prolegomena*, Cap. IV. p. 178.

LECT. II.

Different form of the divine messages.

ᵃ Mat. i. 20

ᵇ ver. 21

This St Matthew relates to us briefly, but with some suggestive and characteristic marks of living truth to which we may for a moment advert.

How very striking is the fact that while to the Virgin the heavenly communication is made directly by an angel, the communication to the handicraftsman of Galilee[1] is made by means of a dream of the nightᵃ. How suggestive is it that while to the loftier spirit of Mary the name of Jesus is revealed with all the prophetic associations of more than David's glories,—to Joseph, perchance the aged Joseph[2], who might have long seen and realized his own spiritual needs, and the needs of those around him, it is specially said, 'thou shalt call His name Jesus: *for He shall save His people from their sins*ᵇ.' Surely, brethren, such things cannot be cunningly devised; such things must work and ought to work conviction; such things must needs make us feel, and feel with truth, that this and the

---

[1] Chrysostom notices the different nature of the heavenly communications, assigning however what scarcely seems the true reason,—the faith of Joseph (πιστὸς ἦν ὁ ἀνήρ, καὶ οὐκ ἐδεῖτο τῆς ὄψεως ταύτης). If we may venture to assign a reason it would rather seem referable, first, to the difference of the subjects of the two revelations—that to the Virgin needing the most distinct external attestation (Euthym.); secondly, to some difference in the respective natures of Joseph and Mary, and in their powers of receiving and appreciating divine communications: comp. Lange, *Leben Jesu*, II. 2. 5, Part I. p. 89.

[2] Without referring to the apocryphal writers, or seeking to specify with the exactness of Epiphanius (πρεσβύτης ὀγδοήκοντα ἐτῶν πλείω ἢ ἐλάσσω, *Hær.* LI. 10), it may perhaps be said that such seems to have been the prevailing opinion of the early Church. That he died in the lifetime of our Lord has been justly inferred from the absence of his name in those passages in the Gospels where allusion is made to the Virgin and the Lord's brethren: see Blunt, *Veracity of Evangelists*, § 8, p. 38; and for notices and ref. as to the supposed age of Joseph at our Lord's birth, see the curious but often very instructive work of Hofmann, *Leben Jesu nach den Apocryphen*, § 10, p. 62.

following holy chapters, so carped at by the doubting spirits both of earlier and of later days,— are verily what the Church has ever held them to be, the special, direct, and undoubted revelations of the Eternal Spirit of God [1].

And now the fulness of time was come. By one of those mysterious workings whereby God makes the very worldliness of man bring about the completion of His own heavenly counsels, the provincial taxing or enrolment of the persons or estates [2] of all that were under the Roman sway—a taxing almost proved by independent historical induction to have been made even as

Journey to Bethlehem, and taxing under Quirinus.

---

[1] It is painful to notice the hardihood with which the genuineness of these chapters has been called in question even by some of the better class of critics; see, for example, Norton, *Genuineness of Gospels*, Note A, § 5, Vol. I. p. 204 sq. When we remember (1) that they are contained in every manuscript, uncial or cursive, and in every version, eastern or western, that most of the early Fathers cite them, and that early enemies of Christianity appealed to them (Orig. *Cels.* I. 38, II. 32)— when we observe (2) the obvious connexion between the beginning of ch. iii. and the end of ch. ii., and between ch. iv. 13 and ii. 23,—and when we remark (3) the exact accordance of diction with that of the remaining chapters of the Gospel,— it becomes almost astonishing that even *à priori* prejudice should not have abstained at any rate from so hopeless a course as that of impugning the genuineness of these chapters. To urge that these chapters were wanting in the mutilated and falsified Gospel of the Ebionites (Epiph. *Hær.* XXX. 13), or that they were cut away by the heretical Tatian (Theodoret, *Hær. Fab.* I. 20), is really to concede their genuineness, and to bewray the reason why it was impugned. For additional notices and arguments, see Griesbach, *Epimetron ad Comment. Crit.* p. 47 sq.; Gersdorf, *Beiträge*, p. 38; and Patritius, *de Evangeliis*, Quæst. VIII. Vol. I. p. 29 sq.

[2] This point is so doubtful and debateable that I prefer adopting this more general form of expression: compare Wieseler, *Chron. Synops.* I. 2, p. 75 sq., and Greswell, *Dissert.* No. XIV. Vol. I. p. 541 sq. On the general lexical distinction between ἀπογραφή and ἀποτίμησις no great reliance can be placed: in Joseph. *Ant.* XVII. 13. 5, XVIII. 1. 1, the words appear used interchangeably; see Wieseler, *l. c.*, and Meyer *in loc.* This much may perhaps be said, that if it was at first only an enrolment *per capita*, it was one that had and perhaps was perfectly well known to have a prospective reference to property.

LECT. II.

ᵃ Lk. ii. 2
ᵇ ver. 4

St Luke relates it[a], during the presidency of Cyrenius[1]—brings the descendants of David to David's own city[b]...Idle and mischievous doubts have sought to question the accuracy of this portion of the Evangelical history, to which we can here pause only to return the briefest an-

---

[1] Without entering at length into this vexed question, we may remark for the benefit of the general reader, that the simple and grammatical meaning of the words, as they appear in all the best MSS. [B. alone omits ἡ before ἀπογραφή], must be this,—'this taxing took place as a first one while Cyrenius was governor of Syria;' and that the difficulty is to reconcile this with the assertion of Tertullian (*contr. Marc.* IV. 19), that the taxing took place under Sentius Saturninus, and with the apparent historical fact that Quirinus did not become President of Syria till nine or ten years afterwards; see the *Cenotaphia Pisana* of Cardinal Norisius, Dissert. II., and the authorities in Greswell, *Dissertations*, No. XIV. Vol. I. p. 446 sq. (ed. 2). There are apparently only *two* sound modes of explaining the apparent contradiction (I dismiss the mode of regarding πρώτη as equivalent to προτέρα as forced and artificial), either by supposing, (a) that ἡγεμονεύοντος is to be taken in a general and not a special sense, and to imply the duties of a commissioner extraordinary,—a view perhaps best and most ably advocated by the Abbé Sanclemente, *de Vulg. Æræ Dionys. Emend* Book IV. ch. 2, but open to the objection arising from the special and localizing term τῆς Συρίας (see Meyer, *Komment. über Luk.* p. 221); or by supposing, (b) that under historical circumstances imperfectly known to us, Quirinus was either *de facto* or *de jure* President of Syria, exactly as St Luke seems to specify. In favour of this latter supposition we have the thrice-repeated assertion of Justin Martyr (Apol. I. § 34, 46, *Trypho,* § 78), that Quirinus *was* President at the time in question, and the interesting fact recently brought to light by Zumpt (*Commentationes Epigraphicæ,* Part II. Berl. 1844), that owing to Cilicia, when separated from Cyprus, being united to Syria, Quirinus, as governor of the first-mentioned province, was really also governor of the last-mentioned,—whether in any kind of association with Saturninus (see Wordsw. *in loc.*) or otherwise, can hardly be ascertained,—and that his subsequent more special connexion with Syria led his earlier and apparently brief connexion to be thus accurately noticed. This last view, to say the least, deserves great consideration, and has been adopted by Merivale, *Hist. of Romans,* Vol. IV. p. 457. The treatises and discussions on this subject are extremely numerous. Those best deserving consideration are perhaps, Greswell, *Dissert.* No. XIV.; Huschke, *über den zur Zeit der Geburt Jes. Chr. gehaltenen Census,* Bresl. 1840; Wieseler, *Chron. Synops.* p. 73 sq. (in these πρώτη is explained away); and Patritius, *de Evangeliis,* Dissert. XVIII. Book III. p. 161, where (a) is advocated.

swers[1]. But this I will presume to say, that I feel certain no fair and honest investigator can study the various political considerations connected with this difficult question, without ultimately coming to the conclusion, not only that the account of St Luke is reconcileable with contemporary history, but that it is confirmed by it in a manner most striking and most persuasive. When we remember that the kingdom of Herod was not yet formally converted into a Roman province, and yet was so dependent upon the imperial city[2] as to be practically amenable to all its provincial edicts, how very striking it is to find,—in the first place, that a taxing took place at a time when such a general edict can be proved to have been in force[3]; and, in the next place, to find that that taxing in Judæa is incidentally described as having taken place according to the yet recognized customs of the country,—that it was, in fact, essentially imperial and Roman in origin, and yet Herodian and Jewish in form. How strictly, how minutely consistent is it with actual historical relations to

---

[1] The main objections that have been urged against this portion of St Luke's narrative are well examined and convincingly refuted by Wieseler, *Chron. Synops.* I. 2, pp. 75—122. The most important work for general reference on the historical and political circumstances connected with this event, beside the above work of Wieseler, is that of Huschke, *über den zur Zeit, u. s. w.* referred to in the foregoing note.

[2] See Wieseler, *Chron. Synops.* I. 2, p. 93 sq. Passages which prove the dependence of Judæa, especially as tributary to the Roman government, are cited by Greswell, *Dissert.* No. XXIII. Vol. II. p. 375. For further facts and references, see Winer, *RWB.* Art. 'Judäa,' Vol. I. p. 630.

[3] See the *Monumentum Ancyranum*, as cited and commented on by Wieseler, *Chron. Synops.* p. 90 sq., and compare Bynæus, *de Natali Jes. Chr.* I. 3, p. 300; Spanheim, *Dub. Evang.* No. VIII. Vol. II. p. 162.

find that Joseph, who under purely Roman law might, *perhaps*, have been enrolled at Nazareth[1], is here described by the Evangelist as journeying to be enrolled at the town of his forefathers, "because he was of the house and lineage[2] of David[a]." This accordance of the sacred narrative with the perplexed political relations of the intensely national, yet all but subject Judæa is so exact and so convincing, that we may even profess ourselves indebted to scepticism for having raised a question to which an answer may be given at once so fair, so explicit, and so conclusive. It seems almost idle to pause further on this portion of the narrative and to seek for reasons why the Virgin accompanied Joseph in this enforced journey to the city of his fathers[3]. Is

[a] Lk. ii. 4

---

[1] This is the objection stated in its usual form; but it seems very doubtful if even on merely general historical data it can be substantiated. In fact Huschke (*über den Cens.* p. 116 sq.) has apparently demonstrated the contrary, and proved that in every Roman census each individual was enrolled where he had his 'forum originis.' This, however, need not be pressed, as the journey of Joseph is so much more plausibly attributed to the Jewish form in accordance with which the census was conducted: comp. Bynæus, *de Natali Jes. Chr.* I. 3, p. 337, and a good article by Winer, *RWB.* 'Schatzung,' Vol. II. p. 398—401.

[2] The terms here used, οἶκος and πατριά, seem to be specially and exactly chosen. The latter is used with reference to the מִשְׁפָּחוֹת or *gentes*, which traced their origin to the twelve patriarchs, the former to the בֵּית אָבוֹת or *familiæ*, of which these latter were composed: see Winer, *RWB.* Art. 'Stämme,' Vol. II. p. 513 sq.

[3] If the census had been purely Roman in its form it would seem that the presence of the Virgin would certainly not have been needed, the giving in of the names of women and children being considered sufficient: comp. Dionys. Halic. IV. 15: Huschke, *über den Cens.* p. 121. As, however, in accordance with the view taken in the text, it is to be considered rather as *Jewish* in form, the presence of Mary is still less to be accounted for on any purely legal reasons. The favourite hypothesis that she was an heiress, and possessor of a real estate at Bethlehem, and so legally bound to appear (Olsh. *in loc.*), is now generally and, as it would seem, rightly given up: see Winer, *RWB.* Art. 'Schatzung,' Vol. II. p. 401.

it positively necessary to ascribe to her some inheritance which required her presence at the enrolment at Bethlehem? Is it really not enough for us that St Luke relates that she *did* take this journey; and is it so strange that at that time of popular gatherings, and perhaps popular excitement[1], she should brave the exhaustion of a long journey, rather than lose the protection of one to whom she must have been bound by ties of the holiest nature, and who shared with her the knowledge of a mystery that had been sealed in silence since the foundations of the world? On such subordinate and bootless inquiries we need, I am sure, delay no longer.

And now the mysterious hour, which an old apocryphal writer has described with such striking yet such curious imagery[2], was nigh at hand. Very soon after the arrival at Bethlehem, perchance on the self-same night, in one of the limestone caverns, —for I see no reason for rejecting the statement of one who was born little more than a century

The Nativity and its attendant circumstances.

---

[1] Compare the sensible remarks of Wieseler, *Chron. Synops.* p. 128.

[2] The sort of pause, as it were, in all things that marked this most momentous period in the world's history is thus curiously described in the *Protevangelium Jacobi*, cap. 18: 'And I Joseph was walking, and yet was not walking; and I looked up into the sky, and I saw the sky in amazement; and I looked up to the pole of heaven, and I saw it standing still, and the birds of the air in tranquil calm; and I directed my gaze on the earth, and I saw a bowl-like table, and labouring men around it, and their hands were in the bowl, and they who had meat in their mouths were not eating, and they that were taking up food raised it not up, and they that were bringing it up to their mouths, were not bringing it up; but the countenances of all were directed upwards. And I saw sheep in the act of being driven, and they were standing still; and the shepherd was raising his hand to smite them, and his arm remained aloft. And I gazed on the torrent-course of a river, and I beheld the kids lowering their heads towards it, and not drinking, and all things in their courses for the moment suspended' (ed. Tisch. pp. 33, 34). Compare Hofmann, *Leben Jesu*, p. 110.

LECT. II.

afterwards and not forty miles from the same spot[1],—in one of the caverns in that narrow ridge of long grey hill on which stands the city of David[2], was the Redeemer born into a world that rejected Him even in His mother's womb.

How brief and how simple are the words that relate these homely circumstances of the Lord's Nativity. How surely does the mother's recital and the mother's stored-up memories come forth in the artless touches of detail[3]. And yet with how much of holy and solemn reserve is that first hour of a world's salvation passed over by the Evangelist. We would indeed fain inquire more into the wonders of that mysterious night; and they are not wholly withheld from us. The same Evangelist that tells us that the mid-day

---

[1] The statement of Justin Martyr, who was born at Sichem, about A.D. 103, is very distinct: Γεννηθέντος δὲ τότε τοῦ παιδίου ἐν Βηθλεέμ, ἐπειδὴ Ἰωσὴφ οὐκ εἶχεν ἐν τῇ κώμῃ ἐκείνῃ τοῦ καταλῦσαι, ἐν σπηλαίῳ τινὶ σύνεγγυς τῆς κώμης κατέλυσε. *Tryph.* cap. 78, Vol. II. p. 264 (ed. Otto). This ancient tradition has been repeated by Origen (*Cels.* I. 51), Eusebius (*Demonstr. Evang.* VII. 2), Jerome (*Epist. ad Marcell.* XXIV.), and other ancient writers, and has been generally admitted by modern writers and travellers, as far from improbable: comp. Stanley, *Palest.* p. 438. Dr Thomson (*The Land and the Book*, Vol. II. p. 507), though admitting the ambiguity of the tradition, opposes it on reasons derived from the context of the sacred narrative, which are however far from convincing. The Virgin might easily have been removed to the οἰκία spo-

cified in Matt. ii. 11, before the arrival of the Magi. For further details and reff. see Thilo, *Codex Apocr.* p. 381 sq.; Hofmann, *Leben Jes.* p. 108; and a very good article by Rev. G. Williams, in the *Ecclesiologist* for 1848.

[2] The reader who may have an interest in the outward aspects of these sacred localities will find a coloured sketch of Bethlehem and its neighbourhood in Roberts's *Holy Land*, Vol. II. Plate 84. The illustrations, however, most strongly recommended by an Oriental traveller of some experience to the writer of this note, as giving the truest idea of the sacred localities, are those of Frith, and the excellent views of Jerusalem and its environs executed by Robertson and Beato (Gambart and Co.).

[3] See above, p. 46, note 1, where this subject is briefly noticed.

sun was darkened during the last hours of the Redeemer's earthly life[a], tells us also that in His first hours the night was turned into more than day, and that heavenly glories shone forth not unwitnessed[b], while angels announce to shepherd-watchers[1] on the grassy slopes of Bethlehem the

[a] Luke xxiii. 44

[b] ii. 9

---

[1] Luke ii. 8, ἀγραυλοῦντες καὶ φυλάσσοντες φυλακὰς τῆς νυκτός; the last words defining the time and qualifying the two preceding participles. The fact here specified has been often used in the debated subject of the exact time of year at which our Lord's birth took place. But little, however, can really be derived from it, as the frequently quoted notice of the Talmudical writers (see Lightfoot *on Luke* ii. 8), that the herds were brought in from the fields about the beginning of November and driven out again about March, is merely general, and might include so many modifications arising from season or locality (see Sepp, *Leben Christi*, Vol. I. p. 213; Wieseler, *Chron. Synops.* p. 146) that it cannot fairly be urged as conclusive against the traditional date in December. Nay, temporary circumstances,—the large afflux of strangers to Bethlehem,—might have easily led to a temporary removal of the cattle into some of the milder valleys to provide an accommodation of which at least the Holy Family were obliged to avail themselves. Still it must be said, the fact viewed simply does seem to incline us towards a period less rigorous than mid-winter; and when we join with this chronological data which appear positively to fix the epoch as subsequent to the beginning of January (see Wieseler, *Chron. Synops.* p. 145), and further, considerations derived from the probable sequence of events, and the times probably occupied by them, we perhaps may slightly lean to the opinion that early in Febr. (most probably A.U.C. 750; Sulpic. Sever. *Hist. Sacr.* Book II. ch. 39) was the time of the Nativity. The question has been discussed from a very early period. In the time of Clement of Alexandria (*Strom.* I. 21, Vol. I. p. 407, ed. Pott.), by whom it appears to have been considered rather a matter of περιεργία, the traditions were anything but unanimous (some selecting Jan. 6, some Jan. 10, others April 20, and even May 20), and it was not till the fourth century that December 25 became generally accepted as the exact date: see the useful table attached to the valuable dissertation of Patritius, *de Evang.* Book III. 19, p. 276. Out of the many treatises and discussions that have been written on this subject the following may be specified: Ittig, *de Fest. Nativ.* Dissert. III.; Jablonsky, *de Origine Fest. Nativ.* Vol. III. p. 317 sq. (ed. te Water); Spanheim, *Dub. Evangel.* XII. Vol. II. p. 208 sq.; Greswell, *Dissert.* XII. Vol. I. p. 381 sq.; Wieseler, *Chron. Synops.* p. 132; compare also Clinton, *Fasti Hell.* Vol. III. p. 256 sq.; and Browne, *Ordo Sæclorum*, § 23 sq., p. 26 sq. A distinct Homily on this subject will be found in Chrysost. *Homil. in Diem Natal.* Vol. II. p. 417 sq. (ed. Bened. 1834).

LECT. II.

^a Lk. ii. 11

tidings of great joy, and proclaim the new-born Saviour^a...How mysterious are the ways of God's dealings with men. The Desire of all nations at length come, the Saviour born into an expectant world, and—announced to village shepherds. What a bathos, what a hopeless bathos to the unbelieving or unmeditative spirit! How noticeable that the Apocryphal writers, who spin out with the most dreary prolixity every other hint supplied by the sacred writers, pass over this in the fewest possible words[1], and as something which they could neither appreciate nor understand. And yet what a divine significance is there in the fact, that to the spiritual descendants of the first type of the Messiah, Abel the keeper of sheep, the announcement is made that the great Shepherd of the lost sheep of humanity is born into the world[2]. What a mysterious fitness that that Gospel, of which the characteristic was that

^b Mat. xi. 5

it was preached unto the poor^b, was first proclaimed neither to the ceremonial Pharisee, who would have questioned it, nor to the worldly Sadducee, who would have despised it, nor to the separatist Essene[3], who would have given it a

---

[1] See *Pseudo-Matth. Evang.* cap. 13; *Evang. Infant. Arab.* cap. 4; and compare Hofmann, *Leben Jesu,* p. 117. Tradition affects to preserve their names—Misael, Acheel, Cynacus, and Stephanus.

[2] "It fell not out amiss that shepherds they were; the news fitted them well. It well agreed to tell shepherds of the yeaning of a strange Lamb, such a Lamb as should 'take away the sins of the world;' such a Lamb as they might

'send to the Ruler of the world for a present,' *mitte Agnum Dominatori terræ,*—Esay's Lamb. Or if ye will, to tell shepherds of the birth of a Shepherd, Ezekiel's shepherd: *Ecce suscitabo vobis pastorem,* 'Behold, I will raise you a Shepherd,' 'the Chief Shepherd,' 'the Great Shepherd,' and 'the Good Shepherd that gave His life for His flock.'" Andrewes, *Serm.* v. Vol. I. p. 65 (A.-C. Libr.).

[3] The spiritual characteristics and

mere sectarian significance, but to men whose simple and susceptible hearts made them come with haste, and see, and believe, and spread abroad the wonders they had been permitted to behold[1]. Shepherds were the first of men who glorified and praised God for their Saviour; shepherds were the first earthly preachers[2] of the Gospel of Christ.

How far their praises and the wonders they had to tell of wrought on the hearts of those who heard them[a] we are not enabled to say. The holy reserve of the Virgin mother, who kept all these sayings[3] and pondered them in her heart[b],

The circumcision and presentation in the Temple.
[a] Lk. ii. 17
[b] ver. 19

---

relations of these three sects are briefly but ably noticed by Lange, *Leben Jes.* II. I. I, Part I. p. 17. The Pharisee corrupted the current and tenor of revelation by ceremonial additions, the Sadducee by reducing it to a mere deistic morality, the Essene by idealizing its historical aspects, or by narrowing its widest principles and precepts into the rigidities of a false and morbid asceticism. Superstition, scepticism, and schism alike found in the cross of Christ a stone of stumbling and a rock of offence. For further notices of these sects and their dissensions, see Jost, *Geschichte des Judenthums*, II. 2. 8, Vol. I. p. 197 sq.

[1] 'Why was it that the Angel went not to Jerusalem, sought not out the Scribes and Pharisees, entered not into the synagogues of the Jews, but found shepherds......and preached the Gospel to them? Because the former were corrupt and ready to be cut to the heart with envy; while these latter were uncorrupt, affecting the old way of living of the patriarchs, and also of Moses, for these men were shepherds.' Origen ap. Cramer, *Caten.* Vol. I. p. 20; compare too Theophylact *in loc.* For some further practical considerations, see Bp Taylor, *Life of Christ*, Part I. *ad* Sect. 4, Vol. I. p. 45 sq. (Lond. 1836).

[2] The first preachers, as Cyril rightly observes (*Comment. on Luke,* Serm. II. Part I. p. 13, Transl., Oxf. 1859), were angels,—a distinction faintly hinted at by the very terms of the original: ὡς ἀπῆλθον ἀπ' αὐτῶν εἰς τὸν οὐρανὸν οἱ ἄγγελοι, καὶ οἱ ἄνθρωποι οἱ ποιμένες εἶπον κ.τ.λ. Here it need scarcely be said we have no mere idle periphrasis ('homo pastor,' Drus.), but an opposition to the preceding term ἄγγελοι; see Meyer *in loc.*

[3] The expression τὰ ῥήματα ταῦτα (Luke ii. 19) is rightly referred by most modern commentators, not to the circumstances generally (τὰ πράγματα ταῦτα, Theoph.), but to the things mentioned by the shepherds: so rightly Euthym. *in loc.*—τὰ παρὰ τῶν ποιμένων λαληθέντα. On the reasonableness of this reserve, see

would lead us to believe that at any rate the history of the miraculous conception was not generally divulged; and that the Lord's earthly parents spake not beyond the small circle of those immediately around them. The circumcision, from the brief notice of the Evangelist[a], would certainly seem to have taken place with all circumstances of privacy and solitude,—in apparent contrast to that of the Forerunner, which appears to have been with gatherings and rejoicings[1], and was marked by marvels that were soon noised abroad throughout all the hill-country of Judæa[b]. Nay, even at the presentation in the temple, more than a month afterwards[2], the Evangelist's remark, that Joseph and Mary marvelled at Simeon's prophecy[c], would seem distinctly to show that no circumstances from without had as yet proved sufficient to prepare them for the mysterious welcome which awaited the infant Saviour in His Father's temple.

But what a welcome that was, and how seemingly at variance with all outward circumstances.

[a] Lk. ii. 21

[b] i. 65

[c] ii. 33

Mill, *on Pantheistic Princ.* II. I. 2, p. 212.

[1] Even if we limit, as perhaps is most grammatically exact, the subject of ἦλθον (Luke i. 59) to those who were to perform the rite of circumcision, the context would certainly seem to show that many were present.

[2] The exact time in the case of a male child (in the case of a female it was double) was 40 days, during 7 of which the mother was to be accounted unclean; during the remaining 33 days she was 'to continue in the blood of her purifying;' she was 'to touch no hallowed thing, nor come into the sanctuary, until the days of her purifying be fulfilled.' Levit. xii. 4. For further information see Michaelis, *Law of Moses*, § 192, Bähr, *Symbolik*, Vol. II. p. 487, Winer, *RWB.* Art. 'Reinigkeit,' Vol. II. p. 315 sq.; and for a good sermon on the subject, Frank, *Serm.* XXII. Vol. I. p. 340 (A.-C. Libr.), and esp. Mill, *Univ. Serm.* XXI. p. 400. The indication of the comparative poverty of the Holy Family supplied by the notice of their offering (Luke ii. 24, Lev. xii. 8) has often been observed by modern, but seldom by ancient, expositors.

The devout, and let us add, inspired^a Simeon[1], whose steps had been led that day to the Temple by the Holy Spirit[2], saw perchance before him no more than two unnoted worshippers[3]. But it was enough. When the eyes of the aged waiter for the consolation of Israel^b saw the Holy Child, he saw all. There in helpless infancy and clad in mortal flesh was the Lord's Christ,—there was the fulfilment of all his mystic revelations^c, the granted issue of all his longings and all his prayers[4]. Can we marvel that his whole soul was stirred to its depths, that he took the Holy Child

^a Lk. ii. 25

^b ver. 25

^c ver. 26

---

[1] The history of this highly favoured man is completely unknown. Some recent attempts (Michaelis, al.) have been made to identify him with Rabban Simeon, the son of Hillel, and father of Gamaliel, who was afterwards president of the Sanhedrin (Lightfoot, *Hor. Hebr. in loc.;* Otho, *Lex. Rabbin.* s. v. 'Simeon,' p. 605): such an identification, however, has nothing in its favour, except the name,—a sufficiently common one, and this against it, that Rabban Simeon could not have been as old as the Simeon of St Luke is apparently represented to be. For some notices of Rabban Simeon, see Sepp, *Leben Christi,* ch. XVII. Vol. II. p. 52 sq.

[2] This seems implied in the words ἦλθεν ἐν τῷ Πνεύματι εἰς τὸ ἱερόν, Luke ii. 27,—the preposition with its case marking the influence in which, and under which he was acting, 'impulsu Spiritus' (Meyer, *on Matth.* xxii. 43), and though not perfectly identical with, yet approximating in force to the instrumental dative; τῷ Πνεύματι τῷ ἁγίῳ κινηθείς, Euthym. *in loc.* So too Origen, even more explicitly,—'Spiritus sanctus eum duxit in templum.' *In Luc.* Hom. XV. Vol. III. p. 949 (ed. Bened.).

[3] One of the Apocryphal writers has represented the scene very differently, and in suggestive contrast to the chaste dignity of the inspired narrative: 'Tum videt illum Simeon senex instar columnae lucis fulgentem, cum domina Maria Virgo mater ejus de eo laetabunda ulnis suis eum gestaret: circumdabant autem cum angeli instar circuli celebrantes tanquam satellites regi adstantes.' *Evang. Infant. Arab.* cap. 6, p. 173 (ed. Tisch.). The *Pseudo-Matth. Evang.* keeps more closely to the inspired narrative: see cap. 15, p. 78.

[4] For an essay on the character of this faithful watcher, see Evans, *Script. Biogr.* Vol. I. p. 326; and for some good comments on his inspired canticle, Patritius, *de Evang.* Dissert. XXVI. Part III. p. 304. In the early Church Simeon appears to have been designated by the title ὁ Θεοδόχος, in memory of the blessing accorded to him: comp. *Menolog. Graec.* Feb. 3, and the oration of Timoth. Hieros. in the *Bibl. Mar. Patrum,* Vol. V. p. 1214.

LECT. II.

^a Lk. ii. 28

in his arms^a, and poured forth, in the full spirit of prophecy¹, that swan-song of the seer of the Old Covenant, to which our Church so justly and befittingly assigns a place in its daily service? Can we marvel that with the Holy Child still in his arms² he blessed the wondering parents, though the spirit of prophecy that was upon him mingled with that blessing words that must have sunk deep into the heart of the Virgin³, words often

---

[1] Προφητικῇ χάριτι τετιμημένος, Cyril Alex. ap. Cramer, *Caten.* Vol. II. p. 23, and *Serm.* IV. Vol. I. p. 25 (Transl.). On the character of this and the other inspired canticles in this part of the Scripture, see the good remarks of Mill, *on Pantheistic Principles*, Part II. L. 3, p. 43 sq.

[2] Though we cannot, with Meyer and others, safely press the meaning of the verb κεῖται as implying 'qui in ulnis meis jacet' (Beng.), it would yet seem highly probable from the context that this blessing was pronounced by the aged Simeon, while still bearing his Saviour in his arms. For a good practical sermon on Simeon's thus receiving our Lord, see Frank, *Serm.* XXIII. Vol. I. p. 360 sq. (A.-C. Libr.), and compare Hackut, *Serm.* X. p. 88 sq. (Lond. 1675).

[3] The prophetic address of Simeon, which it may be observed is directed specially to the Virgin (καὶ εἶπε πρὸς Μαριὰμ τὴν μητέρα αὐτοῦ, Luke ii. 34), has two separate references, the one *general*, to the Jewish nation, and the opposed spiritual attitudes into which the Gospel of Christ would respectively bring those who believed and those who rejected (πτῶσιν μέν, τῶν μὴ πιστευόντων, ἀνάστασιν δέ, τῶν πιστευόντων, Theophylact); the other *special*, to the Virgin personally (καὶ σοῦ δὴ αὐτῆς κ.τ.λ., ver. 35), and to the bitterness of agony with which she should hereafter behold the sufferings of her divine Son. So rightly Euthymius: ῥομφαίαν δὲ ὠνόμασε τὴν τμητικωτάτην καὶ ὀξεῖαν ὀδύνην, ἥτις διῆλθε τὴν καρδίαν τῆς Θεομήτορος, ὅτε ὁ υἱὸς αὐτῆς προσηλώθη τῷ σταυρῷ. Compare also a good comment in Cramer, *Caten.* Vol. II. p. 24, and Mill, *Univ. Serm.* XXI. p. 415. The only remaining exegetical difficulty is the connexion of the final clause, ὅπως ἂν κ.τ.λ. (ver. 35). According to the ordinary punctuation, this would be dependent on ver. 34, the first clause of ver. 35 being enclosed in a parenthesis; according, however, to the best modern interpreters it is regarded as simply dependent on what precedes: the mystery, that the heart of the earthly mother was to be riven with agony at the sufferings of her divine Son, involved as its end and object the bringing out of the true characters and thoughts of men, and making it clear and manifest—τίς μὲν ὁ ἀγαπῶν αὐτόν, καὶ μέχρι θανάτου τὴν εἰς αὐτὸν ἀγάπην ἐνδεικνύμενος. Τίς δὲ ὁ ἐπίπλαστον ἔχων τὴν εἰς αὐτὸν πίστιν, σκανδάλου πληρωθεὶς διὰ τὸν σταυρόν. Cramer, *Caten.* Vol. II. p. 25. So Augustine, in his answer to the

pondered over, yet perchance then only fully understood in all the mystic bitterness of their truth, when, not a thousand paces from where she then was standing, the nails tore the hands that she had but then been holding, and the spear pierced the side she had but then been pressing to her bosom?

Yet man was not alone to welcome the Lord; one sex was not alone to greet Him—in whom there was neither male nor female[a], but all were one. Not one sex only, for at that very instant[b], we are told by St Luke, the aged and tenderly-faithful Anna[1] enters the place she loved so well. Custom[c] rather than Revelation appears to have brought the widowed prophetess into the temple, but she too saw and believed, and returned grateful praise[2] unto the God of her fathers, and of her this special notice has been made by the Evangelist, that "she spake of the Lord to all them that were looking for redemption in Jeru-

[a] Gal. iii. 28
[b] Lk. ii. 38
[c] ver. 37

queries of Paulinus of Nola (*Epist.* CXLIX. 33, Vol. II. p. 644, ed. Migne), except that he unduly limits the πολλῶν καρδιῶν διαλογισμοί to the 'insidiæ Judæorum et discipulorum infirmitas.'

[1] The tenderness and constancy of the aged prophetess to the memory of the husband of her youth is slightly enhanced by the reading of Lachmann and Tischendorf, χήρα ἕως ἐτῶν ὀγδοήκοντα τεσσάρων, Luke ii. 37; but this reading, though supported by A, B, L, the Vulgate, and other versions, is by no means certain. The honour in which the 'univira' was held by the Jews, is shown very distinctly by the comments of Josephus on the persistent widowhood of Antonia: *Antiq.* XVIII. 6. 6. Compare Winer, *RWB.* Art. 'Ehe,' Vol. I. p. 299.

[2] This perhaps is a fairly correct paraphrase of the peculiar term used by St Luke, ἀνθωμολογεῖτο. The remarks of the accurate Winer on this word are as follows: 'Possis existimare de *celebrandi laudandique* significatione;...sed, ut dicam quod sentio, addendum erat, celebrantis istius pietatem mulieris maxime *in gratiarum actione* positam esse...Itaque hæc videtur verbi ἀνθομολογ. vis propria esse, ἀντί enim manifesto referendi rependendique sensum habet, atque ita facile perspicias, quod inter ὁμολογ. Θεῷ et ἀνθομολογ. Θεῷ intersit.' *De Verb. c. Præp.* Fasc. III. p. 20,—a treatise unfortunately never completed.

LECT. II.

ᵃ Lk. ii. 38

salemᵃ." The daughter of Phanuel[1] was the first preacher of Christ in the city of the Great King. And her preaching was not long left unconfirmed. What she was now telling in secret chambers[2] was soon to be proclaimed on the house-tops. The ends of the earth were already sending forth the heralds of the new-born King. The feet of strange pilgrims and worshippers were even now on the mountains of the promised Land.

The visit and adoration of the Magi.

It would seem from the narrative that Joseph and Mary had returned but a few days[3] to their temporary abode at Bethlehem[4], when sages, bear-

[1] The special mention of the father and tribe of Anna was perhaps designed to give to the narrative a still further stamp of historical truth. Anna, the daughter of Phanuel, might have been a name still remembered by many: ἐπιμένει ὁ εὐαγγελιστὴς τῇ περὶ τῆς Ἄννης ἀφηγήσει, καὶ τὸν πατέρα καὶ τὴν φυλὴν καταλέγων, ἵνα μάθωμεν ὅτι ἀληθῆ λέγει, μάρτυρας ὡσανεὶ πολλοὺς προσκαλούμενος. Theoph. *in loc.*

[2] Anna's preaching was not general, but τοῖς προσδεχομένοις λύτρωσιν ἐν Ἱερουσαλήμ, ver. 38. The local addition ἐν Ἱερους. appears to belong specially to the participle τοῖς προσδεχομένοις: see Meyer *in loc.*

[3] According to one MS. of the *Pseudo-Matth. Evangelium* (cap. xvi. p. 79, ed. Tisch.), two *days* afterwards; according to the text adopted by Tischendorf, the completely improbable period of two *years:* see Wieseler, *Chron. Synops.* I. 2, p. 59, note, who, however, himself (see below, p. 73, note 1) seems to press too strongly the ἀπὸ διετοῦς καὶ κατωτέρω, Matth. ii. 16. The *Protev. Jacobi* (cap. 21) makes the visit of the Magi to have been made to the Holy Family while yet in the cave, a statement distinctly at variance with Matth. ii. 11, ἐλθόντες εἰς τὴν οἰκίαν. For chronological considerations substantiating the view taken in the text, see Wieseler, *Chron. Synops.* p. 154 sq.

[4] The narratives of St Matthew and St Luke have been here often regarded as almost wholly irreconcileable; see Meyer and Alford *in loc.* Is this however so certain? Why may not St Luke have studiously omitted what he might possibly have known had been recorded by another Evangelist, and thus have left unnoticed the occurrences which intervened between this visit to the Temple and the return to Nazareth, specified by St Matthew, ch. ii. 23? The reconciliation adopted by Eusebius (*Quæst. ad Marin.* ap. Mai, *Bibl. Patr.* Vol. IV. p. 253), that Joseph and Mary went direct to Nazareth, and afterwards returned to Bethlehem, is not very probable, as no reason can be assigned why the Holy Family should have returned again to a place with which they appear to have had little or no connexion: see Augustine, *de Con-*

ing the already almost generic name of Magi, arrive from some Eastern lands not specified by the Evangelist, but probably remote as the Arabia which one ancient tradition[1], or the Persia which another ancient tradition[2] has fixed upon as their home. Witnesses were they, from whatever clime they came, of the wisdom of God displaying itself in the foolishness or misconceptions of man[3].

sensu Evang. II. 5. 16, Vol. III. p. 1079 (ed. Migne), Wieseler, *Chron. Synops.* p. 156.

[1] Such is the older tradition, noticed and supported by Justin Martyr, *Tryph.* cap. 78, Vol. II. p. 263 (ed. Otto), Tertullian *adv. Jud.* cap. 9, and *adv. Marc.* III. 13. The objection to this view seems to be the term ἀνατολῶν, which, in the New Testament at least, can hardly be regarded as a natural designation of a country which elsewhere is always specified by its regular geographical name: see Winer, *RWB.* Art. 'Stern der Weisen,' Vol. II. p. 523, but also contrast the reff. of Patritius, *de Evang.* Dissert. XXVII. Part III. p. 317.

[2] This somewhat later tradition is maintained by Chrysostom (*in loc.*), Pseudo-Basil (Vol. II. p. 855, ed. Bened.), Ephrem (*Cantic. de Maria et Magis,* Vol. III. p. 601, ed. Assem.), the Christian poet Juvencus, and many other ancient writers,—and with considerable probability, as Persia and the adjoining countries appear always to have been regarded as the chief seat of the Magian philosophy (see the numerous confirmatory reff. in Greswell, *Dissert.* XVIII.), and as the term αἱ ἀνατολαί might naturally and suitably have been applied by the Evangelist to the trans-Euphratean countries of which Persia formed a portion. Such too is the opinion of apparently the majority of the more learned modern writers who have touched upon this subject; we may pause to specify the celebrated Orientalist, Hyde (*de Relig. Vet. Pers.* cap. XXXI. p. 383), who particularly notices their country as Parthia; the learned Dr Thomas Jackson (*Creed,* Book VII. Vol. VI. p. 261, Oxf. 1844), and the no less learned Dr Mill (*Obs. on Pantheistic Principles,* Part II. pp. 365, 375). For further information the student may be referred to Spanheim (*Dub. Evang.* XXIII.—XXIV. Part II. p. 255 sq.), the excellent dissertation of Patritius above referred to (*de Evangeliis,* Part III. pp. 309—354, where every question relating to these sages is fully discussed), Greswell, *Dissert.* XVIII. Vol. II. p. 135 sq., Hofmann, *Leben Jes.* p. 125, and especially the sound and valuable comments of Mill, *on Panth. Princ.* Part II. 3. 1, p. 364.

[3] See the excellent remarks of Mill on the true physical influence and true significancy of the heavenly bodies, and the counterfeit science of astrology with which it was adulterated. *Observations on Pantheistic Principles,* Part II. 3. 2, pp. 364, 365: compare also a learned and not uninteresting dissertation on judicial astrology in Spanheim, *Dub. Evang.* XXXIII. Part II. p. 334 sq.

LECT. II.

The guiding star.

Witnesses were they of the cherished longings of ancient nations[1]; bright examples of a faith that could dignify even superstitions, and of hopes that grew not cold when all must have seemed utter hopelessness.

But what could have brought these first-fruits of the wisdom of the Eastern world from their own distant lands? Even that which was most calculated to work in them the liveliest belief and conviction. A new star[2], which the tenor of the

---

[1] It has long been a matter of discussion what precisely led these Magi to expect a birth so prefigured; see Spanheim, *Dub. Evang.* xxxiv. Part II. p. 366 sq. Was it due to a carefully preserved knowledge of the prophecy of Balaam (Numb. xxiv. 17—19), an opinion maintained by Origen (*contr. Cels.* Book I. p. 46, ed. Spencer), and the majority of the ancient expositors; or was it due to prophecies uttered in their own country, dimly foreshadowing this divine mystery (see the citations from the Zend-Avesta, below, p. 77, note 1, and compare Hyde, *de Relig. Pers.* xxxi. p. 389 sq.)? Perhaps the latter view is the most probable, especially if we associate with it a belief, which the sacred narrative gives us every reason for entertaining (Matth. ii. 12), that these faithful men received a special illumination both to apply rightly what they had remembered, and to recognize its verification in the phenomenon of which they were now the privileged observers: compare Mill, *Observations*, Part II. 3. 2, p. 368.

[2] Thus far, at least, correctly, Origen (*contr. Cels.* Book I. p. 45, ed. Spencer): Τὸν ὀφθέντα ἀστέρα ἐν τῇ ἀνατολῇ καινὸν εἶναι νομίζομεν καὶ μηδενὶ τῶν συνήθων παρα- πλήσιον, οὔτε τῶν ἐν τῇ ἀπλανεῖ οὔτε τῶν ἐν ταῖς κατωτέρω σφαίραις. This great writer seems only to err when in his subsequent remarks he supposes it to be of the nature of a comet. On this star much, and that not always of a satisfactory nature, has been written by both ancient and modern commentators. That it was not a star in the usual astronomical sense (Wieseler, *Chron. Synops.* I. 2, p. 59) seems clear from the special motions apparently attributed to it in the sacred narrative (see Mill, *on Panth. Princ.* Part II. 3. 2, p. 369, note), that it also could not be a mere conjunction of the greater planets (Münter, *Stern der Weisen*, Keppler, and similarly Ideler, *Handbuch der Chronol.* Vol. II. p. 399 sq.,—both following or expanding the older view of Keppler) seems also still more certain from the use of the definite term ἀστήρ. We therefore justly fall back upon the ancient opinion, that it was a luminous body, possibly of a meteoric nature, but subject to special laws regulating its appearance, and perhaps also its motion. The literature of this subject, which is very extensive, will be found in Winer, *RWB.* Art. 'Stern der Weisen,' Vol. II. p. 523 sq.

narrative wholly precludes our deeming aught else than a veritable heavenly body moving apparently in the limits of our own atmosphere, and subject not to astronomical but to special and fore-ordered laws, had suddenly beamed, not many months before[1], upon the eyes of these watchers in their own Eastern lands[2], and, either by cooperating with dormant prophecy or deepseated expectation, leads them to that land, with which either their own science[3], or more probably the whole feeling

[1] The date of the appearance of the star is a question that has been often entertained and cannot easily be decided. Wieseler (*Chron. Synops.* I. 2, p. 59) urges a period of two years previous to the arrival of the Magi, pressing the sort of data afforded by Matth. ii. 16; see above, p. 70. As, however, Greswell (*Dissert.* XVIII. Vol. II. p. 136, ed. 2) has fairly shown that the term ἀπὸ διετοῦς καὶ κατωτέρω need not be understood as necessarily implying the extreme limit, and as it is also probable that Herod would be certain to secure to himself a wide margin, we may, with almost equal plausibility, select any period between thirteen and twenty-four months. Patritius (*de Evang.* Dissert. XXVII. Part III. p. 334) urges with a little show of probability a period of eighteen months, which according to the rough date of the Nativity adopted in these lectures would have to be reduced to sixteen. The time of the miraculous conception seems to commend itself as the exact epoch, but causes us either to reduce somewhat unduly the ἀπὸ διετοῦς, or (with Greswell) to assume an interval of nearly three months between the Presentation and the arrival of the Magi, which is not only improbable in itself, but absolutely incompatible with the date (A.U.C. 750, the death-year of Herod), which we have above fixed upon as the probable year of the Nativity; see p. 63, note 1.

[2] A few interpreters of this passage, and among them our own expositor Hammond (on *Matth.* ii. 2) and the German chronologer Wieseler (*Synops.* p. 59), regard ἐν τῇ ἀνατολῇ as used with an astronomical reference, 'at its rising.' This seems at needless variance with the use of the same words in ver. 9,—where ἐν τῇ ἀνατολῇ and οὗ ἦν τὸ παιδίον seem to stand in a kind of *local* antithesis, and is in opposition to the apparently unanimous opinion of the Vulgate, Syriac, Coptic, and other ancient versions. For yet another view see Jackson, *Creed*, Book VII. Vol. VI. p. 262 (Oxf. 1844).

[3] Much has been said about the astrological association of the constellation of the Fish with the land of Judæa; see Münter, *Stern der Weisen*, p. 55 sq, Ideler, *Handb. der Chronol.* Vol. II. p. 409, and Wieseler, *Chron. Synops.* I. 2, p. 56. As, however, this is more or less associated with the doubtful views as to the nature of the star above alluded to, we make no use of such precarious elucidations.

of the Eastern world[1], tended to associate the mystery of the future. Can we not picture to ourselves the excitement and amazement in Jerusalem as those travel-stained men[2] entered into the city of David with the one question[3] on their lips, 'Where is He that is born King of the Jews[a]?' Can we wonder that the aged man still on the throne of Judæa was filled with strange trouble and perplexity[b]? Can we be surprised at the course that was immediately followed?

[a] Mat. ii. 2
[b] ver. 3

---

[1] This general feeling has been above alluded to; see p. 44, note 2, and compare Mill, *on Panth. Prin.* Part II. 3. 1, p. 366.

[2] Some interesting notices of the probable time which it would have taken the Wise Men to travel from Persia to Jerusalem, will be found in Greswell, *Dissert.* XVIII. Vol. II. p. 138 sq. From the calculations there made it would appear that they could not have been much less than four months on the road. It has been computed by Chrysostom, in reference to the journey of Abraham, that the time occupied in a journey from Palestine no further than to Chaldæa would be about 70 days. *Ad Stagir.* II. 6, Vol. I. p. 188 (cited by Greswell).

[3] The terms of this question deserve some notice, as they serve incidentally to show the firm belief of the Magi that the expected King was now really born into the world, and yet their complete ignorance, not only of the place of His birth, but, as it would seem, also of its mysterious nature and character; comp. Greswell, *Harmony*, Dissert. XVIII. Vol. II. p. 144, but see contra Theoph. *in loc.* They go naturally to Jerusalem, for where, as Jackson says (*Creed*, Book VII. p. 258), 'should they seek the King of the Jews but in His standing court?' and they put forward a question which shows their conviction that a great King had been born in the land they were visiting, though, at present, who or where they knew not (opposed to Theoph. *in loc.*). In the sequel, they were probably permitted to behold some glimpses of the true nature of Him whom they came to reverence; so that, as Bp Taylor well says, 'their custom was changed to grace, and their learning heightened with inspiration; and God crowned all with a spiritual and glorious event.' *Life of Christ*, Part I. 4. 4. Though then in the first προσκυνῆσαι (ver. 2) no more perhaps might have been designed than the outward worshipful reverence of Persian usage (Herod. I. 134), we may well believe that in the subsequent performance of the act (ver. 11) there was something more, and may not incorrectly believe with Tertullian (*adv. Jud.* cap. 9), Origen (*contr. Celsum*, Lib. 1. p. 46, ed. Spencer), and indeed, the whole early Church, that with a deepening though still imperfect consciousness, these faithful men adored the Infant at Bethlehem as God, no less than they prostrated themselves before Him as

Let us only consider the case in its simplest aspects. Here was a question based on celestial appearances coming from the lips of those in whom it would have seemed most portentous,—the Magi of the East, the ancient watchers of the stars. When with this we remember how rife expectation was, and how one perhaps of that very council, which the dying king[1] called together, could tell of his own father's mysterious prophecy of the coming Messiah[2]—when we add to this the strange rumours of the Child of Bethlehem, fast flying from mouth to mouth beyond that narrow circle to which Anna had first proclaimed Him,—can we wonder at all that followed ? How natural the description of the probably hastily-summoned council, and of the question publicly propounded

The extreme naturalness of the sacred narrative.

---

man: see the copious reff. in Patritius, *de Evang.* Dissert. XXVII. 2, Part III. p. 348.

[1] The death of Herod appears *almost* certainly to have taken place a few days before the Passover of the year A. U. C. 750; apparently, if retrospective calculations can be depended on, towards the end of the first week of April; see Wieseler, *Chron. Syn.* p. 57, and comp. Clinton, *Fasti Hell.* Vol. III. p. 254, Browne, *Ordo Sæc.* § 31, p. 31. If then we suppose the Saviour's birth to have been in late winter, say, at the beginning of February, the arrival of the Magi would have taken place about three weeks before Herod's death, and a very few days before his removal to the baths at Callirrhoe (Joseph. *Antiq.* XVII. 6. 5); comp. Browne, *Ordo Sæc.* § 28. If we adopt Dec. 25, A. U. C. 749, a date which, as has been above implied (p. 63, note 1), is perhaps not

quite so probable (compare Wieseler, *Chron. Syn.* p. 134 sq.), the interval between the present event and the death of the wretched king will be proportionately longer, and in *some* respects, it must be admitted, more chronologically convenient.

[2] If, as seems reasonable to suppose, the son of R. Nehumiah ben Hakkana was present at the council, he could scarcely have forgotten the prophecy said to have been uttered by his father,—that the coming of the Messiah could not be delayed more than fifteen years: see Sepp, *Leben Christi*, Vol. II. p. 24, and the curious work of Petrus Galatinus, *de Arcanis Cathol. Verit.* cap. 3, p. 8 (Francof. 1602). The opinion that this was a special meeting of the Sanhedrin (Lightfoot) is perhaps slightly the most probable; the omission of the third element, the πρεσβύτεροι τοῦ λαοῦ, is similarly found in Matth. xvi. 21, xx. 18; see

LECT. II.

^a Mat. ii. 4
^b ver. 7

^c ver. 8

^d ver. 9

to it touching the birth-place of the Messiah^a. How natural too the *private* inquiry about the star's appearance made specially to the Magi^b, and how accordant with all that we know of Herod, the frightful hypocrisy with which they were sent to test and verify the now ascertained declaration of prophecy^c,—and the murderous sequel. How natural also the description of the further journey of the Wise Men, their simple joy when on their evening mission to Bethlehem, they again see[1] the well-remembered star^d, and find that the very powers of the heavens are leading them where Rabbinical wisdom[2] had already sent them. How full must now have been their conviction; with what opening hearts must they have worshipped; with what holy joy must they have spread out

---

Meyer *in loc.* On the γραμματεῖς τοῦ λαοῦ here mentioned, see Spanheim, *Dub. Evang.* XXXVIII. Part II. p. 392 sq., Patritius, *de Evang.* Dissert. XXIX. Part III. p. 366, and on the Sanhedrin generally, Selden, *de Synedriis*, II. 6, Vol. II. p. 1316 sq. Jost, *Gesch. des Judenth.* II. 3. 14, Vol. I. p. 273.

[1] This seems the only natural meaning that we can assign to the words καὶ ἰδού [surely an expression marking the unexpectedness of the reappearance], ὁ ἀστὴρ ὃν εἶδον ἐν τῇ ἀνατολῇ προῆγεν αὐτούς, Matth. ii. 9. Whether the star preceded them the whole way to Jerusalem and then disappeared for a short time, or whether it only appeared to them in their own country, disappeared, and now reappeared, must remain a matter of opinion. The definitive ὃν εἶδον ἐν τῇ ἀνατολῇ, and still more the unusual strength of the expression which describes their joy at again beholding the star,—ἐχάρησαν χαρὰν μεγάλην σφόδρα (ver. 10),—seem strongly in favour of the latter view: so Spanheim, *Dub. Evang.* XXIX. Part II. p. 320, Jackson, *Creed*, Book VII. Vol. VI. p. 261, and Mill, *Observations*, II. 2. 3, p. 369.

[2] The recent revival of the older anti-christian view, that the prophecy of Micah (ch. v. 2), cited by the Evangelist, either refers to Zorobabel (a view unhappily maintained by Theodorus of Mopsuestia), or, if referring to the Messiah, only alludes to His descent from David, whose seat Bethlehem was, has been ably and completely disposed of by Mill, *Observations*, II. 2. 3, pp. 391—402. On this and other supposed difficulties connected with this prophecy, see Spanheim, *Dub. Evang.* XLI.— XLVI. Part II. p. 406; Patritius, *de Evang.* Dissert. XXX. Part III. p. 368 sq.

their costly gifts[a]; how they must now have felt, though perhaps still dimly and imperfectly, that they were kneeling before the hope of the world. One greater than Zoroaster had ever foretold, a truer Redeemer than the Sosiosh of their own ancient creed[1]. No marvel was it, that with prompt obedience they followed the guidance of the visions of the night[b] and returned to their distant home by a way by which they came not.

No sooner had they departed, than the heavenly warning is sent to Joseph[2] to flee on that very night[3] into Egypt from the coming wrath of Herod[c]. And that wrath did not long linger. When the savage king found that his strange messengers had deceived him, with the broad

LECT. II.

[a] Mat. i. 11
[b] ver. 12

Flight into Egypt and murder of the Innocents.

[c] ver. 13

---

[1] According to the statements of Anquetil du Perron, in his Life of Zoroaster, prefixed to his edition of the *Zend-Avesta* (Vol. I. 2, p. 46), Sosiosh was the last of the three posthumous sons of Zoroaster, and was to raise and judge the dead and renovate the earth; see *Ieschts Sadés*, XXVIII., 'Lorsque Sosiosch paroîtra, il fera du bien au monde entier existant' (Vol. II. p. 278); *Boundehesch*, XXXI., 'Sosiosch fera revivre les morts' (Vol. II. p. 411); and similarly, *ib.* XI. (Vol. II. p. 364); *ib.* XXXIII. (Vol. II. p. 420). Whatever may be the faults or inaccuracies of Du Perron's translation (many of which have been noticed in Bournouf's *Commentaire sur le Yaçna*, Paris, 1833), it can at any rate now no longer be doubted, that Zend has its proper place among the primitive languages of the Indo-Germanic family (see Rask's *Essay* translated by Von der Hagen, Berl. 1826), and that the Avesta must have existed in writing previously to the time of Alexander: see Donaldson, *New Cratylus*, § 86, p. 144 sq. (ed. 3).

[2] Again, it will be observed, consistently with the notice of the preceding divine communication vouchsafed to Joseph (Matth. i. 20),—by an angelic visitation in a *dream;* see again ver. 20, and compare the remarks made above, p. 56, note 1. Some curious remarks on the nature of angelic visitations in dreams will be found in the learned work of Bynæus, *de Natali Jes. Chr.* I. 2. 14, p. 210.

[3] Probably on the same *night* that the Magi arrived: for there seems every reason against the view of a commentator in Cramer (*Caten.* Vol. I. p. 14), that the star led them ἐν ἡμέρᾳ μέσῃ. At any rate the Holy family appear to have departed by night: the words, ἐγερθεὶς παράλαβε, seem to enjoin some promptitude,— 'surge accipe,' Syr.

margin that a reckless ferocity left a matter of no moment, he slays every male child in Bethlehem whose age could in any way have accorded with the rough date which the first appearance of the star had been judged to supply[1].

The silence of Josephus.

On this fiendish act we need dwell no further, save to protest against the inferences that have been drawn from the silence of a contemporary historian[2]. What, we may fairly ask, was such an act in the history of a monster whose hand reeked with the blood of whole families and of his nearest and dearest relations? What was the murder of a few children at Bethlehem in the dark history of one who had, perchance but a few days before, burnt alive at Jerusalem above forty hapless zealots who had torn down his golden eagle[3]?

---

[1] See above, p. 73, note 1. As Herod made his savage edict inclusive as regards *locality* (ἐν Βηθλεὲμ καὶ ἐν πᾶσιν τοῖς ὁρίοις αὐτῆς, ver. 16), so did he also in reference to *time:* he killed all the children of two years and under (ἀπὸ διετοῦς, scil. παιδός, not χρόνου, as apparently Vulg., 'a bimatu'), to make sure that he included therein the Divine Infant of Bethlehem; τοὺς μὲν διετεῖς ἀναιρεῖ, ἵνα ἔχῃ πλάτος ὁ χρόνος. Euthym. *in Matth.* ii. 16, p. 81 (ed. Matthæi).

[2] It seems doubtful whether we need go so far as to say, with Dr Mill (*Observations,* II. 3. 1, p. 345), that this silence is remarkable. The concluding days of Herod's life were marked by such an accumulation of barbarities that such an event might easily have been overlooked or forgotten. At any rate the reference of the well-known passage of Macrobius (*Saturnal.* II. 4) to this murder of the Innocents, though often denied or explained away ('aus der christlichen Tradition geflossen ist,' Meyer, *Kommentar,* p. 80), seems now clearly established and vindicated: see Mill, *ib.* p. 349 sq.; and compare Spanheim, *Dub. Evang.* LXXVI. Part II. p. 534 sq. It is worthy of notice that if, as seems nearly certain, the son of Herod alluded to in that passage was Antipater, the date of the murder of the Innocents may be roughly fixed, as not very far distant from that of the execution of the unhappy man referred to, and this latter event, we know, was *five* days before the death of Herod; see Joseph. *Bell. Jud.* I. 33. 8; and compare above, p. 75, note 1.

[3] See Josephus, *Antiq.* XVII. 6. 2, *Bell. Jud.* I. 33. 2. This was an outbreak caused by the harangues of two expounders of the law, Judas and Matthias, and resulted in the

What was the lamentation at Rama[1] compared with that which had been heard in that monster's own palace, and which, if his inhuman orders had been executed, would have been soon heard in every street in Jerusalem[2]? Even doubters have here at least admitted that there is no real difficulty[3]; and why should not we? Is the silence of a prejudiced Jew to be set against the declarations of an inspired Apostle?

The events of this portion of the sacred narrative come to their close with the notice of the divinely-ordered journey back from Egypt on the death of Herod, and the final return to Nazareth. Warned by God in a dream of the death of Herod[a], Joseph at once[4] brings back the Holy Child and

The return to Judæa.

[a] Mat. ii. 19

---

destruction of a large golden eagle of considerable value which Herod had erected over the gate of the temple. From the tenor of the narrative (βασιλεὺς δὲ καταδήσας αὐτοὺς ἐξέπεμπεν εἰς Ἱεριχοῦντα, § 3), and the subsequent oration in the theatre (comp. *Antiq.* xv. 8. 1), it would seem that Herod was at this time in Jerusalem. The date of the execution of these unhappy zealots, which probably almost immediately followed their apprehension, can be fixed with certainty to the night of March 12—13 (A.U.C. 750), as Josephus mentions that on the same night there was an eclipse of the moon (*loc. cit.* § 4): see Ideler, *Handb. der Chronol.* Vol. II. p. 28, and comp. Wieseler, *Chron. Synops.* I. 2, p. 56.

[1] For some excellent critical remarks on the citation from Jeremiah in reference to Rachel weeping for her children, see Mill, *Observations*, II. 3. 1, p. 402 sq.; and for a good sermon on the text, Jackson, *Creed*, Vol. VI. p. 277 (Oxf. 1844).

[2] It is distinctly mentioned by Josephus, that this frantic tyrant had all the principal men of the nation summoned to him at Jericho, and shut up in the hippodrome, and that he gave orders to his sister Salome and her husband Alexas to have them executed immediately he died, that as there would be no mourners *for*, there might be some *at* his death. *Antiq.* XVII. 6. 5.

[3] See Schlosser, *Universalhistor. Uebers. der alten Welt*, Part III. 1, p. 261, referred to by Neander, *Leben Jesu Chr.* p. 45. For several questions connected with the murder of the Innocents, including some characteristically guarded remarks on their number, see Patritius, *de Evang.* Dissert. XXXIII. Part III. p. 375.

[4] If the remark made above (p. 77, note 3) be correct, the same inference must be made in the present case, that the heavenly com-

His mother; and thus after a stay in Egypt of perhaps far fewer days[1] than Israel had there sojourned years, the word of ancient and hitherto unnoted prophecy receives its complete fulfilment[2], the mystic Israel comes up to the land of now more than promise,—out of Egypt God has called His Son[a].

*Mat. ii. 15

To what exact place of abode the blessed Virgin and Joseph were now directing their steps is not specially noticed by the Evangelist. We may, however, perhaps reasonably infer from St Mat-

mand required a similar promptitude on the part of Joseph, and that the faithful guardian delayed not. We may observe, however, that it is now ἐγερθεὶς παράλαβε καὶ πορεύου, not ἐγερθεὶς παράλαβε καὶ φεῦγε, as in ver. 13. This did not escape the observation of Chrysostom.

[1] If the dates we have adopted are approximately correct, it would seem that little more than a fortnight elapsed between the flight into Egypt and the death of Herod, and that consequently we must conceive the stay in Egypt to have been comparatively short. Greswell, by adopting April, A.U.C. 750, as the date of the Nativity, and 751 A.U.C. as the death-year of Herod, is compelled to assume a stay there of about seven months: see *Dissert.* XII. Vol. II. p. 392. The apocryphal writers still more enlarge this period ('exacto vero *triennio* rediit ex Egypto,' *Evang. Inf. Arab.* cap. XXVI.; compare *Pseudo-Matt. Evang.* cap. 26), almost evidently for the purpose of interpolating a series of miracles.

[2] This citation from ancient prophecy has been much discussed. Without entering into the detail of objections which have in many cases

proved as frivolous as they are irreverent, we may observe, (1) that it seems certain that Hosea xi. 1 is the passage referred to: see Jerome *in loc.*, Eusebius, *Eclog. Proph.* p. 46 sq. (ed. Gaisford); and (2) that little doubt can be entertained that the catholic interpretation which makes Israel and the promised Seed stand in typical relations (ἐλέχθη ἐπὶ τῷ λαῷ τυπικῶς, ἐξέβη δὲ εἰς τὸν Χριστὸν ἀληθινῶς, Theoph. *in loc.*, in substance from Chrysostom) is no less true and correct than it is simple and natural. St Matthew, as writing principally to Hebrew readers and to men who felt and knew that the nation to which they belonged was the truest and most veritable type of their Lord, specifies a passage which they had perhaps considered but simple history, but which, with the light of inspiration shed on it, assumes every attribute of mysterious, and, let us add, to them at any rate, of most persuasive typology. For further references and information, the reader may profitably consult Spanheim, *Dub. Evang.* LXII.— LXX. Part II. p. 474 sq., Deyling, *Obs. Sacr.* Vol. IV. p. 769, and Mill, *on Panth. Principles*, II. 3. 1, p. 409.

thew's Gospel that this homeward journey would have terminated at Bethlehem,—that new home now so dear to them from its many marvellous associations,—that home which now might have seemed marked out to them by the very finger of God, had not the tidings which reached Joseph, that the evil son of an evil father[1], the Ethnarch Archelaus, was now ruling over Judæa[a], made that faithful guardian afraid to return to a land so full of hatred and dangers. While thus, perhaps, in doubt and perplexity, the Divine answer is vouchsafed to his anxieties[2], and Joseph and the Virgin are directed to return to the safer obscurity of their old home in the hills of Galilee, and the spirit of ancient prophecy again finds its fulfilment in the designation the Messiah receives from His earthly abode, "He shall be called a Nazarene[3]."

[a] Mat. ii. 22

---

[1] The language of the Jewish deputies to Augustus fully justifies this remark: 'he seemed to be so afraid,' they said, 'lest he should not be deemed Herod's own son, that he took especial care to make his acts prove it:' see Joseph. *Antiq.* XVII. 11. 2.

[2] This seems to lie in the word χρηματισθείς (ver. 22). Though we may not perhaps safely, either here or ver. 12, or indeed in the New Testament generally, press the idea of a definite foregoing question, we may yet so far retain this usual meaning (χρηματίζει· ἀποκρίνεται, Suid.) as to regard the doubts and fears of Joseph as the practical *question* to which the Divine answer was returned: see Suicer, *Thesaur.* s. v. Vol. II. p. 1521.

[3] The very use of the inclusive διὰ τῶν προφητῶν ought to prepare us to expect, what we find to be the case, that this is no citation from any particular prophet, but expresses the declarations of several: 'pluraliter prophetas vocando, Matthæus ostendit non verba de Scripturis a se sumpta sed sensum.' Jerome *in loc.* We seem justified then in assigning to the word Ναζωραῖος all the meanings legitimately belonging to it, by derivation or otherwise, which are concurrent with the declarations of the prophets in reference to our Lord. We may therefore, both with the early Hebrew Christians (see Jerome) and apparently the whole Western Church, trace this prophetic declaration, (*a*) principally and primarily, in all the passages which refer to the Messiah under the title of the Branch (נֵצֶר) of the root of Jesse (Isaiah xi. 1; comp. Jer. xxiii. 5, xxxiii. 15, Zech.

LECT. II.

I must now at once bring this lecture to a close, yet not without two or three sentences of earnest exhortation to you, brethren, who form the younger portion of this audience.

Conclusion.

If there be aught in these hasty outlines of contested portions of Evangelical history that has arrested your attention, and deepened your convictions, I will pray to God that it may yet work more and more in your hearts, and lead you to feel that there is indeed a quick and living truth in every sentence of the blessed Gospel, and that they who read with a loving and reverential spirit shall see it in its clearest manifestations. Pray fervently against the first motions of a spirit of doubting and questioning. By those prayers which you learned at a mother's knees, by that holy history which perchance you first heard from a mother's lips, give not up the first child-like faith of earlier and it may be purer days,—that simple, heroic faith, which such men as Niebuhr[1] and

vi. 12); (*b*) in the allusions to the circumstances of lowliness and obscurity under which that growth was to take place (comp. Isaiah liii. 2); and perhaps further (*c*) in the prophetic notices of a contempt and rejection (Isaiah liii. 3), such as seems to have been the common and, as it would seem in many respects, deserved portion of the inhabitant of rude and ill-reputed Nazareth. See above, p. 47, note 1, and for further information and illustrations, Spanheim, *Dub. Evang.* XC.—XCII. Part II. p. 598 sq., Deyling, *Obs. Sacr.* XL. Vol. I. p. 176, Patritius, *de Evang.* Dissert. XXXVII. Part III. p. 406, Mill, *Observations*, II. 3. 1, p. 422 sq.

[1] It must be regarded as very striking, that the great historian who could express himself with such strength and even bitterness of language against much that, however exaggerated it may have been in the case in question, was really fundamentally sound in pietism (see Letter CCLXXX.), could yet feel it right to educate his son in a way that must have led to the deepest reverence for the very *letter* of the inspired records. These are Niebuhr's own words : 'He [his son] shall believe in the letter of the Old and New Testaments, and I shall nurture in him, from his infancy, a firm faith in all that I have lost, or feel uncertain about.' *Life and Letters*, Vol. II. p. 101 (Transl. 1852).

Neander[1] knew how to appreciate and to glorify, even while they felt its fullest measures could never be their own. Remember that when faith grows cold love soon passes away and hope soon follows it, and believe me that the world cannot exhibit a spectacle more utterly mournful, more full of deepest melancholy, than a young yet doubting, a fresh yet unloving, an eager yet hopeless and forsaken heart.

May these humble words have wrought in you the conviction, that if with a noble and earnest spirit, like the Berœans of old[a], we search the Scriptures, we shall full surely find,—yea verily that we who may go forth weeping to gather up the few scattered ears of truth that might seem all that historical scepticism had now left to us, shall yet return with joy[b], and bring with us the sheaves of accumulated convictions, and the plenitudes of assurance in the everlasting truth of every part and every portion of the Gospel of Jesus Christ.

[a] Acts xvii. 11
[b] Ps. cxxvi. 6

---

[1] After some comments on extreme views as to what is termed, not perhaps very correctly, 'the *old* mechanical view of inspiration,' this thoughtful writer thus proceeds: ' But this [existence of chasms in the Gospel history] only affords room for the exercise of our faith,— a faith whose root is to be found, not in demonstration, but in the humble and self-denying submission of our spirits. Our scientific views may be defective in many points; our knowledge itself may be but fragmentary ; but our religious interests will find all that is necessary to attach them to Christ as the ground of salvation and the archetype of holiness.' *Life of Jesus Christ*, p. 9 (Bohn),—a paraphrastic, but substantially correct representation of the original.

LECTURE III.

THE EARLY JUDÆAN MINISTRY.

St Luke ii. 52.

And Jesus increased in wisdom and stature, and in favour with God and man.

LECT. III.

The early years of our Lord's life.

IN my last lecture, brethren, we concluded with that portion of the sacred narrative which briefly notices the return of the Holy Family to Nazareth, and the fulfilment of the spirit of ancient prophecy in the Redeemer of the world being called a Nazarene. Between that event and the group of events which will form the subject of this afternoon's lecture, and which make up what may be termed our Lord's early Judæan ministry, one solitary occurrence is recorded in the Gospel narrative,—our Lord's second appearance in the Temple at Jerusalem, His second presentation in His Father's house.

Reserve of the Evangelists.

With the single exception of the notice of this deeply interesting event, the whole history of the Saviour's childhood, youth, and even early manhood, is passed over by all the Evangelists with a most solemn reserve. Even he of them who appears to have received so much, directly or indirectly, from the blessed Virgin herself[1], and from whom we might have expected some passing no-

[1] See the remarks above, p. 14, note 1.

tices of that mysterious childhood,—even he would seem to have been specially moved to seal all in silence, and to relate no more than this one event which marks the period when the Holy One was just passing the dividing line between childhood and youth. Both periods, that preceding and that succeeding this epoch, are described in two short verses[a], closely similar in expression, and tending alike to show that the outward and earthly development of our Redeemer was in strict accordance with those laws, by which those He came to save pass from childhood into youth, and from youth into mature age[1].

LECT. III.

[a] Luke ii. 40 and 52

In regard of the first period, that of the childhood, one short clause is graciously added to warn us from unlicensed musings upon the influences of outward things upon the Holy Child[2],—one clause

The brief notice of our Lord's childhood.

---

[1] It is well said by Cyril of Alexandria: 'Examine, I pray you, closely the profoundness of the dispensation; the Word endures to be born in human fashion, although in His Divine nature He has no beginning, nor is subject to time. He who as God is all-perfect submits to bodily growth, the Incorporeal has limbs that advance to the ripeness of manhood...The wise Evangelist did not introduce the Word in His abstract and incorporate nature, and so say of Him that he increased in stature and wisdom and grace, but after having shown that He was born in the flesh of a woman, and took our likeness, he then assigns to Him these human attributes, and calls Him a child, and says that He waxed in stature, as His body grew little by little, in obedience to corporeal laws.' *Comment. on Luke*,

Part I. pp. 29, 30 (Transl.). So too Origen: 'Et crescebat, inquit, humiliaverat enim se, formam servi accipiens, et eadem virtute qua se humiliaverat, crescit.' *In Luc. Hom.* XIX. Vol. III. p. 953 (ed. Bened.).

[2] On this subject see more below, p. 99 sq. Meanwhile we may justly record our protest against the way in which a most serious and profound question is now usually discussed, and the repulsive freedom which many modern writers, not only in Germany, but even in this country, permit themselves to assume when alluding to the mental development of the Holy Child: see for example, the highly objectionable remarks of Hase (*Leben Jesu*, § 31, p. 56), in which this writer plainly tells us at the outset that 'the spiritual development of Jesus depended on fortunate gifts of na-

LECT. III.

ᵃ Lk. ii. 40

Equally brief notice of our Lord's youth.

only, but enough,—'and the grace of God was upon Himᵃ.'

In regard of the second period, that of the Lord's youth and early manhood, one event at its commencement, which shows us how that grace unfolded itself in heavenly wisdom[1], is made fully known to us,—one event, but one only, to which

ture' (*glücklichen Naturgaben*); and that these, though enhanced by the purposes and circumstances of His after-life, still never went beyond the culture of the time and country, and never 'transcended the limits of humanity.' Compare too Von Ammon, *Leben Jesu*, I. 10, Vol. I. p. 236, where the highly questionable views of Theodorus of Mopsuestia find a ready defender; and for an example from writers of our country of eloquent and attractive, but still painfully humanitarian comments on this mysterious subject, see Robertson, *Sermons*, Vol. II. p. 196.

[1] On this subject the following are the sentiments of Gregory of Nazianzus: 'He was making advance, as in stature so also in wisdom and grace. Not by these qualities receiving increase,—for what can be more perfect than that which is so from the very beginning?—but by their being disclosed and revealed by little and little.' *Orat.* XX. p. 343 (Paris, 1609). It may, however, be justly doubted whether these statements,—especially the negative assertion,—though confessedly in close accordance with some expressions of Athanasius (προκόπτοντος τοῦ σώματος προέκοπτεν ἐν αὐτῷ καὶ ἡ φανέρωσις τῆς θεότητος τοῖς ὁρῶσιν. *Adv. Arian.* III. 29. 14), and other orthodox writers, are not unduly restricted, and whether the words of the inspired Evangelist do not clearly

imply (to use the language of Waterland) that our Lord's increase in wisdom is to be understood in a sense as 'literal, as His increasing in stature is literal' (*Script. and Arians compared*, Vol. III. p. 298). While then with these catholic writers we may certainly acknowledge a gradual and progressive *disclosure* of the Lord's *divine* wisdom, we must certainly, with other equally catholic writers, recognize a regular development and *increase* in the wisdom and grace of the *reasonable* soul, *i.e.*,—to speak with psychological accuracy, of the ψυχή and νοῦς; the true and complete statement being,—'Christum secundum sapientiam divinam, hoc est eam, quæ ei competit tanquam Deo, non profecisse; secundum sapientiam autem humanam, hoc est eam, quæ ei ut homini competit, vere profecisse, hominis quidem more, sed tamen supra modum humanum.' Suicer, *Thes.* Vol. II. p. 269 (appy. from Bernh. *de Consid.* Book II.). In a word then, as Cyril of Alexandria (*in loc.*) briefly says, 'the body advances in stature and the [reasonable] soul in wisdom:' see Ambrose, *de Incarn.* cap. 72 sq. Vol. II. 1, p. 837 (ed. Migne), Epiphanius, *Hær.* LXXVII. 26, Vol. I. p. 1019 (Paris, 1622), and the good note of the Oxford Translator (J. H. Newman) of Athanasius, *Select Treatises*, Disc. III. Part II. p. 474 (Libr. of Fathers).

one short verse, that of our text, is added, to teach us how that wisdom waxed momently more full, more deep, more broad, until, like some mighty river seeking the sea, it merged insensibly into the omniscience of His limitless Godhead[1]. One further touch completes the Divine picture,—'in favour with God and man[a],' perchance designed to hint to us that the outward form corresponded to the inner development, that the fulness of heavenly wisdom dwelt in a shrine of outward perfection and beauty[2], and that the ancient tradi-

[a] Lk. ii. 52

---

[1] This simile, though merely intended to illustrate generally a profound mystery, and not to be pressed with dogmatic exactness, is still, as it would seem, substantially correct. The fact of the present verse (Luke ii. 52) being one of those urged by the heretical sect of the Agnoetæ, as tending to show limitations even in our Lord's Divine nature, was not improbably the cause of its having received some interpretations (see above) so rigid, as to favour by inference the Apollinarian statement that the Word itself was in the place of the νοῦς (Pearson, *Creed*, Vol. II. p. 122, ed. Burton). The whole subject, and a scholastic discussion 'de Christi scientia et nescientia et profectu secundum humanitatem,' will be found in Forbes, *Instruc. Hist.-Theol.* Book III. ch. 19, 20: see Petav. *Dogm. Theol.* (*de Incarn.* XI. 2), Vol. VI. p. 39, Suicer, *Thesaur.* s. v. Λόγος, Vol. II. p. 268, and the sensible remarks of Boyse on our Lord's omniscience, *Vindic. of our Saviour's Deity*, Vol. II. p. 23 sq. (Lond. 1728).

[2] Upon this point, it need scarcely be said, nothing certain can be adduced. From the Gospels we seem to be able to infer that our Lord's outward form, on one occasion at least, sensibly struck the beholders with a feeling of the majesty and dignity of Him who condescended to wear the garments of our mortality: comp. John xviii. 6. Perhaps, however, we may go so far as to say, that there was still nothing that merely outwardly marked the Redeemer of the world as *strikingly* different from the general aspect of the men of his own time and country, otherwise it would seem strange that the Apostles who beheld him by the lake of Gennesareth, and to whom He was near enough to be easily heard (John xxi. 4 sq.) did not *instantly* recognize who it was. The similar failure of recognition in the case of the two disciples going to Emmaus (Luke xxiv. 13 sq.) can perhaps hardly be urged, owing to the Evangelist's own remark (ver. 16), and the further illustrative comment of St Mark (ἐν ἑτέρᾳ μορφῇ, ch. xvi. 12). This perhaps is all that can safely be specified. The more distinct descriptions of our Lord's appearance, especially those in the *Epistle of Lentulus* (see Fabricius, *Codex Apocr. N. T.* Vol. I. p. 301

88 The Early Judæan Ministry.

LECT. III.

ᵃ liii. 3

Visit to the Temple when twelve years old.

tion¹ which assigned no form or comeliness to 'the fairest of the children of men²,' was but a narrow and unworthy application of the merely general terms of Isaiah's prophecyᵃ.

Thus waxing strong in spirit and in the grace of His heavenly Father, the Holy Child, when twelve years old, goes up with both His parents

sq.), and the very similar one of Epiphanius Monachus (p. 29, ed. Dressel,—and cited by Winer, *RWB*. Art. 'Jesus,' Vol. I. p. 576, after a better text supplied to him by Tischendorf), appear clearly to be due to the imagination and conceptions of the writers. The statue of our Lord, said by Eusebius (*Hist. Eccl.* VII. 18) to have been erected at Cæsarea Philippi by the woman with the issue of blood (Matth. ix. 20), might perhaps be urged as showing that our Lord's appearance was not unknown to the early Church, if it did not appear probable from historical considerations that the statue in question really never represented our Lord, and was never erected under the alleged circumstances: see the 'Excursus' of Heinichen, in his edition of Eusebius, *H. E.* Vol. III. p. 396 sq. The student who is anxious to pursue further this interesting, but not very profitable subject, will find abundant notices in Winer, *RWB*. Vol. I. p. 576, and especially in Hase, *Leben Jesu*, § 34, p. 62 sq. (ed. 3), Hofmann, *Leben Jesu*, § 67, p. 292 sq.; and may consult the special work of Reiske, *de Imaginibus Christi* (Jen. 1685). Some curious remarks of Origen in reference to a supposed diversity in our Lord's appearance to different persons, will be found in the Latin translation of that great writer's commentaries *on Matth.*

§ 100, Vol. III. p. 906 (ed. Bened.); comp. Norton, *Genuineness of Gospels*, Vol. II. p. 274 (ed. 2).

¹ See Justin Martyr, *Trypho*, cap. 14, Vol. II. p. 52 (ed. Otto): Τῶν τε λόγων τούτων καὶ τοιούτων, εἰρημένων ὑπὸ τῶν προφητῶν, ἔλεγον ᾧ Τρύφων, οἱ μὲν εἴρηνται εἰς τὴν πρώτην παρουσίαν τοῦ Χριστοῦ, ἐν ᾗ καὶ ἄτιμος καὶ ἀειδὴς καὶ θνητὸς φανήσεσθαι κεκηρυγμένος ἐστίν, οἱ δὲ εἰς τὴν δευτέραν αὐτοῦ παρουσίαν. So still more distinctly Clem. Alex. *Pædag.* III. 1. 3: Τὸν δὲ Κύριον αὐτὸν τὴν ὄψιν αἰσχρὸν γεγονέναι διὰ Ἡσαΐου τὸ Πνεῦμα μαρτυρεῖ. Comp. *Strom.* III. 17, 103, Orig. *Cels.* VI. p. 327 (ed. Spencer),—where the concession is made to Celsus, and Tertull. *de Carne Chr.* cap. 9, *adv. Jud.* cap. 14. This opinion, however, soon began to be modified; see Augustine, *Serm.* CXXXVIII. Vol. V. p. 766 (ed. Migne), and Jerome, *Epist.* LXV. Vol. I. p. 380 (ed. Vall.), who well remarks,—' Nisi habuisset et in vultu quiddam oculisque sidereum, nunquam eum statim secuti fuissent Apostoli, nec qui ad comprehendendum eum venerant, corruissent.'

² Chrysostom rightly urges this indirect prophecy: Οὐδὲ γὰρ θαυματουργῶν ἦν θαυμαστὸς μόνον, ἀλλὰ καὶ φαινόμενος πολλῆς ἔγεμε χάριτος, καὶ τοῦτο ὁ προφήτης δηλῶν ἔλεγεν 'Ὡραῖος κάλλει παρὰ τοὺς υἱοὺς τῶν ἀνθρώπων. *Hom. in Matth.* XVIII. 2, Vol. VII. p. 371 (ed. Bened.).

to the Passover at Jerusalem, not however as a worshipper, nor as yet even what Hebrew phraseology has termed, a 'Son of the Law,' though possibly as a partaker in some preparatory rite which ancient custom might have associated with that age of *commencing* puberty[1]. We observe that it is incidentally noticed that the blessed Virgin not only on this occasion, but every year[a], went up with Joseph to the great festival of her nation. Like Hannah of old[b], year after year, though compelled neither by law nor by custom[2], she might have longed to enter into the more immediate presence of the God of Israel, and though but dimly conscious of the eventful future, might have felt with

[a] Lk. ii. 41

[b] 1 Sam. ii. 19; comp. i. 7.

---

[1] This perhaps is the critically exact statement, as it would certainly seem that the age of puberty was not considered as actually attained till the completion of the thirteenth year: see Jost, *Geschichte des Judenth.* III. 3. 11, Vol. I. p. 398 (where the statement of Ewald is rectified); and compare Greswell, *Dissert.* XII. Vol. I. p. 396, and *ib.* XVIII. Vol. II. p. 136. It has been doubted, then, whether on this occasion our Lord was taken up to celebrate the festival, or whether it was merely to appear before the Lord in company with his parents, and perhaps take part in some introductory ceremony. The patristic commentators (*e.g.* Cyril Alex. 'upon the summons of the feast,' Part I. p. 30, and probably Origen, *Hom. in Luc.* XIX.) appear rather to advocate the former opinion, and would lead us to think that our Lord, either in compliance with the wishes of His parents, or more probably in accordance with His own desire (comp. ver. 49), attended the festival as an actual worshipper: the latter opinion, however, seems most correct, and most in accordance with what we know of Jewish customs: see Greswell, *l. c.* Vol. I. p. 397. The rule appears to have been that all males were to attend the three great festivals, 'exceptis surdo, stulto, puerulo...puerulus autem ille dicitur, qui, nisi a patre manu trahatur incedere non valet.' Bartolocci, *Biblioth. Rabbin.* Vol. III. p. 132: compare Lightfoot, *Hor. Hebr.* (*in loc.*) p. 499 (Roterod. 1686)..

[2] See the very distinct quotation adduced by Schoettgen (*Hor. Hebr.* Vol. I. p. 266), from which it would appear that the injunction of Hillel, that women should once attend the passover, was not binding, and indeed self-contradictory. Such a habit on the part of the blessed Virgin must be referred to her piety. Schoettgen quotes from the tract, 'Mechilta,' a similar instance in the case of the wife of Jonah,—'Uxor Jonæ ascendit ad celebranda festa solemnia.' (*loc. cit.*)

LECT. III.

Search for and discovery of the Holy Child.

each revolving year a mysterious call to that Festival, of which the Holy Child beside her was hereafter to be the Lamb and the sacrifice.

After the paschal solemnities were celebrated, most probably on the afternoon of the eighth day[1], the Virgin and Joseph turn their steps backwards to Galilee,—but alone. They deem the Holy Child was in another portion of the large pilgrim-company,—perhaps with contemporaries to whom, after the solemnities they had shared in, ancient custom might have assigned a separate place in the festal caravan[2], and they doubt not that at their evening resting-place among the hills of Benjamin (not improbably that Beeroth which tradition has fixed upon[3]), they shall be sure to find

---

[1] It has been correctly observed by Lightfoot (*Hor. Hebr. in loc.* p. 740), that the expression τελειωσάντων τὰς ἡμέρας (Luke ii. 43), seems certainly to imply that the Holy Family staid the full time of seven days at Jerusalem. During this time it is not improbable that the youthful Saviour had been observed by some of the members of the venerable assemblage among whom he was subsequently found. Perhaps even, with Euthymius, we might further attribute the Lord's prolonged stay to a desire to consort longer with those on whom the words of grace and wisdom which fell from His lips could not but have produced a startling and perhaps long-remembered effect: ὑπέμεινε δέ, εἴτουν ὑπελείφθη ἐν Ἱερουσαλήμ, βουλόμενος συμμίξαι τοῖς διδασκάλοις (Vol. II. p. 279, ed. Matth.).

[2] Greswell urges, on the authority of Maimonides (*de Sacrif. Pasch.* II. 4), that a paschal company could not be composed of 'pueri impuberes.' This would seem certainly correct (comp. *Mishna*, 'Pesachim,' VII. 4, p. 118 of De Sola's transl.); but it does not seem to militate against the assumption in the text, that in returning a separate company might be formed of those who had gone through the preliminary ceremony which Maimonides himself seems to allude to: comp. *de Sacr. Solemn.* II. 3 (cited by Greswell, Vol. I. p. 397).

[3] The usual resting-place for the night appears to have been Sichem, which, though in Samaria, was not forbidden as a temporary station: 'Terra Samaritanorum munda est, et fontes mundi, et mansiones mundae,' *Talm. Hieros.* 'Abodah Zarah,' fol. 44. 4, cited by Sepp, *Leben Christi*, Vol. II. p. 45. But tradition and probability appear to prevail in favour of Beer or Beeroth, a place distant, according to Robinson (*Palest.* Vol. I. p. 452), about

Him. But they find Him not. Full of trouble they turn backwards to Jerusalem; a day is spent in anxious search, perhaps among the travelling companies which now in fast succession would be returning homeward from the Holy City; yet another day they search in vain[1]. On the third they find the Holy Child, but in what an unexpected place, and under circumstances how mysterious and unlooked for. In the precincts of the temple, most probably in one of the rooms[2] where, on Sabbath-days and at the great festivals, the Masters of Israel sat and taught, they find Him they had so long sought for. They find Him sitting in the midst of that venerable circle[a]; sitting[3], yet at no Gamaliel's

[a] Lk. ii. 46

three hours from Jerusalem: comp. Winer, *RWB.* s. v. 'Beer,' Vol. I. p. 146.

[1] The exact manner in which the time specified was spent has been differently estimated. It seems most reasonable to suppose that one day was spent in the return and search on the road, a second in fruitless search in Jerusalem, and that on the third the Holy Child was found. The remark of Bengel is curious: '*Tres.* Numerus mysticus. Totidem dies mortuus a discipulis pro amisso habitus est.' If there be anything in this, we might feel disposed to adopt rather the view of Euthymius: 'One day they spent, when they went a day's journey and sought for Him among their kinsfolk and acquaintance; a second when, in consequence of not having found Him, they returned to Jerusalem seeking Him; in the course of the third day they at length found him.' *Comment. on Luke* ii. 44. The expression μεθ' ἡμέρας τρεῖς, seems, however, rather in favour of the first

view; comp. Meyer *in loc.*

[2] We learn from the Talmudic gloss cited by Lightfoot (*in loc.*), that there was a synagogue 'near the court, in the mountain of the Temple:' comp. Deyling, *Obs. Sacr.* xxx. Vol. III. p. 283, Reland, *Antiq.* I. 8. 6. Here, or in one of the many buildings attached to the Temple, apparently on its eastern side, we may conceive the Holy Child to have been found: see Sepp, *Leben Chr.* I. 16, Vol. II. p. 47, and Just, *Gesch. des Judenth.* II. 1: 2, Vol. I. p. 140.

[3] The Talmudic statement, cited by Lightfoot, that scholars did not sit, but stand ('a diebus Mosis ad Rabban Gamalielem non didicerunt legem nisi *stantes*,' 'Megillah,' fol. 21. 1), is apparently untenable (see Vitringa, *de Synag.* Vol. I. p. 167), and not to be pressed in the present passage. The words καθεζόμενον ἐν μέσῳ τῶν διδασκάλων seem, however, to bear out the view adopted in the text, and are so interpreted by De Wette *in loc.*

feet, but, as the words would seem to imply, spontaneously raised to a position of equal dignity, not the hearer only, but the indirect teacher by the divine depth of His mysterious questions[1]...No wonder that the Evangelist should tell us that His parents when they saw Him 'were amazed[a];' no wonder that even the holy mother when she gazed on that august assemblage, when she saw, as she perchance might have seen[2], the now aged Hillel the looser, and Shammai the binder[3], and the wise sons of Betirah, and Rabban Simeon, Hillel's son, and Jonathan the paraphrast, the greatest of his pupils,—when she saw these and such as these all hanging on the questions of the Divine Child, no wonder that she forgot all

[a] Lk. ii. 48

---

[1] This is the patristic and, as it would seem, correct statement of the exact relation in which the Holy Child now stood to those around Him: 'Quia parvulus erat, invenitur in medio non eos docens, sed interrogans, et hoc pro ætatis officio, ut nos doceret, quid pueris, quamvis sapientes et eruditi sint, conveniret, ut audiant potius magistros, quam docere desiderent, et se varia ostentatione non jactent. Interrogabat inquam magistros, non ut aliquid disceret, sed *ut interrogans crudiret.*' Origen, *in Luc.* Hom. xix. Vol. iii. p. 955 (ed. Bened.). 'Those very questions,' says Bp Hall, were 'instructions, and meant to teach.' *Contempl.* ii. 1. The view taken by Bp Taylor (*Life of Christ*, i. 7), that the present exhibition of learning was little short of miraculous, seems far less natural, and less consonant with the tenor of the sacred text.

[2] The names mentioned in the text belong to men who are known to have been alive at the time, and who occupied conspicuous places among the circle of Jewish Doctors. For further information respecting those here specified, see Sepp, *Leben Christi*, i. 17, Vol. ii. p. 47 sq., and the notices of Petrus Galatinus, *de Arcan. Cath. Ver.* cap. 2, 3, p. 5 sq. (Francof. 1602). There may be some doubt about Hillel being still alive; but if our assumed date of this event (A. U. C. 762) is correct and the dates supplied by Sepp (*loc. cit.*) are to be relied on, we seem justified in believing that that venerable teacher was one of those thus preeminently blessed.

[3] 'Shammai ligat, Hillel solvit;' comp. Lightfoot, *in Matth.* xvi. 19, p. 378. For an account of the general principles of teaching respectively adopted by these celebrated men and their followers, see Jost, *Gesch. des Judenth.* ii. 3. 13, Vol. i. p. 257 sq.

in the strange and unlooked-for circumstances in which she found Him she had so sorrowingly[a] sought for. All the mother speaks out in her half-reproachful address[1], all the consciously incarnate Son in the mysterious simplicity of the answers that reminds the earthly mother that it was in the courts of His heavenly Father's house[2] that the Son must needs be found, that His true home was in the temple of Him whose glories still lingered round the heights of Moriah...And yet with what simple pathos is it noticed by the Evangelist, that 'He went down and came to Nazareth, and was subject to them[b].' As that Holy One left the glories of heaven to tabernacle with men, so now in retrospective shadow and similitude He leaves the blessedness of His Father's temple for the humble home of earthly parents, and remains

[a] Lk. ii. 49

[b] ver. 51

---

[1] The prominence which the Virgin-mother gives to the relation she bore to the Holy One that vouchsafed to be born of her can hardly be accidental,—τέκνον, τί ἐποίησας ἡμῖν οὕτως, ver. 48. The emphatic position of the πρὸς αὐτόν might also almost lead us so far to agree with Bp Hall ('it is like that she reserved this question till she had Him alone,' Contempl. II. 1) as to think that it was addressed to the Divine Child in tones that might not have been heard, or intended to have been heard, by those around. All the patristic expositors comment on the use of the term οἱ γονεῖς αὐτοῦ, and ὁ πατήρ σου in reference to Joseph, and none perhaps with more point than Origen: 'Nec miremur parentes vocatos, quorum altera ob partum, alter ob obsequium, patris et matris meruerunt vocabula.' In Luc. Hom. XIX. Vol. III. p. 955 (ed. Bened.). So Augustine, though with a further and deeper reference : ' Propter quoddam cum ejus matre sanctum et virginale conjugium, etiam ipse [Joseph] parens Christi meruit appellari.' Contr. Faust. Manich. III. 2, Vol. III. p. 214 (ed. Migne).

[2] The exact meaning of the words ἐν τοῖς τοῦ πατρός μου has been differently estimated. Common usage (see exx. in Lobeck, Phrynicus, p. 100), and still more the idea of locality which would seem naturally involved in an answer to the preceding notice of the search that had been made, may incline us to the gloss of Euthymius,—ἐν τῷ οἴκῳ τοῦ πατρός μου. So also the Peshito-Syriac and Armenian versions: the Vulgate, Coptic, and Gothic are equally indeterminate with the original.

94   *The Early Judæan Ministry.*

LECT. III. — with them as the loving and submissive son, the sharer perhaps in His reputed father's earthly labours[1], the consoler and perchance supporter of the widowed Virgin after the righteous son of Jacob, who henceforth appears no more in the history, had been called away to his rest[2].

Frivolous nature of the objections urged against the narrative.   And this is the narrative, this narrative so simple and so true, in which modern scepticism has fancied it can detect inconsistencies and incongruities[3]. And yet what is there so strange, what so inconceivable? Does the age of the Holy Child seem to preclude the possibility of such contact with the Masters of Israel, when the historian Josephus, as he himself tells us[4], was actually consulted by the high priests and principal men of the city at an age but little more advanced than that of the youthful Saviour? Are we to admit

---

[1] This statement is perhaps partially supported by Mark vi. 3, οὐχ οὗτός ἐστιν ὁ τέκτων,—a reading which, even in spite of the assertion of Origen in reply to Celsus, that our Lord is never described in the four Gospels as a carpenter (*Contr. Cels.* VI. 36), must *certainly* be retained: see Tischendorf *in loc.* When we add to this the old tradition preserved by Justin Martyr (*Trypho,* cap. 88), that our Lord made 'ploughs, yokes, and other implements pertaining to husbandry,' we seem fully warranted in believing that our Redeemer vouchsafed to set to us this further example of humility and dutiful love. The silly legends of the apocryphal gospels hardly deserve to be noticed: see, however, *Evang. Thom.* cap. 11, *Evang. Inf. Arab.* cap. 38, 39.

[2] See above, p. 56, note 2. According to a simple comparison of two passages in the apocryphal *Historia Josephi* (cap. 14, 15), this took place in the eighteenth year of our Lord. Upon such authority, however, no further reliance can be placed than perhaps as the expression of a belief in the early Church that Joseph did not, as Ambrose seems distinctly to *imply* (*de Instit. Virg.* cap. 7, Vol. II. 1, p. 318, ed. Migne), survive our Lord, or even the times of His public ministry.

[3] For some notices of these objections, see Ebrard, *Kritik der Evang. Gesch.* § 50, p. 247.

[4] 'Moreover, when I was a child,' says the historian, 'and about fourteen years of age, I was commended by all for the love I had to learning; on which account the highpriests and principal men of the city

such precocity in the case of the son of Matthias and deny it in that of the Son of God? Or again, is the assumed neglect of the parents to be urged against the credibility of the narrative[1], when we know so utterly nothing of the arrangement of these travelling companies, or of the bands and groupings into which on such solemn occasions as the present, custom might have divided the returning worshippers? But I will not pause on such shallow and hapless scepticism; I will not do such dishonour to the audience before which I stand as to assume that it is necessary for me to make formal replies to such unmerited cavillings. I will only presume to make this one mournful comment, —that if a narrative like the present, so full as it is of life-like touches, so exquisitely natural in its details, and so strangely contrasted with the silly fictions of the Apocryphal Infancies[2]—if such a narrative as this is to be regarded as legendary or

---

came then frequently to me together, in order to know my opinion about the accurate understanding of points of the law.' *Life*, ch. 2. Vol. I. p. 2 (Whiston's transl.). Such a statement would seem inconceivable, if it were not remembered that so much, especially of interpretation of the law, turned on opinion and modes of reasoning rather than on accumulations of actual learning: see especially Wotton, *Discourses*, ch. iv. Vol. I. p. 24 sq.

[1] Much has been said by a certain class of writers about the want of proper care for the Holy Child previously evinced by Joseph and Mary. Such remarks are as untenable as they are clearly designed to be mischievous. Even Hase remarks that the Lord's staying behind in Jerusalem is perfectly conceivable without attributing any carelessness to His parents. *Leben Jesu*, § 30, p. 55; comp. Tholuck, *Glaubwürd.* p. 214 sq. Bede (*in loc.* Vol. III. p. 349, ed. Migne) suggests that the women and men returned in different bands, and that Joseph and Mary each thought that the Holy Child was with the other. This, however, seems 'argutius quam verius dictum.'

[2] The simple evangelical narrative of our Lord's interview with the Doctors has, as we might have imagined, called forth not a few apocryphal additions. These will be found in the *Evang. Infant. Arab.* cap. 50—52, pp. 199, 200 (ed. Tisch.).

mythical, then we may indeed shudderingly recognize what is meant by the 'evil heart of unbelief[a],' what it is to have that mind that will excogitate doubts where the very instinctive feelings repudiate them, and will disbelieve where disbelief becomes plainly monstrous and revolting.

And now eighteen years of the Redeemer's earthly life pass silently away[1], a deep veil falls over that mysterious period which even loving and inquiring antiquity has not presumed to raise, save in regard to the brief notice of the Saviour's earthly calling to which an early writer has alluded[2], and to which, both national custom and the examples of the greatest teachers, Hillel not excepted[3], lend considerable plausibility.

Silence of the Evangelists on the next eighteen years of our Lord's life.

[a] Heb. iii 12

---

[1] This would seem the place, in accordance with the arrangement in the Gospel of St Luke, for making a few comments on the genealogies of our Lord as recorded in this Gospel and that of St Matthew. Into this difficult subject, however, it does not seem desirable to enter further, than to remark for the benefit of the general reader, (a) that the most exact recent research tends distinctly to prove the correctness of the almost universally received ancient opinion, that *both* are the genealogies of our Lord's reputed *father;* (b) that the genealogy of St Matthew is not according to lineal descent, but according to the line of *regal* succession from Solomon,—and that in accordance with national and scriptural usage, and possibly for the sake of facilitating memory (Mill, p. 105) it is recorded in an abridged and also symmetrical form; (c) that the genealogy of St Luke exhibits the *natural* descent from David through Nathan; (d) that the two genealogies can be reconciled with one another, and with the genealogy of the house of David preserved in the Old Testament. For a complete substantiation of these assertions, see Mill, *Obs. on Pantheistic Principles,* II. 2. 1, 2, p. 101 sq., Hervey (Lord A.) *Genealogies of our Lord* (Cambr. 1853); and compare August. *de Diversis Quæst.* LXI. Vol. VI. p. 50, and *contra Faust. Manich.* III. 1 sq. Vol. VIII. p. 214 sq.

[2] See above, p. 94 sq.

[3] For numerous citations from the Rabbinical writers confirming the above statement, see Sepp, *Leben Christi,* I. 19, Vol. II. p. 59 sq. The quotation in reference to Hillel is as follows: 'Num forte pauperior eras Hillele? Dixerunt de Hillele seniore quod singulis diebus laborabat, conductus mercede nummi.' Tract 'Joma,' fol. 36. 1: compare Lightfoot, *Hor. Hebr.* p. 444.

On this silence much has been said into which it is here not necessary to enter. Instead of pensive and mistaken longings, it should be to us a subject of rejoicing and thankfulness that in this particular portion of the sacred history Scripture has assumed to itself its prerogative of solemn reserve[1]. Think only, brethren, how the narrative of the simple events of that secluded childhood would have been dealt with by the scoffer and the sceptic. Nay pause to think what a trying effect it might have had even on the better portion of Christianity, how our weak and carnal hearts might have dwelt merely on the human side of the events related, and how hard it might have seemed to have realized the incarnate God in the simple incidents of that early life of duty and love. I ground this observation on the very suggestive fact recorded by St John, that our Lord's brethren 'did not believe on Him[a].' However these words may be interpreted; whether the word 'believe' is to be taken in a more general or more restricted sense,—whether the brethren be regarded as sons of the Virgin, or, as I humbly believe them to be, sons of Mary her sister[2], affects

Providential nature of this silence vindicated and exemplified.

[a] Joh. vii. 5

---

[1] A brief discussion of the question why so great a portion of our Redeemer's life is thus passed over, will be found in Spanheim, *Dub. Evang.* xcvi. Part II. p. 651. The contrast between this holy silence on the part of the Evangelists, and the circumstantial and often irreverent narratives of some of the apocryphal gospels (especially the *Pseudo-Matth. Evangelium*, and the *Evang. Infant. Arabicum*), is singularly striking and suggestive: see further comments, in *Cambr. Essays*, 1856, p. 156 sq.

[2] Upon this vexed question we will here only pause to remark, that the whole subject seems to narrow itself to a consideration of the apparently opposite deductions that have been made from two important texts. On the one hand, if we rest solely on the rigid meaning of the word ἐπίστευον in John vii. 5, and regard οἱ ἀδελφοὶ αὐτοῦ as including all so designated, it would certainly seem to follow that none of them could be apostles, and that consequently James the brother of the Lord was

our present argument but little. This momentous fact these words do place before us, that some of those who stood in the relation of kinsmanship and affinity to the Saviour, who saw Him as the familiar eye saw Him, were among the latest to acquire the fullest measures of faith. Though so many blessed opportunities were vouchsafed to them of seeing the glory of God shining through the veil of mortal flesh, yet they saw it not. Their eyes so rested on the outward tabernacle that they beheld not the Shechinah within. The material and familiar was an hindrance to their recognition of the spiritual,—an hindrance, be it not forgotten, which in their case was ultimately removed[1], but an hindrance, in the case of those

not identical with James the son of Alphæus. On the other hand, if we adopt the only sound grammatical interpretation which the words of Gal. i. 19 can fairly bear, we seem forced to the conclusion that James the Lord's brother *was* an Apostle, and consequently is to be identified with James the son of Alphæus. If this be so, James the Apostle and his brethren, owing to the almost certainly established identity of the names Alphæus and Clopas (Mill, *Observations*, II. 2. 3, p. 236) must be further identified with the children of Mary (Matth. xxvii. 56; Mark xv. 40) the wife of Clopas and aunt of our Lord (John xix. 25), and so His *cousins*. We have thus two texts for consideration, upon the correct interpretation of which the question mainly turns. That Gal. i. 19 cannot be strained to mean 'I saw none of the Apostles, *but* I saw the Lord's brother,' seems almost certain from the regularly exceptive use which εἰ μή appears always to preserve in the New Testament. That ἐπίστευον, however, in John vii. 5, is to be taken in the barest sense of the word, or that οἱ ἀδελφοὶ αὐτοῦ includes all so named, is by no means equally clear. Even if οὐκ ἐπίστευον be understood in a sense in which it could not be applied to an Apostle, we have still two of the ἀδελφοί, and perhaps more (see Mill), who were not Apostles, and who, with the sisters, might form a party that might reasonably be grouped under the roughly inclusive expression οἱ ἀδελφοὶ αὐτοῦ. For further information and references, see notes on *Gal.* i. 20, and especially Mill, *Observations*, II. 2. 3, p. 221 sq.

[1] It has been pertinently observed by Neander, that for this very reason such men are to be accounted still more trustworthy witnesses. The very fact that they who so long resisted the impression wrought upon them by our Lord, did at last yield, and acknowledge Him whom they accounted but as an unnoted re-

who could not have their advantages, which might never have been removed, an obstacle to a true acknowledgment of their Lord's divinity, against which faith might never have been able to prevail.

Much again has been said upon the mental and spiritual development of the Holy Child during these silent years, upon which it is equally unprofitable to enlarge[1]. Whatever speculations, in passive and meditative moments, we may indulge in with regard to these silent years, let us hold this as most fixed and irrefragably true, that our heavenly Master received nothing affecting His Divine purpose and mission from the influences of even the purer and more spiritual teaching of those around Him[2]. With what startling temerity has the converse statement been urged and accepted[3]; and yet is there not tacit blasphemy in the very thought? What was there for example in Pharisaism which could have had its

The mental and spiritual development of our Lord.

lative to be the Messiah and the Son of God, makes their testimony all the more valuable: see *Leben Jes. Chr.* p. 49 (Transl. p. 33).

[1] This subject and the probable 'plan' of our Saviour's ministry are topics which most of the modern lives of our Lord discuss with a very unbecoming freedom: see Hase, *Leben Jesu*, § 31, 40 sq., pp. 56, 69 sq. In reference to the former, and to the true nature of our Lord's advance in wisdom enough has been said above (p. 86, note 1): in reference to the latter it may be sufficient to say, simply and briefly, that the only principle of action by which man may presume to believe the Eternal Son to have been influenced was love toward man co-operating with obedience to the will of the Father (Heb. x. 9),—of Him with whom He Himself was one (John x. 30): comp. Ullmann, *Unsündlichkeit Jesu*, sect. IV. p. 25 (Transl. by Park). Further remarks will be found in Neander, *Life of Christ*, Book IV. p. 80 sq. (Bohn).

[2] Some very valuable comments on the religious views of the leading sects, and of the Jews generally in the time of our Lord, will be found in a recent work by Langen, *Judenthum in Palästina zur Zeit Christi*, pp. 183 sq. (Freiburg, 1866).

[3] The various sources to which ancient and modern sceptical writers have presumed to refer the peculiar characteristics of our Lord's teaching are specified by Hase, *Leben Jesu*, § 31, p. 57.

LECT. III.

influence on Him who so spake against every principle that marked it? What was there in the anti-eudæmonism[1], as it has been termed,—the desire placidly to do good for its own sake, which has been attributed to the original creed of the Sadducee,—that could for one instant be thought to have been assimilated by Him who came to save His own creatures with His sufferings and His blood, and whose ever-operative and redemptive love was the living protest against the coldness and deadness of a merely formal or self-complacent morality? What, lastly, was there in the much-vaunted spirit of Essene teaching that we can trace in the Gospel of Jesus Christ[2]? What was there in the spiritual pride of that secluded sect that sceptical criticism shall think it

---

[1] See Neander, *Life of Christ*, p. 38 (Bohn); and compare Jost, *Gesch. des Judenthums*, II. 2. 8, Vol. I. p. 215. The sentiment ascribed to the so-called founder of this sect is found in the *Mishna* (Tract, 'Pirke Aboth,' I. 3), and is to this effect: 'Be not as servants who serve their master on the condition of receiving a reward; but be as servants who serve on no such a condition, and let the fear of heaven be in you.' It must be observed, however, that though the above appears to have been one of the principles of early and even later Sadducæism, the connexion of the sect with Sadok, and of its doctrines with perversions of the original teaching of Antigonus Socho, is clearly to be regarded as a very questionable hypothesis: see Winer, *RWB.* Art. 'Sadducäer,' Vol. II. p. 352 sq.

[2] The connexion of Christianity with Essene teaching has always been the most popular of these theories: comp. Heubner on Reinhard's *Plan Jesu*, Append. v. How little similarity, however, there really is between the two systems, and how fundamental the differences, is clearly enough shown by Neander, *Life of Christ*, p. 38 (Bohn). For contemporary notices of the habits and tenets of this sect, see Philo, *Quod Omn. Prob.* § 12, Vol. II. p. 457, ib. *de Vit. Contempl.* § 1. Vol. II. p. 471 (ed. Mang.), and Joseph. *Antiq.* XIII. 5, 9, XVI. 1, 5, *Bell. Jud.* II. 8. 2 sq., and for a general estimate of the characteristics of Essene teaching and its relations to Pharisaism, Jost, *Gesch. des Judenth.* II. 2. 8, Vol. I. p. 207 sq. The assumption that the Essenes expected a Messiah who by his sufferings and death was to take away the sins of the world (Stäudlin, Kuinöl, al.) is fully disproved by Langen, *Judenth. zur Zeit Christi,* p. 457, note.

can discern in the active, practical, all-embracing covenant of Love? No, it cannot be. No finite human influences gave tinge to those eternal purposes. No doctrines and traditions of men added aught to the spiritual development of the Holy Child of Nazareth. From that Father in whose bosom[a] He had been from all eternity,—from the fulness of that Godhead of which He Himself was a co-partner,—unmingled and uncontaminated came all forms of that wisdom in which, as man, and as subject to the laws and developments of man's nature, the omniscient Son of God vouchsafed to advance and to make progress.

[a] John i. 18

Thus, O mystery of mysteries, in that green basin in the hills of Galilee[1], amid simple circumstances, and perchance in the exercise of a humble calling, dwelt the everlasting Son of God,—the varied features of that nature which He Himself had made so fair, the permitted media of the impressions of outward things[2]; His oratory the solitary mountains, His purpose the salvation of our race, His will the will of God....Thus silently and thus mysteriously pass away those eighteen years, until at length the hour is come, and the

The secluded youth of the Son of God.

[1] 'The town of Nazareth lies upon the western side of a narrow oblong basin, extending about from S.S.W. to N.N.E., perhaps twenty minutes in length by eight or ten in breadth. The houses stand on the lower part of the slope of the western hill, which rises high and steep above them....Towards the north the hills are less high; on the east and south they are low. In the south-east the basin contracts, and a valley runs out narrow and winding, apparently to the great plain.' Robinson, *Palestine*, Vol. II. p. 333 (ed. 2); see also Thomson, *The Land and the Book*, Vol. II. p. 131, and especially the good description in the new and very able work of Caspari, *Chronologisch-Geographische Einleitung in das Leben Jesu Christi*, p. 51 sq. (Hamburg, 1869).

[2] For a notice of the fair view that must have met the Saviour's eye whenever He ascended the western hill specified in the preceding note, see Robinson, *Palestine*, Vol. II. p. 336 sq., and comp. the photographic view of Frith, *Egypt*, &c., Pt. II.

LECT. III.

The ministry of the Baptist, and its probable effects.

voice of the mystic Elias is now heard sounding in the deserts, and preparing the way for Him that was to come.

On the ministry of the Baptist my limits will permit me to say but little. It would seem to have preceded that of our Lord by some months, and not improbably occupied the greater portion of the sabbatical year, which came to its conclusion three or four months before our Lord had completed His thirtieth year[1]. The effects of the Forerunner's ministry seem to have been of a mingled character. That St John found some partial adherents among the Pharisees and Sadducees[2] seems certain from the express words of St Matthew[a], and that two years after his death he, whom his Master had pronounced as among the greatest of the prophets[b], was to a great degree regarded as such by the fickle multitude at large,

[a] Mat. iii. 7
[b] Lk. vii. 28

---

[1] We have no data for fixing the time when the ministry of the Baptist commenced, unless we urge Luke iii. 1, which, as we shall see below (p. 104, note 1), is more plausibly referred to another period of his history. We are thus thrown on conjectures; the most probable of which seems that as St John was born six months before our Lord, so he might have preceded Him in his public ministrations by a not much greater space of time. The further chronological fact (see Wieseler, *Chron. Synops.* p. 204), that from the autumn of 779 A.U.C. to the autumn of 780 was a sabbatical year, is certainly significant, and may additionally incline us to the opinion that perhaps in the spring or summer of 780 A.U.C. St John's voice was first heard in the wilderness of Judæa. For notices of the outward circumstances under which the Forerunner appeared, the student may be referred to Spanheim, *Dub. Evang.* XCVII—C. Part II. p. 654 sq., Huxtable, *Ministry of St John*, p. 8 sq. (Lond. 1848), and the exhaustive dissertation of Patritius, *de Evang.* XLIII. Book III. 439 sq.

[2] The supposition that the members of these sects came to *oppose* the baptism of St John is just grammatically possible (see Meyer *in loc.*), but wholly contrary to the spirit of the context. They might have come with unworthy motives, from excited feelings, or from curiosity, but certainly not as direct opponents; see Neander, *Life of Christ*, p. 51 sq. (Bohn). Chrysostom perhaps goes too far the other way when he says, οὐ δὲ γὰρ ἁμαρτάνοντας εἶδεν ἀλλὰ μεταβαλλομένους. *Hom. in Matth.* XI. Vol. VII. p. 173 (ed. Bened. 2).

seems equally certain from the Gospel narrative[a]. Yet that the Pharisees as a body rejected his teaching, and that the effect on the great mass of the people was but partial and transitory, seems certain from our Lord's own comments on the generation that would not dance to those that piped unto them[1], and would not lament with those that mourned[b]. We may with reason, then, believe that the harbinger's message might have arrested, aroused, and awakened,—but that the general influence of that baptism of water was comparatively limited, and that its memory would have soon died away if He that baptized with the Holy Ghost and with fire had not invested it with a new and more vital significance. John struck the first chords, but the sounds would have soon died out into silence if a mightier hand had not swept the yet vibrating strings[2].

[a] Mk. xi. 32
[b] Mt. xi. 17
Lk. vii. 32

---

[1] This is also shown clearly by the remark of our Lord to the Jews on their general reception of the Baptist's message, ἠθελήσατε ἀγαλλιαθῆναι πρὸς ὥραν ἐν τῷ φωτὶ αὐτοῦ, John v. 35, where though the chief emphasis probably rests on the ἀγαλλιαθῆναι (as opp. to μετανοῆσαι, see Meyer *in loc.*) the πρὸς ὥραν is not without its special force: 'it marks,' as Chrysostom says, 'their lightmindedness and the quick way in which they fell back from him.' Compare too Matth. xxi. 32, though this perhaps more especially applies to those (οἱ ἀρχιερεῖς καὶ οἱ πρεσβύτεροι τοῦ λαοῦ, ver. 23) to whom our Lord was immediately speaking. On the effect of the Baptist's preaching compare, though with some reserve, the well-expressed estimate of Milman, *History of Christianity*, I. 3, Vol. I. p. 143 sq.

[2] This is the ancient and, as it would seem, correct view of the relations of the ministry of Christ to that of His Forerunner. Though on the one hand we must not rashly dissociate what undoubtedly stood in close relation to one another, we still can scarcely go so far on the other as to say that St John was 'absolutely the counterpart, and merely the forerunner of Christ' (Greswell, *Dissert.* XIX. Vol. II. p. 156). The difference between St John's baptism and christian, though treated as a needless question by Jackson (*Creed*, VII. 41, Vol. VI. p. 380), often occupied the attention of the early Church, and has never been better stated than by Gregory of Nazianzus: 'John also baptized, not however any longer after a Jewish manner, for he baptized, not with water only, but unto repent-

LECT. III.

Journey of our Lord to the Baptism of John.

ᵃ Numb. iv.

It was now probably towards the close of the year of the City 780[1], after more than the time allotted to the Levite's preparation for 'the service of the ministryᵃ' had already passed away[2], that

ance. Still it was not yet after a spiritual manner, for he adds not, "with the Spirit." Jesus baptizes also, but it is with the Spirit.' *Orat.* XXXIX. p. 634 (Paris, 1609): see August. *contr. Litt. Petil.* II. 32. 75, Vol. IX. p. 284 (ed. Migne), where the erroneous opinions of the schismatical bishop on this head are very clearly exposed; comp. also Thorndike, *Laws of the Church*, III. 7. 4, Vol. IV. 1, p. 149 sq. (A.-C. Libr.).

[1] This date, it need scarcely be said, like all the dates in our Redeemer's history, is open to much discussion. It has been selected after a prolonged consideration of the various opinions that have been recently adduced,— and certainly seems plausible. If, as we have supposed, our Lord was born towards the close of January or beginning of February, A.U.C. 750, He would now be 30 years old and some months over,—an age well coinciding with the ὡσεὶ ἐτῶν τριάκοντα ἀρχόμενος of Luke iii. 23. The only difficulty, and it is confessedly a great one, is the date previously specified by Luke, ch. iii. 1, the 15th year of the reign of Tiberius. If we take the first and apparently plain sense of the words, this 15th year can only be conceived to date back from the regular accession of Tiberius at the death of Augustus, and will consequently coincide with A.U.C. 781,—a date which not only involves the awkwardness of positively forcing us to extend the age of our Lord to 31 or more to make His birth *precede* the death of Herod (certainly April, A.U.C.

750), but also forces us to shorten the duration of His ministry very unduly to bring His death either to the year A.D. 29, or A.D. 30, which seem the only ones that fairly satisfy the astronomical elements which have been introduced into the question by Wurm (*Astron. Beiträge*) and others. We must choose then between two modes of obviating the difficulty; either, (*a*) with Creswell (*Dissert.* VII. Vol. I. p. 334 sq.) and more recently Caspari (*Chron.-Geogr. Einleit.* § 34, p. 39), we must suppose the 15 years to include two years during which Tiberius appears to have been associated with Augustus,—a mode of dating, however, both unlikely and unprecedented (see Wieseler, *Chron. Syn.* p. 172, Browne, *Ordo Sæc.* § 71, p. 76 sq.); or (*b*) we must conceive the 15th of Tiberius to coincide, not with the first appearance, but the captivity of John the Baptist,—the epoch, be it observed, from which, in accordance with ancient tradition (Eusebius, *Hist. Eccl.* III. 24), *the narrative of the Synoptical Gospels appears to date* (Matth. iv. 12, 17; Mark i. 14). This latter view has been well supported by Wieseler (*Chron. Syn.* p. 172 sq.) and adopted by Tischendorf (*Synops. Evang.* p. XIV. sq.), and is perhaps slightly the most probable. The opinion of Sanclemente and Browne (§ 85), that the 15th of Tiberius was the year of the Passion, has much less in its favour.

[2] The meaning of the words ὡσεὶ ἐτῶν τριάκοντα ἀρχόμενος (Luke iii. 23) has been much discussed; the doubt being whether the participle is to be referred (*a*) to the age speci-

the holy Jesus, moved we may humbly presume by that Spirit which afterwards directed His feet to the wilderness, leaves the home of His childhood, to return to it no more as His earthly abode, save for the few days[1] that preceded the removal to Capernaum in the spring of the following year.
...It was now winter[2], and the valley of Esdraelon

fied ('incipiebat esse quasi annorum triginta,' Beza, Greswell), or (*b*) to the commencement of the ministry. Whichever position of ἀρχόμενος we adopt (see Tischendorf *in loc.*) it can scarcely be doubted that (*b*) is the correct interpretation (so Origen and Euthym.), and that our Lord's ministry is to be understood to have commenced when He was more than 30, but less than 31 years of age. For arguments (not very strong) in favour of ὡσεί implying, not somewhat above, but somewhat *under* the time specified, see Greswell, *Dissert.* XI. Vol. I. p. 368.

[1] When our Lord returned to Galilee after the Temptation, it would seem that for the short time that preceded the passover He did not stay at Nazareth, but at Capernaum; see John ii. 12. On His next return to Galilee (December, A.U.C. 781), He appears to have gone to and perhaps stayed at Cana (John iv. 46), a place to which some writers have supposed that the Virgin and her kindred had previously retired: see Ewald, *Gesch. Christus*, Vol. V. p. 147. Under any circumstances we have only a short period remaining before the final removal to Capernaum, specified Matth. iv. 13, Luke iv. 31.

[2] The conclusion at which Wieseler arrives after a careful consideration of all the historical data that tend to fix the time of our Lord's baptism, is as follows: Jesus must have been baptized by John not earlier than February 780 A.U.C.

(the extreme 'terminus a quo' supplied by St Luke), nor later than the winter of the same year (the extreme 'terminus ad quem' supplied by St John): see *Chron. Synops.* II. B. 2, p. 201. Wieseler himself fixes upon the spring or summer of 780 A.U.C. as the exact date (p. 202); but to this period there are two objections; *First*, that if, as seems reasonable, we agree (with Wieseler) to fix the deputation to the Baptist (John i. 19 sq.) about the close of February 781 A.U.C., we shall have a period of eight months, viz. from the middle of 780 to the end of the second month of 781 wholly unaccounted for (Wieseler, *Chron. Synops.* p. 258); *secondly*, that it is almost the unanimous tradition of the early church that the baptism of our Lord took place *in winter*, or in the early part of the year: see the numerous ancient authorities in the useful table of Patritius, *Dissert.* XIX. Book III. p. 276, and comp. *Diss.* XLVII. p. 485. The tradition of the Basilideans mentioned by Clement of Alexandria (*Strom.* I. 21, Vol. I. p. 408, ed. Pott.), that the baptism of our Lord took place on the 11th or 15th of Tybi (Jan. 6 or 10) deserves consideration, both from the antiquity of the sect, and from the fact that the baptism of our Lord was in their system an epoch of the highest importance; see Neander, *Church Hist.* Vol. II. p. 102 (Clark). The ordinary objections founded on the season of the year are well and,

was just green with springing corn[1], as the Redeemer's path lay across it towards the desert valley of the Jordan, either to that ancient ford near Succoth, which recent geographical speculation[2] has connected with the Bethabara or rather Bethany of St John, or more probably to the neighbourhood of that more southern ford not far from Jericho, round which traditions yet linger[3], and to which the multitudes that flocked to the Baptist from Judæa and Jerusalem[a] would have found a speedier and more convenient access. There the great Forerunner was baptizing; there he had been but just uttering those words of stern

[a] Mark i. 5

as it would seem, convincingly answered by Greswell, *Dissert.* XI. Vol. I. p. 371 (ed. 2).

[1] The harvest in Palestine ripens at different times in different localities; but as a general rule the barley harvest may be considered as taking place from the middle to the close of April, and the wheat-harvest about a fortnight later; see Robinson, *Palestine*, Vol. I. p. 431 (ed. 2), and compare Stanley, *Palestine*, p. 240, note (ed. 2).

[2] See Stanley, *Palestine*, p. 308, who both pleads for the reading *Bethabara*, and for the more northern position of the scene of the baptism. With regard to the reading, at any rate, there can be no reasonable doubt. All the ancient authorities and nearly all the MSS. in the time of Origen (σχεδὸν πάντα τὰ ἀντίγραφα) adopt the reading *Bethany;* nor would Bethabara have ever found a place in the sacred text, if Origen, moved by geographical considerations, had not given sanction to the change; see Lücke, *Comment. über Joh.* i. 28, and the critical notes of Tischendorf *in loc.* The opinion of Caspari that the scene of St John's baptism is to be transferred to the upper Jordan and to Gaulonitis, though ingeniously maintained, cannot easily be reconciled with the statement of St Mark (Ch. i. 5) or with the probabilities of the case; see *Chron.-Geogr. Einleit.* § 77, p. 96.

[3] The traditional sites adopted by the Latin and Greek churches are not the same, but both not far from Jericho. The bathing-place of the Latin pilgrims is not far from the ruined convent of St John the Baptist, that of the Greek pilgrims two or three miles below it; see Robinson, *Palestine*, Vol. I. p. 536. The objection to the latter, and possibly to the former place, is the steepness of the banks (see Thomson, *The Land and the Book*, Vol. II. p. 445), but this cannot be strongly pressed, as, at the assumed time of year (when as we learn from Robinson [Vol. I. p. 541], the river has not yet been seen by travellers), partial or local overflows might have given greater facilities for the performance of the ceremony; see Greswell, *Dissert.* XIX. Vol. II. p. 184. See, however, Thomson, *The Land and the Book*, Vol. II. p. 452 sq.

The Early Judæan Ministry. 107

warning to the mingled multitude[a], to Pharisee and to Sadducee[1], which are recorded by the first[b] and third Evangelists; there stood around him men with musing hearts, doubting whether that bold speaker were the Christ or no[c], when suddenly, unknown and unrecognized, the very Messiah mingles with those strangely-assorted and expectant multitudes, and with them seeks baptism at the hands of the great Preacher of the desert.

It has been doubted whether that lonely child of the wilderness at once recognized the Holy One that was now meekly standing before him. It is at any rate certain from his own words that his knowledge of our Lord as the Messiah was not due to a previous acquaintance[2], and it is also quite possible that he might not have known his Redeemer even by outward appearance. But if he knew Him not by the seeing of the eye, he must have known of Him by the hearing of the ear, and he must have felt within his soul, as the Lord drew nigh, a sudden and mystic intimation that

LECT. III.
[a] Lk. iii. 7
[b] Mat. iii. 7
[c] Lk. iii. 15

The nature of St John's recognition of our Lord.

---

[1] See above, p. 102, note 2.

[2] This view, which is substantially that taken by the older commentators, has been well defended by Dr Mill against the popular sceptical objections; see *Obss. on Pantheistic Principles*, II. I. 5, p. 79 sq. We certainly seem to gather from the language of St Matthew that the Baptist recognized our Lord, if not distinctly as the Messiah, yet in a degree closely approaching to it, *before* the baptism,—for otherwise how are we to understand the language of Matth. iii. 14? See especially, Chrysost. *in Joann.* Hom. XVI. Whether this was due to a short unrecorded conversation (Mill), or, as suggested in the text, to special revelation (οὐκ ἀπ' ἀνθρωπίνης φιλίας ἦν αὕτη [ἡ μαρτυρία], ἀλλ' ἐξ ἀποκαλύψεως. Ammonius, ap. Cramer, *Caten. in loc.*), cannot be decided. The facts at any rate, as specified by the two Evangelists, are perfectly compatible with each other; on the one hand, St John *did* recognize our Lord *just before* the baptism (Matth. *l. c.*); on the other hand, he himself declares (John *l. c.*) that his personal acquaintance, if such existed, was not in any degree concerned in his subsequent complete recognition of Him as the Christ, the Son of God. So rightly, De Wette, *on John, l. c.*, and similarly, Huxtable, *Ministry of St John*, p. 60.

he was gazing on Him of whose wondrous birth his own mother's lips must oft have told him, and on whose future destinies he might often have mused with a profound and all but consciously-prophetic interest[1] ...With strange memories in his thoughts, and perhaps now still stranger pre-sentiments in his heart, the Baptist pleads[a] against such an inverted relation as the Son of Mary seeking baptism from the son of Elisabeth. He pleads, but he pleads in vain. Overpersuaded and awed by solemn words[b] which he might not have fully understood, the Forerunner descends with his Redeemer into the rapid waters of the now sacred river; when lo! when the inaugural rite is done, the promised sign at length appears, the Baptist beholds the opened heavens, and the embodied form[2] of the descending Spirit[c]; he sees perhaps the kindled fire, apt symbol of the Redeemer's baptism, of which an old writer has made mention[3]; he hears the Father's voice of blessing

---

[a] Mt. iii. 14
[b] ver. 15
[c] Lk. iii. 22

[1] It has been well observed by Mill, that 'the designation to which he bore testimony unconsciously in the womb, and which his mother with entire consciousness of its meaning, expressed reverently to the Virgin Mother of her Lord, cannot have been kept secret from his earliest years: and however the memory of the wonderful facts in question might fade, as would naturally be the case, from the minds of many that heard them,...the tradition of them could not possibly thus pass away from him. Nor would his solitary life in the desert, apart from his kindred, as from mankind in general, tend to impair the recollection but to strengthen it.' *Observations on Panth. Principles*, II. I. 5, p. 80.

[2] The following is the ancient tradition referred to: 'And then when Jesus came to the river Jordan, where John was baptizing, and descended to the water, a fire was kindled over the Jordan.' Justin Martyr, *Trypho*, cap. 88, Vol. II. p. 302 (ed. Otto). So also, somewhat similarly, Epiphanius, *Hær.* XXX. 13, and the writer of a treatise, *de Baptismo Hæreticorum*, prefixed to the works of Cyprian (p. 30, ed. Oxon.), who alludes to the tradition as mentioned in the apocryphal and heretical *Pauli Prædicatio*. Something like it has been noticed in the *Oracula Sibyllæ* (VII. 83) Galland, *Bibl. Vet. Patr.* Vol. I. p. 387 c.

[3] The distinct language of St Luke, σωματικῷ εἴδει ὡσεὶ περιστεράν (ch. iii. 22), must certainly pre-

The Early Judæan Ministry. 109

and love^a,—he sees and hears, and, as he himself tells us, bears witness that this is verily the Son of God^b.

^a Mt. iii. 17
^b John i. 34

And now all righteousness has been fulfilled. Borne away, as it would seem at once, by the motions of the Spirit, either to that lonely and unexplored chain of desert mountains, of which Nebo has been thought to form a part, or to that steep rock on this side of the Jordan which tradition still points out[1],—there amid the wild beasts^c of the thickets and the caverns, in hunger and loneliness, the now inaugurated Messiah confronts in spiritual conflict the fearful adversary of His kingdom and of that race which He came to save.... On the deep secrets of those mysterious forty days it is not meet that speculation should dwell. If we had only the narrative of St Matthew^d, we might think that Satanic temptation only presumed to assail the Holy One when hunger had weakened the energies of the now exhausted body. If again we had only the Gospels of St Mark^e and St Luke^f, we might be led to conclude that the struggle with the powers of darkness extended

The temptation of our Lord: its true nature and circumstances.

^c Mk. i. 13
^d iv. 2
^e i. 13
^f iv. 2

---

clude our accepting any explanatory gloss, referring the holy phenomenon to light shining 'with the rapid and undulating motion of a dove' (Milman, *Hist. of Christianity*, I. 3, Vol. I. p. 151). The form was real. For the opinions of antiquity on the manifestation of the Holy Ghost in this peculiar form, see the learned work of the eloquent Jesuit, Barradius, *Comment. in Harmon.* I. 15, Vol. II. p. 48 (Antw. 1617).

[1] The place which the most current tradition has fixed on as the site of the Temptation, is the mountain Quarantana, which Robinson describes as 'an almost perpendicular wall of rock, twelve or fifteen hundred feet above the plain.' *Palestine*, Vol. I. p. 567 (ed. 2); compare Thomson, *The Land and the Book*, Vol. II. p. 450. It has been asserted by Robinson that this tradition does not appear to be older than the time of the Crusades, but see Mill, *Sermons on the Temptation*, p. 166. The supposition in the text seems better to accord with the probable locality assigned to the baptism, but must be regarded as purely conjectural.

LECT. III.

over the whole period of that lengthened fast. From both, however, combined we may perhaps venture to conclude that those three concentrated forms of Satanic daring, which two evangelists have been moved to record, presented themselves only at the close of that season of mysterious trial[1]. ...Upon the three forms of temptation and their attendant circumstances my limits will not permit me to enlarge. These three remarks only will I presume to make. *First*, I will venture to avow my most solemn conviction that the events here related belong to no trance or dream-land to which, alas! even some better forms of both ancient and modern speculation have presumed to refer them[2],

The temptation no vision or trance.

---

[1] So perhaps Origen, who remarks: 'Quadraginta diebus tentatur Jesus, et quæ fuerint tentamenta nescimus.' *Comment. in Luc.* Hom. XXIX. Vol. III. p. 966 (ed. Bened.). Most of the patristic commentators seem to consider that the hours of hunger and bodily weakness were especially chosen by the Evil One for his most daring and malignant forms of temptation; see Chrysostom, *on Matth.* IV. 2, Cyril. Alex. *on Luke* IV. 3, and compare the excellent remarks of Irenæus, *Hær.* V. 21.

[2] The opinion that, if not the whole, yet that the concluding scenes of the temptation were of the character of a vision, was apparently entertained by Origen (*de Princip.* IV. 16, Vol. I. p. 175, ed. Bened.), Theodore of Mopsuestia (Münter, *Fragm. Patrum,* Fasc. I. p. 107), and the author of a treatise, *de Jeiunio et Tentat. Christi,* annexed to the works of Cyprian (p. 36, Oxon. 1682). This view in a more extended application has been adopted by many modern writers, both English (Farmer, *on Christ's Temptation,* ed. 3, Lond. 1776) and foreign, but it need scarcely be said that all such opinions,—whether the Temptation be supposed a vision especially called up, or a mere significant dream (see Meyer in *Stud. u. Krit.* for 1831, p. 319 sq.),—clearly come into serious collision with the simple yet circumstantial narrative of the first and third Evangelists; in which, not only is there not the faintest hint that could render such an opinion in any degree plausible, but, on the contrary, expressions almost studiously chosen (ἀνήχθη, Matth. iv. 1; ἤγετο, Luke iv. 1; comp. Mark i. 12, ἐκβάλλει; προσελθών, Matth. iv. 3; παραλαμβάνει, ver. 5; ἀναγαγών, Luke iv. 5; ἀπέστη, ver. 13) to mark the complete *objective* character of the whole; see, *thus far,* Fritzsche, *Fritzschior. Opusc.* p. 122 sq., and Meyer, *Komment. über Matth.* p. 114 sq., though in their general estimate of the whole the conclusions of both these writers are distinctly to be rejected. For further notices and

but are to be accepted as real and literal occurrences,—yea, as real and as literal as that final overthrow of Satan's power on Calvary, when the Lord reft away from Him all the thronging hosts of darkness[1], and triumphed over them on His very cross of suffering. *Secondly,* I could as soon doubt my own existence, as doubt the completely outward nature of these forms of temptation[2], and their immediate connexion with the personal agency of the personal Prince of darkness[3]. I could as soon accept the worst statements of the most degraded form of Arian creed as believe that this temptation arose from any internal strugglings or solicitations[4],—I could as soon admit the most

The temptation an assault from without.

---

references on a subject, the literature of which is perplexingly copious, the student may be referred perhaps especially to Andrewes, *Sermons* (*vii*.) *on the Temptation,* Vol. v. p. 479 sq. (A.-C. Libr.), Hacket, *Sermons* (*xxi*.) *on the Temptation,* p. 205 sq. (Lond. 1671), Spanheim, *Dub. Evang.* LI—LXV. Part II. p. 195 sq., Deyling, *Obs. Sacr.* XVII. Part II. p. 354, and Huxtable, *The Temptation of our Lord* (Lond. 1848), and for practical comments on the circumstances and moral intention of the whole, Leo M. *Serm.* XXXIX—L. Vol. I. p. 143 (ed. Ballerin.), Jones (of Nayland), *Works,* Vol. III. p. 157 sq.

[1] For a discussion on the meaning of ἀπεκδυσάμενος in the difficult text here referred to (Col. ii. 15), and for a further elucidation of the view here taken, see *Commentary on Coloss.* p. 161 sq.

[2] One of the popular modes of evading the supposed difficulties in this holy narrative is to assume that the whole series of temptations were really internal, but represented in the description as external; see for example, Ullmann, *Sinlessness of Jesus,* Sect. 7, p. 55 (Transl.). Most of such views arise either from erroneous conceptions in respect of the mysterious question of our Lord's capability of temptation, or from tacit denials of the existence or personal agencies of malignant spirits. On the first of these points, see especially Mill, *Serm.* II. pp. 26—39, and on the second, *Serm.* III. p. 54 sq. Some valuable remarks on these and other questions connected with our Lord's temptation will be found in the curious and learned work of Meyer, *Historia Diaboli,* III. 6, p. 271 sq. (Tubing. 1780).

[3] The monstrous opinion that the Tempter was human, and either the high-priest or one of the Sanhedrin (comp. Feilmoser, *Tübing. Quartalschrift* for 1828) is noticed, but not condemned in the terms which so plain a perversion deserves, by Milman, *Hist. of Christianity,* I. 3, Vol. I. p. 153.

[4] Such conceptions and supposi-

112   *The Early Judæan Ministry.*

LECT. III.

ᵃ Ja. i. 13

The temptation addressed to the three parts of our nature.

ᵇ 1 John ii. 16.

repulsive tenet of a dreary Socinianism as deem that it was enhanced by any self-engendered enticementsᵃ, or hold that it was aught else than the assault of a desperate and demoniacal malice from without[1], that recognized in the nature of man a possibility of falling, and that thus far consistently, though impiously, dared even in the person of the Son of Man to make proof of its hitherto resistless energies. *Thirdly*, I cannot think it an idle speculation that connects the three forms of temptation with those that brought sin into the world[2],—the lust of the flesh, and the lust of the eye, and the pride of lifeᵇ; nor can I deem it unnatural to see in them three spiritual assaults directed against the three portions of our composite nature[3]...To

tions alas! only too often in this humanitarian age secretly entertained, if not always outwardly expressed, are justly censured by Dr Mill (*Serm.* II. p. 38) as degrading and blasphemous. In all speculations on this mysterious subject the student will do well to bear in mind this admirable statement of Augustine: 'Non dicimus nos Christum, felicitate carnis a nostris sensibus sequestratæ, cupiditatem vitiorum sentire non potuisse, sed dicimus, eum perfectione virtutis, et *non per carnis concupiscentiam procreata carne*, cupiditatem non habuisse vitiorum.' *Op. Imperf. contr. Jul.* IV. 48, Vol. X. p. 1366 (ed. Migne),—this great writer's last and unfinished work. In estimating the nature of our Lord's tentability let us never forget the holiness of His humanity, and the eternal truth of His miraculous conception.

[1] On the question as to the form in which the Adversary appeared, whether human or angelical (comp.

Taylor, *Life of Christ*, I. 9. 7, Lange, *Leben Jesu*, II. 3. 6, Part I. p. 217), all speculation is as unnecessary as it is more or less presumptuous. All that we must firmly adhere to is the belief that the presence of the Evil One 'was real, and that it was external to our Lord.' Huxtable, *Temptation of the Lord*, p. 78; compare Mill, *Serm.* III. p. 64.

[2] This is touched upon by Augustine (*Enarr. in Psalm.* VIII. 13, Vol. IV. p. 116, ed. Migne) and others of the earlier writers, but nowhere more clearly and convincingly stated than by Jackson, *Creed*, VIII. 10, Vol. VII. p. 450 sq ; see also Andrewes, *Serm.* II. Vol. V. p. 496 (A.-C. Libr.), Mill, *Serm.* III. p. 60.

[3] For a discussion on the threefold nature of man, and a distinction between the terms *soul* and *spirit;* see *The Destiny of the Creature*, Serm. V. p. 99, and the works there referred to (p. 167). The opinion of Mill that the seat of the second temptation was 'our higher mental nature'

the *body* is presented the temptation of satisfying its wants by a display of power which would have tacitly abjured its dependence on the Father, and its perfect submission to His heavenly will. To the *soul*, the longing, appetitive soul[1] (for I follow the order of St Luke) was addressed the temptation of *Messianic* dominion[2] (mere material dominion would seem by no means so probable) over all the kingdoms of the world, and of accomplishing in a moment of time all for which the incense of the one sacrifice on Golgotha is still rising up on the altar of God. To the *spirit*[3] of our Redeemer, with even more frightful presumption, was addressed the temptation of using that power which belonged to Him as God to vindicate His own eternal nature, and to display by one dazzling miracle the true relation in which Jesus of Nazareth stood to men and to angels and to God[4].

(p. 60), and of the third, the 'highest self-consciousness, by which man becomes to himself the centre of regard' (ib.), is scarcely so simple or so exact as the reference to *soul* and *spirit* adopted in the text.

[1] This we may roughly define with Olshausen as 'vis inferior [in homine] quæ agitur, movetur, in imperio tenetur' (*Opusc.* p. 154), and may in many respects regard as practically identical with καρδία,—the soul's imaginary seat and abiding place: see *Comment. on Phil.* iv. 6, *Destiny of Creature*, v. p. 117, and Beck, *Seelenlehre*, III. 20, p. 63. On the order of the temptations, compare Greswell, *Dissert.* xx. Vol. II. p. 192, Mill, *Serm.* IV. p. 82 sq.

[2] See Lange, *Leben Jesu*, II. 3. 6, Part II. p. 225, and compare Huxtable, *Temptation of the Lord*, p. 87

sq. If with Dr Mill we refer it to worldly dominion generally (*Serm.* IV. p. 105), we must, with the same learned author, suppose that Satan really did not fully know the exact nature of Him whom he impiously dared to tempt (p. 63; comp. Cyril Alex. *on Luke* iv. 3); a view however which does not seem fully consistent with the opening address of the Tempter.

[3] This third and highest part in man we may again roughly define with Olshausen (compare note 1) as 'vis superior, agens, imperans in homine' (*Opusc.* p. 154), and may rightly regard as in many respects identical with νοῦς; see *Comment. on Phil.* iv. 6, *Destiny of Creature*, v. p. 115, and Delitzsch, *Bibl. Psychol.* IV. p. 145.

[4] The third form of temptation,

LECT. III.

The ministering angels, and the return to Galilee.

^a iv. 13

^b ver. 11.

^c i. 29

When every form of temptation was ended, the baffled Tempter departs,—but, as St Luke reminds us, only for a season^a; and straightway those blessed spirits, whose ministry but a few moments before the Devil had tempted Him to command, now tender to their Lord's weakened humanity their loving and unbidden services¹...Sustained by these angelic ministries^b, our Lord would seem at once to have returned backward to the valley of the Jordan in His homeward way to Galilee, and after a *few days*,—for here to assume with a recent chronologer a lapse of several months² is in the highest degree unnatural,—to have had that second and noticeable interview with the Baptist at Bethany or Bethabara, which is recorded to us by St John^c.

that of spiritual presumption, has been thus well paraphrased by Dr Mill: 'Give to the assembled multitudes the surest proof that thou art indeed their expected King,—the Desire of them and of all nations,—at whose coming the Lord shall shake the heavens and the earth, and make this house more glorious than the mysterious Shekinah made the first.' *Serm.* p. 118. The exact spot (τὸ πτερύγιον τοῦ ἱεροῦ, Matth. iv. 5) which was the scene of this temptation is not perfectly certain. The most probable opinion is that it was the topmost ridge of the στοὰ βασιλικὴ on the south side of the temple (observe that in both evangelists it is τὸ πτερύγιον τοῦ ἱεροῦ, not τοῦ ναοῦ), the height of which is thus alluded to by Josephus; 'if any one looked down from the top of the battlements, or down both those altitudes, he would be giddy, while his sight could not reach to such an immense depth.' *Antiq.* xv.

11. 5 (Whiston). This, however, could scarcely be so clearly in the sight of 'the assembled multitudes' (Mill),—if indeed this be a necessary adjunct,—as at other sites that have been proposed; see Middleton, *Greek Art.* p. 135 (ed. Rose), and Meyer, *Komment. üb. 'Matth.* iv. 5, p. 110.

¹ The nature of the services of these blessed spirits, owing to the use of the general term διηκόνουν (Matth. iv. 11), cannot be more exactly specified. If we admit conjectures we may venture to believe that they came to supply sustenance ('allato cibo,' Beng.; comp. 1 Kings xix.), and possibly *also* to administer support and comfort ('ad solatium refero,' Calv.; comp. Luke xxii. 43); see Hacket, *Serm.* xxi. p. 406 (Lond. 1675).

² See Wieseler, *Chron. Synops.* p. 258, and compare the remarks on the chronology of this period made above, p. 105, note 2.

It was but the day before that the Forerunner had borne his testimony to the deputation of Priests and Levites* that had come to him from Jerusalem[1]; and now absorbed, as he well might have been, in thoughts of Him to whom he had so recently borne witness, he raises his eyes and lo! he sees coming to him[b] the very subject of his meditations; he sees his Redeemer[2]; and humbly greets Him as 'the Lamb of God that taketh away the sins of the world[c].' With the same

LECT. III.

The testimony of the Baptist.
ᵃ John. i. 19

ᵇ i. 29

ᶜ i. 29

---

[1] This deputation we are informed by the Evangelist was sent by the Ἰουδαῖοι,—a general name by which St John nearly always designates the Jews in their peculiar aspect as a *hostile community* to our Lord, and as standing in marked contrast to the impressible ὄχλος. The more special and direct senders of this deputation of Priests and their attendant Levites (John i. 19) were perhaps the members of the Sanhedrin, by whom these emissaries might have been directed to inquire into and test the Baptist's pretensions as a public teacher (comp. Matth. xxi. 23), and to gain some accurate information about one who was drawing all Jerusalem and Judæa to his baptism (Matth. iii. 5), and in whom some even deemed that they recognized the expected Messiah (Luke iii. 15). On the message generally, see Lange, *Leben Jesu*, II. 4. 1, Part II. p. 451, Lücke, *Comment. über Joh.* Vol. I. p. 381; and on the particular questions propounded to the Baptist, Origen *in loc.* Vol. IV. p. 108 (ed. Bened.), Greg. Magn. *in Evang.* I. 7, Vol. I. p. 1456 (ed. Bened.).

[2] The circumstances that led to this meeting are wholly unknown to us. That it took place after our Lord's baptism seems certain; and that the preceding interview with the Priests and Levites also took place after the same event seems to follow from the words 'whom ye (ὑμεῖς) know not' (ver. 26),—an expression which may be fairly urged as implying by contrast some knowledge on the part of the speaker. Now as we learn from St Mark (ch. i. 12) that the Temptation followed immediately after the Baptism, we may perhaps reasonably believe that our Lord was now on His homeward way to Galilee after the Temptation (comp. August. *de Consens. Evang.* II. 17), and that He either specially went a little out of His way again to see and greet the Baptist, or that the direction of His journey homeward led Him past the scene of the previous baptism, where John was still preaching and baptizing. If we fix the site of the Temptation at Quarantana, the former supposition will seem most probable, if the mountains of Moab (see above, p. 109, note 1), the latter. The deputation from the Sanhedrin and the close of the Temptation would thus appear to have been closely contemporaneous; see Lücke *on John* i. 19, Vol. I. p. 398, and compare Lampe *in loc.*, and Luthardt, *Joh. Evang.* Vol. I. p. 329.

LECT. III.

ᵃ Joh. i. 35

ᵇ ver. 39

ᶜ ver. 44, 45

The journey to, and miracle at Cana in Galilee.

significant words[1] the Baptist parts from Him on the morrowᵃ,—words that sank so deep into the hearts of two of his disciples, Andrew, and not improbably the Evangelist, who gives the account, that they follow the Lord, and abide with Himᵇ, to return back again no more. On the morrow, with Simon Peter and Philip of Bethsaida, and Nathanael of Canaᶜ added to the small company[2], the Lord directs His steps onward towards the hills of Galilee, perchance by the very path which He had traversed in solitude a few eventful weeks before.

The immediate destination of that small company was doubtless the Lord's earthly home at Nazareth[3]; but there, as we learn from the Evan-

---

[1] Into the exact meaning of these words we will not here enter further than to remark, (a) that the reference seems clearly not to the Paschal Lamb (Lampe, Luthardt, al.), a reference sufficiently appropriate afterwards (1 Cor. v. 7), though not now, but to Isaiah liii. 7 (Origen, VI. 35), a passage, which to one so earnestly expecting the Messiah, as the holy Baptist, must have long been well-known and familiar; (b) that the meaning of αἴρειν has nowhere been better expressed than by Chrysostom, who in referring to a former part of the same prophecy (Isaiah liii. 4) says: "He did not use the expression, 'He ransomed' (ἔλυσεν) but, 'He received and bare' (ἔλαβεν καὶ ἐβάστασεν); which seems to me to have been spoken by the prophet rather in reference to sins, in accordance with the declaration of John, 'Behold the Lamb of God that taketh away the sins of the world.'" *Hom. in Matth.* XXVII. 1, Vol. VII. p. 370 (ed. Bened. 2). For further information on both these points consult the elaborate note of Lücke *in loc.* Vol. I. p. 404 sq.

[2] We can scarcely agree with Greswell (*Dissert.* XXIII. Vol. II. p. 284 sq.) in the inference that the two disciples did not now permanently attach themselves to our Lord. The express terms of the call given the next day to Philip, '*follow me*' (ver. 44), and the certain fact that some disciples were with our Lord the day following (John ii. 2), seem strongly in favour of the opinion that all the five disciples here mentioned *did* formally attach themselves to our Lord, and went with Him into Galilee; see Maldonatus on John i. 43 and ii. 2. The miracle that followed had special reference to these newly-attracted followers; see John ii. 11, and comp. Luthardt, *Johann. Evang.* Vol. I. p. 351.

[3] Unless we accept the not very probable supposition alluded to p. 105, note 1.

The Early Judæan Ministry. 117

gelist, the Lord could not have found the blessed Virgin, as she was now a few miles off at Cana[1], the guest at a marriage festival. How natural then was it that the Lord with His five disciples, one of whom belonged to Cana[a], should at once pass onward to that village to greet her from whom He had been separated several weeks! And how consistent is the narrative that tells us that on the third day[b] after leaving Bethany, the Lord and His followers had become the invited[c] and welcome guests of those with whom the Virgin was now abiding.

marginal notes: LECT. III. — [a] Joh. xxi. — [b] ii. 1 — [c] ver. 2

With the details of the great miracle which on this occasion our Lord was pleased to perform, we are all, I trust, too familiarly acquainted to need any lengthened narrative[2]. We may, however, somewhat profitably pause on one portion of it, the address of the mother of our Lord, and the answer He returned,—which have been thought to involve some passing difficulties, but which a consideration of the previous circumstances combined with a due recognition of Jewish customs tends greatly to elucidate....In the first place let us not forget,—

marginal note: Remarks on the miracle.

---

[1] On the position of Cana, which now appears rightly fixed, not at Kefr Kenna (De Saulcy, *Voyage*, Vol. II. p. 448), but at Kâna el-Jelîl, about 3 hours distant from Nazareth; see Robinson, *Palestine*, Vol. II. p. 346 sq., Vol. III. p. 108 (ed. 2), Thomson, *Land and the Book*, Vol. II. p. 121 sq., and Caspari, *Chron.-Geogr. Einleit.* § 82, p. 100, who similarly decides for the last-mentioned locality.

[2] For details and explanatory remarks the student may be especially referred to the commentaries of Maldonatus, Lücke, and Meyer, to the exquisite contemplation of Bp Hall, Book II. 5, Abp Trench, *Notes on the Miracles*, p. 96 sq., and to the comments of Lange, *Leben Jesu*, II. 4. 4, Part II. p. 475. The supposed typical relations are alluded to in a somewhat striking sermon of Bp Copleston, *Remains*, p. 256: compare with it Augustine, *in Joann.* Tractat. IX. 5, Vol. III. p. 146 (ed. Migne), where very similar views will also be found.

LECT. III.

if we may place any reliance upon modern customs as illustrative of ancient[1],—that the fact of guests adding contributions to an entertainment which extended over several days is by no means singular or unprecedented. With this let us combine the remembrance that the Lord and His five disciples had, as it would appear, come unexpectedly[2], a few hours only before the commencement of the marriage-feast. In the next place let us reflect how more than natural it would be for these disciples,—two of whom, as we are specially told by the Evangelist, had heard[a] the significant announcement of the Baptist, 'Behold the Lamb of God[b],' and another of whom had recognized in our Lord the very One whom prophets had foretold[c],—to have already made such

[a] Joh. i. 37
[b] ver. 36
[c] ver. 45

---

[1] The writer of this note was lately informed by a converted Jew, on whom reliance could be placed, that it was not at all uncommon for the guests at a wedding-feast to make contributions of wine when there seemed likely to be a deficiency, and that such cases had fallen under his own observation. Be this as it may, it seems at any rate clear that the marriage-feasts usually lasted as long as 7 days (Judges xiv. 12, 15; Tobit xi. 10), and it is surely not unreasonable to suppose that in the present case the givers of the feast were of humble fortunes (Lightfoot conjectures it to have been at the house of Mary, the wife of Cleophas; comp. Greswell, *Dissert.* XVII. Vol. II. p. 120), and, as Bp Taylor quaintly says, 'had more company than wine.' *Life of Christ*, II. 10. 5. For further notices and references see Winer, *RWB.* Art. 'Hochzeit,' Vol. I. p. 499 sq.

[2] The only statement that might seem indirectly to militate against this is the comment of St John, ἐκλήθη δὲ καὶ ὁ Ἰησοῦς καὶ οἱ μαθηταὶ αὐτοῦ εἰς γάμον, ch. ii. 2. If however we date the 'third day' (ver. 1), as seems most natural, from the day last-mentioned (ch. i. 44), and estimate the distance from Bethany on the Jordan to Cana, our Lord could scarcely have arrived at the last-mentioned place till the very day specified: compare Wieseler, *Chron. Synops.* II. 3, p. 253. The ἐκλήθη then must be referred to the time when our Lord and His followers arrived, and its introduction accounted for, as slightly distinguishing the newly-arrived and just-invited guests from the Virgin, who had been there perhaps for some little time; comp. Meyer *in loc.*, and Lange, *Leben Jesu*, II. 4. 4, Part II. p. 476, whose date, however, for the τῇ ἡμέρᾳ τῇ τρίτῃ does not seem tenable.

communications to the Lord's mother¹ as might well lead her to expect some display of her Son's changed position and relations. He who a few weeks before had left Galilee the unnoted son of Joseph the carpenter, now returns with five followers the more than accredited teacher, yea, as one of those followers had not hesitated to avow, as the Son of God² and the King of Israel[a]. Wrought upon by these strange tidings, and with all the long-treasured remembrances of her meditative heart[b] brought up freshly before her³, how natural then

[a] Joh. i. 49
[b] Lk. ii. 19

---

¹ Though we are not positively constrained by the tenor of the narrative to fix the miracle on the very day that our Lord arrived (comp. Wordsw. and Lücke *in loc.*), it must be admitted that on the whole such an adjustment seems *slightly* the most probable: comp. ver. 10, in which the remarks of the ἀρχιτρίκλινος seem to have reference to a single festal meal, the beginning and end of which it contrasts. Even in this case, however, the disciples could easily have had time to communicate to the Virgin enough of what they had heard, felt, and observed in reference to their venerated Master to arouse hopes and expectations in the mother's heart; comp. Theophyl. and Euthym. *in loc.*, both of whom, however, slightly over-estimate the Virgin's knowledge of what had recently happened.

² Most modern, and some ancient expositors, explain away the title here given by Nathanael to our Lord as implying no more than 'The Messiah,' or, to use the language of Theophylact, one who ' on account of His virtue was *adopted* as a Son of God' (υἱοθετηθέντα τῷ Θεῷ). Perhaps the further title assigned by Nathanael, and still more our Lord's reply (ver. 51) may *seem* partly to favour this view. It will be well, however, not to forget that this assertion was made by Nathanael after our Lord had evinced a knowledge above that of man (ver. 48), which might well have awakened in the breast of that guileless Israelite some feeling of the true nature of Him who was now speaking with him: so rightly, Cyril Alex. *in loc.*, and Augustine, *in Joann.* Tract. VII. 20, 21.

³ Though we certainly must not adopt the rash and indeed antiscriptural view (comp. John ii. 11) spoken approvingly of by Maldonatus, and even partially adopted by Lücke (p. 470), that the Virgin had previously witnessed miracles performed by our Lord in private, we may yet with reason believe that she ever retained a partial consciousness of the real nature of her Divine Son, and that the mysterious past was ever freshly remembered, when the present served in any way to call it up again: πάντα συνετήρει ἐν τῇ καρδίᾳ αὐτῆς, καὶ ἐκ τούτων ἐλογίζετο τὸν υἱὸν ὑπὲρ ἄνθρωπον δύνασθαι, Theophylact *in loc.* (p. 584, Paris,

becomes that significant comment of the mother 'they have no wine,'—a comment that may have alike implied that the free hand of unexpected guests might supply a want in part occasioned by them[1] (for this the order to the servants may fully justify us attributing to the Virgin), and also may have dimly expressed the hope that the Holy Jesus would use these circumstances of partial publicity for the sake of revealing His true character to the assembled guests[2]. Under these assumptions how full of meaning does the Lord's answer now appear. How solemnly yet how tenderly He reminds the mother that earthly relations

1631),—but with too definite a reference to an expected special θαυματουργία; see below, note 2.

[1] The comments of Luthardt on this exquisitely natural and strikingly characteristic remark of the Lord's mother deserve here to be quoted. 'It is a delicate trait,' says this thoughtful writer, 'that she does no more than call her Son's attention to the deficiency. She feels such confidence in Him, yea, and such reverence towards Him, that she believes that she neither need nor ought to say anything further. Of His benevolent nature she has already had many an experience; and that He is full of wisdom, and can find ways and means, where others mark them not, she knows full well. More, however, was not necessary,—especially when there was this in addition, that the presence of Jesus and His followers had helped to cause the deficiency, —than with humility to direct His attention to it.' *Das Johann. Evang.* Vol. I. p. 115. We may here pause for a moment to advert to the number of the waterpots. Lightfoot (*Hor. Hebr. in loc.*) simply considers the wants of the 'multitudo jam praesens,' and probably rightly; it is, however, worth a passing consideration whether it depended in any way on the *six* newly arrived guests.

[2] This would seem to be a correct estimate of the exact state of feeling in the mother's heart. As Bp Hall well says, 'she had good reason to know the Divine nature and power of her son' (*Contempl.* II. 5): she *felt* that He could display a more than mortal power, and she now *longed* that He would give proof of it. We thus avoid on the one hand the over-statement of the earlier commentators, that this was a definite exhortation to perform a miracle (εἰς τὸ θαῦμα προτρέπει, Cyril); and on the other we avoid the serious understatement of many modern writers (Luthardt even partly included), that it was a request referring merely to assistance to be given in some natural way,—how, the speaker knew not: see, for example, Meyer *in loc.*

must now give place to heavenly[1], and that the times and seasons in which the Eternal Son is to display His true nature are not to be hastened even by the longings of maternal love. The Lord's manifestation, however, takes place, the miracle is performed, and its immediate effect is to confirm the faith[a] of the five disciples who now appear before us as the first-fruits of the in-gathering of the Church.

Joh. ii. 11

Immediately after the performance of this first miracle the Lord with His mother, His brethren, and His disciples go down to Capernaum[2], a place, which as the residence of one of His followers, but still more as a convenient point for joining the pilgrim-companies now forming for the

Brief stay at Capernaum, and journey to Jerusalem.

who states this latter view in a very objectionable form.

[1] It has been remarked by Luthardt (*loc. cit.*), and before him by Bp Hall (*Contempl. l. c.*), that in His answer our Lord here addresses the Virgin as γύναι (ver. 4), and not μῆτερ,—a term which, though marking all respect, and subsequently used by our Lord in a last display of tenderness and love (John xix. 26), still seems to indicate the now changed relation between the Messiah and Mary of Nazareth. That our Lord's words contained a tender reproof is certain, and that it was felt so is probable; but, as the Virgin's direction to the servants clearly shows, it could not repress the longings of the mother, or alter the convictions of the all but conscious Deipara.

[2] The exact site of Capernaum has been much contested: see Robinson, *Palestine*, Vol. III. p. 348 sq. (ed. 2), where the question is discussed at considerable length, and the site fixed at Khân Minyeh, a place not far from the shore of the lake and at the northern extremity of the plain of Gennesareth; comp. Vol. II. p. 403. On the whole, however, the name, ruins, position, and prevailing tradition seem justly to incline us to fix the site at Tell Hûm, a ruin-bestrewed and slightly elevated spot on a small projecting curve of the shore, about one hour in distance nearer the head of the lake than Khân Minyeh: see esp. Thomson, *Land and the Book*, Vol. I. p. 542 sq., Ritter, *Erdkunde*, Vol. XV. p. 339, Van de Velde, *Memoir* (accompanying map), p. 302, and Williams in Smith's *Dict. of Geogr.* s. v. Vol. I. p. 504. Caspari in his recent work argues strongly against Tell Hûm as the site of Capernaum, and in favour of the vicinity of Ain Medawarah (*Chron.-Geogr. Einleit.* § 63, p. 69); recent exploration, however, appears somewhat decisively to substantiate the opinion adopted above.

LECT. III.

*Joh. ii. 12

The expulsion of the traders from the Temple.

paschal journey to Jerusalem, would at this time be more suitable for a temporary sojourn than the secluded Nazareth[1]. After a stay of but a few days*, our Lord and His disciples now bend their steps to Jerusalem, to celebrate the passover[2]— the first passover of our Lord's public ministry.

The first act is one of great significance, the expulsion of the buyers and sellers from the temple,—an act repeated two years afterwards with similar circumstances of holy zeal for the sanctity of His Father's house[3]. How strange

---

[1] This observation seems justified by the fact that the western shores of the lake of Gennesareth were at that time extremely populous and scenes of a bustle and activity of life that could be found nowhere else in Palestine, except at Jerusalem (see Stanley, *Palestine*, chap. x. p. 370); and further by the fact that there were at least *three* routes of considerable importance that led from the neighbourhood of the lake to the south. The traveller of that day might join the great Egypt and Damascus road, where it passes nearest to the lake (near Khân Minyeh: see Robinson, *Palestine*, Vol. II. p. 405, Van de Velde, *Memoir*, p. 226), and leaving it 2 or 3 miles W.S.W. of Nain proceed south through Samaria; or *secondly*, he might journey along the lake to Scythopolis (Beisan), and thence by the ancient Egypt and Midian road to Ginæa (see Winer, *RWB*. Art. 'Strassen,' Vol. II. p. 539, Van de Velde, *Memoir*, p. 238), and so onward by the Jerusalem and Galilee road to Shechem and the south; or *thirdly*, he might take the then more frequented, but now little known route from the south end of the lake through Peræa (comp. Van de Velde, *Memoir*, p. 233, Ritter, *Erdkunde (Palästina)*, § 13, Part XV. p. 1001 sq.), and across the Jordan to Jericho, and so to Jerusalem. For further information on this somewhat important subject, the student may be referred to Reland, *Palæstina*, II. 3; Vol. I. p. 404 (Traject. 1714); Winer, *RWB*. (*loc. cit.*), the various itineraries in Ritter, *Erdkunde (Palästina)*, Part XV.; and the useful list of routes in Van de Velde, *Memoir*, pp. 183—258.

[2] It is not mentioned positively that the disciples accompanied our Lord, but it is certain that they were present at Jerusalem and witnessed the purgation of the temple: see John ii. 17, where the ἐμνήσθησαν is not to be referred to any future time (Olsh.), but to the period in question; see Meyer *in loc.*, and comp. Origen, *in Joann.* Tom. X. 16, Vol. IV. p. 186 (ed. Bened.).

[3] That this is not to be identified with the purgation of the temple mentioned by the Synoptical Evangelists (Matth. xxi. 12 sq., Mark xi. 15 sq., Luke xix. 45 sq.), is the opinion of the patristic writers (see Origen, *in Joann.* Tom. X. 15, Chrysost. *in*

it is that the thoughtful Origen should have found any difficulties in this authoritative act of the Messiah, or should have deemed incongruous and unsuited to the dignity of his Master what in the narrative of the Evangelist appears to be so natural and intelligible[1]. If we closely consider the words of the original, we have presented to us only the very natural picture of the Redeemer driving out from the court of the Gentiles the sheep and oxen that base huckstering and traffic had brought within the sacred inclosure. What is there here unseemly, what is there startling in finding that the Lord of the Temple not only drives forth the animals[2], but

---

Matth. Hom. LXVII. init., and August. *de Consensu Evang.* II. 67), and is rightly maintained in the majority of the best recent expositors: see Meyer *in loc.*, and Ebrard, *Ev. Gesch.* p. 488.

[1] These difficulties are stated very clearly in his *Commentary on St John*, Book X. 16, Vol. IV. p. 185 sq. (ed. Bened.), and yet disposed of by no one better than himself, when he indicates how actions which in a mere child of man, however authorized, would have been met with resentment and resistance, were in the case of our Lord viewed with a startled and perhaps reverential awe, —an awe due to that θειοτέρα τοῦ Ἰησοῦ δύναμις οἵον τε ὄντος ὅτε ἐβούλετο, καὶ θυμὸν ἐχθρῶν ἀναπτόμενον σβέσαι, καὶ μυριάδων θείᾳ χάριτι περιγενέσθαι, καὶ λογισμοὺς θορυβούντων διασκεδάσαι. loc. cit. p. 186: comp. Jerome, *in Matth.* xxi. 15. Vol. VII. p. 166 (ed. Vallars.). See some good comments on this impressive act in Milman, *Hist. of Christianity*, I. 3, Vol. I. p. 164 sq.,

and a quaint but sound practical sermon by Bp Lake, *Serm.* Part IV. p. 122 sq.

[2] It seems not improbable that Meyer (*in loc.*) is right in referring πάντας (ver. 15) to τά τε πρόβατα καὶ τοὺς βόας, and that the translation should not be 'and the sheep and the oxen' (Auth. Ver.), but, 'both the sheep and the oxen,' as in the *Revised Transl. of St John*, p. 5. The true force of the τε—καὶ is thus preserved (comp. Winer, *Gr.* § 53. 4, p. 389), and the sacred narrative freed from one at least of the objections which others beside Origen have felt in the Saviour's use of the φραγέλλιον against the sellers as well as against the animals they sold. It may be observed that our Lord *speaks* to the 'sellers of doves,' not perhaps that He regarded them with greater consideration (De Wette), —for compare Matth. xxi. 12, Mark xi. 15,—but simply because the animals could be driven forth, while these latter offerings could only be removed.

LECT. III.

*Joh. ii. 19

Impression made by this and other acts.

overthrows the tables of so-called sacred coin[1], tables of unholy and usurious gains, and with a voice and attitude of command sternly addresses even the sellers of the offerings of the poor,— offerings such as His own mother had once presented,—and bids them take them hence, and make not the house of His Father a house of Mammon and merchandize? The half-astonished, half-assenting bystanders ask for a sign that might justify or accredit such an assumption of authority, and a sign is not withheld[a]; a sign which, though not understood at the time, appears from subsequent notices to have made no slight impression on those that heard it[2], and to have been lovingly remembered and verified when the dissolved Temple of their Master's body was reared up again on the predicted day.

But not only by this authoritative act and

[1] Every Israelite was bound to pay half a shekel annually to the temple, in the month of Adar; see *Mishna (Shekalim,* I. 3). Gifts were also presented at other seasons, and especially at the Passover; see Caspari, *Chron.-Geogr. Einleit.* § 84, p. 102.

[2] That these words of our Lord referred to His body, which stood to the Temple in the relation of type to antitype, is the distinct declaration of the inspired Evangelist (John ii. 21), and has justly been regarded by all the older expositors as the only true and possible interpretation of the words. To assert, then, that the reference was simply to the breaking up of the older form of religious worship and the substitution of a purer form in its place

(Herder, Lücke, De Wette), is plainly to contradict that Evangelist who was blessed with the deepest insight into the mind of his Divine Master, and further to substitute what is illogical and inexact for what is clear, simple, and consistent: see esp. Meyer *in loc.* (p. 95, ed. 2), who has ably vindicated the authentic interpretation of the words. See also Stier, *Disc. of our Lord,* Vol. I. p. 72 sq.; and on the eternal truth that our Lord did raise Himself, Pearson, *Creed,* Art. v. Vol. I. p. 302 sq. (ed. Burt.). The futile objection founded on the supposed enigmatical character of the declaration is well disposed of by Chrysostom *in loc.* Vol. VIII. p. 155 E (ed. Bened. 2).

these words of mystery, but, as St John has specially recorded, by the display of signs and wonders during the celebration of the festival^a, the deep heart of the people was stirred. Many believed, and among that many was one of the members of the Sanhedrin[1] whose name is not unhonoured in the Gospel history. He who at this passover sought the Lord under cover of night, and to whom the Lord was pleased to unfold the mystery of the new birth[2], was so blessed by the regenerating power of the Spirit as to be emboldened at a later period to plead for the Lord in the open day^b, and to do honour to His crucified body^c....On that mysterious interview, which probably took place towards the end of the paschal week, I cannot here enlarge[3]; but I may ven-

^aii. 23

^bJn. vii. 50

^cxix. 39
The discourse of our Lord with Nicodemus.

---

[1] Of this timid yet faithful man nothing certain is known beyond the notices in St John's Gospel, here and ch. vii. 50, xix. 39. The title he here bears, ἄρχων τῶν Ἰουδαίων (iii. 1), seems to show that he was a member of the Sanhedrin (comp. ch. vii. 26, 50, Luke xxiv. 20; Joseph. *Antiq.* xx. 2. 2.); and the further comment of our Lord (ὁ διδάσκαλος τοῦ Ἰσραήλ, ver. 10) may favour the supposition that he belonged to that portion of the venerable body which was not of Levitical or priestly descent, but is spoken of in the Gospels under the title of γραμματεῖς τοῦ λαοῦ: see Knapp, *Scripta Var. Argum.* Vol. I. p. 200, note; and comp. Lightfoot, *Hor. Hebr. in Matth.* ii. 4. Vol. II. p. 260 (Roterod. 1686). Tradition says that Nicodemus was afterwards baptized by St Peter and St John, and expelled from his office and from the city: see Photius, *Biblioth.* § 171.

[2] Whether the word ἄνωθεν (ver. 3) is to be taken (a) in a *temporal* reference, and translated 'anew' with the Vulgate, Pesh.-Syriac, Coptic, and Ethiopic Versions, and with Chrysostom (who, however, gives the other view) and Euthymius, or (b) to be taken in a *local* reference, and translated 'from above,' with the Gothic and Armenian Versions, and with Origen and Cyril, it is very hard to decide. The latter is perhaps most in accordance with the usage (ver. 31) and general teaching of St John (see Meyer *in loc.*), the former with the apparent tenor of the dialogue.

[3] For a good general exposition of this mysterious discourse of our Lord with the timid ruler, see generally, of the older writers, Chrysostom, *in Joann.* Hom. XXIV.—XXVIII., Cyril Alex. *in Joann.* Vol. IV. p. 145—156, Augustine, *in Joann.* Tractat. XII. cap. 3, Euthymius and Theophylact *in loc.*; and of the modern expositors, Knapp, *Script. Var. Ar.*

LECT. III.
ture to make one remark to those who desire to enter more deeply into the meaning of our Lord's words,—and it is this, that if we remember, as I said in my first lecture[1], that in St John's Gospel our Lord especially appears before us as the reader of the human heart, we shall be prepared to find, as apparently we do find, that He often answers rather the *thoughts* than the words of the speaker, and alludes to the hidden feeling rather than the expressed sentiment[2]. If we bear this in mind, I verily believe that, by the help of God, we shall be enabled to gain some clue to understanding the more difficult parts of this most solemn and profound revelation.

---

gum. Vol. I. p. 199—254, Meyer, *Kommentar*, p. 101 sq., Stier, *Disc. of our Lord*, Vol. IV. p. 359 sq. (Clark), and the excellent work of Luthardt, *Johan. Evang.* Vol. I. p. 364 sq. Some good remarks on the character of Nicodemus will be found in Evans, *Scripture Biography*, Vol. II. p. 233 sq.; and an ingenious but not satisfactory defence of his timidity in Niemeyer, *Charakt.* Vol. I. p. 113 sq. Caspari conceives St John to have been present at the interview, and deems it not improbable that our Lord was now in the house of the Apostle; see *Chron.-Geogr. Einleit.* § 85, p. 103, and comp. p. 93. The subsequent presence of the Apostle with his brother and their father Zebedee at the lake of Gennesareth is accounted for on the supposition that they were temporarily there for fishing; see *ib.* § 105, p. 123.

[1] See p. 32, note 1.

[2] Thus, for example, at the very outset, our Lord's first words can scarcely be considered an answer to the words with which Nicodemus first addresses Him, but may very suitably be conceived an answer to the question of his heart, which seems rather to have related to the mode of gaining an entrance into the kingdom of God. Was the lowly but wonder-working Teacher whom he addressed the veritable Way, the Truth, and the Light,—or was there some other way still compatible with the old and familiar tenets of Judaism? Chrysostom seems rather to imply that our Lord regards Nicodemus as not yet to have passed even into the outer porch of true knowledge (ὅτι οὐδὲ τῶν προθύρων τῆς προσηκούσης γνώσεως ἐπέβη), and that He does not so much address Nicodemus as state generally a mystic truth, which he know not of, but which might well arrest and engage his thoughts. *Comment. in Joann.* XXIV. Vol. VIII. p. 161 (ed. Bened. 2). The very different views that have been taken of these opening words will be seen in the commentaries above referred to.

The Early Judæan Ministry. 127

With this interview the occurrences of this eventful passover appear to have closed. Our Lord perceiving by that same knowledge of the human heart, to which I have just alluded, that He could no longer trust Himself[a] even with those who had heard His teaching and beheld His miracles, now leaves Jerusalem[b], most probably for the North Eastern portion of Judæa[1], in the vicinity of the Jordan, where we seem to have good grounds for supposing that He was pleased to abide till nearly the end of the year. There the sacred narrative[c] tells us He baptized by the hands of His disciples[2], and so wrought upon the hearts of the people that He eventually gathered round Him believers and disciples[3] which outnum-

LECT. III.

Our Lord leaves Jerusalem and retires to the N. E. parts of Judæa.
[a] Joh. ii. 24
[b] iii. 22
[c] Joh. iv. 2

---

[1] The Evangelist only says, ἦλθεν ὁ Ἰησοῦς καὶ οἱ μαθηταὶ αὐτοῦ εἰς τὴν Ἰουδαίαν γῆν (ch. iii. 22); but from the closely-connected mention of the administration of baptism, it does not seem unreasonable to suppose, with Chrysostom, that our Lord retired to the Jordan (ἐπὶ τὸν Ἰορδάνην πολλάκις ἤρχετο) and perhaps sought again the place where He Himself had been baptized by John (see p. 106, note 3), and to which numbers might still be thronging. Lightfoot suggests a place more exactly to the north of Jerusalem, and closer to the direct route to Galilee: see *Harmon. Quat. Evang.* Vol. I. p. 446 (Roterod. 1686).

[2] The reason why our Lord did not Himself baptize has formed a subject of comment since the days of Tertullian. We can, however, scarcely adopt that early writer's view that it was owing to the difficulty of our Lord baptizing in His own name (*de Baptism.* cap. 11), but may plausibly adopt the opinion hinted at by the poetical paraphrast Nonnus (οὐ γὰρ ἄναξ βάπτιζεν ἐν ὕδατι, p. 30, ed. Passow), and well expressed by Augustine ('præbebant discipuli ministerium corporis, præbebat ille adjutorium majestatis,' *in Joann.* Tract. xv. 4. 3),—that baptism was a ministerial act, and thus more suitably performed by disciples than by their Lord: compare Acts x. 48, 1 Cor. i. 17.

[3] We can of course form no exact estimate of the actual numbers of disciples which John might have now gathered round him. As, however, the inspired narrative distinctly specifies the multitudes that came to his baptism (Matth. iii. 5; Mark i. 5; Luke iii. 7), and alludes to the different classes and callings of which they were composed (Luke iii. 12), we may reasonably infer that the number of his actual disciples and followers could by no means have been inconsiderable.

LECT. III.

ᵃ ver. 1
The final testimony of the Baptist.
ᵇ John iii. 33.

ᶜ John iii. 27—36

bered those of Johnᵃ, many as there seems reason for supposing them now to have become. The Baptist was still free. He was now at Ænon[1] near Salim, a place of watersᵇ in the Northern portion of the Valley of the Jordan[2], and from which he might afterwards have passed by the fords of Succoth into the territory of the licentious Antipas. At this spot was delivered his final testimony to the Redeemerᶜ,—a testimony perhaps directed against a jealousy on the part of his disciples[3], which might have been recently called out by the Jew[4] with whom they

---

[1] Some plausible but purely contextual arguments for fixing the site of Ænon in the wilderness of Judæa will be found in Wieseler, *Chron. Synops.* p. 249 sq. Such arguments, however, cannot safely be urged against the direct statements of early writers: see next note.

[2] There seems good reason for identifying the Salim, near to which the Evangelist tells us John was baptizing, with some ruins at the northern base of Tell Ridghah, near to which is a beautiful spring, and a Wely (Saint's tomb), called Sheikh Sâlim: see Van de Velde, *Memoir,* p. 345. Robinson appears to doubt this (*Palestine,* Vol. III. p. 333, ed. 2), but without sufficient reason. The mere coincidence of name might perhaps be an unsafe argument, if the position of the place did not accord with the position of Salim as fixed by Jerome in his *Onomasticon* (Art. 'Ænon'), where Ænon and Salim are both noticed as being eight Roman miles from Scythopolis: see Van de Velde, *Syria and Palestine,* Vol. II. p. 345 sq., Caspari, *Chron.-Geogr. Einleit.* § 87, p. 104.

[3] The words of the sacred text (John iii. 26) give us some grounds for supposing it possible that feelings of doubt or jealousy might have been shown by some of St John's disciples,—feelings which perhaps might have remained even to a later period, and might have been one of the causes which led to the mission of the two disciples recorded in Matth. xi. 2 sq., Luke vii. 18 sq. There is an expression of something unlooked for, and perhaps not wholly approved of, in the ἴδε οὗτος βαπτίζει καὶ πάντες ἔρχονται πρὸς αὐτόν. So Augustine ('moti sunt discipuli Johannis; concurrebatur ad Christum, veniebatur ad Johannem'), and still more distinctly Chrysost. *in loc.*

[4] There seems no reasonable doubt that the true reading is Ἰουδαίου, and not Ἰουδαίων (*Rec.*). The evidence for the former, which includes eleven uncial MSS. in addition to the Alexandrian and Vatican, will be found in the new edition of Tischendorf's *New Test.* Vol. I. p. 564. What the exact subject of the contention was we are not told, further than that it was περὶ καθαρισμοῦ (ver. 25): it might well have arisen,

had been contending on the subject of purifying[a]. That testimony was in one respect mournfully prophetic. He had now begun, even as he himself said[b], to decrease; his ministry was over; the Bridegroom had come, and the friend of the bridegroom had heard his voice, and the joy of that faithful friend was now completed and full[c]. Thus it was that apparently at the close of this year, or according to a recent chronologer, two or three months later[1], the fearless rebuker of sin, though it be in kings' palaces, is seized on by the irritated yet superstitious Antipas[d], and after a short imprisonment in the dungeons of Ma-

[a] Joh. iii. 25
[b] ver. 30
[c] ver. 29
[d] Lk. iii. 19, compared with Mark vi. 20

as Augustine suggests, from the statement on the part of the Jews [August. adopts the plural],—'majorem esse Christum, et ad ejus baptismum debere concurri.' *In Joann. Tract.* XIII. 3. 8.

[1] The exact date of the captivity of the Baptist is a question of great difficulty, and perhaps can never be settled: see Winer, *RWB.* Art. 'Johannes der Täufer,' Vol. I. p. 590. Wieseler, in a very elaborate discussion (*Chron. Synops.* p. 223—251), has endeavoured to show that it took place about the feast of Purim in the following year (March 19, A.U.C. 782), and that he was beheaded a few days before the Passover (April 17) of the same year. The latter date seems made out (see *Chron. Synops.* p. 292 sq.), but the former is open to many objections, two of which may be specified, (a) the way in which our Lord speaks of the Baptist (John v. 33); and (b) the brief space of time that is thus necessarily assigned to his captivity, —a time apparently as unduly short, as that assigned by Greswell is unnecessarily long; see *Dissert.* X. (Append.) Vol. III. p. 425. It seems then, on the whole, safer to adopt the first view in the text, and to suppose that St John was put into prison shortly before our Lord's present departure into Galilee, and that the ἀναχώρησις into that country specified by the Synoptical Evangelists (Matth. iv. 12; Mark i. 14; Luke iv. 14) coincides with that here specified by St John. For a brief consideration of the difficulties this view has been supposed to involve, see Lect. IV. p. 149, note 3, and compare the remarks of Tischendorf, *Synops. Evang.* p. xxv. The most recent writer on the Chronology of our Lord's life (Caspari) fixes the date as somewhere between the Passover of A.U.C. 781 and the September of the same year, but this rests on the assumption that the ἑορτή (John v. 1) was the festal season beginning with the day of Atonement, on which hypothesis see below p. 136, note 2: see also Caspari, *Chron.-Geogr. Einleit.* § 96, p. 112.

LECT. III.

chærus[1], falls a victim to the arts of the vengeful Herodias.

This capture of the Baptist, if we adopt the earlier date, might perhaps have soon become known to our Lord, and might have suggested some thoughts of danger to Himself and to His infant Church from which now He might have deemed it meet to withdraw. Perhaps with this feeling, but certainly, as St John specially tells us, with the knowledge that the blessed results and success of His ministry had reached the ears of the male- volent Pharisees[a], our Lord suspends His first ministry in Judæa, a ministry that had now lasted eight months, and prepares to return by the shortest route, through Samaria[2], to the safe retirement of the hills of Galilee.

[a] Joh. iv. 1

Our Lord's journey through Samaria.

It was now late in December[3], four months

---

[1] See Josephus, *Antiq.* XVIII. 5. 2; and for a description of the place, ib. *Bell. Jud.* VII. 6. 2. From this latter passage, and especially from the notice of the fine palace built there, we may *perhaps* suppose it to have been the scene of the festival (Matth. xiv. 6; Mark vi. 21) which preceded the Baptist's murder: see, however, Wieseler, *Chron. Synops.* p. 250 sq., who places the scene at Livias. The site of Machærus is supposed by Seetzen to be now occupied by a ruined fortress on the north end of Jebel Attârûs, which is said still to bear the name of M'kauer: see Ritter, *Erdkunde*, Part XV. 1, p. 577.

[2] Our Lord was now probably in the north-eastern, or as the ἔδει δὲ αὐτὸν κ.τ.λ. (John iv. 4) may be thought to suggest, more northerly portions of Judæa. Thither He might have gradually moved from the more immediate neighbourhood of the Jordan, towards which He seems first to have gone: see above, p. 128. Our Lord on one occasion at least (Luke ix. 51 sq.) adopted the route through Samaria in preference to the route through Peræa. At a later time the journey through Samaria was occasionally rendered unsafe by the open hostility of the Samaritans (see Joseph. *Antiq.* XX. 6. 2), some traces of which we find even in our Lord's time: comp. Luke ix. 53; and see Lightfoot, *Harm.* Part III. Vol. I. p. 460 (Roterod. 1686).

[3] Stanley (*Palestine*, ch. V. p. 240, note, ed. 2) fixes it in January or February, but in opposition to Robinson, *Harmony*, p. 19 (Tract Society), who adopts an earlier date: see above, p. 106, note 1.

as the narrative indirectly reminds us from the harvest[1], when the Lord crossed the rich plain that skirts the southern and eastern bases of Ebal and Gerizim, and weary with travel rested on His way by a well which even now the modern pilgrim can confidently identify[2]. His disciples had gone forward up the beautiful but narrow valley[3] to the ancient neighbouring city, to which, as it would seem, Jewish prejudice had long since given the name of Sychar[4], when the grace of

---

[1] See John iv. 35, οὐχ ὑμεῖς λέγετε ὅτι ἔτι τετράμηνός ἐστιν καὶ ὁ θερισμὸς ἔρχεται,—a passage which, from the distinctness and precision of the language (observe the ἔτι and compare it with ἤδη which follows), has been rightly pressed by some of the best expositors as affording a note of time: see Meyer *in loc.*, and especially Wieseler, *Chron. Synops.* p. 214 sq. This note of time must, as Caspari rightly observes, be referred either to the time of sowing or of harvest. The context certainly seems very distinctly in favour of the former, but it may be conceded that the latter is possible; see the remarks in the preface, and Caspari, *Chron.-Geogr. Einleit.* § 86, p. 104. The arguments in favour of its being merely a proverbial expression, and not at all of a chronological nature, deserve some consideration, but appear to have been fairly disposed of by Wieseler, *loc. cit.* A different, and very improbable note of time is deduced from the passage by Greswell, *Dissert.* IX. (Append.). Vol. III. p. 408.

[2] For a good description of Jacob's Well, see Robinson, *Palestine*, Vol. II. p. 286 sq.: compare also Van de Velde, *Syria and Palestine*, Vol. I. p. 399, Caspari, *Chron.-Geogr. Einleit.* § 89, p. 106, and Thomson, *The Land and the Book*, Vol. II. p. 206, where a sketch is given of this profoundly interesting spot. For a possible identification of this well with the עֵין סוֹכַר of the Talmudical writers, see Lightfoot, *Chorogr.* Vol. II. p. 586 sq. (Roterod. 1686), and compare Wieseler, *Chron. Synops.* p. 256, note.

[3] For a description of this valley, see Van de Velde, *Syria and Palestine*, Vol. I. p. 386 sq., and compare Stanley, *Palestine*, ch. v. p. 232.

[4] The name of Sychar (not Sichar; see Tischendorf *in loc.*) does not appear to have arisen from a mere corruption of the ancient name of Shechem (Olsh., al.), but from a studiedly contemptuous change with reference either to שֶׁקֶר, 'falsehood,' *i. e.* idol-worship (comp. Hab. ii. 18, and Reland, *Dissert. Misc.* Vol. I. p. 241), or to שִׁכּוֹר, 'drunkard' (comp. Isaiah xxviii. 1, and Lightfoot, *Chorogr.* Vol. II. p. 586, ed. Roterod.), and in the time of St John had become the regular name of the place; compare, however, Acts vii. 16, where Stephen perhaps designedly recurs to the ancient name, and Wieseler, *Chron. Synops.*

God brings one poor sinful woman either from the city or the fields to draw water at Jacob's well. We well remember the memorable converse that followed: how the conviction of sin began to work within, and how the amazed woman became the Lord's first herald in Sychem,—the first-fruits of the great harvest that but a few years afterwards was to be gathered in by Philip the Deacon[1].

The faith of the Samaritans. The faith of these Samaritans and the effect produced on them, even when contrasted with that produced by our Lord during His ministry in Judæa, deserves more than a passing notice. In Judæa our Lord had abode eight months; in Sychem He spends but two days. In Judæa He works many miracles[a]; in Samaria He works none[2].

[a] Joh. ii. 23

---

p. 256 sq. (note), where the name is connected, *apparently* less probably, with שָׂכַר=סָכַר, 'to hire,' in reference to Gen. xxxiii. 19. It is now called Nabulus, by a contraction from the name of Neapolis afterwards given it by the Romans; but it seems probable that the ancient city was larger and extended nearer to Jacob's Well: see Robinson, *Palestine*, Vol. II. p. 292 (ed. 2), where there will be found a full and excellent description of the place and its vicinity. Compare also Thomson, *The Land and the Book*, Vol. II. p. 200 sq.,—where a sketch will be found of the entrance into the city, Van de Velde, *Syria and Palestine*, Vol. I. p. 386 sq., and a photographic view by Frith, *Egypt and Palestine*, Part IV. 3. It has been recently urged by Caspari, with some plausibility, that Sychar is to be identified with El Askar, a hamlet not above ten minutes' walk from the well; see *Chron.-Geogr. Einleit.* § 90,

p. 107. The above assumption, however (the greater extent of the ancient city) seems best to reconcile difficulties.

[1] See Acts viii. 5 sq., where the thankful reception of the Gospel on the part of the Samaritans is especially noticed; and compare Baumgarten, *in loc.* § 14, Vol. I. p. 184 sq. (Clark). That the 'city of Samaria,' to which the Deacon went down from Jerusalem, was the city of Sychem, does not appear *certain* (Meyer, *on Acts* viii. 5), though it may reasonably be considered highly probable.

[2] On the faith of these Samaritans see Horsley, *Serm.* XXIV.—XXVI., and on its contrast with that of the Jews, Chrysost. *in loc.* It seems, however, a little rhetorical to say that the latter 'were doing everything to expel Him from their country,' while the former were entreating Him to stay: see *Hom. in Joann.* XXXV. Vol. VIII. p. 232. The

The Early Judæan Ministry.

And yet we read that in Sychem many believed even the vague tidings of the heart-stricken woman[a], and hastened forth to welcome Him, whom, in the fulness of a faith that overstepped all narrow national prejudices, they believed in and acknowledged as the true Messiah, the Restorer, or perhaps rather Converter, as He was termed in their own dialect[1], the Saviour, as they indirectly avow not of Samaria only, but of all the scattered families of the children of men[b].

LECT. III.

[a] Joh. iv. 39

[b] ver. 42

But faith astonishing even as that of Samaria might not detain Him who came to the lost sheep of the house of Israel. After a stay of two memorable days, which the people of Sychem would

The further journey of our Lord to Galilee.

multitudes in Judæa or elsewhere appear almost always to have gladly received our Lord, except when instigated to a contrary course by His true and bitter enemies, the ruling and hierarchical party (the Ἰουδαῖοι of St John; see Meyer, *on John* xi. 19) and their various satellites: comp. Matth. xvii. 20, Mark xv. 11.

[1] Much has been written about the expectation of a Messiah on the part of the Samaritans. It is not improbable that, as their own letters in modern times assert (see Hengstenberg, *Christol.* Vol. I. p. 66, Clark), they derived it from such passages in the Pentateuch as Gen. xlix. 10, Numb. xxiv. 17, Deut. xviii. 15; and that, though really foreigners by descent (comp. Robinson, *Palestine*, Vol. II. p. 289), they still maintained this belief in common with their hated neighbours, the Jews. At any rate it seems certain that an expectation of a Restorer or Converter under the title of הַשָּׁהֵב or הַתָּהֵב, was enter-

tained among them at an earlier period of their history (see Gesenius, *Samar. Theol.* p. 41 sq., and the curious doctrinal hymns published by the same learned editor under the title *Carmina Samaritana*, p. 75 sq.); and we learn from Robinson that even to this day, under the name of el-*Muhdy* (the Guide), the Messiah is still looked for by this singular people: see *Palestine*, Vol. II. p. 278, and p. 297 sq., where an account is given of the celebrated correspondence maintained at intervals between the Samaritans and Joseph Scaliger, Marshall, and other scholars of the West: compare also Winer, *RWB.* Art. 'Samaritaner,' Vol. II. p. 273. The exact meaning of הַתָּהֵב is discussed by Gesenius in the Berlin *Jahrb. für Wissensch. Krit.* for 1830, p. 651 sq. Some interesting remarks on this subject and on the Messianic expectations of the Samaritans generally will be found in Langen, *Judenthum in Palästina zur Zeit Christi*, p. 407 sq.

gladly have had prolonged[a], the Lord returns to a country that now vouchsafed to receive its prophet[1] only because His miracles at Jerusalem had been such as could not be denied[b]. Signs and wonders were all that dull-hearted Galilee could appreciate. Signs and wonders they must see, or, as our Lord mournfully says, 'they would not believe[c].' We may observe then how consistent is the narrative which represents our Lord as having chosen the scene of His first miracle as His temporary resting-place[2]. He returns to Cana in Galilee, where as St John significantly adds, 'He made the water wine[d].' There He yet again performs a second miracle[e] in bringing back to life the dying son of the Capernaite nobleman[3],—

LECT. III.
[a] Joh. iv. 40
[b] ver. 45
[c] ver. 48
[d] ver. 46
[e] ver. 54

[1] The exact meaning of our Lord's comment, John iv. 44, αὐτὸς γὰρ Ἰησοῦς κ.τ.λ., is not perfectly clear, owing to the apparent difficulty caused by the argumentative γάρ, and the doubtful application of πατρίδι. That this latter word does not refer to Judæa (Origen, and recently Wieseler, Chron. Synops. p. 45) but to Galilee, seems almost certain from the mention of Γαλιλαία both in the preceding and succeeding verses. The force of the γάρ is, however, less easy to decide upon, but is perhaps to be sought for in the fact that our Lord stayed so short a time with the Samaritans, and avoided rather than courted popularity. It is true that He found it in Galilee (ver. 45), but that was because He brought it as it were from another country. The Galilæans did not honour the Lord as their own prophet, but as One whom they had seen work wonders at Jerusalem. The explanatory force adopted by Lücke and others does not harmonize with the simplicity of the context.

[2] See John iv. 46, ἦλθεν οὖν [ὁ Ἰησοῦς] πάλιν εἰς τὴν Κανᾶ,—where the οὖν seems to imply that the visit of our Lord was in consequence of this disposition on the part of the Galilæans. He sees the effect which miracles produced upon the people, and is pleased so far to condescend to their infirmities as to sojourn for a time at the scene of a miracle that must have made a great impression on those who witnessed it, and the memory of which His presence among them might savingly revive and reanimate : see Chrysostom in loc. Hom. XXV. Vol. VIII. p. 235.

[3] From the instances from Josephus of the use of the term βασιλικός, that have been collected by Krebs (Obs. in Nov. Test. p. 144), we may perhaps reasonably conclude that the person here specified was not a relative (Chrys. 1.), but in the service of Herod Antipas ('in famulitio

a miracle which wrought its blessed effects on the father and his whole household[a], and may thus perchance have had some influence in leading our Lord three months afterwards, when rejected by the wretched madmen of Nazareth[b], to make Capernaum His earthly home[1].

[a] Joh. iv. 53
[b] Lk. iv. 29

Our present portion of the Evangelical history contains but one more event,—the journey of our Lord to Jerusalem, and His miraculous cure of the infirm man at the pool of Bethesda[c]. Here, I need scarcely remind you, we at once find ourselves encountered by a question, on the answer to which our whole system of Gospel-harmony mainly depends, and on which we find, both in ancient[2] and modern times, the most marked diversity of opinions. The question is,—what festival does St John refer to at the beginning of the fifth

Our Lord's return to Jerusalem at the feast of Purim.

[c] John v. 1 sq.

---

et ministerio regis,' Krebs, *l. c.*),—in what capacity, however, cannot be determined. The opinion that this miracle was identical with that of the healing of the Centurion's servant (Matth. viii. 5 sq., Luke vii. 1 sq.) is mentioned both by Origen (*in Joann.* Tom. XIII. 60) and Chrysostom (*in Joann.* Hom. XXXV. 2), but very properly rejected by them. Nothing really is identical in the two miracles except the locality of the sufferer, and the fact that our Saviour did not see him: see especially Theophylact and Euthymius *in loc.*

[1] For some good comments on the details of this miracle,—one of the characteristics of which is the performance of the cure by our Lord, not only without His seeing (as in the case of the Centurion's servant), but when at a distance of some miles from the sufferer,—see the commentaries of Origen, Chrysostom, Cyril Alex., Theophylact, and Euthymius; and for a general view of the whole, Hall, *Contempl.* III. 2, and Trench, *Miracles*, p. 117 sq.: compare also Lange, *Leben Jesu*, II. 4. 10, Part II. p. 552 sq.

[2] The differences of opinion as to the festival mentioned in John v. 1, are not confined to modern writers. Irenæus says that it was at the Passover (*Hær.* II. 39), but as we cannot ascertain what reading (ἑορτή or ἡ ἑορτή, see next note) was adopted by this ancient writer, his opinion must be received with some reserve. Chrysostom, Cyril of Alexandria, and after them Theophylact and Euthymius, with more plausibility, suppose it to have been the feast of Pentecost: see, however, p. 136, note 2.

LECT. III.

*Joh. v. 1

chapter of his Gospel, when he tells us that 'there was a feast of the Jews, and Jesus went up to Jerusalem[a]'? The various answers I will not now pause to discuss, but will say briefly, that after a prolonged consideration of this difficult subject, I venture to think that as the language of St John, according to the best text[1], and when duly considered, does seem distinctly unfavourable to this festival being considered as either the Passover or one of the three greater festivals[2], we may, not

[1] The true reading appears to be ἑορτὴ τῶν Ἰουδαίων (*Rec.*), without the article. It has, in addition to secondary authorities, the support of three out of the five leading uncial MSS. (ABD; opposed to ℵ and C), is specially commented on in the *Chronicon Paschale* (p. 405 sq., ed. Dindorf), and is adopted by Lachmann, Tischendorf, and the best recent editors.

[2] The principal arguments are as follow, and seem of some weight: (*a*) the omission of the article,—which though sometimes observed when a verb substant. precedes (Middleton, *Greek Art.;* comp. Neander, *Life of Christ*, p. 234, note, Bohn), or when a strictly defining or possessive genitive follows (see exx. in Winer, *Gramm.* § 19. 2. *b*), cannot possibly be urged in the case of a merely inverted sentence like the present, and where the gen. has no such special and defining force: see Winer, *Gramm. l. c.* p. 232, note. [The answer to this in Robinson, *Harmony*, p. 199 (Tract Soc.), has no force, as the cases adduced are not out of St John, wholly different, and easily to be accounted for.] To this we may add (*b*) the absence of the name of the festival, whereas St John seems always to specify it: compare ch. ii. 13, vii. 2, and even (in the case of the ἐγκαίνια) x. 22. Again (*c*) it seems now generally agreed upon that it was not the Pentecost; that if it be a Passover, our Lord would then have been as long a time as eighteen months absent from Jerusalem (see Wieseler, *Chron. Synops.* p. 217); and that if it be the Feast of Tabernacles, we then, according to Ebrard (*Kritik der Ev. Gesch.* § 37, p. 157), *must* adopt the highly improbable view that it was not the σκηνοπηγία that followed the Passover mentioned ch. ii. 13, but that followed a second Passover, which St John, usually so accurate on this point (see ch. vi. 4), has not specified. It is just however to say that this view of Ebrard does not seem so certainly clear as he regards it. We may with Caspari (*Chron.-Geogr. Einleit.* § 96, p. 112) apparently regard this festival, as far as other chronological considerations are concerned, as the Day of Atonement after the *first* Passover, but if we accept the view taken above (p. 131, n. 1) of the supposed note of time in John iv. 35, then this *would* be the σκηνοπηγία after a second Passover, and our chronology would become hopelessly embarrassed.

without many plausible arguments, adopt the view of the best recent harmonists and commentators, and regard it as the Feast of Purim[1],—the commemorative feast of Esther's pleading and Haman's overthrow. This festival, it would appear by backward computation, must have taken place in this present year of our Lord's life (A. U. C. 782), on the 19th of March[2], and, as we may reasonably infer from the narrative, a Sabbath-day,—a day on which, according to the ancient, though not according to the modern calendar of the Jews, this festival could apparently have been celebrated[3],

---

[1] The arguments in favour of this particular festival, though sufficiently strong to have gained the assent of a decided majority of the best recent expositors, are still of a dependent and negative character. They are as follow: (*a*) if the note of time derived from John iv. 35 be correct, then the festival here mentioned clearly falls between the end of one year and the Passover of the one following (ch. vi. 4), and consequently can be no other than the Feast of Purim, which was celebrated on the 14th and 15th of the month Adar (Esth. ix. 21); (*b*) if, as seems shown in the above note, strong critical as well as exegetical objections can be urged against any and all of the other festivals that have been proposed, then a remaining festival which is only open to objections of a weaker and more general character (see below, note 3) deserves serious consideration; (*c*) if this date be fixed upon, the chronology of the period between it and the following Passover not only admits of an easy adjustment, but also, as will be seen in the course of the narrative, involves some striking coincidences and harmonies which reflect great additional plausibility upon the supposition. For additional notices and arguments, see Anger, *de Temp. in Act. Apost.* I. p. 24 sq., Wieseler, *Chron. Synops.* pp. 205—222, Lange, *Leben Jesu*, Book II. Part I. p. 9; and for perhaps the strongest statement of the counter-arguments, Hengstenberg, *Christology*, Vol. III. p. 244 sq. (Clark).

[2] For the principles on which this computation rests, see Wieseler, *Chron. Synops.* p. 206 sq., compared with p. 219: compare also the useful table in Tischendorf, *Synops. Evang.* p. LI.; and for general tables for facilitating such calculations, see Browne, *Ordo Sæcl.* § 452—455, p. 499 sq.

[3] This *seems* to be made out by Wieseler, *Chron. Synops.* p. 219 sq., but is so strongly questioned by Hengstenberg (*Christology*, Vol. III. p. 248),—who refers for proofs to Reland, *Antiq. Sacr.* IV. 9, and the special treatise of Shickard, on this festival, reprinted in the *Critici Sacri*, Vol. II. p. 1183 (ed. Amsteled. 1698—1732),—that a few comments

138   The Early Judæan Ministry.

LECT. III.

and, singularly enough, the only instance in which a Sabbath could fall upon any one of the festivals of the year in question[1].

Main objections to this opinion.

It has I know been urged that our Lord would never have gone up to a festival of mere earthly rejoicing and revelry[2]. In answer to this, without

must be made on the subject. Much seems to turn on the question whether the 14th of Adar, or, as Hengstenberg urges, the day on which the roll of Esther was read,—a day, as will be seen from the *Mishna*, made variable for convenience,—was the true day of the festival? With the opening sections of the Tract 'Megillah' before us, we shall probably (with Wieseler) decide for the former, especially when we compare with the preceding sections the close of sect. 3, where it is said in answer to the general question, 'when the Megillah may be read before its proper time,' that an exception is to be made for places where it is customary for [the country people] to assemble on Mondays and Thursdays, but that ' where that does not take place it may only be read *on its proper day*' (אין קורין אותה אלא בזמנה). *Mishna*, p. 182 (De Sola and Raphall's Transl.). The question is here noticed as of some interest, but it may be observed that though it is *probable* from the sacred narrative that the Sabbath on which the miracle was performed coincided with the festival, it is not expressly said so; and that even if the Feast of Purim could not fall on a Sabbath, the main question would remain wholly unaffected by it: see Meyer, *on John* v. 1, p. 143.

[1] See Wieseler, *Chron. Synops.* p. 219, and compare the table in Tischendorf, *Synops. Evang.* p. LI.

It may be observed that the year now in question was a leap year, and had a second month of Adar,— hence the difference between this calendar and that in Browne, *Ordo Sæcl.* § 594, p. 647, where this fact is not observed. For exact information on the difficult subject of the Jewish calendar, see Ideler, *Handbuch der Chronol.* Vol. I. p. 477 sq., the special work of Ben-David, *Gesch. des Jud. Kalend.* (Berl. 1817); compare also the good Excursus of Wieseler, *Chron. Synops.* p. 437 sq., and Browne, *Ordo Sæclorum,* § 403 sq.

[2] This objection is urged, though not with much cogency, by Trench, *Miracles,* p. 245. For a full account of the ceremonies at this festival, see the work of Shickard, *de Festo Purim* (Tubing. 1634) above alluded to (p. 137, note 3), and compare Winer, *RWB.* Art. 'Purim,' Vol. II. p. 589. The objection that has been founded on St John's omission of the special name of this festival, contrasted with his usual habit in similar cases (ch. vii. 2, x. 22), is fairly met by Anger, who remarks that while the names of other festivals (*e.g.* σκηνοπηγια and ἐγκαίνια) partially explained themselves, that of the Feast of Purim, under its Grecized title (τῶν φρουραί or φουραί, or τῆς Μαρδοχαικῆς ἡμέρας), was probably felt by the Evangelist as likely to prove unintelligible to the general readers for whom the Gos-

pausing to compare this merely negative statement with the positive arguments which have been advanced on the contrary side, let us simply reply, that at this festival, in which the hard lot of the poor and needy received a passing alleviation, the Divine presence of Him who came to preach the Gospel to the poor might not seem either strange or inappropriate[1]. In addition to this, let us not forget that, in the year now under consideration, the Passover would take place only a month afterwards, and that our Lord might well have thought it meet to fix His abode at Jerusalem and to commence His preaching before the hurried influx of the multitudes that came up to the solemnities of the great yearly festival[2].

But let us now return to our narrative, and with sadness observe how the malice and wickedness of man was permitted to counteract those counsels of mercy, and to shorten that mission of love.

The miracle at the pool of Bethesda.

On this Sabbath-day by the waters of that healing pool[3], which ancient tradition as well as

---

pel was designed. *De Temp. in Act. Apost.* p. 27 sq.

[1] See Wieseler, *Chron. Synops.* p. 222,—vigorously, though not very convincingly, opposed by Hengstenberg, who seems to take a somewhat extreme view of the revelry and license which prevailed at the festival; see *Christology*, Vol. III. p. 247.

[2] A partial illustration of this is supplied by John xi. 55, where it is expressly said that 'mary went out of the country up to Jerusalem *before the Passover*, to purify themselves.' The ἵνα ἁγνίσωσιν of course does not apply in the present case,

but the general fact that there was such a habit of going up before the festival is not without significance.

[3] It may be considered somewhat doubtful whether ver. 4 is really an integral portion of the Sacred Text, or a later addition. It is omitted by Tischendorf with B, the first hand of C, D (to which we may now add ‎א), and a few ancient versions, —the valuable Curetonian Syriac (but see Roberts, *On Lang. of St Matth. Gospel*, p. 122) being of the number. This is undoubtedly authority of much weight, but as prejudice or reluctance to accept the

recent investigation seems to have correctly identified with the large, but now ruined reservoir in the vicinity of St Stephen's gate[1], the Lord performs a miracle on one poor sufferer, who had long lingered in that House of Mercy[2], unpitied and friendless. That miracle was accompanied with a sign of great significance. Not only does

---

fact specified might have something to do with the removal of the verse, we shall *perhaps* be justified in following the judgment of Lachmann, and, with one first-class and nearly all the second-class uncial MSS., in retaining the verse. It must not be disguised, however, that these authorities differ greatly with one another in the separate words,—a further argument of some importance; compare Meyer, *Komment.* p. 141 sq. (ed. 2). The attempts, in which strangely enough a note of Hammond is to be included, to explain away the miraculous portion of the statement are very unsatisfactory. If the verse is a part of the Sacred Text, then undoubtedly the ultimate agency, however *outwardly* exhibited, whether by gaseous exhalations or intermittent currents, was *angelical*: see Wordsworth *in loc.*, and comp. Lange, *Leben Jesu*, II. 2. 2, Part I. p. 50, and some curious comments and quotations in Sepp, *Leben Christi*, IV. 5, Vol. II. p. 315 sq.

[1] This, it must be conceded, is a debated point, as there are arguments of some weight in favour of this reservoir being regarded as a portion of the ancient fosse which protected the temple and the fort of Antonia: see Robinson, *Palestine*, Vol. I. p. 293 sq. (ed. 2). The traditional site, however, and its identification with the pool of Bethesda,

mentioned in the ancient *Jerusalem Itinerary* (p. 589), seems fairly maintained by Williams, *Holy City*, II. 5, Vol. II. p. 483, though doubted by Winer, *RWB.* Vol. I. p. 170. Under any circumstances the suggestion of Robinson (apparently favoured by Trench, *Miracles*, p. 247), that Bethesda is perhaps to be identified with the Fountain of the Virgin, is pronounced by an unbiassed traveller who has seen that deeply excavated fountain (see vignette in Williams, Vol. II. p. xi), as plainly incompatible with what we must infer from the details of the sacred narrative as to the nature of the locality where the miracle was performed. For a good view of the traditional site, see Robertson and Beato, *Views of Jerusalem*, No. 12, and for some useful comments, Caspari, *Chron.-Geogr. Einleit.* § 98, p. 114.

[2] This appears to be the correct meaning: the true etymology not being בֵּית אִשְׁדָּא 'the house of effusion or washing' (Bochart, Reland, al., followed by Williams, *Holy City*, Vol. II. p. 487), but בֵּית חֶסְדָּא,—an etymology strongly confirmed by the Peshito-Syriac, which here resolves the Grecized form back again into its original elements (*beth chesdo*): see Wolf, *Curæ Philolog.* (*in loc.*) Vol. II. p. 835.

our Lord restore the helpless paralytic[1], but commands him to rise up and bear his bed[a], and thus practically evince not only his own completed recovery, but the true lordship of the Son of Man over Sabbatical restrictions and ceremonial rest[2]. He that a year before had shown that He was Lord of the Temple[b], now shows that He is Lord also of the Sabbath. But this was what Pharisaical hypocrisy could not brook. This act, merciful and miraculous as it was, involved a violation of what Scribe and Pharisee affected to hold most dear; and it could not and must not be tolerated. The Jews or,—as that term nearly always implies in St John,—the adherents of the Sanhedrin[3], who had been informed by the man who it was that

LECT. III.

[a] Joh. v. 8

[b] ii. 19

---

[1] For an explanation of the various details of the miracle, the student must be referred to the standard commentaries, especially those of Chrysostom, Cyril of Alexandria, Theophylact, and Euthymius; and among more modern writers, those of Maldonatus, Lücke, Meyer, and Alford. See also the fragmentary homily of Cyril of Jerusalem (*Works*, p. 336, ed. Bened.), Hall, *Contemplations*, IV. 11, and Trench, *Notes on the Miracles*, p. 243.

[2] It would certainly seem, as Lightfoot suggests (*Hor. Hebr. in loc.* Vol. II. p. 622), that our Lord desired by this command to show His power over the Sabbath, and to exhibit openly His condemnation of the ceremonial restrictions with which it was then encumbered. For some striking instances of these, see especially the *Mishna*, Tract, 'Sabbath,' p. 37 sq. (De Sola and Raphall),—where the case of an act of charity (relieving a mendicant) forms the subject of discussion. We may infer what must have been the amount of glosses with which the law respecting the Sabbath was now encumbered, when in the above formal collection of the precepts of the oral law, committed to writing little more than 150 years afterwards, we find that 'a tailor must not go out with his needle near dusk [on the Sabbath eve], lest he forget and carry it out with him, [during the Sabbath].' *Mishna*, Tract, 'Sabbath,' I. 3, p. 38 (De Sola and Raphall).

[3] See above, p. 115, note 1. The only and indeed obvious exception to this is when the term Ἰουδαῖοι is used with a national reference (John ii. 6, 13, iii. 1, iv. 9, al.); in all other cases the term in St John's Gospel seems to mark the hostile and hierarchical party that especially opposed our blessed Lord's teaching and ministry.

LECT. III. had healed him[1], and some of whom had perhaps witnessed the miracle, at once begin to exhibit a vengeful[2] hatred[a], which only deepens in its implacability when, in that sublime discourse at the close of the chapter on which we are meditating, the fifth chapter of St John, the Lord declares not only His unity in working[b], but His unity in dignity and honour[c] with the Eternal Father[3].

[a] Joh. v. 16
[b] ver. 17
[c] ver. 23

Distinctive character of this epoch.

This is the turning point in the Gospel history. Up to this time the preaching of our Lord at Jerusalem and in Judæa has met with a certain degree of toleration, and in many cases even of acceptance[4]: but after this all becomes changed.

---

[1] There does not seem *sufficient* reason for supposing that the man made the communication from gratitude, or from a desire to commend our Lord to the rulers (comp. Chrys., Cyril Alex.); still less was it from any evil motive (comp. Lange, p. 769). It probably arose simply from a desire to justify his performance of the command (ver. 9) by specifying the authority under which he had acted; comp. Meyer *in loc.*, and Luthardt, *Joh. Evang.* Part II. pp. 6, 7.

[2] This perhaps is the strongest term that we are fairly justified in using, as the words καὶ ἐζήτουν αὐτὸν ἀποκτεῖναι (ver. 16) are omitted by three out of the four leading uncial MSS.: see Tischendorf *in loc.* Vol. I. p. 577.

[3] A very careful investigation into the connexion and evolution of thought in this divine discourse,— the main subject of which is the Person, Mission, and Offices of the eternal Son of the eternal Father, and the testimony by which they are confirmed,— will be found in Luthardt, *Johann. Evang.* Part II.

p. 10 sq.; see also Stier, *Words of our Lord*, Vol. v. p. 83 sq. (Clark), and Lange, *Leben Jesu*, II. 5. 1, Part II. pp. 770—775. The whole is ably expanded and enlarged upon by Augustine, *in Joann.* Tract. XVIII.— XXIII. Vol. III. p. 1355 sq.

[4] See John ii. 23, iv. 1. In estimating the degree of reception that our Lord's teaching met with, we must carefully distinguish between the general mass of the people, whether in Judæa or Galilee, which commonly 'heard him gladly' (Mark xii. 37), and the Pharisaical and hierarchical party, which both disbelieved themselves, and, commonly acting from Jerusalem as a centre (see esp. Matth. xv. 1, Mark iii. 22, vii. 1), readily organized co-operation in other quarters; comp. Luke v. 17. Their present state of feeling deserves particular notice, as preparing us for their future machinations, and as leading us to expect no such prolonged duration of our Lord's ministry as the supposition that this feast was a passover would force us to assume. The fearful re-

Henceforth the city of David is no meet or safe abode for the Son of David; the earthly house of His heavenly Father is no longer a secure hall of audience for the preaching of the Eternal Son. Henceforth the Judæan or, more strictly speaking, the Jerusalem ministry narrows itself into two efforts, the one made seven the other nine months afterwards[1], and both marked by a similar vindictive animosity[a], on the part of the hostile Jewish section, to that which now first comes into such melancholy prominence....Abruptly as it would seem, perhaps only a day or two after this eventful Sabbath[2], the Lord leaves Jerusalem, to return to His old home in Galilee,—there alas! to meet with a yet sadder rejection[b], and to withdraw from hands more savage and murderous[c] than those even of the Pharisees of Jerusalem.

[a] John viii. 59; x. 31, 39
[b] Luke iv. 16 sq.
[c] iv. 28

With this return to Galilee, which is implied in the interval between the 5th and 6th chapters of St John, and which has been supposed, though I cannot think correctly[3], by a recent sacred chronologer[4], as identical with the departure or return

The termination of the early Judæan ministry.

solve to *kill our Lord*, though perhaps not officially expressed, had nevertheless now been distinctly formed, and was being acted upon: see John v. 18, and comp. Lange, *Leben Jesu,* II. 5. 1. Part II. p. 769 sq.

[1] The first of these was at our Lord's visit to Jerusalem, during the Feast of Tabernacles, towards the middle of October in the present year, A.U.C. 782 (John vii. 1 sq., comp. Luke ix. 51 sq.); the second at His appearance in Jerusalem at the Feast of the Dedication, in the December of the same year (John x. 22 sq.).

[2] When our Lord left Jerusalem is not mentioned or even implied, but after the impious efforts directed against His life, we may reasonably conclude that it was immediately,—the very day perhaps after the present Sabbath, and thus with fully sufficient time to reach Galilee and Nazareth before the Sabbath which succeeded: comp. Wieseler, *Chron. Synops.* p. 222, 260 sq.

[3] See above, p. 129, note 1, and the beginning of the next Lecture, where this question is noticed more at length.

[4] See Wieseler, *Chron. Synops.* p. 161 sq., compared with p. 223. This

LECT. III.

[a] Mt. iv. 12
Mark i. 14
Lk. iv. 14

to Galilee specified by all the three Synoptical Evangelists[a],—this portion of our history comes to its conclusion.

Thus then what has been roughly termed the Judæan ministry,—a ministry extending continuously from the March to the December of the preceding year (A.U.C. 781),—and resumed only to be abruptly broken off in the March of the present year (A.U.C. 782),—may be considered as now practically ended[1]. This is immediately succeeded by the ministry in Galilee and in the neighbouring districts to the North and East,—a ministry, be it again observed, to which the principal portion of the Synoptical Gospels, especially of the first and second[2], is nearly exclusively confined. If we

opportunity may properly be taken of especially recommending to the attention of every thoughtful student, who may be acquainted with the language in which it is written, this able treatise on the succession of the events in the Gospel-history. The more recent *Synopsis Evangelica* of Tischendorf is based nearly entirely upon the researches and deductions of this keen-sighted writer, and the present work owes a very large part of what may be thought plausible or probable in its chronological arrangement to the same intelligent guide. It is just to state that nothing has been accepted without independent and very deliberate investigation, and that many modifications, and, as it would seem, rectifications, have been introduced. The clue, however, even where it has been judged to lead off in a different direction, has in most cases, I again most gratefully acknowledge, either been indicated or supplied by this excellent work. A translation of it has, I am glad to say, recently appeared. The most recent work on the subject is one already quoted several times, and to which I very confidently refer the student,—the *Chronologisch-Geographische Einleitung in das Leben Jesu Christi* of C. E. Caspari, Hamburg, 1869.

[1] The short period of two months which intervenes between the Feast of Tabernacles and the Feast of the Dedication was probably spent in Judæa (see Lecture VI.), and thus might properly be considered a portion of the Judæan ministry. The general reader, however, will find it more convenient to regard the main Judæan ministry as now past, the Galilæan ministry as about to follow, and to be succeeded by a period of broken and interrupted ministrations, of removals and journeys, which terminate with the last Passover: see above, Lect. II. p. 39.

[2] It seems necessary to make this

only steadily bear in mind that the Synoptical Gospels mainly relate to us the events of the ministry in Galilee, the rough starting-point of which is the Baptist's captivity[1], we shall, I venture to feel confident, find but little difficulty in appreciating the true relations to one another of the four Gospels, and in mastering the general outline of the succeeding portions of the Evangelical narrative.

And now let me close this lecture with the earnest prayer that these hasty and fleeting sketches[2] may have in some degree served to bring this portion of the history of our Redeemer before our minds with increased measures of freshness and coherence. Hard it has been, very hard, to adjust the many questions of contested history; harder still to know where to enlarge or where to be brief only in unfolding the connexion of

Concluding remarks and exhortation.

---

[1] See above, p. 129, note 1. The ancient tradition on which this very reasonable opinion mainly rests is cited below, p. 151, note 1. The reason why the Synoptical Evangelists leave unnoticed the early ministry in Judæa cannot perhaps be readily assigned. As, however, it seems certain that nearly every system of chronology must, in a greater or less degree, concede the fact, we may, with all humility and reverence, perhaps hazard the opinion that these Evangelists were specially directed and guided mainly to confine their narrative to the period of the ministry in Galilee,—a period so marked, not only by the founding of the Church, but by the exhibition of many and mighty miracles, and the communication of varied and manifold forms of heavenly teaching. Compare Wieseler, *Chron. Synops.* p. 261.

[2] This is the term which is most appropriate to these Lectures, and which would have appeared on the very title-page if it had not been deemed unsuitable to place a term, so purely belonging to mere human things, in connexion with the most holy name of Our Lord and Saviour Jesus Christ.

LECT. III.

events which are still regarded by the wise and meditative as in uncertain dependence, or in more than precarious sequence. Yet I trust all has not been in vain; I trust that in you, my younger brethren, more especially[1], I have awakened some desire to search the Scriptures, and to muse on the events of your Redeemer's life with a fresher and more vital interest. Remember, I beseech you, that though chronologies may seem perplexing and events intermingled, yet still that every earnest effort to bring before your hearts the living picture of your Redeemer's life will be blessed by His Spirit[2]. Be not discouraged by the difficulty of the task: though here perchance we may wander,—there miss the right clue, yet if with a true and living faith we seek to bring home to our hearts the great features of the Evangelical history,—to journey with our Master over the lonely mountains of Galilee, to sit with

[1] Some experience as a public examiner in the New Testament, both in this University and elsewhere, has served to teach me that few points connected with the exposition of the four Gospels are less known or less attended to, by the young, than the study of the probable order of events, and the relations and degrees of interdependence existing between the records of the four inspired writers.

[2] It is well and truly observed by Bishop Taylor, in his noble introduction to his greatest work, *The Life of Christ*, that every true and sincere effort to set before our souls the life of our Master both ought to, and, with God's blessing, must needs end in imitation. 'He that considers,' says the Chrysostom of our Church, in reference to one particular aspect of our Lord's life, 'with what effusions of love Jesus prayed; what fervours and assiduity, what innocency of wish, what modesty of posture, what subordination to His Father, and conformity to the Divine pleasure, were in all His devotions, is taught and excited to holy and religious prayer. The rare sweetness of His deportment in all temptations and violences of His passion, His charity to His enemies, His sharp reprehension of the Scribes and Pharisees, His ingenuity towards all men, are living and effectual sermons to teach us patience, and humility, and zeal, and candid simplicity and justice in all our actions.' *Life of Christ*, Prelim. Exhort. § 15, Vol. I. p. 25 (Lond. 1836).

The Early Judæan Ministry. 147

Him beside the busy waters of the lake of Gennesareth,—to follow His footsteps into remote and half-pagan lands[1], or to hang on His lips in the courts of His Father's house,—we shall not seek in vain.

The history of the Gospels will be more and more to us a living history; one Divine Image ever waxing clearer and brighter, shedding its light on lonely hours, coming up before us in solitary walks,—ever fresher, ever dearer, until at length all things will seem so close, so near, so true, that our faith in Jesus and Him crucified will be such as no sophistry can weaken, no doubtfulness becloud[2].

For that vivid interest in the history of Jesus let us all pray to our heavenly Father, and in the name of Him on whom we have been meditating, let us conclude with the prayer of His chosen ones, 'Lord, increase our faith[a].'

[a] Lk. xvii. 5

---

[1] This striking and commonly too much overlooked portion of our Lord's ministry will be found noticed especially in Lect. v.

[2] For an expansion of these passing comments on the unspeakable blessedness of this form of meditative union with our adorable Saviour, the student may profitably be referred to one of the most eloquent devotional treatises ever written in our language,—the *Christ Mystical* of Bp Hall (*Works*, Vol. VII. p. 225. Talboys, 1837).

LECTURE IV.

THE MINISTRY IN EASTERN GALILEE.

St Mark i. 14.

Now after that John was put in prison, Jesus came into Galilee, preaching the Gospel of the Kingdom of God.

LECT. IV.

Resumption of the subject.

IN resuming my course of Lectures upon those events in the Life of our Lord and Master which are recorded to us in the Gospels it will be perhaps well for me, both in consideration of the time that has elapsed since my last Lecture[1], and with the remembrance that some may now be present who did not hear the former portion of this course[2], so far to recapitulate as to remind you briefly of our present position in the Gospel-history, and of the events which appear to have just preceded our present starting-point.

Brief recapitulation of the events of the Judæan ministry.

It may perhaps be remembered that our last meditations were devoted to what we agreed to term our Lord's early Judæan ministry[3],—a ministry

---

[1] The first three Lectures of this course were delivered in the month of April, the present and the two following not till the succeeding October. The brief recapitulation in the text could thus hardly be dispensed with when so long an interval had elapsed between the two portions of the Course. In the form in which the Lectures now appear it is not so necessary; as, however, it has seemed probable that, in a subject like the present, a brief recapitulation might be of benefit even to the general reader, the Lecture has been left in the same state in which it was delivered.

[2] This refers to the new comers in the October Term. See the remarks in Lecture I. p. 2.

[3] See Lecture II. p. 39, and compare p. 144, note I.

which commenced with the cleansing of the Temple at our Lord's first Passover (March A.U.C. 781)[1], and extended continuously to the December of that year when our Lord returned to Galilee through Samaria, and performed the second and, as it would seem, isolated miracle of healing the son of the nobleman of Capernaum[2]. It may be further remembered that after a brief stay in Galilee of which we have no further record than the passing comment of St Luke, that 'He taught in their synagogues, being glorified of all[a],'[3] and

[a iv. 15]

---

[1] If the tables constructed by Wieseler (*Chron. Synops.* p. 482 sq.; reprinted in Tischendorf, *Synops. Evang.* p. LI) on the basis of the astronomical data supplied by Wurm (*Astron. Beitrage*) are to be relied on as exact, the first day of this Passover, *i.e.* according to popular usage, the 14th of Nisan, took place on the 29th of March. One day earlier (March 28) is the date specified by Browne (*Ordo Sæcl.* § 64), but the Tables from which it appears to have been derived (§ 448) are admitted to involve sufficient error to account for the difference: see the examples on p. 497.

[2] See above, Lecture III. p. 134.

[3] This text appears to illustrate, if not confirm, the opinion previously advanced (see above, p. 129, note 1), that the return of our Lord specified by the three Synoptical Evangelists (Matth. iv. 12, Mark i. 14, Luke iv. 14) does not coincide with the interval between the 5th and 6th chapters of St John, but with the return specified by that Evangelist in the 4th chapter. The words of St Luke just seem to give that passing notice of the two-month residence in Galilee, which preceded the Feast of Purim, that we might naturally expect. The chief feature which probably marked that period,—preaching and teaching in the synagogues, is briefly specified, while in the words δοξαζόμενος ὑπὸ πάντων it is just possible that there may be an oblique allusion to the miracle which we know from St John (ch. iv. 44) was performed during that interval. The force of the main objection,—that the synoptical narrative does not thus, as it would seem to profess to do, commence immediately after that return of our Lord to Galilee, but really two months later, is thus so far weakened, that when we further observe—(*a*) that of two returns to Galilee, St John pauses carefully to specify one, and leaves the other almost unnoticed (comp. ch. vi. 1), and again (*b*) that in ch. v. 35 our Lord *seems* to speak of John's ministry as something now quite belonging to the past,—it appears difficult to resist the conviction that the distinctly-mentioned ἀναχώρησις into Galilee of the Synoptical writers, immediately after John's captivity, is identical with the carefully specified journey recorded in the 4th chapter of St John: see Tischendorf,

LECT. IV.

a iv. 17
b i. 15

the similarly brief notices of St Matthew[a], and St Mark[b], that the burden of that teaching was repentance, our Lord went up to Jerusalem at the time of a festival, which it was judged highly probable was that of Purim, with the apparent intention of staying over the Passover[1], but that, owing to the malignity of the more hostile sections of the Jews, He appears to have left the city almost immediately, and again to have returned to Galilee.

Here our present section begins, and with it what may be termed the Lord's Galilæan or extra-Judæan ministry, a ministry which in itself lasted about six months, but which, combined with the journeys and interrupted ministries which succeeded, occupied as nearly as possible a single year[2],—the 'acceptable year' of that ancient pro-

---

Synopsis Evangelica, p. xxv. and for the arguments (not very strong) in favour of the identity of the above return with that implied in John vi. 1, Wieseler, Chron. Synops. p. 161 sq. The attempt of Lange (Leben Jesu, Part II.), and others to interpolate a considerable portion of the events of the present earlier Galilæan ministry between the return through Samaria and the Feast of Purim, has been well considered, and been found to involve chronological difficulties wholly insurmountable.

[1] See above, p. 139, note 2.

[2] The ministry of our Lord would thus seem to have lasted about two years and three months, i. e. from His baptism at the close of 27 A.D. (780 A.U.C.) or beginning of 28 A.D. to the last Passover in 30 A.D. The opinions on this subject have been apparently as much divided in ancient as in modern times. Several early writers, among whom may be specified Clement of Alexandria (Strom. I. 21, § 145), Origen (de Princip. IV. 5, in Levit. Hom. IX., in Luc. Hom. XXXII.—but see below), Archelaus of Mesopotamia (Routh, Reliq. Sacr. Vol. IV. p. 218), and, according to apparently fair inferences, Julius Africanus (Greswell, Dissert. XIII. Vol. I. p. 46), suppose our Lord's ministry to have lasted little more than one year. Others again of equal or even greater antiquity, such as Melito of Sardis (Routh, Reliq. Sacr. Vol. I. p. 115), Irenæus (Hær. II. 39,—but see below), and, according to correct inferences, Tertullian (see Kaye, Eccl. Hist. ch. II. p. 159, and comp. Browne, Ordo Sæcl. § 86. 3), and, later in life, Origen (Cels. II. 12, οὐδὲ τρία ἔτη) have fixed the duration as three years, or, as Irenæus (l. c.) implies, even more. A calm consi-

phecy[a] which our Lord Himself proclaimed in the synagogue at Nazareth as now receiving its fulfilment[b],—the year to which a most trustworthy tradition preserved by Eusebius confines the narrative of the three Synoptical Gospels[1].

[a] Is. lxi. 2
[b] Lk. iv. 21

Two preliminary observations.

Before we enter upon the details of the inspired history, let me pause to make two preliminary observations, the *first* in reference to the space of time which it is convenient to consider in the present Lecture,—the *second* in reference to the variations of order in the events as related in this portion of the Synoptical Gospels.

With regard to the *first* point, we may observe deration of these and other passages from early writers will show that they cannot be strongly pressed on either side. Several of them involve references to prophecy, which in some cases evidently swayed the opinion of the writer (comp. Euseb. *Dem. Evang.* VIII. 400 B); some (as the passage of Irenæus) are called out by the counter-opinion of heretics, while others again are mere *obiter dicta*, that cannot fairly be urged as giving a really deliberate opinion. After a review of the whole evidence the most reasonable opinion, and one which tends in a great degree to harmonize these citations, is this,—that the general feeling of antiquity was that our Lord's *entire* ministry lasted for a period, speaking roughly, of about *three* years, but that the more active part, *i.e.* that with which the synoptical narrative practically commences, lasted *one*. If this be correct, the statement at the beginning of the note has to a certain extent the united support of all antiquity, and sufficiently nearly accords with the three years of the significant parable (Luke xiii. 6 sq.), which has, perhaps rightly, been pressed into this controversy; see Wieseler, *Chron. Synops.* p. 202; and for further general information, Greswell, *Dissert.* XIII. Vol. I. p. 438 sq., Browne, *Ordo Sæcl.* § 85 sq., and the acute comments of Anger, *de Temp. in Act. Apost.* p. 23 sq.

[1] The valuable tradition above alluded to is as follows : ' When the three first written Gospels had been now delivered into the hands of all, and of John too as well, they say that he approved of them and bore witness to their truth, and that thus all that the history lacked was an account of the things done by Christ at first and at the beginning of His preaching. And the account is certainly true. For it is easily seen that the other three Evangelists have only written an account of what was done by our Saviour *in the space of one year after the imprisonment of John the Baptist*, and that they have intimated the same at the beginning of their history.' Eusebius, *Hist. Eccl.* III. 24; comp. Wieseler, *Chron. Synops.* p. 163.

LECT. IV.

The exact period of time embraced in the present Lecture.

that we have now before us the events of a year and a few days[1], distributed, however, very unequally in the Gospel-narrative. Of the events of the first portion, which, as will be seen, are included in a period of little more than three weeks, we have an ample and almost continuous history; of the events of the whole remaining period (excluding the final week of our Lord's ministry), more isolated and detached notices, and a somewhat altered mode of narration....This being the case, I venture to think that we shall both distribute our incidents more equably, and, what is more important, keep distinct from one another portions of the Gospels which appear to be dissimilar in their general characteristics[2], if on the present occasion we confine ourselves solely to the events of the three weeks above alluded to, and reserve for the remaining Lectures the events

[1] The first event is the rejection of our Lord on his appearance in the synagogue at Nazareth (Luke iv. 16). This we know was on the sabbath day, the exact date of which, —if Wieseler's Tables (see above, p. 149, note 1) are fully to be relied on, *and* if the Feast of Purim fell, as it appears to have done, on the sabbath when our Lord healed the man at the pool of Bethesda (see Lect. III. p. 137),—would be March 26. The Passover of the succeeding year we learn from the same authority commenced on April 6. We have then exactly a year and eleven days. The calculation, by which the weekday answering to any given date is arrived at, will be greatly facilitated by Tables IV. and V. in Browne's *Ordo Sæcl.* p. 502 sq. In the present case it will be found by independent computation that, as above asserted, March 26 coincided with a Saturday.

[2] This statement will be substantiated by the succeeding comments upon the variations of order in the first three Evangelists (p. 154), and by the introductory remarks at the commencement of Lecture IV. The main points to be observed are that up to the Feeding of the 5000 the order of events in St Matthew appears intentionally modified, after that period, mainly regular and systematic; and that up to the same point St Luke is full and explicit, while to the six months between that period and the journey to Jerusalem at the Feast of Tabernacles he only devotes about 30 verses. The arrangement of the events in their order will be found in a convenient form in Caspari, *Chron.-Geogr. Einleit.* p. 116 sq.

of the longer portion. The dividing epoch, let it be observed, is that of the Feeding of the five thousand,—an epoch by no means arbitrarily chosen, but, as a brief chronological notice in St John's Gospel[a] warrants our asserting, an epoch closely coincident with that Passover of the present year[1] which the savage and impious designs of the Jewish party at Jerusalem appear to have prevented our Lord from celebrating in the Holy City[2]. Estimating them roughly by festivals, our present period extends from the Feast of Purim (March 19, A.U.C. 782) to the Passover-eve (April 14)—at which point our present meditations will conveniently come to their close.

With regard to the *second* point,—the order of the events in these three weeks, let me briefly observe that the period we are now engaged in presents the utmost difficulty to the harmonist[3],

[a] Joh. vi. 4

The variations of order in the three Synoptical Gospels.

---

[1] This useful conciliatory date is commented upon by Wieseler, *Chron. Synops.* p. 273. To set aside the words τὸ πάσχα as a gloss (Mann. *True Year of our Lord's Birth*, p. 161; comp. Browne, *Ordo Sæcl.* § 89) is arbitrary, and not justified by any external evidence.

[2] See above, p. 142, note 2.

[3] These discrepancies perhaps can never be wholly cleared up, especially in those cases where there are partial notes of place which augment the already existing difficulties in regard of time. To take an example: in the case of the Healing of the Leper recorded in the three Synoptical Gospels, independent of all the difficulties arising from the difference in time, the scene of the miracle as defined by St Matthew, καταβάντι δὲ αὐτῷ ἀπὸ τοῦ ὄρους, (ch. viii. 1) does not *seem* to accord with the ἐν μιᾷ τῶν πόλεων of St Luke (ch. v. 12). We can of course imagine several ways in which the two accounts *could* be harmonized, but we must be satisfied with merely putting them forward as tentative and conjectural. At first sight it might be thought judicious in a case like the present to consider the special notice of St Matthew as contrasted with the more general notices of St Mark and St Luke as *definitely fixing* both the time and place (comp. Alford, *on Matth.* viii. 2), but a remembrance of the principle of grouping, which appears almost evidently to have been followed in this portion of the record of the first Evangelist (comp. Lecture I. p. 21), warns us at once that all such eclectic modes of harmonizing can never be relied on, and that even with St Matthew's accessory definitions the order

LECT. IV.

arising from this simple fact, that though all the first three Evangelists record more or less the same facts, St Matthew relates them in an order so signally and palpably different from that adopted by St Mark and St Luke,—that all efforts to combine the two must be pronounced simply *hopeless*[1]. Either for those three weeks we must accept the order of St Matthew and adapt that of St Mark and St Luke to it, or we must adopt the converse course. The third alternative, that of constructing a harmony of our own out of all three,—an alternative that has only too often been adopted by the ingenious and the speculative,—is in a high degree precarious, and as far as I am able to judge, has not led to any other than debateable and unsatisfactory results.

The order of St Mark and St Luke followed in these Lectures.

Without here entering into details which delivered orally would prove both wearisome and perplexing[2] I will simply say, that after long and

of the events he relates must to the last remain a matter of uncertainty.

[1] Let the student either make for himself, with the proper notes of time and place, three lists of the events in their order as related by the first three Evangelists, or refer to those drawn up by others, as, for instance, by Wieseler (*Chron. Synops.* pp. 280, 297), Browne (*Ordo Sæcl.* § 586), or any of the better harmonizers of this portion of the inspired narrative, and he will feel the truth of this remark. For example, if 1......26 represent in order the events *of this period* as collected from St Mark *and* St Luke, the order in St Matthew will be found as follows: 1, 2, 3, 5, 12, 6, 13, 4, 19, 20, 7, 8, 21, 23, 15, 9, 10, 18, 17, 22, 25, 26. Such a result speaks for itself.

[2] To conduct such an inquiry properly, we must endeavour (*a*) to form a correct idea of the general object of the Gospel in question, and to observe how far this admits of its being made the basis of a regular and continuous Gospel-history; (*b*) to collect all the passages which in any degree indicate the principles anecdotal or historical, on which the Evangelist appears to have drawn up his narrative; (*c*) to note carefully the nature and amount of the irregularities which can be detected, —either from a comparison of different portions of the same Gospel with one another, or with parallel accounts in the other Gospels; (*d*) to classify the notes of *time* and *place*, and to observe where they are precise and definitive, and where merely

careful consideration, and with a full sense of the great responsibility of making distinct assertions on such difficult questions before an audience like the present, I have come to the determination of following the order of events as given by St Mark and St Luke rather than that given by St Matthew—and that for these general but weighty reasons. *First*, that in cases of clear discrepancy in the order of narration between two of the sacred writers, we seem bound to follow the one who himself tells us[1], if words mean anything, that it has been his care to draw up his history with general reference to the order of events.... *Secondly*, that the order of St Luke in the first part of our present portion is strikingly confirmed by the order of events in St Mark, from which

First reason.

Second reason.

vague and indefinite; lastly, (e) to investigate the nature of the formulæ which link together the successive paragraphs, and to distinguish between those which mark immediate connexion, and those which indicate mere general sequence. The first of these heads is partially illustrated in Lect. I. p. 20: the rest are best left to independent observation. If assistance be needed; in reference to (b), see Davidson, *Introd. to N. T.* Vol. I. p. 56, or Credner, *Einleitung*, § 37, p. 63 sq.; in ref. to (c), Greswell, *Dissert.* III. Vol. I. p. 195 sq.; in ref. to (d), the table in Wieseler, *Chron. Synops.* p. 297 sq.; and in ref. to (e), Ebrard, *Kritik der Ev. Gesch.* § 23, pp. 88—94.

[1] The exact meaning of some of the expressions in this introduction, especially ἀπ' ἀρχῆς, παρηκολουθηκότι, ἄνωθεν, and most of all καθεξῆς, has been abundantly discussed. The most correct view seems to be as follows; that ἀρχή refers to the beginning of the πραγμάτων previously alluded to, scil. τῶν θαυμάτων καὶ τῶν πραγμάτων, Euthymius *in loc.*; that παρηκολουθηκότι, in accordance both with its use and derivation, marks research as evinced in *tracing along*, and as it were mentally accompanying the events in question; that ἄνωθεν refers to a commencement from the *very* beginning,—from the birth of the Baptist; and lastly that καθεξῆς, like ἐφεξῆς, can only imply an adherence to the natural *order* of the events related,—ἐξῆς, ὡς ἕκαστα ἐγένετο, Thucyd. II. 1, v. 26 : see Meyer, *in loc.*, and compare Greswell, *Dissert.* I. Vol. I. p. 9. In a word, in this preface we are assured by the inspired writer that we are to expect in what follows, fidelity, accuracy, research, and *order*,—and we find them: compare Lange, *Leben Jesu*, I. 6. 3. Introd. p. 220.

LECT. IV.

Third reason.

Fourth reason.

it only differs in two or three instances[1], which have been satisfactorily accounted for and adjusted....*Thirdly*, that the chronology of St Luke in this portion of the Gospel history can be shown to harmonize with that supplied indirectly by St John in a very striking manner[2]....*Fourthly*, that the seeming want of order in St Matthew can be very readily accounted for by observing that, in this portion of his Gospel, the Evangelist appears to have wittingly adopted a peculiar arrangement, viz. a separation into different groups of the discourses of our Lord and the historical events with which they stood in connexion, and that such an arrangement almost necessarily precludes strict chronological adjustments. However perplexing we may deem such a phenomenon in a Gospel that in other parts appears mainly to follow a regular and chronological order,—however we may be tempted to speculate on the causes which led to it[3], this much appears certain, that such an

---

[1] These are, the calling of the four Apostles (Luke v. 1—11, compared with Mark i. 16—20), the arrival of the mother and brethren of our Lord (Luke viii. 19—21, compared with Mark iii. 31—35), and *apparently* the calumnies of the Pharisees (Mark iii. 20 sq., compared with Luke xi. 15 sq.), and the parable of the Grain of Mustard (Luke xiii. 18 sq., compared with Mark iv. 30 sq.)—though both these might well have been repeated on two different occasions. For a good adjustment of the two main differences, see Wieseler, *Chron. Synops.* p. 284 sq., and in respect of the first of them, compare also Augustine, *de Consens. Ev.* II. 17, and Spanheim,

Dub. Evang. LXII. 2, p. 341 sq.

[2] For a careful investigation into the confirmatory elucidations of the order of this portion of St Luke's Gospel as supplied by that of St John, see Wieseler, *Chron. Synops.* III. 2 A, p. 271 sq.

[3] Though it is ever both unwise and unbecoming to speculate too freely about the origin and composition of an inspired document, the opinion may perhaps be hazarded that this peculiarity in St Matthew's Gospel may be due to the incorporation by the Evangelist of an earlier (Hebrew) narrative in this later and more complete (Greek) Gospel. If such a conjecture be received, we can not only explain

arrangement *does* exist and can be easily verified, if we examine the peculiar structure of the portion of the Gospel which begins with the fifth and closes with the thirteenth chapter. We see for example, that on the one hand we have three large portions containing discourses, viz. the Sermon on the Mount, the apparently grouped and collected instructions which our Lord addressed to the Twelve previous to their mission, and the collection of the parables in the thirteenth chapter[1]; and, on the other hand, that we have a large collection of miracles related in the eighth and ninth chapters, which comprise, with scarcely any exception, the scattered events of the period preceding

the present peculiarity, but can also account for, on the one hand, the positive statements of antiquity that the first Evangelist composed his Gospel originally in Hebrew (Papias ap. Euseb. *Hist. Eccl.* III. 39, Irenæus, *Hær.* III. 1, al.), and on the other, the universal reception of the Greek Gospel as the veritable and undoubted work of the Evangelist: see Wieseler, *Synops.* p. 304. The portion to which we are alluding *may* thus have been a part of the λόγια which Papias says were drawn up by St Matthew, and the meaning of the doubtful word λόγια *may* be so far correctly modified, as to point to a predominance in that treatise of the τὰ ὑπὸ Χριστοῦ λεχθέντα over the πραχθέντα which appears also included in the term; see above, Lect. I. p. 12, note 2. That St Matthew originally wrote in Hebrew can scarcely be doubted if we are to place any reliance on external testimony, and that the present Greek Gospel came from his hand, and not from that of an editor or compiler, seems almost equally clear from internal and external testimony combined;—how then can we adjust the two apparent facts without assuming an earlier and a later treatise? And if so, is it strange that the first should have been incorporated in the second, and thus so effectually superseded as to have soon passed out of notice? The pretensions of the Curetonian Syriac (as put forward by its laborious editor) to represent more nearly the words of St Matthew than any other extant document would in some degree affect the present question, if it had not apparently been demonstrated that such pretensions are untenable; see, thus far, the recent investigation of Roberts, *Original Lang. of St Matthew's Gospel*, ch. IV. 3, p. 122 sq., and compare Donaldson, *New Crat.* § 15, p. 23, note (ed. 3).

[1] For a brief notice of these, see Lect. I. p. 21, note 2, and for a specification of the miracles in the 8th and 9th chapters, *ib.*, note 3.

the sending out of the Twelve,—after which the narrative proceeds in strict chronological order.... When we add to this the concluding observation, that singularly enough, we find in several instances careful notices of *place* exactly where the order of *time* seems most disarranged[1], it seems almost impossible to resist the conviction that the first Evangelist was by no means unacquainted with the correct order of events, but that he designedly departed from it, and directed his first attention to his Master's preaching during this momentous period, and then grouped together the nearly contemporary events and miracles[2] with such notices of place as should guard against any possibility of misconception.

Relying on these sober and apparently convincing reasons for following the order of St Mark and St Luke rather than that of St Matthew, let us now again take up the thread of the inspired narrative.

---

[1] Compare for example ch. viii. 5, εἰσελθόντι δὲ αὐτῷ εἰς Καπερναούμ; ver. 14, ἐλθὼν εἰς τὴν οἰκίαν Πέτρου; ver. 18, εἰς τὸ πέραν; ver. 28, ἐλθόντι εἰς τὸ πέραν εἰς τὴν χώραν τῶν Γεργεσηνῶν; ch. ix. 1, ἦλθεν εἰς τὴν ἰδίαν πόλιν; ch. xii. 9, ἦλθεν εἰς τὴν συναγωγὴν αὐτῶν; xiii. 1, ἐξελθὼν ἀπὸ τῆς οἰκίας ἐκάθητο παρὰ τὴν θάλασσαν. See also Wieseler, *Chron. Synops.* p. 307.

[2] The want of regularity in St Matthew's Gospel, arising from this mode of construction, is acknowledged by nearly all impartial inquirers of recent times; see Greswell, *Dissert.* III. p. 194—238; Browne, *Ordo Sæcl.* § 590,—whose theory of a Redactor, however, is neither satisfactory nor plausible. Attention was formerly called to it by Lightfoot (*Harmony*, Vol. I. p. 503, Roterod. 1686), and also by Whiston (*Harmony of Gospels*, p. 100 sq., Lond. 1702), but accounted for by the latter in a way (misarrangement by a translator of fragmentary scraps) which Browne (p. 644, note) properly designates as palpably absurd. He was answered by Jones, *Vindic. of St Matth.* Lond. 1719. The latest writer on the chronology of the Lord's life (Caspari) similarly decides against the order of the first Evangelist, and in favour of that of St Mark; see *Chron. Geogr. Einleit.* p. 119 sq.

After a hasty departure from Jerusalem our Lord returns to His old home at Nazareth, where some, if not all, of the kindred of the Lord appear to have been still residing[1], and on the Sabbath-day which immediately succeeded His return entered into the Synagogue[a], as had now become His custom[b], to read and to teach.... What a vivid picture has the inspired Evangelist St Luke been moved to present to us of that memorable morning. Prayer and the reading of the law was now over[2] and the reading of the prophets was to begin, and the reading of the season was from the old Evangelist Isaiah. The Redeemer stands up to read[c], and with the sanction of the now not improbably expectant ruler of that house of prayer[3],

LECT. IV.

Appearance of our Lord in the synagogue at Nazareth.
[a] Lk. iv. 16
[b] ver. 16

[c] ver. 16

---

[1] It has been supposed that the Virgin and her family had retired to Cana (see above, p. 105, note 1), but apparently not on sufficient grounds. That the ἀδελφοί of the Lord were now living at Nazareth seems certain from Matth. xiii. 56, Mark vi. 3, and that the Virgin and the brethren were there also is not improbable. The way, however, in which the residence of the ἀδελφοί is specified *seems* rather to imply the contrary, and may lead us to conjecture that the Virgin and her other kindred were now at Capernaum,—a place which they might have selected for their abode a year before (John ii. 12): consider Matth. xii. 46 sq., Mark iii. 31 sq., Luke viii. 19 sq., and John vii. 3. The commonly assumed identity of this visit to Nazareth with that mentioned Matth. xiii. 54 sq., Mark vi. 1 sq., is convincingly disproved by Wieseler, *Chron. Synops.* p. 284.

[2] The service of the Synagogue commenced with praise and prayer; then a portion of the law was read aloud, and after this a portion from the prophets; see Jost, *Gesch. des Judenth.* II. 1. 6, Vol. I. p. 173 sq., the special treatise of Vitringa (*de Synag.*), the more modern work of Zunz (*Gottesdienst. Vorträge der Juden*, p. 329 sq.), and for useful references illustrative of the whole passage, compare Lightfoot, *Hor. Hebr.* Vol. II. p. 508 sq. (Roterod. 1686).

[3] It would appear that our Lord by *rising* indicated that, as a member of the Synagogue of Nazareth, He desired on the present occasion to undertake the office of *Maphtir*, or reader of the lesson from the prophets; comp. Vitringa, *de Synag.* III. 1. 7, Part II. p. 696 sq. Though not called upon by the ruler of the Synagogue (comp. *Mishna*, Tract 'Megillah,' IV. 4), assent is at once given, as both the ruler and the congregation appear to have heard

the roll is delivered to Him by the attendant. He unfolds it and reads that striking passage which His own Divine wisdom and foreknowledge had moved Him to select[1],—that passage which both in its specifications of time[a] and circumstances was now being so exactly fulfilled.

Such words might well have aroused the attention of those that heard it, nor can we wonder that our Lord's explanations[2] were looked for with interest[b], and at first received with a kind of amazed approval[c]. But what a fearful sequel! When grave yet gracious words of warning[3] were directed against those feelings of distrust and

[a] ver. 19; see above, p. 150.

The impious sequel.

[b] ver. 20
[c] ver. 22

---

of the comparatively recent miracle at Capernaum (Luke iv. 23; comp. Wieseler, *Chron. Synops.* p. 271), and as the context shows (ver. 20), were full of expectation; see Lightfoot, *in loc.* Vol. II. p. 508.

[1] It seems probable that the reading of the season was from Isaiah (Lightfoot), and that our Lord received accordingly that portion of Scripture from the attendant keeper of the sacred books (comp. Vitringa, *Synagog.* III. 2. 2, p. 899), but that, with the privilege which the oral law conceded in the case of the lesson from the prophets (*Mishna*, 'Megillah,' IV. 4), He either passed over from the section of the day to the beginning of the 61st chap., or else an 'Lord of the Sabbath,' specially selected that portion; see Lightfoot, *Hor. Hebr.* Vol. II. p. 509, and comp. Meyer *in loc.* The supposition, that on our Lord's opening the roll this passage providentially met His eye (comp. De Wette), is not improbable, but apparently less in accordance with the ἀναπτύξας, which, as Lightfoot remarks, seems something more than the mere 'explicuit or aperuit librum' (*l. c.* p. 510).

[2] After having read such a portion of the passage as by custom was deemed sufficient ('si fuerit Sabbato interpres, legunt in Propheta versiculos tres aut quinque aut septem, et non sunt solliciti de versiculis viginti uno,' *Massecheth Soph.* cap. 12), our Lord took upon Himself the office of interpreter, and according to custom *sat down* to perform it: comp. Zunz, *Gottesd. Vorträge der Juden,* p. 337, and Sepp, *Leben Christi,* II. 10, Part II. p. 122.

[3] The objections that have been urged against the general character of this address are most idle and irreverent. Our Lord, who knew the human heart, saw here unbelief, and the ordinary Galilæan estimate of His Divine mission (John iv. 45) in their worst forms, and accordingly adopts the language of merciful warning and reproof. On the whole incident, see some useful comments in Lange, *Leben Jesu,* II. 4. 9, Part II. p. 541 sq.

unbelief into which even now these dull-hearted men of Nazareth were fast falling back again, we remember with horror what followed,—how these wretched men dared to do what even the gainsayers at Jerusalem a week before had only begun to think of doing, how they thrust Him forth not only from their synagogue and their town[a], but led Him to a neighbouring declivity, which modern travellers have not doubtfully identified[1], to cast Him down headlong, and how by an exercise of His Divine power[2] He escaped[b] their impious and vengeful hands.

LECT. IV.

[a] ver. 29

[b] ver. 30

Henceforth that quiet home in the bosom of the green hills of Galilee was no longer to be the Lord's earthly resting-place. His Divine steps were now turned to more busy scenes, and in accordance with the voice of ancient prophecy[c], to the

Departure to, and abode at Capernaum.

[c] Is. ix. 1 sq.

---

[1] The exact place to which these wretched and infatuated people endeavoured to lead our Lord was certainly not the traditional Mount of Precipitation overlooking the vale of Esdraelon and two miles distant, but apparently one of the precipices of the western hill which flanks the town,—perhaps that by the present Maronite Church: see Robinson, *Palestine*, Vol. II. p. 335 (ed. 2)'; and compare Stanley, *Sinai and Palestine*, p. 363 (ed. 2), Thomson, *The Land and the Book*, Vol. II. p. 135. In the photograph of Frith (*Syria and Palestine*, Part II.) this portion of the western hill is not included: see Roberts, *Holy Land*, Vol. II. Plate 29.

[2] There does not seem sufficient reason for assuming with Robinson and others that in this there was no exercise of that miraculous power which most of the ancient writers (Ambrose, Euthymius, al.) recognize in our Lord's thus passing through the infuriated throng: so also and rightly, Alford *in loc.* In all these things He manifested alike the exercise of His Divine wisdom and His Divine power; of the former in defining the time in which He vouchsafed to suffer, and of the latter in preventing that time being hurried by the impiety and violence of men. As Cyril of Alexandria well says, 'it depended on Him to suffer, or not to suffer; for He is the Lord of times as well as of things.' *Comment. on St Luke*, Part I. p. 64,—where, however, it is just to observe that there is no distinct reference to an exercise of miraculous power, but rather of overawing majesty: so also Lange, *Leben Jesu*, II. 4. 9, Part II. p. 548.

LECT. IV.

Special call to the four disciples.

ᵃ Joh.iv.46

ᵇ v. 1

ᶜ Lk. v. 10

people that sat in the darkness the Light came; and in Capernaum, at but little distance¹ from that fair and populous plain of 'Gennesar' which a nearly contemporary visitor has so eloquently described², the rejected One of Nazareth found a more thankful and believing home....... More thankful, and more believing; for not perhaps without a fresh recollection of the miracle performed on one who had lain sick among them a few weeks beforeᵃ, the people we are told by St Luke 'pressed upon Him to hear the word of Godᵇ;' and we may well conceive that it was not without the deep consciousness and foreknowledge of the active ministry that was now to be vouchsafed amid the populous towns of Gennesareth³, that He called the four disciples, who had already been with Him for above a year, to leave, on this occasion, for ever their earthly occupations, and to become the 'fishers of menᶜ.' And we know how readily that call was obeyed; we know how St Peter and his brother, and the two sons of Thun-

---

¹ As to the supposed position of Capernaum, see Lect. III. p. 121, note 2.

² See Josephus, *Bell. Jud.* III. 10. 8,—according to Robinson (*Palestine*, Vol. II. p. 402), an overdrawn picture. Thomson, with more judgment, draws a distinction between what the land then was, and what it has become now: comp. *The Land and the Book*, Vol. I. p. 536.

³ A very good description of what was probably the state of this populous district in the time of our Lord is given by Stanley, *Sinai and Palestine*, p. 371 sq. (ed. 2). The remark that 'it was to the Roman Palestine almost what the manufacturing districts are to England,' is apparently borne out by the indirect allusions in the inspired narrative to the populous nature of the district, and by what we can infer from the ruins which are still found scattered about on the western shores of the lake: compare Robinson, *Palestine*, Vol. II. p. 403. The traces of buildings which appear to have been used in the operations of trade, and may be the remains of ancient potteries, tanneries, &c. have been observed by Dr Thomson at Tabiga, —which he terms 'the grand manufacturing suburb of Capernaum.' *The Land and the Book*, Vol. I. p. 547.

der, wrought upon by that miracle that showed how the creatures that the hand of the Lord had made could gather together at His will ᵃ,—that miracle that brought the impressible Peter on his knees[1], and filled all with amazement ᵇ,—obeyed the heavenly voice, and left father and earthly callings, nets and vessels, forsook all, and followed Him[2].

ᵃ Lk. v. 6

ᵇ ver. 9

LECT. IV.

This prompt adhesion of men so well known in Capernaum as two at least of the four must have been[3], this ready giving up of everything to follow Jesus of Nazareth, could not have been without its effect on the people of Capernaum and its neighbourhood. The report too of the miracle,

Healing of a demoniac in the synagogue at Capernaum.

---

[1] The effect which the miracle produced on St Peter is well commented upon by Olshausen (*in loc.* Vol. I. p. 299, Clark), and by Ewald, *Gesch. Christus*¹, p. 252. The contrast between his own conscious unholiness and the holy majesty and power of Him who had just wrought the mighty miracle made the fervid disciple both on the one hand offer his spontaneous adoration, and on the other to beseech his pure sinless Lord to depart from one who felt and knew in his own bosom what sin was. On the whole miracle, see Olshausen, *Commentary*, Vol. I. p. 292 sq. (Clark), Trench, *Miracles*, p. 126; and compare Lange, *Leben Jesu*, II. 4. 11, Part II. p. 562 sq.

[2] There seems no reason for doubting that the call of the four disciples mentioned by St Matthew (ch. iv. 18 sq.) and St Mark (ch. i. 16 sq.) was contemporaneous with the above call mentioned by St Luke. The only difficulty is, that St Luke makes it *subsequent* to the healing of the demoniac, and of St Peter's mother-in-law, while St Mark places it *before*. The order of the latter is confirmed by St Matthew, and distinctly to be preferred, especially as the change of order in St Luke can be partly accounted for by the desire of the Evangelist to place in immediate contrast the reception in the synagogue at Capernaum, with the rejection a week before at Nazareth: see Wieseler, *Chron. Synops.* p. 285 sq.

[3] From the notice of the hired servants (Mark i. 20), the two vessels employed (Luke v. 7), and the subsequent mention of St John's acquaintance with one in so high a position as the high-priest (John xviii. 15), it has been reasonably inferred that Zebedee, if not a wealthy man (Jerome, *in Matth.* iv. 12, opp. to Chrys. *in Joann.* Hom. II. 1), was at any rate of some position in Capernaum. As has already been noticed, Caspari considers that Zebedee belonged to Jerusalem and came only from time to time to the lake: see *Chron.-Geogr. Einleit.* p. 123.

though perhaps as yet not fully understood or appreciated, had probably soon passed from mouth to mouth, among the fishers and boatmen on the lake, and might well have added to the prevailing expectation and excitement. We may readily imagine then the eagerness and gladness with which on the following Sabbath[a] the Redeemer's preaching was listened to in the synagogue, and we know the mighty effect that was produced by it, enhanced as it was by the subsequent healing of the demoniac within its walls[1]. ...How startling must have been that scene when the spirits of darkness, driven by the wild antagonisms of their fears[b] and malignities, broke out amid that mingled concourse into cries alike of reprobation and of confession[2], 'Let us alone—I know thee who thou art; the Holy One of God[c].' What amazement was there then when those frightful voices were silenced, and the wretched sufferer, whose frail body had been the tenement of those hellish occupants, though rent and con-

[a] Mk. i. 21
[b] Lk. iv. 34
[c] Mk. i. 24
Lk. iv. 34

---

[1] See especially Mark i. 27 (*Tisch.*), in which this amazement both at the teaching and the miracle is expressed in the strongest terms:—Τί ἐστιν τοῦτο; διδαχὴ καινὴ κατ' ἐξουσίαν· καὶ τοῖς πνεύμασιν τοῖς ἀκαθάρτοις ἐπιτάσσει, καὶ ὑπακούουσιν αὐτῷ.

[2] In the circumstances connected with this and other miracles performed on demoniacs, three things are worthy of notice: (1) the lost consciousness of personality on the part of the sufferer, the man becoming, as it were, identified with, and at times the mouthpiece of the devil within him (Mark v. 7, Luke viii. 28); (2) the terror-stricken recognition on the part of the devils of Jesus as the Son of God and their future Judge (Matth. viii. 29, Mark iii. 11, v. 7, Luke viii. 28),—enhanced in the present narrative by the awful ἔα! (Luke iv. 34) of the recoiling demon; (3) the prohibition from speaking on the part of our Lord (Mark i. 34, iii. 12, Luke iv. 41),—possibly that the multitude might not believe in their Redeemer on the testimony of devils: comp. Cyril Alex. *on Luke* iv. 41, Part I. p. 71 (Transl.). Hence, perhaps, the omission of the prohibition in the case of the demoniacs of Gadara or Gergesa, when only those were present whose faith was already firm, and convictions true and settled.

vulsed by the final paroxysm[a], yet a moment afterwards stood both freed and unharmed[b] before them[1]. There were as yet none among those simple-hearted men to object to healings on the Sabbath[c]. There were as yet none to make the blasphemous assertion that such power after all was only due to some league with the prince of those spirits[d] that had been commanded with such authority, and had obeyed with such terror. These men of Capernaum had no such doubts; they saw and believed, yea and as two Evangelists record, soon spread the fame of the great Healer not only through all the neighbouring villages and towns[e], but in all the regions round about Galilee[f].

Mk. i. 26
Lk. iv. 36
vi. 7
Mt. xii. 24
Mk. iii. 22
Lk. iv. 37
Mk i. 28: see Meyer.

But the wonders of this first Sabbath at Capernaum, this day of which the events are so specially and so minutely told us by two Evangelists, had not yet come to their close. Immediately after that amazing scene in the synagogue, probably about mid-day[2], our Lord with His four freshly-called disciples round Him[g] enters into the common dwelling of two of the number[h], and graciously vouchsafes to that small home-circle, on the person of the mother-in-law of St Peter, ano-

Continued performance of miracles on the same day.
Mk. i. 29
ver. 29

---

[1] For further comments on this miracle, see Trench, *Miracles*, p. 230, and for some thoughtful observations on the case of demoniacal possessions generally, Olshausen, *Commentary*, p. 305; compare also Deyling, *Obs. Sacr.* XXVIII. Part II. p. 373 sq.

[2] It would seem from a passage in Josephus, that on the Sabbath-day the usual hour for the meal of which our Lord appears afterwards to have partaken in the house of the two brothers was mid-day: ἕκτη ὥρα καθ' ἣν τοῖς σάββασιν ἀριστοποιεῖσθαι νόμιμον ἐστὶν ἡμῖν. *De Vita Sua*, cap. 54. The service in the synagogue, the forms and hours of which appear to have been studiously conformed to those in the temple-worship (Vitringa, *de Synag.* p. 42, Jost, *Gesch. des Judenth.* Vol. I. p. 170), would in all probability have commenced about 9 o'clock, and ended some time before mid-day.

ther merciful display of those healing powers, of which a whole synagogue had but lately been witness. There, perhaps in the low and crowded suburb[1], the mother-in-law of the Apostle Peter was laid and sick, as the physician-Evangelist characteristically notices, of a *great* fever[2]. But the Healer was now nigh at hand. Anxiously they tell Him of her state, anxiously they beseech His help; and with power and majesty that help is bestowed. With His voice the Lord rebukes[3] the evil influence of the disease[a], with His hand He touches the sufferer[b],—and she who a moment before lay subdued and powerless, now rises supported by the Divine hand[c], and, as all the three Synoptical Evangelists especially notice, ministers unto them[4], and with wonted strength and health

[a] Lk. iv. 39
[b] Mt. viii. 15
[c] Mk. i. 31

---

[1] The conjecture of Dr Thomson above alluded to (p. 162, note 3), that Tabiga is the site of what was the manufacturing suburb of Capernaum, derives some support from the above incident, there being marshy land in the vicinity which might account for the 'great fever' under which St Peter's mother-in-law was suffering: see *The Land and the Book*, Vol. I. p. 547. There may be also a slight hint at the season of the year; as we learn from modern travellers that in the East fevers prevail in *spring* and autumn, dysentery in the summer: compare Winer, *RWB*. Art. 'Krankheiten,' Vol. I. p. 673.

[2] This passage has been often referred to as illustrating not only the accuracy, but the profession of St Luke. We learn from the Greek medical writers that there was a recognized distinction between 'great' and 'small' fevers: see Galen, *de Different. Febr.* 1. cited by Wetstein *in loc.*

[3] The exact expression in the original should not be overlooked, ἐπετίμησεν τῷ πυρετῷ (Luke iv. 39), according to which the disease, like the boisterous wind and stirred-up sea in the miracle on the lake (Matth. viii. 26, Mark iv. 39, Luke viii. 24), is treated as a hostile potency. Deductions as to the presence of spiritual agencies in similar cases, must be made with caution, but the expression is remarkable, and has not been left unnoticed by the early expositors: see especially Cyril Alex. *in loc.* Part I. p. 69 (Transl.).

[4] 'Not only doth He cure her from her disease,' says Theophylact, 'but also infuses in her full strength and power, enabling her to minister.' *In Luc.* iv. 39, p. 334 (Paris, 1631); compare also Chrysost. *in loc.* For some very good remarks on the manner in which this miracle was

prepares for our Lord and His followers the Sabbath mid-day meal....And yet the record of that eventful day is not concluded. A few hours later, at sun-set[1], the whole city[a], with all its sick, gathers at the door of the house, and ancient prophecy[b] again finds its fulfilment in that exercise of Divine power that raised the sick and healed demoniacs, and yet chained in silence the driven-forth spirits[2], who with the recognition of terror both knew Him[c] and would have proclaimed Him as man's Redeemer and their own Judge.

[a] Mk. i. 33
[b] Is. liii. 4
[c] Mk. i. 34

What an insight does the account of this day, so marked by deeds of love and mercy, give us into the nature of our Lord's ministry in Galilee! What holy activities, what ceaseless acts of mercies! Such a picture does it give us of their actual nature and amount, that we may well conceive that the single day, with all its quickly-succeeding events, has been thus minutely portrayed, to show us what our Redeemer's ministerial life really was[3], and to justify, if need be, the

The nature of our Lord's ministerial labours as indicated by this one day.

---

performed, see Cyril Alex. *in loc.* Part I. p. 70 sq. (Transl.): compare also Trench, *Miracles*, p. 234.

[1] This note of time, supplied both by St Mark (i. 32) and St Luke (iv. 40), serves to mark that the Sabbath was over, after which the sick and suffering could legally be brought to our Lord: see Lightfoot, *Hor. Hebr.* Vol. I. p. 306 (Roterod. 1686). So rightly Theophylact (*in Marc.* i. 32), and the Scholiast in Cramer, *Catena*. Vol. I. p. 278.

[2] The comment of Cyril Alex. (referred to above, p. 164, note 2) seems correct and pertinent: 'He would not permit the unclean demons to confess Him, for it was not fitting for them to usurp the glory of the Apostolic office, nor with impure tongue to talk of the mystery of Christ.' Part I. p. 71 (Trans.): see also Theophyl. *in Luc.* iv. 41 (1st interpr.), who subjoins the good practical remark,—οὐχ ὡραῖος αἶνος ἐν στόματι ἁμαρτωλῶν.

[3] The incidents of this first Sabbath at Capernaum are well noticed by Ewald (*Gesch. Christus'*, p. 254 sq.), as showing what the nature of our Lord's holy labours really was: comp. Lange, *Leben Jesu*, II. 4. 11, p. 559 sq. The occurrence of so many events on a single day makes the short duration of the present ministry in Galilee less improbable.

noble hyperbole of the beloved Apostle, that if the things which Jesus did should be written every one, 'the world itself could not contain the books that should be written[a].'...... What a day too had this been for Capernaum! What manifestations of Divine power had been vouchsafed to them in their synagogue! what mercies had been showered down upon them in their streets[b]! Could they, and did they, remain insensible to such displays of omnipotence?—It would have been indeed impossible; and it is not with surprise that we find that in the dawn[1] of the following morning the multitudes, conducted as it would seem by Peter and the newly-called disciples, tracked out the great Healer to the lonely place[c] whither He had withdrawn to commune with His Father, broke in upon His very prayers, and strove to prevent Him leaving those whom He had now so pre-eminently blessed[d]. But it might not be. That request could not be granted in the exclusive manner in which it had been urged. Though the faith of these men of Capernaum was subsequently rewarded by our Lord's vouchsafing soon to return again, and by His gracious choice of Capernaum as His principal place of abode, yet now, as He alike tells both them and His disciples[e], He must fulfil His heavenly mission by preaching to others

---

[1] We learn from St Mark that our Lord retired before day broke to some lonely spot, apparently at no great distance from Capernaum (comp. Stanley, *Sinai and Palestine*, ch. x. p. 374), and was there praying; see ch. i. 35. From the tenses used and the special note of time, ἔννυχα λίαν (*Lachm., Tisch.*), it would seem that He had been there some little time before He was discovered by St Peter and those with him, who appear to have thus eagerly followed our Lord (κατεδίωξαν αὐτόν) at the instigation of the multitude: see Luke iv. 42, and compare Lange, *Leben Jesu*, II. 4. 11, Part II. p. 561.

as well as unto them. The blessings of the Gospel were to be extended to the other towns and villages by those peopled shores[1], and thither, with His small company of followers, the Lord departed, 'healing,' as St Matthew tells us[a], 'all manner of sickness, and all manner of disease among the people.'

[a] iv. 23

Probable duration of this circuit.

How long this circuit lasted we are not specially informed, but as one incident only, the healing of the earnest and adoring leper[2], *appears* to belong to this journey, we may perhaps, not without some probability, believe that the present circuit lasted but a few days, and that the return to Capernaum[b] took place on the day before the Sabbath of that week,—a Sabbath of which we have some special notices[3].

[b] Mk. ii. 1

---

[1] The expression used by St Mark (ch. i. 38) is τὰς ἐχομένας κωμοπόλεις (St Luke adopts the more general term, ταῖς ἑτέραις πόλεσιν), which seems to mark the sort of 'village-towns' (compare Strabo, *Geogr.* XII. pp. 537, 557) with which the whole adjacent plain of Gennesareth was closely studded; compare Stanley, *Sinai and Palest.* ch. X. p. 370.

[2] It seems right to speak guardedly, as St Matthew (ch. viii. 1) here *appears* to add a note of time, καταβάντι δὲ αὐτῷ ἀπὸ τοῦ ὄρους (*Rec.*, Tisch.). As, however, there is really nothing *very* definitely connective in the καὶ ἰδοὺ λεπρὸς προσελθὼν κ.τ.λ. —as St Mark and St Luke both agree in their position of the miracle,—and as the place it occupies in St Matthew's Gospel can be reasonably accounted for (see Lightfoot, *Harmony*, Vol. I. p. 512), we seem justified in adhering to the order of St Mark and St Luke; comp. Wieseler, *Chron. Synops.* p. 306 sq., and Caspari, *Chron.-Geogr. Einleit.* p. 124. On the miracle itself, one of the most remarkable characteristics of which was, that, as the three Evangelists all specify (Matth. viii. 13, Mark i. 41, Luke v. 13), our Lord *touched* the sufferer (δεικνὺς ὅτι ἡ ἁγία αὐτοῦ σὰρξ ἁγιασμοῦ μετεδίδου, Theoph. *in Matth. l. c.*),—see Trench, *Miracles*, p. 210; and for some good notices on the nature of the disease, Von Ammon, *Leben Jesu*, Vol. I. p. 111, and the frightful account in Thomson, *Land and the Book*, Vol. II. p. 516. The subject is treated very fully and completely in Winer, *RWB.* Art. 'Aussatz,' Vol. I. p. 114 sq.

[3] As the circuit was probably confined to the 'village-towns' on the western shores of the lake and in the vicinity of Capernaum (see above, note 1), we have an additional reason for thinking that it

LECT. IV.

The return to Capernaum, and healing of the faithful paralytic.

ᵃ Lk. v. 17

Meanwhile Capernaum had not forgotten its Healer and Redeemer, though evil men from other parts of Galilee, and, as it is significantly added, of Judæa and *Jerusalem*ᵃ, had now come in among them[1],—men, as it would seem, specially sent to collect charges against our Lord, and to mature the savage counsels which, we have already seen[2], had been taken by the party of the Sanhedrin. No sooner was it noised abroad that he had returned, than we find the whole city flocking to

did not last more than four or five days, and that thus our Lord might easily and naturally be found at Capernaum on the following Sabbath,—which, as we shall see below, has a definite and distinctive date. No objection against this chronological arrangement can be founded on the fact that our Lord 'preached in their synagogues' (Mark i. 39, Luke iv. 44), as it appears certain, setting aside extraordinary days (of which there would seem to have been one in this very week,—the New Moon of Nisan), there were services on the Mondays and Thursdays (comp. *Mishna*, Tract 'Megillah,' I. 2), in which the law was read and *probably* expounded, and to which the Talmudists (on 'Baba Bathra,' 4) assigned as great an antiquity as the days of Ezra: see Lightfoot, *Harmony*, Vol. I. p. 476 (Roterod. 1686), Vitringa, *de Synag.* I. 2. 2, p. 287, and compare Jost, *Gesch. des Judenth.* Vol. I. p. 168 sq. Some valuable observations on the subject of our Lord and His Apostles preaching in synagogues will be found in Vitringa, *de Synag.* III. 1. 7, p. 696 sq.

[1] We owe the important notice of the precise quarter from which these evil men came solely to St Luke. From the other two Synoptical Evangelists we only learn that the objectors were Scribes (Matth. ix. 3, Mark ii. 6), and that they appear to have come there with a sinister intent. The allusion, however, to Judæa and Jerusalem (especially when compared with Mark iii. 22, γραμματεῖς οἱ ἀπὸ Ἱεροσολύμων καταβάντες), throws a light upon the whole, and gives some plausibility to the supposition that the 'Scribes and Pharisees' we here meet with for the first time in Galilee were emissaries from the hostile party at Jerusalem. These men, promptly uniting themselves with others that they found to be likeminded in Galilee, formed a settled plan of collecting charges against our Lord, and the sequel shows with what feelings and in what spirit they were acting. For a while they wear the mask; they reason (Luke v. 21), they murmur (ver. 30), they insidiously watch (ch. vi. 7). Soon, however, all disguise is thrown aside; a deed of mercy on the sabbath, in spite of their tacit protest, hurries them on to their ruthless decision. That decision is at Capernaum what it had already been at Jerusalem (John v. 18),—death: see Matth. xii. 14, Mark iii. 6.

[2] See above, Lect. III. p. 142.

the house, so that as St Mark, with one of his graphic notices tells us, 'there was no room to receive them, no not so much as about the door^a.' But there were some without who would not be sent away. One sinful¹ but heart-touched paralytic there was, whose body and soul alike needed healing, and whose faith was such that when entry in the usual way was found to be impracticable, he prevailed on friends to bear him up the outside staircase, and let him down through the roof into the upper chamber, where, as it would seem from the narrative, our Lord was preaching to the mingled multitude both around Him and in the courtyard below²......And we remember well how that faith prevailed, and how the soul was healed first^b and then the palsied body^c, and how the last act was made use of, as it were, to justify the first

[a] ii. 2
[b] Lk. v. 20
[c] ver. 24

---

¹ We may infer this from the declaration of our Lord recorded by all the three Synoptical Evangelists,—ἀφέωνταί σου αἱ ἁμαρτίαι, Matth. ix. 2, Mark ii. 5; comp. Luke v. 20. The disease of the man, as Neander observes, may have been due to sinful excesses; and the consciousness, if not of this connexion, yet of the guilt within him was such that spirit and body reacted on each other, and an assurance of forgiveness was first needed, before the sensible pledge of it extended to him by his cure could be fully and properly appreciated: see *Life of Christ*, p. 272 (Bohn), and compare Olshausen, *Commentary*, Vol. I. p. 300 sq. (Clark).

² The course adopted was as follows: As the bearers could not enter the house on account of the press (Mark ii. 4), they ascend by the outside staircase that led from the street to the roof (Winer, *RWB*. Art. 'Dach,' Vol. I. p. 242), proceeding thereon till they come to the spot over which they judged our Lord to be. They then remove the tiles or thin stone slabs, which are sometimes used even at this day (see Thomson, cited below), and make an opening (Mark ii. 4, Luke v. 19; comp. Joseph. *Antiq.* XIV. 15. 12), through which, perhaps assisted by those below, they let the man down into the ὑπερῷον, or large and commonly *low* chamber beneath, in which, or perhaps rather under the verandah of which, the Lord then was: see Thomson, *The Land and the Book*, Vol. II. p. 7 sq., Meyer, *Komment. über Mark.* p. 24 sq., and compare the good article in Kitto, *Bibl. Cyclop.* Vol. I. p. 874 sq., especially p. 877.

LECT. IV.

in the eyes of those scribes and Pharisees who had stolen in among the simple-hearted men of Capernaum, and were finding blasphemy in the exercise of the Divine power and prerogatives of the Son of God. But this time at least those intruders were silenced, for when the sufferer obeyed his Lord's command, and showed the completeness of his restored powers[1] by bearing his bed, and walking through that now yielding throng, not only amazement, but as St Matthew[a] and St Luke[b] both notice, *fear* found its way into their hearts, and made the lips confess 'that they had seen strange things that day.'

[a] ix. 2 (see Tisch.).
[b] v. 26

The call of St Matthew and the feast at his house.

But another opportunity soon offered itself to these captious and malignant emissaries. Every prejudice was to be rudely shocked, when, as it would seem, on the very same day, our Lord called from his very toll-booth by the side of the lake[c], a publican, Matthew[2],—a publican, to be one of His followers and disciples. Here was an infrac-

[c] Mt. ix. 9
Mk. ii. 14

---

[1] 'He saith to the paralytic, Rise, and take up thy bed, to add a greater confirmation to the miracle, as not being in appearance only; and at the same time to show that He not only healed him, but infused power into him.' Theophylact, *on Mark* ii. 11. The command on the former occasion that it was given (John v. 8) probably also involved a reference to Christ's lordship over the Sabbath: comp. Lect. III. p. 141. For further comments on this miracle, see Olshausen, *Commentary*, Vol. I. p. 326 sq., Lange, *Leben Jesu*, II. 4. 14, Part II. p. 666 sq., Trench, *Notes on the Miracles*, p. 199 sq.; and for some curious allegorical applications, Theophylact, *loc. cit.* p. 199 (Paris, 1631).

[2] There seems no reason for calling in question the opinion of most of the more ancient writers (see *Const. Apost.* VIII. 22, and Coteler *in loc.*; contrast, however, Heracleon ap. Clem. Alex. *Strom.* IV. 11), that Levi (Mark ii. 14, Luke v. 27) and Matthew (Matth. ix. 9) are names of one and the same person. In favour of this identity, we have (1) the perfect agreement, both as to place and all attendant circumstances, of the narrative of the calling of Matthew (Matth. ix. 10) with that of the calling of Levi (Mark ii. 15, Luke v. 29); (2) the absence on the lists of the Apostles of any trace of the name Levi (the attempted identification with Lebbæus is in the highest degree improbable), while

The Ministry in Eastern Galilee. 173

tion of all that Pharisaical prejudice held to be most clear and recognized, an infraction too against which they were soon able to inveigh openly, when at the feast which the grateful publican made in honour of his Lord, and to which, perhaps by way of farewell, many of his old associates were summoned[1], the great Teacher openly sat down to meat 'with publicans and sinners.' This was an opportunity that could not be neglected. The disciples are taxed with their own and their Master's laxity, to which the Lord vouchsafes an answer turning against these gainsayers the very term in which their prejudice had expressed itself. The Redeemer, He tells them, had 'not come to call the righteous, but *sinners*, to repentance[a].' If the publicans were sinners, then to them must He vouchsafe His presence, then with them was it meet that He should be found. It was in vain that they

LECT. IV.

[a] Mt. ix. 13

the name of Matthew occurs in all, and is specified by the first Evangelist (ch. x. 3) as of that earthly calling which is here *definitely* ascribed by the second Evangelist to Levi. It is far from improbable that after and in memory of his call, the grateful publican changed his name to one more appropriate and significant. He was now no longer לֵוִי but מַתִּיָה, not Levi but Theodore,—one who might well deem both himself and all his future life a veritable 'gift of God:' see Winer, *RWB.* s. v. 'Name,' Vol. II. p. 135.

[1] This supposition, which is due to Neander (*Life of Christ*, p. 230, Bohn), is not without some probability; at the same time the specially inserted dative αὐτῷ (Luke v. 29) seems clearly to imply that St Matthew's first object in giving the entertainment was to do honour to our Lord, and thereby to commemorate his own now highly-favoured lot: compare Hall, *Contempl.* IV. 4. The attempt to show that the feast mentioned by St Matthew is not that mentioned by St Mark and St Luke (Greswell, *Dissert.* XXV. Vol. II. p. 397) is by no means successful; still less the attempt of Meyer (*Komment. üb. Matth.* p. 195) to establish a discrepancy between the first and the other two Synoptical Evangelists as to the locality of the feast. That ἐν τῇ οἰκίᾳ (Matth. ix. 10) refers to the house of St Matthew (ἐν τῇ οἰκίᾳ τῇ ἐκείνου, Chrys.) is not only grammatically possible, but in a high degree natural and probable: the general expression is studiedly used by the Apostle as keeping in the background the fact of his own grateful hospitality: see Blunt, *Veracity of Evangelists*, § 5. p. 30 sq.

shifted their ground and brought forward the stern practices of John's disciples, some of whom it is noticed were present^a, and some of whom seem to have been speakers^b. *They* were not worldly, *they* fasted; the prophet of Nazareth feasted. Yea but the very garments worn by those around and the very wine they were drinking suggested a simile that conveyed the true answer,—the New and the Old could not be brought together[1]; the spirit of the new dispensation was incompatible with the dead formalities of a dispensation that now, with all that marked it, was gone and passed away for ever.

Further charges: the plucking of the ears of corn.

The day that followed was apparently a Sabbath[2], the second-first Sabbath as it is especially defined by St Luke,—the first Sabbath, as it is now most plausibly explained, of a year that stood second in a sabbatical cycle[3]—when again the same

^a Mk. ii. 18
^b Mt. ix. 14

---

[1] Some good comments on this text, of which the above is a summary, will be found in Cyril Alex. *Comment. on St Luke*, Part II. p. 89 (Oxf. 1859).

[2] This assertion rests, not on the ἐν ἐκείνῳ τῷ καιρῷ (ch. xii. 1) of St Matthew, which is only a general note of time, but on the apparent close connexion in point of time between the different charges of the Pharisees and their adherents. The Passover was nigh at hand, and time was pressing.

[3] There are four explanations of this difficult word that deserve consideration: (*a*) that of Theophylact (*in loc.*), that it was a Sabbath that immediately succeeded a festival, which from falling on the παρασκευή, was observed as a regular Sabbath; (*b*) that of Scaliger (*de Emend. Temp.* p. 557), that it was the Sabbath that succeeded the second day of the Passover; (*c*) that of Hitzig (*Ost. u. Pfingst.* p. 19), that it was the 15th of Nisan, the 14th being, *it is asserted*, always coincident with a Sabbath; (*d*) that of Wieseler (*Chron. Synops.* p. 231 sq.), as stated in the text. Of these (*a*) is open to the decisive objection that such concurrences must have been frequent, and that if such was the custom, and such the designation, we must have found some trace of it elsewhere: (*c*) involves an assumption not historically demonstrable (see Wieseler, *Chron. Synops.* p. 353 sq.), and, equally with (*b*), labours under the formidable objection that as the event here specified is thus *at*, and not, as every reasonable system of chronology appears to suggest, *before* a Passover, the Passover at the feeding of the 5000 (John vi. 4) must be referred to a succeeding year, and an interval of more than

bitter spirit of Pharisaical malice finds opportunity for displaying itself. Yesterday the social privacy of the publican's feast, to-day the peace and rest of the year's first Sabbath[1], is broken in upon by the malignity of that same gathered company of Pharisees whom Judæa and Jerusalem and alas too Galilee[a] had sent forth to forejudge and to condemn. With the full sanction of the Mosaic law[b] the disciples were plucking the ears of ripening corn, and rubbing them in their hands. The act was permissible, but the day was holy[2], and the charge, partly in the way of rebuke to

[a] Lk. v. 17

[b] Deut. xxiii. 25: see *Mishna* ('Peab,' ch. 2).

a year assumed to exist between the 5th and 6th chapters of St John. We adopt then (*d*), as open to no serious objections, as involving no chronological difficulties, and as apparently having some slight historical basis to rest upon, viz. that at this period years appear to have been reckoned by their place in a Sabbatical cycle: comp. Joseph. *Antiq.* XIV. 10. 6. In the recent work of Caspari a somewhat different view is taken. The uncertainty as to the exact length of the month (29 or 30 days) is supposed to have involved the necessity of observing two consecutive days as Sabbaths, so as to ensure Nisan being duly observed: the first of these was called σάββατον πρῶτον, the second σάββατον δευτερόπρωτον; *Chron.-Geogr. Einleit.* § 102, p. 120. The view is ingenious and plausible, but has but little evidence to rest on. The word is omitted in the important MSS. BLN, and a few ancient versions (see Tischend. *in loc.*), but seems certainly genuine, there being an obvious reason for its omission, and none for its insertion.

[1] The exact date of this Sabbath, according to our present calendar, if we can rely on the tables of Wurm and Wieseler, would seem to be April 9,—a date when the corn would be forward enough in many localities to be rubbed in the hands; see Wieseler, *Chron. Syn.* p. 225 sq., and compare Lect. III. p. 106, note 1.

[2] The act was regarded as a kind of petty harvesting, and as such was regarded by the ceremonial Pharisee as forbidden, if not by the written yet by the oral law: 'Metens sabbato vel tantillum reus est. Et vellere spicas est species messionis.' Maimonides, Tit. 'Shabbath,' ch. IX. cited by Lightfoot (*Hor. Hebr. in Matth.* xii. 2, Vol. II. p. 320), who further reminds us that, according to the traditional law, the punishment for the offence was capital, the action being one of those 'per quæ reus fit homo lapidationis atque excisionis.' Maimon. *ib.* ch. VII. It is not probable that at this period such a penalty would ever have been pressed; still it is not unreasonable to suppose that the legally grave nature of the supposed offence may have tended to call forth from our Lord that full and explicit vindication of his disciples which the Evangelists have recorded.

the disciples, partly in the way of complaint to our Lord who was tacitly sanctioning their act, is promptly made with every assumption of offended piety,—'Why do ye do that which it is not lawful to do on the Sabbath[a]?' why indeed! The reason was obvious: the justification immediate. Did not the history of the man after God's own heart justify such an act[b]? Did not the unblamed acts of the great type of Him who stood before them supply the substance, as did ancient prophecy[c] the exact terms of the answer that was vouchsafed, 'I will have mercy, and not sacrifice'? Mercy, and not sacrifice,— words uttered already the day before[d], but now accompanied with a striking declaration, which some of those standing by might have remembered had been practically illustrated three weeks before in Jerusalem, by a deed of mercy and power[1], even 'that the Son of man is Lord also of the Sabbath[e],' and of all its alleged restrictions.

[a] Lk. vi. 2
[b] 1 Sam. xxi. 6
[c] Hos. vi. 6
[d] Mt. ix. 13
[e] Lk. vi. 5

The healing of a man with a withered hand on a Sabbath.

And now hostility deepens. On the next, or apparently next day but one[2], which in the case of the year we are considering (A.U.C. 782) computation would *seem* to fix as the seventh day of the first month, and which we may infer from a passage in Ezekiel was specially regarded as a holy day[3], we almost detect traces of a regular

---

[1] See Lect. III. p. 140.

[2] See below, p. 193, note 1, from which it would seem that there is an error of a day in the tables of Wurm and Wieseler.

[3] After speaking of the first month and the sacrifices to be observed therein, the prophet adds (ch. xlv. 20),—'And so thou shalt do the *seventh day of the month* for every one that erreth, and for him that is simple: so shall ye reconcile the house.' From these words, when coupled with the similar notice of the solemn first day of Nisan in the verses that precede, and the notice of the still more solemn 14th day in the verses that follow, it has been apparently rightly inferred that the 7th of Nisan was regarded as

stratagem. A man in the synagogue afflicted with a withered right hand[a], placed perchance in a prominent position, forms the subject of a question which these wretched spies not only entertain in their hearts[b], but even presume openly to propound to our Lord,—'was it lawful to heal on the Sabbath-day[c]?' The answer was prompt and practical, first the command to the sufferer to rise from his place and stand forth in the midst[d]; then the all-embracing gaze[1] of grief and anger[e], and lastly after a few reproving words, the immediate performance of the miracle[2]. But such an answer malice and infidelity could neither receive nor endure. The flame of savage vengeance at once breaks out. 'They were filled with madness' are the remarkable words of St Luke[f]; they go forth from the synagogue, they hold a hasty council[g], yea they join with their very political opponents, the followers of Herod

[a] Lk. vi. 6
[b] vi. 7, 8
[c] Mt. xii. 10
[d] Lk. vi. 8
[e] Mk. iii. 5
[f] vi. 11
[g] Mt. xii. 14

holy, and might appropriately be designated by St Luke (ch. vi. 6) as ἕτερον σάββατον: compare Wieseler, *Chron. Syn.* p. 237. It seems difficult to regard these words as marking the remainder of the day which began at even with the incident in the cornfields: so however, Caspari, *Chron.-Geogr. Einleit.* § 106, p. 125.

[1] Not only St Mark, but St Luke notices this act of our Lord's both using the same expressive word, περιβλεψάμενος. On the use of this term by St Mark, comp. p. 25, note 1.

[2] The present miracle forms one of the seven which are particularly noticed as having been performed on the Sabbath (see John v. 9, Mark i. 21, Mark i. 29, John ix. 14, Luke xiii. 14, Luke xiv. 1,

and comp. *Crit. Sacr. Thesaur. Nov.* Vol. II. p. 196), and is specially the one before the performance of which the Lord vouchsafes to vindicate the lawfulness (Matth. xii. 12) of such acts of mercy, by an appeal to recognized principles of justice and mercy which even the Pharisees could not reject or deny. For some comments on the miracle, the nature of which was the immediate restoration of the nutritive powers of nature to a part where they had perhaps by degrees, but now permanently ceased to act (Winer, *RWB.* Art. 'Krankheiten,' Vol. I. p. 674), compare Hook, *Serm. on the Miracles*, Vol. I. p. 135 sq., and especially see Trench, *Notes on the Miracles*, p. 312 sq.

178   *The Ministry in Eastern Galilee.*

LECT. IV.

[a] Mk. iii. 6

[b] Lk. v. 21

Antipas[1], as St Mark has been moved to record[a], and now deliberately lay plans to slay the great Healer. The cup in their eyes is full. Two days since blasphemy, as they deemed it, had been spoken[b]; this however they might have borne with; but publicans have been received, the rest of a weekly Sabbath infringed upon, and now worst of all, a *legal* Sabbath has been profaned by—beneficence; that profanity must be washed out by blood. As but a short time before in Jerusalem, so now in Galilee the fearful determination is distinctly formed of compassing the death of One whose life-giving words their own ears had heard, and whose deeds of mercy their own eyes had been permitted to behold.

Choice of the twelve Apostles, and Sermon on the Mount.

This is a very important turning-point in the Gospel-history, and it prepares us for the event which followed perhaps only a day or two afterwards[2],—and which the now deepening ani-

---

[1] There seems no reason to dissent from the conjecturally expressed opinion of Origen (*Comm. in Matth.* Tom. XVII. 26) that the Herodians were a political sect who, as their name implies, were partisans of Herod Antipas (οἱ τὰ Ἡρώδου φρονοῦντες, Joseph. *Antiq.* XIV. 15. 10), and, by consequence, of the Roman government, so far as it tended to maintain his influence: comp. Ewald, *Gesch. Christus*' (Vol. V.), p. 43 sq. Thus they were really, as Meyer (*Komment. üb. Matth.* xxii. 16) defines them, royalists as opposed to maintainers of theocratic principles; still, being members of a political and not a religious sect, they might easily be found in coalitions with one of the latter sects for temporary objects which might affect, or be thought to affect, the interests of both: comp. Matth. xxii. 16, Mark xii. 13, where they again appear in temporary union with the Pharisees. For further comments, see Winer, *RWB.* s. v. Vol. I. p. 486, Herzog, *Real-Encycl.* s. v. Vol. VII. p. 14, and compare Lightfoot, *Harm. Evang.* § 16, Vol. I. p. 470.

[2] The only note of time is ἐν ταῖς ἡμέραις ταύταις (Luke vi. 12), which, though far too general to be quoted in support of the above supposition, does not in any way seem opposed to it. There appears much in favour of a close connexion in point of time between the formal choice of the Apostles, and these murderous determinations of the hierarchical party and their adherents: comp. Ewald, *Gesch. Christus*' (Vol. V.), p. 270 sq.

mosities against the sacred person of our Redeemer rendered in a high degree natural and appropriate,—a retirement into the lonely hills on the western side of the lake, and the choice of twelve pillars for the not yet consolidated, yet already endangered Church. There, on that horned hill of Hattin, which a late tradition does not in this case appear to have erroneously selected[1], was the scene of the formal compacting and framing together of the spiritual temple of God; there too was heard that heavenly summary of the life and practice of Christianity which age after age has regarded as the most sacred heritage that God has vouchsafed unto His Church[2].

I must here be tempted into no digressions,—for there are several events yet before us for

Probable form of the Sermon on the Mount.

---

[1] See Robinson, *Palestine*, Vol. II. p. 370 sq. (ed. 2), who admits that, though this appears to be only a late tradition of the Latin Church, 'there is nothing in the form or circumstances of the hill itself to contradict the supposition.' So far, indeed, it may be added, is this from being the case, that Dr Stanley finds the conformation of the hill so strikingly in accordance with what we read in the Gospel narrative, 'as almost to force the inference that in this instance the eye of those who selected the spot was for once rightly guided.' *Sinai and Palestine*, p. 364 (ed. 2); comp. Caspari, *Chron.-Geogr. Einlcit.* § 107, p. 126. Thomson (*The Land and the Book*, Vol. II. p. 118) speaks far more slightingly than is usual with that agreeable and observant writer.

[2] Of the many expository works on this divine discourse the following may be selected as appearing, perhaps more particularly, to deserve the attention of the student:—the exposition of Chrysostom in his *Commentary on St Matthew;* Augustine, *de Sermone Domini*, Vol. III. p. 1229 sq. (Migne), and with it Trench, *Serm. on the Mount* (ed. 2); Pott, *de Indole Orat. Mont.* (Helmst. 1788),—whose general conclusion, however, as to the nature of the Sermon does not appear plausible; the exegetical comments of Stier (*Disc. of our Lord*, Vol. I. p. 90, Clark), and Maldonatus (*Comment.* p. 95); the special work of Tholuck, *Bergpredigt* (translated in Edinb. Cabinet Libr.); and lastly, the more directly practical comments and discourses of Bp Blackall (Lond. 1717), and *James* Blair (Lond. 1740,—with a commendatory preface by Waterland); to which may be added the comments in Taylor, *Life of Christ*, II. 12, Vol. I. p. 190 (Lond. 1836), and in Lange, *Leben Jesu*, II. 4. 12, Part II. p. 566 sq.

LECT. IV.

consideration,—still, at such an important point in our history, it does seem almost wrong to suppress the humble statement of an opinion on a most serious and yet most contested question in reference to this Divine discourse. Let me say then with that brevity that our limits demand,—*First*, that there seem greatly preponderant reasons for believing the sermon recorded by St Luke to be substantially the same with that recited by St Matthew[1];—*Secondly*, that the divine unity which pervades the whole totally precludes our believing that St Matthew is here presenting us only with a general collection of discourses uttered at different times, and leads us distinctly to maintain the more natural and reasonable opinion, that this holy and blessed Sermon was uttered as it is here delivered to us[2];—*Thirdly*, that of the modes of reconciliation proposed between the two forms of this Sermon vouchsafed to us by the Holy Ghost, two deserve considera-

---

[1] The main arguments are,—that the beginning and end of the Sermon are nearly identical in both Gospels; that the precepts, as recited by St Luke, are in the same general order as those in St Matthew, and that they are often expressed in nearly the same words; and lastly, that each Evangelist specifies the same miracle, viz. the healing of the centurion's servant, as having taken place shortly after the Sermon, on our Lord's entry into Capernaum: comp. Matth. viii. 5, Luke vii. 2 sq., and see Tholuck, *Sermon on the Mount*, Vol. I. p. 5 sq. (Clark).

[2] This opinion, improbable as it is now commonly felt to be, was adopted by as good an interpreter as Calvin (*Harm. Evang.* Vol. I. p. 135, ed. Tholuck), and has been lately advanced in a slightly changed form by Neander, who attributes to the Greek editor (?) of St Matthew the insertion of those expressions of our Lord which are found in other collocations in St Luke's Gospel: see *Life of Christ*, p. 241 (Bohn). There is nothing however, unnatural in the supposition that our blessed Lord vouchsafed to use the same words and give the same precepts on more occasions than one: compare Matth. v. 25 and Luke xii. 58, Matth. vi. 19—21 and Luke xii. 33, Matth. vi. 24 and Luke xvi. 13, Matth. vii. 13 and Luke xiii. 24, Matth. vii. 22 and Luke xiii. 25—27.

tion, (*a*) that which represents St Luke's as a condensed recital of what St Matthew has related more at length, and (*b*) that which attributes the condensation to our Lord Himself, who on the summit of the hill delivered the longer but, as it has been doubtfully termed, *esoteric* sermon to His Apostles, and perhaps disciples, and on the level piece of ground, a little distance below, delivered the shortened and more popular form to the mixed multitude[1].

But let us now pass onward. On the Lord's return to Capernaum, which it does not seem unreasonable to suppose took place on the evening of the same day, the elders of the synagogue of Capernaum meet our Lord with a petition from one who shared in the faith, though he was not of the lineage of Abraham.—This petition, and the way in which it was made, deserve a passing notice. We see, on the one hand, the different feelings with which as yet the leading party at Capernaum were animated when contrasted with

The healing of the centurion's servant, and raising of the widow's son.

---

[1] Of these two opinions, the second, though noticed with some approval by Augustine (*de Consensu Evang.* II. 19), and convenient for reconciling the slight differences as to locality and audience which appear in the records of the two Evangelists (see Lange, *Leben Jes.* II. 4. Part II. p. 568 sq.), has so much the appearance of having been formed simply to reconcile these differences, and involves so much that is unlikely and indeed unnatural, that we can hardly hesitate to adopt the first; so too, as it would seem, Augustine, *loc. cit.* ad fin.: comp. Trench, *Expos. of Serm. on Mount*, p. 160 (ed. 2). A fair comparison of the two inspired records seems to confirm this judgment, and satisfactorily to show that St Luke's record is here a compendium, or rather selection, of the leading precepts which appear in that of St Matthew. No extract, it may be observed, is made from chap. vi. (Matth.), as the duties there specified (almsgiving, prayer, fasting, &c.) are mainly considered in reference to their due performance in the sight of God, while St Luke appears to have been moved to specify those which relate more directly to our neighbour. For further notices and comments, see Tholuck, *Serm. on Mount*, Vol. I. p. 1 sq. (Clark).

LECT. IV.

the emissaries from Jerusalem; and on the other we recognize the profound humility of the God-fearing soldier who, it would seem from St Luke's account[a], twice preferred his petition by the mouths of others, before he presumed himself to speak in behalf of his suffering servant. Then followed, probably from his own lips, words of faith that moved the wonder of our Lord Himself, and forthwith came the reward of that faith,—the healing of apparently the first Gentile sufferer[1]... But the morrow was to see yet greater things; for, as St Luke[b] tells us, on the following day, during the course of a short excursion into the vale of Esdraelon, the Lord of Life comes into first conflict with the powers of death. At the brow of that steep ascent, up which the modern traveller to the hamlet of *Nain* has still to pass[2], the Saviour, begirt with a numerous company of His disciples and a large attendant multitude[c], beholds a sad and pity-moving sight. The only son of a widow was being borne out to his last resting-place, followed by the poor weeping mother and a large and, as it would seem, sympathizing crowd[d]. But there was One now nigh at hand who no sooner beheld than He pitied[e],

[a] vii. 3, 6
[b] vii. 11 sq.
[c] Lk. vii. 11
[d] ver. 12
[e] ver. 13

---

[1] For comments on this miracle, one of the characteristics of which is, that, as in the case of the nobleman's son, our Lord vouchsafed the cure without seeing or visiting the sufferer, see Bp Hall, *Contempl.* II. 6, Trench, *Miracles*, p. 222, and compare Lange, *Leben Jesu*, II. 4. 13, Part II. p. 645 sq.

[2] See Stanley, *Sinai and Palestine*, ch. IX. p. 352 (ed. 2). The Dutch traveller Van de Velde remarks that the rock on the west side of Nain is full of sepulchral caves, and infers from this that our Lord approached Nain on its western side: *Syria and Palestine*, Vol. II. p. 382. A sketch of the wretched-looking but finely situated hamlet that still bears the name of Nain or Nein (Robinson, *Palest.* Vol. II. p. 361) will be found in Thomson, *The Land and the Book*, Vol. II. p. 159.

and with whom to pity was to bless. The words of power were uttered[a], the dead at once rose up to life and speech[b], and was given to the widow's arms, while the amazed multitude glorified God, and welcomed as a mighty prophet[c] Him who had done before their eyes what their memories might have connected with the greatest of the prophets of the past[1]....It is here *perhaps*, or at one of the towns in the neighbourhood, that we are to fix the memorable and affecting scene at the house of Simon the Pharisee[d], when the poor sinful woman pressed unbidden among the guests to anoint not the head[e], like the pure Mary of Bethany, but the *feet* of the Virgin's Son, and whose passionate repentance and special and preeminent faith[f] was blessed with acceptance and pardon[2].

[a] Lk. vii. 14
[b] ver. 15
[c] ver. 16
[d] ver. 36
[e] ver. 38.
[f] ver. 50

---

[1] For some further comments on this miracle, see Cyril Alex. *on St Luke*, Serm. xxxvi. Part I. p. 132 sq. (Transl.), Bp Hall, *Contempl.* II. 1, and Trench, *Notes on the Miracles*, p. 239. Compare also Augustine, *Serm.* xcviii. Vol. v. p. 591 sq. (ed. Migne), and Lange, *Leben Jesu*, II. 4. 16, Part II. p. 740 sq.

[2] With regard to this anointing of our Lord, we may briefly remark, (*a*) that it certainly is not identical with that which is specified by the other three Evangelists (Matth. xxvi. 6 sq., Mark xiv. 3 sq., John xii. 1 sq.). Everything is different,—the time, the place, the chief actor, and the circumstances; see Meyer, *on Matth.* xxvi. 6, p. 483, and Lange, *Leben Jesu*, II. 4. 16, Part II. p. 736. We may further remark, (*b*) that there seems no just ground for identifying the repentant sinner here mentioned with Mary Magdalene, who, though a victim to Satanic influence, and that too in a fearful and aggravated form (Luke viii. 2), is not necessarily to be considered guilty of sins of impurity. Nay more, the very description of the affliction of Mary Magdalene seems in itself sufficient to distinguish her from one whom no hint of the Evangelist leads us to suppose was then or formerly had been a demoniac. The contrary opinion has been firmly maintained by Sepp (*Leben Christi*, III. 23, Vol. II. p. 285), but on the authority of Rabbinical traditions, which are curious rather than convincing. On the incident generally, see Greg. M. *Hom. in Evang.* xxxiii., Augustine, *Serm.* xcix., and especially Bp Hall, *Contempl.* IV. 16.

LECT. IV.

The Baptist's message of inquiry.

It is about the same time too, and, as appears by no means improbable, but a very few days before the tragical end of their Master's life[1], that the two disciples of John the Baptist come to our Lord with the formal question which the, so to say, dying man commissioned them to ask,—whether the great Healer, the fame of whose deeds had penetrated into the dungeons of Machærus, were truly He that was to come, or whether another were yet to be expected[a]....The exact purpose of this mission will perhaps remain to the end of time a subject of controversy[2], but it has ever been fairly, and, as it would seem, convincingly urged, that he whose eyes, scarce sixteen months before, had beheld the descending Spirit, whose ears had heard the voice of Paternal love and benediction, and who now again had but recently been told of acts of omnipotent power, could himself have never really doubted the truth of his own declaration[3], that

[a] Mt. xi. 3 Lk. vii. 19

---

[1] The most probable period to which the murder of the Baptist is to be assigned would seem to be the week preceding the Passover of the second year of our Lord's ministry, April 10—17, A.U.C. 782. For the arguments on which this rests, consult Wieseler, *Chron. Synops.* p. 292 sq., and see below, p. 196, note 1.

[2] The three different states of feeling (doubt, impatience, desire to convince his disciples) which have been attributed to the Baptist, as having given rise to this mission, are noticed and commented on by Ebrard, *Kritik der Evang. Gesch.* § 73, p. 367 sq. For a full discussion of the subject, however, see the calm and learned comments of Jackson, *on the Creed*, Vol. VI. p. 310 sq. Compare also, but with caution, Lange, *Leben Jesu*, II. 4. 17, Part II. p. 745 sq.

[3] The utmost that can be said is, that the Baptist required the comfort of accumulated conviction (see Jackson, *Creed*, Vol. VI. p. 314): that he entertained distrust, or wavered in faith in these last days of his life, seems wholly incredible. To convince his disciples (Cyril Alex. *in loc.*) fully and completely before his death, was the *primary* object of the mission; to derive some incidental comforts from the answer he foresaw they would return with, may possibly have been the *secondary* object.

this was indeed 'the Lamb of God that taketh away the sins of the world^a.'

Almost immediately after the marvellous scene at Nain, our Lord accompanied not only by His twelve Apostles, but, as it is specially recorded, by pious and grateful women^b, chief among whom stands the miraculously healed Mary of Magdala, passed onward from city to city and village to village preaching the kingdom of God. That circuit could not have lasted much above a day or two after the miracle at Nain[1], and as the words of the second Evangelist seem to imply terminated at Capernaum, which as we already know had now become our Lord's temporary home. On their return two parties anxiously awaited them; on the one hand the multitude, which, St Mark^c tells us, gathered so hastily round the yet unrested company, that either the disciples, or, as seems more probable from the sequel^d, the mother and brethren of our Lord, deemed themselves called upon to interpose[2], and to plead

^a Joh. i. 29 *Short circuit; fresh charges of the Pharisees.*

^b Lk. viii. 2

^c iii. 20

^d see ch. iii. 31 sq.

---

[1] It has been already observed (p. 169, note 1), that the villages and even towns were so numerous in some parts of Galilee, that the words of the Evangelist (διώδευεν κατὰ πόλιν καὶ κώμην κηρύσσων, Luke viii. 1) need not be pressed as necessarily implying a lengthened circuit. It may be indeed doubted whether these notices of circuits, which it is confessedly *very* difficult to reconcile with other notes of time, may not be general descriptions of our Lord's ministry at the time rather than special notices of special journeys. That the circuit had a homeward direction and terminated at Capernaum, we gather from Matth. xiii. 1, which, in specifying the place (παρὰ τὴν θάλασσαν), marks the day as the same with that on which the visit of our Lord's mother and brethren took place, and so connects us with Mark iii. 19 sq., which seems to refer to the return from the circuit (Luke viii. 1 sq.) which we are now considering.

[2] A little difficulty has been felt (a) in the exact reference of the words οἱ παρ' αὐτοῦ (Mark iii. 21), and (b) in the fact that St Luke places the visit of our Lord's mother and brethren *after* the delivery of the parables rather than before them. With regard to the first point,—οἱ

against what they could not but deem an almost inconsiderate enthusiasm [a]. On the other hand, we still find there the hostile party of Scribes and Pharisees from Jerusalem, whom we have already noticed, and who yet lingered, though the passover was so nigh, in hopes that they might find further and more definite grounds of accusation. An opportunity, if not for preferring a charge, yet for attempting to check the growing belief of the amazed multitude [b], and for enlisting the worst feelings against the very acts of mercy which our Lord vouchsafed to perform, soon presented itself at the miraculous cure of a blind and dumb demoniac, which appears to belong to this portion of the sacred narrative [1]. Then was it that the embittered hatred of these prejudiced and hardened men showed itself in the frightful blasphemy,—repeated, it would seem, more than once [2], that attributed the wonder-working power

[a] Mk. iii. 21
[b] Mt. xii. 23

παρ' αὐτοῦ seems clearly to imply not the Apostles, but our Lord's relatives ('propinqui ejus,' Syr.), who are noticed here as going forth (probably from some temporary abode at Capernaum; see p. 159, note 1), and a few verses later (Mark iii. 31) as having now arrived at the house where our Lord then was. With regard to (*b*), it seems enough to say that St Luke clearly agrees with St Matthew in placing the event in question on the same day, but from having here omitted the discourse which preceded the arrival (Mark iii. 22 sq.), he mentions it a little out of its true chronological order, to prevent its being referred to some one of the towns on the circuit, and to connect it with the right place and time,—Capernaum, and the day of the return.

[1] There seems reason for placing the narrative of the healing of the demoniac, recorded in Matth. xii. 22 sq., between Mark iii. 21 and Mark iii. 22, as the substance of the words which follow in both Gospels are so closely alike, and as the narrative of the miracle in St Matthew follows that of other miracles which certainly appear to belong to a period shortly preceding the one now under consideration.

[2] Compare Luke xi. 17 sq., where we meet with, in what seems clearly a later portion of the history, the same impious declaration on the part of the Pharisees, which St Mark (ch. iii. 22 sq.) and apparently St Mat-

of the eternal Son of God to the energy of Satan[a]; and then too was it that our Lord called them to him[b], and mercifully revealed to them the appalling nature of their sin, which was now fast approaching the fearful climax of sin against the Holy Ghost,—that sin for which there was no forgiveness[1], 'neither in this world, neither in that which is to come[c].' The afternoon or early evening of that day was spent by the shores of the lake. The eager multitude, augmented by others who had come in from the neighbouring towns[d], had now become so large that, as it would seem, for the sake of more conveniently addressing them, our Lord was pleased to go on board one of the fishing vessels, and thence with the multitude before Him, and with His divine eyes perchance resting on some one of those patches of varied and undulating corn-field which modern travellers have noticed as in some cases on the very margin of the lake[2],—with the earthly and

[a] Mt. xii. 24
[b] Mk. iii. 23

[c] Mt. xii. 32
The teaching by parables.

[d] Lk. viii. 4

---

thew (ch. xii. 24) refer to the present place. That such statements should have been made more than once, when suggested by similar miracles, is every way natural and probable: compare Matth. ix. 34 and xii. 22 sq., and see Wieseler, *Chron. Synops.* p. 287 sq.

[1] On this highest and most frightful enhancement of sin in the individual,—of which the essential characteristic appears to be, an *outward expression* (see Waterland) of an inward hatred of that which is recognized and felt to be divine, and the irremissible nature of which depends, not on the refusal of grace, but on the now lost ability of fulfilling the conditions required for forgiveness,—see the able remarks of Müller, *Doctrine of Sin*, Book v. Vol. II. p. 475 (Clark), and the good sermon of Waterland, *Serm.* XXVIII. Vol. V. p. 707. For further comments on this profound subject, see Augustine, *Serm.* LXXI. Vol. V. p. 445 sq. (ed. Migne), the special work on the subject by Schaff (Halle, 1841), and the article by Tholuck, in the *Studien u. Kritiken* for 1836, compared with the earlier articles in the same periodical by Grashoff (1833), and Gurlitt (1834).

[2] See the interesting and illustrative remarks of Stanley, *Sinai and Palestine*, ch. XIII. p. 421 sq.; and, in reference to the parable, compare the elucidations, from local

the heavenly harvest-field thus alike before Him, —He delivered to that listening concourse the wondrous series of parables beginning with that appropriately chosen subject, specified alike by all the three Synoptical Evangelists,—the Sower and the seed[1].

The passage across, and storm on the lake.

And now, as St Mark specifies, the evening had come, and after that long and exhausting day the Holy One needed retirement and repose, and nowhere could it be more readily obtained than in the solitudes of the eastern shore[a].... The multitudes still linger; but the Apostles bear away their wearied Master, 'as He was,' says the graphic St Mark[b], in the vessel from which He had been preaching. As they sail the Lord slumbers, when from one of the deep clefts of the surrounding hills[2] a storm of wind bursts upon the lake[c], and the stirred-up waters beat in upon the boat[d]. Terror-stricken the disciples awaken their sleeping Master, and He, who only a few hours before had driven forth devils[e], now quells by His word[f] the lesser potencies of wind and storm[3].

[a] Mk. iv. 35
[b] ver. 36
[c] Lk. viii. 23
[d] Mk. iv. 37
[e] Mt. xii. 22
[f] Mk. iv. 39

observation, of Thomson, *The Land and the Book*, Vol. I. p. 115 sq.

[1] On the connexion of the parables, of which this forms the first, see Lect. I. p. 21, note 2.

[2] 'To understand,' says Dr Thomson, who himself witnessed on the very spot a storm of similar violence, and that lasted as long as *three days*, 'the causes of these sudden and violent tempests, we must remember that the lake lies low [hence κατέβη λαῖλαψ, Luke viii. 23],—six hundred feet lower than the ocean; that the vast and naked platenus of Jaulan rise to a great height, spreading backward to the wilds of the Hauran, and upward to snowy Hermon; that the water-courses have cut out profound ravines and wild gorges, converging to the head of this lake, and that these act like gigantic funnels to draw down the winds from the mountains.' *The Land and the Book*, Vol. II. pp. 32, 33. See also Ritter, *Erdkunde*, Part XV. 1, p. 308 sq., where the peculiar nature of these storm-winds is briefly noticed.

[3] For further comments on this miracle, one of the more striking features of which is the Saviour's

The Ministry in Eastern Galilee.

When they reached the opposite side, which might have been late that evening, or more probably studiously delayed till the dawn of the following day, our Lord had no sooner gone out of the vessel than He was met by the hapless Gergesene[1] demoniac or demoniacs[2], whose home was in the tombs* that can still be traced in more than one of the ravines that open out upon the Lake on its eastern side[3]. There, and in the

LECT. IV.

The Gergesene demoniacs.

* Mk. v. 3

rebuke to the warring elements, the very words of which, as addressed to the storm-tost waters (καὶ εἶπε τῇ θαλάσσῃ, Σιώπα, πεφίμωσο, Mark iv. 39), have been specially recorded by the second Evangelist,—see the expository remarks of Chrysostom, in *Matth.* Hom. XXVIII., the typical and practical application of Augustine, *Serm.* LXIII. (ed. Migne), Trench, *Notes on the Miracles*, p. 143 sq., and compare Hook, *Serm. on the Miracles*, Vol. I. p. 207 sq.

[1] Whether the true reading in Matth. viii. 28 be Γεργεσηνῶν, Γαδαρηνῶν, or Γερασηνῶν, is a question which cannot easily be answered. On the whole, however, if we assign due weight not only to the evidence of manuscripts, but also to recent geographical discovery, we shall perhaps be led to adopt the first reading in St Matthew and the second in St Mark and St Luke. The grounds on which this decision rests are as follows: (1) The amount of external evidence in favour of Γεργεσηνῶν in Matth. viii. 28 (see Tischendorf *in loc.*) is much too great to be due solely to the correction of Origen; (2) Origen plainly tells us that there *was* a place in his time so named, and that the exact site of the miracle was pointed out to that day; (3) ruins have been recently discovered by Dr Thomson in Wady Semak, still bearing the name of Kerza or Gerza, which are pronounced to fulfil every requirement of the narrative. See especially, *The Land and the Book*, Vol. II. p. 33 sq., and compare Van de Velde, *Memoir to Map*, p. 311. The probable reading in St Mark and St Luke (Γαδαρηνῶν) may be accounted for by supposing that they were content with indicating *generally* the scene of the miracle, while St Matthew, whose knowledge of the shores of the lake whereon he was a collector of dues would naturally be precise, specifies the *exact* spot.

[2] Of the current explanations of the seeming difficulty that St Matthew names *two* and St Mark and St Luke *one* demoniac, that of Chrysostom (*in loc.*) and Augustine (*de Consensu Evang.* II. 24) seems most satisfactory, viz. that one of the demoniacs took so entirely the prominent part as to cause two of the narrators to omit all mention of his companion. We have no reason for inferring from St Matthew that the second of the sufferers did more than join in the opening cry of deprecation; see Matth. viii. 29.

[3] See Thomson, *The Land and the Book*, Vol. II. p. 35. Tombs

solitudes of the desert mountains behind, dwelt the wretched, and, as it would seem, sinful man, who by his Lord's own Divine command[a] was hereafter to be Christ's first preacher in his own household, and who told abroad the blessings he had received through the surrounding land of Decapolis[b]. How he was healed, the astonishing and most convincing way in which every line of the narrative sets before us the awful kind of double or rather manifold personality[c], the kneeling man of the one moment[d] and the shouting demoniac of the next[e], the startling yet all-wise permission given to the devils[1], and the overpowered instinct of self-preservation in the possessed swine,—all this our present limits preclude me from pausing fully to delineate, but

[a] Lk. viii. 39
[b] Mk. v. 20
[c] ver. 9
[d] ver. 6
[e] Comp. p. 164, note.

have also been observed in Wady Fik on the side of the road leading up from the lake (Stanley, *Palestine*, ch. x. p. 376), the position of which has perhaps led to that ravine being usually selected as the scene of the miracle; if, however, the above identification of Γέργεσα and *Gerza* be accepted, the scene of the miracle must be transferred to the more northern Wady Semak.

[1] On this much debated subject we may briefly observe, (*a*) that the *permission* to enter into the herd of swine may have been deemed necessary by our Lord (πολλὰ ἐντεῦθεν οἰκονομῶν, Chrys.) to convince the sufferer of his cure (Chrys. 1.); (*b*) that it may also stand in connexion with some unknown laws of demoniacal possession generally, and more particularly with that which the demons dreaded, deprecated, and perhaps foresaw,—a return to the abyss (Luke viii. 31). It may be that to defer that return they ask to be suffered to enter into fresh objects in that district to which they so mysteriously clung (Mark v. 10), and it may be too that the very permitted entry by destroying the instinct of self-preservation in the swine brought about, even in a more ruinous way, the issue they so much dreaded. That this was (*c*) further designed to punish the people for keeping swine is not perfectly clear, as the inhabitants of those parts were mainly Gentile: comp. Joseph. *Antiq.* XVII. 11. 4. The supposition that the swine were driven down the precipice by the demoniacs (Kuinoel, followed by Milman, *Hist. of Christianity*, Vol. I. p. 238) is not only in the highest degree improbable, but wholly at variance with the express statements of the inspired writers.

this one comment I will venture to make, that with this miracle before us, with expressions so unqualified, and terms so distinct, a denial of the reality of demoniacal possession on the part of any one who believes the Gospel narrative to be true and inspired, may justly be regarded as simply and plainly inconceivable[1].

On the Lord's return to the western side, *The raising of Jairus' daughter.* which took place immediately in consequence of the request of the terror-stricken inhabitants of the neighbouring city[a], He found the multitude [a]Mt.viii.34 eagerly waiting to receive Him[b], and among them [b]Lk.viii.40 one anxious and heart-stricken man, Jairus, whose daughter lay dying, and who besought our Lord with all the passion of a father's love to save his child. But the crowd hung round the Lord[c], and [c]ver. 42 the case of the suffering woman[d], who touched her [d]ver.43sq. Saviour's garments with the touch of faith[2], added to the delay, and the daughter of the ruler of the synagogue had breathed her last before the Lord could reach the father's house[3]. So they tell Him

---

[1] For some good remarks on this subject see Olshausen, *Commentary*, Vol. I. p. 305 sq. (Clark), Trench, *Notes on the Miracles*, p. 151 sq., Alford, *on Matth.* viii. 32, and compare Kitto, *Journal of Sacr. Lit.* No. VII. p. 1 sq., No. XIV. p. 394 sq. In addition to these, on the miracle generally, see Chrysostom, *on Matth.* Hom. XXVII., the good comments of Maldonatus, *on Matth. l.c.*, Bp Hall, *Contempl.* III. 5, and compare Jones of Nayland, *Works*, Vol. V. p. 72 sq., and Bp Wilberforce, *Serm.* p. 107.

[2] On this miracle, the characteristics of which are the great faith of the sufferer, and the indirect though not unconscious performance of the cure, see Hall, *Contempl.* IV. 7, Trench, *Notes on the Miracles*, p. 189 sq., Hook, *Serm. on the Miracles*, Vol. I. p. 242 sq.; and compare Lange, *Leben Jesu*, IV. 4. 14, Part II. p. 681.

[3] The slight difference between the narrative of St Matthew in which the father speaks of his daughter as now dead (ch. ix. 18), and that of St Mark, where he speaks of her as being at the last gasp (ch. v. 23), has been accounted for most reasonably by Augustine (*de Consens. Evang.* II. 2), Theophylact (1st alternative), and others, by the supposition that Jairus spoke from what

LECT. IV.

ᵃ Mk. v. 35
Lk. viii. 49

ᵇ vii. 11

ᶜ Mk. v. 43

that all was overᵃ. But now was the glory of God to be revealed. Yet again a second time, as once on the bier, so now on the bed, did the Lord loose the bands of death—with however this very striking and peculiar difference, that what a few days before was done in the sight of all Nainᵇ, was here done in strict privacy with three chosen Apostles and the father and mother alone present, and with the special and urgentᶜ command to those present not to raise the veil of the solemn scene they had been permitted to witness[1].

The second visit to the synagogue at Nazareth.

Soon after this, perhaps on the same day, our Lord accompanied by His disciples leaves Capernaum, and on the Sabbath which immediately followed again appeared in the synagogue at His own town of Nazareth[2]....The feeling there is now in some degree better than it was three

his fear suggested, and that he regarded the death of his daughter as by that time having actually taken place; comp. Greswell, *Dissert.* III. Vol. I. p. 217.

[1] This command, which Meyer (on *Mark* v. 43) most rashly considers a mere unauthorized addition of later tradition, is perfectly in harmony with the private manner in which the miracle was performed. The reason *why* it was given can, however, only be conjectured. It can scarcely have been on account of the Jews (διὰ τὸν φθόνον τάχα τῶν Ἰουδαίων, Theophyl. *on Luke* viii. 56), but may very probably have been suggested by a desire to avoid undue publicity, and perhaps also by merciful considerations of what the Lord knew to be best for the maiden and her relatives; compare

Olshausen, *Commentary on Gospels*, Vol. I. p. 276 (Clark). On the miracle itself see the good comments of Chrysost. *in Matth.* Hom. XXXI., Bp Hall, *Contempl.* IV. 8, Lardner's vindication, *Works*, Vol. XI. p. 1 sq., Trench, *Notes on the Miracles*, p. 179, and Lange, *Leben Jesu*, II. 4. 14, Part II. p. 683 sq.

[2] That this visit to Nazareth is not identical with that recorded by St Luke (ch. iv. 16) is rightly maintained by Meyer, *on Matth.* xiii. 54. The only argument for the identity is our Lord's use of the same proverb on both occasions; but is there anything strange in such a repetition, especially when the conduct of the people of Nazareth on each occasion rendered such a proverb most mournfully pertinent? See Wieseler, *Chron. Syn.* p. 284 sq.

weeks before[a]. The fame that spread all through Galilee had produced some effect even at Nazareth, and had disposed them to give ear a second time to Him whose wisdom and even miraculous powers[b] they were forced to recognize and to confess. But the inward heart of the men of Nazareth was unchanged as ever. Though there was now no longer that open indignation and murderous rage[c] that was so frightfully manifested at the former visit, there was a similar vexed spirit of amazement and incredulity, and a similar and even more scornfully-worded appeal to family connexions of low estate, and to kindred that had long lived humbly among them; 'Is not this the carpenter, the son of Mary and the brother of James and Joses and Judas and Simon[d]?' It is now however offence rather than positive rejection—yet offence that sprang from a deep heart of unbelief, which stayed the Saviour's healing hands[e], and made Him who knew full well what it was to meet with rejection and want of faith, to marvel at the exceeding measures of Nazarene unbelief[f]. On the eve of that day, or more probably early on the morrow, our Lord appears to have commenced a short circuit of Galilee, but, as we must conclude from our general notes of time[1], in the direction of Capernaum, and at this

[a] Luke iv. 16 sq.
[b] Mk. vi. 2
[c] Lk. iv. 28
[d] Mk. vi. 3
[e] Mt. xiii. 58
[f] Mk. vi. 6
The sending forth of the Twelve Apostles.

---

[1] The sabbath on which our Lord preached at Nazareth would certainly seem to be the sabbath which succeeded the σάββατον δευτερόπρωτον (Luke vi. 1), and consequently according to our explanation of the latter term, the second Sabbath of Nisan. Now if we turn to our tables (Wieseler, *Chron. Synops.* p. 484), we find that our present Sabbath answers to Nisan 13, and therefore must conclude that both our Lord and His Apostles returned to Capernaum from their respective missionary journeys on the following day, there being good reason for fixing the Feeding of the 5000 on the Passover-eve, Nisan 14; see be-

LECT. IV.

ᵃ Mk. vi. 1

ᵇ vi. 12

ᶜ Mt. x. 5 sq.

same time also it would certainly appear that He sent forth the twelve Apostles (who we know accompanied Him to Nazareth)ᵃ, by two and two, probably in different directions, and perhaps with an order, after having made a brief trial of the powersᵇ with which they had been intrusted, to join their Master at Capernaum. Thither they must have returned, it would seem, not more than two days afterwards¹.... Such a statement may at first seem startling. It may be urged that so short an absence on the part of the Apostles is hardly compatible with the instructions given to them by our Lord, as recorded by the first Evangelistᶜ, wherein distant and continued journeyings would seem rather to be contemplated than the limited circuit which our present chronology suggests². The objection is

low, and compare John vi. 4. Such a result can hardly be conceived natural. The difficulty, however, may be in some degree removed by taking into consideration the fact that the first day of the Jewish month was fixed by *observation*, and that the day of the Julian calendar with which it agrees can hardly be determined with perfect certainty. In the case of Nisan 1 in the present year the correct time of new moon was about 7 o'clock in the evening of April 2; the new moon would then probably be observed on the evening of April 4 (see Wieseler, *Chron. Synops.* p. 446). But the Jewish day begins after 6 o'clock; Nisan 1 would then *begin* on April 4 but really coincide with April 5, and not with April 4 as Wieseler and Wurm suppose. The date of our present Sabbath would then be

Nisan 12 and not Nisan 11, and we should have two whole days for the absence of the Apostles, a time not improbably short: see below. Such niceties and difficulties may well teach us caution, and may justly make us *very* diffident as to our ability to assign each event in this portion of the sacred narrative to the true day on which it occurred.

¹ See the preceding note.

² Another objection may perhaps be founded on the declaration of St Mark that our Lord 'went round about the villages, teaching' (ch. vi. 6; comp. Matth. ix. 35). This is also of some weight, but as we find no special note of time serving to define it as subsequent to the visit to Nazareth, and prior to the sending forth of the Twelve, we may perhaps justly and correctly regard it either (*a*) as serving only to mark

certainly not without force, and is useful in warning us not to be too confident either on the construction of our chronological tables, or in the correctness of our collocation of individual events. Still when we consider,—*First*, that it is far from improbable that St Matthew has incorporated in this address to the Apostles instructions given to them by our Lord at other periods of His ministry[1]; *Secondly*, that the address whether in its longer or its shorter form may reasonably be supposed to extend far beyond the present time[a], and to refer to periods of missionary labour as yet still distant; *Thirdly*, that it does not seem probable that our Lord would have long dispensed with the attendance of those to whom His blessed presence was so vital and so essential[2]—when we consider all these points, it will perhaps seem less improbable, that this first missionary journey was but short, and that the Apostles returned

[a] Comp. Mt. x. 23

that our Lord's ministry was continuous; that He did not remain at Nazareth, but was extending His blessings to other places, or, still more simply (*b*) as merely specifying the work in which our Lord was then engaged, and as preparing the reader for a transition to other subjects (ver. 7—29); see above, p. 185, note 1.

[1] When we remember that St Matthew does not notice the sending forth of the Seventy, and further, when we compare the instructions delivered to them, as recorded by St Luke (ch. x. 2), with those which are here recorded by St Matthew, as delivered to the Twelve (ch. x. 2 sq.), it seems hard to resist the conviction that as the first Evangelist was moved in the preceding chapters to group miracles together, so in the present case he is presenting in a collected form all our Lord's instructions on the subject of missionary duties and labours generally. See a comparison of the parallel passages in Wieseler, *Chron. Synops.* p. 303.

[2] It is right to remember that the formal appointment of the Twelve can scarcely be placed further back than a week or ten days from the present time. Some of the number, we know, had been already long enough with our Lord as disciples for us to conceive that they might have been enabled to teach and preach for some time without being sustained by His presence, but this can hardly be felt in reference to all the Apostles.

to Capernaum as early as the evening of the second day. The return was nearly, it would seem, contemporaneous with the arrival of the tidings of the Baptist's murder[1], and it was perhaps partly on this account[a], and partly for the sake of communing in stillness with His chosen ones after their first missionary efforts[b], that our Lord thought it meet to avoid the many comers and goers[c] which a time so close to the Passover would be sure to set in motion, and to seek rest and privacy by retiring with His Apostles to the solitudes of the further side of the lake.

The Feeding of the five thousand. But rest and privacy were not to be obtained. A very short time, especially when we remember the probable vicinity of the city of Bethsaida-Julias[2], and the numbers that might now have been moving about the country, would have served to have brought the Five thousand round our Lord; and there on the green table-lands on

---

[1] It seems probable that the death of the Baptist took place somewhere about a week before the time now under consideration; see Wieseler, *Chron. Synops.* p. 292 sq. Much however turns on the meaning assigned to the term γενέσια (Matth. xiv. 6, Mark vi. 21). If it refers to the festival in honour of the *birthday* of Herod Antipas (Meyer) no precise date for the murder of the Baptist can be obtained from this portion of the narrative; if, however, as seems not unlikely, it refers to the festival in honour of the *commencement of Herod's reign*, then an approximately close date can easily be arrived at, as Herod the Great, whom Herod Antipas succeeded in the government of Galilee (Joseph. *Antiq.* XVII. 8. 1), is known to have died a few days before the Passover, A.U.C. 750; see Lect. II. p. 75, note 1.

[2] This appears to have been a place of some size and importance. It was transformed by Philip from a mere village into a populous and handsome town (see Joseph. *Antiq.* XVIII. 2. 1), of which some traces are thought to have been found on some rising ground on the east side of the Jordan and not far from the head of the lake; see Robinson, *Palestine*, Vol. II. p. 413, Thomson, *The Land and the Book*, Vol. II. p. 9, and compare Winer, *RWB.* Vol. II. p. 174.

the north eastern corner of the lake, or amid the 'green grass^a' of the rich plain near the mouth of the Jordan¹, must we place the memorable scene of the miraculous feeding of that vast multitude. Memorable indeed: memorable for the display of the creative power of the eternal Son that was then made before more^b than five thousand witnesses; memorable too for the strange coincidence that on the very eve that the Paschal lambs were being offered up in the temple-courts of Jerusalem, the eternal Lamb of God was feeding His people in the wilderness with the bread which His own Divine hands had multiplied².

<small>LECT. IV.
^a Mk. vi. 39

^b Mt. xiv. 21</small>

And now I must draw these words and this portion of our Master's life at once to a close, yet not without the prayer that this effort to set forth the narrative of a most solemn and eventful period,—the period of the Lord's founding His Church,—may be blessed by His Spirit. To be confident of the accuracy of details either of time or place, where not only the connexion of individual events but the arrangement of the whole period is a matter of the utmost doubt and difficulty,

<small>*Concluding remarks.*</small>

<small>¹ See Stanley, *Palestine*, ch. x. p. 377, and especially Thomson, *The Land and the Book*, Vol. II. p. 29, where it is stated that the exact site of the miracle may almost confidently be identified. For a confutation of the rashly advanced opinion that St Luke places the scene of the miracle on the western shore (De Wette, comp. Winer, *RWB*. Vol. I. p. 175), see Meyer, *on Luke* ix. 10.

² On this miracle, which, as has been often observed, is the only one found in *all* the four Gospels, and which, when compared with the miracle of turning the water into wine (John ii. 1 sq.), shows our Lord's creative powers in reference to *quantity*, as the latter does His transforming powers as to *quality*, see Origen, *in Matth.* xi. 1, Vol. III. p. 476 sq. (ed. Bened.), Augustine, *in Joann.* Tract. XXIV. Vol. III. p. 1592 sq. (ed. Migne), Bp Hall, *Contempl.* IV. 5, Trench, *Notes on the Miracles*, p. 261, and a good sermon by Mill, *Univ. Serm.* XVI. p. 301.</small>

would indeed argue a rash and self-satisfied spirit; yet this I will presume to say, that if certain chronological data and reasonings be approximately correct,—and after manifold testings correct *in the main* I do verily believe them to be,—then the general picture can hardly be much otherwise than as it has been here sketched out. Be this however as it may, I count all as nought if only I have succeeded in the great object which these Lectures are intended to promote, if only, by presenting some sketches of the continued life of the Saviour, I may have been enabled to bring that Saviour nearer to one heart in this Church. On that holy life, on all its Divine harmonies, on all its holy mysteries, may we be moved more and more to dwell. By meditating on the inspired records may we daily acquire increasing measures of that fulness of conviction, to have which in its most complete proportions is to enjoy the greatest earthly blessing which the Lord has reserved for those that love Him....This is indeed to dwell with the Lord on earth[1], this is indeed to feel His spiritual presence around us and about us, and yet to feel, with no ascetic severity but in sober truth, that we have here no abiding city, but

---

[1] 'Do not then,' says the wise and eloquent Bp Hall, 'conceive of this union as some imaginary thing that hath no existence but in the brain, or as if it were merely an accidental or metaphorical union by way of figurative resemblance; but know that this is a real and substantial union, whereby the believer is indissolubly united to the glorious person of the Son of God. Know that this union is not more mystical than certain, that in natural unions there may be more evidence but cannot be more truth. Neither is there so firm and close a union betwixt the soul and body as there is betwixt Christ and the believing soul; for as much as that may be severed by death but this cannot.' *Christ Mystical*, ch. II.; see above, Lect. III. p. 147, note 2.

that there, where He is, is our true and everlasting home: there, by the shores of that crystal sea[a] our heavenly Gennesareth, there that new Jerusalem, whose light is the light of the Lamb[b], —the 'city which has foundations, whose builder and maker is God[c].'

[a] Rev. iv. 6
[b] Rev. xxi. 23
[c] Heb. xi. 10

LECTURE V.

THE MINISTRY IN NORTHERN GALILEE.

St Luke iv. 43.

And He said unto them, I must preach the kingdom of God to other cities also: for therefore am I sent.

LECT. V.

I have chosen these words, brethren, which really belong to a slightly earlier period[1] than that which we are now about to consider, as nevertheless a very suitable text for that part of our Master's history which will occupy our attention this afternoon.

General features of this part of our Lord's history.

In the portion of the inspired narrative now before us, we have the brief yet deeply interesting notices of more widely extended journeys and more prolonged circuits. We find the clear traces of missionary travel to the West and to the East and to the North, and we read the holy record of deeds of mercy performed in remote regions both of Galilee and the lands across the Jordan[2],

---

[1] The exact time when these words were uttered by our Lord was the morning following the first Sabbath at Capernaum, when the amazed but grateful multitudes were pressing Him not to leave the place He had so greatly blessed; see Lect. IV. p. 168.

[2] It has not been easy to select a single term which should correctly describe the principal scene of the ministerial labours of our Lord which come before us in this Lecture. The known geographical divisions of Upper and Lower Galilee (Joseph. *Bell. Jud.* III. 3. 1) would naturally have suggested the adoption of the former term in reference to the present, and the latter in reference to the preceding portion of the sacred narrative, if it were not apparently an established fact that Capernaum

The Ministry in Northern Galilee.

which the Lord had not, as it would appear, yet blessed with His Divine presence. Hitherto the plain of Gennesareth and the nearer portions of Galilee, 'the land of Zabulon and the land of Nephthalim^a,' had been almost exclusively blest with the glory of the great Light; now Phœnice and Decapolis were to behold its rays. Hitherto the lake of the East, 'the way of the sea beyond Jordan^b,' had been the chief theatre of the Redeemer's teaching and miracles; now the dwellers round Tyre and Sidon were all^c to hear, even in their own remote lands, the tidings of salvation, yea and to bear their witness to victories over the powers of that kingdom of darkness which had so long been seated on those heathen and idolatrous shores.

Such is the general character of the very remarkable portion of the sacred narrative on which we are now about to dwell. Remarkable is it for the glimpses it vouchsafes to us of the unwearied activities of our Lord's ministerial life; remarkable for the notices it supplies to us of the extended spheres to which those holy energies were directed[1]; remarkable too for the contrasted

LECT. V.

^a Mt. iv. 15

^b ver. 15

^c Comp. Mark iii. 8 Luke vi. 17

Special contrasts and characteristics.

---

belonged, not as it might be thought to Lower (Kitto, *Bibl. Cycl.* Art. 'Galilee,' Vol. I. p. 727), but to Upper Galilee; comp. Euseb. *Onomast.* Art. 'Capharnaum,' and Smith, *Dict. of Bible*, Art. 'Galilee,' Vol. I. p. 646. The title above has thus been chosen, though it is confessedly not exact, as failing to include the districts across the Jordan, which, as will be seen from the narrative, were the scenes of some part of the ministry that we are now considering.

[1] The peculiar character of these distant missionary journeys of our Lord, and the considerable portion of time which they appear to have occupied, have been too much overlooked by modern writers of the Life of our Lord; compare, for example, Hase, *Leben Jesu*, § 85, and even to some extent Lange, *Leben Jesu*, II. 5. 10, Part II. p. 864, neither of whom seems properly to recognize the important place which

LECT. V.

Chronological limits of the present portion.

relations in which it stands to that portion of the Gospel history which claimed so much of our attention last Sunday. To these contrasts and characteristics let us devote a few preliminary thoughts.

First, however, let us specify the limits of the section to which we are about to confine our attention....These seem, almost at once, to suggest themselves to the meditative reader, and serve to separate the evangelical narrative into simple and natural divisions. Our section, it will be remembered, commences with the events which immediately succeeded the Feeding of the five thousand on the Passover eve[1], and naturally and appropriately concludes with the return of our Lord to Capernaum a very short time previous to His journey to Jerusalem at the feast of Tabernacles, towards the middle of October. We have thus as nearly as possible a period of six months[2], a period bounded by two great festivals, and, as I have already said, marked off from the preceding portion of our Lord's history by some striking contrasts and characteristics. On these let us briefly pause to make a few observations which the nature of the subject appears to demand.

these journeys really occupy in our Lord's ministry; see below, p. 203. Ewald on the contrary has correctly devoted a separate section to this portion of the Gospel history; see *Gesch. Christus'*, p. 331 sq.

[1] See above, Lect. IV. p. 197. The opinion there advanced, of the exact coincidence of the day on which the multitudes were fed with that on which the paschal lamb was slain, derives some slight support from the subject of our Lord's discourse (the bread of life, John vi. 22 sq.) at Capernaum on the following day, which, it does not appear at all unlikely, was suggested by the festal season; see below, p. 211.

[2] If we are correct in our general chronology, the present year would be 782 A.U.C., and in this year the Passover would begin April 17 or 18 (see above, p. 193, note 1), and the feast of Tabernacles October 19; see the tables in Wieseler, *Chron. Synops.* p. 483.

One of the most striking features of the present section is the glimpse it affords us of the *progressive* nature, if I may venture to use such an expression, of our Lord's ministerial labours, and the prophetic indications, as it were, which it supplies of the future universal diffusion of the Gospel. At first we have seen that our blessed Master was mercifully pleased to confine His teaching and His deeds of love and mercy mainly to that province which could now alone be reckoned as the land of the old theocracy. In Judæa He was pleased to dwell continuously more than eight months[1]; in Judæa He gathered round Him disciples more numerous than those of John[a], and from Judæa He departed only when the malignity of Scribe and Pharisee rendered that favoured land no longer a safe resting-place for its Redeemer and its God[b]. Then, and not till then, followed the ministry in the eastern and as it would seem more Judaized[2] portion of Galilee.

LECT. V.

Progressive nature of our Lord's ministry.

[a] Joh. iv. 1

[b] ver. 3

---

[1] This ministry began with the Passover of the year 781 A. U. C. (March 29), and concluded with our Lord's departure to Galilee through Samaria, which, as we have seen above, may be fixed approximately as late in December: see Lect. III. p. 130, note 3.

[2] This last epithet may perhaps be questioned, but is apparently borne out by the essentially Jewish character of the district which the sacred narrative seems to reveal. The population of the great city of the district, Tiberias, though mixed (Joseph. *Antiq.* XVIII. 2. 3), appears to have included a considerable and probably preponderant number of Jews, as we find it mentioned as in revolt against the Romans (Joseph. *Vit.* 9), while the other large city of Galilee, Sepphoris, did not swerve from its allegiance. Capernaum too, if we agree to identify it with Tell Hûm (p. 121, note 2), must have had a large population of Jews at a time not very distant from the Christian era, otherwise we can hardly account for the extensive ruins, apparently of a synagogue of unusual magnificence, which have been observed at that place by modern travellers; see Robinson, *Palestine*, Vol. III. p. 346 (ed. 2), Thomson, *Land and the Book*, Vol. I. p. 540. As to the supposed early date of the building, compare the remarks of Robinson, *Palest.* Vol. III. p. 74.

LECT. V.

In due and mysterious order succeeded those missionary labours in frontier lands where the Gentile element was mainly, if not in some cases exclusively prevalent. This gradual enlargement of the field of holy labour does indeed seem both striking and suggestive; this we may perhaps venture to regard as a result from our present system of harmonizing the Gospel narrative, which reflects on that system no small degree of plausibility.

Contrasts between this and the preceding portions of the narrative.

But there are *contrasts* too between the narrative of this present portion of our Lord's history and that which has preceded, which seem to illustrate the foregoing remarks, and are in themselves both interesting and instructive. Though the portion of time vouchsafed to the ministry in Capernaum and its vicinity was so short, yet with what minute accuracy is it detailed to us by the three Synoptical Evangelists! How numerous the miracles, how varied and impressive the teaching! Three continuous weeks only[1], yet

---

[1] Assuming our general dates to be right, our Lord's first appearance in the synagogue at Nazareth would be on a Sabbath corresponding with the 21st day of the intercalated month Beadar, or, according to the Julian Calendar, March 26 or 27. The Passover, as we have already seen, commenced on April 17 or 18. We have thus for the portion of our Lord's ministry on which we dave commented in the preceding Lecture only a period of about twenty-two days. It may be urged that this is far shorter than we could have inferred from the narrative; but it may be answered,—that *if* the feast mentioned by St John (ch. v. 1) be Purim, and *if* we consider, as we seem fairly justified in doing, the Feeding of the five thousand coincident with the Passover-eve of the same year (see p. 153, note 1), then our Lord's ministry in Eastern Galilee cannot readily be shown to have lasted longer than has here been supposed. It is by no means disguised that there are in this, as in every other system of chronology that has yet been proposed, many difficulties, and much that may make us very doubtful of our power of fixing the exact epochs of many events (see above, p. 193, note 1); still, if the extreme chronological limits appear rightly fixed, we seem bound to accept the fair results of such an arrangement, if

The Ministry in Northern Galilee. 205

in that short time one signal instance of the Lord's controlling power over the elements[1], two records of triumphs over the power of death, three notable accounts of a stern sovereignty exercised over the spirits of perdition[2], the formal founding of the Church, and the promulgation of all its deepest teaching....But in our present section when we follow our Lord's steps into half-heathen lands, though the time spent was so much greater, how few the recorded miracles, how isolated and detached the notices of them!

Nay more, our very inspired authorities seem to change their relations, and yet suggest by the very change that local teaching and preaching[3] rather than display of miraculous power was the chief characteristic of these six months of the Lord's ministerial life. I ground this opinion on the easily verified fact that the professed *historian*

LECT. V.

Teaching and preaching rather than miracles characteristic of this period.

---

not as certainly true, yet at least as consistent with what has been judged to be so, and thus far as claiming our assent. For some remarks tending in some measure to dilute the force of *à priori* arguments founded on the apparent shortness of the time, see Wieseler, *Chron. Synops.* p. 288.

[1] We might have almost said *two*, as the miracle of walking on the water (Matth. xiv. 25, Mark vi. 48, John vi. 19), though placed in the portion on which we are now commenting, obviously belongs to the ministry in Eastern Galilee.

[2] These are, (1) the striking instance in the synagogue at Capernaum (Mark i. 23 sq., Luke iv. 33 sq.), which so greatly amazed those who witnessed it; (2) the instance of healing the blind and deaf demoniac (Matth. xii. 22), which provoked the impious declarations of the Jerusalem scribes and Pharisees; and (3) the Gergesene demoniacs (Matth. viii. 28 sq., Mark v. 1 sq., Luke viii. 26 sq.).

[3] The statement of Chrysostom (*in Matth.* Hom. LII. Vol. VII. p. 596, ed. Bened. 2), that our Lord did not journey to the borders of Tyre and Sidon for the purpose of preaching there (οὐδὲ ὡς κηρύξων ἀπῆλθεν), seems doubtful. From St Mark, as Chrysostom urges, we learn that our Lord sought privacy 'and would have no man know' (ch. vii. 24), but this, from the immediate context and, as it were, contrasted miracle, would seem to indicate a desire for *partial* rather than absolute concealment, a temporary laying aside of His merciful displays of Divine power rather than a suspension of His ministry.

of his Master's life, he who made it his duty to set in order the narrative which eye-witnesses had delivered[a], and who records to us events rather than discourses[1], has assigned to this six months' period only some thirty or more verses[2], while to the brief but eventful period that preceded he has devoted at least seven times as much of his inspired record. Our principal authority, as we might almost expect, is St Matthew; yet not exclusively, as about 150 verses of St Mark's Gospel relate to the same period[3]. The events however recorded by both evangelists taken together are so very few, that again the inference would seem reasonable, that if two of those who were eye-witnesses,—for in St Mark we have the testimony of St Peter,—have related so little, our Lord's miracles during this time could scarcely have been numerous. Miracles, as we know, *were* performed, but it was probably less by their influence than by the calm but persuasive influence of teaching and preaching that the Lord was pleased to touch and test the rude, yet apparently receptive hearts of the dwellers in the remote uplands of Galilee, or in the borders of Hellenic Decapolis[4].

---

[1] On the nature and characteristics of this Gospel, see Lect. I. p. 27 sq.

[2] The only portion of St Luke's Gospel which appears to relate to this period of our Lord's ministry, if we except a very few verses which may perhaps belong to discourses during this period (ch. xv. 3—7: xvii. 1, 3), begins ch. ix. 18, and concludes with the 50th verse of the same chapter: comp. Wieseler, *Chron. Synops.* p. 314.

[3] The portion of St Mark's Gospel that refers to this period of our Lord's ministry begins ch. vi. 45, and seems to conclude with the last verse of ch. ix. The next chapter describes our Lord as journeying into Judæa by way of Peræa, and consequently is describing the last journey to Jerusalem; see Lecture VI.

[4] The district, or, more strictly speaking, confederation bearing this name, seems to have been made up of cities and the villages round them (Joseph. *Vit.* § 65), of which the

This is exactly what we might have presumed to expect from the circumstances of the case, and from what has been incidentally revealed to us of the conditions on which the performance of the Lord's miracles in a great measure depended. From the comment which both St Matthew and St Mark have made upon the repressing influence of the unbelief of the people of Nazareth[a], we seem justified in asserting that our Redeemer's miracles were in a great degree contingent upon the faith of those, to whom the message of the Gospel was offered[1]. How persuasively true then does that narrative appear which on the one hand represents the appeal to miracles most frequent and continuous in Eastern Galilee, where the receptivity was great and the contravening influences mainly due to alien emissaries[2],—and, on the other, leaves us to infer, by its few and isolated notices, that amid the darkness and necessarily

LECT. V.

Such a difference probable from the nature of the case.

[a] Mt. xiii. 58
Mk. vi. 5

---

population was nearly entirely Gentile: two of the cities, Hippos and Gadara are distinctly termed by Josephus (*Antiq.* XII. 11. 4) Ἑλληνίδες πόλεις. The geographical limits of Decapolis can scarcely be defined; we seem, however, justified in considering that *nearly* all the cities included in the confederation were across the Jordan, and on the eastern side of the lake of Gennesareth; comp. Euseb. *Onomast.* s. v. 'Decapolis,' Winer, *RWB.* Art. 'Decapolis,' Vol. I. p. 263, and the detailed account of the district and its cities in Caspari, *Chron.-Geogr. Einleit.* § 72, p. 83 sq.

[1] The following comment of Origen is clear and pertinent: 'From these words (Matth. xiii. 58) we are taught that miracles were performed among the believing, since "to every one that hath it shall be given and shall be made to abound," but among unbelievers miracles not only were not, but, as St Mark has recorded, even could not be performed. For attend to that "He could not perform any miracle there;" he did not say "He *would* not," but "He *could* not," implying that there is an accessory co-operation with the miraculous power supplied by the faith of him towards whom the miracle is being performed, but that there is a positive hindrance caused by unbelief.' *In Matth.* x. 18, Vol. III. p. 466 (ed. Bened.); see also Euthym. *Matth.* xiii. 58.

[2] See above, Lecture IV. p. 170, note 1.

LECT. V.

The return across the lake. Our Lord walks on the waters.

imperfect belief of the frontier lands that appeal was comparatively limited and exceptional.

But it is now time for us to resume the thread of the inspired history. On that Passover-eve with which our narrative commences, our Lord after having fed the Five thousand remains Himself behind on the eastern shore to dismiss the yet lingering multitudes[a], but directs the disciples to cross over the lake to Bethsaida. From some supposed discordant notices in the accounts given of the circumstances which followed, it has been urged that this Bethsaida was the town of that name, known also by the name of Julias, not far from the head of the lake[1], and with this supposition it may be conceded that there are some

[a] Mt. xiv. 22
Mk. vi. 45

---

[1] This view, which is perhaps originally due to Lightfoot (*Chron. Temp.* § 47, Vol. II. p. 30, Roterod. 1686), is very elaborately maintained by Wieseler (*Chron. Synops.* p. 274, note), and has also found a recent advocate in Dr Thomson (*The Land and the Book*, Vol. II. p. 30 sq.), who conceives that there was really only one Bethsaida, viz. the town at the north-eastern corner of the lake. In opposition to Lightfoot and Wieseler we may justly urge, *first*, the distinct words of St Matthew, describing the position of the vessel on its return, τὸ δὲ πλοῖον ἤδη μέσον τῆς θαλάσσης ἦν (ch. xiv. 24; comp. Mark vi. 47); and *secondly*, the words of St Mark προάγειν εἰς τὸ πέραν πρὸς Βηθσαϊδάν (ch. vi. 45), which, when coupled with the above notice of the position of the vessel, it does seem impossible to explain otherwise than as specifying a direct course across the lake : compare also John vi. 17.

With regard to Dr Thomson's opinion it may be observed that all modern writers seem rightly to acquiesce in the opinion of Reland that there *was* a place of that name on the western coast, very near Capernaum. Robinson fixes its site as at the modern et-Tabighah (*Palestine*, Vol. III. p. 359, ed. 2), but there seems good reason for agreeing with Ritter in placing it at Khân Minyeh, and in fully admitting the statement of Seetzen, that this last-mentioned place was also known by the local name of Bât-Szaida: see *Erdkunde*, Part XV. p. 333 sq., and the comments of Caspari, *Chron.-Geogr. Einleit.* § 66, p. 75 sq. That there should be two places called Bethsaida ('House of Fish') on or near a lake so well-known not only for the peculiar varieties (Joseph. *Bell. Jud.* III. 10. 8) but the great abundance of its fish as that of Gennesareth, cannot justly be considered at all improbable.

statements in the sacred narrative that at first sight seem to be fairly accordant: as however the supposed discordances and difficulties are really only imaginary, there seems no sufficient reason for departing from the ordinarily received opinion that this was the village on the western side. Nay more, the scarcely doubtful direction of the gale from the south-west[1], which would bring, as we are afterwards told, vessels from Tiberias to the north-eastern coast[a], but would greatly delay a passage in the contrary direction, seems to make against such a supposition, and to lead us decidedly to believe that Bethsaida on the western coast was the point which the Apostles were trying to reach,—and trying to reach in vain. Though they had started in the evening[2], they

[a Joh. vi. 23]

---

[1] See Blunt, *Veracity of Evangelists*, No. xx. p. 82, who appears rightly to connect with the mention of the gale the incidental notice of the passage of boats from Tiberias to the N. E. corner of the lake. For a description of these sudden and often *lasting* gales, see Thomson, *Land and the Book*, Vol. II. p. 32, and comp. p. 188, note 2.

[2] Some little difficulty has been found in the specifications of time in the narrative owing to the inclusive nature of the term ὀψία. The following remarks will perhaps adjust the seeming discrepancies. From St Matthew (ch. xiv. 15) we learn that it was ὀψία before the men sat down. This we may reasonably suppose roughly specifies some time in the *first* evening (3 P.M.—6 P.M.), which again the ὥρα πολλή of St Mark (ch. vi. 35) would seem more nearly to define as rather towards the close than the commencement of that ὀψία. At the beginning of the *second* evening, probably soon after 6 o'clock, the disciples embark (John vi. 16), and ere this ὀψία, which extended from sunset to darkness, had quite concluded, the disciples had reached the middle of the lake (Mark vi. 47; comp. Matth. xiv. 24), and were now experiencing the full force of a gale, which probably commencing soon after sunset (comp. Thomson, *Land and the Book*, Vol. II. p. 32) was now becoming hourly more wild. For some hours they contend against it, but without making more than a few stadia (comp. John vi. 19: the lake was about forty stadia broad; Joseph. *Bell. Jud.* III. 10. 7), when in the fourth watch (Matth. xiv. 25) they beheld our Lord walking on the waters, and approaching the vessel. On the first and second evenings, see Gesenius, *Lex.* s. v. עֶרֶב, p. DCLII (Bagster), Jahn, *Archæol. Bibl.* § 101.

had not crossed the lake by the time of the fourth watch[a]; still were they toiling against the stirred-up waters and tempestuous wind, when to their bewilderment they see the Lord walking on those storm-tost waves, and as it were leading the way[1] to the haven they had so long been striving to reach. We well remember the incident of the striking but, alas! soon failing faith of St Peter[b], the ceasing of the wind, and the speedy arrival of the vessel at the land whither they were going[c]; and we have perhaps not forgotten that this miracle produced a greater impression on the Apostles than any they had yet witnessed[2]. The miracle of the multiplied loaves they could not fully appreciate. Though, as we well know, it had produced a profound effect upon those for whose sake it had been performed[d], and had caused them to confess that this was 'of a truth that prophet that should come into the world[e],' and though we cannot doubt that in such a confession the Apostles had also silently shared, yet we are plainly told by the second Evangelist[f], that their hearts were too hard and too dull to understand fully the mighty miracle at which they themselves had been permitted to minister. Here, however,

[a] Mt. xiv. 25
Mk. vi. 48

[b] Mt. xiv. 28 sq.

[c] Joh. vi. 21

[d] Joh. vi. 15

[e] ver. 14

[f] vi. 52

---

[1] See Mark vi. 48, καὶ ἤθελεν παρελθεῖν αὐτούς; and compare Lange, Leben Jesu, II. 5. 3, Part II. p. 788.

[2] On this miracle, which is one of the seven selected by St John (comp. Ewald, Gesch. Christus', p. 359, note), and which, as the Greek commentators rightly observe (see Chrysost. and Euthymius, in Matth. xiv. 33), evinces even more distinctly than the Stilling of the tempest our Lord's power over the laws that govern the material world,—see some novel, though too allegorically applied comments in Origen, in Matth. xi. 5, Vol. III. p. 484 sq. (ed. Bened.), and in Augustine, Serm. LXXV. LXXVI. Vol. V. p. 474 sq. More general comments will be found in Hall, Contempl. IV. 6, Trench, Miracles, p. 274 sq.; and notices of difficulties in this and the accompanying narrative, in Ebrard, Kritik der Evang. Geschichte, § 76, p. 391.

was something that produced on them a far deeper impression; here was something that appealed to those hardy boatmen as nought else could have appealed, and made them both with their lips and by their outward and unforbidden posture of worship^a avow for the first time collectively, that their Master was what one of them had long since separately declared Him to be^b, not only 'the king of Israel,' but 'the Son of God¹.'

^a Mt. xiv. 33
^b Joh. i. 49

Return to Capernaum; our Lord's discourse in the synagogue.

The morning brings back to the western side many² of those who had been miraculously fed the evening before, and to them in the synagogue at Capernaum (for it was the fifteenth of Nisan and a day of solemn service³) the Lord utters that sublime discourse recorded by St John, so strikingly in accordance not only with the past miracle but with the present Passover-season, wherein He declares Himself to be the Bread of Life. The whole discourse is worthy of deep attention⁴,

---

¹ On the full signification of the title 'Son of God,' as applied to our Lord in the New Testament, see the valuable remarks of Wilson, *Illustr. of the New Test.* ch. II. p. 10 sq. In the present case it is impossible to doubt that it was aught else than a full and complete recognition, not merely of our Saviour's Messiahship (Meyer), which would here be wholly out of place, but of His Divine nature and prerogatives.

² Unnecessary difficulties have been made about the transit of the multitude. Without unduly pressing ὁ ἑστηκώς (Stier), as specially implying those who remained, in contrast with those that went away, it still seems obvious from the tenor of the narrative that those who followed our Lord were only the more earnest and deeply impressed portion of the multitude. Boats they would find in abundance, as the traffic on the lake was great, and the gale would have driven boats in a direction *from* Tiberias, and obliged them to seek shelter on the north-eastern shores; see above, p. 209, note 1, and comp. Sepp, *Leben Christi*, v. 7, Vol. III. 16.

³ See Lev. xxiii. 7, Deut. xxviii. 18, from both of which passages we learn that there was to be a holy convocation on the day, and no servile work done thereon.

⁴ For good and copious comments on this discourse, the subject of

LECT. V.

as serving to confirm, perhaps in a somewhat striking way, some of the views which we were led to adopt last Sunday in regard to the spiritual state of the people of Capernaum and its neighbourhood. It seemed almost clear, you may remember, that the hostility and unbelief which the Lord met with at Capernaum was in a great degree to be traced to malignant emissaries from Jerusalem[a], subsequently joined by some Galilæan Pharisees[1]. We may reasonably conceive that these evil men had now left Galilee to celebrate the Passover, and we may in consequence be led to expect far fewer exhibitions of hatred and hostility when our Lord vouchsafes to preach in the synagogue from which they were temporarily absent. And this is exactly what we do find recorded by the fourth Evangelist. We detect traces of doubt and suspended belief in some of the assembled hearers[b], nay, we are told of murmurings from the more hostile section then present[2], when our Lord declares that He Himself was 'the bread which came down from heaven[c];' we observe too strivings[d] among themselves as to the true meaning of His weighty words[3], but we are shocked by

[a] Luke v. 17; comp. Mk. iii. 22
[b] Joh. vi. 30
[c] ver. 41
[d] ver. 52

which is the mysterious relation of our Lord to His people as the Bread of Life, and as the spiritual sustenance of believers,—see Chrysostom, in Joann. Hom. XLIV.—XLVII., Cyril Alex. in Joann. Vol. IV. pp. 295—372 (ed. Aubert), Augustine, in Joann. Tractat. XXV. XXVI. and among modern writers in Luthardt, das Johann. Evang. Part II. pp. 49—64, and Stier, Disc. of our Lord, Vol. V. pp. 149—205 (Clark).

[1] See above, p. 170, note 1.

[2] It deserves notice that the speakers are now not, as above, some of the multitude who had followed our Lord, and whose questions had received the solemn answers recorded in the earlier portion of the discourse, but are specially noticed as Ἰουδαῖοι; i. e. according to what seems St John's regular use of the term, adherents of the party that was specially hostile to our Lord: see above, p. 141, note 3.

[3] These strivings, though in a dif-

none of those outbursts of maddened hatred which on an earlier occasion[a] marked the presence of the intruders from Jerusalem. It is clear, however, that evil seed had been sown and was springing up; it is plain that our Lord's words caused offence, and that not merely to the general multitude, but, alas! to some unspiritual disciples, who, St John tells us shortly but sadly, 'went back, and walked with Him no more[b].'...But the holy Twelve were true and firm: they who a few hours before on the dark waters of the solitary lake had confessed their Master's divinity[c], now again in the face of all men declare by the mouth of St Peter[1], that they believed and were sure that 'He was Christ the Son of the living God[d].'

LECT. V.

[a] Luke vi. 11; comp. ver. 7

[b] vi. 66

[c] Mt. xiv. 33

[d] Joh. vi. 69

ferent and better spirit, have continued to this very day. Without entering deeply into the contested question of the reference of the words καὶ ὁ ἄρτος κ.τ.λ. (ver. 51), we may remark generally (1) that the allusion in ver. 50 is clearly to the Incarnation, which at the commencement of ver. 51 is more fully unfolded, and in the conclusion of that verse seems also further (καὶ ὁ ἄρτος δέ, κ.τ.λ.) followed out to its last most gracious purpose,—the giving up of the human flesh thus assumed, to atone for the sins of mankind: ἀποθνήσκω φησίν, ὑπὲρ πάντων, ἵνα πάντας ζωοποιήσω δι' ἐμαυτοῦ, Cyril Alex. in loc. Vol. IV. p. 353. This supposition, thus derived from the context, is strongly confirmed by the word σάρξ, which, especially in its present connexion, seems intended still more definitely to point to our Lord's atoning death; comp. Eph. ii. 15, Col. i. 22, 1 Pet. iii. 18. To which we may add (2) that the idea pervading the whole verse,— Christ the bread of the world, and the further explanations which our Lord Himself vouchsafes (ver. 53)— fully warrant a reference, not directly and exclusively but indirectly and inclusively, to the Holy Communion of our Lord's body and blood. For an account of the various conflicting views, see Lücke, Comment. über Joh. Vol. II. p. 152 sq. (ed. 3), Meyer, ib. p. 209 (ed. 3),—but to ascertain the *exact* opinion of the patristic writers there referred to, the student will be wise to consult the original writers.

[1] This confession of St Peter, which, as Chrysostom rightly remarks, was said in behalf of all (οὐ γὰρ εἶπεν 'ἔγνωκα,' ἀλλ' 'ἐγνώκαμεν'), is certainly not to be regarded as identical with that recorded in Matth. xvi. 16: contrast Wieseler, Chron. Synops. p. 277. Time, place and circumstances seem so clearly different that we can hardly fail to

LECT. V.

Healings in Gennesareth, and return of the Jewish emissaries.

ᵃ Mt. xiv. 35
Mk. vi. 55

ᵇ Mt. xiv. 3
Mk. vi. 56

ᶜ xv. 1
ᵈ vii. 1

Of the miraculous events that immediately followed we can only speak in general terms. Both St Matthew and St Mark here expressly mention numerous healings which were performed in the plain of Gennesareth. Both speak of the great confluence of the sick and the suffering[a]; both specify the mightiness of the power with which they were healed[b]. To the performance of these deeds of mercy a short time,—a few days perhaps,—may reasonably be assigned[1], but it was a short time only. Those healing hands were, alas! soon to be stayed. Old enemies were by this time on their way back again to bring charges and to condemn; the human agents of the kingdom of darkness were again arraying themselves against the Lord of the kingdom of Light. St Matthew[c] and St Mark[d] both relate the arrival of

admit, what is in itself highly natural, that the fervid apostle twice made a similar confession. Such seems distinctly the opinion of Chrysostom (*in loc.*), who alludes to the other confession as ἀλλαχοῦ. The exact words of the confession are not perfectly certain. We have followed above the Received Text, but as there seems *some* probability of alteration from Matth. xvi. 16 (see Meyer and Alford *in loc.*) it may be fairly questioned whether the reading of BC¹DL,ℵ,—ὁ ἅγιος τοῦ Θεοῦ, is not to be preferred.

[1] In the narrative of St Matthew there is nothing to guide us. The remark, however, of St Mark, ὅπου ἂν εἰσεπορεύετο εἰς κώμας ἢ εἰς πόλεις ἢ εἰς ἀγρούς (ch. vi. 56), seems to indicate a continued ministry in the neighbourhood of Capernaum, of at least a few days' duration. Wieseler (*Chron. Synops.* p. 311, note) seems to refer not only all these events but also the reply of our Lord to the Pharisees on the subject of eating with unwashen hands (Matth. xv. 1 sq., Mark vii. 1 sq.) to the same day as that on which the discourse on the Bread of Life was delivered, *i. e.* on Nisan 15. This, however, is by no means probable. The Pharisees and Scribes, who are specified both by the first and second Evangelists as having come *from Jerusalem*, would hardly have left the city till the festival of the Passover was fully concluded. Origen (*in Matth.* Tom. XI. 8) comments on the τότε (Matth. xv. 1) as marking a general coincidence in point of time with the healings in Gennesareth, but gives no precise opinion as to the exact time when the emissaries reappeared.

The Ministry in Northern Galilee. 215

Scribes and Pharisees from Jerusalem[1]—beyond all doubt those whose machinations we noticed in our last lecture, and who now, with the true spirit of the sect to which they belonged, had formally observed their Passover at Jerusalem, and had hastened back, as it were from the presence of the God of justice and truth, to take counsel against innocent blood. Ground of accusation is soon found out. These base men had perhaps insidiously crept into the social meetings of the disciples, and marked with malignant eyes the freedom of early evangelical life, and the charge is soon made: 'Why walk not thy disciples according to the tradition of the elders, but eat bread with unwashen hands[a]?' Stern and crushing indeed is the answer which is returned, startling the application of prophecy[b], plain the principle, declared openly and plainly to the throng of bystanders[2], that defilement is not from without but from within[c]. Complete indeed was the vindication, but dangerous in its very completeness. The Pharisees, as we learn incidentally, were now still more deeply offended[d]; their malevolence was

LECT. V.

[a] Mt. xv. 2 Mk. vii. 5

[b] Mk. vii. 6

[c] Mt. xv. 11

[d] ver. 12

---

[1] Chrysostom (*in Matth.* xv. 1) has noticed the special mention of the place whence they had come, remarking that the Scribes and Pharisees from the capital were both actuated by a worse spirit and held more in repute than those from other parts of Judæa. Hom. LI. Vol. VII. p. 585 (ed. Bened. 2); see Euthymius, *in loc.* Vol. I. p. 605.

[2] Both St Matthew and St Mark notice the fact that our Lord called the mixed multitude round Him (Matth. xv. 10, καὶ προσκαλεσάμενος τὸν ὄχλον; comp. Mark vii. 14)

and declared more especially to them (τρέπει τὸν λόγον πρὸς τὸν ὄχλον ὡς ἀξιολογώτερον, Euthym.) the principle, which the Pharisees would have been slow to admit, that defilement was from within and not from without. It would seem, however, that this was uttered in the hearing of the Pharisees, and that, as Euthymius rightly suggests, this was the λόγος (Matth. xv. 12) at which, both from its sentiment and the publicity given to it, the Pharisees were so much offended; comp. Meyer, *in loc.* p. 306 (ed. 4).

assuming hourly a more implacable form, and, not improbably, hourly becoming more and more contagious. Doubts, suspicion, and perhaps aversion[1], were now not improbably fast springing up in the minds even of those who once[a] would fain have prevented the Lord from ever leaving their highly-favoured land. Nor was this all. Other evil influences were at work not only among the people but among their rulers; for we may remember that it was but a short time before that the evil and superstitious Herod Antipas[2] had evinced a strong desire[b] to see One of whom he had heard tidings that filled him with uneasiness and perplexity[c]. And such a desire on the part of the murderer of the Baptist, we may well infer, could bode nothing but ill against One who his fears had made him believe was his victim come back again from the grave[3]. All the Lord's secret

[a] Lk. iv. 42
[b] Lk. ix. 9
[c] ver. 7

---

[1] This seems in some measure to transpire in St John's account of our Lord's recent preaching at Capernaum, especially in those expressions of thorough Nazarene unbelief (Luke iv. 22, Mark vi. 3) which followed our Lord's declaration that He was the 'Bread which came down from heaven' (John vi. 41 sq.). Though it is right to remember that these expressions came from a hostile section (see above, p. 212, note 2), yet the very presence of such a section in a synagogue where a very short time before the only feeling was amazement (Mark i. 22, Luke iv. 32) seems to show that some change of feeling was beginning decidedly to show itself.

[2] What little we know of the character of this Tetrarch is chiefly derived from what is recorded of him in the Gospels, especially in that of St Luke. Josephus notices chiefly his love of ease and expense (*Antiq.* XVIII. 7. 1 sq.), but in the sacred writers, beside the mention of his adultery, and murder of the Baptist, we also find allusions that prove him to have been a thoroughly bad man; comp. Luke iii. 19, and Nolde, *Historia Idum.* p. 251 sq.

[3] In the account given by the three Synoptical Evangelists (Matth. xiv. 1 sq., Mark vi. 14 sq., Luke ix. 7 sq.) we have the workings of a bad conscience plainly set before us. Observe the emphatic ἐγώ (Luke ix. 9), and the desire expressed to see our Lord so as to satisfy himself that the general opinion (Luke ix. 7) in which he himself seems to have shared (Matth. xiv. 2, Mark vi. 16, comp. Chrysost. *in Matth. l. c.*) was

or avowed enemies thus seemed unconsciously working together: danger was on every side, and eastern Galilee was probably fast becoming as unsafe an abode for the Redeemer and His Apostles as Judæa had been a few months before.

Journey to Tyre and Sidon, and the miracle performed there.

However this may be, the blessing of the Lord's presence was now to be vouchsafed to other lands. In the remote West and in the confines[1] of Tyre the Lord was now pleased to seek, if not for a security that was denied at Capernaum, yet for a seclusion[a] that might have been needed for a yet further instruction of the Apostles in the things pertaining to the kingdom of God. But, as St Mark records, 'He could not be hid[b].' There was faith even in those darkened and heathen lands, and a faith that in one instance at least was proved and was blessed. No sooner was it known that the Lord was there than one poor woman at once crossed the frontier[c] which as yet the Redeemer had not passed, and with those strange words on heathen lips, 'Have mercy on me, Lord, thou Son of David[d],' called upon the Lord with importunate energy to heal her demoniac daughter. The whole tenor of the narrative

[a] Mk. vii. 24
[b] ib. ver. 24
[c] Mt. xv. 22
[d] ver. 22

---

not true after all. There seems no reason for ascribing to the Tetrarch a belief in any form of transmigration of souls; (comp. Grotius *in loc.*); his words were merely the natural accents of guilty fear.

[1] This seems the correct inference from the words of St Mark (τὰ μεθόρια Τύρου, ch. vii. 24) coupled with the incidental comment of St Matthew (ἀπὸ τῶν ὁρίων ἐκείνων ἐξελθοῦσα, ch. xv. 22). At present, it would seem, our Lord had not actually crossed into the territory of Tyre, but was in the district closely contiguous to it. Origen (*in Matth.* Tom. XI. 16) rightly connects this journey with the offence given to the Pharisees by our Lord's declaration to the multitudes on the subject of inward and outward pollution (Matth. xv. 11, Mark vii. 15); comp. also Greswell, *Dissert.* XXIII. Vol. II. p. 354. That it was *also* for quiet and repose (Euthym.) is to be inferred from Mark vii. 24.

of both the Evangelists who relate the incidents seems clearly to show that this passionate call and these wildly-uttered words at first met with no response[1]. Our Lord was silent. When, however, that suppliant drew nigh, when she fell at her Redeemer's feet, and uttered those pity-moving words of truest faith, 'Lord, help me[a],' then was it that the all-merciful One beheld and vouchsafed to accept a faith that was permitted to extend the very sphere of His own mission. The Canaanite was heard, the descendant of ancient idolaters[2] was practically accounted as one of the lost sheep of the house of Israel; the devil was cast out, and the child was healed[3].

Mt. xv. 25

---

[1] See Matthew xv. 23. That this silence on the part of our Lord was designed to prove the faith of the woman is the opinion of the ancient commentators (see Chrys. *in Matth.* Hom. LII. 2), and seems certainly borne out by the trying answer of our Lord (Matth. xv. 26, Mark vii. 27) which was vouchsafed to her second entreaty. To suppose that our Lord was here condescending to the prejudices of the apostles (Milman, *Hist. of Christianity*, Vol. I. p. 253) is not probable or satisfactory; still less so is the supposition that He was simply overcome by her faithful importunity (De Wette, Meyer): as Chrysostom properly says, Εἰ μὴ δοῦναι ἔμελλεν, οὐδ' ἂν μετὰ ταῦτα ἔδωκεν. Vol. VII. p. 598 (ed. Bened. 2).

[2] The term Χαναναία, used by St Matthew (ch. xv. 22), seems fully to justify this statement. She is termed Ἑλληνίς (*i. e.* a heathen, not of Jewish descent), Συροφοινίκισσα (*Lachm.*) or Σύρα Φοινίκισσα (*Tisch.*) τῷ γένει by St Mark (ch. vii. 26), a definition perfectly accordant with that of St Matthew, as these Syro-Phœnicians probably derived their origin from the remains of old Canaanite nations which had withdrawn on the conquest of Palestine to the extreme northern coasts; comp. Winer, *RWB.* Art. 'Cananiter,' Vol. I. p. 210.

[3] On this miracle, the characteristics of which are that it was performed on one of heathen descent, at a distance from the sufferer (comp. p. 135, note 1), and in consequence of the great faith of the petitioner ('vox humilis, sed celsa fides,' Sedulius), see Chrysost. *in Matth.* Hom. LII., Augustine, *Serm.* LXXVII. Vol. V. p. 483 (ed. Migne), Bp Hall, *Contempl.* IV. 1, Trench, *Miracles*, p. 339 sq., and Lange, *Leben Jesu*, II. 5. 10, Part II. p. 865 sq. The allegorical reference according to which the woman represents the Gentile Church, and her daughter τὴν πρᾶξιν κυριευομένην ὑπὸ δαιμόνων, is briefly but perspicuously noticed by Euthymius, *in Matth.* xv. 28.

The Ministry in Northern Galilee. 219

How long our Lord abode in these regions we know not; but as this touching miracle is the only incident recorded by the Evangelists, and as the privacy which our Lord sought for, was now still less likely to be maintained, we may, perhaps, not unreasonably conclude that after a short stay, yet probably long enough for His enemies to have dispersed and returned to Jerusalem, our Lord turned His steps backward, passing through the midst of the semi-pagan Decapolis[1], and ultimately approaching the sea of Galilee, as it would seem, from the further side of the Jordan[a]. Equally, or nearly equally ignorant are we of the extent of this northern journey: if, however, we adopt a reading which now finds a place in most critical editions[2], we are certainly led to extend this journey beyond the Tyrian frontier, and further to draw the interesting inference, that our Lord, moved probably by the great faith of the Syro-Phœnician woman, actually passed into the heathen territory, visited ancient and idolatrous Sidon[3], and from the neighbourhood of that city commenced His south-easterly circuit toward De-

LECT. V.

Return towards Decapolis, and the eastern shore of the lake.

[a] Comp. Mk. vii. 31

---

[1] See above, p. 206, note 4, where the character of this confederation is briefly noticed.

[2] The reading in question is ἦλθεν διὰ Σιδῶνος (Mark vii. 31), which is found in the Codex Vaticanus and Codex Bezæ, in the valuable MS. marked L, in ℵ, Δ (Cod. Sangall.), and in several ancient versions of considerable critical value, e.g. the Old Latin, Vulgate, Coptic, and Ethiopic. It has been adopted by Lachmann, Tischendorf, Fritzsche, Meyer, Alford, and Tregelles, and appears certainly to deserve the preference which these critics and commentators have thus unanimously given to it: see Meyer, *Komment. üb. Mark.* p. 80 (ed. 3).

[3] It is not safe to enlarge upon a point which rests only on a probable reading; but, if we accept this reading, it must be acknowledged as a fact of the greatest significance in reference to the subsequent diffusion of the Gospel, that the City of Baal and of Astarte was visited by the Redeemer of mankind; see above, p. 201. This question is worthy of further consideration.

capolis and the further shore of the sea of Gennesareth.

Return to Decapolis; healing of a deaf and dumb man.

On that shore He was not now to be a strange and unwelcome [a] visitor. There, in that region of Decapolis, lips by which devils once had spoken had already proclaimed [b] the power and majesty of Him that had now vouchsafed to journey through that darkened land;—and there too those lips had not spoken in vain. No sooner had the Lord appeared among them, than, as St Mark relates to us [c], His healing powers are besought for a deaf and all but dumb man who is brought to Him, and brought only to be healed [1].... It is worthy of a moment's notice that both this, and a miracle performed shortly afterwards on a blind man at Bethsaida-Julias [d], were accompanied with a withdrawal of the sufferer from the throng of bystanders, special outward signs, and, in the case of the latter miracle, a more gradual process of restoration. All these differences it is undoubtedly right to connect with something peculiar in the individual cases of those on whom the miracle was performed [2]; yet still it does not seem improper to take into consideration the general fact that these were miracles performed in lands which

[a] Contrast Mt. viii. 34
[b] Mk. v. 20 Lk. viii. 39
[c] vii. 32
[d] Mk. viii. 22

---

[1] On this miracle, the characteristics of which are alluded to in the text, see the comments of Maldonatus and Olshausen, Hook, *Serm. on the Miracles*, Vol. II. p. 49 sq., Trench, *Notes on the Miracles*, p. 348 sq., and Hare (Jul.), *Serm.* XIV. Vol. I. p. 245.

[2] See Olshausen *on the Gospels*, Vol. II. p. 206 (Clark), who comments at some length on the peculiarities in the performance of this miracle, and in that of the Healing of the blind man at Bethsaida. Some good comments will also be found in Maldonatus, *Comment. in Marc.* vii. 33. The withdrawal from the crowd is ascribed by the scholiast in Cramer's *Catenæ* (Vol. I. p. 338) to a desire on the part of our Lord to avoid display (ἵνα μὴ δόξῃ ἐπιδεικτικῶς ἐπιτελεῖν τὰς θεοσημίας); but this, in the present case, seems very doubtful.

the Lord had not before traversed,—lands where the nature of His healing powers might have been wholly misunderstood, and to which, for the spiritual benefit of the sufferers, it was judged meet that their earnest and deliberate attention[1] should be especially directed. Both these miracles, we may also observe, were accompanied with a command to preserve silence[2],—but in the case of the present miracle it was signally disobeyed[a]. So widely indeed was the fame of it spread abroad that great multitudes, as we are told by St Matthew[b], brought their sick unto the Lord; and He, who as He Himself had but recently declared[c], was not come 'save to the lost sheep of the house of Israel,' nevertheless sought His Father's glory even amidst half-Gentile Decapolis; so that it is not perhaps without deep meaning that the first Evangelist[d] tells us that 'they glorified the God of Israel[3].' And they were yet to glorify Him more, and to be the witnesses of the creative as well as of the healing powers of His beloved Son....Those eager-hearted men had now so swelled in numbers that four thousand, without

[a] Mk. vii. 36
[b] xv. 30
[c] ver. 24
[d] xv. 31

The Feeding of the four thousand.

---

[1] So in effect Maldonatus: 'Quia ergo qui surdi sunt, videntur re aliquâ obturatas habere aures, mittit digitum in aures surdi, quasi clausas et obturatas terebraturus, aut impedimentum, quod in illis erat, ablaturus digito. Et quia qui muti sunt, videntur ligatam nimiâ siccitate habere linguam (?), palatoque adhærentem, ideoque loqui non posse...mittit salivam in os muti, quasi ejus linguam humectaturus.' Vol. I. p. 762 (Mogunt. 1611).

[2] See above, p. 192, note 1.

[3] This did not escape the notice of Origen (*in Matth.* Tom. XI. 18), who remarks as follows: 'Yea, they glorify Him, being persuaded that the Father of Him who healed the man above mentioned is one and the same God with the God of Israel; for God is not the God of the Jews only but also of the Gentiles.' Vol. III. p. 508 (ed. Bened.). Theophylact (*in Matth.* xv. 29) places the scene in Galilee, but, as the parallel passage in St Mark (ch. vii. 31 sq.) seems clearly to prove, not correctly; compare Robinson, *Palestine*, Vol. II. p. 397, note 2.

counting women and children^a, were gathered round the Lord and His Apostles, and He who had so pitied and relieved their afflictions, now pitied and relieved their wants. They had come from far^b; they were faint and weary, and were to be miraculously refreshed. Seven loaves feed the four thousand, just as, a few weeks before, and perhaps not far from the same spot[1], five loaves had fed a great number: 'they did all eat,' says the first Evangelist, 'and were filled, and they took up of the broken meat that was left seven baskets full^c.'

Mt. xv. 38
Mk. viii. 3
Mt. xv. 37

Not identical with the Feeding of the five thousand.

We may here pause, yet for a moment only, to make our decided protest against that shallow criticism which would persuade us that this distinctive miracle is merely an ill-remembered reproduction of the Feeding of the five thousand a few weeks before[2]. Few opinions can be met more easily; few of the many misstatements that have been made in reference to the miracles of our Redeemer can be disposed of more readily and more satisfactorily. Let it be observed only that everything that might seem most clearly to specify and to characterize is different in the two miracles.

---

[1] The locality is not very clearly defined. That it was an uninhabited place appears from Matth. xv. 33, and that it was on the high ground east of the lake may be inferred from ver. 29. As the spot to which our Lord crosses over is situated about the middle of the western coast, we may perhaps consider the high ground in the neighbourhood of the ravine nearly opposite to Magdala, which is now called Wady Semak, as not very improbably the site of the present miracle.

[2] See for example, De Wette, *on Matth.* xv. 29, and Neander, *Life of Christ*, p. 287, note (Bohn). The remarks in the text seem sufficiently to demonstrate that such a view is wholly untenable; see more in Olshausen, *Comment.* Vol. II. p. 209 sq. (Clark), Ebrard, *Kritik der Ev. Gesch.* § 86, p. 433; and compare Origen, *in Matth.* xi. 19, Vol. III. p. 509 (ed. Bened.), Alford, *Commentary*, Vol. I. p. 157 (ed. 4).

The number of loaves in the latter miracle is greater; the number of fish greater; the remnants collected less; the people fewer; the time they had tarried longer; their behaviour in the sequel noticeably different. The more excitable inhabitants of the coast-villages of the North and the West[1], we are distinctly told, would have borne away our Lord and made Him a king[a], if He had not withdrawn into the mountains; the men of Decapolis and the eastern shores permit the Lord to leave them without any recorded excitement or demonstration. Let all these things be fairly considered, and there will, I firmly believe, be found few indeed who will question our Lord's own declarations[b], or raise any difficulty as to the separate and distinct nature of this second manifestation of His creative beneficence[2]. Immediately after this miracle our Lord leaves a land which seems to

[a] Joh. vi. 15

[b] Mt. xvi. 9 sq.

Return to the western side of the lake.

---

[1] The recipients in the case of the former miracle appear to have come mainly from the western side; comp. Mark vi. 33. They followed our Lord, we are told, on foot (Matth. xiv. 13), and would consequently have passed round the northern extremity of the lake, receiving probably, as they went, additions from Bethsaida-Julias and the places in its vicinity. Chrysostom (*in Matth.* Hom. LIII. 2) seems to imply that the effect produced by this miracle was as great as that produced by the former miracle; this may have been so, but it certainly cannot be inferred from the words of the sacred narrative.

[2] On the miracle itself, which Origen (*in Matth.* Tom. XI. 19), though on somewhat insufficient reasons, considers as even greater than that of the Feeding of the five thousand, see Origen, *l. c.*, Hilary, *in Matth.* Can. XV. p. 342 (Paris, 1631), Augustine, *Serm.* LXXXI. Append. (but apparently rightly regarded by Trench as genuine), Vol. V. p. 1902 (ed. Migne), Hook, *Serm. on the Miracles*, Vol. II. p. 66, Trench, *Notes on the Miracles*, p. 355. The idea of Hilary (*loc. cit.*) that the former miracle has reference mainly to the Jews, the present miracle to the Gentiles, is perhaps not wholly fanciful; the multitude in the present case we may reasonably conceive to have been collected nearly entirely from Decapolis, and so mainly Gentile; the multitude in the former case, as we have observed, was apparently from Capernaum and its vicinity, and probably mainly Jewish; compare p. 203. note 2.

have displayed somewhat striking faith, and on which His Divine visit could hardly have failed to have exercised a permanent spiritual influence, for the familiar shores on the opposite side of the lake. He crosses over to Magdala[1], or perhaps to some village close to the high ground in its vicinity, which seems alluded to in the designation Dalmanutha[2], as specified by the second Evangelist[a]. But there His abode was short. The evil wrought by the emissaries from Jerusalem was now only too mournfully apparent. No sooner was the Lord arrived than Pharisees, now for the first time leagued with Sadducees, as once before they had combined with Herodians[b], come to Him with the sceptical demand of a sign from heaven[c]. Amid such faithless and probably malevolent hearts the Lord vouchsafes not to tarry, but, as it would seem immediately, enters

[a] viii. 10

[b] Mk. iii. 6

[c] Mt. xvi. 1

---

[1] This place is now unanimously regarded by recent travellers as situated, not on the eastern side of the lake (Lightfoot, *Decas Chorographica Marco præmissa*, cap. v. 1), but on the western side, and at the miserable collection of huts now known by the name of 'el-Medjel;' see Robinson, *Palestine*, Vol. II. p. 397 (ed. 2), Thomson, *Land and the Book*, Vol. II. p. 108, where there is a sketch of this forlorn village, and Van de Velde, *Memoir*, p. 334. It is proper to observe that some MSS. and versions of importance (BD; Vulg., Old Lat., al.) read Μαγαδάν, and that this reading has been adopted by some recent editors: see Caspari, *Chron.-Geogr. Einleit.* § 73, p. 90. Of this latter place nothing seems to be known; the identification with Megiddo (Ewald, *Drei Erst. Evv.* p. 268, *Gesch. Christus*', p. 333) does not seem very probable.

[2] The exact locality of Dalmanutha is difficult to trace. It must clearly have been near to Magdala, as St Mark (ch. viii. 10) specifies it as the place into the neighbourhood of which our Lord arrived in the transit across the lake which we are now considering. If we accept the not improbable derivation of דָרב 'was pointed' (Wieseler, *Chron. Synops.* p. 312), we may fix the locality as close to or among the cliffs (see Thomson's sketch) which rise at a short distance from Magdala. Porter identifies Dalmanutha with 'Ain el-Bârideh' (Smith, *Dict. of Bible*, Vol. I. p. 381), situated at the mouth of a narrow glen a mile south of Magdala; but this appears only to rest on the fact that ruins are found there.

The Ministry in Northern Galilee. 225

the vessel in which he had come[1], and with warning words to them[a], and a special caution to His disciples against the leaven of their teaching[b], crosses over to Bethsaida-Julias, and there performs the progressively-developed miracle of healing the blind man to which we have recently alluded[2].

From thence we trace the Lord's steps northward to the towns and villages in the neighbourhood of the remote city of Cæsarea Philippi[3], near which it is just possible that he might have passed in His circuit from Sidon a very few weeks before....Of the exact purpose of this journey or of the special events connected with it we have no certain knowledge, though we may reasonably infer, from the incidental mention of a formal address to the multitude[c] as well as to the disciples, that public teaching and preaching rather than

LECT. V.

[a] Mt. xv. 2 sq.
[b] xvi. 6 Mk. viii. 15

Journey northward to Cæsarea Philippi.

[c] Mk. viii. 34

---

[1] The words of St Mark are here so very distinct (πάλιν ἐμβὰς ἀπῆλθεν, ch. viii. 13) that the supposition of Fritzsche, that our Lord crossed over alone to the place where He was questioned by the Pharisees, and that he was afterwards joined by His disciples (Matth. xvi. 6), must be pronounced wholly untenable. The disciples are mentioned specially and by themselves (Matth. xvi. 5), simply because they alone form the subject of the ἐπελάθοντο, and because this act indirectly gave rise to the warning instructions which follow.

[2] On this miracle, the chief characteristic of which is the very gradual and progressive nature of the cure, see the comments of Olshausen above alluded to (*Comment.* Vol. II. p. 206, Clark), Trench, *Notes on the Miracles*, p. 359, Hook, *Serm. on the Miracles*, Vol. II. p. 20. The Bethsaida here mentioned is clearly not the village on the western side (comp. Theophylact *in loc.*) but Bethsaida-Julias, by which the Lord would naturally have passed in his northward journey to Cæsarea Philippi.

[3] This picturesquely placed city, formerly called Panium (Joseph. *Antiq.* XV. 10. 3) or Paneas, from a cavern sacred to Pan in its vicinity (see Winer, *RWB.* Vol. I. p. 207, Stanley, *Palest.* p. 394), received its subsequent name from the Tetrarch Philip, by whom it was enlarged and beautified (Joseph. *Antiq.* XVIII. 2. 1, *Bell. Jud.* II. 9. 1). For a description of its site see Robinson, *Palestine*, Vol. III. p. 408 sq. (ed. 2), Caspari, *Chron.-Geogr. Einleit.* § 122, p. 139, and compare Thomson, *Land and the Book*, Vol. I. p. 344 sq., where there is a sketch of the singular cavern above alluded to.

seclusion was the object of this extended circuit. However this may be, with those regions we connect three circumstances of considerable moment; *First*, the remarkable profession of faith in Christ as the Son of the living God uttered by St Peter as the ready spokesman of the rest of the Apostles, accompanied by the remarkable charge on the part of the Lord that they should tell it to no man[1]; *Secondly*, and as it would seem almost immediately afterwards, the Lord's first formal prediction of His own sufferings and death—a prediction which jarred strangely on the ears of men who now seem to have begun to realize more fully the Divine nature and Messiahship of their beloved Master[2]; *Thirdly*, the Transfiguration, which a precise note of time supplied by two Evangelists[a] fixes as six days from some epoch not defined, but which the more general comment of St Luke[b] seems to imply was that of the above-mentioned confession, and of the discourses associated with it[3].

[a] Mt. xvii. 1
Mk. ix. 2

[b] ix. 28

---

[1] The true reason for this strict command (διεστείλατο, Matth. xvi. 20), at which Origen (*in Matth.* Tom. xii. 15) appears to have felt some difficulty, would seem to be one which almost naturally suggests itself; viz. that our Lord's time was not yet come, and that expectations were not to be roused among those who would have sought to realize them in tumults and popular excitement. As Cyril of Alexandria well says, 'He commanded them to guard the mystery by a seasonable silence, until the whole plan of the dispensation should arrive at a suitable conclusion.' *Comment. on St Luke*, Part I. p. 220.

[2] On this prediction, see a good sermon by Horsley, *Serm.* XIX. Vol. II. p. 121 (Dundee, 1810).

[3] The six days are regarded by Lightfoot (*Chron. Temp.* LIII.) as dating from the words last spoken by our Lord. This view differs but little from that adopted in the text, as the confession of St Peter seems to stand in close connexion with the Lord's announcement of His own sufferings (see Luke ix. 21, 22), and this last announcement to have suggested what follows. A more inclusive reference, however, as well to the important confession as to what followed, appears, on the whole, more simple and more probable. The ώσεί of St Luke (ch. ix. 28) shows that there is no necessity to

The Ministry in Northern Galilee. 227

On the mysteries connected with this third event,—the glorified aspect of Him whose very garments shone bright as the snows of the mountain on which He was standing[a],—the personal presence of Moses and Elias,—the Divine voice, not only of paternal love, but of exhortation and command, 'Hear ye Him[b],'—and the injunction of the Saviour to seal all in silence till the Son of Man be risen from the dead[c],—on all this our present limits will not permit me to enlarge. Let me only remark, first, as to *locality*,—that there seems every reason for fixing the scene of the Transfiguration, not on the more southern Tabor, but on one of the lofty spurs of the snow-capt Hermon[1]; Secondly, as to its *meaning* and *significance*,—that we may, not without reason, regard the whole as in mysterious connexion both with St Peter's profession of faith and with that saddening prediction which followed it, and which, it has been specially revealed, formed the subject of the mystic converse between the Lord and His two attendant saints[d]. That the Transfiguration appears generally to have had, what may be termed,

LECT. V.

The locality and significance of the Transfiguration.

[a] Mk. ix. 3
[b] Mt. xvii. 5; contrast iii. 17
[c] Mk. ix. 9

[d] Lk. ix. 31

attempt a formal reconciliation (see Chrysost. *in loc.*) of his note of time with that supplied by St Matthew and St Mark.
[1] So rightly Lightfoot (*Hor. Hebr. in Marc.* ix. 2), Reland (*Palæst.* p. 334 sq.), and apparently the majority of the best recent commentators. The objections of Lightfoot to the traditional site, founded on the high improbability of so sudden a change of place, are nearly conclusive; and when we add to this that the summit of Tabor was then occupied by a fortified town (see Robinson, *Palestine*, Vol. II. p. 359) we seem certainly warranted in rejecting a tradition though as old as the 6th century: see also Caspari, *Chron.-Geogr. Einleit.* § 125, p. 142. The incidental simile, ὡς χιών, of the graphic St Mark (ch. ix. 3) might well have been supplied to him by one to whom the snow-capt mountain suggested it; the reading, however, though fairly probable (see Meyer, *Komm. üb. Mark.* p. 97) is not certain, ὡς χιών not being found in two of the four leading manuscripts.

15—2

LECT. V.

a *theological* aspect, and was designed to show that the Law and the Prophets had now become a part of the Gospel, cannot reasonably be doubted; but that it was also designed to confirm the faith of the Apostles who witnessed it, and to supply them with spiritual strength against those hours of suffering and trial which our Lord had recently predicted, seems pressed upon us by the position it occupies in the sacred narrative[1].

The healing of a demoniac boy.

And the practical faith of the Apostles was verily still weak, for, on the very day that followed, their want of spiritual strength to heal a deaf and dumb[a] demoniac afforded an opportunity, only too readily seized, to some Scribes who were present, of making it fully known to the gathering multitudes. They were in the very act, St Mark tells us, of questioning with the disciples[b], when the Lord, with His face perchance still reflecting

[a] Mk. ix. 25
[b] ver. 14

---

[1] This view seems certainly to have been considered probable by Chrysostom, who states as a fifth reason why Moses and Elias appeared in attendance on the Lord, that it was 'to comfort Peter and those who regarded with fear the (Lord's) suffering, and to raise up their thoughts,' in *Matth.* Hom. LI. 2, Vol. VII. p. 638 (ed. Bened. 2); comp. Cyril Alex. *on St Luke,* Serm. LI. Part II. p. 227 (Transl.). The last-mentioned writer, it is proper to be observed, also clearly states the reason alluded to in the text for the appearance of Moses and Elias (*ib.* p. 228), and so, as we might imagine, does Origen, who briefly but pertinently says, 'Moses the Law and Elias the Prophets are become one, and united with Jesus the Gospel.' *In Matth.* Tom. XII. 43, Vol. III. p. 565 (ed. Bened.). On the subject generally, besides the writers above referred to, see August. *Serm.* LXXVIII. Vol. V. p. 490 (ed. Migne), Hall, *Contempl.* IV. 12, Hacket, *VII. Serm.* p. 441 sq. (Lond. 1675), Frank, *Serm.* XLVII. Vol. II. p. 318 (A.-C. L.), Lange, *Leben Jesu,* II. 512, Part II. p. 902, and Olshausen, *Commentary,* Vol. II. p. 228 sq. (Clark). The opinion that this holy mystery was a sleeping or waking vision (comp. Milman, *Hist. of Christianity,* Vol. I. p. 258), though as old as the days of Tertullian (*contr. Marc.* IV. 22), is at once to be rejected, as plainly at variance with the clear, distinct, objective statements of the three inspired narrators: see Caspari, *Chron.-Geogr. Einleit.* § 124, p. 141.

the glories of the past night[1], comes among the disputing and amazed[a] throng. After a general rebuke for the want of faith shown by all around[2], the Lord commands the hapless lad to be brought to Him....The recital of what followed from the pen of St Mark is here in the highest degree graphic and sublime. The whole scene seems at once to come up before us: the paroxysm of demoniacal violence brought on by proximity to the Redeemer[3],—the foaming and wallowing sufferer[b], —the retarded cure till the faith of the father is made fully apparent[c],—the crowding multitude[d]; and then the word of power, the last struggle of the departing demon[e], the prostration of the lad after

LECT. V.
[a] Mk. ix. 15
[b] ver. 20
[c] ver. 23
[d] ver. 25
[e] ver. 26

---

[1] This, as Euthymius (2d altern.) suggests, may perhaps be inferred from, and be the natural explanation of, the strong word ἐξεθαμβήθησαν (καὶ γὰρ εἰκὸς ἐφέλκεσθαί τινα χάριν ἐκ τῆς μεταμορφώσεως), with which St Mark (ch. ix. 15), whose account of this miracle is peculiarly full and graphic (see Da Costa, *The Four Witnesses*, p. 78 sq.), describes the feelings of the multitude when they beheld our Lord; compare also Bengel *in loc.*

[2] The αὐτοῖς (Mark ix. 19, Lachm., Tisch.) may refer only to the disciples (Meyer), but our Lord's use of the strong term, 'perverted' as well as 'faithless' (ὦ γενεὰ ἄπιστος καὶ διεστραμμένη), specified both by St Matthew and St Luke, would seem to show that the address is to both parties, if indeed not principally to the disputing Scribes. Perverted feelings were far more at work in the συζήτησις of the Scribes than in the exhibition of the imperfect faith of the disciples that probably tended to provoke it: see Lightfoot, *Hor.*

Hebr. in Matth. xvii. 17.

[3] This seems implied in the words καὶ ἰδὼν [sc. ὁ δαιμονιζόμενος; see Meyer *in loc.*] αὐτόν, τὸ πνεῦμα εὐθὺς ἐσπάραξεν αὐτόν (Mark ix. 20). Something similar may be observed in the case of the demoniac in the synagogue at Capernaum (Luke iv. 34 ; comp. Lect. IV. p. 164) and that of the Gergesene demoniacs (Mark v. 6 sq., Luke viii. 28). Lange (*Leben Jesu*, II. 5. 13, Part II. p. 921) considers the paroxysm as an evidence that the power of our Lord was already working upon the lad, but the view adopted in the text seems more simple and natural. For further comments on this miracle, see Origen, *in Matth.* xiii. 3 sq. Vol. III. p. 574 (ed. Bened.), Cyril Alex. *Comment. on St Luke*, Serm. LII. Part I. p. 231 sq. (Transl.), Bp Hall, *Contempl.* IV. 19, Trench, *Notes on the Miracles*, p. 362 sq., and the careful exposition of the whole narrative in Olshausen, *Commentary on the Gospels*, Vol. II. p. 238 sq. (Clark).

LECT. V.

ᵃ Mk. ix. 27

Return to and probably temporary seclusion at Capernaum.

the fierceness of the reaction, and the upraising hand of the great Healerᵃ,—all tend to make up one of those striking pictures which so noticeably diversify the inspired narrative of the second Evangelist, and which could have only come originally from one who heard, and saw, and believed¹.

Our Lord's steps appear now to have been again turned southward, through Galilee towards Capernaum, at which place the next recorded event is the miraculous payment of the tribute-money. If, as seems most natural both from the peculiar use of the term (τὰ δίδραχμα), and still more from the context, we retain the old opinion that it was the half-shekel for the Temple-service², we must attribute the present tardy

---

¹ It is scarcely necessary to remark that reference is here made to the early and universally received tradition that St Mark's Gospel was written under the guidance of St Peter, and embodies the substance, if not in some cases the very words, of that Apostle's teaching. The principal testimonies of antiquity on which this assertion rests have been already referred to (Lect. I. p. 13, note 4), to which we may add Tertullian, *contr. Marc.* IV. 5. See further, if necessary, Guerike (*Einleitung in das N. T.* § 39, 2, p. 254 ed. 2), and the introductory comments of Meyer (*Komment.* p. 3), who seems fairly to admit the truth of the ancient tradition.

² This sum was to be paid every year for the service of the sanctuary (Exod. xxx. 13; comp. 2 Kings xii. 4, 2 Chron. xxiv. 6, 9) by every male who had attained the age of twenty years (see Winer, *RWB.* Art. 'Abgaben,' Vol. I. p. 4), and as we learn from the *Mishna* ('Shekalim,'

1, 3), was levied in the month Adar. We seem therefore obliged to have recourse to some supposition like that advanced in the text; compare Lightfoot, *Hor. Heb. in loc.* Vol. II. p. 341 sq. (Roterod. 1686), and see Greswell, *Dissert.* XXIII. Vol. II. p. 377, who gives some reason for thinking that the tax might have been regularly *paid* about the feast of Tabernacles. Caspari refers the event to a later period in the history, and places it after the feast of Dedication; see *Chron.-Geogr. Einleit.* § 136, p. 154. This however involves a greater dislocation of the order in St Matthew's Gospel than seems warranted by the general narrative. The opinion of most of the ancient expositors that the reference is here to a tribute which each male had to pay to the *Roman* government ('tributum Cæsarcum,' Sedulius) is noticed, not disapprovingly, by Lightfoot, and has been zealously defended by Wieseler (*Chron. Synops.* p. 264 sq.), but

demand of a tax levied some months before, either to the Lord's frequent absences from Capernaum, or to some habit of delayed collection which may very likely have prevailed in places remote from Jerusalem, but which, from deficient knowledge of local customs, we are unable formally to substantiate[1].... The present stay at Capernaum was probably short, and, as far as we can infer from the Lord's desire expressed on His homeward journey to remain unobserved[a], one of comparative seclusion. He had now to prepare the minds of His chosen ones for the heavy trials through which they must soon pass when their Master was delivered up into the hands of men, and when their longings for a triumphant Messiah were to be changed into the avowal of a crucified Saviour. On their late return through Galilee, when their hearts were dwelling most on their Lord's powers[b], their elation was checked by a renewal of the sad prediction which they first heard near Cæsarea Philippi; and now again, in the quiet of home[c], the same holy anxiety may be traced to check that pride of spirit which seems to have been sen-

[a] Mk. ix. 30

[b] Lk. ix. 43

[c] Mk. ix. 33

to such a view the words of our Lord (Matth. xvii. 25, 26) seem distinctly opposed. What our Lord implies by His question to St Peter, and His comment on the Apostle's answer, seems clearly this:—as Son of Him to whom the temple was dedicated, and, indeed as Himself the Lord thereof, He had fullest claim to be exempted from the tribute, but still He would not avail Himself of His undoubted prerogatives: see Hammond *in loc.*, whose discussion of this passage is both clear and convincing.

[1] On the remarkable miracle by which the half-shekel was paid, the design of which, we may humbly conceive, was still further to illustrate and substantiate what was implied in the address to the Apostle ('in medio actu submissionis emicat majestas.' Bengel),—see the extremely good comments of Trench, *Notes on the Miracles*, p. 372. The older expositors cannot here be referred to with advantage, as they nearly all adopt the apparently erroneous opinion above alluded to, that it was a tribute which was paid to the *Roman* government, and adapt their comments accordingly.

sibly manifesting itself in the apostolic company. Such manifestations were apparently of a mixed character, and were probably due to very different influences. On the one hand, we may connect them with a more real conviction of their Lord's Divine nature and Messiahship; on the other hand, we cannot fail to observe that they involved much that was merely carnal and worldly. This pride of spirit showed itself, as we are especially informed, in unbecoming contentions among themselves about future preeminence[a], and led them overhastily to forbid some yet undeclared disciple[1] who was casting out devils in their Master's name from continuing to do, what they might have remembered they themselves could not do, a week or two before, when an agonized father called to them for help, and when Scribes stood by and scoffed. Humility[b], forbearance[c], avoidance of all grounds of offence[d], love towards their Master's little ones[e], gentleness, and forgiveness, the lost sheep[f], and the debtor of the ten thousand talents[g], were the wise and loving lessons which the Lord now specially vouchsafed to them in this brief period of tranquillity and seclusion.

Marginalia: Lk. ix. 46; [b] Mk. ix. 33; [c] ver. 38; [d] Mt. xviii. 6; [e] ver. 10; [f] ver. 12 sq.; [g] ver. 23 sq.

---

[1] It would seem clear from our Lord's words that the man was no deceiver or exorcist, but one, who, as Cyril of Alexandria observes, though 'not numbered among the holy Apostles, was yet crowned with apostolic powers.' *Comment. on St Luke*, Serm. LV. Part 1. p. 249 (Transl.), where there are some other good comments on this very suggestive incident. The connexion of thought between the notice of this occurrence on the part of St John and the words of our Lord which preceded is perhaps more clearly to be traced in St Mark (ch. ix. 37, 38) than in St Luke (ch. ix. 49). Our Lord's declaration, ὃς ἂν ἓν τῶν τοιούτων παιδίων δέξηται ἐπὶ τῷ ὀνόματί μου ἐμὲ δέχεται, seems to bring to the remembrance of St John a recent case which appeared at variance with his Master's words, viz. that of one who used the Lord's *name* and yet did not evince his *reception* of Him by becoming an avowed disciple. The remembrance, coupled perhaps, as Theophylact suggests, with the feeling that their treatment of that case had not been right, gives rise to the mention of it to our Lord.

And here this portion of our meditations comes to a natural and suitable close[1]. Yet ere we part let us spend a few moments in recapitulation and retrospect.

We have considered this afternoon what I think we cannot but deem a most interesting part of our Redeemer's ministry, and yet one which does not perhaps always so distinctly present itself to the general reader as other and more sharply defined portions of the Gospel history. We have perhaps been led to admit the appearance of a gradual enlargement of the sphere of our Master's personal ministries; we have journeyed with Him in half-heathen lands; we have seen saving mercies extended to those who were not of the stock of Abraham; we have seen that Divine presence not withheld from the dwellers in Decapolis; nay more, we have seemed to see[2] that priceless bless

Lect. V.

Conclusion and recapitulation.

---

[1] After this period, as will be seen in the following Lecture, the nature of our Lord's ministerial labours and the character of His missionary journeys appear to assume a completely different aspect. The whole wears the character of being what St Luke very fitly terms it,—αἱ ἡμέραι τῆς ἀναλήψεως (ch. ix. 51). Though Jerusalem is the point towards which the journeys tend, and Judæa the land to which a portion of the ministry is confined, yet the whole period is so marked by interruptions and removals, that we can hardly consider it as standing in ministerial connexion with any former period: see above Lect. III. p. 144, note 1.

[2] Here, as it has already been observed, it is our duty to speak with caution. That our Lord approached that portion of Palestine which was termed the 'confines of Tyre' (τὰ μεθόρια Τύρου, Mark vii. 24,—if with Tischendorf we adopt the shorter reading), or, with more latitude, the 'parts of Tyre and Sidon' (τὰ μέρη Τύρου καὶ Σιδῶνος, Matth. xv. 21), is indisputable, but that He was pleased actually to cross the frontier rests really upon a probable though contested reading: see above, p. 218, note 2. Modern writers appear often to have felt a difficulty in the supposition that our Lord went beyond the Jewish border (comp. Meyer, üb. Matth. xv. 21), but this feeling does not seem to have prevailed equally among the earlier writers, some of whom, as Chrysostom, in Matth. Hom. LII. 1, not only speak of our Lord's having departed εἰς ὁδὸν ἐθνῶν, but endeavour to account for His having acted contrary to a command which

LECT. V.

*Matt. xxviii. 19

ing vouchsafed to strictly pagan regions; the land of Baal and of Ashtoreth; yea, we have beheld as it were the Lord's prophetic performance of His own subsequent command^a, that the message of mercy should be published not only in Judæa and Jerusalem but even to the uttermost bounds of the wide heathen world. All this we have seen and dwelt upon,—and I trust not dwelt upon wholly in vain....To some perchance the grouping of events which I have ventured to advocate may seem to wear the aspect of partial novelty; to others again I may have seemed to press unduly characteristics to which they may feel disposed to assign a different or a modified application. Be this, however, as it may; whether such a survey of this portion of our Lord's life be regarded as plausible or improbable; whether such an endeavour to trace the connexion of events during a period where connexion is doubtful be deemed hopeful or precarious, matters but little provided only it may have so far arrested the student's attention as to lead him to examine for himself, patiently and thoughtfully, the harmonies in the narrative of his Master's life[1]. Yea, I will joy-

He Himself gave to His Apostles; compare Matth. x. 5.

[1] It is much to be feared that the tendency of our more modern study of the Gospels is to regard every attempt to harmonize the sacred narrative with indifference, if not sometimes even with suspicion. We may concede that recent harmonistic efforts, viewed generally, though made with the most loyal feelings towards the inspired Word, have in many cases been such as cannot stand the test of criticism. Nay we may go farther and say, that the modern tendency to study each Gospel by itself, rather than in connexion with the rest, is undoubtedly just and right, so long as the object proposed is a more complete realization of the view of our Lord's life as presented by each of the sacred writers, and so long as it is considered preparatory to further combinations. All this we may willingly concede, and yet we may with justice most strongly urge the extreme importance, not only in a

fully count all as nought, if only I have been enabled by the help of God to stir up in others a desire to look more closely into the connexion of the inspired record, and have helped to strengthen the belief that the earnest student may unceasingly derive from it fresh subjects for meditation, and that the seeker may verily hope to find.

May God move us all to dwell upon such things with an ever fresh and ever renewing interest. May His eternal Spirit guide us into all truth; and may He on whose blessed words and deeds we have mused this afternoon, lovingly draw us, heart and soul and spirit, to Himself. May we really feel that to commune with Him here on earth is the most blessed privilege that the Lord has reserved for those that love Him;—yea, that it is a very antepast of the joys of those realms where He now is,—a very foretaste of that blessed and final union, when, whether summoned forth from the holy calm of Paradise, or borne aloft from earth by upbearing clouds[1], the servants of Jesus shall enter into their Redeemer's presence, and dwell with Him, for ever and for ever.

---

mere critical, but even in a devotional point of view, of obtaining as complete and connected a view of our Lord's life and ministry as can possibly be obtained from our existing inspired records. And this, let it be remembered, can only be done by that patient and thoughtful comparison of Scripture with Scripture which finds such very little favour with so many theologians of our present day. The general principle on which such comparisons ought to be made we have already endeavoured to indicate: see Lect. I. p. 17 sq.

[1] See 1 Thess. iv. 17, ἁρπαγησόμεθα ἐν νεφέλαις,—on which we here pause only to make the passing comment, that the sublime picture the inspired words present is commonly missed by the general reader, and perhaps obscured by the collocation of words and insertion of the article in our Authorized Version. The Greek text appears to imply that the clouds are, as it were, the triumphal chariots in which the holy living, and as it would seem also, the holy dead, will be borne aloft to meet their coming Lord: see *Commentary on* 1 *Thess.* p. 66.

LECTURE VI.

THE JOURNEYINGS TOWARD JERUSALEM.

St Luke ix. 58.

And Jesus said unto him, Foxes have holes, and birds of the air have nests: but the Son of Man hath not where to lay His head.

LECT. VI.

General character of the present portion of the inspired narrative.

THESE mournful and affecting words, which were uttered nearly at the commencement of the period which we are now about to consider, form I think a very suitable text for our present meditations.

The scene now strikingly changes. Last Sunday we had before us the deeply interesting record of missionary journeys into heathen and half-heathen lands. We seemed to follow our Lord's steps to the very gates of idolatrous Sidon[1], we beheld His miracles in half-Gentile Decapolis, we traced His deeds of mercy in the remote uplands of Galilee, and we again heard His loving words and touching parables in the short seclusion[2] in His

---

[1] See, however, the observations on this point, p. 233, note 2.

[2] How long our Lord remained at Capernaum after His return from the district of Cæsarea Philippi and the northern parts of Galilee is in no way specified. As, however, St Luke passes at once from his notice of the contention among the Apostles (which we know took place before they had actually come to Capernaum; see Mark ix. 33) to the journey of our Lord to Jerusalem, we are perhaps correct in supposing that the stay was short. It is not improbable that the approaching celebration of the feast of Tabernacles led to the return from the North, and induced our Lord to come back to Capernaum, not only as being His temporary home, but as being a convenient starting-

earthly home at Capernaum. But now that earthly home is to receive Him no more. Six months of anxious wanderings in Judæa and the lands on the further side of Jordan, interrupted only by brief sojourns in remote frontier-towns, now claim our attention;—six months of ceaseless activities and unresting labour, of mighty deeds and momentous teaching, yet six months if not of actual flight, yet of ever-recurring avoidance of implacable and murderous designs[1] that were now fast approaching their appalling and impious climax.

Limits of the present section.

What I have just said serves indirectly to define the limits of our present section. These, however, for the sake of clearness, I will specify more exactly, as commencing with the Lord's journey in October to the feast of Tabernacles and concluding with His arrival at Bethany six days before the Passover.

Harmonistic and chronological difficulties.

This period I need scarcely remind you presents to the harmonist and chronologer difficulties so

point for the journey to Jerusalem: see above, Lect. III. p. 121, and p. 122, note 1.

[1] It would seem probable that a resolution to kill our Redeemer had been secretly formed among the leading members of the hierarchical party at Jerusalem, perhaps some months before the present time. If we are correct in the view we have taken in Lect. IV., that the machinations against our Lord in Galilee were due to emissaries from Jerusalem, it does not seem wholly improbable that the vengeful feelings of the Pharisaical party, which first definitely showed themselves at the feast of Purim (see above, p. 121), had been from time to time fostered by these emissaries, and were now issuing in designs so far matured as to have become the subject of frequent comment, and of almost general notoriety; see especially John vii. 25. It is at the beginning of the present period that we meet with the first open and formal attempt on the part of the authorities to lay their sacrilegious hands on the person of our Lord; see John vii. 32,—where it will be observed that the imperfectly organized attempt noticed two or three verses before (ἐζήτουν, ver. 30) is recommenced under official sanction; compare Meyer, *Komment. üb. Joh.* p. 236 (ed. 3), and Greswell, *Dissert.* xxx. Vol. II. p. 489.

unusually great[1], that it has been frequently considered a matter of simple impossibility to adjust in their probable order the events which belong to this portion of the narrative. It has been urged that the Evangelist, to whom we owe the recital of so many of the circumstances and discourses which belong to this period, has here failed in his deliberately announced design[a] of relating in order[2] the events of his Master's life, and has here blended in one incoherent narrative the distinctive features and elements of the last three journeys of our Redeemer to Judæa and Jerusalem[3]. We may

[a] Lk. i. 3

---

[1] The precise nature of these difficulties is explained below, p. 240. Some considerations on the nature of that portion of St Luke's Gospel with which these difficulties are chiefly connected, will be found in Greswell, *Dissert.* XXXI. Vol. II. p. 517 sq., but the results at which the learned writer arrives, viz. that Luke ix. 51—xviii. 14 refers to our Lord's last journey to Jerusalem, and that to doubt it is 'the perfection of scepticism and incredulity' (p. 540), are such as may be most justly called into question. Some useful observations on this portion of the Gospel narrative will be found in Robinson, *Harmony of Gospels*, p. 92 (Tract Society); compare also the remarks of Abp Thomson in Smith's *Dictionary of the Bible*, Vol. I. p. 1061.

[2] Some comments on the apparent meaning of this and other expressions used by St Luke in the introduction to his Gospel will be found above, Lect. IV. p. 155, note 1.

[3] See for instance the very sweeping and objectionable remarks of De Wette, who speaks of the necessity of recognizing in this portion of the Evangelist's record 'eine unchronologische und unhistorische Zusammenstellung' (*Erkl. des Luk.* p. 76), and conceives that it resulted from St Luke's having had a certain amount of matter before him relating to our Lord's ministry which he did not know how otherwise to dispose of. The opinion of Schleiermacher, and after him of Olshausen, Neander and others, that we have in this portion of St Luke's Gospel the accounts of *two* journeys, the one terminating at the Feast of Dedication, the second at the Passover, is at first sight more reasonable. It will be found, however, to involve assumptions,—viz. (*a*) that the two narratives of the two journeys were blended by some one ignorant of the exact circumstances, and in this state inserted by St Luke in his Gospel (Schleierm.),—or (*b*) that St Luke re-wrote the accounts and himself helped to blend them (comp. Olshausen, *Commentary*, Vol. II. p. 282 sq.),—which must be pronounced by every sober interpreter to be as untenable in principle, as they will be found on examination to be unsupported by facts.

indeed be thankful to feel and know that such opinions, which in fact carry with them their own condemnation, are now beginning to belong to the past. We may with good reason rejoice that of late years a far more reverent as well as critical spirit has been at work among the chronologers and expositors of the sacred histories. We may gladly observe that order and connexion have been found where there was once deemed to be only confusion and incoherence,—that the inspired narratives are regarded no longer as discrepant but as self-explanatory,—and that honest investigation is showing more and more clearly that what one inspired writer has left unrecorded another has often supplied with an incidental preciseness of adjustment, which is all the more convincing from being seen and felt to be undesigned. All this it is cheering to feel and know[1]; yet still I must not and ought not to disguise from you that the difficulties in our present portion of the Gospel-

---

[1] We may observe, by way of example, the working of these sounder principles in the manner in which the peculiar portion of St Luke's Gospel to which we have been alluding is discussed in the best recent commentaries: see for instance Meyer, *Komment. üb. Luk.* p. 326 sq. (ed. 3), and in our own country, Alford, *on Luke* ix. 51, both of whom, though too scrupulously declining every attempt to reconcile the narrative with that of St John, clearly recognize (Meyer in a less degree) its unity of historical importance. The assertion, however, of the latter writer, that St Luke 'has completely by his connecting words in many places *disclaimed*' any chronological arrangement in this portion of his Gospel, seems certainly much too strong. The utmost that can be said is that the absence of notes of time precludes our determining the precise epoch at which the events specified took place, and the intervals of time between them, but that we have no reason whatever to doubt that in *nearly* all cases the right sequence is preserved. In other words, though we have no *chronology* in this portion of the third Evangelist's Gospel, we have no reason to doubt that we have *order*. On this distinction see Ebrard, *Kritik der Evang. Gesch.* § 11, p. 46, and compare Wieseler, *Chron. Synops.* p. 327 sq.

LECT. VI.

Precise nature of these difficulties.

history,—difficulties, however, which I firmly believe have been of late correctly cleared up,—are still such as must sensibly strike the general reader, and must claim from me a few, yet only a few, explanatory and introductory comments.

The facts are these. Above three hundred verses of St Luke's Gospel, or from the end of the ninth to nearly the middle of the eighteenth chapter, clearly belong to the period that we are now about to consider[1], but stand, so to speak, isolated and alone. To this portion the two other Synoptical Gospels scarcely supply more than two or three parallel notices, though with what follows they again become fully accordant, and again present the most exact coincidences with the narrative of the third Evangelist[2],—coincidences as striking as the former absence of them, and the former comparative silence. But this is not all: these three hundred verses of St Luke's Gospel have somewhat remarkable characteristics. They are very rich in their recital of our Lord's

---

[1] A few sections may perhaps belong to an earlier portion of the narrative, e.g. Luke xi. 17 sq. compared with Mark iii. 20 sq., Luke xiii. 18 sq. with Mark iv. 30 sq.,— if indeed it be not more probable that the substance of both the above sections was repeated on two different occasions; comp. Wieseler, *Chron. Synops.* p. 288.

[2] The first point of resumed connexion between St Luke and the first and second Evangelists is apparently to be found in Luke xvii. 11 compared with Matth. xix. 1, 2, and Mark x. 1,—St Luke alluding to the journey (from Ephraim; see John xi. 54) through Samaria and Galilee, and St Matthew and St Mark the continuation of it through Peræa to Judæa and Jerusalem. The more distinct point of union, however, is the narrative of the young children being brought to our Lord, which begins ch. xviii. 15, and stands in strict parallelism with Matthew xix. 13 sq. and Mark x. 13 sq. After this, for the few remaining sections, the narrative of the Synoptical Evangelists proceeds harmoniously onward to the close of the portion now before us: compare the table in Wieseler, *Chron. Synops.* p. 331, and in Caspari, *Chron.-Geogr. Einleit.* § 134, p. 150 sq.

discourses, especially of those which were suggested by passing occurrences, but they contain but few of those notices of *time* and *place*[1], which we so naturally associate with the narrative of the historian Evangelist.

Now what would be the opinion of any calm, reasonable, and reverent man upon the phenomenon thus presented to him? Why clearly this. In the first place, he would at once conclude that here was but another of the almost countless instances which the holy Gospels present to us of the mercy and wisdom of Almighty God, whose Eternal Spirit moved one Evangelist to relate what the others had left unrecorded[2]. In the second place, he would here recognize, on the one hand, an indirect verification of that careful research which was openly professed by the third

---

[1] This remark will be best verified by an inspection of the chapters in question. We may, however, pause to specify the following very undefined notices of chronological connexion, μετὰ δὲ ταῦτα, ch. x. 1; καὶ ἰδού, ch. x. 25; ἐγένετο δέ, ch. x. 38; καὶ ἐγένετο, ch. xi. 1; simply καί, ch. xi. 14, xiii. 22; ἐν δὲ τῷ λαλῆσαι, ch. xi. 37; ἐν οἷς, ch. xii. 1; εἶπεν δέ, ch. xii. 22, and comp. xiii. 6, xvi. 1, xvii. 1, xviii. 1; καὶ ἐγένετο, ch. xiv. 1; καὶ εἰσερχομένου αὐτοῦ εἴς τινα κώμην, ch. xvii. 12. The only really definite expressions in reference to time are apparently confined to ch. xiii. 1, 31, and even these are of little use to us, owing to the events with which they stand in connexion themselves being undefined as to time. With regard to *place*, for examples of a similarly undefined character, compare ch. x.

38, xi. 1, xiii. 10, 22, xiv. 1, xvii. 12. It may be admitted that we can find instances of a similar absence of definite notices of time and place in other portions of St Luke's Gospel, but in none so regularly and continuously as in the portion now before us: see the table in Ebrard, *Kritik der Ev. Gesch.* § 32, p. 131 sq.

[2] The supplementary relations in which the earlier-written Gospels appear to stand to the later-written are noticed at some length by Greswell, *Dissert.* I. Vol. I. p. 15. The popular objection, that we have no intimations in the sacred records themselves by which we can infer where one is to be regarded defective and others supplementary to it, is considered and reasonably answered in the Appendix, *Dissert.* I. Vol. III. p. 321 sq.

LECT. VI.

Evangelist[1]; and on the other, a direct proof of that faithfulness that made him adopt less special notices of the strict connexion of events when the sources of information, oral or written, to which he had been moved to refer, had not fully or distinctly supplied them.

Comparison of this portion of St Luke's Gospel with that of St John.

Now suppose such a reasonable thinker had observed, as he could scarcely fail to have observed, that the fourth Evangelist, true to the supplementary character, which we seem to have very sufficient grounds for ascribing to several portions of his Gospel[2], had supplied three distinct chronological notices of three journeys taken *toward* if not all actually *to* Jerusalem during this period we are about to consider[3]—would he not at once turn back to St Luke to discover some trace, however slight, of journeys so clearly

---

[1] This seems a fair representation of what the Evangelist designed to imply by παρηκολουθηκότι ἄνωθεν πᾶσιν ἀκριβῶς (ch. i. 3): see the comments on this passage in Lect. IV. p. 155, note 1. The view of the ancient Syriac translator, according to which πᾶσι is masculine, and παρηκολουθ. implies *proximity*, and personal attendance (see also von Gumpach in Kitto, *Journal of Sacred Lit.* for 1849, No. VIII. p. 301), deserves attention from its antiquity, but is apparently rightly rejected by all the best modern expositors.

[2] See above, Lect. I. p. 14, note 4, and compare the illustrations supplied by Greswell, *Dissert.* XXI.—XXIII. Vol. II. p. 196 sq., *Dissert.* XXX. Vol. II. p. 482 sq.: compare also Ebrard, *Kritik der Ev. Gesch.* § 37, p. 150 sq.

[3] The objection that if we include our Lord's visit to Jerusalem at the Feast of Dedication, we might seem to have *four* journeys to Jerusalem (see the synopsis of Lampe) is readily removed by observing that the way in which St John mentions the festival and our Lord's appearance at it (John x. 22), combined with the fact that there is no previous mention of any departure from Judæa (contrast John x. 40), leads us certainly to suppose that during the interval between the feast of Tabernacles and that of the Dedication our Lord confined His ministry to Judæa; see p. 256. If this be so, the visit to the latter festival is not to be regarded as due to a separate or second journey, but only as a sequel of the first: compare Bengel's more correct synopsis, *Gnomon*, Vol. I. p. 351, and see Wieseler, *Chronol. Synops.* p. 318, note 1.

defined by another Evangelist? And would he turn back there in vain? Would he find no break in the narrative, no indications of journeys to Jerusalem beside that with which this portion of his Gospel commences? Most assuredly not. Instead of all seeming, as it might once have seemed, the confused recital of the circumstances of but one journey, he would now be led to identify the journey of the ninth chapter of St Luke with the journey to the feast of Tabernacles specified by St John[1]; he would again have his attention arrested by the break a little past the middle of the thirteenth chapter[a], and would see how strikingly it agreed with St John's notice of

LECT. VI.

[a] ver. 22

---

[1] The main argument *for* the identity of the journey specified John vii. 10 with that mentioned Luke ix. 51 rests on the two facts, (*a*) that the journey specified by the third Evangelist was through Samaria (Luke ix. 52), and (*b*) that the inhabitants of that country at once inferred that our Lord's destination was Jerusalem (ver. 53). The first of these facts is in complete harmony with the avoidance of observation specified in John vii. 10; the second is in equally complete harmony with St John's statement of the object of that journey (ἀνέβη εἰς τὴν ἑορτήν, ib. ver. 10). It was the knowledge on the part of the Samaritans that the feast of Tabernacles was now going on that made them so readily notice and recognize the direction to which the Lord's face was now turned; see below, p. 249. The main objection *against* the identity lies in St Luke's rough note of time, ἐν τῷ συμπληροῦσθαι τὰς ἡμέρας τῆς ἀναλήψεως (ch. ix. 51), which, it is urged, the use of the peculiar term ἀνάληψις clearly shows can only belong to a last journey (see Meyer *in loc.*, and compare Greswell, *Dissert.* XXXI. Vol. II. p. 522). Why, however, may not the very general term, αἱ ἡμέραι τῆς ἀναλήψεως (ὁ καιρὸς ὁ ἀφορισθεὶς μέχρι τῆς ἀναλήψεως, Euthym.), suitably apply to the period between the conclusion of the regular ministry of our Lord and the last Passover,—a period which was ushered in by special prophecies of such an ἀνάληψις (Mark ix. 30), and which throughout wears the character of being a season of preparation for that final issue? compare p. 233, note 1. The interpretation of the words proposed by Wieseler (*Chron. Synops.* p. 324; comp. Lange, *Leben Jesu*, II. 5. 12, Part II. p. 1054),—'the days of His having found acceptance with men,' is contrary to the New Testament use of the verb (Mark xvi. 19, Acts i. 2, xi. 22, 1 Tim. iii. 16), and completely untenable.

16—2

LECT. VI.

the second journey toward Jerusalem, that reached no further than Bethany[1]; and lastly, he could not fail to pause at the special notice of a third journey towards the beginning of the seventeenth chapter[a], and would naturally connect it not only with the express statements of St Matthew[b] and St Mark[c], but with the previous retirement to Ephraim so distinctly specified by St John[2]... Such would be the result of a fair and reasonable investigation into the narrative of St Luke,—and such too is the result arrived at, in part by the learned Lightfoot[3], and more distinctly by a recent investigator, whose elaborate treatise on the chronology of the Gospel history may justly be classed among the most successful efforts in that department of theology that have appeared in our own times[4].

[a] ver. 11
[b] xix. 1
[c] x. 1

---

[1] For further considerations in favour of this connexion of Luke xiii. 22 with St John's notice of our Lord's withdrawal πέραν τοῦ Ἰορδάνου (ch. x. 40), and the same Apostle's notice of the journey to Bethany (ch. xi. 1), see below, p. 262 sq., and compare Wieseler, *Chron. Synops.* p. 321, and Caspari, *Chron.-Geogr. Einleit.* § 135, p. 153.

[2] With John xi. 54 we seem rightly to connect Luke xvii. 11, διήρχετο διὰ μέσου Σαμαρείας καὶ Γαλιλαίας, where the confirmatory hint supplied by the notice of the direction of the journey should not be overlooked; see below, p. 269, note 5.

[3] The following appears to be the arrangement of this able harmonist as indicated in his *Chronica Temporum* (Vol. II. p. 36 sq. Roterod. 1686): (1) he connects (sect. 57) Luke ix. 51 and John vii. 10; (2) he places (sect. 60) Luke x. 17—xiii. 23 before John ix. 1—x. 42; (3) he refers Luke xvii. 11 to our Lord's last journey to Jerusalem, connecting it, however, with John x. 42 rather than with John xi. 55; see sect. 62. The main differences between this and the view adopted in the text are the identification of Luke xiii. 22 with the visit to Jerusalem at the feast of Dedication (see above, p. 242, note 3), and the reference of John ix. 1—x. 21 to the visit at the feast of Dedication other than, as seems much more natural, to that at the feast of Tabernacles; contrast Wieseler, *Chron. Synops.* p. 329.

[4] It is scarcely necessary to observe that reference is here made to the *Chronologische Synopse der Vier Evangelien* of Karl Wieseler,—a treatise of which the importance has been already commented on; see p. 143, note 4. It is to be regretted that in a few important pas-

If we rest satisfied with this result, and I verily believe it will commend itself to us each step we advance forward in the history, we have before us, to speak broadly and generally, the record of the circumstances connected with *three* journeys to or toward Jerusalem, the first being at the feast of Tabernacles, the second, three months or more afterwards, the last a short time before the ensuing Passover[1].

Let us now proceed to a brief but orderly recital of the recorded events.

The last circumstance on which we dwelt was the return of our Lord to Capernaum after His

Results of the above considerations.

Brief stay at Capernaum: worldly request of our Lord's brethren.

sages Wieseler has been tempted to propound novel interpretations (see above, p. 243, note 1) which have been almost universally pronounced to be untenable. This has led hasty readers to rate this able work much below its real merits: compare Kitto, *Journal of Sacr. Lit.* for 1850, No. XI. p. 75.

[1] The date of the commencement of the second and third journeys and their duration can only be fixed roughly and approximately. The data for forming a calculation are as follow. The feast of the Dedication took place on the 25th of Kislev (Dec. 20), and lasted 8 days (Joseph. *Antiq.* XII. 7. 7; comp. Jahn, *Archæol.* § 359): at this, as we know from St John, our Lord was present. Very soon afterwards our Lord retires to the Peræan Bethany (John x. 40), and there abides long enough for many to believe on Him (John x. 42). At the end of this stay the *second* journey towards Jerusalem (Luke xiii. 22; comp. John xi. 7) is commenced, which for the time terminates at Bethany, but which, owing to the machinations of the Jews (John xi. 47), is very shortly afterwards directed to Ephraim (John xi. 54). From this place the *third* journey is commenced, which appears to have extended through Samaria, Galilee, and Peræa, and to have been temporarily arrested at Bethany near Jerusalem 6 days before the Passover, or, in the year in question (A.U.C. 783), somewhere about April 1. If we now reckon backward, and assign at least a fortnight to this journey, a month or 5 weeks to the stay at Ephraim, and a week or more to the second journey, — which though much shorter than the third *seems* at first to have been leisurely performed (comp. Luke xiii. 22, and see below, p. 262, note 2), — we shall then leave about a month or 5 weeks for the stay in the neighbourhood of the Peræan Bethany. The second journey according to this view would have commenced about the beginning of February, and the third about the middle of March.

LECT. VI.

long missionary journeys, and His impressive teaching to His Apostles during that brief period of apparent tranquillity and seclusion[1]. That time of holy rest seems soon to have come to an end. The feast of Tabernacles was nigh at hand, and the Lord's brethren[2], who now come prominently before us, and who in spite of their practical unbelief[3] appear to have distinctly shared in similar feelings of pride and expectancy to those which we seem to have already traced in the Apostles, now urge Him to display His wonder-working powers amid circumstances of greater publicity[a],—to challenge and to command adhesion, and that not in remote Galilee but in the busy thoroughfares of Jerusalem[4], and among the

[a] Joh. vii. 3

---

[1] See Lecture v. p. 231, and compare p. 236, note 2.

[2] For a brief consideration of the probable meaning of this much contested appellation see above, p. 97, note 2, and for examples of the various senses of the word ἀδελφός according to Hebrew usage, see Greswell, *Dissert.* XVII. Vol. II. p. 117.

[3] That the words οὐδὲ ἐπίστευον (John vii. 5), though probably implying a disbelief in our Lord's Godhead (ὡς εἰς Θεόν, Euthym.), did not imply a disbelief in His mighty works, and perhaps not even in His claims to be regarded a divinely accredited teacher, seems clear from the context; see ver. 3, and compare Lect. III. p. 98, note. Chrysostom (*in loc.*) rightly remarks that the address, though marked by bitterness, still clearly came from friends (δοκεῖ ἡ ἀξίωσις δῆθεν φίλων εἶναι; contrast Euthymius *in loc.*): we may pause, however, before we agree with that able expositor in his further remark that James the brother of the Lord was one of the speakers: compare Greswell, *Dissert.* XVII. Vol. II. p. 116.

[4] The exact meaning of the address of our Lord's brethren, especially of the confirmatory clause (οὐδεὶς γὰρ ἐν κρυπτῷ τι ποιεῖ καὶ ζητεῖ αὐτὸς ἐν παρρησίᾳ εἶναι, John vii. 4) is not at first sight perfectly clear. What the brethren appear to say is this: 'Go to Judæa that Thy disciples, whether dwelling there or come there to the festival, may behold the works which Thou art doing here in comparative secrecy: it is needful that Thou seek this publicity if true to Thy character, for no man doeth his works in secret, and seeks personally (αὐτός) to be before the world,—as Thou who claimest to be the Messiah must necessarily desire to be. Hidden though wondrous works and personal acceptance by the world

thronging worshippers in its Temple courts.... The apparent contradiction that has here been found between our Lord's words and His subsequent acts vanishes at once when we pause to observe that here, as so often in the narrative of the fourth Evangelist, He is revealed to us as the reader of the heart, and as answering its thoughts and imaginations, rather than the words by which those feelings were disguised[1]. It is to the spirit and meaning of this worldly and self-seeking request rather than to the mere outward terms in which it was couched that the Lord answers His brethren, even as He had once before answered a mother's tacit importunity, that 'His time is not yet come[a],' and that He goeth not up to the feast. He does indeed *not* go up to the feast in the sense in which those carnal-minded men presumed to counsel Him. He joins now no festal companies; He takes now no prominent part in festal solemnities[2]; if He be found in Jerusalem and in the

[a] Joh. vii. 6

---

at large are things not compatible.' The whole is the speech of shrewd and worldly-minded, but not treacherous or designing men; compare Lücke *in loc.* Vol. II. p. 189 (ed. 3).

[1] See above, Lect. I. p. 32, note 1, and compare p. 126. note 2. The supposition of Meyer that our Lord here states His intention and afterwards *alters* it, is neither borne out by the context nor rendered admissible by any parallel case (Matth. xv. 26 sq. is certainly not in point) in the whole sacred narrative. The miserable effort of Porphyry to fix on our Lord the charge of fraudulent representations and deliberate inconstancy is noticed and refuted by Jerome, *contr. Pelag.* II. 6.

[2] That this is the true meaning of the words was apparently *felt* by the earlier expositors (οὐ γὰρ ἀναβαίνει συνεορτάσων νουθετήσων δὲ μᾶλλον, Cyril Alex. *in loc.* p. 404 B), and has been distinctly asserted by many of the sounder modern writers. So rightly Luthardt ('nicht an diesem Feste wird er *so wie sie meinen* hinauf- und einziehn in Jerusalem.' *Das Johann. Evang.* Part II. p. 77), Stier (*Disc. of our Lord*, Vol. v. p. 242, Clark), and somewhat similarly, Lücke *in loc.* The explanation of De Wette and Alford that the true reading οὐκ ἀναβαίνω is *practically* equivalent to the οὔπω ἀναβαίνω of the Received Text, is *perhaps* defensible on the ground

courts of His Father's House, it is not as the wonder-worker or Messianic king, but as the persecuted Redeemer who will yet again brave the malice of Scribe and Pharisee that He may still fulfil His mission to those lost sheep of the house of Israel whom the festival may gather together.

Journey to Jerusalem through Samaria.

Thus it was, that perhaps scarcely before the very day on which the festival actually commenced[1], our Lord, and as the sequel seems to show[a], His Apostles, directed their steps to Jerusalem; but, as it were, in secret. Their way, as we might have expected, and as the apparently coincident notice of St Luke distinctly substantiates[b], lay through Samaria[2]. But Samaria now

[a] Comp. Lk. ix. 54
[b] ix. 52

---

that the succeeding οὕτω may be thought to reflect a kind of temporal limitation on the foregoing negative, but seems neither so simple nor so natural as that which has been adopted in the text.

[1] That our Lord did not arrive at Jerusalem till the middle of the Feast is certainly not positively to be deduced from John vii. 14, which may only imply that up to that day, though in Jerusalem, He remained in concealment (Meyer). Still the use of the term ἀνέβη, especially viewed in connexion with its use a few verses before, seems to involve the idea of a preceding journey, and may possibly have been chosen as serving to imply that on His arrival our Lord proceeded at once to the Temple, — that it was in fact the true goal of the present journey. Cyril of Alexandria calls attention to the word ἀνέβη (οὐχ ἁπλῶς εἰσῆλθεν, ἀλλὰ ἀνέβη, φησίν, εἰς τὸ ἱερόν, *in loc.* p. 409 E) but apparently refers it to the solemn and formal nature of the entry.

[2] Even if we hesitate to regard the journey mentioned by St Luke (ch. ix. 51) as identical with that here specified by St John, — which indeed, as we have shown above, we seem to have no sufficient reason for doing, — we can scarcely doubt that the journey was through Samaria. By this route our Lord would be able to make His journey more completely ὡς ἐν κρυπτῷ (John vii. 10), and would also apparently be able to reach Jerusalem more quickly than if He had taken the usual and longer route through Peræa: see above, Lect. III. p. 122, note 1. The assertion of Meyer (*in loc.*) that ὡς ἐν κρυπτῷ simply implies that our Lord joined no festal caravan, but affords no indication of the way He was pleased to take, may justly be questioned. If our Lord was accompanied by His Apostles, — which, from St John's Gospel alone, seems certainly more probable than the contrary, — could a company of thirteen have travelled ὡς ἐν κρυπτῷ by any but a little-frequented route?

receives not its Saviour as it had received Him nine months before[a]. Then the Lord's face was turned towards Galilee, now it is turned towards Jerusalem; then His journey was made more leisurely, now it is in haste; then there was no apparent reason why the route through Samaria had been chosen rather than any other, now it is self-evident. The peculiar season of the year at once reminds the jealous Samaritan whither those hurried steps were being directed, and tells him plainly enough what must be the true reason which now has brought that hastening company through their commonly avoided land. So when messengers[b] are sent forward to expedite the journey, and make preparation for the coming Master, He whom the city of Sychar had once welcomed is now rejected[c] by the churlish village that lay in His way. The Sons of Thunder[1] would

[a] Joh. iv. 40

[b] Lk. ix. 52

[c] ver. 53

---

[1] The incident mentioned in this passage deserves particular attention as tending to correct a very popular and prevailing error in reference to the character of one of the actors. Does the present passage, especially when combined with Luke ix. 49, and Mark x. 38, and further illustrated by the most natural and obvious interpretation of the term 'Son of Thunder' (Mark iii. 17; see Meyer *in loc.* p. 39), at all justify our regarding St John as the Apostolic type of that almost feminine softness and meditative tranquillity (see Olshausen, *Comment. on the Gospels*, Vol. III. p. 304) which is so popularly ascribed to him? Is it not much more correct to say that the notices of the Beloved Apostle recorded in the Gospels, when estimated in connexion with the name given to him by his Master, present to us the scarcely doubtful traces of an ardent love, zeal, and confidence (Mark x. 39), which, like the thunder to which the character was compared, was sometimes shown forth in outspokenness and outburst? This characteristic ardour, this glowing while loving zeal, is not obscurely evinced in the outspokenness, and honest denunciation of falsehood and heresy that marks the first, and, even more clearly, the short remaining Epistles of this inspired writer; compare 2 John 10, 3 John 10. The misconception of the character of the Apostle is apparently of early date, and perhaps stands in some degree of connexion with his own simple yet affecting notice of the love and confidence vouchsafed towards him by our Redeemer during

have had fire called down from heaven, but their intemperate zeal is rebuked by their Lord, yea and practically rebuked by a striking proof that even now Samaria was not utterly faithless. One at least, there *seems* to have been[1], who was ready to cast in his lot with that travel-worn company[a], and to him it was answered in the words of our text, and with a striking and pathetic appropriateness, that though the creatures that His own Divine hands had made had their allotted places of shelter and rest, 'the Son of Man had not where to lay His head.'

Our Lord's arrival and preaching at Jerusalem.
[a] Lk. ix. 57
[b] Joh. vii. 11

The Lord soon reaches Jerusalem, where it would seem He was partially expected[b], and about the middle of the feast enters the Temple, and teaches in its now crowded courts. And that teaching was not in vain. Though some of the mere dwellers in Jerusalem[2] paused only to specu-

the Last Supper (John xiii. 23). Let us not forget, however, that he, who in memory of this, was lovingly called ὁ ἐπιστήθιος by the early Church, was called by his own Master the 'Son of Thunder.' The patristic explanation of this latter title will be found in Suicer, *Thesaur.* s. v. βροντή, Vol. I. p. 712 sq., but is not sufficiently distinctive.

[1] It seems proper here to speak with caution, as the present case and that of the man who, when called by our Lord, requested leave first to go and bury his father, are placed by St Matthew in a totally different connexion: see ch. viii. 19—21. To account for this is difficult, though we can have no difficulty in believing that it *could* be readily accounted for if we knew *all* the circumstances. It is not, for example, unreasonable to suppose that the incident of the self-offering follower might have happened *twice*, and that St Matthew, in accordance with his habit of connecting together what was similar (see Lect. I. p. 20 sq.), might have associated with the first occurrence of that incident, an incident which in point of time really belonged to the second.

[2] It is worthy of notice that St John here places before us the views and comments of a party that clearly must be regarded as different from the general ὄχλος (ver. 20) on the one hand, and the more hostile Ἰουδαῖοι (ver. 15) on the other. We have here the remarks of some of the *residents* in the city. They evidently are perfectly acquainted with the general designs of the party of the Sanhedrin, and are full of

The Journeyings toward Jerusalem. 251

late on the policy of their spiritual rulers in permitting One whom they were seeking to kill now to speak with such openness and freedom[a], the effect on the collected multitude was clearly different. Many we are told believed on our Lord[b]; many saw in His miracles an evidence of a Messiahship which it seemed now no longer possible either to doubt or to deny[c]. The sequel, however, we might easily have foreseen. An effort is at once made by the party of the Sanhedrin to lay hands on our Lord[d], but is frustrated, perhaps partly, by the multitude, and certainly also in great measure by the convictions of the very men that were sent to take Him[1]. The savage spirit of the Sanhedrin is now, however, distinctly shown, and now is it that for the first time *publicly*, though darkly, the Lord speaks of that departure,—of that 'being sought for and not found[e],' on which He had already spoken twice before to His disciples with such saddening explicitness. Yet He will not leave those heart-touched multitudes that were now hanging on His words. Yet again on the last day of the festival[f], the Lord preaches publicly with a most solemn and appropriate reference to the living waters of the Spirit which should

LECT. VI.

[a] Joh. vii. 25
[b] ver. 31
[c] ver. 31
[d] ver. 32
[e] ver. 34
[f] ver. 37

---

natural wonder that they should have permitted this free speaking on the part of One whom they had resolved, and whom it was obviously their interest, to silence. The incidental notice of the sort of halfknowledge these 'Ιεροσολυμῖται had acquired is in the highest degree natural and characteristic: see Stier, *Disc. of our Lord*, Vol. v. p. 267.

[1] This transpires afterwards: see John vii. 45, 46. It would seem that when these ὑπηρέται were sent forth with orders to seize our Lord, it was left to their discretion to watch for a good opportunity and a reasonable pretext. At the next session of the Sanhedrin they make a report of what they had done, or rather left undone, and are exposed accordingly to the scornful inquiries and practical censure of the council (ver. 47). Further proceedings, it would seem, are at present, if not arrested, yet impeded by the question of Nicodemus (ver. 51).

flow forth when He was glorified[1]. Again a desire is manifested by the party of the Sanhedrin to lay hands on Him[a]; again, as it would seem, a meeting of the Sanhedrin is held, and again their proposals are encountered by a just opposition; not however on this occasion by the tacit and merely passive opposition of their reluctant satellites, but by the open pleading of one of its most important members, the timid yet faithful Nicodemus[2]—the only one among the rulers of the Jews, who was found to urge the observance of that law of Moses[b], which its hypocritical guardians were now seeking to pervert or to violate.

The woman taken in adultery: probable place of the incident in the Gospel history.

To this same period, if we conceive the narrative in question to be written by St John, must be assigned the memorable, and most certainly in-

[a] Joh. vii. 44
[b] ver. 51

---

[1] There seems no sufficient reason for rejecting the generally received opinion, that allusion is here made to the custom of bringing water from the well of Siloam and pouring it on the altar, which appears to have been observed on every day of this Festival,—the *eighth* (according to R. Judah in 'Succah,' IV. 9) also included; see especially Lightfoot, *Hor. Hebr. in loc.* Vol. II. p. 632 (Roterod. 1686), and the good article in Winer, *RWB.* 'Laubhüttenfest,' Vol. II. p. 8. Whether this 'great day' of the Festival is to be regarded as the 7th or as the 8th is a matter of some doubt. If it be true, as urged by Winer, that the opinion of Rabbi Judah above cited is only that of an individual, and that the prevailing practice was to offer libations only on 7 days ('Succah,' IV. 1), and if it be further supposed that our Lord's words were called forth by the actual performance of the rite,—then 'the great day' must be the 7th day. As, however, it appears from the written Law that the 8th day was regarded as a Sabbath (Lev. xxiii. 36; comp. Joseph. *Antiq.* III. 10. 4), and as peculiar solemnities are specified in the oral law as celebrated on that day (see Lightfoot, *loc. cit.*), it seems more correct to regard the 8th as 'the great day;' and if it be conceded that there was no libation on that day, to suppose our Lord's words were called forth, not by the act itself, but by a remembrance of the custom observed on the preceding days: see Meyer *in loc.* p. 239 (ed. 3), and the elaborate comments of Lücke, Vol. II. p. 223 sq. (ed. 3). Some good remarks on the festival will be found in Caspari, *Chron.-Geogr. Einleit.* § 127, p. 144 sq.

[2] Compare Lect. III. p. 125, note 3 ad fin.

spired history of the woman taken in adultery; but as I venture to entertain, somewhat decidedly, the opinion that it was not written by that Evangelist[1], and that it does not in any way blend naturally with the *present* portion of the Redeemer's history, I will not here pause on it, but will only notice in passing the great plausibility and historical fitness with which three or four of the cursive manuscripts insert it at the end of the twenty-first chapter of St Luke[2].

But the Lord still lingers at Jerusalem in spite of the vengeful storm that was fast gathering round Him....To the first Sabbath after the festival we must apparently[3] assign the discourse on

Further teaching and preaching at Jerusalem.

---

[1] The limits and general character of these notes wholly preclude our attempting to enter upon a formal discussion of this difficult question. It may be briefly observed, however, that the opinion expressed in the text rests on the following considerations; (1) The absence of the passage from (*a*) four out of the five first-class MSS. and the valuable MS. marked L,—(*b*) several ancient versions, among which are some early Latin versions of great importance, and apparently the Peshito-Syriac, — (*c*) several early and important patristic writers; Origen, Tertullian, Cyprian, and Chrysostom being of the number: (2) The *striking* number of variations of reading among the documents that retain the passage, there being not less than 80 variations of reading in 183 words: (3) The almost equally striking difference of style, both in the connecting particles and other words, from that of St John, and the apparent similarity in style to that of St Luke. From these reasons, external and internal, we seem justified in removing the passage *from the place* it now occupies in the Received Text, though there appears *every* reason for believing it a portion of the Gospel history. It cannot be too strongly impressed on the general reader that no reasonable critic throws doubt on the incident, but only on its present place in the sacred narrative. For critical details see the new (7th) edition of Tischendorf's *Greek Test.* Vol. I. p. 602, and Meyer, *Komment. üb. Joh.* p. 247 (ed. 3).

[2] These manuscripts are numbered 13, 69, 124, 346; one of these (69) being the well-known Codex Leicestrensis, and the other three MSS. of the Alexandrian family. It cannot apparently be asserted that the passage *exactly* fits on after Luke xxi. 38, but it certainly does seem rightly attached to that chapter generally, and properly to find a place among the incidents there related: see more in Lect VII.

[3] It may be doubted whether we

254 The Journeyings toward Jerusalem.

LECT. VI.

[a] John viii. 12—20.
[b] ver. 25 sq.
[c] ver. 30
[d] ver. 33
[e] ver. 59

His own and His Father's testimony[a], and the striking declarations of His mission from Him that was true[b], and of His union with the eternal Father,—declarations, which we know so wrought upon our Lord's very opponents that many of them[1], as St John tells us, believed on Him as He thus spake unto them[c], though alas! as the sequel seems to show, that belief was soon exchanged for captious[d] questioning, and at last even for the frightful violences of blinded religious zeal[e]. To this same Sabbath we must certainly assign the performance of the deeply interesting miracle of giving sight to the beggar[2] who had grown up

---

are to assign the discourses recorded by St John in ch. viii. to the last day of the feast of Tabernacles (John vii. 37), or to the Sabbath on which the blind man was healed (John x. 14). The latter appears to be the more probable connexion. The beginning of chap. ix. seems closely linked with the concluding verse of chap. viii.,—a chapter which really commences with ver. 12, and contains the record of a series of apparently continuous discourses; comp. Origen, *in Joann.* XIX. 2, Vol. IV. p. 292 (ed. Bened.). Between this chapter and the close of chap. vii. there seems a break, which in the received Text is filled up with the narrative of the woman taken in adultery. On the connexion of this portion, see Wieseler, *Chron. Synops.* p. 329, and compare the remarks of Meyer, *Komment. üb. Joh.* p. 289 sq. (ed. 3)—who, however, does not seem correct in separating John viii. 21 sq. from what precedes, and in assigning the discourse to a following day.

[1] It is worthy of notice that the Evangelist seems desirous that it should be clearly observed that the πολλοί who believed (John viii. 30) belonged to the hostile party, the Ἰουδαῖοι (see p. 115, note 1), as he specially adds that the address beginning ch. viii. 31 was directed πρὸς τοὺς πεπιστευκότας αὐτῷ Ἰουδαίους. On the whole discourse and the melancholy fluctuations in the minds of these sadly imperfect believers, see the exceedingly good comments of Stier, *Disc. of our Lord*, Vol. IV. p. 349 sq. (Clark).

[2] See John ix. 8, where the true reading seems undoubtedly, not ὅτι τυφλὸς ἦν (*Rec.*), but ὅτι προσαίτης ἦν, which has the support of four principal MSS., the Syriac, Latin, Coptic, and other ancient versions, and is rightly adopted by most recent editors. On the miracle itself,—the characteristics of which are, our Lord's being pleased to impart His healing powers by an outward medium (ver. 5), a deferred (comp. Mark viii. 23) or rather suspended cure, and its divinely ordered dependence on the sufferer's perform-

to manhood in blindness[a], and who believed in, yea and worshipped as the Son of God[b] Him by whose merciful hands he received his sight[1]. With the sublime discourse on the Good Shepherd[c], —the Good Shepherd that even now, with stones every moment ready to be cast upon Him[d], was giving His very life for His sheep, the memorable occurrences on this eventful Sabbath[2] and during our Lord's present stay in Jerusalem appear to have come to their close. At no preceding festival had our Lord made a deeper impression on the minds of those whom He had vouchsafed to address. At no former visit was such an effect produced on the feelings, not only of the more friendly multitudes[e] but even of open or concealed foes[f],—and that too, as far as we can infer from the inspired narrative, not so much by mighty

[a] John ix. 1 sq.
[b] ver. 38
[c] x. 1 sq.
[d] comp. viii. 59
[e] vii. 31, 40
[f] comp. vii. 15

ance of a prescribed act (2 Kings v. 10),—see the comments of Cyril Alex. and Chrysostom *in loc.*, August. *in Joann.* Tractat. XLIV., Bp Hall, *Contempl.* IV. 8, and Trench, *Notes on the Miracles*, p. 288.

[1] Some modern expositors endeavour to dilute the nature of the blind man's belief in our Lord as 'the Son of God.' Why, however, are we to say that this title must have had a theocratic (Meyer) rather than a Christian meaning to the mind of the recent sufferer, when it is so possible, and even so probable from his conduct before the Pharisees, that He who had given light to his bodily eye had vouchsafed a special illuminating influence (see Euthym. *in loc.*) to the inner eye of the mind? What else are we to understand from his prompt act of accepted adoration than a recognition of the Divine nature of Him before whom he was standing? As Augustine well says, 'Agnoscit eum non filium hominis tantum, quod ante crediderat, sed jam filium Dei qui carnem susceperat.' *In Joann.* Tractat. XLIV. 15, Vol. III. p. 1718 (ed. Migne). On the meaning ascribed to the title 'Son of God,' compare Lect. III. p. 119, note 2, Lect. V. p. 211, note 1.

[2] Some expositors place an interval of one or more days after John ix. 34, and before John x. 1 (see Stier, *Disc. of our Lord*, Vol. V. pp. 445, 448), and so extend the events over a greater space of time. This may be so; but the above assumption, that all took place on the Sabbath mentioned ch. ix. 14, seems on the whole rather more in accordance with the general tenor of the text.

works^a, as by powerful and persuasive teaching. All seem alike to have felt, and in some degree alike to have yielded to the influence of the gracious words that proceeded from the Redeemer's mouth. The impression was general; the testimony all but unanimous. The mixed multitude, the dwellers at Jerusalem^b, the officials of the Temple^c, and to some extent even the hostile Jewish party^d bore witness to the more than mortal power of the teaching of Jesus of Nazareth.

Departure from Jerusalem and mission of the Seventy.

Whither our Lord now went is not specified, and must remain only a matter of conjecture. It may be remarked, however, that the silence of St John, who commonly indicates whenever our Lord's ministry was transferred from Judæa, seems to give us very good grounds for supposing that our Lord, as once before after His first passover, so now again, remained still within the frontier of Judæa, and again partially resumed a ministry there which had been suspended in the December of the preceding year. If this be so, it is to this country, and apparently also to this period[1] that we must refer the sending forth of the seventy disciples^e,—those seventy whose very number hinted at the future destination of the Gospel for the wide world and the seventy nations into which the Jews divided it[2], even as the mission of the

---

[1] The exact period of the mission of the Seventy has been much debated by harmonists of this portion of Scripture. Wieseler fixes it as during the journey through Samaria, and finds a special appropriateness in the choice of that country: see *Chron. Synops.* p. 326, note. As, however, the journey through Samaria was apparently in haste, and as the whole of Luke x. seems to refer to events which succeeded that journey (comp. De Wette *in loc.*), the place here assigned to the mission is perhaps more probable.

[2] See Eisenmenger, *Entd. Ju-*

The Journeyings toward Jerusalem.

twelve Apostles not obscurely hinted at the first offer of the Gospel to the now merged twelve tribes of God's own peculiar people.

LECT. VI.

During this same period,—this interval between the feast of Tabernacles and the feast of the Dedication,—we may also with considerable probability place the visit of our Lord to Martha and Mary at Bethany[a], when Martha was so cumbered with much serving; and to this same interval we may assign that instructive series of discourses[1] which extend from the middle of the tenth to the middle of the thirteenth chapter of St Luke, the few incidents connecting which seem admirably to agree with the arrangement that would refer them to Judæa and to this particular period of our Lord's ministry[2]. Though

Further incidents in Judæa recorded by St Luke.

[a] Lk. x. 38

---

denthum, Vol. II. p. 736 sq., and especially the interesting Rabbinical citations in Lightfoot (*Hor. Hebr. in Joann.* vii. 37), which we may further use as indirectly confirming our present chronological arrangement. If the custom, alluded to in those passages, of offering sacrifices at the feast of Tabernacles for the 70 nations of the heathen world was as old as the time of our Saviour,—and this there seems no reason to doubt,—it does not seem wholly fanciful to connect this mission of 70 men, whose destination, though not defined, does not at any rate appear to have had any specified limits assigned to it (contrast Matth. x. 5), with a period shortly succeeding a festival where the needs of the heathen world were not forgotten even by the Jews.

[1] This interesting portion of St Luke's Gospel opens with the parable of the Good Samaritan (ch. x.

25 sq.) and closes with the miracle performed on the woman bowed by a spirit of infirmity (ch. xiii. 10—17). The two striking parables of the Rich Fool (ch. xii. 16 sq.) and the Barren Fig-tree (ch. xiii. 6 sq.) belong to this period, and present the characteristics of so many of the parables recorded by St Luke, viz. that of springing from or being suggested by some preceding event; see Da Costa, *The Four Witnesses*, p. 211 sq.

[2] The healing of the two blind men (Matth. ix. 27 sq.) is inserted by Tischendorf (*Synops. Evang.* p. xxxix.) in the present portion of the narrative on the ground that according to St Matthew it stands in close connexion with the cure of a deaf and dumb demoniac (ver. 32 sq.), which again, according to Luke xi. 14 sq., must belong to the present period of the history. On the whole, however, it seems better to conceive

LECT. VI.

devoid of all notices of place[1] which might enable us to give some circumstantial touches to the few interspersed incidents, or sketch them out in a connected narrative, they still serve to show us very clearly,—on the one hand, that the effect produced by our Lord's present ministry in Judæa was very great, that His hearers were now un-usually numerous[a], and showed as earnest a desire to hear the words of Life as was ever shown even in Galilee; and on the other hand, that the enmity of the Pharisees and hierarchical party was deepening in its implacability[b],—and that too more especially, as our Lord did not now repress His solemn and open denunciations[c] of the hypocrisy and bloodthirsty spirit of these miserable and blinded men....The last incident of the period in question, the cure on a Sabbath-day of a woman weakened and bowed down by demoniacal influence[2], brings both parties very clearly before us,

[a] Lk. xii. 1; comp. xi. 29

[b] xi. 53 sq.

[c] see ver. 39 sq.

that the incident of curing a deaf and dumb demoniac and the blasphemy it evoked (Matth. ix. 34, Luke xi. 15) happened twice, than to detach Matth. ix. 27 sq. *so far* from the period to which it certainly seems to belong. The blasphemous comment might well have been first made by the Pharisees (Matth. ix. 34), and then afterwards have been imitated and reiterated by others; compare Luke xi. 15, where observe that the speakers are not defined.

[1] Compare ch. x. 38, where even the well-known Bethany [Greswell's arguments (*Dissert.* XXXII.) against this identification seem wholly invalid] is no more nearly defined than as a κώμη τις. Compare also ch. xi. 1, ἐν τῷ εἶναι ἐν τόπῳ τινί, xiii. 10, ἐν μιᾷ τῶν συναγωγῶν, and see above,

p. 241, note 1.

[2] This miracle, it may be observed, also took place in a synagogue (Luke xiii. 10), and in this respect was the counterpart in Judæa of the similar healings on the Sabbath in the synagogue at Capernaum (Mark i. 21 sq., Luke iv. 31 sq.; and again, Matth. xii. 9 sq., Mark iii. 1 sq., Luke vi. 6 sq.). On the first occasion we find no expression of complaint or indignation; on the second occasion, evil thoughts are at work but no demonstration is made; here however the ruler of the synagogue himself interposes and addresses the multitude in terms specially intended to reflect censure on our Lord (ver. 14). On the miracle itself, the peculiar nature of which was the removal of a contraction of the body, pro-

The Journeyings toward Jerusalem.

the adversaries and their shamed silence[a], and the people, that, as the Evangelist tells us, 'rejoiced for all the glorious things[b]' that were done by their great Healer.

At the end of this two-month ministry in Judæa, and, as computation seems to warrant our saying, about the 20th of December[1], St John distinctly specifies that our Lord was present in Jerusalem at the annual festival which commemorated the purification and re-dedication of the Temple under Judas Maccabeus[2]. Though threatened by every form of danger, the Good Shepherd yet went once again, as His own Divine words seem partially to suggest, to tend His sheep,—the sheep which heard His voice and had been given to Him by that eternal Father with whom He

LECT. VI.
[a] Lk.xiii.17
[b] ver. 17

Our Lord's visit to Jerusalem at the feast of Dedication.

duced by demoniacal influence (ver. 16), that had continued as long as 18 years,—see Augustine, *Serm.* cx. Vol. v. p. 638 sq. (ed. Migne), Hook, *Serm. on the Miracles*, Vol. II. p. 102, and Trench, *Notes on the Miracles*, p. 324.

[1] The feast of Dedication regularly commenced on the 25th of Chislev. This date in the year we are now considering (A.U.C. 782) will coincide, according to the tables of Wurm and Wieseler, with Tuesday, December 20; see *Chron. Synops.* p. 484, or Tischendorf, *Synops. Evang.* p. LII.

[2] This festival, more fully specified in the Books of Maccabees as ὁ ἐγκαινισμὸς τοῦ θυσιαστηρίου (1 Macc. iv. 56, 59), ὁ καθαρισμὸς τοῦ ναοῦ (2 Macc. x. 5), and further distinguished by the name φῶτα, in consequence, according to Josephus (*Antiq.* XII. 7. 7), of unlooked-for deliverance, was instituted by Judas Maccabeus after his victories over the generals of Antiochus Epiphanes, and designed to commemorate the purification of the temple after its pollution by that frantic and cruel man (1 Macc. i. 20, Joseph. *Antiq.* XII. 5. 4). It lasted 8 days, and appears to have been a time of great festivity, and rejoicing: see Otho, *Lex. Rabbin.* p. 238 sq., and Lightfoot, *Hor. Hebr. in Joann.* x. 22, where quotations are given from the *Mishna* which seem to show that the practice of illuminating the city during the festival, and perhaps also the title φῶτα, was derived from a legendary account of a miraculous multiplication of pure oil for lighting the sacred lamps, which occurred at the first celebration of the festival; see however Winer, *RWB.* Art. 'Kirchweihfest,' Vol. I. p. 659, and comp. Caspari, *Chron.- Geogr. Einleit.* § 131, p. 148.

LECT. VI.

ᵃ Joh. x. 30
ᵇ Mt. xvi. 20

ᶜ John x. 24, 25

now solemnly and explicitly declared Himself to be oneᵃ. He who but a few months before in the remote uplands of Galilee had commanded His disciples not to divulge His Messiahshipᵇ, now in Solomon's porch[1] and in the face of bitter foes proclaims His divinity: He who even now vouchsafed not fully to answer the question of the excited people whether He were the Christ or noᶜ, nevertheless avows before all men that He is the Son of God[2]. That title which to the misbelieving Jew would have been but the symbol of earthly and carnal hope or the watchword of sedition, He merges in the higher designation that betokened His eternity and Godhead[3]....We can

---

[1] The comment, χειμὼν ἦν (ch. x. 22), which St John prefixes to his notice of the exact locality in which our Lord then was, seems designed to remind the reader why He was pleased to select this covered place ('ut captaret calorem,' Lightfoot) rather than the open courts in which, it would seem, He more usually taught the multitudes; comp. Winer, *RWB.*, Art. 'Tempel,' Vol. II. p. 586. The porch or cloister in question, we learn from Josephus (*Antiq.* xx. 9. 7), was on the east side of the Temple,—hence also known by the name of the στοὰ ἀνατολικῆ,—and appears to have been a veritable portion of the ancient temple of Solomon, which either wholly or in part escaped when the rest of the building was burnt by Nebuchadnezzar, 2 Kings xxv. 9 (Joseph. *Antiq.* x. 8. 5). It formed one, and that apparently the most splendid of the noble cloisters which surrounded the temple-enclosure: see Lightfoot, *Descr. Templi,* cap. 8, Vol. I. p. 565 (Roterod. 1686), and the valuable comments of Caspari, *Chron.-Geogr. Einleit,* p. 255 sq.

[2] On this title, which here, as in other places, has been explained away by many recent writers, see the following note, and compare above, p. 119, note 2, and p. 211, note 1. Some good comments on this particular passage will be found in Wilson, *Illustr. of the N. T.* ch. II. p. 37 sq., and a defence of the true meaning of the title in opposition to Dorner, in Stier, *Disc. of our Lord,* Vol. v. p. 496 sq.

[3] The popular assumption that the term 'Son of God' was regarded by the Jews in the time of our Lord as one of the appropriate titles of the Messiah, is carefully investigated by Wilson in the work referred to above (chap. IV. p. 56 sq.), and the conclusion arrived at is stated as follows: "With no direct testimony whatever on one side, and with the testimony of Origen (*contr. Cels.* I. p. 38, ed. Spencer), supported by a strong body of probable evidence deduced from the New Testament,

perhaps scarcely wonder at what followed. If nine months before, at the feast of Purim, the same bitter and prejudiced men had sought to kill our Lord for claiming to be the Son of God[a]; if again at the recent feast of Tabernacles the declaration of an existence before Abraham had made them snatch up stones to cast at Him[b], it could scarcely be otherwise now, when the eternal Son was claiming a oneness of essence with the eternal Father[c]. Savage hands soon take up the stones that lay round those ancient cloisters[1]: wild voices charge the Holy One with blasphemy. With blasphemy! when the very language of Scripture[d] proved that Shiloh was only laying claim to prerogatives and titles that were verily His own[e]. Blasphemy! when the very works to which our Lord appealed were living proofs that He was in the Father, and the Father in Him[f]. But the hearts of those wretched men were hardened, and their ears could not hear. Fain would they have used the stones they were now holding in their hands[2], fain would they have seized on

[a] Joh. v. 18
[b] viii. 59
[c] x. 30
[d] Psalm lxxxii. 6
[e] Joh. x. 36
[f] ver. 38

---

on the other, it seems necessary to conclude that custom had not appropriated this title, to the Messiah of the Jews, near the time of Jesus Christ.' *Illustr. of N. T.* p. 74.

[1] The idle question, how stones would be found in such a locality, may be most easily disposed of by observing, not only that general repairs and restoration in and about the temple were going on to a considerable extent until after the time of our Lord (Joseph. *Antiq.* xx. 9. 7; comp. Lightfoot, *Hor. Hebr.* Vol. II. p. 638), but that these very cloisters had not improbably suffered greatly in the fire during the revolt against Sabinus (*Antiq.* XVII. 10. 2), and might not even yet have been completely restored. At any rate a proposal was made to rebuild them in the time of Agrippa (*Antiq.* x. 9. 7). For an account of stones being freely used in an uproar in the temple-courts, see *Antiq.* XVII. 9. 3.

[2] We seem justified in pressing the present tense (διὰ ποῖον αὐτῶν ἔργον με λιθάζετε; John x. 32): the Jews had taken up stones, and were standing ready to carry out their blinded impiety; compare Winer, *Gram.* § 40. 2, p. 237 (ed. 6). Stier (*Disc. of our Lord*, Vol. V. p. 494, Clark) contrasts the

LECT. VI.

a Joh. x. 40

b ver. 41

c Lk. xiii. 22

their Redeemer, and carried out, even where they were, their lawless and impious designs, when that Holy One at once left both the temple and the city, and withdrew to those secluded districts across the Jordan*ª*, where the Baptist had commenced his ministry[1]. There the Lord found both faith and reception*ᵇ*, and there, as it would seem, He vouchsafed to abide until the commencement of His second and subsequent journey*ᶜ* to Bethany and to the neighbourhood of Jerusalem.

The Lord's message to Herod, and preparation to leave Peræa.

But even in those secluded districts hypocrisy and malice soon found an opportunity for co-operation. After our Lord had now, as it would seem, commenced His journey toward Jerusalem, and as His steps were leading Him perhaps through one of the Peræan villages or towns in the neighbourhood of His former abode[2], Pharisees come

---

ἐβάστασαν λίθους in the present case with the ἦραν λίθους in ch. viii. 59, urging that the former word marks a more deliberate rolling up of larger stones, the latter a more hasty and impetuous snatching up of any stones that chanced to lie in their way. The explanation of ἦραν may possibly be correct, but the ἐβάστασαν seems rather to imply, what the context seems to confirm, both the act of taking up the stones and *also* that of holding them in their hands, so as to be ready for use.

[1] For a rough estimate both of the time (4 or 5 weeks) which our Lord may be supposed to have now spent in Peræa, and of the date of the commencement of the second journey, see above, p. 245, note 1. The place we may observe is particularly specified as 'where John at first baptized' (John x. 40), i.e. Bethabara or (according to the correct reading) Bethany, which would seem to have been situated not very far from the ford over the Jordan in the neighbourhood of Jericho; see above, Lect. III. p. 106, note 3. Here and in the adjoining districts of Peræa our Lord remained till the second journey toward Jerusalem, which at first might have assumed the character of a partial missionary circuit, with the Holy City as its *ultimate* goal (see the following note), and which at first might have been leisurely, but which afterwards, as the sequel shows, was speedy.

[2] It would seem, as has been suggested in the preceding note, that our Lord's present journey was not at first direct. St Luke's very words διδάσκων καὶ πορείαν ποιούμενος εἰς

with plausible words to expedite His departure, and to rid themselves of One, whose successful preaching and teaching they had probably already observed with anxiety and hatred. They affect to give Him friendly warning; they urge Him to depart,—because Herod was seeking to kill Him^a. ^a Lk. xiii. 31
Because Herod was seeking to kill Him! O double-sided stratagem! O cunning co-operation of evil men! 'Twas Herod who was wishing Him to depart; 'twas Pharisees who were wishing to kill Him. That weak, wicked, and selfish Tetrarch[1] was probably anxious to get out of his territory One whose fame was daily spreading, and whom he knew not whether to honour or to persecute. He was embarrassed, but soon both sought and found useful tools in the Pharisees[2], who were only too ready to urge our Lord to leave a land where His life was comparatively safe, for one where as they well knew it was now in extremest jeopardy. But the Divine Reader of the heart, as His message to Herod seems to prove, and His

'Ιερουσαλήμ (ch. xiii. 22) appear almost studiously both to mark a more deliberate progress and to point to Jerusalem, not as the immediate destination, but as the place *toward* which the journey was tending; see Wieseler, *Chron. Synops.* p. 321.

[1] See Lect. v. p. 216, note 2.

[2] The above explanation is the only one which appears to satisfy the context and the plain meaning of the terms used. Our Lord sees through the stratagem, and sends a message to Herod, which in the peculiar term used (τῇ ἀλώπεκι ταύτῃ, Luke xiii. 32) implies that the Tetrarch's craftiness had not escaped notice, and in the distinct specifica-

tions of time (σήμερον καὶ αὔριον καὶ τῇ τρίτῃ) seems to imply not mere general and undefined periods, but literal and actual days (see Meyer and Alford *in loc.*), two of which would be spent in the territory of the evil man to whom the message was sent, and devoted to miraculous works of mercy. That our Lord really designed the message not for Herod but for the Pharisees (Stier, *Disc. of our Lord*, Vol. IV. p. 61, Clark; comp. also Cyril Alex. *in loc.*, and the Scholiast in Cramer, *Caten.* Vol. II. p. 110), seems highly improbable, and contrary to the plain tenor of very simple and very explicit words.

LECT. VI.

Probable events during the last two days in Peræa.

ᵃ Joh. xi. 54

mournful address to Jerusalem¹, which immediately follows, serves indirectly to confirm, saw in an instant through that combination of cunning and malevolence. Works of mercy were yet to be done, miraculous cures were to be vouchsafed to-day and to-morrow even in the borders of that wily ruler's province; on the third was to begin the journey, that though recommenced from Ephraimᵃ, was the last made actually *to* Jerusalem,—that journey that closed with Golgotha and its perfected sacrifice².

Whether the difficult words which have just

¹ The position which this address to Jerusalem occupies in St Luke's Gospel (ch. xiii. 34) as compared with that in St Matthew's Gospel (see ch. xxiii. 37 sq.), and the interpretation which is to be given to the words, are points which have been much discussed. With regard to the *first*, the natural coherence with what precedes wholly precludes our believing that St Luke has misplaced the words. Nearly as much may be urged for the position of the words in St Matthew. It appears then not unreasonable to suppose that the words were uttered on two different occasions,—a supposition further supported by some slight diversities of language in the two places: see Alford *on Luke* xiii. 34. With regard to the *second* point, while it seems difficult to believe that the words have no reference to the time when the very terms here specified were actually used (see Mark xi. 9), it seems equally difficult to believe that their meaning was then exhausted. We may thus, perhaps with some reason, believe with modern chronologers (comp.

Wieseler, *Chron. Synops.* p. 322) that the words had a first and perhaps immediate reference to the Triumphal Entry, and with the ancient writers (Theophylact, al.) that they had a further reference to the Lord's second Advent.

² The meaning and reference of τελειοῦμαι (Luke xiii. 32) is perhaps slightly doubtful. That it is a present *passive* (Syr., Vulg.), not a pres. middle (Meyer), and that the meaning is 'consummor' (Syr., Vulg.), seems clearly to follow from the regular usage of the verb in the N. Test. (comp. esp. Phil. iii. 12); and that the reference is to an action soon and certainly (Winer, *Gr.* § 40. 2) to be commenced, and also to be continued, seems a just inference from the tense. Combining these observations we may perhaps rightly refer it as above to our Lord's perfected sacrifice ('the passion upon the cross for the salvation of the world,' Cyr. Alex.), which was consummated in Golgotha, but the onward course to which was commenced when our Lord left the borders of Peræa.

been paraphrased apply definitely to the period of the history now before us, whether they are merely proverbial, or whether they involve a special note of time, cannot confidently be decided. The latter, as we have already implied, seems the more natural view, and is most in accordance with the precise nature of the inspired language,—but more than this cannot be positively asserted. One thing seems perfectly clear, that in the succeeding portion of St Luke's Gospel there is nothing which is opposed to such a view, and that in St John's Gospel, as we shall hereafter see[1], there is something in its favour. That our Lord preached and performed miracles[2] during the brief remainder of His stay in Peræa, can scarcely be doubted. That He healed a man afflicted with dropsy[3] at the house of a leader of the Pharisees[a], where He was invited, as it would seem, only to be watched, and uttered there the appropriate parable of the Great Supper[b],—that publicans[4] and sinners crowded round Him[c],—

[a] Lk. xiv. 1
[b] ver. 16
[c] Lk. xv. 1

---

[1] See below, pp. 267, 268.

[2] The prominent declaration in our Lord's message to Herod is that there will still be a continuance of miraculous works of mercy 'to-day and to-morrow.' Of these St Luke only mentions the healing of a man afflicted with dropsy; but as we may observe that in this portion of his Gospel he was clearly moved rather to record the teaching of our Lord than to specify His mighty works, we cannot fairly press the omission of other miracles that might have taken place on these concluding days.

[3] On this miracle, which forms one of the seven performed on the Sabbath (see above, p. 177, note 2), compare some comments by Anselm, *Hom.* x. p. 180 (Paris, 1675), a few remarks by Stier, *Disc. of our Lord*, Vol. IV. p. 67 (Clark), and Trench, *Notes on the Miracles*, p. 329. The miracle was performed at the house of an ἄρχων τῶν Φαρισαίων (Luke xiv. 1),—a general title, as it would seem, implying some leadership or pre-eminence in the sect; see Meyer *in loc.*

[4] The peculiar reference which St Luke here makes to 'all the publicans' (πάντες οἱ τελῶναι, Luke xv. 1) appears to deserve attention as something more than a merely general or 'popularly hyperbolical'

LECT. VI.

^a Lk. xv. 4
^b ver. 8
^c ver. 11
^d xvi. 14
^e ver. 1
^f ver. 19

and that when Scribes and Pharisees murmured thereat, He uttered the parables of the Lost Sheep[a], the Lost Coin[b], the Prodigal Son[c], and subsequently, to His disciples, though in the hearing of the Pharisees[d], the parables of the Unjust Steward[e], and of Lazarus[1] and the Rich Man[f], seems almost certain from the place which these discourses occupy in the present portion of St Luke's narrative. That all this might have been done in the two days, the 'to-day and to-morrow' which our

^g xiii. 32, 33

Lord twice[g] so distinctly specifies, and that on the third He might have crossed the Jordan and commenced a journey, which though, as we have already observed, not the last to Judæa[2], was not-

(Meyer) form of expression. If our Lord was now near one of the fords of the Jordan and not far from Jericho he would be on the borders of a district in which, owing to its great productiveness (Robinson, *Palestine*, Vol. I. p. 559), these tax-collectors would probably have been very numerous: comp. Luke xix. 2, and see Lange, *Leben Jesu*, II. 6. 1, Part III. p. 1159.

[1] From the general connexion of Luke xvi. 1 (ἔλεγεν δὲ καὶ πρὸς τοὺς μαθητάς) with ch. xv., and the apparent connexion of subject between ch. xvi. 19—31 with ver. 9—13 (see Meyer *in loc.* p. 421, ed. 3) we may perhaps infer that this parable was uttered on the same day that so many of the publicans came to hear our Lord's teaching (ch. xv. 1), and probably at the close of the last day in Peræa, or at the beginning of the next, when our Lord might have been in the district of Jericho; see above, p. 262, note 1. If this be so and we agree to combine with this portion of St Luke's Gospel the narrative in John xi. 1 sq. (see below), this parable would have been uttered only a day or two after our Lord had received the message about Lazarus. May not then the name of the sufferer in the parable have been suggested by the name of Lazarus of Bethany, on whom our Lord's thoughts might now have been dwelling, and in whose history there may have been *possibly* some circumstances of resemblance to that of the Lazarus of the parable? The opinions of early writers were divided in reference to this parable, some (Irenæus, Tertullian, Chrysostom, al.) conceiving it to be an actual history, some of equal antiquity (Clem. Alex., Theophilus, Asterius, al.) more plausibly regarding it a parable; see especially the citations in Suicer, *Thesaur.* s.v. Ἀδ{ζ}αρος, Vol. II. p. 206 sq.

[2] The journey from Ephraim, which apparently lay through Samaria, Galilee, and Peræa, was the last to Judæa, but in reference to Jerusalem may be considered a part of

withstanding the last estimated with reference to the final goal, Jerusalem,—is a supposition which seems to coincide fully with the language and notices of St Luke[1].

LECT. VI.

And with this too the narrative of St John does indeed appear very strikingly to harmonize. The next event recorded by that Evangelist, after the notice of the withdrawal to and preaching in Peræa[a], is the message sent by the afflicted sisters of Lazarus,—accompanied by the special note of time that the Lord abode *two* days where he then was. Now as two days more would easily bring our Lord from Peræa to Bethany[2], and as we also know that Lazarus was summoned from the tomb after he had lain there *four* days[b], how very plausible is the supposition that the Lord was in Peræa when He received the message from the sisters of Lazarus[3], and that the two days during

Apparently confirmatory notice in St John.

[a] x. 40

[b] xi. 39

the second. On these journeys see above, p. 242 sq., and compare p. 245, note 1.

[1] Compare the notice of this second journey, πορείαν ποιούμενος εἰς Ἰερουσαλήμ (Luke xiii. 22), with the notice of what seems the third journey, ἐν τῷ πορεύεσθαι αὐτὸν εἰς Ἰερουσαλήμ, καὶ αὐτὸς διήρχετο διὰ μέσου Σαμαρείας καὶ Γαλιλαίας (Luke xvii. 11),—between which passages there is just the connexion we might expect, on the hypothesis that the first refers to a journey which did not reach Jerusalem, and that the second refers to its continuation or recommencement.

[2] According to the Jerusalem Itinerary the distance from Jerusalem to Jericho was 18 miles, and from Jericho to the Jordan 5 more, in all 23 miles. The same distances are specified by Josephus (*Bell. Jud.* IV. 8. 3) as 150 and 60 stades respectively, or in all 210 stades; see Greswell, *Dissert.* XXXVIII. Vol. III. p. 60. Whichever calculation be adopted, our Lord clearly could have reached Bethany from the Jordan in as little as one day, and with ease in two, even if He had been some little distance on the other side of the river. On the rate of a day's journey, see Greswell, *Dissert.* XXVI. (Append.) Vol. IV. p. 525 sq.

[3] The message only announced that Lazarus was sick, but the supposition is not improbable that by the time the messenger reached our Lord, Lazarus had died. It may be observed that two days afterwards when our Lord speaks of the death of Lazarus he uses the aorist

268   *The Journeyings toward Jerusalem.*

LECT. VI.

[a] ver. 6

[b] Lk.xiii.31

[c] See p. 266, note 1

which 'He abode in the place where He was[a]' were the two last days in Peræa, the 'to-day and to-morrow' of which He spake when the Pharisees came with the hypocritical warning about the designs of Herod[b]. This seeming coincidence of the notes of time supplied by the fourth Evangelist with those hinted at by St Luke, combined with the further very curious fact already alluded to[c], that the not very common name of Lazarus[1] appears in a parable delivered by our Lord just at a time, when it may be thought to have been suggested by the message which St John tells us was sent to our Lord about the actual Lazarus of Bethany,—all this does indeed seem to support our view of the chronology of the present period, and to reflect some probability on our explanation of the ambiguous 'to-day and to-morrow' of the third Evangelist[2].

But let us pass onward.

Effect produced by the raising of Lazarus.

[d] Joh. xi. 45

[e] xii. 9

On the mighty but familiar miracle of the raising of Lazarus, I will not pause save to remark that the effect it produced was immense. It gathered in believers even from the ranks of opponents[d]; it afterwards brought multitudes from Jerusalem to see the risen man[e], and swelled the

---

ἀπέθανεν (John xi. 14), which seems to refer the death to some period, undefined indeed, but now past: see Fritz. *de Aoristi Vi,* p. 17, and compare notes *on* 1 *Thess.* ii. 16. On the adjustments of time mentioned in the narrative of St John, see Meyer *on John* xi. 17, p. 331 (ed. 3).

[1] Lazarus appears to be a shortened form of the more familiar Eleazer; see especially the learned investigation of Bynæus, *de Morte*

Christi, III. 8, Vol. I. p. 180 sq., and comp. Lightfoot, *Hor. Hebr. in Joann.* xi. 1.

[2] We may perhaps recognize a further point of contact between the τῇ τρίτῃ τελειοῦμαι of St Luke (ch. xiii. 32) and the remarks of the Apostles (John xi. 8, 16) on our Lord's proposal to go into Judæa: they regard that journey, as it truly proved to be, a journey of which τὸ τετελειῶσθαι was the issue.

The Journeyings toward Jerusalem. 269

triumph of the Lord's entry[1]; and alas! it also now stirred up enemies to delay no longer[a], and made a High Priest pervert the mysterious gift of prophecy[2] by using it to hurry on the members of his council to plot against innocent blood[b]. So avowed were now the savage counsels, that our Lord at once withdrew to the town of Ephraim[c] on the borders of Samaria[3], and there after an abode of perhaps a very few weeks[4] commenced the last, and as we may perhaps venture to term it, the farewell-journey described by all the three Synoptical Evangelists[d], and specially noticed by St Luke as being directed 'through the midst of *Samaria* and Galilee[5].' The striking harmony

LECT. VI.

[a] Joh. xi. 47
[b] ver. 49 sq.
[c] xi. 54
[d] Mt. xix. 1
Mark x. 1
Lk. xvii. 11

---

[1] See John xii. 17, 18. On this mighty miracle, in which our Lord not only appears, as previously, the conqueror of death, but even of corruption (John xi. 39), see the commentaries of Origen [the part preceding ver. 39 is lost], Chrysostom, Cyril Alex. and Augustine (*in Joann.* Tractat. XLIX.), Bp Hall, *Contempl.* IV. 23, 24, the very good comments in Stier, *Disc. of our Lord*, Vol. VI. p. 1 sq. (Clark), the vindication of Lardner, *Works*, Vol. XI. p. 1, and Trench, *Notes on the Miracles*, p. 389.

[2] It has often been discussed whether this was conscious or unconscious prophecy. The tenor of the context seems clearly to show that it can only be regarded in the latter view. Caiaphas was only consciously stating what he deemed politically advisable, but he was nevertheless, as the inspired Evangelist distinctly tells us, at the time actually prophesying; κατὰ τοῦ Ἰησοῦ ἀγωνιζόμενος οὐδὲν ἧττον προεφήτευσεν. Origen, *in Joann.*

Tom. XI. 12,—where the nature of this prophecy is considered at great length: compare *Thesaur. Nov. (Crit. Sacr.)* Vol. II. p. 525.

[3] There seems reason for believing that this place was identical with Ophrah, and corresponds with the modern village of *Taiyibeh*, which according to Robinson occupies a commanding site on the top of a conical hill, whence a fine view is to be obtained of the eastern mountains, the valley of the Jordan, and the Dead Sea: *Palestine*, Vol. I. p. 444, 447. It is about 6h. 20m. (1 hour = 3 Roman miles) distant from Jerusalem (see *ib.* Vol. II. p. 568),—a distance very closely agreeing with that specified by Jerome (*Onomast.* s. v.), who makes it 20 miles. Caspari attempts to identify it with a place now called El Faria or El-Farah, about 2 hours N. E. of Nablus,—but not successfully: see *Chron.-Geogr. Einleit.* § 139, p. 158.

[4] See above, p. 245, note 1.

[5] The interpretation of Meyer (comp. Alford *in loc.*, Lange, *Leben*

between this notice of direction and the abode in the frontier town of Ephraim specified by St John may well give us confidence in our foregoing arrangement, and add strength to our belief in the general chronological accuracy of the latter as well as of the former portions of the narrative of the third Evangelist.

Incidents in the last journey to Judæa.

The incidents in this last journey are not many. Possibly on the frontiers of Samaria we may fix the scene of the Healing of the ten lepers[1], and of the gratitude of the single sufferer that belonged to the despised land[a]. To the period of the transit through Galilee we may *perhaps* assign the notice of the solemn answer to the probably treacherous inquiry of the Pharisees when the kingdom of God should come[b], and to the same period[2] the parable of the Unjust Judge[c],—a parable that gains much of its force and solemnity from the previous mention of a

[a] Luke xvii. 16

[b] ver. 20

[c] xviii. 1 sq.

Jesu, Part II. p. 1065, Caspari, *Chron.-Geogr. Einleit.* p. 159), according to which διὰ μέσου Σαμαρείας καὶ Γαλιλαίας (Luke xvii. 11) is to be understood as implying the frontier district lying between these two provinces *along* which our Lord journeyed from west to east, is apparently grammatically defensible (see Xen. *Anab.* I. 4. 4), but certainly not very natural or probable. The plain and obvious meaning surely is that our Lord went, not merely 'per Samaritanos in Galilæam,' Syr.-Pesh., but through the middle of both countries; see Lightfoot, *Chron. Temp.* § 62, and comp. Wieseler, *Chron. Synops.* p. 322.

[1] On this miracle, the characteristic of which is its deferred working till the faith of the sufferers was shown by their obedience to the Lord's command, see Bp Hall, *Contempl.* IV. 10, Trench, *Notes on the Miracles*, p. 332,—who, however, has adopted the not very probable interpretation referred to in the preceding note; and compare Hook, *Serm. on the Miracles*, Vol. II. p. 140, and a good practical sermon by Hare (A. W.), *Sermons*, Vol. II. p. 457.

[2] It is very doubtful whether these incidents are to be assigned to the portion of the journey through Galilee, or to that through Peræa. The latter view is adopted by Greswell, *Dissert.* XXXI. Vol. II. p. 542; the former, however, seems slightly the most probable: see Lightfoot, *Chron. Temp.* § 62, 63, Vol. II. p. 40 (Roterod. 1686).

time of terrible trial and perplexity[1]. From Galilee we seem fully justified, by the distinct notices both of St Matthew[a] and St Mark[b], in tracing our Lord's steps to the lands across the Jordan[2]. Whether this journey extended to the more northern parts of Peræa, where it will be remembered a few months before the Four thousand were fed, and where the name of the God of Israel was so magnified[c], we cannot determine. The expressions of St Matthew[d] would rather lead us to the contrary opinion, and to the supposition that our Lord passed directly onward to the portions nearer Judæa[3] in which he had preached a few weeks before, and to which we shall apparently be right in confining the few remaining

LECT. VI.

[a] xix. 1
[b] x. 1

[c] Mt. xv. 3

[d] xix. 1

---

[1] There seems no reason for supposing with Olshausen and others that some intermediate remarks connecting this parable more closely with what precedes are here omitted. On the contrary, as ver. 7 seems to prove, the connexion is close and immediate. When the Lord comes, He comes to avenge His own and free them from their foes,—and that full surely: if an unjust earthly judge avenged her who called upon him, shall not a righteous heavenly Judge avenge the elect of God! See Meyer, *in loc.* p. 441 (ed. 3), and on the parable generally, compare Greswell, *Exposition of the Parables*, Vol. IV. p. 213 sq., Trench, *Notes on the Parables*, p. 439.

[2] Caspari does not admit this. He urges that we have no notice of our Lord having crossed the Jordan, and that we are rather to suppose that our Lord approached Jericho by the road leading from Scythopolis to that city: see *Chron.-Geogr.* *Einleit.* § 140, p. 159. This view however rather depends on his interpretation of Luke xvii. 11; see above, p. 269, note 5.

[3] There is some little difficulty in the words ἦλθεν εἰς τὰ ὅρια τῆς Ἰουδαίας πέραν τοῦ Ἰορδάνου (Matth. xix. 1). Viewed simply, and with the remembrance that an insertion of the article before πέραν is not positively necessary (see Winer, *Gr.* § 20. 2), they would seem in accordance with the statement of Ptolemy (*Geogr.* v. 16. 9) that a certain portion of the province of Judæa actually lay on the *eastern* side of the Jordan: viewed however in connexion with Mark x. 1, they seem rather to mark the general direction of our Lord's journey, and might be paraphrased,—'He came to the frontiers of Judæa (οὐκ ἐπὶ τὰ μέσα, ἀλλ᾽ οἱονεὶ τὰ ἄκρα, Origen), His route lying on the other side of the Jordan;' comp. Greswell, *Dissert.* XXXI. Vol. II. p. 542.

incidents which we meet with in this part of the inspired narrative[1]. We observed there just what we should have expected from our remembrance of our Lord's former sojourn in that country. We trace the same characteristics displayed by the two classes of our Lord's hearers with which we are so familiar in earlier parts of the Gospel-history,— thankful and even enthusiastic reception on the part of the multitude[a], craft and malignity on the part of the Pharisees and their various adherents. The latter feelings are soon displayed in the insidious inquiry about the lawfulness of divorce[b],— a question studiously chosen to place our Lord in antagonism either with the school of Hillel or with the school of Shammai, and thus to bring upon Him the hostility of one or other of two influential parties, if not also in some degree to involve Him with the adulterous Tetrarch in whose territory He then was[2]. In these same districts and in touching contrast to all this craft were the young children brought to our Lord[c], and

[a] Mt. xix. 2
[b] xix. 3 sq. Mk. x. 2 sq.
[c] Mt. xix. 13

---

[1] In this arrangement nearly all harmonists are agreed; the only doubt, as has been observed (p. 270, note 2), is whether these are the *only* incidents which belong to the journey through Peræa. Greswell urges the apparent consecutive character of the discourses, Luke xvii. 20—xviii. 14, but it may be said that there is really no greater break between Luke xvii. 19 and Luke xvii. 20, which Greswell disconnects, than between Luke xviii. 14 and Luke xviii. 15, which he unites. It must remain then a matter of opinion, the few arguments in favour of one arrangement being nearly of equal weight with those in favour of the other.

[2] Compare De Wette *on Matth.* xix. 3, to whom the hint is due. The main design, however, as St Matthew's addition κατὰ πᾶσαν αἰτίαν (practically the language of the school of Hillel) seems clearly to show, was to induce our Lord to decide upon a question that was much in debate between two large parties, the school of Hillel adopting the lax view, the school of Shammai the more strict: 'schola Shammæana, non permisit repudia nisi in causâ adulterii, Hilleliana aliter.' Lightfoot, *in loc.* Vol. II. p. 345; compare Jost, *Gesch. des Judenth.* II. 3, 13, Vol. I. p. 257.

The Journeyings toward Jerusalem.

blessed with the outward signs and tokens of His Divine love[1]. Here too was the home of that rich young man whom Jesus looked on and loved[a], and of whom the melancholy notice[b] is left that worldly possessions kept him back from the kingdom of God[2].

[a] Mk. x. 21
[b] ver. 22

LECT. VI.

And now every step was leading our Lord and His Apostles nearer to Jerusalem, and every step calls forth in the very outward demeanour of the Lord a manifestation of a dauntless resolution which awes and amazes[3] that shrinking and now foreboding company. The Lord now heads His band of followers, as St Mark graphically mentions[c], and leads the onward way. To the general company of disciples, augmented as it now well might have been by many a worshipper that the festival was bringing up to Jerusalem, the Lord is silent; but to the chosen Twelve[4] He now again

Onward progress toward Jerusalem.

[c] x. 32

---

[1] We are distinctly told by St Matthew the two blessings which the bringers of the children hope to receive for them at the hands of our Lord,—ἵνα τὰς χεῖρας ἐπιθῇ αὐτοῖς καὶ προσεύξηται (ch. xix. 13). The former act, the imposition of hands, was probably regarded to some extent what it truly was, the outward sign of the conveyance of inward gifts and blessings (τὴν φρουρητικὴν ἑαυτοῦ δύναμιν, Euthym.; comp. Origen, *in Matth.* Tom. xv. 6); the latter was regarded and apparently not uncommonly sought for (see Buxtorf, *Synag.* cap. vii. p. 138, Basil, 1661) as adding to the former the efficacies of holy and prevailing prayer. Rightly did the early Church see in this an argument for infant baptism: compare Augustine, *Serm.* cxv. 4, Vol. v.

p. 657 (ed. Migne).

[2] That this young man was not a hypocrite, but one whom wealth and worldliness held in a thraldom that kept him from Christ, is justly maintained by Chrysostom (*in Matth.* Hom. LXIII.), who bases his opinion on Mark x. 21. The apocryphal version of the incident, said to come from the *Evang. secundum Hebræos*, is given by Origen, *in Matth.* (*Vet. Interpr.*) Tom. xv. 14; see Hofmann, *Leben Jesu*, § 71, p. 306.

[3] The second reason assigned by Euthymius (*on Mark* x. 32) seems certainly the true one: 'They were amazed,—either at what He was saying, or because of His own accord He was going onward to His passion' (διότι ηὐτομόλει πρὸς τὸ πάθος).

[4] It is distinctly told us by St Matthew (ch. xx. 17) that this

LECT. VI.

*Mt. xx. 18
b Lk. ix. 46

c Matt. xx. 20 sq.
Mark x. 35 sq.

Arrival at Jericho.

for the third time speaks of the future that awaited Him^a. Yet they could not or they would not understand. Nay, they seem, as on a former occasion^b, almost to have put a counter-interpretation on the words; for strange as indeed it appears, this we learn was the hour that the sons of Zebedee and their mother preferred their ambitious request^c, and in fancy were enthroning themselves on the right hand and the left hand of their triumphant Master[1].

Jericho is soon reached; and there as it would seem at the entrance into the city, one or, as St Matthew specifies, *two* blind men[2] hail the Lord

---

mournful communication was made privately (κατ' ἰδίαν) to the Apostles; comp. Mark x. 32, Luke xviii. 31. The two other occasions on which the same sad future had been announced to them was in the neighbourhood of Cæsarea Philippi, immediately after St Peter's confession (Matth. xvi. 21 sq., Mark viii. 30 sq., Luke ix. 21 sq.), and not very long afterwards during the subsequent return to Capernaum (Matth. xvii. 22 sq., Mark ix. 30 sq., Luke ix. 43 sq.). The reason for the private manner in which the communication was made is perhaps rightly given by Euthymius,—to avoid giving grounds of offence to the attendant multitudes.

[1] It is worthy of notice that the request is made by one from whom according to our common estimate of his character we should not have expected it,—St John, the disciple whom Jesus loved. The attempt of Olshausen to explain away the request as a petition hereafter to enjoy the same privilege of nearness to our Lord (*Comment. on Gospels*,

Vol. III. p. 121, Clark) must certainly be rejected: such a desire was doubtless present, but the request itself was plainly one for προεδρία (Chrys.), a genuine characteristic of the glowing hearts of the Sons of Thunder: see above, p. 249, note 1. According to St Matthew (ch. xx. 20) the request was preferred by their mother, Salome. The explanation is obvious: the mother was the actual speaker, the two apostles were the instigators; αἰσχυνόμενοι προβάλλονται τὴν τεκοῦσαν, Chrysost. *in Matth.* Hom. LXV. Vol. VII. p. 645 (ed. Bened. 2).

[2] It is difficult to account for this seeming discrepancy, as there is not only a difference between St Matthew and the second and third Evangelists as to *number*, but between St Luke and the first and second as to *time*. Perhaps, as seemed likely in the similar case of the Gadarene demoniacs (see above, p. 189, note 2), one of the blind men, Bartimæus, was better known (Augustine), and thus his cure more particularly specified; see Mark x. 46 sq.

with the same title that a few days afterwardsᵃ was heard from a thousand voices on the slopes of Olivet. They call unto the Son of Davidᵇ whom as yet they saw not: they call and they are healed. Begirt by the now-increasing and glorifying multitude the Lord enters the city. But praises soon change to general murmuringsᶜ when the just and faithful Zacchæus is called down from the sycamore-tree to entertain Him, on whose Divine form he would have rejoiced only to have gazed afar off[1], but whom now he was to be so blest as to welcome under the shadow of his roofᵈ. Still the heart of the people was moved. Wild hopes and expectations still pervade all hearts; and it is to allay them, that the Lord now utters both to the disciples and the multitude the solemn parable of the Pounds,—that parable which, as St Luke tells usᵉ, was specially designed to check the hope that God's kingdom was speedily to be revealed[2].

ᵃ Mt. xxi. 9
ᵇ Mk. x. 47
ᶜ Lk. xix. 7
ᵈ ver. 5
ᵉ xix. 11

If we add to this the further supposition, that the one who is mentioned at our Lord's entry into Jericho as having learnt from the crowd who it was that was coming into the city (Luke xviii. 37), was not healed *then*, but, in company with another sufferer, when our Lord was leaving the city (Maldonatus, Bengel),—we have perhaps the most probable solution of the difficulty that has yet been proposed. On this point and the miracle generally, see Trench, *Notes on the Miracles*, p. 428 sq., and compare Origen, *in Matth.* Tom. XVI. 9,—who adopts an allegorical mode of reconciliation, Augustine, *de Consens. Evang.* II. 65, Vol. III. p. 1167, *Serm.* LXXXVIII. Vol. V. p. 539 (ed. Migne), and Lange, *Leben Jesu*, II. 6. I, Part III. p. 1158.

[1] The language of St Luke (ἐζήτει ἰδεῖν τὸν Ἰησοῦν τίς ἐστιν, ch. xix. 3) would seem to imply that Zacchæus was anxious to behold the person and outward form of our Lord, and distinguish it from that of the bystanders. That this was not from curiosity but from a far deeper feeling,—perhaps presentiment, seems clear from what followed: εἶδεν αὐτὸν τοῖς ὀφθαλμοῖς τῆς ἀνθρωπότητος προεῖδε γὰρ αὐτὸν τοῖς ὀφθαλμοῖς τῆς θεότητος, Euthymius, *in loc.* On the title ἀρχιτελώνης, compare p. 20, note 1.

[2] Apparently two reasons are given by St Luke why our Lord uttered this parable,—'because He was nigh to Jerusalem,' and 'because the kingdom of God should immediately appear' (ch. xix. 11). The

LECT. VI.

ᵃ Lk. xix. 11

ᵇ Joh. xii. 1

In the same noticeable attitude,—as is again specially mentionedᵃ,—at the head of His followers, the Lord soon journeys onward towards Jerusalem, and reaches Bethany six days¹ before His last Passoverᵇ.

two reasons however really only amount to one, our Lord's journey to Jerusalem being connected in the mind of the populace (as was fully shown two or three days later) with the establishment there of His future kingdom: 'they deemed,' says Euthymius, 'that for this cause He was now going up that He might reign therein.' On the parable itself, which is obviously very similar to, but not on that account to be regarded as identical with, the parable of the Talents (Matth. xxv. 14), see Greswell, *Exposition of the Parables*, Vol. IV. p. 418 sq., Trench, *Notes on the Parables*, p. 234 sq.

¹ There is some little difficulty as to the date of our Lord's arrival at Bethany. It is definitely fixed by St John as πρὸ ἓξ ἡμερῶν τοῦ πάσχα (ch. xii. 1), and thus, according to the ordinary meaning of the words and the usual mode of reckoning, would seem to be Nisan 8, the passover being Nisan 14. Now as it seems certain that our Lord suffered on a Friday, and as it is scarcely less certain that *according to St John* (ch. xiii. 1, xviii. 28, xix. 14) the Passover was eaten on that same day, it will follow that Nisan 8 or the day of our Lord's arrival at Bethany, will coincide with the preceding Saturday or with the Jewish sabbath. Of this difficulty various solutions have been proposed, the most elaborate of which is that of Greswell (*Dissert.* XXXVIII. Vol. III. p. 51 sq.), according to which our Lord came from Jericho to a place a few miles from Bethany, assumed to be the house of Zacchæus, on Friday eve, and on Saturday eve after sunset went onward to Bethany. This appears so complicated that it is better either (a) to admit that our Lord arrived on Nisan 8, but to leave the circumstances and time of the arrival unexplained (Lücke, Meyer, Alford), or (b) to conceive that St John, writing generally, does not here include the days *from* which and *to* which the six days are reckoned, and that thus our Lord arrived at Bethany on Friday, Nisan 7: compare Tischendorf, *Syn. Evang.* p. XLIII. It is worthy of consideration, however, whether (c) our Lord might not have arrived on Friday eve *just* after the Sabbath commenced, so that the day of His arrival was really according to Jewish reckoning Nisan 8. Caspari adopts the opinion that our Lord arrived at Bethany on the Sunday, and that the supper prepared for Him was in the evening of that day, but this, though in some respects a convenient chronological hypothesis for the arrangement of incidents during the remaining days, is at variance with the ancient tradition that the Triumphal Entry was on the Sunday; see *Chron.-Geogr. Einleit.* § 165, p. 186 sq. Discussions of this question will be found in the various commentaries; compare also Bynæus, *de Morte Christi*, I. 3. 12, Vol. I. p. 188 sq., Schneckenburger, *Beiträge*, p. 14.

And here our present section, and our extended though, alas! hasty survey of the concluding year of our Lord's ministry comes to its close. *LECT. VI.*

I will delay you with no practical comments,—for the time is far spent,—but I will conclude with the deep and earnest prayer that I may have awakened in some hearts a fresh desire to ponder over for themselves the connexions of the blessed history of their own and the world's redemption. The close study of it may require all our highest powers, and tax all our freshest energies, but believe me, brethren, the consolations of that study no tongue of man or angels can fully tell. While we are so engaged we do indeed feel the deep meaning of what an apostle has called the 'comfort' of the word of God[a]. Though at times we may seem as yet in doubtfulness or perplexity, yet soon, very soon, all becomes clear and comforting. Lights break around our path; assurance becomes more sure; hopes burn brighter; love waxes warmer; sorrows become joys; and joys the reflections of the unending felicities of the kingdom of Christ. Around us and about us we feel the deepening influence of the Eternal Son. All inward things, yea too, all outward things appear to us verily transfigured and changed. We cast our eyes abroad on earth: 'tis the earth that *He* trod, and earth seems bright and blessed. We raise our eyes to the Heavens, and we know that He is there,—we gaze, and faith rolls back those everlasting doors; yea, we seem to see the vision of beauty[b], and in our spirit we behold our God. *Conclusion.*

[a] Rom. xv. 4
[b] Isai. xxxiii. 17

LECTURE VII.

THE LAST PASSOVER.

St Luke xviii. 31.

Behold, we go up to Jerusalem, and all things that are written by the prophets concerning the Son of Man shall be accomplished.

WE have now entered upon a portion of the inspired narrative, which, no less in its general and outward features than in the subjects on which it treats, is strikingly different from any other portion that we have yet attempted to consider. Hitherto in only a very few, and those scattered parts of the sacred history, has the united testimony of the four Evangelists been vouchsafed to us in reference to the same facts[1]. Sometimes one

---

[1] In the large portion of the Gospel-history which we have now considered, apparently not more than three or four cases can be found in which the same speech, subject, or event is specified by *all* the four sacred writers. The *first* instance perhaps is the declaration of the Baptist as to the relation in which he stood to our Lord: with Matth. iii. 11 sq., Mark i. 7 sq., Luke iii. 16 sq., compare John i. 26, but observe that the words which are approximately the same in the four narratives were uttered on more than one occasion and to different hearers. The *second* instance is the narrative of our Lord's baptism, which, as related by the Baptist (John i. 32), may be compared with the notices of the Synoptical writers (Matth. iii. 16 sq., Mark i. 10 sq., Luke iii. 21 sq.). The *third* is the account of the Feeding of the five thousand, where John vi. 1 sq. is clearly parallel with Matth. xiv. 13 sq., Mark vi. 32 sq., Luke ix. 10 sq. St Peter's profession of faith in our Lord may perhaps be considered a *fourth* case, but it must be remembered that the occasions were different; the first profession (John vi. 68) being made at Capernaum, the second (Matth. xvi. 16, Mark viii.

of the inspired writers has been our principal guide, sometimes another; what one has left unnoticed another has often been moved to record, but seldom have all related to us the same events, or even dwelt in equal proportions upon the same general divisions of the Gospel-history. Not unfrequently indeed we have enjoyed the privilege of the combined testimony of two of the sacred writers, and not much less frequently even of the first three[1]; but at present anything like a continuously concurrent testimony, even in the case of the Synoptical Gospels, has rarely presented itself except for very limited periods of the time over which their records extend.

Characteristics of the preceding portion of the narrative.

We may verify this by a brief retrospect. We may remember, for instance, how in the earliest portions of the Gospel-history the appointed witness

29, Luke ix. 20) in the neighbourhood of Cæsarea Philippi; see above, Lect. v. p. 213, note 1.

[1] The exact numerical proportions in which the discourses, subjects, or events specified by three of the Evangelists stand with respect to those related only by two can hardly be satisfactorily stated, owing to the differences of opinion about some of these coincidences, and still more to the obvious fact that the relations between the three Synoptical Gospels are continually changing. As a general statement however it may be said that the combined testimony of the first *three* Evangelists preponderates in the narrative of the ministry in Eastern Galilee, but that in the narrative of the north-Galilæan ministry the instances are not many where we have the testimony of more than *two*,—principally St Matthew; see above, Lect. v. p. 206. The whole question of these correspondences is one of great importance, as affecting our opinion of the origin and relations of the first three Gospels, but far too long to be comprised in the limits of a single note. The attention of the student may, however, be called to the fact that exact verbal coincidences are much more frequent in the *recital of words spoken* than in merely *narrative portions*, and, again, that the ratio of coincidence in *narrative* to that in *recital* is strikingly different in the first three Evangelists, the ratio in St Matthew being as 1 to a little more than 2, in St Mark as 1 to 4, and in St Luke as 1 to 10. See especially the good discussion in Norton, *Evidences of the Genuineness of the Gospels*, Vol. I. p. 239 (ed. 2), where the consideration of these numerical relations appears to lead to satisfactory results.

LECT. VII.

seemed to be, pre-eminently though not exclusively, St Luke, and how again in the brief narrative of the early ministry in Judæa, almost our only guide was found to be St John[1]. It may be remembered further, that of portions of our Lord's ministry in Eastern Galilee we often had the blessing of three records, but that in reference to the order of the events, we appeared to have reasons for relying more on the narrative of the second and third Evangelists, than on that of the more grouped records of St Matthew[2]. Of the ministry in northern Galilee, we have seen that but little has been recorded by the historian-Evangelist St Luke, but again that of our Lord's concluding ministry in Judæa and Peræa we should have known almost nothing, if he had not been specially moved to record that striking series of connected events and discourses[3] which occupied our attention in the concluding part of the foregoing Lecture.

Characteristics of the present portion.

Thus varied would seem to be the general aspect of those parts of the inspired narrative to which we have hitherto confined our meditations.

---

[1] See above the important quotation from Eusebius, Lect. IV. p. 151, note 1.

[2] See above, Lect. IV. p. 155 sq., where a statement will be found of the four principal reasons for adopting the order of St Mark and St Luke rather than that of St Matthew: compare also Lect. I. p. 20 sq.

[3] It has been already implied, but may be more distinctly stated that the great peculiarity of the large portion of St Luke's Gospel extending from the end of the 9th to the middle of the 19th chapter is the close connexion that appears to exist between the incidents mentioned or alluded to and the discourses which followed. It would seem almost as if the former were only noticed as serving to introduce and give force to the weighty words which followed: compare Luke xi. 37 sq., xii. 1 sq., xiii. 1 sq., 23 sq., xiv. 1 sq., xv. 1 sq., al. Some careful comments on this portion of St Luke's Gospel, though not always such as can be fully accepted, will be found in Greswell, *Dissert.* XXXI. Vol. II. p. 517 sq.

Now, however, we meet with a striking and yet not unlooked-for change. If all the three solemn predictions of our Lord's sufferings were thought to be of such moment that they have been specially recorded by all the three Synoptical Evangelists[1], surely it would not be too much to expect that the mournful record of the verification of those prophecies should be given, not by two only or by three, but by all. The history of the sufferings whereby mankind was redeemed must be told by no fewer in number than the holy Four[2]. The fulfilment of type and shadow, of the hopes of patriarchs, of the expectations of prophets, yea and of the dim longings of a whole lost and sinful world, must be declared by the whole Evangelistic company; the four streams that go forth to water the earth[3] must here meet in a common channel; the four winds of the Spirit of life[4] must here be united and one.

---

[1] The prediction uttered near Cæsarea Philippi is specified in Matth. xvi. 21 sq., Mark viii. 30 sq., and Luke ix. 21 sq.; the prediction near or on the way to Capernaum, in Matth. xvii. 22 sq., Mark ix. 31 sq., Luke ix. 44; the prediction in Peræa on the way to Jericho, in Matth. xx. 17 sq., Mark x. 32 sq., Luke xviii. 31 sq.

[2] It may be noticed as a matter of curiosity, that the Apocryphal Gospels which we have long lost sight of, now again come before us. With the exception of an account of our Lord's appearance in the Temple when twelve years old (*Evang. Inf. Arab.* cap. 50 sq., *Evang. Thom.* cap. 19), a few scattered notices of our Lord's baptism (see Hofmann, *Leben Jesu,* § 69, p. 299), and the narrative of the Rich young man (see above, p. 273, note 2), we meet with no attempts to add anything to the Gospel-history since the period of the infancy. Now, however, in the *Evangelium Nicodemi* we find the apocryphal narrative resumed, and are furnished with accounts (not *wholly* undeserving of notice) of our Lord's trial, and of the events which followed; see Tischendorf, *Evang. Apocr.* p. 203 sq., and compare Hofmann, *Leben Jesu,* § 78 sq.

[3] Jerome, *Præf. in Matth.* cap. 4, Vol. VII. p. 18 (ed. Migne).

[4] This second simile is a modification of one which occurs in a curious passage in Irenæus, which though not very convincing, may bear citation as also incidentally showing how completely at that

LECT. VII.

For such a dispensation of wisdom and grace, ere we presume to dwell upon it, let us offer up our adoring thanks. Let us bless God for this fourfold heritage, let us praise the Eternal Spirit that thus moved the hearts and guided the pens of these appointed witnesses, and then with all lowliness and reverence address ourselves to the momentous task of attempting so far to combine their holy narratives, as to bring before our minds, in all its fulness and completeness, the record of the six concluding days of the Lord's earthly ministry, the six days in which a world was re-created, and the last fearful efforts of the rulers of its darkness[a] met, quelled, and triumphed over for evermore.

[a] Eph. vi. 12

The journey to and supper at Bethany.

The last incident, it will be remembered, to which we alluded in the preceding Lecture, was the short stay of our Lord at Jericho, and the subsequent journey to Bethany. He had now again[b] passed along the wild and unsafe road[1] that leads from the plain of Jericho to the uplands of

[b] Comp. Joh. xi. 7

---

early age the *four*, and only the *four* Gospels were accepted throughout the Church. 'Since there are four regions of the world,' says this ancient writer, 'in which we live, and four cardinal winds, and the Church has become spread over the whole earth, and the Gospel is the pillar and support of the Church, and the breath of life; it is meet that it should have four pillars breathing on all sides incorruption and refreshing mankind.' *Adv. Hær.* III. 11, p. 221 (ed. Grabe).

[1] This road, though connecting two places of great importance, seems almost always to have been infested by robbers (Jerome *on Jerem.* iii. 2), and to have been deemed notoriously dangerous to the traveller: see Light-foot, *Hor. Hebr. in Luc.* x. 30. It was the scene of the striking parable of the Good Samaritan, and was now being traversed, apparently for the second time (the first being on the occasion of the sickness and death of Lazarus), by Him whom several writers of the early Church (Origen, Ambrose, Augustine, al.) regarded as shadowed forth by the merciful stranger of His own parable. For an account of the road see Thomson, *The Land and the Book*, Vol. II. p. 440 sq., Caspari, *Chron.-Geogr. Einleit.* § 142, p. 160 sq., and for a very powerful sketch of a wild portion of it, with the plain of Jericho below, see Roberts, *Holy Land*, Vol. II. Plate 15.

Judæa, and was now, possibly late on the Friday evening[1], in the abode of that highly-favoured household, which, as the fourth Evangelist tells us, our Lord vouchsafed to regard with feelings of affection and love[a]. There in the retirement of that mountain-hamlet of Bethany[2],—a retirement soon to be broken in upon[b],—the Redeemer of the world may with reason be supposed to have spent His last earthly sabbath. There too, either in their own house or, as seems more probable, in the house of one who probably owed to our Lord his return to the society of his fellow-men[3], did that loving household 'make a supper[c]' for their Divine Guest. Joyfully and thankfully did each one of that loving family instinctively do that which might seem most to tend to the honour and glorification of Him whom one of them had declared to be, and whom they all knew to be, the

[a] Joh. xi. 5
[b] Joh. xii. 9
[c] Joh. xii. 2

---

[1] See above, p. 276, note 1.

[2] The village of Bethany (according to Lightfoot, בֵּית הִינֵי 'house of dates') lies on the eastern slope of Olivet in a shallow and partially wooded valley, and in a direction about E.S.E. from Jerusalem, and at a distance of about fifteen furlongs (John xi. 18), or between half and three-quarters of an hour in time. It is now called 'el-'Aziriyeh' from the tomb of Lazarus which is still pretended to be shown there, and is described by travellers as a poor and somewhat forlorn hamlet of about twenty houses: see Robinson, *Palestine*, Vol. I. p. 432 (ed. 2), Thomson, *The Land and the Book*, Vol. II. p. 599, Stanley, *Palestine*, p. 188, Caspari, *Chron.-Geogr. Einleit.* § 142, p. 161, and for views of it, Roberts, *Holy Land*, Vol. II. Plate 13, Robertson and Beato, *Views of Jerusalem*, No. 30, and Frith, *Egypt and Palestine*, Part XXIV. 3.

[3] It has been conjectured, and perhaps rightly, that Simon 'the Leper,' at whose house the supper would seem to have been prepared (Matth. xxvi. 6, Mark xiv. 3), had formerly suffered under this frightful disease, and had been healed by our Lord; compare Meyer, *on Matth.* xxvi. 6. The connexion in which he stood to Lazarus and his sisters is wholly unknown to us; according to Theophylact he was the father (comp. Ewald, *Gesch. Christus*', p. 357), according to some modern writers the husband of Martha (Greswell, *Dissert.* Vol. II. p. 554), or, as seems perhaps slightly more probable, a friend of the family.

LECT. VII.

^a Joh. xi. 27
^b xii. 2

^c ver. 3

^d Mt. xxvi. 8
Mk. xiv. 4

^e Matt. xxvi. 13

The Triumphal entry into Jerusalem (Sunday).

Son of God[1] that was to come into the world^a. So Martha serves; Lazarus it is specially noticed takes his place at the table^b, the visible living proof of the omnipotence of his Lord; Mary performs the tender office of a mournfully foreseeing love, that thought nought too pure or too costly^c for its God,—that tender office, which though grudgingly rebuked by Judas and, alas! others than Judas^d, who could not appreciate the depths of such a devotion, nevertheless received a praise which it has been declared^e shall evermore hold its place on the pages of the Book of Life[2].

But that sabbath soon passed away. Ere night came on, numbers even of those who were seldom favourably disposed to our Lord, now[3] came to see both Him and the living monument of His mer-

[1] On the title 'Son of God' see above, Lect. V. p. 211, note 1, and also Lect. VI. p. 260, note 3. It can scarcely be doubted that on the occasion referred to (John xi. 27) Martha had a general if not a theologically precise belief in our Lord's divinity. Now that belief would naturally have become still clearer and fuller, and probably evinced itself in all these acts of duteous and loving service.

[2] For the arguments by which it would appear almost *certain* that the present anointing is not identical with that in the house of Simon the Pharisee (Luke vii. 36), see above, p. 183, note 2, and compare Ebrard, *Kritik der Evang. Gesch.* § 96, p. 473. The incident is related by St Matthew and St Mark *after* the triumphal entry,—not as having happened then, but as standing in suitable connexion with the mention of the betrayal of Judas, the workings of whose evil heart, as we know from St John, were fully displayed on the occasion of this supper; see Wieseler, *Synops.* p. 391 sq.

[3] It seems reasonable to suppose that at a time of such large popular gatherings, the strict observance of the Sabbath day's journey might in some measure have been relaxed. Even however without this assumption, we may suppose these eager visitants to have arrived at Bethany, soon after the Sabbath was over, having performed the permitted part of the distance (5 or 6 stades) before the Sabbath legally ended, and the rest afterwards. The news that our Lord was there could easily have been spread by those who journeyed with Him from Jericho on the Friday, and who themselves went on direct to Jerusalem. On the length of a Sabbath day's journey, see Winer, *RWB.* Art. 'Sabbathsweg,' Vol. II. p. 351, Greswell, *Dissert.* XXXVIII. Vol. III. p. 70.'

ciful omnipotence^a. The morrow probably brought more of these half-curious, half-awed, yet, as it would now seem, in a great measure believing^b visitants. The deep heart of the people was stirred, and the time was fully come when ancient prophecy^c was to receive its fulfilment, and the daughter of Zion was to welcome her King¹. Yea and in kingly state shall He come. Begirt not only by the smaller band of His own disciples but by the great and now hourly increasing multitude, our Lord leaves the little wooded vale that had ministered to Him its sabbath-day of seclusion and repose, and directs his way onward to Jerusalem. As yet, however, in but humble guise and as a pilgrim among pilgrims He traverses the rough mountain-track which the modern traveller can even now somewhat hopefully identify²; every step bringing Him nearer to the

^a Joh. xii. 9
^b ver. 11
^c Zec. ix. 9

---

[1] This prophecy, we are told distinctly by St John (ch. xii. 16), was not understood by the disciples as now being fulfilled till after our Lord had been glorified. The illumination of the Holy Ghost then enabled them both to call to mind the words of this particular prophecy (observe the thrice-repeated ταῦτα) and to recognize the occasion on which it was thus signally fulfilled; see Meyer, *on John* xii. 16.

[2] See Stanley, *Sinai and Palestine*, p. 189 sq., where this triumphal entry is extremely well described and illustrated. In deference to the opinion and arguments of this observant traveller, who has himself seen and considered the locality in reference to the very event we are now considering, it has been assumed in the text that our Lord proceeded, not by the traditional route over the summit of Olivet, but by the most southern of the three routes from Bethany to Jerusalem. We must not, however, forget that the present appearance of the city from Olivet and the appearance of the city in the time of our Lord, when the eastern wall certainly ran much within the present line of wall (see the plans by Fergusson in Smith, *Dict. of Bible*, Vol. I. pp. 1028, 1032), must certainly have been different, and that the statements of the modern traveller must always be subjected to this correction. Views of the city from Olivet are very numerous; see however especially, Williams, *Holy City*, Vol. I. Frontispiece, Roberts, *Holy Land*,

ridge of Olivet, and to that hamlet or district of Bethphage, the exact site of which it is so hard to fix, but which was separated perhaps only by some narrow valley from the road along which the procession was now wending its way[1]. But the Son of David must not solemnly enter the city of David as a scarcely distinguishable wayfarer amid a mixed and wayfaring throng. Prophecy must have its full and exact fulfilment; the King must approach the city of the King with some meek symbols of kingly majesty. With haste, it would seem, two disciples are despatched to the village over against them, to bring to Him 'who had need of it[a]' the colt 'whereon yet never man sat[b]:' with haste the zealous followers cast upon it their garments[c], and all-unconscious of the significant nature of their act, place thereon their Master[d],— the coming King. Strange it would have been if feelings such as now were eagerly stirring in every heart had not found vent in words. Strange indeed if, with the Hill of Zion now breaking upon

[a] Mt. xxi. 3
[b] Lk. xix. 30
[c] ver. 35
[d] ver. 39

Vol. I. Plate 4, 16, Frith, *Egypt and Palestine*, Part XVIII. 1, 2, and for a view of the roads down the side of Olivet, Williams, Vol. I. p. 318, and compare Stanley, *Palestine*, p. 156.

[1] The site of this village or district has not yet been satisfactorily determined; see Robinson, *Palestine*, Vol. I. p. 433, but compare also Van de Velde, *Memoir to Map*, p. 297. The most reasonable view seems to be that Bethphage (בֵּית פַּגֵּא, 'house of figs') was a village or hamlet not far from Bethany, but nearer to Jerusalem (hence the order in Mark xi. 1; compare Luke xix. 29), and situated at no great distance from one of the roads connecting these two places; compare Matth. xxi. 2, τὴν κώμην τὴν ἀπέναντι ὑμῶν; Mark xi. 2, τὴν κώμην τὴν κατέναντι ὑμῶν; Luke xix. 30, τὴν κατέναντι κώμην,—in all which places Bethphage appears to be referred to. The apparently less probable supposition that it was a district rather than a village has been advocated by Lightfoot, *Cent. Chorogr. in Matth.* cap. 37, Vol. II. p. 198 (Roterod. 1686); comp. also Williams, *Holy City*, Vol. II. p. 412 sq., and Caspari, *Chron.-Geogr. Einleit.* § 143, p. 162.

their view[1], the long prophetic past had not seemed to mingle with the present, and evoke those shouts of mysterious welcome and praise, which, first beginning with the disciples[a] and those immediately round our Lord[2], soon were heard from every mouth of that glorifying multitude. And not from them alone. Numberless others there were fast streaming up Olivet, a palm-branch in every hand[b], to greet the raiser of Lazarus, and the Conqueror of Death; and now all join. One common feeling of holy enthusiasm now pervades that mighty multitude, and displays itself in befitting acts. Garments are torn off and cast down[3] before the Holy One[c]; green boughs bestrew the way[d]; Zion's King rides onward in meek majesty, a

[a] ver. 37

[b] Joh. xii. 13

[c] Mt. xxi. 8
[d] ver. 8

---

[1] See Stanley, *Sinai and Palestine*, p. 190, where it is stated that on reaching the ridge of the southern slope of Olivet, by the road above alluded to, the traveller obtains a view of Mount Zion and that portion of Jerusalem which was more especially connected with the memory of David, as the site of his palace. The Temple and the more northern parts would not be seen at present, being hid from view by an intervening slope on the right: see Caspari, *Einleit.* § 142, p. 161.

[2] This would seem to be the correct reconciliation of Luke xix. 37, with Matth. xxi. 9 and Mark xi. 9. The disciples that were round our Lord first raise the jubilant shouts, the multitudes both before and behind (Matth. *l. c.*) take them up immediately afterwards. St John specifies some of the acclamations, but more particularly gives us the subject of the testimony which the multitude publicly bare to our Lord, viz. that He had raised Lazarus from the dead (ch. xii. 17), and thus incidentally supplies the reason why they so readily joined in these shouts of triumph: compare Ewald, *Gesch. Christus'*, p. 384.

[3] Most of the recent expositors of this passage have appropriately referred to the curious incident mentioned by Dr Robinson (*Palestine*, Vol. I. p. 473, ed. 2) of the people of Bethlehem casting their garments on the way before the horses of the English Consul of Damascus when supplicating his assistance and intercession. The same writer briefly illustrates by modern usage the act of the disciples casting their cloaks (the plaid-like pieces of coarse woollen cloth, which formed the outer garment, Smith's *Dict. of Bible*, Vol. I. p. 455) upon the foal to serve as a saddle; *Palestine*, Vol. II. p. 219. Such is the enduring nature of Eastern habits.

thousand voices before, and a thousand voices behind rising up to heaven with Hosannas and with mingled words of magnifying acclamation, some of which once had been sung to the Psalmist's harp[a], and some heard even from angelic tongues[b]......But the hour of triumph was the hour of deepest and most touching compassion. If, as we have ventured to believe, the suddenly opening view of Zion may have caused the excited feelings of that thronging multitude to pour themselves forth in words of exalted and triumphant praise, full surely we know from the inspired narrative, that on our Redeemer's nearer approach[c] to the city, as it rose up, perhaps suddenly[1], in all its extent and magnificence before Him who even now beheld the trenches cast about it[d], and Roman legions mustering round its fated walls, tears fell from those Divine eyes,—yea, the Saviour of the world wept over the city wherein He had come to suffer and to die......The lengthening procession again moves onward, slowly descending into the deep valley of the Cedron, and slowly winding up the opposite slope, until at length by one of

[a] Psalm cxviii. 26
[b] Lk. ii. 14
[c] Lk. xix. 41
[d] ver. 43

[1] We learn from Dr Stanley (*Sinai and Palestine*, p. 191), that at a particular point of the southern road the traveller reaches a ledge of smooth rock from which the whole city rising up, as it were, 'out of a deep abyss' is suddenly beheld in all its extent: compare the view in Williams, *Holy City*, Vol. I. Frontispiece, which seems to illustrate this description. It seems too much to venture with Dr Stanley positively to identify this spot with that where the Saviour paused and wept, especially as it is by no means certain (see above, p. 285, note 2) that this was the route actually taken, still we may perhaps permit ourselves to believe that our Saviour's affecting address was synchronous with and perhaps suggested by the sudden opening out of some widely extended view of the magnificent city. The view from the summit of Olivet is noticed by Dr Robinson, and described as 'not particularly interesting,' and as embracing little more than a 'dull mixed mass of roofs and domes.' *Palestine*, Vol. I. p. 236 (ed. 2).

the Eastern gates it passes into one of the now crowded[1] thoroughfares of the Holy City.

Such was the Triumphal Entry into Jerusalem; such the most striking event, considered with reference to the nation, on which we have as yet meditated. It was no less than a public recognition of Jesus of Nazareth as the long looked-for Messiah, the long and passionately expected theocratic King. Though, as the sequel shows, only transitory and evanescent, it was still a recognition, plain, distinct, and historical, and exactly of such a nature as tends to increase in the highest degree our convictions of the living truth of the inspired narrative. Let us pause a moment only to observe how marvellously it sets forth no less the sacred dignity than the holy decorum of the

Reflections on the striking credibility of the narrative.

---

[1] It is now hardly possible to form a just conception of the appearance which Jerusalem and its vicinity must have presented at the season of the Passover. All the open ground near the city and perhaps the sides of the very hill down which our Lord had recently passed were now, probably, being covered with the tents and temporarily erected structures of the gathering multitudes, who even thus early would have most likely found every available abode in the city completely full. We are not left without some data of the actual amount of the gathered numbers, as we have a calculation of Josephus based upon the number of lambs sacrificed (256,500), according to which it would appear that even at the very low estimate of 10 persons to each lamb the number of people assembled must have been little short of 2,700,000, without taking into consideration those that were present but incapacitated by legal impurities from being partakers in the sacrifice; see *Bell. Jud.* VI. 9. 3, and compare *Bell. Jud.* II. 14. 3, where the number is with more probability set down at about three millions. There would thus have been present not much short of half of the probable population of Judæa and Galilee: see Greswell, *Dissert.* XXIII. Append. Vol. IV. p. 494. These observations are not without importance considered theologically. They show that our Lord's rejection and death is not merely to be laid to the malevolence of the party of the Sanhedrin and to the wild clamours of a city mob, but may justly be considered, though done in partial ignorance (Acts iii. 17), the act of the nation. When Pilate made his proposal it was to the multitude (Mark xv. 9), and that multitude we know was unanimous (John xviii. 40).

accepted homage. Let us only observe with wonder and reverence how not a single prerogative of the Messiah was waived or foregone, and how not even the most bitter opponent of the truth[1] can dare with any show of reason or justice to assert that the faintest appeal was here made to the prejudices or passions of the multitude. Let us mark, on the one hand, how ere the multitude begin to greet their Lord with the words of a Messianic psalm[2], He Himself vouchsafes them a Messianic sign, and how when the Pharisees urge our Lord to silence the commencing acclamations[a], He refuses with an answer at once decided and sublime. Let us mark again, on the other hand, how the object of all that jubilant reverence shows in the plainest way the spiritual nature of His triumph and of His kingdom, when on His nearer approach He pauses and weeps over the city to which He was advancing with such kingly majesty. Was this the way to appeal to the political passions of the multitude? Was this what worldly prudence would have suggested as the most hope-

[a] Lk. xix. 39

---

[1] The various objections in detail which modern scepticism has endeavoured to bring against the inspired narrative do not appear in any way to deserve our attention or require any further confutation than they have already received; for notices of them, and short but sufficient answers, see Ebrard, *Kritik der Evang. Gesch.* § 97, p. 476. The general objection, however, or rather false representation, alluded to, and briefly discussed in the text, deserves a passing notice and exposure. It was advanced towards the close of the last century by the compiler of the notorious Wolfenbüttel Fragments, and has often been repeated in later sceptical writings. When we read the inspired accounts and observe how they incidentally disclose everything that was most opposed to political demonstration, it may seem doubtful whether the impiety of such a theory is not even exceeded by its improbability and its total want of all historical credibility.

[2] The comment of Hilary is not without point: 'Laudationis verba redemptionis in eo exprimunt potestatem, nam Osanna Hebraico sermone significatur redemptio [domus David].' *Comment. in Matth.* Canon XXI. p. 567 (Paris, 1631).

ful mode of assuming the attributes of such a Messiah as was then looked for by popular enthusiasm[1]? No, it cannot be. Here at least let scepticism fairly own that it is at fault, plainly, palpably at fault. If it affects to value truth let it own that here at least there is a sober reality wholly irreconcileable with assumptions of mistaken enthusiasm or political adventure, here a life and a truth with which the subtlest combinations of thought could never have animated a mythical narrative.

But let us pass onward. No sooner had our Lord entered the city than all was amazed inquiry and commotion. The recognition, as far as we can infer from the sacred narrative, would seem to have been speedy and general[2]; not indeed in those exalted strains which had just been heard on Olivet, yet still in a manner which probably served to show how true was the bitter admission of the Pharisees one to another, that the whole

Our Lord's entry into Jerusalem.

---

[1] It perhaps cannot be doubted that at the present time numbers trusted that they beheld in our Lord the mighty Deliverer and Restorer, whose advent was so earnestly and so eagerly looked for; see Luke xxiv. 21, and compare Acts i. 6. Still it seems by no means improbable that with all this there was also such a growing feeling that the expected kingdom was to be at least as much of a spiritual as of a temporal nature (compare Luke xix. 11), that even the most enthusiastic did not perhaps generally associate with the Lord's present triumphal entry many well-defined expectations of *purely* political results and successes; compare Ewald, *Gesch. Christus*¹, p. 381. The nature of their acclamations seems confirmatory of this view.

[2] We may observe the characteristic way in which the inquiry is made and the answer returned. The people in the city at present share but little in the enthusiasm of the entering multitudes; their only question is, Τίς ἐστιν οὗτος (Matth. xxi. 10). The answer is given by the ὄχλοι,—mainly as it would seem, though probably not exclusively those who were now accompanying our Lord,—and not perhaps without a tinge of provincial and local pride: Οὗτός ἐστιν ὁ προφήτης Ἰησοῦς [*Rec.* Ἰησοῦς ὁ προφήτης] ὁ ἀπὸ Ναζαρὲθ τῆς Γαλιλαίας; see Meyer, *in loc.* p. 389 (ed. 4).

LECT. VII.

ᵃ Jn. xii. 19

ᵇ Mk. xi. 11

ᶜ ver. 11

The cursing of the barren fig-tree (Monday).

ᵈ xxi. 18
ᵉ xi. 12

'world had gone after Himᵃ,' and that all their efforts were at present of no avail. Yet by no outward acts, if we adopt what seems on the whole the most probable connexion of the sacred narrative[1], did our Lord as yet respond to those excited feelings. All we read is that He entered the Templeᵇ, and in one comprehending gaze[2] beheld all things,—all the mercenary desecration to which the needs of the festal season had given fresh impulse[3], and which on the morrow must solemnly be purged away. When all was surveyed evening was now comeᶜ, and with the small company of the Twelve our Lord returned to the quiet of the upland village which He had left with such a mighty multitude but a few hours before.

Early on the following morning, as we learn from a comparison of the narratives of St Matthewᵈ and St Markᵉ, our Lord set forth from

---

[1] It seems slightly doubtful whether with Robinson we are to place the cleansing of the Temple on the same day as our Lord's triumphal entry, or whether with Lightfoot, Wieseler, al., we are to refer it to the following day. The former view is most in accordance with the connexion of St Matthew's narrative, and is partially supported by the notice of the children crying in the Temple, which might seem but a continuation of what had happened on the way. Still the very distinct note of time (τῇ ἐπαύριον, ch. xi. 12) supplied by St Mark, coupled with his precise notice of the lateness of the hour when our Lord finished His survey the preceding evening (ch. xi. 11), leads us here to adopt the generally safe rule, in cases of disputed order, of giving the preference to the narrative of that Evangelist who has been moved to supply a special rather than a merely general note of the time when any event occurred. The hypothesis that the cleansing of the Temple commenced on the afternoon of the Sunday and was continued on the following day, is noticed, but rightly rejected by Greswell, *Dissert.* XXXIX. Vol. III. p. 99 sq.

[2] On the use of this peculiar term by St Mark, see Da Costa, *Four Witnesses*, p. 122, and compare Lect. I. p. 25, note I.

[3] See Lightfoot, *Hor. Hebr. in Matth.* xxi. 12, who mentions that the place where this traffic was carried on was called חניות ('Tabernæ'), and was in the spacious court of the Gentiles. Compare *Descr. Templ.* cap. IX. Vol. I. p. 565.

Bethany, with the intention, we may humbly presume, of reaching the temple before any great influx of worshippers could have been found in its courts. The inspection of the preceding day[a] had shown only too clearly that the sanctity of His Father's House must again be vindicated, and that the unholy and usurious[1] traffic which was now being carried on within its walls must again[2] be purged out of the hallowed precincts. On the way, He who was truly flesh of our flesh and bone of our bone, felt the weakness of the nature He vouchsafed to assume. He hungered, we are told by the first two Evangelists[b], and turned to a way-side fig-tree[c] to see if haply there was the fruit thereon of which the early show of leaves though not the season of the year[3] gave such

[a] ver. 11

[b] Mt. xxi. 18 Mk. xi. 12

[c] Mt. xxi. 19

---

[1] See Lightfoot, *Hor. Hebr. in Matth.* xxi. 12, where there are some valuable Rabbinical citations illustrative of the κολλυβισταί and their practices. The following seems to show that the agio exacted in changing common money into sacred, or the shekel into two half-shekels, was great: 'Quanti valoris est istud lucrum? Tunc temporis cum denarios persolverent pro Hemisiclo, Kolbon [vel, lucrosus reditus nummulario pensus] fuit dimidium Meæ, hoc est pars duodecima denarii: et nunquam minus.' *Talm.* 'Shekalim,' cap. 3. For a description of the sacred shekel, compare Friedlieb, *Archäol.* § 15, p. 37.

[2] The purging of the temple mentioned by St John (ch. ii. 13 sq.) is rightly regarded by Chrysostom, most of the older, and nearly all the best recent expositors as different from the present. The Apostle having once mentioned the incident, now, very naturally, does not again specify it: see Caspari, *Chron.-Geogr. Einleit.* § 165, p. 187. It took place at the Passover, A.U.C. 781, or two years before the present time: see above, Lect. III. p. 122. The vindication of the sanctity and honour of His Father's house was thus one of our Lord's earliest as well as one of His latest public acts. On the difficulties which some interpreters have felt in the performance of this authoritative act by our Lord, especially on the first occasion, see above, p. 123, note 1.

[3] Much difficulty has been felt at the partially parenthetical clause, Mark xi. 13, ὁ γὰρ καιρὸς οὐκ ἦν σύκων (Tisch.), or οὐ γὰρ ἦν καιρὸς σύκων (Rec.). From this it has been urged, we are to conclude that our Lord could not have expected to find figs on the tree, and consequently that the curse pronounced on it is less easy to be accounted

LECT. VII.

ostentatious promise. Hapless tree, emblem of a still more hapless nation! The dews of heaven had fallen upon it, the sun-light had fostered it, the sheltering hill-side had protected it; all seasonable influences had ministered to it, and, even as it had been with the mercies of Jehovah to His chosen people, all had been utterly in vain. Nay worse than in vain; the issue was a barrenness that told not merely of frustrated but of perverted influences; gifts from the God of nature received only to issue forth in unprofitable and deceptive produce; not in the fruit of His appointment, but in pretentious and unseasonable leaves.

for. A close attention to the exact words of the original combined with the notices of modern travellers seems completely to remove all difficulty. St Mark tells us distinctly that our Lord saw a fig-tree ἔχουσαν φύλλα (ver. 13), *i. e.* affording the usual, though in the present case, extremely early evidence that fruit was certainly to be looked for, the latter regularly preceding the leaves: see Thomson, *The Land and the Book*, Vol. I. p. 538, from whom we learn that in a sheltered spot figs of an early kind may occasionally be found ripe as soon as the beginning of April; compare also Winer, *RWB.* Art. 'Feigenbaum,' Vol. I. p. 367, Greswell, *Dissert.* XXXIX. Vol. III. p. 91. Our Lord approaches the tree to see εἰ ἄρα, —if, as was reasonable to expect under such circumstances (Klotz, *Devar.* p. 178 sq.), fruit was to be found. He finds nothing except leaves—leaves not fruit, whereas if it had been later and the regular season He would have found fruit and not leaves, and would not have been attracted by the unseasonable appearance of the tree; see Meyer, *Komment. üb. Mark.* p. 134, whose general explanation of the passage is reasonable and satisfactory. The ordinary supposition that these were leaves of the preceding year and that what our Lord expected was fruit of the same year (see Lightfoot, *Hor. Hebr. in Matth.* xxi. 19), is by no means probable, as the connexion between the presence of leaves and absence of fruit is thus wholly lost, the curse not accounted for (the tree might have once had figs which others had now plucked off), and lastly the force of the clause οὐ γὰρ κ. τ. λ. either explained away ('Non stricte et solum rationem reddit, cur ficus non invenerit; sed rationem reddit totius actionis, cur scilicet in monte isto, ficubus abundanti, unam tantum viderit, cui folia talia,' Lightfoot) or completely lost. Explanations such as those of Lange (*Leben Jesu*, Part II. p. 321), Sepp (*Leben Christi*, Vol. III. p. 219) and others, according to which καιρὸς is amplified to mean 'favourable season' or 'favourable locality' appear wholly untenable.

Why then are we to pause for reasons, or to seek about for any further explanation of what is at once so suggestive and so intelligible? Why marvel we that, like the watered earth 'that bringeth not forth herbs meet for the use of man[a],' but beareth only thorns and briars, that emblematic tree was now 'nigh unto cursing' and that its end was to be burned[1]?

[a] Heb. vi. 7

It was probably still early when our Lord reached the Temple. Its present desecration might possibly not have been so great in every respect as it had been two years before. Still it is clear that nearly every evil practice had been resumed. Buyers and sellers were there, usurious money-changers were there; all was well nigh as of old. Meet then was it that by authoritative acts no less than in inspired words[b] it should be proclaimed in the face of all men that God's House was not for thievish gains[2] but for worship, not for Jewish buying and selling but for the prayers of all the scattered children of God[3]. Meet was it that as

The cleansing of the Temple and works of mercy performed there.

[b] Is. lvi. 7
Jer. vii. 11

---

[1] The above comments seem fully sufficient to meet the open or tacit objections against this 'destructive act,—and that on a tree by the wayside, the common property,' (Milman, *Hist. of Christianity*, ch. VII. Vol. I. p. 309). Those who advance such objections would do well to remember the sensible remarks of Chrysostom: 'Whenever any such act takes place either in respect of places, plants, or things without reason, be not over precise in thy comments, and do not say, "How then with justice was the fig-tree made to wither away?"...for it is the extreme of folly to make such remarks. Look rather at the miracle, and admire and glorify Him who wrought it.' *In Matth.* Hom. LXVII. Vol. VII. p. 746. On the miracle generally, see the good comments of Hall, *Contempl.* IV. 26, and Trench, *Notes on the Miracles*, p. 435.

[2] See above, p. 293, note 1.

[3] It is worthy of notice that the words πᾶσι τοῖς ἔθνεσιν, which duly express the spirit of the prophecy referred to, are only found in St Mark (ch. xi. 17). The addition would not seem due to any greater care in St Mark's mode of citation (De Wette), but as suggested by the general character of his Gospel and its more general destination for Gentile readers.

LECT. VII.

at the first Passover of our Lord's ministry so at His last the majesty of the eternal Father should be thus openly glorified by the acts of His eternal Son. And not by these only. Deeds of mercy followed deeds of necessity. The blind came to Him and received their sight; the lame walked[a],—yea even before the unbelieving eyes of the very chief priests and scribes, who, as we learn from St Mark[b], had heard of the Lord's presence in the Temple, and were now seeking to find an opportunity of destroying Him[1] whom now, more than ever, they were regarding with mingled hatred and apprehension. At present it was in vain. The children round them glorifying the son of David[c], the attentive and awe-stricken multitude[d] hanging on the words and deeds of Him whom they had welcomed yesterday with cries that their children were now reiterating, all clearly told the party of the Sanhedrin, that their hour,—the hour of the powers of darkness[e],—had not yet come. One effort they make; reproachfully they ask Him if He hears, if He accepts these cries of homage[f], plainly implying what the Pharisees had

[a] Mt. xxi. 14
[b] ch. xi. 18
[c] Mt. xxi. 15
[d] Mk. xiv. 18
[e] Lk. xxii. 53
[f] Mt. xxi. 16

---

[1] It is perhaps scarcely safe to make definite historical deductions from finer shades of grammatical distinction which may not have been fully recognized by the writers; still the student's attention may be called to Mark xi. 18, ἐζήτουν [οἱ ἀρχιερεῖς καὶ οἱ γραμματεῖς] πῶς αὐτὸν ἀπολέσωσιν, where the tense adopted, ἀπολέσωσιν (Tisch., Lachm., with the four leading MSS.) or ἀπολέσουσιν (Rec. with later MSS.), will modify the view taken of the conduct of the members of the Sanhedrin. If we adopt the subjunctive the meaning will simply be 'how they should kill Him,' how they should carry out the design they were now entertaining: if the future,—which, however, critically considered seems less probable,—the meaning will be, 'how they shall kill Him,' how they shall accomplish a design, already definitely formed and agreed upon, and now considered only in reference to the 'modus operandi.' On this distinction see Winer, Gr. § 41. a, p. 266 (ed. 6), and compare Stallbaum on Plato, Sympos. p. 225.

openly demanded on the Mount of Olives the day before[a], that such demonstrations should be silenced[1]. But neither then nor now is it meet that the jubilant accents, whether of loving or of innocent lips, should be hushed and checked. Nay prophecy must have its fulfilment. With the pertinent words of a Psalm[b], of which the deeper meaning and application was now fully disclosed, our Lord leaves the Temple and city and returns again to Bethany.

On the morrow, and, as St Mark tells us[c], early in the day, our Lord and His disciples take their way to Jerusalem. Much there awaited them. The day preceding had been marked by manifestations of Divine power as shown forth in deeds and wondrous works; the present day was to be the witness of Divine wisdom as shown forth in words and discourses. It was a day that our

LECT. VII.
[a] *Lk. xix. 39*
[b] *Ps. viii. 2*
Answers to the deputation from the Sanhedrin (Tuesday).
[c] *ch. xi. 20*

---

[1] The present feelings of these evil men are very distinctly put before us by the comment of St Mark,—ἐφοβοῦντο γὰρ αὐτόν, ch. xi. 18. Formerly it was the hostility of an hypocrisy, which saw its real principles of action exposed, and of a party spirit which deemed its prerogatives interfered with or disregarded. Now there is a positive *apprehension*, founded, probably, on the recent reception of our Lord by the populace, that their own power will be soon wholly set aside, and that the prophet of Nazareth will become the theocratic leader of the nation. Even the heathen Pilate recognized the true motive of their actions; ᾔδει γὰρ ὅτι διὰ φθόνον παρέδωκαν αὐτόν, Matth. xxvii. 18. The present behaviour of the people, as Cyril of Alexandria has well observed, ought to have led to a very different result: 'And does not this then make the punishment of the scribes and Pharisees and all the rulers of the Jewish ranks more heavy? that the whole people, consisting of unlearned persons, hung upon the sacred doctrines, and drank in the saving word as the rain, and were ready to bring forth also the fruits of faith, and place their neck under His commandments: but they whose office it was to urge on their people to this very thing, savagely rebelled, and wickedly sought the opportunity for murder, and with unbridled violence ran upon the rocks, not accepting the faith and wickedly hindering others also.' *Commentary on St Luke*, Serm. cxxxii. Part II. p. 615 (Transl.).

298   *The Last Passover.*

LECT. VII.

Lord foreknew would be marked by rapidly changing incidents[1], by every varied form of stratagem, by hypocritical questionings and insidious inquiry; it was to be a day of last and most solemn warnings, of deepest and most momentous prophecies; early must it needs be that He go, late that He return. Ere they reach Jerusalem the hapless emblem of that city and its people meets the eyes of the disciples: the fig-tree, as the graphic St Mark tells us, was withered from its very roots[a]. The wondering question that was called forth by such an exhibition of the power of their Master over the material world, receives its practical answer in the solemn reiteration of words first uttered by way of gentle reproof some months before[b], and now again, by way of instruction, declaring the omnipotence of perfect and unwavering faith[2].

[a] ch. xi. 20

[b] Mt. xvii. 20

[1] To the present day (Tuesday) are assigned by most of the leading harmonists all the events and discourses comprised in Matth. xxi. 20—xxv. 46, Mark xi. 20—xiii. 37, Luke xx. 1—xxi. 38, and apparently (see below, p. 315), John xii. 20—36, with the recapitulatory remarks and citations of the Evangelist ver. 37—50. We have thus on this important day, the answer to the deputation from the Sanhedrin, and the three parables which followed it; the answer to the Pharisees and Herodians about the tribute-money, to the Sadducees about the woman with seven husbands, and to the scribe about the greatest commandment; the question put to the Pharisees about the Messiah, and the severely reproving discourse in reference to them and the scribes; the praise of the poor widow; the words uttered in the presence of the Greeks who sought to see our Lord, and the last prophecies in reference to the destruction of Jerusalem and the end of the world, with the accompanying parable of the Ten Virgins. See Wieseler, *Chron. Synops.* p. 393 sq., and Greswell, *Dissert.* XL. Vol. III. p. 109 sq., who, however, conceives the day to be Wednesday (so also Caspari, *Chron.-Geogr. Einleit.* §165), and also differs in fixing the incident of the Greeks on the day of the Triumphal Entry. The view of Milman (*Hist. of Christianity,* Vol. I. p. 311, note) that some of the discourses *e.g.* the answer to the Pharisees and Herodians and what followed, belong to a day subsequent to that on which the answer was made to the deputation from the Sanhedrin, has very little in its favour.

[2] The addition of the verse in St Mark (ch. xi. 25) on the duty and

The Last Passover. 299

They pass onward to the Temple, where already, early as it was[a], many were gathered together to hear the teaching of Life and those glad-tidings of the Gospel, which now, as St Luke[b] incidentally informs us, formed the subject of our Lord's addresses to His eager[c] and wondering[d] hearers. But, as since, so then was the Gospel to some a savour of death unto death[e]. The Lord's preaching is broken in upon by a formal deputation from the Sanhedrin[1], with two questions fair and specious in their general form, and yet most mischievously calculated to call forth an answer that might be twisted into a charge,—'By what authority was He doing these things[2]?' and

LECT. VII.

[a] See Mk. xi. 20, and compare Lk. xxi. 38
[b] ch. xx. 20
[c] Lk. xix. 48
[d] Mk. xi. 18
[e] 2 Cor. ii. 16

necessity of showing a forgiving spirit especially when offering up prayer to God (compare Matth. vi. 14) has been judged by Meyer and others as due to the Evangelist, and as not forming a part of our Lord's present words. This seems a very uncalled-for assumption. The preceding declaration of the prevailing nature of the prayer of faith leads our Lord to add a warning, which a possible misunderstanding of the miracle just performed might suggest as necessary,—viz. that this efficacy of prayer was not to be used against others even though they might be thought justly to deserve our animadversion: compare Stier, *Disc. of our Lord*, Vol. III. p. 105, Lange, *Leben Jesu*, III. 6. 6, p. 1212. That our Lord should have uttered the same words on another and earlier occasion, and should now be pleased to repeat them, involves nothing that is either unlikely or even unusual; see Lect. IV. p. 180, note 2.

[1] This seems clearly implied by St Mark's mention of the three component parts of the supreme court,—ἔρχονται πρὸς αὐτὸν οἱ ἀρχιερεῖς καὶ οἱ γραμματεῖς καὶ οἱ πρεσβύτεροι, ch. xi. 27; compare Matth. xxi. 23, Luke xx. 1. For a good account of these three sections of the Sanhedrin, the first of which was composed of priests (*perhaps* heads of the 24 classes,—not deposed High-priests), the second of expounders and transcribers of the law (see Lightfoot, *Hor. Hebr. in Matth.* ii. 4), the third of the heads of the principal families of Israel, see Friedlieb, *Archäol.* § 8, p. 15 sq.

[2] In the question proposed by the deputation, Ἐν ποίᾳ ἐξουσίᾳ ταῦτα ποιεῖς (Mark xi. 28), the ταῦτα appears to refer, not to the previous teaching of our Lord (Bengel, comp. Chrys.), but to the authoritative purging of the Temple the day before (Cyril Alex., Euthym.) and apparently also to the miracles on the blind and the lame, of which some of the speakers had been witnesses; see Matth. xxi. 15.

LECT. VII.

ᵃMt.xxi.23

'From whom did He receive itᵃ?' But question must be met by question. Ere the Messiah declares the nature of His mission, He must be told in what aspects the mission of His Forerunner was regarded. Was that without higher sanction, unaccredited, unauthorized,—from men or from heaven? Let the spiritual rulers of the nation answer that question, and then in turn shall answer be made to them. The sequel we well remember; the shrewdly-weighed alternativesᵇ, the necessary admission—'they could not tellᶜ,' the consequent refusal of our Lord to give them an answer¹, and yet the mercy, with which, by means of two parablesᵈ, their conduct both in its individual and in its official aspects is placed clearly before them², with all its issues of shame and condemnation.

ᵇ ver. 25
ᶜ ver. 27

ᵈver.28,32, 33—46

The probable design was to induce our Lord to lay such claim to Divine powers as might be turned into a charge against Him.

¹ The question proposed by our Lord had close reference to Himself as Him of whom John had spoken, and that too to a similar deputation (John i. 19 sq.) to the present. The Sanhedrin had heard two years ago from the mouth of the Baptist an indirect answer to the very question they were now proposing: meet then was it that they should first declare the estimation in which they held him who had so spoken to them.

² In the first of the two parables, the Two Sons sent into the Vineyard, the general course of conduct of the Pharisaical party is put in contrast with that of the publicans and harlots (ver. 31), and thus more clearly shown in its true character. By their general habits this latter class practically said οὐ θέλω to the Divine command, but afterwards repented at the preaching of John. The Pharisaical party, on the contrary, at once said ἐγώ κύριε with all affected readiness, but as their conduct to this very hour showed clearly enough, never even attempted to fulfil the promise: they were the Second son of the parable, the harlots and publicans (not the Gentiles, as Chrysost. and the principal patristic expositors) the First; compare Lange, *Leben Jesu*, II. 6. 6, Part III. p. 1215, Greswell, *Dissert.* XL. Vol. III. p. 113, and see De Wette and Meyer *in loc.* In the second parable,—the Husbandmen who slew the Heir, the conduct of the Pharisaical party, as Stier (*Disc. of our Lord*, Vol. III. p. 107) rightly

The drift of the two parables, especially of the second, they failed not clearly to perceive. They knew that our Lord was speaking with reference to them[a], but they heed not, nay they renew their efforts against Him with greater implacability, and are only restrained from open acts by their fear of the populace[b]. With words of last and merciful warning[1], as expressed in the parable of the Marriage of the King's Son[c], they depart for a season to organize some plan how they may ensnare the Holy One in His speech[d]; how they may force Him or beguile Him into admissions which may afford a colourable pretext for giving Him up to the stern man[2] that then bore the sword in Jerusalem.

They choose fit instruments for such an at-

LECT. VII.

Continued efforts on the part of the deputation.
[a] Mk. xii. 12
[b] Mt. xxvi. 46
[c] xxii. 1 sq.
[d] Mt. xx. 15 Mk. xii. 13

The question about the duty of

observes, is set forth more in reference to its official characteristics, and to the position of the rejecting party as representatives of the nation. At the same time also the punishment that awaited them (ἐπήγαγε καὶ τὰς κολάσεις, Chrys.), which was only hinted at in the first parable (Matth. xxi. 21), is now expressly declared; see Matth. xxi. 41. On these parables generally, see Stier, *l. c.*, Trench, *Notes on the Parables*, p. 160 sq., 173 sq., and comp. Greswell, *Parables*, Vol. v. p. 1 sq.

[1] There seems no just reason for thinking with Olshausen and others that Matth. xxi. 45, 46 conclude the previous scene. The words only depict the general state of feeling of the adverse party,—viz. that they both perceived the application of the parable and were only restrained from open violence by fear of the multitude,—and thus in fact prepare the reader for the further act of mercy on the part of our Lord in addressing yet another parable to these malignant enemies: compare Chrysost. *in Matth.* Hom. LXIX. init., Lange, *Leben Jesu*, II. 6. 6, Part III. p. 1217.

[2] Such certainly seems to have been the general character of Pilate as Procurator of Judæa: see Luke xiii. 1, and compare Joseph. *Antiq.* XVIII. 3. 1 sq., *Bell. Jud.* II. 9. 2 sq. There are some proofs that this sternness was not always pushed to an extreme (see Friedlieb, *Archäol.* § 34, p. 122, note), but it is still equally clear that his general conduct towards the refractory province of which he was Procurator was by no means marked by leniency or forbearance. The consideration of his conduct as a public officer forms the subject of a separate treatise by J. C. S. Germar, Thorun. 1785; see Winer, *RWB.* Art. 'Pilatus,' Vol. II. p. 262.

LECT. VII.

ᵃ Mt. xxii. 16
ᵇ Mk. iii. 6

ᶜ xx. 20

tempt,—their own disciples associated with Herodiansᵃ, men at variance in many points¹ but united in one, and ready enough now, as they had been once beforeᵇ, to combine in any attempt to compass the destruction of one who was alike hateful to both. 'Twas a well-arranged combination; religious hypocrisy and political craft; hierarchical prejudice and royalist sympathies; each party scarcely tolerating the other except for temporary and special purposes, and yet both of them for the time and the occasion working harmoniously together², and concurring in the proposal of the most perplexing and dangerous question that could then have been devised,—the tributary relations of a conquered to a conquering people. Let us pause for a moment to consider the exact nature of the attempt, and the true difficulties of the question proposed...A party of men with every appearance, as the third Evangelist impliesᶜ, of being right-minded and thoroughly in earnest, come, as it would seem, with a case of conscience³, 'Was it meet and right to

---

¹ On the general characteristics of the political sect of the Herodians, see Lect. IV. p. 178, note 1.

² The temporary bond of union between the two parties was now probably a common fear caused by the attitude which they conceived our Lord to have recently assumed. The triumphal entry into Jerusalem and the authoritative acts in the Temple would have been easily represented by the Pharisees, though happening in Judæa, as boding danger to the authority of Herod when the Prophet should return back to His home in Galilee. To regard the Herodians as 'soldiers of Herod' (Chrysost.), and sent only as witnesses (εἴ τι κατὰ τοῦ Καίσαρος ἀποκριθείη, Euthym.), does not seem either natural or accordant with the expressions of the sacred narrative, which seem rather to imply that both parties joined in the question; see Mark xii. 14.

³ The question, it will be observed, was so worded as to show that it affected to be considered as something more than one of mere political duty or expediency. The inquiry was not whether it was advisable to give tribute to Cæsar, but whether it was *lawful* to do so (ἔξεστιν δοῦναι, Matth. xxii. 17, Mark xii. 14, Luke xx. 22), whether it was consistent with an acknowledgment

give tribute to Cæsar or no.' To such a question even if proposed by honest men, it would have been hard to have returned a blameless answer at such a time and in such a place,—during the tumultuous passover-season, and in the very presence of the symbols of these conflicting claims; when round the speakers spread the Temple-courts and the thronging worshippers of the God of Israel, when yonder stood the palace of the first Herod, and in front rose the frowning tower of Antonia[1]. Hard indeed would it have been in such a case to have answered honest men without causing offence; but plainly, as it would have seemed, impossible, when those who put the question were avowed hypocrites, of differing religious sympathies and of discordant political creeds. If the Lord answered as they might have hoped and expected[2], standing as now He did in the very

of God as their king. The seditious enterprise of Judas of Gamala (Acts v. 37) put this forward as one of the principles which it pretended to vindicate,—μόνον ἡγεμόνα καὶ δεσπότην τὸν Θεὸν εἶναι, Joseph. Antiq. XVIII. 1. 6; compare Lightfoot, Hor. Hebr. in Matth. xxii. 20, Sepp, Leben Christi, VI. 17, Vol. III. p. 256.

[1] This fortress was rebuilt by the first Herod towards the beginning of his reign (Joseph. Antiq. XVIII. 4. 3) and was situated at the N. W. corner of the Temple enclosure, with which it was connected by an underground gallery (Joseph. Antiq. XV. 11. 7). Its situation and the full view it commanded of the outer courts made it a convenient place for the Roman garrison by which, when Judæa came under the jurisdiction of a Procurator, it was regularly occupied: see Winer, RWB. Art. 'Tempel,' Vol. II. p. 586, compare Friedlieb, Archäol. § 28, p. 98 sq.

[2] 'They expected,' says Chrysostom, 'that they should catch Him whichever way He might answer; they hoped, however, that He would answer against the Herodians.' In Matth. Hom. LXX.: compare Euthym. in loc. This also, as Cyril of Alexandria observes, seems clearly to transpire from the words of St Luke (ἵνα ἐπιλάβωνται αὐτοῦ λόγου, ὥστε παραδοῦναι αὐτὸν τῇ ἀρχῇ καὶ τῇ ἐξουσίᾳ τοῦ ἡγεμόνος, ch. xx. 20), and probably suggested the insidious comment (οὐ βλέπεις εἰς πρόσωπον ἀνθρώπων, Matth. xxii. 16, Mark xii. 14; compare Luke xx. 21) with which they accosted our Lord. 'This too they say, inciting Him not to entertain any reverence fo

LECT. VII.

centre of Judaism, and laying claim to represent all that was most distinctive in its expectations,— if He answered, Nay, their most eager wish was realized; they could at once, with a fair show of reason and justice, deliver Him up to the Roman government as an advocate of sedition, a Galilæan of avowed Galilæan sympathies, one whose blood they knew Pilate would now as readily shed at the very altar, as he had shed that of his countrymen[a] but a short time before[1]. Did He, however, contrary to expectation answer, Yea,—then He stood forth to the multitude as the practical opponent of the theocratic aspirations they so dearly cherished; and to the Herodians, as the Jewish subject of a Jewish prince, who scrupled not to sanction the payment of tribute to heathens and to strangers.

[a] Lk. xiii. 1

Exposure and frustration of the stratagem.

Such was the most artful and complex stratagem ever laid against the Saviour[2]; and yet with what Divine simplicity was it frustrated. A word

Cæsar, and not from any fear to withhold an answer to the inquiry.' Euthymius *on Matth.* xxii. 16.

[1] The exact time and circumstances under which the act here alluded to took place is not known. The way in which it was told to our Lord (παρῆσαν δέ τινες ἐν αὐτῷ τῷ καιρῷ ἀπαγγέλλοντες, Luke xiii. 1) would seem to imply that it had happened recently, and the mention of the country to which the victims belonged would also seem to render it likely that it was one of those movements in which the Galilæans were so often implicated; compare Joseph. *Vit.* § 17, and *Antiq.* XVII. 9. 3. That they were actual adherents of the party which Judas of Gamala had formerly headed (Theophyl.) is possible, but not very probable: see Lightfoot, *Hor. Hebr.* in *Luc.* xiii. 1.

[2] It is not without point that Cyril of Alexandria alludes to the way in which they who strove to involve the innocent Saviour with the Roman government themselves became involved with that nation in the most tragic way. After quoting Psalm xxxv. 7 and showing its application in the present case he adds: 'For so verily they did fall; for because they delivered Jesus unto Pilate, they were themselves given over to destruction, and the Roman host consumed them with fire and sword, and burnt up all their land, and even the glorious temple that was among them.' *Commentary on Luke*, Serm. CXXXV. Part II. p. 633 (Transl.).

lays bare the true character of the affected case of conscience and of those who proposed it[1]; a single command that the tribute-money be brought[a], and a single inquiry whose image it bore[b],—and the whole web of cunning and hypocrisy is rent in a moment :—'All that by God's appointment belongs unto Cæsar must be rendered unto Cæsar, and all that be God's unto God, and to Him alone[2].'...On receiving such an answer no marvel is it that we read[c] that the very inquirers

[a] Mk. xii. 15
[b] Matt. xxii. 20 Lk. xx. 24
[c] Matt. xxii. 22

---

[1] It is very distinctly specified by all the three Synoptical Evangelists that our Lord saw into the hearts and characters of those who came with the question; compare Matth. xxii. 18, γνοὺς δὲ ὁ Ἰησοῦς τὴν πονηρίαν; Mark xii. 15, εἰδὼς αὐτῶν τὴν ὑπόκρισιν; Luke xx. 23, κατανοήσας δὲ αὐτῶν τὴν πανουργίαν. We are told by St Luke that they were ἐγκαθέτους ὑποκρινομένους ἑαυτοὺς δικαίους εἶναι (ch. xx. 20); this our Lord confirms and exposes by His address as recorded by St Matthew [the reading in St Mark and St Luke is doubtful],—Τί με πειράζετε ὑποκριταί, ch. xxii. 18.

[2] The exact force of this declaration has been somewhat differently estimated, in consequence of the different meanings that have been assigned to τὰ τοῦ Θεοῦ. Most of them, however, e.g. 'the Temple-tribute' (Milman, *Hist. of Christianity*, Vol. L p. 313), 'the inner life' (Lange, *Leben Jesu*, Part III. 1220; comp. Tertull. *contr. Marc.* IV. 38), &c., seem wholly inconsistent with the general form of the expression, and give a mere special and partial aspect to what was designedly inclusive and comprehensive. If with Chrysostom (*in Matth.* Hom. LXX. Vol. VII. p. 776) we explain the expression as simply and generally, τὰ τῷ Θεῷ παρ' ἡμῶν ὀφειλόμενα, the meaning of the whole appears perfectly clear: 'Give to Cæsar what rightly belongs to him (οὐ γάρ ἐστι τοῦτο δοῦναι, ἀλλ' ἀποδοῦναι, Chrys.), as to one ordained of God (Rom. xiii. 1), and to God, all that be His,—all that is due to Him, as your King and your God.' Thus then, far from separating what is political from what is religious, or accepting the question in the *alternative* form (δοῦναι ἢ οὔ i.e. in point of fact, 'Cæsar or God'?) in which it was proposed, our Lord graciously returns an answer which shows that it was not a question for either Yea or Nay; that obedience to Cæsar and duty to God were not things to be put in competition with each other but to be united,—the latter supplying, where necessary, the true, regulating, and limiting principle of the former (see Chrys. *in loc.*), and the former, thus regulated and defined, becoming a very part of the latter,—duty to Him by whom Cæsar was Cæsar, and from whom are 'the powers that be.' For practical applications of this text, see Andrews, *Serm.* VI. Vol. v. p. 127 (A.-C. Libr.), and a sermon by Mill, *Univ. Serm.* I. p. 1 sq.

LECT. VII.

ᵃ Lk. xx. 26

The question of the Sadducees touching the Resurrection.

ᵇ xxii. 23

tendered to Him the reluctant homage of their wonder¹, that they were silent*ᵃ* and went their way.

But if a question as to civil duties and relations has been thus answered and thus foiled, might not a question as to religious differences prove more successful? Was there not some hope in stirring a controversy that had long separated two important sects? Might not the Sadducee succeed where the Pharisee and Herodian had failed? The trial we know was made. On that same day, as St Matthew*ᵇ* particularly specifies, a party of the Sadducees², probably acting under the instructions of the same supreme court, approach our Lord with a hypothetical case of religious difficulty,—the woman that had seven husbands in this world; to whom was she to belong in that world to come in which those worldly and self-sufficient speakers so utterly disbelieved³? The question was coarsely devised and

---

¹ This, not improbably, would have been increased by the recognition of the determination of their own schools ('Ubicunque numisma regis alicujus obtinet, illic incolæ regem istum pro domino agnoscunt.' Maimon. in 'Gezelah,' cap. 5), which the Lord was in part here actually propounding to them: see Lightfoot, *Hor. Hebr. in Matth.* xxii. 20.

² These Sadducees might have been and perhaps actually were a portion of the Sanhedrin, the religious opinions of the sect being no bar to their election as members of the supreme court; see Acts xxiii. 6, and compare Friedlieb, *Archäol.* § 8, p. 19. There seems no reason for supposing with Lightfoot (*in Matth.* xxii. 23) that there was any connexion in point of religious creed between the present party and the Herodians who had just gone away. Some of the Herodians might possibly have been Sadducees, but to draw definitely such a conclusion from Matth. xvi. 6 compared with Mark viii. 15 seems certainly precarious, especially when we remember that Herod can hardly be conceived himself to have had much in common with the peculiar tenets of the Sadducees; see Matth. xiv. 2.

³ See Lightfoot, *Hor. Hebr. in Matth.* xii. 32. The statement of the Sadducee was, 'Deficit nubes, atque abit; sic descendens in sepul-

coarsely propounded; but the attempt to drive our Lord into some admissions that might compromise Him either with the Pharisees or with the multitude was rendered thereby all the more hopeful. To such a question our Lord vouchsafes to return no answer; but to the evil heart of unbelief from which it came He speaks out clearly and plainly. With all their affected wisdom and philosophic calm, He tells them they do err[a], and that they know not, either the Scriptures, which clearly teach the doctrine of the future state that they so confidently denied, or the power of God, which shall make man the equal of angels and the inheritor of incorruption[1]. So clear was the vindication of God's truth, so weighty the censure, so final the answer, that we can scarcely wonder that the impressible multitudes were stricken with amazement[b], and that some even of the number of

[a] Matt. xx. 29
Mk. xii. 24

[b] Matt. xxii. 33

chrum non redit.' Tanchum, fol. 3, 1, cited by Lightfoot, in *Matth.* xxii. 23. They appeared to have believed that the soul perished with the body (Σαδδυκαίοις τὰς ψυχὰς ὁ λόγος συναφανίζει τοῖς σώμασι, Joseph. *Antiq.* XVIII. 1. 4), and thus as a matter of course denied the doctrine of the Resurrection, and of Future rewards and punishments; compare Joseph. *Bell. Jud.* II. 8. 14. On the origin and peculiarities of this sect, see Lightfoot, in *Matth.* iii. 7, Jost, *Gesch. des Judenth.* II. 2. 8, Vol. I. p. 215, and a good article by Winer, *RWB.* Vol. II. p. 352.

[1] Our Lord does not notice the mere question of the Sadducees but the erroneous belief that suggested it (οὐ πρὸς τὰ ῥήματα ἀλλὰ πρὸς τὴν γνώμην ἱστάμενος, Chrysost.); this He shows was due to their ignorance of two things, (1) the Scriptures, (2) the power of God. Their ignorance of the *latter* is shown first (Matth. xxii. 30, Mark xii. 25, Luke xx. 35, 36), by a declaration of the characteristics of the life after death, and the change of the natural body into a spiritual body (1 Cor. xv. 44; comp. Phil. iii. 21); the ignorance of the *former* by a declaration of the doctrine really contained in the Scriptures, and more especially in one of the books (Exod. iii. 6) of that very portion (the Pentateuch) that contained the passage on which they had based their question: ἐπειδήπερ ἐκεῖνοι τὸν Μωϋσέα προεβάλοντο λοιπὸν καὶ αὐτὸς ἀπὸ τῆς Μωσαϊκῆς γραφῆς τούτους ἐπιστομίζει. Euthymius, in *Matth.* xxii. 31, closely following Chrysost. *in luc.*, Vol. VII. p. 778 (ed. Bened.).

308   *The Last Passover.*

LECT. VII.

ᵃ Lk. xx. 39

The question of the lawyer about the greatest commandment.

ᵇ xxii. 35

our Lord's opponents could not forbear declaring that He had 'well spokenᵃ,' that the discomfiture of the impugners of the future state was complete and overwhelming¹. One at least of that number was so struck by the Divine wisdom of our Lord's last answer, that though, as it would seem from the narrative of St Matthewᵇ, he came forward with the hope of retrieving the honour of the sect to which we know that he belonged², the partisan seems to have been merged in the interested inquirer;

---

¹ It has commonly been alleged both by ancient (Origen, *contr. Cels.* I. 49, expressly,—compare also Tertull. *Præscr. Hær.* cap. 45) and modern writers that the Sadducees only acknowledged the authority of the Pentateuch, and that in consequence our Lord specially appealed to that portion of Scripture. This, however, is now as it would seem rightly called in question, there being no confirmation of such an opinion in the notices of the sect supplied by Josephus (compare *Antiq.* XIII. 10. 6, XVIII. 1. 4, *Bell. Jud.* II. 8), and a reasonable probability that the Sadducees could not have had the share in the civil and religious government of the nation, which it can be proved they had, if they had openly differed from the rest of their countrymen on a point of such fundamental importance as the canon of Scripture. The correct statement appears to be, that they rejected all tradition, and received only the written law, and that this special adherence to the latter, though merely in contradistinction to the former, gave rise to the opinion that this was the only part of *Scripture* that they accepted as canonical: see esp.

Joseph. *Antiq.* XIII. 10. 6, and Winer, *RWB.* Art. 'Sadducäer,' Vol. II. p. 353.

² According to St Matthew (ch. xxii. 35 sq.) the lawyer forms one of a party of Pharisees who were collected together after the defeat of the Sadducees, and comes forward with a trying and probably insidious question (πειράζων αὐτόν): according to St Mark (ch. xii. 28 sq.) he puts the question after observing how well our Lord had answered. The slight apparent difference between these accounts admits of this natural explanation, that the man was put forward by his party for the purpose of ensnaring our Lord, and that he acquiesced, but that he was also really inspired by a sincere desire to hear the opinion of one whose wisdom he respected. St Matthew exhibits him in the former light, and in reference to his party; St Mark in the latter, and as an individual: compare Lange, *Leben Jesu,* II. 6. 6, Part II. p. 1232. The reconciliation adopted by Euthymius (see Chrysostom),—that the designs of the man at first were bad, but were changed by our Lord's answer, seems scarcely so natural.

party spirit seems to have given way to a genuine desire to learn from the wise Teacher His opinion on one perhaps of the questions of the time[1],—the relative greatness and precedence of the leading commandments of the law. At the same time the question was one that would not be disapproved of by the adherents of the party to which the inquiry belonged, as involving probably more than one answer which might seriously compromise our Lord with some of the Rabbinical schools of the day[2]. In the inquirer's concluding comment his better feelings still more clearly prevail: a sort of consciousness of the idle nature of all that casuistry and formality of which his own question was the exponent breaks out in words, and obtains for him from the Redeemer's lips the gracious declaration[3], that 'he was not far from the kingdom of God[a].'

[a] Mk. xii. 34

---

[1] Somewhat similar questions are noticed by Schoettgen, *in Matth.* xxii. 36, and by Wetstein in his notes on ch. v. 19 and xxiii. 23. According to Lightfoot (in *Marc.* xii. 28) the inquiry turned upon the importance of the ceremonial as compared with the moral law: this however seems less probable.

[2] It is not easy to specify in what particular way the question was calculated to ensnare our Lord, though, from the nature of the controversies and casuistry of the day, it is not difficult to imagine that there were known differences of opinion on the subject in which it might have been thought our Lord could not escape becoming involved. It is worthy of notice that on an earlier occasion when our Lord puts an inquiry to a lawyer who had a similar but stronger design against Him (ἀνέστη ἐκπειράζων αὐτόν, Luke x. 25), 'What is written in the law?' (compare Matth. xxii. 36, ποία ἐντολὴ μεγάλη ἐν τῷ νόμῳ) the answer was promptly given in terms but little different to the present, and was approved of by our Lord (Luke x. 28). The present question then might have been intended to lead Him to give the prominence to some single command; the answer given, however, was one which our Lord had commended as an answer to a more general question, and which involved the substance of no single command but of all. The opinion of Chrysostom and others, that it was to tempt our Lord to say something about His own Godhead, is apparently not very probable.

[3] We cannot say with Milman that the lawyer 'did not hesitate

LECT. VII.

The question relative to the woman taken in adultery.

And was this the last attempt to ensnare our Lord which was made on this eventful day? So indeed it would seem from the tenor of the present portion of the inspired narrative. But are we not in some degree justified in again[1] advancing the conjecture that the incident of the woman taken in adultery belongs to the history of the present day? Such a view, it may be remembered, has the support of some slight amount of external evidence in addition to the very strong internal arguments on which it principally rests[2]. What, save the deeply-laid stratagem of the tribute-money, could have seemed more hopeful than the proposal of a case for decision which must apparently have involved our Lord either with the Roman governor or the Sanhedrin. Did He decide, as they seem to have hoped, in favour of carrying out the Mosaic law[3],

---

openly to espouse our Lord's doctrines,' and that the Pharisees 'were paralysed by this desertion' (*Hist. of Christianity*, Vol. I. p. 315), as there is nothing in the sacred text to substantiate such an inference. The declaration that 'he was not far from the kingdom of God,' gives hope that he was afterwards admitted into it; but as Chrysostom correctly observes, δείκνυσιν ἔτι ἀπέχοντα ἵνα ζητήσῃ τὸ λεῖπον. *In Matth.* Hom. LXXI.

[1] See above, Lect. VI. p. 253.

[2] The external evidence is specified above, p. 253, note 1. The internal arguments are, on the *negative* side, (*a*) the striking dissimilarity of the language from that of St John especially in the particles, (*b*) the forced nature of the connexion with the close of John vii. (see Luthardt, *Johann. Evang.* Part II. p. 93), and (*c*) the total want of union with what follows: and on the *positive* side, (*d*) the similarity in language to that of the Synoptical Gospels (compare Meyer, *on John* viii. 1—3), especially of St Luke, and lastly, (*e*) the striking similarity between the attempt and those recorded as having been made on the day we are now considering: compare Lange, *Leben Jesu*, II. 6. 6, Part III. p. 1222, and the introductory critical comments of Meyer, *Kommentar*, p. 247 sq. (ed. 3).

[3] Some little difficulty has been felt in the mention of 'stoning' (ver. 5), as the general punishment of death was decreed against those convicted of adultery (Lev. xx. 20, Deut. xxii. 22), the special punishment of stoning being apparently reserved for the case of unfaithfulness in one betrothed (Deut. xxii.

then He was at once committed to antagonism not only with Roman customs, but with the exclusive power which Rome seems to have reserved to herself in all capital cases[1]. Did He decide in favour of mercy to the sinner, then He stood forth, both before the Sanhedrin and the populace, as a daring innovator that publicly sanctioned the abrogation of a decree of the Mosaic law. But, as in all the preceding cases, the same heavenly wisdom displays itself in the answer that was vouchsafed. The law of Moses was tacitly maintained, but its execution limited to those who were free from all such sins of uncleanness[2] as those of the guilty woman who

---

23, 24). It is not improbable that the woman in the present case might have been one of the latter class (Lightfoot, *Hor. Hebr. in Joann.* v. 5), especially as the Rabbinical law seems to have specified that the adulteress was to be *strangled* (see Lightfoot, *in loc.*); still as this last point does not appear certain (see Ewald, *Alterth.* pp. 218, 232, and comp. Michael. *Mos. Recht*, § 262), and as 'stoning' is mentioned in the *Law*, and in close connexion with adultery, it is perhaps more probable that such was generally regarded as the prescribed mode of death, and that this was a case of μοιχεία in the ordinary acceptation of the word.

[1] This question has been much debated. The most reasonable view appears to be, that though, in hurried cases like that of St Stephen's martyrdom, the punishment of death might have been tumultuously inflicted, still that the declaration of the party of the Sanhedrin that 'it was not lawful for them to put any one to death' (John xviii. 31) was strictly true, and that the supreme court lost the power of formally carrying out their sentence, even in religious cases, probably about the time that Judæa became attached to Syria, and placed under a Roman Procurator: see Friedlieb, *Archäol.* § 28, p. 96 sq. and Winer, *RWB.* Art. 'Synedr.' Vol. II. p. 553. The statements of the Talmudical writers that the loss of this power was really owing to the Sanhedrin ceasing to sit in the room or hall called 'Gazith' (see Lightfoot, *Hor. Hebr. in Joann.* xviii. 31, and compare Selden, *de Synedr.* II. 15), is now justly considered an evasion to cover the true state of the case, viz. that they had been deprived of it by the Romans: see Friedlieb, § 10, p. 22 sq.

[2] The context and circumstances of the case seem to suggest that the term ἀναμάρτητος (a ἅπαξ λεγόμ. in the N.T.) is not here to be understood in reference to sin generally (Luthardt, *Johann. Evang.* Part II. p. 96), but in reference to the class of sins of which the case in question was an instance, *i. e.* sins of the

LECT. VII.

*Jn. viii. 9

stood before them. No wonder is it that we read that they went out one by one convicted by their consciences[a], and left the sinner standing in the midst, in the solitary presence of her sinless yet merciful Judge. If this be the true position of the narrative, our blessed Lord would now have been subjected to the most trying questions that the subtlety of man could excogitate,—the first relative to the authority of His public acts, the second of a political nature, the third relating to doctrine, the fourth to speculative teaching, the last-mentioned to discipline[1].

Our Lord's question respecting the Son of David.

[b] Matt. xxii. 46
Mk. xii. 34
Lk. xx. 40

And now all those malicious attempts had been openly and triumphantly frustrated; so triumphantly, that all the three Synoptical Evangelists tell us that no man henceforth had the hardihood to propose any further question[b]. One final display of meek victory alone was wanting, and that must be seen in the interrogated now assuming the character of the interrogator, and receiving only the answer of shamed silence. The last question mentioned in the narratives of St Matthew and St Mark had been proposed by a Scribe, and to them and to the Pharisees with whom he was united[2], and to whose sect he probably belonged,

---

flesh: compare μηκέτι ἁμάρτανε, ver. 11, and the limited meaning of ἁμαρτωλός, Luke vii. 37. It may be remarked that, according to the text of the Codex Bezæ, the woman is actually described as ἐπὶ ἁμαρτίᾳ γυναῖκα εἰλημμένην (ver. 3).

[1] The position in which this attempt stands with reference to the others cannot of course be determined. The cursive manuscripts (see above, p. 253, note 2) which place it after Luke xxi. 38 probably only intended to imply that the incident was judged to belong to the portion of the Gospel which immediately preceded, not that it formed the last of the attempts in historical order. Of mere conjectures the most probable seems that which places it after the question about the tribute-money: compare Lange, *Leben Jesu*, II. 6. 6, Part III. p. 1222.

[2] According to St Matthew the

does our Lord now turn with the inquiry, how, when according to the teaching of the Scribes Christ is the Son of David, David while speaking under the influence of the Spirit nevertheless calls Him Lord[a]. How can He be both his Lord and his Son[1]? To that profound question, so clearly pointing to the mystery of the Divine and human natures of Him who stood before them[2], no answer is even attempted. By silence[b] they acknowledge their defeat; and in silence they now receive that warning though merciful chastisement of their meek victor recorded to us by the first Evangelist, which forms the subject of the whole of the 23rd chapter of his Gospel. There our Lord with a just severity lays bare the practices of Scribe and Pharisee[c], concluding with an apostrophe to Jerusalem[d], which it would seem had been uttered on an

[a] Ps. cx. 1

[b] Matt. xxii. 46

[c] ver. 13 sq.

[d] ver. 37 sq.

---

question was proposed to the Pharisees (ch. xxii. 41); according to St Luke, who omits the question about the chief commandment, *to* [not *concerning*, Grot., Alford *on Matth.* xxii. 41] the Scribes (ch. xx. 39); according to St Mark it was uttered in the hearing of the people (ch. xii. 35, 37), and as a sort of answer (ver. 35) to the silence of the opponents. All these accounts admit of the obvious explanation, that the question of our Lord was proposed openly, and to those who had last questioned Him, viz. Pharisees in regard to their sect, but several of whom were scribes and lawyers by profession; compare Luke xx. 39 with Mark xii. 28.

[1] It has been popularly urged by modern expositors that the Psalm was not written *by* David but *to* David (Ewald, Meyer, al.), and that our Lord conformed His language to the generally received views of the time (De Wette). This latter assumption, though a very favourite one in our popular theology, is always *very* precarious, if no worse: in the present case it is even out of place, as there are strong reasons for believing, from a fair critical consideration of the Psalm in question, that it *was* written *by* David, as is here expressly declared: comp. Hengstenberg, *Comment. on Psalms*, Vol. III. p. 316 sq. (Clark), Phillips, *ib.* Vol. II. p. 416, and on the Messianic character of the Psalm and its reference to 2 Sam. vii. 1 sq., 1 Chron. xvii. 1 sq., see Ebrard, *Kritik der Evang. Gesch.* § 100, p. 490.

[2] As Euthymius briefly but clearly expresses it,—'He is said to be his Son, as having sprung from his root, according to His human generation;

LECT. VII.

ª ver. 38

The offering of the poor widow.

ᵇ Mk. xii. 40 Lk. xx. 47

earlier occasion¹, but was now appropriately repeated, as declaring in language of the deepest pathos that desolation was nigh at handª, that the hour of mercy had at length passed away, and that justice, temporal and eternal, must now be the portion of the city that had poured out the blood of Jehovah's prophets, and was thirsting for the blood of His Son².

The scene changes with a marvellous truthfulness and appropriateness. After our Lord had uttered His last words of solemn denunciation against the Scribes and Pharisees,—the consumers of *widows'* housesᵇ, the rapacious, the hypocritical and the bloodthirsty, He turns His steps toward the place where free gifts and contributions for the various ministrations of the Temple were offered by the worshippers, and sits there marking the varied and variously-minded multitude that was

but his Lord, as being his God.' *In Matth.* xxii. 45, Vol. I. p. 869.

¹ An address scarcely differing from the present except in the particle that connects the last verse with what precedes (γάρ, Matth. xxiii. 39; δέ, Luke xiii. 35) is specified by St Luke as having been uttered by our Lord after receiving the message about Herod's designs as communicated by the Pharisees; see above, Lect. VI. p. 264. There does not seem any reason, either for agreeing with Meyer (*on Luke* xiii. 34), who asserts that the original and proper position of the words is that assigned by St Matthew, or with Wieseler(*Chron. Synops.* p. 322; comp. Credner, *Einleit.* pp. 67, 136), who regards the words in their present position as interpolated from St Luke. As we have elsewhere, and

as it would seem, justly urged the probability of a repetition of the same words on different occasions, when called forth by something similar, so in the present instance does it seem reasonable to suppose that the similarity of the subject which in both cases precedes the words (the slaughter of the righteous in Jerusalem) called forth in both the pathetic address to the bloodthirsty and now forlorn city; compare Lect. IV. p. 180, note 2, p. 192, note 2.

² The concluding words οὐ μή με ἴδητε κ.τ.λ. (Matth. xxiii. 39) had reference, on the former occasion that they were uttered, primarily to the Triumphal Entry, and secondarily to the second Advent (see above, p. 264, note 1): in the present the reference is exclusively to the latter. 'Then,' as Euthymius well remarks,

now clustering round the numerous chests¹. There He beholds one of those hapless ones of whom He had but so lately spoken as the victim of the extortionate Scribe,—in her penury casting in her two mites[a], her all. And she departed not unblest. That act caused the Redeemer of the world to call up to Him His disciples[b], and to declare to them that the poor desolate one had cast in more than all[c]; yea, and one at least of the hearers did so bear witness[d], that by the record of two Evangelists, the widow's gift, like the piety of Mary of Bethany, shall be known and remembered wheresoever the Gospel shall be preached unto men².

While, as it would seem, our Lord was still teaching within³, a strange message is brought

LECT. VII.

[a] Mk. xii. 42
Lk. xxi. 2
[b] Mk. xii. 43
[c] ver. 44
[d] St Peter; see p. 13, note 4.

The request of the Greek proselytes.

'will they say this,—willingly, never; but unwillingly, at the time of His second Advent, when He shall come with 'power and great glory,' and when their recognition shall be of no avail.' *In Matth.* xxiii. 39.

¹ These we learn from Lightfoot (*Decas Chorogr. in Marc.* cap. 3, § 4) were thirteen in number, called by the Talmudical writers שׁוֹפָרוֹת (from the trumpet-like shape of the openings into which the money was dropped,—'angustæ supra latæ infra, propter deceptores.' Gemara on *Mishna*, 'Shekalim,' II. 1), and stood in the Court of the Women: see Reland, *Antiq.* I. 8. 14, and compare Winer, *RWB.* Art. 'Tempel,' Vol. II. p. 583.

² As Lightfoot pertinently says, —'Hæc paupercula duobus minutis æternam sibi famam coemit.' *In Marc.* xii. 42. The grounds of the Divine commendation are distinctly specified,—she gave all; she might have given one of the *two* λεπτά

[the Rabbinical citation in Schoettgen *in loc.*, and Sepp, *Leben Chr.* Vol. III. p. 311, does not seem to refer to contributions like the present], but she gives *both:* 'The woman offered two farthings; but she possessed nothing more than what she offered; she had nothing left: with empty hand, but a hand bountiful of the little she possessed, she went away from the treasury.' Cyril Alex. *Comment. on St Luke*, Serm. CXXXVIII. Part II. p. 647.

³ The suggestion of Greswell (*Dissert.* XL. Vol. III. p. 123, note) that our Lord sat and taught in the Court of the Women, in order 'that the female Israelites might have access to Him, as well as the male,' is not without probability. It must be remembered, however, that the Court of the Women (γυναικωνῖτις, Joseph. *Bell. Jud.* VI. 9. 2) was so called not because it was especially designed for their use, but because it was the furthest court into which

LECT. VII.

ᵃ Jn. ii. 20

ᵇ ver. 21

from the court without. Some Greek proselytes of the gate, who had come up to Jerusalem to worship the God of the Jew and the Gentile[a] at the feast of the Passover, prefer by the mouths of the Apostles, Andrew and Philip[b], a request to see Him of whom every tongue in Jerusalem now was speaking, and towards whom perchance deep-seated presentiment had mysteriously attracted these God-fearing Gentiles[1]. Deeply moved by a request which He felt to be yet another token of His own approaching glorification, and of the declaration of His name to the wide heathen world of which these were the earliest fruits, our Lord, as it would seem, accedes to the wish[2]. In their hearing and

they were permitted to enter; see Lightfoot, *Decas Chorogr. in Marc.* cap. 3, § 5. The incident that follows is also assigned by Greswell to the day of our Lord's Triumphal Entry; the words καὶ ἀπελθὼν ἐκρύβη ἀπ' αὐτῶν (Joh. xii. 36) seem, however, much more in favour of its present position: compare Wieseler, *Chron. Synops.* p. 396.

[1] The Ἕλληνες here mentioned by St John are rightly considered by the majority of modern expositors not to have been, on the one hand, purely heathens (Chrys., Euthym.), nor again on the other, Hellenists (Ewald, *Gesch. Chr.* p. 392), but, in accordance with the usual meaning of the word in the N. T., *Greeks*, whom, however, the clause ἀναβαινόντων, κ.τ.λ. (observe the pres. part.) seems further to specify as *habitual* worshippers, and so probably, as is stated in the text, 'proselytes of the gate,' many of whom attended the great feasts; see Acts viii. 27, Joseph. *Bell. Jud.* VI. 9. 3, and compare Lightfoot, *Hor. Hebr.*

in Joann. xii. 20. The reason why they peculiarly addressed themselves to the Apostle Philip can only be a matter of conjecture. It has been supposed that they may have come from Galilee (De Wette, Meyer) and from the neighbourhood of Bethsaida, to which place it is here *again* (see John i. 45) specially noticed that the Apostle originally belonged. It is, however, perhaps, equally probable that they were complete strangers, but attracted to Philip by his Grecized name. The conduct of the Apostle on the present occasion and his application to Andrew ('cum sodali audet,' Beng.) has been rightly judged to indicate a cautious, wise, and circumspect nature; comp. Luthardt, *Johan. Evang.* Part I. p. 102.

[2] This has been considered doubtful. It is, however, reasonable to suppose that such a request, thus sanctioned by two Apostles, would not be refused by our Lord, especially as the character of the applicants (ἀναβαινόντων ἵνα προσκυνήσουσιν ἐν τῇ ἑορτῇ, ver. 20) seems to

in that of the people around He reveals, by means of a similitude[a] appropriately taken from the teaching of nature, that truth which it was so hard for the Greek mind with its deifying love of the living and the beautiful to conceive or to realize,—that unto man the pathway to true Life lay through the dreaded gates of death and decay. And if to man, so also, by the mystery of redeeming love, in a certain measure to the Son of Man Himself,—a thought which so moved the depths of the Saviour's soul[1], and called forth from His Divine lips such words of self-devotion and prayer[b], that now

[a] ver. 24
[b] ver. 27

show that it did not result from mere curiosity. The first portion of our Lord's reply (ver. 23) may have been addressed only to the two Apostles on the way to the outer court, the rest uttered in the hearing of the Greeks and the multitude (ver. 29). On the whole incident, see Lange, *Leben Jesu*, II. 6. 5, Part III. p. 1200 sq.

[1] It is worthy of notice that as in the more awful scene in Gethsemane (Matth. xxvi. 38, Mark xiv. 34), the Evangelist has been specially moved to record that the *soul* of the Saviour, —that human ψυχή of which the earlier Apollinarians seem at first even to have denied the existence (Pearson, *Creed*, Vol. II. p. 205, ed. Burton),—was moved and troubled (ver. 27). On the scriptural meaning of the term, and its prevailing reference to the *feelings* and *affections*, rather than to the thoughts or imaginations, see Olshausen, *Opuscula*, p. 153 sq., and compare notes on 1 Tim. iii. 16, and *Destiny of the Creature*, Serm. V. p. 99. It is perhaps scarcely necessary to add that the present troubled state of the Saviour's soul is not for a moment to be referred to the mere apprehension of physical death (comp. Lücke *in loc.*), still less, of the wrath of the devil (Lightfoot, *in Joann.* xii. 28), but to the profound consciousness of the close connexion of death with sin. In dying for us the sinless Saviour vouchsafed to bow to a dispensation which was the wages of sin (Rom. vi. 23); and it was the contemplation of such a contact on the part of the all-Pure and all-Holy with every thing that was most alien to the Divine nature,— sin, darkness, and death, that called forth the Saviour's present words (ver. 27), that heightened the agonies of Gethsemane, and found its deepest utterance in that cry of unimaginable suffering (Matth. xxvii. 46, Mark xv. 34), which was heard from Golgotha, when all that was contemplated was approaching its appalling realization. See Luthardt, *das Johann. Evang.* Part II. p. 252, and compare Pearson, *On the Creed*, Vol. I. p. 234 (Burton), Jackson, *Comment. on the Creed*, VIII. 14, Vol. VII. p. 502 sq.

LECT. VII.

ᵃ Mt. iii. 17
ᵇ Lk. ix. 35
ᶜ Jn. xii. 30

again in the Court of the Gentiles as once by the banks of the Jordanᵃ and on the Mount of the Transfigurationᵇ, the answer of Paternal love was vouchsafed, for the sake of those who stood aroundᶜ, in audible accents of acceptance and promise¹.

The departure from the Temple and the last prophecies.
ᵈ ver. 36
ᵉ ver. 37
ᶠ Mk. xiii. 1
ᵍ ver. 2
Mt. xxiv. 2
Lk. xxi. 6

And now the day was far spent, and our Lord prepares to leave His Father's house, and for a short space to conceal Himselfᵈ both from His enemies, and from the thronging multitudes that hung on His words and beheld His miracles, and yet did not and could not fully believeᵉ. While leaving the Temple a few words from one of the disciplesᶠ, suggested perhaps by a remembrance of an expression² in our Lord's recent apostrophe to Jerusalem, call forth from Him a declaration of the terrible futureᵍ that awaited all the grandeur and magnificence of the sumptuous structure from which He was now taking His final departure.

---

¹ All the best commentators now admit what indeed there never ought to have been any doubt of,—the real and objective nature of the voice from heaven. It may be observed that those who heard appear to be divisible into three classes: (1) the more dull-hearted who heard the *sound*, recognized from whence it came, but mistook it for thunder; (2) the more susceptible hearers who perceived it to be a *voice*, and imagined it to be angelical, but were unable to distinguish what was uttered; (3) the smaller circle, of which the Apostle who relates the occurrence was one, who both heard the voice, knew whence it came, and were enabled to understand the *words* that were spoken. See the note of Meyer, *in loc.* p. 361 (ed. 3), and the brief but good comment of Chrysostom, *in Joann.* Hom. LXVII. Vol. VIII. p. 461 (ed. Bened. 2), who has noticed the first and second class of hearers.

² The opinion of Chrysostom, Theophylact, and others, that the disciples were led to call our Lord's attention to the solidity of structure (Mark xiii. 1) and general magnificence (Luke xxi. 5) of the temple from a remembrance of his recent declaration ἰδοὺ ἀφίεται ὑμῖν ὁ οἶκος ὑμῶν ἔρημος (Matth. xxiii. 38) seems highly probable. A declaration of speedy and all but present desolation (ἀφίεται) when all around was so grand and so stable appeared to them wholly inexplicable. On the nature of the buildings, see Joseph. *Antiq.* xv. 11. 5, *Bell. Jud.* v. 5. 6, and comp. Lightfoot, *Hor. Hebr. in Matth.* xxiv. 1.

Such boding words called for yet fuller explanation. On their homeward journey as the Lord was sitting on the mount of Olives[a], to contemplate perchance yet again the doomed city and temple of which the desolation had even now begun, four of His Apostles[1], Peter and James and John and Andrew[b], come to Him with the solemn inquiry when this mournful prophecy was to be fulfilled, and when the end of this earthly state of things, which they could not but connect with the end of the theocracy[2], was to be looked for by the children of men[c]. In a manner strikingly and appropriately similar to that in which the question was proposed does our Lord return His answer. In a prophecy in which at first the fate of the Holy City and the end of the world are mysteriously blended[3], but which gradually, by

[a] Matt. xxiv. 3 Mk. xiii. 3

[b] Mk. xiii. 3

[c] Matt. xxiv. 3 Mk. xiii. 4 Lk. xxi. 7

---

[1] According to St Matthew the question was proposed by the μαθηταί generally,—a statement which, when coupled with the further remark of both Evangelists that it was proposed *privately* (Matth. xxiv. 3, Mark xiii. 3), admits of the easy and obvious explanation, that none except the chosen Twelve were present when the question was proposed, and that the four Apostles mentioned by St Mark acted as spokesmen for the rest. A good description of the scene and its accessories will be found in Milman, *Hist. of Christianity*, Vol. I. p. 317 sq.

[2] It has been correctly observed (comp. Lange, *Leben Jesu*, Part III. p. 1257, note) that the two questions proposed to our Lord ought not to be separated too sharply, or regarded as definitely referring to separate and distinct periods, but only as referring generally to the period when the destruction recently foretold by our Lord was actually to take place: with this event they instinctively connect the Advent of the Messiah (compare Matth. xxiv. 3 with Mark xiii. 4 and Luke xxi. 7), and of this they not unnaturally ask for the prevenient sign. The connexion of these two events in the mind of the Apostles was not improbably due to a share in the 'sententia apud gentem receptissimâ de חבלי משיח, *Doloribus Messiæ*, [comp. Hos. xiii. 13], id est, de calamitatibus, quas expectarunt futuras ad adventum Messiæ.' Lightfoot, *Hor. Hebr. in Marc.* xiii. 9. Compare also Schoettgen, *loc. cit.* Vol. II. p. 550.

[3] The limits and general character of these notes preclude any regular discussion of this solemn and diffi-

LECT. VII.

ᵃ Matt. xxv. 1 sq.
ᵇ xxv. 14; see p. 275, note 2, ad fin.

means of the solemn parables of the Ten Virgins ᵃ and the Talents ᵇ, and the revelation that follows, unfolds itself into a distinct declaration of the circumstances of the Last Judgment, the Saviour of the world vouchsafes an explicit answer to the questions of His amazed hearers,—yea, too, and on the slopes of that very mountain where mysterious prophecy¹ *seems* to indicate that He who then spake as our Redeemer will hereafter appear as our King and our Judge.

Consultation of the Sanhedrin and treachery of Judas (Wednesday).
ᶜ xii. 36

The day that followed was spent in that holy retirement, into which, as it would seem from St John ᶜ, our Lord now solemnly withdrew, and appears only to have been marked by two events, first the formal and deliberate consultation of the Sanhedrin how they might best carry out their

cult prophecy. It may be remarked, however, (*a*) that it appears exegetically correct, with the majority of modern expositors, to recognize a change of subject at Matth. xxiv. 29 (not, with Chrys., at ver. 23), so that what has preceded is to be referred mainly, but not exclusively to the destruction of Jerusalem,— what follows, mainly but not exclusively (see below) to our Lord's Second Advent and the final judgment; (*b*) that the difficult word εὐθέως (ὁμοῦ γὰρ σχεδὸν ἅπαντα γίνεται, Chrys.) is to be explained by the apparent fact that towards the close of the former part of the prophecy the description of the events connected with the fall of Jerusalem becomes identical with, and gradually (ver. 27, 28) passes into that of the end of the world ; (*c*) that the appended parable (ver. 32 sq.) refers to *both* events, the πάντα ταῦτα (ver. 34) belonging exclusively to the events preceding the fall of Jerusalem, and standing in clear contrast to the ἡμέρα ἐκείνη (ver. 36) which obviously refers exclusively to the end of the world. For more special explanations the student may be referred to the excellent comments of Chrysostom, *in Matth.* Hom. LXXV—LXXVII, Stier, *Disc. of our Lord,* Vol. III. p. 244 sq. (Clark), Lange, *Leben Jesu,* II. 6, 7, Part III. p. 1253, and, with reservations, to the special treatises of Dorner (*de Orat. Chr. Eschatolog.* Stuttg. 1844), E. J. Meyer (*Komment. zu Matth.* xxiv. xxv., Frankf. 1857, and the commentary of Meyer (H. W.), p. 433 sq. (ed. 4).

¹ On the prophetic declaration of the appearance of the Lord on Olivet (Zech. xiv. 4), and its supposed reference to the circumstances of His second Advent, and to the locality of His seat of judgment, see Jackson, *On the Creed,* Vol. X. p. 196.

designs[a], and secondly their compact with the traitor Judas, who perhaps might have availed himself of this very retirement of our Lord for seeking out the chief priests, and for bringing the designs of his now satanically possessed heart[b] to their awful and impious completion.

On the next day, and, as we may perhaps with some reason be led to think, so near its close[1], as to be really on the commencement (according to Jewish reckoning) of the fourteenth of Nisan, the day on which the paschal lamb was to be killed[c] and preparation made for the celebration of the Passover, we are told by the three Synoptical Evangelists that our Lord answers the inquiry of His disciples, where He would have preparation made for eating the passover, by sending Peter and John[d] to the house of a believing follower[2] with a special message and with orders

---

[1] See Greswell, *Dissert.* XLI. Vol. III. p. 170 sq., where it is shown on the authority of Maimonides and Apollinarius of Laodicea that the proper beginning of any feast-day was reckoned from the night [eve] which preceded it; see also Caspari, *Chron.-Geogr. Einleit.* § 148. The *fourteenth* of Nisan though not, strictly considered, a portion of the festival (comp. Joseph. *Antiq.* III. 10. 5), was popularly regarded as such, and, from the putting away of leaven which took place immediately it commenced and the cessation from servile labour (comp. *Mishna*, 'Pesach.' IV. 5), was usually spoken of as the 'first day of unleavened bread' (Matth. xxvi. 17, Mark xiv. 12: see Joseph. *Antiq.* II. 15. 1, who speaks of the festival as lasting *eight* days, and compare Lightfoot,

in *Marc.* xiv. 12, Friedlieb, *Archäol.* § 17, p. 42).

[2] This supposition seems justified by the peculiar use of the words specified by all the three Synoptical Evangelists ὁ διδάσκαλος λέγει (Matth. xxvi. 18, Mark xiv. 14, Luke xxii. 11), and still more by the peculiar and confidential terms of the message: compare Kahnis, *Lehre vom Abendm.* p. 5. When we further remember that the bearers of the message were our Lord's most chosen Apostles, we shall feel less difficulty in admitting the apparently inevitable conclusion (see below) that the supper was prepared *within* what we have seen were popularly considered the limits of the festival, but perhaps one day before the usual time.

[a] Matt. xxvi. 3
[b] Lk. xxii. 3
The celebration of the Last Supper (Thursday).
[c] Mk. xiv. 12 Lk. xxii. 7
[d] Lk. xxii. 8

there to make ready. Thither it would seem our Lord shortly afterwards followed them with the rest of the disciples, and partook of a supper which the distinct expressions of the first three Evangelists[1] leave us no ground for doubting was a *paschal* supper, but which the equally distinct expressions of the fourth Evangelist[2], combined with the peculiar nature of our Lord's message to the householder[a], give us every reason for believing was celebrated twenty-four hours earlier than the time

[a] Matt. xxvi. 18

---

[1] These are especially φαγεῖν τὸ πάσχα (Matth. xxvi. 17, Mark xiv. 12, Luke xxii. 7) and ἑτοιμάζειν τὸ πάσχα (Matth. xxvi. 19, Mark xiv. 16, Luke xxii. 13), both of which no sound principles of interpretation allow us to refer, either here or John xviii. 28 (opp. to Wieseler, *Chron. Synops.* p. 381 sq.), to aught else than the paschal supper : comp. Gesenius, *Thesaur.* Vol. II. p. 1115. Whether, however, the term φαγεῖν τὸ πάσχα necessarily implies the presence of the lamb is by no means so certain. Caspari has investigated the question with great care, and seems fairly to have shown that the paschal supper did not necessarily involve the presence of a lamb. The lamb must have been killed in the Temple, and at a fixed time : where from absence from Jerusalem or any other grave reason this could not be done, then the supper consisted of unleavened bread (which seems to have been the *essential* characteristic of the paschal season and its introductory supper), and the other prescribed accompaniments, viz. bitter herbs, sauce, and two dishes of cooked food; comp. *Mishna*, 'Pesach.' x. 3. This probably was the supper on the present occasion; see esp. Caspari, *Chron.-Geogr. Einleit.*

§ 158, p. 173 sq.

[2] These are (a) ἵνα φάγωσιν τὸ πάσχα (ch. xviii. 28) alluded to in the above note, and referred to the day following that which we are now considering; (b) the special note of time (ch. xiii. 1) in reference to a supper which it seems nearly impossible (opp. to Lightfoot, *in Matth.* xxvi. 6) to regard as different from that referred to by the Synoptical Evangelists ; (c) the definition of time παρασκευὴ τοῦ πάσχα (ch. xix. 14), which it seems equally impossible (opp. to Wieseler, *Chron. Synops.* p. 336) in the language of the N. T. to understand otherwise than as 'the preparation' or day preceding the Passover; see Meyer *in loc.* p. 478 (ed. 3), and Kitto, *Journal of Sacr. Lit.* for 1850, XI. p. 75 sq.; (d) the statement that the Sabbath in the Passover week was 'a high day' (ch. xix. 31), which admits of no easy or natural explanation except that of a coincidence of the important Nisan 15 with the weekly Sabbath. The statements are so clear, that to attempt with Wieseler (*Chron. Synops.*), Robinson (*Biblioth. Sacr.* for Aug. 1845), and others to explain them away must be regarded as arbitrary and hopeless.

when it was celebrated by the chief priests and Pharisees* and apparently the whole body of the nation[1]. While they are taking their places at the [LECT. VII. *John xviii. 28]

[1] From what is here said and the above notes it will be seen that we adopt the view of the Greek Fathers, and indeed of the primitive Church generally (see the quotations in Greswell, *Dissert.* XLI. Vol. III. p. 168 sq., and add Clem. Alex. *on St Luke*, Serm. CXLI. Part II. p. 660, Transl.), that, even as Talmudical tradition (*Babyl.* 'Sanhedr.' VI. 2) also asserts, our Lord *suffered on Nisan* 14, and that He ate the paschal supper on the eve with which that day commenced. In favour of this opinion we may briefly urge on the *positive* side, (*a*) the statements of St John above alluded to; (*b*) the peculiar nature of the message sent to the οἰκοδεσπότης, which seems to refer to something special and unusual: see above, p. 321, note 2; (*c*) the words τοῦτο τὸ πάσχα (Luke xxii. 15), and the desire expressed by our Lord (ib.), both of which well coincide with the assumption of a peculiar celebration; (*d*) several apparent hints in the Synoptical Gospels that the day on which our Lord suffered was not marked by the Sabbatical rest which belonged to Nisan 15; Matth. xxvii. 59 sq., Mark xv. 21 (?), 42, 46, Luke xxiii. 26 (?), 54, 56; (*e*) the anti-typical relation of our Lord to the paschal lamb (1 Cor. v. 7),—in accordance with which, the death of our Redeemer on the very day and hour when the paschal lamb was sacrificed must be reverently regarded as a coincidence of high probability: see Euthym. *in Matth.* xxvi. 20. On the *negative* side, we may observe (*f*) that the main objection founded on the necessity of the lamb being killed in the Temple (Lightfoot, *in Matth.* xxvi. 19, Friedlieb, *Archäol.* § 18, p. 47) rests entirely on the assumption that a lamb must have been present at the Last Supper, which seems by no means certain (see above, and Caspari, *Einleit.* § 161, p. 178), and further, that even if there had been a lamb, the above objection is much modified by the language of Philo adduced by Greswell, *l. c.*, p. 146, and still more so by the probability that the time specified for killing the lamb, viz. 'between the two evenings' (Exod. xii. 6, Lev. xxiii. 3, Numb. ix. 3), *might* have been understood to mean between the eves of Nisan 14 and Nisan 15 (see Lee, *Serm. on Sabb.* p. 22),— and that more especially at a time when the worshippers had become so numerous that above 256,000 lambs (see above, p. 289, note 1) would have had to be sacrificed in about two hours, if the ordinary interpretation of the בֵּין הָעַרְבַּיִם had been rigorously observed. Again (*g*) the silence of St John as to the paschal nature of the supper is in no way more singular than his silence as to its Eucharistic character. Both were well-known features, which it did not fall in with his divinely ordered plan here to specify. All that it was necessary to add so as to obviate all misapprehension he does add, viz. that the supper was *before* the Passover: ch. xiii. 1. Lastly, (*h*) if we accept the *highly* probable statement that our Lord suffered A.D. 30, and the nearly certain statement that the day of the week was Friday (see Wieseler, *Chron. Synops.* p. 334 sq.), then beyond all reason-

LECT. VII.

^a See p. 274

^b John xiii. 4, 5

table the same unbecoming contention for priority, which we have already noticed on previous occasions[a], again shows itself, called forth perhaps in the present case by a desire to occupy the places nearest One towards whom every hour was now deepening their love and devotion. But such demonstrations were unmeet for the disciples of Jesus Christ; such contentions, though not without some excuse, must still be calmly repressed. And in no way could this be more tenderly done than by the performance of every part[b] of an office,—that of washing the feet of those about to sit down to meat,—which usually fell to the lot of a servant[1], but was now solemnly completed in the case of each one of them, yea, the traitor not excepted,

able doubt He suffered on Nisan 14 and ate the Passover on the first hours of that day the eve before,—calculation clearly showing that in that year the new moon of Nisan was on Wednesday, March 22, at 8h. 8m. in the *evening*, and that consequently, if we allow the usual two days for the phase (see Greswell, *Dissert.* Vol. I. p. 320), Nisan 1 commenced (according to Jewish reckoning) on Friday evening March 24, but really coincided as to daylight with Saturday March 25, or Nisan 14 with *Friday*, April 7. Compare Wieseler, *Chron. Synops.* p. 446, whose own tables (independently proved to be accurate) may thus be used against him; see also above, p. 193, note 1, and the very clear table in Caspari, *Chron.-Geogr. Einleit.* § 153, p. 170. More might be urged, but the above considerations may perhaps lead us to pause before we reject a mode of reconciliation so ancient, so free from all forcings of language, and apparently so reasonable and trustworthy. For notices of the many different treatises on this difficult subject, see Winer, *RWB.* Art. 'Pascha,' Vol. II. p. 202, and Meyer, *Komment. üb. Joh.* xviii. 28, p. 463 sq. (ed. 3).

[1] See Friedlieb, *Archäol.* § 20, p. 64, and Meyer *in loc.* p. 375 (ed. 3). It may be observed that there is some little difficulty in arranging the circumstances of the Last Supper in their exact order, as the narrative of St Luke is not in strict harmony with that of St Matthew and St Mark. Of the various possible arrangements, the connexion adopted in the text, which is closely in accordance with that of the best recent harmonists, seems, on the whole, the most satisfactory; see Wieseler, *Chron. Synops.* p. 398 sq., Robinson, *Harmony,* p. 153 (Tract Soc.), and compare Greswell, *Dissert.* XLII. Vol. III. p. 179 sq.

by Him whom they called and rightly called their Master and their Lord^a....And now the supper had commenced[1], and round the Saviour were gathered, for the last time, those whom He loved so well, and loved even unto the end^b. And yet the hand of the betrayer was on the table,—a thought we are told that so moved the very inward spirit of the Lord^c that He solemnly announced it, and brought it home by a general indication[2] to that small and saddened^d company that sat around Him, and that now asked Him, each one of them in the deep trouble of his heart, whether it were possible that it could be he. After a more special and private indication had been vouchsafed^e, and the self-convicted son of perdi-

^a ver. 13
^b ver. 1
^c ver. 21
^d Matt. xxvi. 22
^e Jn. xiii. 26

---

[1] There seems some reason for accepting with Tischendorf the reading of BLXℵ; Cant.; Orig. (4), δείπνου γινομένου (John xiii. 2), according to which the time would seem to be indicated when our Lord and His Apostles were just in the act of sitting down; comp. Meyer *in loc.* Even, however, if we retain the Received Text γενομένου, the meaning cannot be 'supper being ended' (Auth. Ver.; comp. Friedlieb, *Archäol.* p. 64); for compare ver. 4, 12, 26, but, 'when supper had begun, had now taken place;' compare Lücke, *Commentar über Joh.* Vol. II. p. 548 (ed. 3).

[2] It seems incorrect and uncritical to confuse the general indication specified in the Synoptical Gospels, ὁ ἐμβάψας μετ' ἐμοῦ τὴν χεῖρα (Matth. xxvi. 23) or ὁ ἐμβαπτόμενος κ.τ.λ. (Mark xiv. 20), with the more particular one John xiii. 26. The first merely indicates what is in fact stated by St John in ver. 18, that the betrayer was one of those who were now eating with our Lord: the second is a special indication more particularly vouchsafed to St John, though perhaps in some degree felt to be significant by the rest of the Apostles; see Stier, *Disc. of Our Lord*, Vol. VII. p. 49 (Clark). The change of tense in St Mark ὁ ἐμβαπτόμενος ('the dipper with me &c.') has been alluded to by Meyer (*in loc.*) as indicating that Judas sat in close proximity to our Lord. This does not seem improbable (comp. John xiii. 26), and may be thought to favour the idea that St John was on one side of our Lord, and the traitor on the other. If, however, we accept the reading of Lachmann and Tischendorf in ver. 24, νεύει οὖν Σίμων Πέτρος καὶ λέγει αὐτῷ Εἰπὲ τίς ἐστιν, the usually received opinion that St Peter was on the other side of our Lord will then seem most natural.

LECT. VII.

[a] ver. 30
[b] Matt. xxvi. 29
Mk. xiv. 25

tion had gone forth into the night[a], followed in due and solemn order the institution of the Eucharist[1], and with it those mysterious words[b] that seem to imply that that most Holy Sacrament was to have relation not only to the past but to the future, that it was not only to be commemorative of the sad but blessed hour that then was passing, but prophetic of that hour of holy joy when all should again be gathered together, and the Lord should drink with His chosen ones the new paschal wine in the kingdom of God[2]. After a few melancholy words on the dispersion and failing faith of all of those who were then around, yea, and even more particularly of him who said in the warmth of his own glowing heart that he would lay down his life for his Master[c] and follow Him to prison and to death[d], our Lord

[c] Jn. xiii. 37
[d] Luke xxii. 33

---

[1] This would seem not to have taken place till the traitor went out. The strongly affirmative σὺ εἶπας of St Matthew (ch. xxvi. 25; compare Schoettg. *in loc.*) appears to agree so well with the second and distinct indication of the traitor in John xiii. 26, after which we know that he went out, that we can hardly imagine that Judas was present at what followed. Again John *l. c.* seems to imply that the supper was going on, whereas it is certain that the Cup was blessed μετὰ τὸ δειπνῆσαι, Luke xxii. 20, 1 Cor. xi. 25. If this view be correct we must suppose that the departure of the traitor took place after Matth. xxvi. 25, and that ver. 26 ἐσθιόντων δὲ αὐτῶν refers to a resumption of the supper after the interruption caused by his leaving the apartment.

[2] The meaning of this mysterious declaration can only be humbly surmised. It would appear, however, from the peculiar distinctness of the expressions (τούτου τοῦ γεννήματος τῆς ἀμπέλου, Matth. xxvi. 29) that there is a reference to some future participation in elements which a glorified creation may supply (comp. Rev. xxii. 2), perchance at that mystic marriage-supper of the Lamb (Rev. xix. 9), when the Lord and those that love Him shall be visibly united in the Kingdom of God, nevermore to part. The reference to our Lord's companionship with His disciples after the resurrection (Theophyl., Euthym.) can never be accepted as an adequate explanation of this most mysterious yet most exalting promise. See especially, Stier, *Disc. of Our Lord*, Vol. VII. p. 166 sq., and compare Krummacher, *The Suffering Saviour*, ch. v. p. 44 (Clark).

appears to have uttered the longer and reassuring address which forms the fourteenth chapter of the Gospel of St John, and which ceased only to be resumed again[a], perchance while all were standing in attitude to depart[1], in the sublime chapters which follow. With the high-priestly prayer in the seventeenth chapter, in which, as it were in rapt and holy retrospect the Lord contemplates and dedicates to His heavenly Father His completed work[2], the solemn scene comes to its exalted close.

margin: LECT. VII.
[a] Jn. xv. 1

Still followed by the yet undispersed Eleven,

margin: The agony in Gethsemane (Thursday night).

---

[1] It scarcely seems probable that John xv. 1 sq. was uttered in a different and safer place (comp. Chrysost. *in loc.*) than that in which the preceding discourse had been delivered, still less that it was uttered on the way to Gethsemane. The view adopted by Luthardt (*das Johann. Evang.* Part II. p. 321), Stier (*Disc. of Our Lord*, Vol. VI. p. 266), and other recent expositors, viz. that our Lord uttered the discourses in the 15th and two following chapters in the paschal apartment, on the point of departure, and with the disciples standing round Him, seems much more natural. The reference to the vine (ver. 1) has led to several arbitrary assumptions, *e. g.* that it was suggested by the vineyards through which they are to be supposed to have been passing (Lange, *Leben Jesu*, Part II. p. 1347), or by the vine on the door of the Holy place (Joseph. *Antiq.* XV. 11. 3), to which it has been thought allusion may have been made (Lampe *in loc.*). If we are to presume that this heavenly discourse was suggested by any thing outward, 'the fruit of the vine' of which all had so solemnly partaken would seem to be the more natural object that gave rise to the comparison: see Grotius *in loc.*, and Stier, *Disc. of Our Lord*, Vol. VI. p. 269 (Clark).

[2] Though it is right to be cautious in pressing grammatical distinctions, it still seems probable that the significant aorists in John xvii. 4 sq., ἐδόξασα, ἐτελείωσα, ἐφανέρωσα κ.τ.λ., point to a contemplation, on the part of the Saviour, of His work on earth as now completed and concluded. He now stands as it were at the goal, and in holy retrospect commends both His work and those loved ones who had been permitted to witness it to the Eternal Father in a prayer, which has been rightly regarded by all deeper expositors as the most affecting and most sublime outpouring of love and devotion that stands recorded on the pages of the Book of Life. See Luthardt, *das Johann. Evang.* Part II. p. 354, and the admirable exposition of Stier, *Disc. of our Lord*, Vol. VI. p. 421 sq.

LECT. VII.

Our Lord now leaves that upper room which had been the witness of such adorable mysteries, and, passing out of the city and down the deep gorge on its eastern side, crosses over the Kedron[a] to a garden at the foot of the Mount of Olives, where, as we learn from St John, He was often wont to resort[b], and to which the produce of the adjacent hill gave the name of Gethsemane[1]. Arrived at the spot the Lord leaves the greater part of His saddened[c] Apostles in the outskirts of the garden[d], while with His three more especially chosen attendants, Peter and the two sons of Zebedee, He Himself advances farther into the solitude and gloom[2]. And now was solemnly disclosed a mystery of unimaginable sufferings and woe. Removed from the three Apostles[e], but only at such a distance that their eyes might still behold, and their poor human hearts strive to sympathize[3],

[a] Jn. xviii. 1
[b] xviii. 2 Comp. Lk. xxiii. 39
[c] Comp. Lk. xxvi. 45
[d] Mt. xxvi. 36
[e] Matt. xxvi. 39

---

[1] The most probable derivation appears to be גַּת שֶׁמֶן ('oil-press'); see Winer, *RWB.* Vol. I. p. 424, and compare Bynæus, *de Morte Christi*, II. 2. 6, Part II. p. 73. For an account of the place with which Gethsemane has been identified by modern travellers see Robinson, *Palestine*, Vol. I. p. 234 sq. (ed. 2), Smith, *Dict. of Bible*, Vol. I. p. 684, but comp. Thomson, *Land and the Book*, Vol. II. p. 483. For a representation, see Robertson and Beato, *Views of Jerusalem*, No. 20.

[2] The conjecture of Dean Alford that our Lord retired with the three Apostles into a portion of the garden from which the moonlight might have been intercepted by the rocks and buildings on the opposite side of the gorge does not seem improbable, or at variance with the supposed site: comp. Robinson, *Palestine*, Vol. I. p. 235.

[3] While with the older expositors we may reasonably believe that our Lord was pleased to take the three Apostles with Him that they might be eye-witnesses to His church of His mysterious Agony (ὥστε ἐνδείξασθαι αὐτοῖς τὰ τῆς λύπης, Euthym. in Matth. xxvi. 37), we may perhaps also, with the best modern expositors, presume to infer from the special exhortation γρηγορεῖτε μετ' ἐμοῦ (Matth. xxvi. 38) that the Redeemer of the world vouchsafed to desire the human sympathy of these His chosen followers : see Stier, *Disc. of Our Lord*, Vol. VII. p. 225, where the practical aspects of this opinion are fittingly alluded to, and compare

with the now consciously deepening^a agony of their beloved Master, the Eternal Son kneels^b, bows, and falls forward on the earth^c. Twice did the prayer pass those suffering lips, that if it were possible,—if it were compatible with His Father's glory and the world's salvation,—this cup, this cup of a present anguish, in which in an awful and indivisible unity all the future was included, might pass from Him[1]; and twice with words of meekest resignation^d did He yield Himself to the heavenly will of Him with whom He Himself was One. Twice did He return to the three chosen ones whom He had bidden to watch with Him^e in this awful hour of uttermost conflict, and twice did He find Himself bereft even of human sympathy, unwatched with, unheeded, alone. Yet a third time, if we here[2] incorporate the narrative

marginal notes: LECT. VII. — a ver. 37, 38 b Lk. xxii. 41 c Mk. xiv. 35 d Mt. xxvi. 39, 42 e ver. 38

Krummacher, *The Suffering Christ*, § 12, p. 96 (Clark), Ewald, *Gesch. Christus*, p. 414.

[1] To regard this most holy prayer as merely expressive of that shrinking from death and suffering (Meyer, al.), which belongs to the nature our Lord was pleased to assume, is as unfitting on the one hand, as it is precarious on the other, to refer the anguish and amazement that preceded it either to the visible appearance ('in formâ scilicet aliquâ dirâ et horrendâ,' Lightfoot, *Hor. Hebr. in loc.*) of the Prince of darkness, or to a sense of the *punitive* withdrawal of the Paternal presence (Krummacher, p. 97,—in language unwarrantably strong) from Him who, though now feeling the full pressure of the burden of a world's sin, not only could say but did say, 'Abba, Father;' see Stier, *Disc. of Our Lord*, Vol. VII. p. 237. Heavy indeed was the burden of sin, for it bowed the Saviour to the *earth* (Mark xiv. 35); fearful the assaults of the powers of evil, for their hour was at hand (Luke xxii. 53); but it was to the vivid clearness of the Saviour's knowledge of the awful affinity between death, sin, and the powers of darkness (see p. 317, note 1) that we may humbly presume to refer the truest bitterness of the cup of Gethsemane; see Beck, *Lehrwissenschaft*, p. 514 (cited by Stier), and compare Pearson, *Creed*, Vol. I. p. 234 (ed. Burt.), Jackson, *Creed*, VIII. 12. 4, Vol. VII. p. 472 sq.

[2] It is perhaps doubtful whether we are to consider the appearance of the sustaining angel recorded by St Luke as after the first or after the second prayer. However this may be, it seems right closely to connect

of the third Evangelist[a], even while the ministry of the sustaining angel, and the thick falling drops of bloody sweat[1] alike bore witness to an agony fast transcending the powers of our common humanity,—yet a third time was that prayer offered to the Eternal Father, and again was it answered by the meek resignation of the Eternal Son. For the last time the Lord returns to His slumbering Apostles[b], and now with words that sadly remind them that the holy privilege of watching with their suffering Master is finally lost and forfeited[2],

[a] Mt. xxii. 42
[b] Mark xiv. 41

---

[1] the angelical ministration and the agony recorded in the next verse. The infused *physical* strength (ἐνισχύων αὐτόν, ver. 43; comp. Matth. iv. 11) was exhibited in the more agonized fervency of the prayer (ἐκτενέστερον προσηύχετο, ver. 44) but in a manner that showed that the exhaustion of the human and bodily powers of the Redeemer had now reached its uttermost limit. The omission of this verse (ver. 43) and of that which follows in some manuscripts [AB; 13. 69. 124], and the marks of suspicion attached to them in others (see Tisch. *in loc.*), are apparently only due to the mistaken opinion that the nature of the contents of the verses was not consistent with the doctrine of our Lord's divinity.

[1] It has been considered doubtful whether the comparison of the sweat to falling drops of blood was only designed to specify the thickness and greatness of the drops (Theophyl., Euthym., Bynæus), or whether it also implies, that the sweat was tinged with actual blood, forced forth from the pores of that sacred body (comp. Pearson, *Creed*, Vol. I. p. 233, ed. Burt.) in the agony of the struggle. The latter opinion seems most probable, and most coincident with the language of the inspired writer. If the use of ὡσεὶ shows that what fell were not drops of blood, but of sweat, the special addition of αἵματος seems certainly to indicate the peculiar nature of the sweat, viz. as an ἱδρὼς αἱματοειδής (Diod. Sic. *Hist.* XVII. 90), and to direct attention to that with which it was tinged and commingled: see Meyer, *on Luke* xxii. 44, and for notices of partial analogies, Jackson, *Creed*, Vol. VII. p. 483, Bynæus, *de Morte Christi*, Part II. p. 133.

[2] The exact meaning of the words καθεύδετε τὸ λοιπὸν καὶ ἀναπαύεσθε (Matth. xxvi. 45) has been somewhat differently estimated. To find in them a sort of mournful *irony* (Meyer, *in loc.*) is, to use the mildest term, psychologically unnatural, and to take them in an interrogative sense (Greswell, *Dissert.* XLII. Vol. III. p. 194) in a high degree improbable. We must then either supply an εἰ δύνασθε with Euthymius, or, as seems much more natural, regard the words as spoken with a kind of

He forewarns them that the hour is come[a], and the traitor nigh at hand.

Nigh indeed he was, for even now as the Lord was speaking[b] an armed heathen[1] and Jewish band with torches and lanterns[c], led by the lost Apostle[d], arrives before the entrance of the garden. While they pause perchance, and stand consulting how they may best provide against every possibility of escape, He whom they were seeking, with all the holy calm of prescience[e], comes forth from the enclosure and stands face to face with the apostate and his company....And now follows a scene of rapidly succeeding incidents, the traitor's kiss[2],—the Lord's question to the soldiers, and

[a] Matt. xxvi. 45
The betrayal of our Lord.
[b] Mark xiv. 43
[c] John xviii. 3
[d] Luke xxii. 47
[e] John xviii. 4

---

permissive force (Winer, *Gram.* § 43, p. 278), and in tones in which merciful reproach was blended with calm resignation: δεικνύς, ὅτι οὐδὲν τῆς αὐτῶν δεῖται βοηθείας, καὶ ὅτι δεῖ πάντως αὐτὸν παραδοθῆναι. Chrys. *in loc.* Hom. LXXXIII. With this the ἐγείρεσθε, ἄγωμεν (verse 46) that follows seems in no way inconsistent. The former words were rather in the accents of a pensive contemplation; the latter in the tones of exhortation and command. Compare Mark xiv. 41, where the inserted ἀπέχει seems exactly to mark the change in tone and expression.

[1] From the term σπεῖρα used by St John (ch. xviii. 3) and the separate mention of ὑπηρέται ἐκ τῶν ἀρχιερέων καὶ Φαρισαίων we must certainly conclude that a portion of the Roman *cohort* (comp. Valcken. *Schol.* Vol. I. p. 458), with which the fortress of Antonia was usually garrisoned, was now placed at the service of the chief-priestly party,— probably for the sake of at once quelling any opposition that might be offered, and thus of avoiding all chance of uproar at a time when public tranquillity was always liable to be disturbed; see Friedlieb, *Archäol.* § 21, p. 67. The notice of the 'torches and lanterns' (John xviii. 3) that were brought, though it was now the time of full moon, shows the deliberate nature of the plan, and the determination to preclude every possibility of escape: comp. Luthardt, *das Johann. Evang.* Part II. p. 378.

[2] It may be observed that both St Matthew (ch. xxvi. 49) and St Mark (ch. xiv. 45) specially use the compound form κατεφίλησεν. To assert that this 'is only another word for ἐφίλησεν' (Alford) seems very precarious, especially when the nature of the case would render a *studied* manner of salutation highly probable. Meyer appropriately cites Xenoph. *Mem.* II. 6. 33, ὡς τοὺς καλοὺς φιλήσαντός μου, τοὺς δ' ἀγαθοὺς καταφιλήσαντος.

332 *The Last Passover.*

LECT. VII.

ᵃ Jo. xviii. 5
ᵇ ver. 8
ᶜ Luke xxii. 38
ᵈ ver. 49
ᵉ xxii. 51

ᶠ John xviii. 12

avowal of Himself as Him whom they were seeking ᵃ,—the involuntary homage of the terror-stricken band¹,—the tender solicitude of the Lord for His Apostles ᵇ, and their reciprocated readiness to defend Him, scantily armed as they were ᶜ, even to the death ᵈ,—the rash sword-stroke of Peter, and the healing touch of the Divine hand ᵉ,—the Lord's words of meek protest to the chief-priests² and multitude,—the flight of the terrified Apostles,—the binding and leading away of the now forsaken Redeemer ᶠ,—all of which we must here not fail thus briefly to enumerate, but on the details of which our present limits will not permit us to enlarge, especially as there is still so much before us that requires our more close and concentrated attention.

The preliminary examination before Annas.

It was now deep in the night, when that mixed Jewish and Gentile multitude returned to the city with Him whom the party of the Sanhedrin had so long and so eagerly desired to seize. Directed probably by those who sent them forth or by some

---

¹ The statement of Stier, that there was here 'no specific miracle apart from the standing miracle of our Lord's personality itself' (*Disc. of our Lord*, Vol. VII. p. 271), may very justly be called in question. It seems much more correct to suppose with the older expositors that the mighty words ἐγώ εἰμι (compare Mark vi. 50) were permitted to exercise their full miraculous force, in order that alike to friends and foes the voluntary nature of the Lord's surrender of Himself might be fully declared; see Chrysostom *in loc.*, and compare the curious remarks of Origen, *in Matth.* § 100, Vol. III.

p. 906 (ed. Bened.).

² It seems clear from the inclusive terms of Luke xxii. 52, that not only some of the Temple-officers, but that some even of the members of the Sanhedrin had either come with or recently joined (Euthym.) the crowd, and were now taking a prominent part in the proceedings. To call this a 'Verirrung der Tradition' (Meyer, *üb. Luk.* p. 486) is as arbitrary as it is presumptuous. Such a fact is neither unlikely in itself nor incompatible with the statements of the other Evangelists.

of the chief priests and elders, who we know were among the multitude^a, the soldiers and Jewish officers[1] that were with them^b lead our Lord away to the well-known and influential Annas[2], who, if not as president of the Sanhedrin, yet certainly as the father-in-law of the acting High-priest^c, was the fittest person[3] with whom to leave our Lord till the Sanhedrin could be formally assembled.... The locality of the examination that followed is confessedly *most* difficult to decide upon, as the first and fourth Evangelists *seem* here to specify

^a See p. 332, note 2.
^b John xviii. 12
^c ver. 13

---

[1] The very distinct enumeration of those that took part in the present acts (John xviii. 12) may *perhaps* hint at the impression produced by the preceding events, which now led *all* to help (Luthardt), but is more probably only intended to mark that Gentiles and Jews alike took part in the heinous act, ἡ σπεῖρα καὶ ὁ χιλίαρχος forming a natural designation of the one part, οἱ ὑπηρέται τῶν Ἰουδαίων, of the other.

[2] This successful man was appointed High-priest by Quirinus A.D. 12, and after holding the office for several years was deposed by Valerius Gratus, the Procurator of Judæa who preceded Pilate; comp. Joseph. *Antiq.* XVIII. 2. 1 sq. He appears, however, to have possessed vast influence, as he not only obtained the high-priesthood for his son Eleazar, and his son-in-law Caiaphas, but subsequently for four other sons, under the last of whom James the Brother of our Lord was put to death: comp. Joseph. *Antiq.* XX. 9. 1. It is thus highly probable that besides having the title of ἀρχιερεὺς merely as one who had filled the office, he to a great degree retained the powers he had formerly exercised, and came to be regarded practically as a kind of *de jure* High-priest. The opinion of Lightfoot that he was *Sagan* is not consistent with the position of his name before Caiaphas, Luke iii. 2 (see Vitringa, *Obs. Sacr.* VI. p. 529), and much less probable than the supposition of Selden (revived and ably put forward by Wieseler, *Chron. Synops.* p. 186 sq.) that he was the *Nasi* or President of the Sanhedrin, an office not always held by the High-priest; compare Friedlieb, *Archäol.* § 7, p. 12. The latter view would well account for the preliminary examination, but is not fully made out, and hardly in accordance with John xviii. 13; see below.

[3] The words ἦν γὰρ πενθερὸς κ.τ.λ. (John xviii. 13) seem certainly to point to the degree of *relationship* as the cause of the sending. They are thus, to say the least, not inconsistent with the supposition that Caiaphas was wholly in the hands of his powerful father-in-law; compare (thus far) Sepp, *Leben Christi*, VI. 48, Vol. III. p. 463 sq.

LECT. VII.

ᵃ Matt. xxvi. 57
Jn. xviii. 13

two different placesᵃ, though indeed it requires but the simple and reasonable supposition that Annas and Caiaphas occupied a common official residence, to unite their testimony, and to remove many of the difficulties with which this portion of the sacred narrative is specially marked[1]. Be this as it may, we can scarcely doubt from the clear state-

ᵇ xviii. 13—24

ments in St John's Gospelᵇ that a preliminary examination of an inquisitorial nature, in which the Lord was questioned, perhaps conversationally,

ᶜ xviii. 19
ᵈ ver. 22

about His followers and His teachingᶜ, and which the brutal conduct of one of the attendants presentᵈ seems to show was private and informal, took place in the palace of Annas. Here too, it would seem, we must also place the three denials of St Peter[2], the last of which, by the sort of note of

---

[1] So Euthymius, *in Matth.* xxvi. 58,—a very reasonable conjecture which has been accepted by several of the best modern expositors; see Stier, *Disc. of Our Lord*, Vol. VII. p. 306 (Clark), and the more recent comments of Caspari, *Chron.-Geogr. Einleit.* § 170, p. 191.

[2] The difficult question of the harmony of the various accounts cannot here be fully entered into. If we allow ourselves to conceive that in the narrative of St John the first and second denials are transposed, and that the first took place at going *out*, rather than coming *in*, there would seem to result this very natural account,—that the *first* denial took place at the fire (Matth. xxvi. 69, Mark xiv. 66 sq., Luke xxii. 56, John xviii. 25), and was caused by the fixed recognition (Luke xxii. 56) of the maid who admitted St Peter; that the *second* took place at or near the door leading out of the court, to which fear might have driven the Apostle (Matth. xxvi. 71, Mark xiv. 68 sq., Luke xxii. 58, John xviii. 17); and that the *third* took place in the court about an hour afterwards (Luke xxii. 59) before several witnesses who urged the peculiar nature of the Apostle's harsh Galilæan pronunciation (see Friedlieb, *Archäol.* § 25, Sepp, *Leben Chr.* Vol. III. p. 478 sq.), and near enough to our Lord for Him to turn and gaze upon His now heart-touched and repentant follower. Minor discordances, as to the number and identity of the recognizers still remain, but these when properly considered will only be found such as serve the more clearly to show not only the independence of the inspired witnesses, but the living truth of the occurrence. For further details see a good note of Alford, *on Matth.* xxvi. 69, Robinson, *Harmony*, p. 166 note (Tract Society), and

time afforded by the mention of the second cock-crowing[a], must have occurred not very long before the first dawning of day[1], and not improbably at the very time that the Saviour was being led away bound to Caiaphas[b] across the court where the Apostle was then standing.

And now day was beginning to draw nigh; yet, as it would seem, before its earliest rays the whole body of the Sanhedrin had assembled, as it was a case that required secrecy and despatch, at the house of the High-priest Caiaphas[c], whither the Lord had recently been brought[2]. The Holy One is now placed before His prejudiced and embittered judges, and proceedings at once commenced. These were probably not gravely irregular. Though neither the time nor perhaps the place of meeting were strictly legal in the case of a capital trial like the present, there still does not seem any reason for supposing that the council departed widely from the outward rules of their court[3]. With vengeance in their hearts,

Marginal notes: [a] Mk. xiv. 72   [b] John xviii. 24   *The examination before the Sanhedrin.*   [c] Comp. Mt. xxvi. 3

---

compare Lichtenstein, *Lebensgesch. Jes.* p. 427 sq.

[1] From a consideration of passages in ancient writers (esp. Ammian. Marcellinus, *Hist.* XXII. 14) Friedlieb shows that the second cock-crowing must be assigned to the beginning of the fourth watch, and consequently to a time somewhere between the hours of 3 and 4 in the morning; see *Archäol.* § 24, p. 79, Wieseler, *Chron. Synops.* p. 406, and compare Greswell, *Dissert.* XLII. Vol. III. p. 211 sq.

[2] From the above narration it will be seen that the contested ἀπέστειλεν (John xviii. 24) is taken in its simple aoristic sense, and as defining the end of the preliminary examination before Annas, of which the fourth Evangelist, true to the supplemental nature of his Gospel (see p. 14, note 4), alone gives an account. The usual pluperfect translation ('miserat') is open, in a case like the present, to serious objection in a mere grammatical point of view (consider the examples in Winer, *Gr.* § 40, p. 246), especially as the verb has a pluperfect in regular use; even, however, if these be waived the exegetical arguments against it seem plainly irresistible: see Stier, *Disc. of Our Lord*, Vol. VII. p. 307 (Clark).

[3] As the council had now it

LECT. VII.

^a Matt. xxvi. 60

^b Mk. xiv. 56

^c ver. 55

^d Matt. xxvi. 63

^e ver. 61

yet, as it would seem, with all show of legal formality they forthwith proceed to receive and investigate the many suborned witnesses^a that were now in readiness to bear their testimony. But conviction is not easy. The wretched men, as we may remember, so gainsaid each other^b that something further seemed required before the bloody sentence^c, which so many present had now ready on their lips, could with any decency be pronounced. Meanwhile the Lord was silent^d. The witnesses were left to confute or contradict each other[1]; even the two^e that affected to repeat words actually spoken, and even in this could

---

would seem (Lightfoot, *Hor. Hebr. in Matth.* xxvi. 3) ceased to occupy its formal hall of meeting on the south side of the temple, called Gazith (לשכת הגזית) conclave cæsi lapidis), and had moved elsewhere (see Friedlieb, *Archäol.* § 5, p. 10, Caspari, *Einleit.* § 144, p. 163; and correct accordingly Milman, *Hist. of Christianity*, chap. VII. Vol. I. p. 336, note and p. 344), meetings in the city and in the house of the Highpriest may have become less out of order. The time, however, was not in accordance with the principle, 'judicia capitalia transigunt interdiu, et finiunt interdiu' (*Gem. Babyl.* 'Sanhedr.' IV. 1), as the comment of St Luke ὡς ἐγένετο ἡμέρα (ch. xxii. 66) would appear to refer to the concluding part of the trial, of the whole of which he only gives a summary; compare Meyer *in loc.* p. 488. The preceding part of the trial would thus seem to have been in the night. In other respects it is probable that the prescribed forms were complied with. The Sanhedrists were doubtless resolved to condemn our Lord to death at all hazards; it still however seems clear from the sacred narrative (Matth. xxvi. 60, 61) that they observed the general principles of the laws relating to evidence: see Wilson, *Illustr. of the New Test.* ch. V. p. 77, and for a description of the regular mode of conducting a trial, compare Friedlieb, *Archäol.* § 26, and the rabbinical quotations in Sepp, *Leben Christi*, VI. 48 sq., Vol. III. p. 464 sq.

[1] The difference of our blessed Lord's deportment before His different judges is worthy of notice. Before Annas, where the examination was mainly conversational, He vouchsafes to answer, though, as Stier remarks, with dignified repulsion. Before the injustice of the Sanhedrin and the mockery of Herod He is profoundly silent. Before Pilate, when apart from the chief priests and elders (contrast Matth. xxvii. 12—14), He vouchsafes to answer with gracious forbearance, and to bear testimony unto the truth: see Stier, *Disc. of Our Lord*, Vol. VII. p. 311 (Clark).

not agree[a], were dismissed without one question being put to them by the meek Sufferer who, even as ancient prophecy had foretold[b], still preserved His solemn and impressive silence. Foiled and perplexed the High-priest himself becomes interrogator[c]. With a formal adjuration[d], which had the effect of putting the accused under the obligation of an oath[e], he puts a question[1], which if answered in the affirmative would probably at once ensure the Lord's condemnation as a false Messiah[2], and as one against whom the law relating to the false prophet[f] might be plausibly brought to bear. And the answer was given. He that spake avowed Himself to be both the Christ and the Son of God[g],—yea the Son of God in no modified or theocratic sense[3], but

[a] Mk. xiv. 59
[b] Is. liii. 7
[c] Mark xiv. 60
[d] Matt. xxvi. 63
[e] Comp. Lev. v. 1
[f] Deut. xiii. 5; xviii. 20
[g] Mk. xiv. 62

---

[1] The question, it has been not improbably supposed, was partially suggested by the previous testimony about our Lord's destroying the Temple, there being an ancient rabbinical tradition that when the *Messiah* came, He was to construct a much more glorious temple than the one then existing: see especially Sepp, *Leben Christi*, VI. 48, Vol. III. p. 468 sq.

[2] When the High-priest asked our Lord whether He were 'the Christ the Son of God (Matth. xxvi. 63) or 'the Christ the Son of the Blessed' (Mark xiv. 61) he was probably using with design a title of the Messiah which, though not appropriated by custom to the Messiah (see p. 260, note 3), was not *wholly* unprecedented, and in the present case was particularly well calculated to lead to some answer which might justify condemnation. If our Lord had answered that He was truly the Messiah, it is possible the intention might have been to put further questions as to His relation with the Father, and so lead Him to declare before the Sanhedrin what they perhaps knew He had declared before the people (John x. 30). It is, however, not improbable that the formal avowal of Messiahship would have been deemed enough to justify condemnation according to the law alluded to in the text; see the following note. A slightly different explanation is given by Wilson, *Illustr. of New Test.* ch. IV. p. 64.

[3] Whatever may have been the design of the High-priest in putting the question to our Lord in the peculiar terms in which we find it specified both by St Matthew and St Mark,—whether it was merely a formal though unusual title, or one chosen for sinister purposes,—the

LECT. VII.

whom their own eyes should behold sitting on the right hand of Him with whom equality was now both implied and understood, and riding on the clouds of heaven[a]. With those words all was uproar and confusion. The High-priest, possibly with no pretended horror[1], rent his clothes[b]; the excited council put the question in the new form which it had now assumed. Was it even so? Did the seeming mortal that stood before them declare that He was *the Son of God*[c]? Yea verily He did[2]. Then His blood be on His head. Worse, a thousand times worse than false prophet or false Messiah,—a blasphemer, and that before the High-priest and great council of the nation, let Him die the death[d].

After our Lord was removed from the chamber, or perhaps even in the presence of the San-

[a] Mt. xxvi. 64
Mk. xiv. 62
[b] Mt. xxvi. 65
[c] Luke xxii. 70
[d] Matt. xxvi. 66
Mk. xiv. 64

The brutal mockery of the attendants.

fact remains the same, that our Lord gave marked prominence to the second portion of the title, using a known synonym and well-remembered passage (Dan. vii. 13) to make the meaning in which He used it still more explicit, and that it was for claiming this that He was condemned: see John xix. 7, and the very clear statements of Wilson, *Illustr. of the N. T.* p. 5 sq.

[1] There seems no good reason for supposing this was either a 'stage trick' (Krummacher), or the result of a concerted plan. The declaration of our Lord following the formally assenting Σὺ εἶπας (Matth. xxvi. 64), introduced as it is by the forcible πλήν ('besides my assertion, you shall have the testimony of your own eyes;' comp. Klotz, *Devar.* Vol. II. p. 725), seems to have filled the wretched Caiaphas with mingled rage and horror. He gives full prominence to the last, that he may better satiate the first. On the ceremony of rending garments, which we learn was to be performed standing (comp. Matth. xxvi. 65), and so that the rent was to be from the neck straight downwards ('fit stando; a collo anterius non posterius.' Maimon. ap. Buxtorf, *Lex. Talm.* p. 2146), see Friedlieb, *Archäol.* § 26, p. 92, Sepp, *Leben Christi,* VI. 48, Vol. III. p. 473, note.

[2] In the words ὑμεῖς λέγετε, ὅτι ἐγώ εἰμι (Luke xxii. 70) the ὅτι is rightly taken by the best expositors as argumentative ('*because* I am'), the sentence here being, to use the language of grammarians, not *objective* but *causal*: comp. Donald. *Gr. Gram.* § 584, 615.

hedrin, began a fearful scene of brutal ferocity in which, possibly not for the first time in that dreadful night[1], the menial wretches that held the Lord[a] now all took their satanic part, and in which the terms used showed that the recent declaration of our Lord was used as a pretext for indignities and shameless violence that verily belonged to the hour of the powers of darkness[b]. Meanwhile the confused court was again reassembled[c], and after some consultation how their sentence could most hopefully be carried into effect[2], they again bind our Lord[d], and lead Him to Pontius Pilate who was now in his official residence in Herod's palace[3], and had as usual come to Jerusalem to preserve order during the great yearly festival.

[a] Luke xxii. 63

[b] ver. 53

[c] Matt. xxvi. 1 Mk. xv. 1

[d] Matt. xxvii. 2

[1] It is extremely doubtful whether Luke xxii. 63—65 is to be conceived as placed a little out of its exact order, or as referring to insults and mockery in the court of Annas. The exact similarity of the incidents with those specified, Matth. xxvi. 67 sq., Mark xiv. 65, make the first supposition perhaps slightly the most probable.

[2] The meeting of the council alluded to Matth. xxvii. 1, Mark xv. 1 (compare Luke xxiii. 1, John xviii. 28), and defined by the second Evangelist as ἐπὶ τὸ πρωΐ ('about morning;' Winer, Gr. § 49, p. 363), was clearly not a new meeting, but as the language both of St Matthew and St Mark seems clearly to imply, a continued session of the former meeting, and that too in its full numbers (καὶ ὅλον τὸ συνέδριον, Mark xv. 1). The question now before the meeting was, how best to consummate the judicial murder to which they had recently agreed.

[3] Here appears to have been the regular residence of the Procurators when in Jerusalem; see Joseph. Bell. Jud. II. 14. 8 (compared with II. 15. 5), Philo, Leg. ad Cai. § 38 (compared with § 39), and see Winer, RWB. Art. 'Richthaus,' Vol. II. p. 329. This has been denied by Ewald (Gesch. Christus', p. 12), who states that the temporary residence of the Procurators was in an older palace nearer to the fort of Antonia,—a statement more recently supported by Caspari (Chron.-Geogr. Einleit. § 172, p. 192),—but scarcely on sufficient grounds. For a description of Herod's palace and notices of the size and splendour of its apartments, see Joseph. Bell. Jud. V. 4. 4, Antiq. xv. 9. 3, and compare Sepp, Leben Chr. VI. 53, Vol. III. p. 496 sq., Ewald, Gesch. des Volk. Isr. Vol. IV. p. 493.

LECT. VII.

The fate of Judas Iscariot.

We may here pause for a moment to observe that, from the connexion in this portion of St Matthew's narrative, it would certainly seem reasonable to suppose that it was this last act on the part of the Sanhedrin that served suddenly to open the eyes of the traitor Judas to the real issues of his appalling sin. Covetousness had lured him on; Satan had blinded him; and he could not and would not look forward to all that must inevitably follow. But now the lost man sees all. The priests[1], at whose feet he casts the blood-money, jibe him[a] in language almost fiendish; his soul is filled with bitterness, darkness, despair, and death. The son of perdition[2] goes to his own place[b].

[a] Matt. xxvii. 4

[b] Acts i. 25

---

[1] The use of the definite terms ἐν τῷ ναῷ (Matth. xxvii. 5) would certainly seem to imply that the wretched traitor forced his way into the inner portion of the temple, where the priests would now have been preparing for the approaching festival (comp. Sepp, *Leben Chr.* VI. 78, Vol. III. p. 609), and there flung down the price of blood. With regard to his end, it is plainly impossible to interpret the explicit term ἀπήγξατο (Matth. xxvii. 5) in any other way than as specifying a self-inflicted death by hanging; compare the exx. in Greswell, *Dissert.* XLII. Vol. III. p. 220, note. The notice in Acts i. 18 in no way opposes this, but only states a frightful sequel which was observed to have taken place by those probably who found the body. The explanation of Lightfoot (*Hor. Hebr. in Matth. l. c.*), according to which ἀπήγξατο is to be translated 'strangulatus est, a Diabolo scilicet,' is obviously unten- able. We may say truly with Chrysostom that it was the mediate work of Satan (ἀναιρεῖ πείσας ἑαυτὸν ἀπολέσαι), but must refer the immediate perpetration of the deed to Judas himself. For further accounts, all exaggerated or legendary, see the notices in Hofmann, *Leben Jesu,* p. 333.

[2] This title given to the wretched man by our Lord Himself in His solemn high-priestly prayer (John xvii. 12; comp. vi. 70), coupled with His previous declaration, Καλὸν ἦν αὐτῷ εἰ οὐκ ἐγεννήθη ὁ ἄνθρωπος ἐκεῖνος (Matth. xxvi. 24; compare hereon Krummacher, *The Suffering Saviour,* p. 69), will always be regarded by sound thinkers as a practical protest against all the antichristian attempts of later historical criticism (see the reff. in Meyer, *Komment. üb. Matth.* p. 487) to palliate the traitor's inexpiable crime, and to make it appear that he only wished to force our Lord to declare

But let us return to the further circumstances of our Lord's trial. The Redeemer now stood before the gates of him who bore the sword in Jerusalem, awaiting the message which the Sanhedrists, men who shrank from leaven[a] though they shrank not from blood, had sent into the palace of the Procurator, demanding, as it would seem, that our Lord should at once be put to death as a dangerous malefactor. With ready political tact the Roman comes forth at their summons, but, with a Roman's instinctive respect for the recognized forms of justice, demands the nature of the charge[b] brought against the man on whom his eyes now fell, and whose aspect proclaimed His innocence. The accusers at first answer evasively[c]; but soon, as it would seem from the narrative of St Luke[d], find an answer that they calculated could not fail in appealing to a Procurator of Judæa. With satanically prompted cunning they carefully suppress the real grounds on which they had condemned the Saviour, and heap up charges of a purely *political* nature[1]; chief among which were specified, in all their familiar sequence to the Procurator's ear, seditious agitation, attempted

Our Lord's first appearance before Pilate.
[a] John xviii. 28
[b] ver. 29
[c] ver. 30
[d] ch. xxiii. 2

His true nature, and betrayed Him as the best means of ensuring it. Whether such motives did or did not mingle with the traitor's besetting sin of covetousness (comp. Ewald, *Gesch. Chr.* p. 398 sq.) we pause not to inquire; we only see in his fearful end the most dread instance of the regular development and enhancement of sin in the individual (see Müller, *Doctr. of Sin*, Book v. Vol. II. p. 461, Clark) that is contained in the history of man, and with awe we behold in him the only one who received his sentence in person before the last day: see Stier, *Disc. of our Lord*, Vol. VII. p. 56 sq., and a practical sermon by Pusey, *Paroch. Serm.* XII. Vol. II. p. 197.

[1] This fact has been alluded to by Wilson, *Illustr. of the New Test.* p. 5, and has been urged by Blunt, *Veracity of Gospels*, § 13, p. 50 sq. (Lond. 1831). It did not escape the notice of Cyril Alex., who has some good comments upon the changed character of the charges. *Comment. on St Luke*, Part II. p. 709.

LECT. VII.

prohibition of the payment of the tribute-money, and assumption of the mixed civil and religious title of King of the Jews[1]. It seems, however, clear that from the very first the sharp-sighted Roman plainly perceived that it was no case for his tribunal,—that it was wholly a matter of religious differences and religious hate, and that the meek prisoner who stood before him, was at least innocent of the political crimes that had been laid to His charge with such an unwonted and suspicious zeal[2]. The prescribed forms must however be gone through: the accused must be examined, and be dealt with according to the facts which the examination may elicit. That examination[a], which (we may observe in passing) was conducted by the Procurator in person[3], served to deepen Pilate's impressions, and to convince him that the exalted sufferer, whose mien and words seem alike to have awed and attracted him, was guiltless of everything save an enthusiasm which the practical Roman might deem hopeless

[a] John xviii. 33

---

[1] There are no sufficient grounds for rejecting with Meyer (*üb. Joh.* p. 470, ed. 3) the usual and very reasonable supposition that St Luke's mention of the charges preferred by the Sanhedrin (ch. xxiii. 2) is to be connected with Pilate's question as recorded by St John (ch. xviii. 29). It would seem that at first the Sanhedrists hoped to urge the Procurator to accept the decision of their own court without further inquiry, but finding this promptly and even tauntingly (John xviii. 38) rejected, they then are driven to prefer specific charges; compare Lange, *Leben Jesu*, II. 7. 7, Part II. p. 1504 sq. On the nature of these charges see Stier, *Disc. of our Lord*, Vol. VII. p. 346 (Clark).

[2] The remark of Pfenninger (cited by Stier) is just and pertinent, that 'Pilate knew too much about Jewish expectations to suppose that the Sanhedrin would hate and persecute one who would free them from Roman authority.'

[3] Pilate being only a Procurator, though a Procurator *cum potestate*, had no Quæstor to conduct the examinations; and thus, as the Gospels most accurately record, performs that office himself: compare Friedlieb, *Archäol.* § 31, p. 105.

and visionary[1], but which it was in no way meet to punish with the sword of civil justice. And the yet righteous judge acts on his convictions. He goes forth to the Jews and declares the Lord's innocence[a], and only so far listens to the clamours of the accusers, as to use their mention of the name of Galilee[b] as a pretext for sending our Lord to the Tetrarch of that country [2], who was now in Jerusalem[c] as a so-called worshipper at the paschal festival....This course the dexterous Procurator failed not to perceive had two great advantages; it enabled him, in the first place, to rid himself of all further responsibility, and in the next it gave him an opportunity of exercising the true Roman state-craft of propitiating by a trifling act of political courtesy a native ruler with whom he had been previously at enmity[3], and with

[a] John xviii. 38
[b] Lk. xxiii. 5
[c] ver. 7

---

[1] On the character of Pilate see below, p. 350, note 2. His memorable question, 'What is truth?' (John xviii. 38) which occurred in the present part of the examination, must apparently neither be regarded with the older writers as the expression of a desire to know what truth really was (Chrys., al.), nor again with some recent expositors as the cheerless query of the wearied and baffled searcher (Olshaus., al.), but simply as the half-pitying question of the practical man of the world, who felt that truth was a phantom, a word that had no political import, and regarded the attempt to connect it with a kingdom and matters of real life as a delusion of harmless though pitiable enthusiasm; see Meyer *in loc.* p. 472, Stier, *Disc. of our Lord*, Vol. VII. p. 376 sq. (Clark), and compare Luthardt, *Johann. Evang.* Part II. p. 400.

[2] Pilate here availed himself of a practice occasionally adopted in criminal cases, viz. that of sending away (Luke xxiii. 7, ἀνέπεμψεν, *remisit*) the accused from the *forum apprehensionis* to his *forum originis;* compare the partly similar case in reference to St Paul (Acts xxv. 9 sq.), and the conduct of Vespasian towards the prisoners who were subjects of Agrippa; Josephus, *Bell. Jud.* III. 10. 10. See Friedlieb, *Archäol.* § 32, p. 107.

[3] The cause of the enmity is not known, but is probably to be referred to some acts on the part of the Procurator, which were considered by Herod undue assumptions of authority. It is possible that the recent slaughter of the Galilæans mentioned Luke xiii. 1, if it did not give rise to, may still have added

LECT. VII.

The dismissal of our Lord to Herod.
a Lk. xxiii. 8

b ver. 9

c ver. 11

d ver. 11

whose authority he had probably often come in collision.

The sinful man[1] before whom our Lord now was brought, had, we are told by St Luke[a], long desired to see Him, and is now rejoiced to have the wonder-worker before him[2]. He puts many questions[b], all probably superstitious or profane, but is met only by a calm and holy silence. Superstitious curiosity soon changes to scorn. With a frightful and shameless profanity, the wretched man after mocking and setting at nought[c] Him whom a moment before, if any response had been vouchsafed to his curiosity, he would, with equal levity, have honoured as a prophet, now sends the Lord back to Pilate, clad in a shining[3] kingly robe[d], as if to intimate that

to the ill-feeling. The discreditable attempts to throw doubt upon the whole incident, as being mentioned only by one Evangelist, require no other answer than the narrative itself, which exhibits every clearest mark of truth and originality; comp. Meyer, *Komment. üb. Luk.* p. 493 (ed. 3), Krummacher, *The Suffering Christ*, ch. XXXI. p. 268.

[1] On the character of this Tetrarch, which seems to have been a compound of cunning, levity, and licentiousness, see above, p. 216, note 2.

[2] The key to the present conduct of this profane man is apparently supplied us by the observant comment (comp. p. 28, note 2) of the thoughtful Evangelist, καὶ ἤλπιζέν τι σημεῖον ἰδεῖν ὑπ' αὐτοῦ γενόμενον, Luke xxii. 8. As long as there seemed any chance of this desire being gratified, Herod treated our Lord with forbearance; when it became evident that he was neither to see nor hear anything wonderful, he gave rein to his wretched levity, and avenged his disappointment by mockery. On the incident generally, see Lange, *Leben Jesu*, II. 7. 7, Part III. p. 1512 sq.

[3] It has been thought that by the use of the terms ἐσθῆτα λαμπρὰν (Luke xxiii. 11) the Evangelist intended to denote a *white* robe, and that the point of the profane mockery was, that our Lord was to be deemed a 'candidatus;' see Friedlieb, *Archäol.* § 32, p. 109, Lange, *Leben Jesu*, Part III. p. 1515. This seems very doubtful; the word λαμπρὸς does not necessarily involve the idea of *whiteness* (the primary idea is 'visibility' [λάω]; see Donaldson, *Crat.* § 452), nor would the dress of a 'candidate' imply the contempt which Herod designed to express for the pretensions of this King so well as the 'gorgeous robe' (Auth. Ver.) of caricatured royalty. The

for such pretenders to the throne of David neither the Tetrarch of Galilee nor the Procurator of Judæa need reserve any heavier punishment than their ridicule and contempt.

We may well conceive that Pilate was much perplexed at seeing our Lord again before his own tribunal. In the present appearance, however, of the Saviour the Procurator plainly saw a practical exhibition of Herod's sentiments, and at once resolved to set free One, who he was now more than ever convinced was a harmless enthusiast, wholly and entirely innocent of the crimes that had been laid to His charge. So too he tells[a] the assembled chief-priests and people[1]. But alas! for Roman justice, he seeks to secure their assent by a promise of inflicting punishment[b], lighter indeed by very far than had been demanded[2], yet still by his own previous declarations undeserved and unjust. But this, though a most unrighteous concession, was far from satisfying the bitter and bloodthirsty men to whom it was made. Something perchance in their countenances or gestures[3] drove the now anxious

Second appearance before Pilate: his efforts to set our Lord free.

[a] Luke xxiii. 15

[b] ver. 16

---

remark too of Lightfoot seems fully in point, 'de veste albâ cum aliis intellexerim, nisi quod videam hunc Evangelistam, cum de veste albâ habet sermonem, *albam* eam vocare in terminis;' cap. ix. 29, Acts i. 10. *Hor. Hebr. in Luc.* xxiii. 7.

[1] We may observe that St Luke specially notices that on the return of our Lord from Herod, Pilate assembled not only the chief priests and rulers but the *people* also (ch. xxiii. 13); he probably had already resolved to make an appeal to *them*, if his present proposal (ver. 16) were not accepted. See above, p. 289, note 1.

[2] The punishment implied in the term παιδεύσας (Luke xxiii. 16) is left undefined. It was, however, probably no severer than scourging; compare Hammond *in loc.* Here was Pilate's first concession, and first betrayal of a desire, if possible, to meet the wishes of the accusers. This was not lost on men so subtle and so malignant as the Sanhedrists.

[3] There is a slight difficulty in the fact that according to St Luke (xxiii. 18; ver. 17 is of doubtful authority) the request in reference to Barabbas comes first from the

judge to an appeal to the people, who, he might have heard and even observed, were for the most part on the side of the Prophet of Nazareth, and whose clamorous requests[a] now reminded him of a custom, not improbably instituted by himself or his predecessors[1], which offered a ready mode of subterfuge :—He will offer to release to them one of two, the seditious and bloodstained robber[b] Barabbas[2], or Jesus who was called, and whom but lately so many of those present had triumphantly hailed as the Christ. The choice cannot be doubtful. Meanwhile he will ascend his tribunal formally to accept and formally to ratify the judgment of the popular voice. Unhappy man! No sooner has he taken his seat[3] than a fresh appeal comes

[a] Mk. xv. 8

[b] Luke xxiii. 19

---

people, and in St Matthew (ch. xxvii. 17) that the proposal is made by Pilate. All, however, seems made clear by the narrative of St Mark (ch. xv. 8), who represents the people as making the request in general terms, and Pilate as availing himself of it in the present emergency of this particular case.

[1] The origin of the custom here alluded to is wholly unknown. If Luke xxiii. 17 were an unquestioned reading, it might seem as if it were some ancient (Jewish) custom (comp. John xviii. 39) to which the Procurator was practically obliged (ἀνάγκην εἶχεν) to adhere. As, however, the verse has some appearance of being a gloss, and as the other Evangelists seem to refer the custom to the ἡγεμών (Matth. xxvii. 15), or to Pilate personally (Mark xv. 6, 8; comp. John xviii. 39), we may perhaps best consider it as due to the shrewd Roman policy of one of the early Procurators, by which a not unusual pagan custom (see Winer, RWB. Vol. II. p. 202, ed. 3) was adopted as a contribution to the general festivities and solemnities of the Passover; compare Friedlieb, Archäol. § 33, and for general information on the subject Bynæus, de Morte Chr. III. 3, Vol. III. p. 57 sq. and the copious reff. in Hofmann, Leben Jesu, § 83, p. 360.

[2] Nothing more is known of this insurgent than is specified in the Gospels. From them we learn that his seditious movements took place in Jerusalem (Luke xxiii. 19), that he had comrades in his undertaking (Mark xv. 7), and had also acquired some notoriety (Matth. xxvii. 16). The reading which makes the name to have been Jesus Barabbas is adopted by Ewald, Meyer and others, but has very far from sufficient external support, and is now rightly rejected by Tischendorf in his last edition; see Vol. I. p. 154.

[3] Compare Matth. xxvii. 19, καθη-

to him^a in the form of a message from his mysteriously warned wife[1], bidding him not to condemn the Just One who stands before him. But^a the agents of the priestly party are doing their work^b. Many a fiendish whisper is running through the crowd that the Nazarene was a blasphemer, yea, a blasphemer in the face of the elderhood of Israel, one who had claimed the incommunicable attributes of Jehovah, and who Jehovah's word had said must expiate His profanity by His blood^c. It was enough: the worst passions of the rabble multitude were now stirred up[2]: the question is no sooner formally proposed than the answer is returned with a fearful unanimity—'Not this man,

LECT. VII.

^a Matt. xxvii. 19

^b ver. 20

^c Lev. xxiv. 16

μένου δὲ αὐτοῦ ἐπὶ τοῦ βήματος. This βῆμα was a portable tribunal which was placed where the magistrate might direct, and from which judgment was formally and finally delivered. In the present case, as we learn from St John (ch. xix. 13), it was erected on a (tesselated) pavement, the position of which is unknown, but which was called in Greek Λιθόστρωτον and in Hebrew (probably from the slight ridge [גב] on which it may have been laid) Gabbatha, and perhaps formed the front of the Procurator's residence; see Friedlieb, *Archäol.* § 31, p. 105, Winer, *RWB.* Art. 'Lithostroton,' Vol. II. p. 29.

[1] According to tradition, her name was Procla, or Claudia Procula, and her sympathies Jewish: see *Evang. Nicod.* cap. 2, and the good comments of Hofmann, *Leben Jesu*, § 79, p. 340 sq. The dream, which is specified by the Evangelist as of a disturbing and harrowing nature (πολλὰ ἔπαθον, Matth. xxvii.

19), may well be supposed with some of the early expositors to have been *divinely* sent, though this need not preclude the further supposition that the woman had previously heard of our Lord, and was now more than ever impressed with a feeling of His holiness and innocence. Most expositors here rightly call attention to the fact that former laws by which Roman magistrates might have been prohibited from taking their wives with them were not now observed; see cap. Tacit. *Annal.* III. 33, 34, and comp. Sepp, *Leben Chr.* VI. 56, Vol. III. p. 507.

[2] The strong word ἀνέσεισαν (Mark xv. 11) seems to show the determined way in which the priestly party were now endeavouring to turn the current of popular feeling against our Lord. It was in consequence of this that we have that tutored unanimity of clamour which is specially noticed by three of the Evangelists; comp. Matth. xxvii. 22, Luke xxiii. 18, John xviii. 40.

LECT. VII.

^a John xviii. 40
^b Luke xxiii. 22
^c ver. 23

but Barabbas[a].' The astounded Procurator for a moment tries to reason with them[b], but now it is all in vain. The rabble and their satanic instigators press their advantage; wild voices are heard on every side[c]; tumult is imminent; the unhappy and unrighteous judge gives way, and by an act, which was probably as fully understood[1] as it was contemptuously disregarded, strives to transfer the guilt of innocent blood to the infuriate throng around him. Fearfully and frantically they accept it[d], but their end is now gained: Barabbas is set free[2]; the holy Jesus is given up to their will.

^d Matt. xxvii. 25

Scourging of our Lord: renewed efforts of Pilate.

^e Mk. xv. 15

Now followed the scourging preliminary to crucifixion[e], the crown of thorns[3], the scarlet robe[4], and

---

[1] It has been doubted whether Pilate in washing his hands (according to the apocryphal *Evang. Nicodemi*, cap. 9, 'before the sun') was following a heathen or a Jewish custom. The latter view, which is that adopted by the sensible commentator Euthymius, seems on the whole most probable; see Deut. xxi. 6, and compare Thilo, *Cod. Apocr.* p. 573 sq., Hofmann, *Leben Jesu*, § 83, p. 361.

[2] It has been thought by some modern writers (Sepp, *Leben Chr.* Vol. III. p. 502, Wratislaw, *Serm. and Dissert.* p. 8) that this has an antitypical reference to the ceremony of the Scape Goat. This seems in itself in a high degree doubtful; and that more especially as the ancient interpreters all rightly consider the two goats as *both* typifying Christ, the one in His death, the other in His resurrection; see Barnab. *Epist.* cap. 7, Ephrem. Syr. *in Lev.* xvi. 20, Vol. I. p. 244 sq. (Romæ, 1737).

[3] The question of the exact species of the thorn it is here not necessary to discuss: the *rhamnus nabeca* (Hasselquist) and the *lycium spinosum* (Sieber) have both been specified by competent observers as not unfitted for the purpose, but of these the latter seems the more probable; see Friedlieb, *Archäol.* § 34, p. 119, Hofmann, *Leben Jesu*, § 84, p. 373. As *mockery* seems to have been the primary object (τῷ στεφάνῳ τῶν ἀκανθῶν καθύβριζον, Chrys.), the choice of the plant was not suggested by the sharpness of its thorns: the soldiers took what first came to hand utterly careless whether it was likely to inflict pain or no.

[4] The robe appears to have been the usual cloak of scarlet cloth worn both by the common soldiers and those in command. In the latter case it was longer and of better wool: see Friedlieb, *Archäol.* § 34, p. 118, and compare Winer, *RWB.* Art. 'Kleider,' Vol. I. p. 664.

all the horrible mockery of the brutal soldiery^a, the Gentile counterpart of the appalling scenes of fiendish derision in which Jews had taken part scarcely two hours before^b. The heart of the hapless Pilate was perhaps in some degree touched; and judging from what even a Roman could feel for one of the stubborn nation over which he ruled, he strove to make one last appeal to the wild Jewish multitude without[1], by showing to them, with the garb of mockery flung around that lacerated and bleeding form, THE MAN^c,—the man of their own race and nation, whom they had given up to such sufferings and such shame. But even this last appeal was utterly in vain. Nay, worse than in vain. That pity-moving sight only calls from the priestly party fresh outbursts of ferocity^d; the charge is only the more vehemently repeated,— 'By our law ought He to die^e,' because 'He made Himself the Son of God^f.' The Son of God! That title spake with strange significance to one pagan heart in that vast concourse. The awed[2] and now

LECT. VII.

^a Matt. xxvii. 28 sq.
^b Mark xiv. 65
^c Joh. xix. 5
^d ver. 6
^e Comp. Lev. xxiv. 16
^f Joh. xix. 7

---

[1] Though Pilate appears to have sanctioned or, to say the very least, failed to interfere with the mockery and indeed brutalities (John xix. 3) of the soldiers, he is still rightly considered by the older expositors to have here made an effort to arouse some feelings of pity in the priests and people; see Lange, *Leben Jesu*, II. 7. 7, Part III. p. 1525. The ἴδε ὁ ἄνθρωπος (ver. 5) was thus said in a tone of commiseration, and certainly without any of the bitterness which seems plainly to mark the ἴδε ὁ βασιλεὺς ὑμῶν of ver. 14; comp. Luthardt, *das Johann. Evang.* Part II. p. 413.

[2] The fear which Pilate now felt, even more than before (μᾶλλον ἐφοβήθη, John xix. 8), when he heard that our Lord had represented Himself as υἱὸς Θεοῦ, would naturally arise from his conceiving such a title to imply a Divine descent or parentage, which the analogy of the heroes and demigods of ancient story might predispose him to believe possible in the present case; comp. Luthardt, *Johann. Evang.* Part II. p. 405. The message from his wife might have already aroused some apprehensions: these the present declaration greatly augments. The unjust judge begins to fear he may

LECT. VII.

[a] John xix. 9

unnerved Procurator again returns into his palace to question the Holy Sufferer[a], and comes forth again, yet once more to make a last effort to save One whose mysterious[1] words had now strangely moved his very inmost soul. What a moment for that hapless pagan! One expression of an honest and bold determination to take a responsibility on himself from which no Roman magistrate ought ever to have shrunk; one righteous resolve to follow the dictates of his conscience, and the name of Pilate would never have held its melancholy place in the Christian's creed as that of the irresolute and unjust judge who, against his own most solemn convictions, gave up to a death of agony and shame One whom he knew to be innocent, and even dimly felt to be Divine[2]. But that word was never

---

be braving the wrath of some unknown deity, and now anxiously puts the question πόθεν εἶ σύ; (ver. 9),—'Was His descent indeed such as the mysterious title might be understood to imply?' To this the ἄνωθεν (ver. 11) forms, and probably was felt by Pilate to form a kind of indirect answer: see Stier, *Disc. of our Lord*, Vol. VII. p. 391 sq. (Clark), where the last question is well explained; comp. Lange, *Leben Jesu*, II. 7. 7, Part III. p. 1527.

[1] The difficult words διὰ τοῦτο ὁ παραδιδούς μέ σοι κ.τ.λ. (John xix. 11), which the Evangelist notices as having still more caused (ἐκ τούτου ἐζήτει) Pilate to renew his efforts, appear to refer to Caiaphas as the official representative of those who formally *gave over* our Lord to the Roman governor (Matth. xxvii. 2, Mark xv. 1), and to imply—that his guilt was greater, because, when he had no power granted him from above against our Lord, he gave the Lord up to one who had, and whose power was plenary. In a word, Pilate, the instrument in God's hands, the bearer of the sword, is guilty because he acts against his convictions, but he who gave up the Lord to this bearer of the sword is more guilty, because he knew what he was doing, and was acting against clearer knowledge and fuller light.

[2] The character of Pilate though often discussed, has not always been correctly estimated. The fair statement seems to be that he was a thorough and complete type of the later-Roman man of the world. Stern, but not relentless (see Friedlieb, *Archäol.* § 34, p. 122), shrewd, and world-worn, prompt and practical, haughtily just, and yet, as the early writers correctly perceived,

spoken. Cries now smote upon Pilate's ears at which every previous impression was forgotten. Instinctive sense of justice, convictions, prepossessions, apprehensions were all swallowed up in an instant, when he heard himself denounced before the multitude, before the Sanhedrin, and before his own soldiers as 'no friend to Cæsar¹,' if he let go one who by His assumptions had practically spoken against that dreaded name[a]. 'No friend to Cæsar.' Already in imagination the wretched man saw himself in the presence of his gloomy and suspicious master, informed against, condemned, degraded, banished². It was enough: Pilate must

[a] Joh. xix. 12

---

self-seeking and cowardly (ἄνανδρος σφόδρα, Chrys.; comp. *Const. Apos.* v. 14), able to perceive what was right, but without moral strength to follow it out,—the sixth Procurator of Judæa stands forth a sad and terrible instance of a man whom the fear of endangered self-interest drove not only to act against the deliberate convictions of his heart and his conscience, but further to commit an act of the utmost cruelty and injustice even after those convictions had been deepened by warnings and strengthened by presentiment. Compare Niemeyer, *Charakt.* Vol. I. p. 121 sq., Luthardt, *Johann. Evang.* Part I. p. 128 sq., Winer, *RWB.* Art. 'Pilatus,' Vol. II. p. 262, and for references to various treatises on this subject, Hase, *Leben Jesu*, § 117, p. 198.

¹ See John xix. 12, οὐκ εἶ φίλος τοῦ Καίσαρος. This appellation was probably not here used in its formal and semi-official sense 'amicus Cæsaris' (Sepp, *Leben Chr.* VI. 60, Vol. III. p. 519), but in its more simple meaning of 'friendly and true to the interests of Cæsar.' The concluding words πᾶς ὁ βασιλέα κ.τ.λ. must also have had their full effect on the Procurator, who probably knew full well how truly in those times 'majestatis crimen omnium accusationum complementum erat.' Tacit. *Annal.* III. 38.

² All that the unhappy man was now probably dreading in imagination finally came upon him. On the complaint of some Samaritans, Vitellius, the President of Syria, sent his friend Marcellus to administer the affairs of Judæa, and ordered Pilate to go to Rome to answer the charges preferred against him; see Joseph. *Antiq.* XVIII. 4. 2. This deposition appears to have taken place in the lifetime of Tiberius (see Winer, *RWB.* Art. 'Pilatus,' Vol. II. p. 261), and about Easter, A.D. 36. The sequel is said to have been disgrace and misfortunes (Euseb.), and not long afterwards, death by his own hand; see Euseb. *Hist. Eccl.* II. 7. For a good account of his political life, see Ewald, *Gesch. Christus*³, p. 30 sq.

not come to this dishonour; the Galilæan must die; it remains only to pronounce the sentence. The Roman again ascends the tribunal, now determined, yet with words of jibing bitterness towards his tempters[a], which show the still enduring struggle in his unhappy soul; but again the ominous rejoinder 'We have no king but Cæsar[b],' and the struggle is ended. The sentence is pronounced, and the Saviour is led forth to Golgotha[1].

On that concluding scene our words must be guarded and few. The last sufferings of the Eternal Son are no meet subject for lengthened description, however solemn and reverential be the language in which it is attempted to be conveyed. Let us then presume only with all brevity to illustrate the outward connexion of events which the inspired writers have been moved to record......The Chief Priests and Scribes now at length have Him for whose blood they were thirsting formally delivered over[c] into their murderous hands. With the aid of the Roman soldiery[2] who had now

---

[a] Joh. xix. 15
[b] Ib.
[c] Joh. xix. 16

THE CRUCIFIXION.

---

[1] Into the difficult questions relating to the site of this place we cannot here enter further than to remark (a) that the name (Chald. גֻּלְגָּלְתָּא) is *perhaps* more plausibly understood as referring to the general form of the place (Cyril of Jerus., al., but see Caspari, *Chron.-Geogr. Einleit.* § 176),—possibly a low, rounded, bare hill (Ewald, *Gesch. Chr.* p. 434)—than to the skulls of the criminals executed there (Jerome, al.); (b) that it *appears* to have been in the vicinity of some thoroughfare (Matth. xxvii. 39), and lastly (c),—if it be not presumptuous to express an opinion on a question of such extreme difficulty,—that the arguments in favour of its proximity (at any rate) to the present traditional site, appear to preponderate: see, on the one hand, the able arguments of Williams, *Holy City*, Vol. II. p. 13 sq., and on the other Robinson, *Palestine*, Vol. I. p. 407 sq., to which add an article by Fergusson in Smith, *Dict. of Bible*, Vol. I. p. 1017 sq. The nearness of the assumed site to that of Herod's palace is a fact of some importance.

[2] In John xix. 17 sq. the grammatical subject would seem to be the same as the αὐτοῖς of the preceding verse, *i. e.* the ἀρχιερεῖς ver.

removed from Him the garb of mockery[a], they led the Saviour without the gate to a spot of slightly rising ground, known by a name which the shape of the rounded summit may perhaps have suggested,—Golgotha or the place of a skull. Ere, however, they arrive there, two touching incidents are specified by the Evangelists,—the unrestrained lamentation and weeping of the women[1] that formed part of the vast attendant multitude, and the substitution of Simon of Cyrene[2] as bearer of the cross in the place of the now exhausted Redeemer. The low hill is soon reached; the cross is fixed; the stupefying drink is offered and refused[b]; ruthless hands strip away the garments[3];

[a] Matt. xxvii. 31
[b] ch. xxvii. 34

---

[15] The soldiers seem first specially mentioned ver. 23, but, from the distinctly specified ὅτε ἐσταύρωσαν (ib.) and the statements of the other Evangelists, were obviously throughout the *instruments* by which the sentence was carried out. The party of the Sanhedrin are, however, still clearly put forward as the leading *actors*: *they* crucified our Lord (John xix. 18, Acts v. 30); Roman hands drove in the nails.

[1] This incident is only specified by St Luke (ch. xxiii. 27 sq.), who as we have already had occasion to remark, mentions the ministrations of *women* more frequently than any of the other Evangelists; see Lect. I. p. 30, note 1.

[2] He is said both by St Mark (ch. xv. 21) and St Luke (ch. xxiii. 26) to have now been ἐρχόμενος ἀπὸ ἀγροῦ,—a comment which may perhaps imply that he had been labouring there, and was now returning ('onustus ligno,' Lightfoot, *Hor. Hebr. in Marc. l. c.*)

some time before the hour when (if the day was the παρασκευὴ τοῦ πάσχα) servile work would commonly cease; comp. Friedlieb, *Archäol.* § 17, p. 41. If this be the meaning of the words, they may be urged as supplying a subsidiary proof that the day was Nisan 14 and not Nisan 15: see p. 322, note 1, where this and a few similar passages are briefly specified.

[3] See Matth. xxvii. 35, Mark xv. 24, Luke xxiii. 34, John xix. 23. None of these passages are opposed to the ancient belief that a linen cloth was bound round the sacred loins, as the apocryphal *Evang. Nicodemi* (cap. 10) cursorily, and so perhaps with a greater probability of truth, mentions in its narrative of the crucifixion. What we know of the prevailing custom has been thought to imply the contrary (see Lipsius, *de Cruce*, II. 7); still as this is by no means certain, the undoubted antiquity of the apocryphal writing to which we have referred

the holy and lacerated body is raised aloft; the hands are nailed to the transverse beam; the feet are *separately* nailed[1] to the lower part of the upright beam; the bitterly worded accusation is fixed up above the sacred head[a]; the soldiers divide up and cast lots for the garments, and then, as St Matthew has paused to specify[b], sit watching, the stolid impassive spectators of their fearful and now completed work.

It was now, as we learn from St Mark[c], about the third hour[2], and to the interval between this and mid-day must we assign the mockeries of the passers by[d], the brutalities of the soldiery[e], and the display of inhuman malignity on the part of the members of the Sanhedrin[f], who now were striving, Chief-priests and Elders of Israel as they

[a] Matt. xxvii. 37
[b] ver. 36
[c] ch. xv. 25
[d] ch. xxvii. 39
[e] Luke xxiii. 36
[f] Matt. xxvii. 41

Occurrences from the third to the sixth hour.

---

may justly be allowed to have some weight; see Hofmann, *Leben Jesu*, § 84, p. 373, and compare Hug, *Freib. Zeitschr.* VII. p. 161 sq. (cited by Winer).

[1] This is a very debated point. The arguments, however, in favour of the opinion advanced in the text, viz. that not *three* (Nonnus, p. 176, ed. Passow) but *four* nails were used, seem perhaps distinctly to preponderate: see Friedlieb, *Archäol.* § 41, p. 144 sq., Hofmann, *Leben Jesu*, p. 375. The attempt to show that it is doubtful even whether the feet were nailed *at all* (comp. Winer, *de Pedum Affixione*, Lips. 1845, and *RWB.* Vol. I. p. 678) must be pronounced plainly futile, and is well disposed of by Meyer, *Komment. üb. Matth.* xxvii. 35, p. 533 sq. For a full account of the form of the cross, which, in the present case, owing to the τίτλος fixed thereon (John xix. 19), was probably that of the *crux immissa* (✝), not of the *crux commissa* (T), see esp. Friedlieb, *Archäol.* § 36, p. 130,—and for the assertion that the holy body was raised, and then nailed, *ib.* § 41, pp. 142, 144.

[2] This again is a doubtful point owing to the distinct statement of St John, who specifies it as ὥρα ὡς ἕκτη (ch. xix. 14). As the supposition that the fourth Evangelist here was reckoning from midnight (comp. Wieseler, *Chron. Synops.* p. 410 sq. Greswell, *Dissert.* XLII. Vol. III. p. 229) does not seem satisfactorily made out, and the old assumption of an erratum (ς´ for γ´; see Caspari, *Einleit.* § 174, and comp. Alford *in loc.*) extremely precarious, we must either leave the difference as we find it, or, what is not unreasonable, suppose that the hour of crucifixion was somewhere between the two broad divisions, the 3rd and 6th hours, and that the one Evangelist specified the hither, the other the farther terminus.

were, by every fiendish taunt and jibe to add to the agonies of the crucified Lord, when even, as it would seem[a], the rude multitude stood around in wistful and perhaps commiserating silence. To the same period also must we refer the narrative of the mercy extended to the penitent malefactor[b], and St John's affecting notice of our Lord's tender care for the forlorn Virgin-mother[c], who with her sister[1], and the faithful Mary of Magdala, was remaining up to this fearful hour nigh to the Redeemer's cross, but who now, it would seem, yielded to what she might have either inferred or perceived was the desire of her Lord, and was led away by the beloved Apostle[2].

[a] Comp. Luke xxiii. 35
[b] ver. 39
[c] ch. xix. 26

---

[1] It has recently been considered doubtful whether *three* or *four* women are here specified, *i.e.* whether the sister of the blessed Virgin is to be regarded as identical with the wife of Clopas, or whether we have in fact two pairs, Mary and her sister, Mary the wife of Clopas and Mary Magdalene. The latter opinion has been maintained by Wieseler (*Stud. u. Krit.* for 1840, p. 648 sq.) and adopted by Lange (*Leben Jesu*, Part II. p. 1558), Ewald (*Gesch. Chr.* p. 438), Meyer (*in loc.*) and others, but on grounds that seem wholly insufficient to overcome (*a*) the improbability that the sister of the Virgin should have been thus vaguely mentioned in a passage which appears studiedly explicit and distinct, and (*b*) the improbability arising from the general style of St John that καὶ should have been omitted (the Syr.-Pesh. inserts it), and the women thus enumerated in pairs; contrast John ii. 12, where we might have almost expected such a separation, and ch. xxi. 2. Wieseler conceives the unnamed ἀδελφή to have been Salome, and Meyer finds in the passage a trace of the Apostle's peculiarity not directly to name himself or *his kindred;* but as ch. i. 42 (where Meyer *asserts* that James was then called though not mentioned) proves utterly nothing, and ch. xxi. 2 proves the contrary, we seem to have full reason for adhering to the usual acceptation of the passage, and for believing that the sister of the Virgin was the wife of Clopas: see Luthardt, *das Johann. Evang.* Part II. p. 419, Ebrard, *Kritik der Evang. Gesch.* § 108, p. 555.

[2] This seems a reasonable inference from John xix. 27, the ἀπ' ἐκείνης ὥρας appearing to mark that the Apostle at once and on the spot manifested his loving obedience by leading away the Virgin-mother to his own home. After this (μετὰ τοῦτο, ver. 28), and during the three-hour interval of darkness the Apostle would have returned, and thus have been the witness of what he has recorded, ver. 28 sq. In con-

LECT. VII.

The darkness from the 6th to the 9th hour.
[a] Matt. xxvii. 45
Mk. xv. 33

[b] Lect. II. p. 63

[c] Matt. xxvii. 45
Mk. xv. 33
Lk. xxiii. 44

But could all these scenes of agony and woe thus fearfully succeed each other, and nature remain impassive and unmoved? The sixth hour now had come[a]. Was there to be no outward sign, no visible token that earth and heaven were sympathizing in the agonies of Him by whose hands they had been made and fashioned? No verily, it could not be. If one Evangelist, as we have already observed[b], tells us that on the night of the Lord's birth a heavenly brightness and glory shone forth amid the gloom, three inspired witnesses now tell us that a pall of darkness was spread over the whole land[1] from the sixth to the ninth hour[c]. But while they thus specially notice the interval, it may be observed that they maintain the most solemn reserve as to the incidents by which it was marked. Though full and explicit as to the circumstances of the agony in the Garden, they are here profoundly silent. The mysteries of those hours of darkness, when with the sufferings of the

---

firmation of this view it may be noticed, that among the women specified as beholding afar off (Matth. xxvii. 56, Mark xv. 40) the Virgin is not mentioned; comp. Greswell, *Dissert.* XLII. Vol. III. p. 249, Stier, *Disc. of Our Lord*, Vol. VII. p. 479 (Clark).

[1] This darkness, as now seems properly admitted by all the best expositors, was neither due to any species of eclipse, nor to the deepened gloom which in some cases precedes an earthquake (comp. Milman, *Hist. of Chr.* Vol. I. p. 363), but was strictly *supernatural*,—the appointed testimony of sympathizing nature: 'Yea, creation itself,' as it has been well said, 'bewailed its Lord, for

the sun was darkened, and the rocks were rent.' Cyril Alex. *Comment. on St Luke*, Serm. CLIII. Part II. p. 722,—where reference is made to Amos (ch. viii. 9, *not* v. 8, as having foretold it: compare Bauer, *de Mirac. obscurati solis*, Wittenb. 1741. External heathen testimony appears not to have been wanting (see Tertull. *Apologet.* cap. 21), though as recent chronologers have properly shown, the constantly-cited notice of the freedman Phlegon (apud Syncell. *Chronogr.* Vol. I. p. 614, ed. Bonn) has no reference to the present miracle, but to an ordinary eclipse the year before; see Ideler, *Handb. der Chronol.* Vol. II. p. 417, Wieseler, *Chron. Synops.* p. 388.

agonized body mingled the sufferings of the sacred soul, the struggles with sinking nature, the accumulating pressure of the burden of the world's sin, the momently more and more embittered foretastings of that which was its wages and its penalty, the clinging desperation of the last assaults of Satan and his mustered hosts[1], the withdrawal and darkening of the Paternal presence,—mysteries such as these, so deep and so dread, it was not meet that even the tongues of Apostles should be moved to speak of, or the pens of Evangelists to record. Nay, the very outward eye of man might now gaze no further. All man might know was by the hearing of the ear. One loud cry revealed all and more than all that it is possible for our nature to conceive,—one loud cry of unfathomable woe, and uttermost desolation[2], and yet even as its very accents imply of achieved and consummated victory. Even from the lowest depths of a tortured, tempted, sin-burthened, and now forsaken

---

[1] It is worthy of consideration whether the important and difficult passage, Col. ii. 15, may not have some reference to this awful period. If, as now seems grammatically certain, ἀπεκδυσάμενος is to be taken in its usual and proper *middle* sense, may not the 'stripping off from Himself of Powers and Principalities' have stood in some connexion as to time with the hours when the dying but victorious Lord, even out of the darkness, called unto His God, and by His holy surrender of Himself into the hands of His Eternal Father quelled Satanic assaults, which though not recorded, and scarcely hinted at (compare however Luke xxii. 53, and observe Luke iv. 13), we may still presume to think would then have been made with fearfully renewed energies: see *Commentary on Col. l. c.* p. 161.

[2] On the words of our Lord here referred to,—which are indeed far far from being 'perhaps a phrase in common use in extreme distress,' as Milman coldly terms them (*Hist. of Chr.* Vol. I. p. 364), and which the two inspired witnesses who record them have retained even in the very form and accents in which they were uttered,—see esp. the thoughtful comments of Stier, *Disc. of our Lord*, Vol. VII. p. 483 sq., Lange, *Leben Jesu*, II. 7. 9, Part III. p. 1573, and compare *Thesaur. Theol.* (*Crit. Sacr.*) Vol. II. 247 sq.

LECT. VII.

humanity,—even from the remotest bound, as it were, of a nature thus traversed to its extremest limits[1], and thus feelingly realized in all the measures of its infirmity for man's salvation, the Saviour cried unto God as *His* God[a]; the Son called unto Him with whom—even in this hour of dereliction and abandonment—He felt and knew that He was eternally one,—yea, and as the language of inspiration has declared, He 'was heard in that He feared[b].' With the utterance of that loud cry, or, perhaps, more probably, not till the Lord had resigned His spirit, the clouds of darkness gradually rolled away and the light broke forth[2]....However this may be, these awful moments were profaned by a mockery and a malignity on which it is fearful to dwell. We shudder as we read that the words of that harrowing exclamation, words first spoken by the prophetic Psalmist[c] and the outward mean-

[a] Matt. xxvii. 46
Mk. xv. 34

[b] Heb. v. 7

[c] Ps. xxii. 1

---

[1] Compare Cyril Alex.: 'He who excels all created things, and shares the Father's throne, humbled Himself unto emptying, and took the form of a slave, *and endured the limits of human nature*, that He might fulfil the promise made of God to the forefathers of the Jews.' *Commentary on St Luke*, Serm. CLIII. Part II. p. 722.

[2] It seems most consistent with the deep mysteries of these hours to conceive that the darkness had not passed away when the Lord uttered the opening words of Psalm xxii. 1. Whether the light returned immediately afterwards (Stier, *Disc. of Our Lord*, Vol. VII. p. 483, Clark), or not till after the occurrence of the other supernatural phenomena, cannot be ascertained. Under any circumstances, we must certainly maintain that these words of Psalm xxii. were not, as asserted by Milman (*Hist. of Christianity*, Vol. I. p. 364), our Lord's 'last words,' it being perfectly clear from St Matthew that after the 'Ελωί, 'Ελωί, κ.τ.λ. our Lord uttered *at least* another cry (πάλιν κράξας, ch. xxvii. 50). The received opinion seems undoubtedly the right one; according to which the sixth word from the cross was Τετέλεσται (John xix. 30), the *last* words Πάτερ, εἰς τὰς χεῖράς σου παρατίθεμαι τὸ πνεῦμά μου [compare παρέδωκεν τὸ πνεῦμα, John xix. 30], as recorded by St Luke (ch. xxiii. 46): compare, if necessary, Stier, *Disc. of Our Lord*, Vol. VIII. p. 28 (Clark), Meyer, *üb. Luk.* p. 498 (ed. 3).

ing of which no Jew could possibly have misunderstood, were studiously perverted by a satanic malice[1], and that the most holy name of the Eternal Father was used by the Jewish reprobates that stood around as that wherewith they now dared to make a mock at the Eternal Son[a]. But the end had now come. One solitary act of instinctive compassion[2] was yet to be performed; the sponge of vinegar was pressed to the parching lips; the dying Lord received it, and with a loud cry of consciously completed victory for man, and of most loving resignation unto God[3], bowed meekly His Divine head and gave up the ghost.

Jesus was dead. Can we marvel, then, when we read that the most awful moment in the history of the world was marked by mighty and significant portents,—that the veil[b], that symbolically separated sinful man from his offended God, was now rent in twain[4], that the earth quaked[c], that the

margin notes:
LECT. VII.
[a] Matt. xxvii. 47 Mk. xv. 35
The portents that followed our Lord's death.
[b] Matt. xxvii. 51 Mk. xv. 38
[c] Matt. xxvii. 51.

---

[1] There is no reason for thinking with Euthymius (*in Matth.* xxvii. 47) that those who said 'Ηλίαν φωνεῖ (Matth. *l. c.*) were Roman soldiers (τὴν Ἑβραΐδα φωνὴν ἀγνοοῦντες), who only caught the sound of the words uttered. There was here neither misunderstanding nor imperfect hearing, but only a mockery which had now become verily demoniacal.

[2] This would seem to be the correct statement, as we learn from Mark xv. 36 that the poor wretch joined in the mockery of the rest, and yet must apparently infer from Matth. xxvii. 49, that his present act was regarded as one of mercy which his companions sought to restrain. It may be true, as has been suggested by some expositors, that the man was really touched by the Saviour's suffering, now perhaps made more apparent by the διψῶ of John xix. 28, and that under the cover of mockery he still persisted in performing this last act of compassion. At any rate the δραμών (Matth. xxvii. 48, Mark xv. 36) and ἄφετε (Mark xv. 36,—not improbably 'let me alone') seem very fairly to accord with such a supposition.

[3] The remark of Draseke (cited by Stier) is perhaps not wholly fanciful,—that the *It is finished* was more especially directed to men, as the farewell greeting to earth, and that the *Father, into thine hands* was, as it were, 'His entrance-greeting to heaven.' *Disc. of Our Lord*, Vol. VIII. p. 28 (Clark).

[4] That the veil of the Temple here specified was that which sepa-

rocks were rent and the graves opened[a], and that by the vivifying power of the Lord's death they that slumbered therein arose, and after their Saviour's resurrection were seen by many witnesses[1]. Such things were known, patent, and recognized; they were seen by Jews and by Gentiles; by the centurion on Golgotha[b], and by the priest in the temple; by the multitudes that now beat their breasts in amazed and unavailing sorrow[c], and by the women and kinsmen that stood gazing afar off[d]; they were believed in and they stand recorded; yea, and in spite of all the negative criticism that the unbelief of later days has dared to

LECT. VII.
[a] Matt. xxvii. 52
[b] ver. 54 Luke xxiii. 47
[c] Luke xxiii. 48
[d] ver. 49

---

rated, not the Holy place from the rest of the Temple (Hug), but the Holy place from the Holy of Holies, seems most clearly shown not so much by the mere term used (καταπέτασμα not κάλυμμα; Friedlieb, Archäol. § 47, p. 172), as by the authentic elucidations supplied by the inspired author of the Epistle to the Hebrews; see ch. ix. 7 sq., x. 20. The remark of Lightfoot (*Hor. Hebr. in Matth.* xxvii. 51) that according to custom the High-priest entered on one *side* of the inner veil, may *perhaps* illustrate the full meaning of the sign: the veil now, as we are distinctly told by St Luke, was rent in the *midst* (ἐσχίσθη μέσον, ch. xxiii. 45), a statement made still more explicit by the ἐσχίσθη ἀπὸ ἄνωθεν ἕως κάτω εἰς δύο of St Matthew (ch. xxvii. 51) and St Mark (ch. xv. 38).

[1] Nothing can be more unwarrantable than to speak of this statement of the inspired Evangelist as the mythical conversion into actual history of the sign of the rent graves (Meyer, *üb. Matth.* xxvii. 52), nor less in harmony with sound principles of interpretation than to term these resurrections (ἠγέρθησαν, ver. 52) visionary appearances of the spirits (contrast πολλὰ σώματα, ver. 52) of deceased brethren confined to the *minds* of our Lord's followers (Milman, *Hist. of Chr.* Vol. I. p. 365), when the words of St Matthew are so particularly definite and explicit; compare ver. 52, 53. We are plainly told that at the Lord's death the bodies of slumbering saints arose (φωνὴ αὐτοὺς ἤγειρε, Chrys.; but!); and we are as plainly told, with the addition of a special and appropriate note of time, that *after* our Lord's resurrection they entered into the Holy City and were seen there by many. Into particulars it is unwise and precarious to enter; if, however, further comments be needed, the student may be referred to the special dissertation of Calmet; see *Journal of Sacr. Lit.* for 1848, p. 112, and comp. Lardner, *Works*, Vol. X. p. 340.

bring against them[1], they remain and will remain even unto the end of time, as the solemn testimony of nature to the truth of the mighty mystery of redeeming Love.

And now the day was beginning to wane, and within Jerusalem all was preparation for paschal solemnities which henceforth were to lose their deepest and truest significance. Eager bands of householders[2] were now streaming into the Temple, each one to slay his victim, and to make ready for the feast. It was a Passover of great solemnity[a]. The morrow was a high day, a double Sabbath, a day which was alike the solemn fifteenth of Nisan and the weekly festival[3]. Not unna-

LECT. VII.

The removal from the cross and burial of the Lord's body.

[a] Jo. xix. 31

---

[1] Some critical writers have ventured to consider Matthew xxvii. 52 an interpolation; see Norton, *Introd. to the Gospels*, Vol. I. p. 216, and compare Gersdorf, *Beiträge*, p. 149. Such a statement is wholly unsupported by external evidence, and is rejected even by those who regard this portion of the narrative as mythical: see Meyer, *Komment. üb. Matth.* p. 542 (ed. 4). Reference has been freely made by this last-mentioned writer and others to the *Evang. Nicodem.* cap. 17 sq. as containing the further development of the incident. This statement, probably designed to be mischievous, is not wholly correct. The notices of the event in question are really very slight, and in language closely resembling that of St Matthew (see *Evang. Nicod.* cap. 11); in fact the only use made of the incident by the apocryphal writer is to introduce the narrative of Carinus and Leucius, which refers nearly exclusively to the Lord's descent into Hades and appearance in the under-world.

If the *Evang. Nicod.* tends to prove anything, it is this, that the ancient writer of that document regarded Matth. xxvii. 52 as an authentic statement, and as one which no current traditions enabled him to embellish, but which was adopted as a convenient starting-point for his legendary narrative.

[2] See especially Friedlieb, *Archäol.* § 18, p. 47 sq., where this and other ceremonies connected with the Passover are very fully illustrated.

[3] The efforts of those writers who regard this Saturday as Nisan 16 cannot be considered successful in proving it to have been a 'high day' (John xix. 31). The principal fact adduced in favour of such an opinion is that on this day the first-fruits were presented in the Temple; see Wieseler, *Chron. Synops.* p. 385, Robinson, *Harmony*, p. 150 (Tract Society). If on the contrary the day be regarded as Nisan 15, then all becomes intelligible and self-explanatory, the solemn character of Nisan 15 being so well-known and

tural then was it that petition should be made to Pilate for the prompt removal from the cross of the bodies of those who had been crucified in the forenoon, that the approaching day might not be legally profaned. The petition is granted; the legs of the two malefactors are broken[a] to hasten their death[1], but no bone is broken of that sacred body which now hung lifeless between them. A spear is thrust into the holy side[b], perchance in the neighbourhood of the heart, to make sure that life is extinct, and forthwith a two-fold sign was vouchsafed, whether natural or supernatural we know not[2], but which the fourth Evangelist was specially moved to record and in which we may, with all the best interpreters of the ancient Church, not perhaps unfitly recognize the sacramental

---

[a] Jo. xix. 32
[b] ver. 34

so distinctly defined; see Exod. xii. 16, Lev. xxiii. 7.

[1] The breaking of the legs has been thought to include a *coup de grace* (see Friedlieb, *Archäol.* § 48, and compare Hug, *Freib. Zeitschr.* III. p. 67 sq.), as the *crurifragium* would not seem sufficient in itself to extinguish life. As, however, such an expansion of the term has not been made out (Amm. Marcell. *Hist.* XIV. 9 is certainly not sufficient to prove it), and as the present passage seems to show that it had reference to the death of the sufferer (comp. John xix. 33), we must conclude that it was found by experience to bring death, possibly slowly, but thus not unconformably with the fearful nature of the punishment.

[2] The emphatic language of St John (ch. xix. 34) seems to favour the opinion that it was a supernatural sign. The use made of this incident by Dr Stroud (*Physical Death of Christ*, Lond. 1849) and others to prove that our Lord died of a ruptured vessel of the heart is ingenious, but seems precarious. Without in any way availing ourselves of the ancient statement that our Lord's death was hastened supernaturally (see Greswell, *Dissert.* XLII. Vol. III. p. 251), we may perhaps reasonably ascribe it to the exhausting pains of body (see Richter quoted by Friedlieb, *Archäol.* § 44), which though in ordinary cases not sufficient to bring such speedy death, did so in the present, when there had been not only great physical suffering previously, but agonies of mind which human thought cannot conceive, and which clearly appear (comp. Matth. xxvii. 46) to have endured unto the very end.

symbol both of the communion of our Master's body and blood, and of the baptismal laver of regenerating grace.... The sacred body was taken from the cross and was still in the custody of the soldiers, when a secret disciple, the wealthy Joseph of Arimathea, who as a member of the supreme court would know that the bodies were to be removed, now came to Golgotha[1], and after finding that the Procurator's permission was carried out, emboldened himself[a] so far as to beg personally for the Lord's body from that unrighteous judge. The request is freely granted[2], and the holy body is borne by the pious Joseph to a garden nigh at hand[b], which was probably his own property, and in which was a tomb that he had hewn out of the rock[c], wherein man had never yet been laid[d]. Aided by one who at first came secretly to the Lord under cover of night, but now feared not to bring his princely offering[3] of

[a] Mk. xv. 42
[b] Jo. xix. 41
[c] Matt. xxvii. 60
[d] Luke xxiii. 53

---

[1] See Matth. xxvii. 57, where the ἦλθεν would seem naturally to have reference to the scene of the incidents last mentioned, *i. e.* to the place of crucifixion. While the soldiers were waiting for the sequel of the *crurifragium* (John xix. 32) Joseph would easily have had time to go to the Prætorium and prefer his request to Pilate. The touch supplied by the τολμήσας of the graphic St Mark (ch. xv. 43) should not be left unnoticed.

[2] It is not improbable that the term ἐδωρήσατο was designedly used by St Mark (ch. xv. 45), as implying that Pilate gave up the holy body without demanding money for it; see Wetstein *in loc.* Had not Joseph been moved to perform this pious office, it would seem that the Lord's body would have been removed to one of two common sepulchres reserved for those who had suffered capital punishment,— 'unum occisis gladio et strangulatis, alterum lapidatis [qui etiam suspendebantur] et combustis.' 'Sanhedr.' vi. 5, cited by Lightfoot, *in Matth.* xxvii. 58; comp. Sepp, *Leben Christi*, vi. 76, Vol. iii. p. 602.

[3] This we learn from St John was of the weight of 100 pounds (ch. xix. 39), and did indeed display what Chrysostom rightly calls the μεγαλοψυχίαν τὴν ἐν τοῖς χρήμασι (*in Matth.* Hom. LXXXVIII.) of the faithful and true-hearted ruler. The myrrh and aloes were probably mixed, and in the form of a coarse

364   *The Last Passover.*

LECT. VII.

ᵃ Jo. xix. 38

ᵇ Luke xxiii. 51

ᶜ Matt. xxvii. 61
ᵈ Luke xxiii. 56

myrrh and aloes openly, and in the light of day, the faithful disciple^a solemnly performs every rite of honouring sepulture. Yea the hands of two members of that very council that had condemned the Lord to death, but one at least of whom had no part in their crime^b, are those that now tenderly place the Redeemer's body in the new rock-hewn tomb.... And now all is done, and the Sabbath well nigh begun. The King's Son is laid in His sleeping chamber; the faithful Mary Magdalene and the mother of Joses[1], who in their deep grief had remained sitting beside the tomb^c, now return to the city to buy spices and ointments^d, and make preparations for doing more completely what had now necessarily been done in haste; the great stone is rolled against the opening of the tomb[2];

---

powder freely sprinkled between the ὀθόνια with which the body was swathed: see John xix. 40. For further details see Friedlieb, *Archäol.* § 50, p. 171 sq. and Winer, *RWB.* Art. 'Leichen,' Vol. II. p. 15.

[1] The reading is somewhat doubtful (*Lachmann, Tregelles, Tischend.*, ἡ Ἰωσῆτος, — apparently rightly), though the person designated is not, Ἰωσῆτος being only the Greek form of the more familiar Ἰωσῆ. Wieseler (*Chron. Synops.* p. 426, note) adopts the reading of the Alexandrian MS., ἡ Ἰωσήφ, and considers the Mary here mentioned to have been the daughter of the honourable man who bore that name; this, however, has been rightly judged by recent critics to be open to objections which, combined with the small amount of external evidence on which the reading rests, are decisive against it; see Meyer *üb. Mark.*

p. 180 (ed. 3). With regard to the two women, it would seem from Matth. xxvii. 61 (καθήμεναι ἀπέναντι τοῦ τάφου), compared with Mark xv. 47, Luke xxiii. 55, that at present they took but little part, but sat by, stupefied with grief, while the two rulers (John xix. 40, ἔλαβον, ἔδησαν) performed the principal rites of sepulture.

[2] The tombs were then probably as now, either (*a*) with steps and a descent in a perpendicular direction, or (*b*) in the face of the rock and with an entry in a sloping or horizontal direction. The tomb of our Lord would seem to have been of the latter description; tombs of the former kind are perhaps alluded to Luke xi. 44. The stone which was rolled against the opening and in this case appears to have completely filled it up (comp. John xx. 1, ἐκ τοῦ μνημείου, and see Meyer

The Last Passover.

the two pious rulers turn their steps to Jerusalem, and all rest on the sabbath-day 'according to the commandment[a].'

With the first Evangelist's notice of the request preferred by the members of the Sanhedrin that the sepulchre should be guarded[b], and with a brief mention of the Procurator's curtly expressed permission[c], the sealing of the stone, and the setting of the watch[1], this lengthened portion of the inspired narrative now comes to its close.

And here our Lecture shall at once conclude. Practical reflections on events so numerous, and of such momentous interest, would far exceed the limits that must be prescribed to this work[2], and would necessarily involve recapitulations which, in a narrative so simple and continuous as that here given by the Evangelists, might reasonably be deemed to a certain degree unnecessary and undesirable. Into such varied reflections then it may not now be wholly suitable to enter. Yet let us at least bear one truth which this portion

LECT. VII.

[a] Luke xxiii. 56
[b] Matt. xxvii. 64
[c] ver. 66

Conclusion.

---

in loc.) was technically termed *Golal* (גולל; see Sepp, *Leben Chr.* VI. 77, Vol. III. p. 608), and was usually of considerable size (Mark xvi. 4): see Pearson, *Creed*, Art. IV. Vol. II. p. 187 sq. (ed. Burton), and on the subject generally, the special work of Nicolai in Ugolini, *Thesaur.* Vol. XXXIII., and Winer, *RWB.* Art. 'Gräber,' Vol. I. p. 443 sq.

[1] See Matth. xxvii. 65, where the verb ἔχετε would seem more naturally imperative than indicative, as in the latter case the reference could only be to such a κουστωδία as the Chief-priests had at their disposal, *i. e.* templo-guards, whereas the actual watchers were Roman soldiers;

see Matth. xxviii. 14. In the former case permission is given in the form of a brusquely expressed command, means being supplied for it to be carried out.

[2] It may again be noticed (see above, p. 39, note 2) that both this and the following Lecture were not *preached*, the number required, owing to recent changes, being only six. The omission of practical comments or hortatory application will thus seem perhaps not only natural but desirable, as such addresses if merely of a general character, and not made to a special audience, can rarely be satisfactory.

of our subject has presented to us, practically, vitally, and savingly, in mind,—even the everlasting truth, that our sins have been atoned for, that they have been borne by our Lord on His cross, and that by His stripes we have been healed[a]. God grant that this belief of our fathers and our forefathers, and of the holiest and the wisest of every age in the Church of Christ may not at length become modified and diluted. Let words of controversy here appear not. Let no terms of party-strife appear at the close of a narrative of a love boundless as the universe, and of a sacrifice of which the sweet-smelling savour[b] has pervaded every realm of being,—let none such meet the eye of the reader of these concluding lines. Yet let the prayer be offered with all lowliness and humility that these weak words may have been permitted to strengthen belief in the Atonement, to convince the fair and candid reader of the written Word, that here there is something more than the perfection of a self-denial, something more than a great moral spectacle at which we may gaze in a perplexed wonder, but of which the benefits to us are but indirect, the realities but exemplary.

No, it cannot be. That blood, which as it were, we have beheld falling drop by drop on Golgotha fell not thus fruitlessly to the earth. Those curtains of darkness shrouded something more than the manifestation of a moral sublimity. That cry of agony and desolation told of something more than a sense of merely personal suffering, or the closing exhaustions of a distressed humanity. The very outward circumstances of the harrowing his-

[a] 1 Pet. ii. 24

[b] Eph. v. 2

tory raise their voices against such a bleak and cheerless theosophy. The very details of the varied scenes of agony and woe plead meekly yet persuasively against such an estimate of the sufferings of an Incarnate God. May deeper meditation on these things bring conviction. May those who yet believe in the perfections of their humanity, and doubt the efficacies of their Redeemer's blood unlearn that joyless creed. May the speculators here cease to speculate; may the casuist learn to adore. Yea to us all may fuller measures of faith and of saving assurance yet be ministered, that with heart and mind, and soul and spirit we may verily and indeed believe that 'Christ was once offered to bear the sins of many[a],' and that even as the beloved Apostle has said, 'He is the propitiation for our sins, and not for ours only, but for the sins of the whole world[b].'

[a] Heb. ix. 28
[b] 1 Joh. ii. 2

LECTURE VIII.

THE FORTY DAYS.

St John xx. 17.

Go to my brethren, and say unto them, I ascend unto my Father, and your Father; and to my God, and your God.

LECT. VIII.

Introductory comments.

THE portion of the inspired narrative at which we have now arrived is the shortest, but by no means the least important of the divisions into which it has appeared convenient to separate the Gospel-history. In some respects indeed, it may be rightly termed the most important, as containing the account of that which was in fact the foundation of all apostolical preaching, and which, when alluding to the subject generally, St Paul has not scrupled to speak of[a] as that which alone gives a reality to our faith here and to our hope of what shall be hereafter[1]. The resurrection of Jesus Christ, of Him whom Joseph and Nicodemus laid in the new rock-hewn tomb, is no less the solemn guarantee to us of the truth of that in which we have believed, than also the holy

[a] 1 Cor. xv. 14

---

[1] The nature of the Apostle's argument, and the reciprocal inferences, viz. 'that Christ's resurrection from the dead is the necessary cause of our resurrection,' and 'that our future resurrection necessarily infers Christ's resurrection from the dead,' so that 'the denial or doubt of our resurrection infers a doubt or denial of His resurrection,' are well discussed by the learned Jackson, in his valuable *Commentaries on the Creed*, xi. 16. 1, Vol. x. p. 307 sq. (Oxford, 1844).

The Forty Days.

pledge to us of our own future victory over death and corruption.

On the history of such an adorable manifestation of the Divine power and majesty of Him who saved us, and who has thus given an infallible proof that He had as much the power[1] to take His life again[a] as He had the mercy to lay it down,—on such a history, meet indeed will it be for us to dwell with thoughtfulness, precision, and care. Meet indeed will it be to strive to bring into one every ray of Divine truth as vouchsafed to us in this portion of the Evangelical history, to miss no hint, to overlook no inference whereby our faith in our risen and ascended Lord may become more real and more vital, and our conviction of our own resurrection more assured and more complete[2].

And not of our own resurrection only, but

LECT. VIII.

Doctrinal questions involved in this portion of the history.

[a] Joh. x. 18

---

[1] The Catholic doctrine on the agency by which Christ was raised from the dead is nowhere better or more clearly stated than by Bp. Pearson, who, while stating the general truth 'that the Father, Son, and Holy Ghost raised Christ from the dead,' shows also that the special truth 'that the Lord raised Himself' is distinct and irrefragable, as resting on our Lord's own words (John ii. 22) and the way in which those words were understood by the Apostles: 'If upon the resurrection of Christ the Apostles believed those words of Christ, "Destroy this temple, and I will raise it up again," then did they believe that Christ raised Himself; for in those words there is a person mentioned which raised Christ, and no other person mentioned but Himself.' *Exposition of the Creed*, Art. v. Vol. I. p. 303 (ed. Burton).

[2] It has been well said by Dr Thomas Jackson, that 'Every man is bound to believe that all true believers of Christ's resurrection from the dead shall be undoubted partakers of that endless and immortal glory into which Christ hath been raised. But no man is bound to believe his own resurrection in particular into such glory any further, or upon more certain terms, than he can (upon just and deliberate examination) find that himself doth steadfastly believe this fundamental article of Christ's resurrection from the dead.' *Commentaries on the Creed*, XI. 16. 11, Vol. X. p. 326 sq., where there is also a short but excellent practical application of the doctrine.

LECT. VIII.

even of what lies beyond. Yea, hints there are of partial answers not only to the question, 'How are the dead raised?' but even to that further and more special question, 'With what body do they come?' which so perplexed the doubters of Corinth, and remains even to this day such a subject of controversy and debate. Into such questions the general character of my present undertaking will wholly preclude me from entering either formally or at length; nay, in a professed recital of events it will scarcely be convenient to call away the attention of the reader from a simple consideration of facts to their probable use as bases for speculative meditation; still it will not be unsuitable or inappropriate to bestow such a careful consideration on those parts of the subject which need it on their own account, as will also incidentally prove suggestive of fruitful thoughts in reference to our future state, our hopes and our expectations. The remembrance that our risen Lord was the veritable firstfruits of them that slept, that as He rose we shall rise, will always press upon us the thought that the nature of His resurrection-body[1] must involve something, at any rate, remotely

[1] This difficult subject will not be formally discussed in the text, but in every case comments will be made upon the nature of those appearances which seem to require more special consideration. From these, and above all from a sound exegetical discussion of the passages in question the student will perhaps be enabled to arrive at some opinion upon a very important subject. Meanwhile, without anticipating what will be best considered separately and in detail, it may be well to notice that there have been, roughly speaking, *three* opinions on the subject,—(a) that our Lord's body was the same natural body of flesh and blood that had been crucified and laid in the tomb; (b) that it was wholly changed at the resurrection, and became simply an ethereal body,—something between matter and spirit (ὥσπερεί ἐν μεθορίῳ τινὶ τῆς παχύτητος τῆς πρὸ τοῦ πάθους σώματος καὶ τοῦ γυμνὴν τοιούτου σώματος φαίνεσθαι ψυχήν. Origen, contr. Cels. II. 62); (c) that it was

The Forty Days.

analogous to the nature of the future bodies of His glorified servants, and must insensibly lead us to dwell with thoughtful care upon all the circumstances and details relating to those appearances which we are now about to recount. Let us then address ourselves to this important portion of the inspired history with all earnestness and sobriety. Never was there a time when meditations on the history of the risen yet not ascended Lord were more likely to be useful than now; never was there an age when it was more necessary to set forth events that not only imply but practically prove the Resurrection of the body[1], and that not only suggest but confirm that teaching of the Church in reference to the future state, which it is the obvious tendency of the speculations of our own times to explain away, to modify, or to deny[2].

the same as before, but endued with new powers, properties, and attributes. Of these views (*a*) is open to very serious objections arising from the many passages which seem clearly to imply either (1) that there was a change in the outward appearance of our Lord's body, or (2) that its appearances and disappearances involved something supernatural. Again (*b*) seems plainly irreconcileable with our Lord's own declaration (Luke xxiv. 39), and with the fact that His holy body was touched, handled, and proved experimentally to be real. Between these two extremes (*c*) seems soberly to mediate, and is the opinion maintained by Irenæus, Tertullian, Hilary, Augustine (but not exclusively), and other sound writers of the early church. As will be seen from what follows, it appears best to reconcile all apparent differences in the accounts of the Lord's appearances, and, to say the very least, deserves the student's most thoughtful consideration. For a very complete article on this subject, see the *Bibliotheca Sacra*, for 1845, Vol. II. p. 292. The writer (Dr Robinson) advocates (*a*), but supplies much interesting matter and many useful quotations in reference to the other opinions.

[1] Some of the more popular *quasi*-scientific objections to the received doctrine of the Resurrection of the body are noticed, discussed, and fairly answered in an article by Prof. Goodwin in the *Bibliotheca Sacra*, for 1852, Vol. IX. p. 1 sq. For earlier objections, see Jackson, *Creed*, XI. 15, Vol. X. p. 283 sq.

[2] Information is so often sought for

LECT. VIII.

Characteristics of the present portion of the narrative.

Ere, however, we proceed to the regular and orderly recital of the events of this portion of the evangelical history, let us pause for a moment to make a few brief comments on the general character of the different records of the inspired narrators.

Number of the accounts.

ⁿ See p. 281

With regard to the number of those holy records, the same remarks that were made at the beginning of the last Lecture* may here be repeated, as equally applicable to the portion of the sacred history now before us. Events of such a momentous nature as those which followed our Lord's death and burial were not to be told by one but by all. If all relate how the holy body of the Lord was laid in the tomb, surely all shall relate how on the third morning the tomb was found empty, and how angelical witnesses[1] declared that the Lord had risen. If all relate how holy women were spectators of their Redeemer's suffering, shall not all relate how some at least of this ministering company[2] were first to hear the glad-

in vain on the subject of the general teaching of the best writers of the early Church on the Doctrine of the Last Things (Eschatology, as it is now called), that we may pause to refer the student to a learned volume now nearly forgotten, Burnet, *de Statu Mortuorum et Resurgentium*, London, 1728.

[1] The first point, the fact that the tomb was empty and the body not there, is very distinctly put forward by all the four Evangelists; compare Matth. xxviii. 6, Mark xvi. 6, Luke xxiv. 3, John xx. 2, 6, 7. The second point, the angelical testimony is, strictly considered, only specified by the first three Evangelists: St John relates the appearance of two angels, and their address to Mary Magdalene (ch. xx. 13), but the testimony which they deliver to the women (Matth. xxviii. 6, Mark xvi. 6, Luke xxiv. 6), is, in the case of Mary Magdalene, practically delivered by the Lord Himself.

[2] The women mentioned as having visited the sepulchre were not the same even in the case of the first three Evangelists. This, however, can cause no real difficulty, as the fact that St Matthew only mentions Mary Magdalene and 'the other Mary' (the wife of Clopas or Alphæus, and sister of the Virgin; see above, p. 355, note 1) in no way implies that

tidings of His victory over the grave, and to proclaim it to His doubting Apostles? If all, as we have seen in the last Lecture, have so minutely described the various scenes of the Passion, can we wonder that all were moved to record some of the more striking scenes of the great Forty days that followed, and that afforded to the disciples the visible proofs of the Lord's resurrection[1]. It could not indeed be otherwise. These things must be told by all, though, as in other portions of the Gospel-history, all have not been moved to specify exactly the same incidents.

LECT. VIII.

Nay, when we come to consider the precise nature and character of the four holy records we meet with some striking and instructive differences[2]. The first two Evangelists devote no more

Their peculiarities and differences.

others were not with her. From St Mark (ch. xvi. 1) we learn that Salome was also present; and from St Luke (ch. xxiv. 1 compared with ch. xxiii. 49 and 55) we should naturally draw the same inference; when, however, the Evangelist pauses a little later to specify by name, Salome is not mentioned but Joanna (ch. xxiv. 10), the αἱ λοιπαὶ σὺν αὐταῖς including Salome and, as it would appear, others not named by any of the Evangelists. The attempt of Greswell (*Dissert.* XLIII. Vol. III. p. 264 sq.) to prove that there were two parties of women, tho one the party of Salome, and the other the party of Joanna, is very artificial, and really does but little to remove the difficulties which seem to have given rise to the hypothesis.

[1] So rightly Augustine; 'Ergo ad eorum [discipulorum] confirmationem dignatus est post resurrectionem vivere cum illis quadraginta diebus integris, ab ipso die passionis suæ usque in hodiernum diem [fest. Ascensionis], intrans et exiens, manducans et bibens, sicut dicit Scriptura [Act. i. 3, 4], confirmans hoc redditum esse oculis eorum post resurrectionem, quod ablatum erat per crucem.' *Serm.* CCLXIV. Vol v. p. 1212 (ed. Migne). The reasons suggested by the same author (p. 1211, 1216) why the interval was exactly *forty* days are ingenious, but scarcely satisfactory.

[2] These differences when studiously collected and paraded out (see De Wette, *Erkl. des Evang. Matth.* p. 306, ed. 3) at first *seem* very startling and irreconcileable. They cease, however, at once to appear so, when we only pause to observe the brevity of the sacred writers, and remember that an additional knowledge of perhaps no more than two or three particulars would enable us at once to reconcile all that

than twenty verses each to the history of this period, and are but brief in their notices of the appearances of the risen Lord, though explicit as to the circumstances under which the first witnesses of the Resurrection were enabled to give their testimony. The third and fourth Evangelists, on the other hand, have each given a record nearly three times as long, and have each related with great exactness the circumstances of selected instances of the Redeemer's manifestation of Himself, wherein He more especially vouchsafed to show that He had raised again the same body that had been laid in Joseph's sepulchre, that it was indeed He Himself[a], their very own adorable Master and Lord. And yet both in this and other differences we can hardly fail to be struck by the Divine harmony that pervades the whole, and must again be led to recognize in this portion of the history, with all its seeming discrepancies, what we have so often already observed in earlier portions,—how strikingly the Evangelical accounts illustrate by their differences, and how the very omissions in one or two of the sacred records will sometimes be found to place even in a clearer light, and to reflect a fuller and truer significance on what others have been moved to record. If, for example, two Evangelists would thus appear to dwell simply upon the fact of the Resurrection, the other two, we observe, were specially guided to set forth the proofs of its true nature, its reality

[a] Luke xxiv. 39

---

seems discordant: see the careful comments of Caspari, *Chron.-Geogr. Einl.* § 186, p. 203, and a good article by Robinson in the *Bibliotheca Sacra* for 1845, Vol. II. p. 162. At the end (p. 189) will be found a useful selected list of treatises both on the subject of the Resurrection and on the principal events connected therewith.

and its certainty[1]. If again we might be induced to think from the words of the first and second Evangelists that Galilee was to be more especially the land blessed by the appearances of the risen Saviour, the two others direct our thoughts more to Judæa, and yet one of these joins the testimony of an eyewitness to that of the first two by his explicit and most undoubtedly genuine[2] account of the Lord's appearance at the most favoured scene of His Galilæan ministry[3]. If lastly, two only of

---

[1] It can hardly escape the notice of the observant reader that while the first and second Evangelists dwell mainly on the fact that the Lord was risen from the dead, the third and fourth Evangelists dwell most upon the reality of the body that was raised (Luke xxiv. 30, 39, 41 sq.; comp. Acts i. 3) and its identity with that which was crucified; compare John xx. 20, 27. The, so to speak, crucial test of eating is alone referred to by these Evangelists,—being definitely specified, Luke xxiv. 43, and perhaps implied, John xxi. 12 sq.

[2] On this point it is not necessary to dwell at length. There is not a vestige of *external* evidence to lead us to think that the early Church entertained the slightest doubt of John xxi. being written by the *Apostle* St John. *Internal* evidence has nothing else whatever to rest upon than the two seeming conclusions, ch. xx. 30 sq., and ch. xxi. 24 sq.; it being now admitted by the best recent critics of the Apostle's language (see esp. Meyer, *Komment.* p. 510) that ch. xxi. came from his hand. On such evidence or rather absence of evidence we shall, probably, be slow to believe with Wieseler (comp. *Chron. Synops.* p. 418,

and his special dissertation on the subject) that John xxi. was written by John the *Presbyter*.

[3] Few points have been dwelt upon more studiously by sceptical and semi-sceptical writers than the assumed fact that St Matthew and St Mark (ch. xvi. 9—20 being presupposed to be not genuine) regard *Galilee* as the scene of the Lord's appearances (Matth. xxviii. 7, 10, 16 sq.; Mark xvi. 7), while St Luke and St John (ch. xxi. is commonly assumed by such writers to be not genuine) place them in *Judæa*; compare Wieseler, *Chron. Synops.* p. 421 sq. Now in the first place such a statement rests on two assumptions, the first of which is open to some doubt (see above, p. 26, note 1), and the second of which is inconsistent with evidence (see the preceding note); and in the second place, even if we concede these two assumptions, what more can be fairly said than this,—that St Matthew relates two appearances only, one confessedly in Galilee (ch. xxviii. 16), but one most certainly in Judæa (ch. xxviii. 9, 10); that St Mark's Gospel is according to assumption imperfect, and cannot be pleaded for either side; that St Luke and St John (ch. xx.) have recorded special

LECT. VIII.

[a] Mark xvi. 19
Luke xxiv. 51
Acts i. 9

the four witnesses[a] have been moved to record the Ascension, the other two have taught us by their very silence, in the first place, to view that last event of the Gospel-history in its true light,—as so entirely the necessary and natural sequel of what preceded that Apostles could leave it unrecorded; and in the second place thus to realize more deeply the true mystery of the Resurrection, to see and to feel how it included and involved all that followed, and how it truly was that one great victory over sin and death that made every minor conquest over earthly relations a matter of certain and inevitable sequence[1]. If, on the one hand, St Luke has told us how the Lord 'was carried up into heaven[b],' and St Mark[2] has followed Him with the eye of faith even up to the

[b] Luke xxiv. 51

appearances of a highly important nature in reference to the object which they seem mainly to have had in view (see p. 375, note 1); and that these from the nature of the case would be very soon after the Resurrection, and by consequence in Judæa? Even then with the two concessions above alluded to our opponents cannot be regarded as having done much to impair the harmony of the Evangelical records, or to establish the favourite theory of different 'traditions' of the Resurrection; compare Meyer, *Komment. üb. Matth.* p. 553,—where this untenable hypothesis is put forward and defended.

[1] It may be remarked how comparatively little the Ascension of our Lord is dwelt upon by the early writers compared with their references to the Resurrection, and it may also be observed that the special festival, though undoubtedly of great antiquity (see Augustine, *Epist. ad Januar.* LIV. Vol. II. p. 200, ed. Migne), and certainly regarded in the fourth century as one of the great festivals (*Const. Apost.* VIII. 33), is still not alluded to by any of the earliest writers, Justin Martyr, Irenæus, Clement of Alexandria, and Cyprian, and is not included in the list of festivals enumerated by Origen (*contr. Cels.* VIII. 21, 22); see Riddle, *Christian Antiq.* p. 678. The preaching of the Apostles was preeminently the *resurrection* of Christ (Acts ii. 31, iv. 33, al.), as that which included in it everything besides: it was from this that the early Church derived all its fullest grounds of assurance; compare Clem. Rom. *Epist. ad Cor.* cap. 42.

[2] For a brief discussion of the arguments in favour of the genuineness of the concluding verses of St Mark's Gospel, see above, Lect. I. p. 26, note, and comp. Caspari, *Chron.-Geogr. Einleit.* § 184, p. 202 sq.

moment of His session at the right hand of God[a], no less, on the other, is our text a most significant testimony from the beloved Apostle, that when the Lord arose, that ascension had virtually commenced, that He rose to ascend, and that in the early dawning of that Easter morn the Lord's return to the throne of Omnipotence was already begun[1] :—' I ascend to my Father and your Father, and to my God and your God[b].'

[a] Mark xvi. 19

[b] Joh. xx. 17

We might extend these observations, but enough perhaps has been said to indicate the general character of this portion of the inspired narrative, and the general nature of the difficulties we may expect to meet with. We must now turn to its subject matter, and to a consideration of the few but notable events which marked this concluding part of our Redeemer's history.

Resumption of the narrative.

One of the last events in the preceding portion of our narrative is that which connects us with the present, and unites the Friday eve with the Easter morn. This we observe especially in the Gospel of the historian Evangelist, who, without any break or marked transition, relates to us how the ministering women of Galilee now come to perform the pious work for which they had made preparations on the Friday evening. They had bought spices and ointments ere the Sabbath had commenced[c],

Visit of the women to the sepulchre.

[c] Luke xxiii. 56

---

[1] Though the use of the present ἀναβαίνω (John xx. 17) *may* be regarded as *ethical, i. e.* as indicating what was soon and certainly to take place (see Winer, *Gram.* § 40, 2, p. 237, ed. 6), it seems here more simple to regard it as *temporal,*—as indicating a process which had in fact already begun. The extreme view of this text as indicating that an ascension of our Lord took place on the same day that He rose (Kinkel, in *Stud. u. Krit.* for 1841,—translated in *Biblioth. Sacra,* Vol. I. p. 152 sq.) is, it is needless to say, plainly to be rejected, as inconsistent with Acts i. 3, and numerous other passages in all the four Gospels.

and again, as it would seem, after its legal conclusion, on the Saturday evening^a. Every preparation was thus fully made, and it remained only that with the earliest light of the coming day, they should bear their offering to the sepulchre, and tenderly anoint that sacred body[1] which they had seen laid in haste, though with all reverence and honour, in the new rock-hewn tomb. It was still dark when they set out, and their hearts were as sad and as gloomy as the shadows of the night that were still lingering around them[2]. But the mere needs of the present were what now mainly occupied their thoughts;—who was to roll away for them the great stone[b] they had seen but two nights before so closely fitted in its appointed place[3]? Where were the strong and zealous hands

LECT. VIII.
^a Mk. xvi. 1
^b ver. 3

---

[1] The object is more definitely stated by St Mark than by St Matthew. The first Evangelist says generally that it was θεωρῆσαι τὸν τάφον (ch. xxviii. 1); the second specifies more exactly that it was ἵνα ἀλείψωσιν αὐτόν (ch. xvi. 1). It will be remembered that when our Lord was interred, spices were only strewn between the folds of the swathing bands (John xix. 40; compare p. 363, note 3); the object of the women was now to spread over the sacred body the customary liquid perfumes; see Greswell, *Dissert.* XLIII. Vol. III. p. 260.

[2] Some little difficulty has arisen from the apparently different definitions of the time of the visit to the sepulchre, as specified in the four Evangelists, the two extreme being, that of St John, σκοτίας ἔτι οὔσης (ch. xx. 1), and the second of St Mark, ἀνατείλαντος τοῦ ἡλίου (ch. xvi. 2). Were these the only notes of time we might have been led to suppose that the first referred to the time of starting, the second of arriving at the sepulchre. As, however, St Mark has another note of time λίαν πρωΐ (ver. 2), and as this is supported by the τῇ ἐπιφωσκούσῃ [κς. ἡμέρᾳ] εἰς μίαν σαββάτων of St Matthew (ch. xxviii. 1) and the ὄρθρου βαθέως of St Luke (ch. xxiv. 1), the most natural conclusion is, that the ἀνατειλ. τοῦ ἡλίου is not to be referred to the actual phenomenon (Meyer, al.) but to be regarded only as a general definition of time: see Robinson, *Biblioth. Sacra*, Vol. II. p. 168, where examples are given from the Septuagint which dilute the objection arising from the use of the aorist.

[3] This, as has already been suggested (p. 364, note 2), is perhaps to be inferred from the ἠρμένον ἐκ τοῦ μνημείου of John xx. 1, the preposition seeming to imply that the stone

that were to open that door that would lead them to their Lord? While thus musing, and as yet, as it would seem, at some distance from the sepulchre, lo! the ground around them quakes[a] under their feet[1]; the angel of the Lord descends from heaven[b], the heathen watchers at the tomb fall prostrate with fear[c] as the glory of that celestial appearance smites upon their eyes; the great stone is rolled away from the already empty sepulchre[2]; men now may perceive what angels know, that THE LORD IS RISEN. Meanwhile the women, who probably were still too distant to see distinctly, perhaps pause bewildered and irresolute, doubtful whether to go onward or to return. But all is now again the wonted calm of early dawn; the earth has ceased to tremble; the strange flashing light has faded

LECT. VIII.

[a] Matt. xxviii. 2
[b] ver. 2
[c] ver. 4

was not only rolled against the door, but fitted into the cavity.

[1] It is very difficult to decide whether the women actually beheld the miraculous circumstances mentioned Matth. xxviii. 1 sq., or not. The definite expression, καὶ ἰδοὺ (ver. 2), the address of the angel (ver. 5), and the contrasting ὑμεῖς (ver. 5; comp. Chrys. *in loc.*) seem most distinctly in favour of the *affirmative*, while the silence of the other Evangelists, and even St Matthew's very indirect notice of the impression produced on the women by the wondrous sight strongly suggest the *negative*. In this difficulty the mediating view of the text,—that they beheld it partially and at a distance, has been adopted as in some degree reconciling the two impressions produced by a consideration of this portion of the narrative. The terrified guards would also probably have been unable to have *wholly* suppressed some account of an event (Matth. xxviii. 13) which so greatly terrified them, and thus partly from them and partly from the women the occurrence would have become gradually but completely known.

[2] The exact moment when the Lord issued from the tomb is left wholly undefined. The prevailing view of the early writers is that it preceded the events specified by the Evangelist (μετὰ τὴν ἀνάστασιν ἦλθεν ἄγγελος, Chrysost. *in Matth.* xxviii. 1), and that the appearance of the angel and removal of the stone were to announce what had already taken place and to demonstrate its reality: comp. Hacket, *Serm. v. on Resurr.* p. 592 sq. (Lond. 1675). All we can know of the circumstances of the holy mystery is to be gathered from John xx. 6 sq.; from which we may perhaps presume to say that it took place with all the adjuncts of holy order, deliberation, and peace: comp. Robinson, *Bibl. Sacra*, Vol. II. p. 166.

LECT. VIII.

away; they will yet pursue their way; they will enter the quiet garden; they will strive to find entrance into the tomb; they will do that for which they are come. As they draw nearer, they see to their joy that the stone is rolled away, resting perhaps on one side of the rocky portal[1]; they take heart and press onward, yea they enter, as St Luke tells us[a], into the tomb itself, and by the seeing of the eye are assured that the holy body they themselves had beheld securely laid there, is now there no longer. The tomb is empty; they have searched and have not found, and now stand sadly gazing on each other in utter bewilderment and perplexity[b]. But one there was among them more rapid in the inferences of her fears, and more prompt in action. Ere, as it would seem, the rest had entered the sepulchre and commenced their search, Mary Magdalene was already on her way to Jerusalem[2]. She who owed to Him that died

[a] xxiv. 3

[b] ver. 4

---

[1] Some little difficulty has been felt in the clause ἦν γὰρ μέγας σφόδρα (Mark xvi. 4), as it might seem rather to give a reason why the women meditated how the stone should be removed, than why they perceive that what they mused on had happened. If, however, we make the assumption in the text or some similar one as to the position of the stone, all seems clear; while the women are yet at a little distance they perceive that the stone is not in its place, it being of large size, and its changed position readily seen. This harmonizes with the supposition that Mary Magdalene went away first, and at once: compare John xx. 1, 2, βλέπει κ.τ.λ. Τρέχει οὖν κ.τ.λ., where the οὖν must not be left unnoticed.

[2] The common supposition is that Mary ran first to the sepulchre without waiting for the rest; to this, however, there are objections arising from the fact that St Matthew specifies that there was at least another with her when she went (ch. xxviii. 1), and that St Luke implies that she acted in some degree of concert with the other women; compare Wieseler, Chron. Synops. p. 430, and see below, p. 381, note 2. The primary difficulty that St John names no other woman than Mary, must be *cut*, if not solved, by the reasonable assertion that St John was moved to notice her case particularly, and by the fair principle of Le Clerc, which so often claims our recognition in this part of the inspired narrative,—'qui

on Golgotha a freedom from a state worse than death[a], and who loved even as she had been blessed, no sooner beholds the stone removed from the doorway of her Lord's resting-place than she sees or seems to see all. She whose whole present thought was only how she might do honour to her buried Master, how best strew the spices around the holy body, how most tenderly spread the ointment on the sacred temples of the sleeping head, now at a glance perceives that others have been before her; she sees it and at once fears the worst,— her Lord's sepulchre violated, His holy body borne away to some dishonoured grave[1], or exposed to shame and indignities which it was fearful even to think of. Help and counsel must at once be sought, and that of a more effectual kind than weak women could provide. Perhaps with a few hasty words to those around[2], she runs with all speed to the Lord's most chosen followers, Peter and John[b], and in artless language, which incidentally shows that she had not been the sole visitant

[a] Lk. viii. 2

[b] Joh. xx. 2

plura narrat, pauciora complectitur; qui pauciora memorat, plura non negat.' *Harmon.* p. 525, Can. XII. fin. (cited by Robinson).

[1] See above, p. 363, note 2.

[2] This supposition, though not positively required by any of the succeeding incidents, is still hazarded, as serving to indicate how it might have happened that the women did not meet St Peter as he was coming up to the sepulchre. Knowing that one of their party had gone to him, the women possibly went off in different directions to the abodes of the other Apostles. Though they were all assembled together in the evening (Luke xxiv. 33, John xx. 19), it does not follow that they were now all occupying a common abode; comp. Griesbach, *Opusc. Acad.* Vol. II. p. 243. If further objections are worth making, it does not seem wholly improbable that St Peter might have been now in the abode that contained St John and the Virgin (John xix. 27). The psychological truth in Mary's running for help to *men* is noticed by Luthardt, *Johann. Evang.* Part II. p. 435. It is, however, quite as useful in illustrating the reason why Mary did not *remain* with those unable to help, as why (on Luthardt's hypothesis) she did not *run back* to them.

LECT. VIII.

[a Joh. xx. 2]
[b ver. 3]
[c ver. 11]

of the tomb[1], at once tells them the mournful tidings,—'they have taken away the Lord out of the sepulchre, and *we* know not where they have laid Him[a].' The two Apostles promptly attend to the message and hasten to the sepulchre[b], followed, as it would seem, by her who brought the tidings, and who, it appears from the context[c], must have arrived there not long afterwards.

The appearance of the angels to the women at the sepulchre.

[d Matt. xxviii. 8]
[e ver. 8]
[f Luke xxiv. 4]
[g Ib.]
[h Mark xvi. 5; comp. Matt. xxviii. 5]

Ere, however, the two Apostles had reached the tomb, other messengers, filled indeed with an awe and amazement that sealed their lips to every one they met[2], but filled also with a deep feeling of holy[d] joy that quickened their steps[e] to the city, were now seeking out the rest of the Eleven. Shortly after Mary Magdalene had left the other ministering women, and while as it would seem, they were standing bewildered in the tomb[f], *two*[g] or, as some of these perturbed beholders might have specified[3], *one*[h] of the heavenly host, announce

---

[1] This deduction from the plural οἴδαμεν (John xx. 2) is objected to by Meyer (*in loc.*), who urges the οἶδα (ver. 13) as fully counterbalancing the plural in the present case. This does not seem satisfactory. The first statement was made under different feelings to the second; now she had but lately left others and speaks under the natural consciousness of the fact; afterwards she feels left alone in her sorrow, and speaks accordingly; see below, p. 386, note 2.

[2] It seems unreasonable in Meyer (*on Mark* xvi. 8) and others to press the οὐδενὶ οὐδὲν εἶπον of the second Evangelist, as implying that the women did not obey the angel's command, and that it was only afterwards that they mentioned it. Surely it is reasonable on psychological grounds (to borrow a favourite mode of argument in modern writers) to think that the women would not, individually, much less collectively, disobey a command of such a kind, and uttered by such a speaker. Fear sealed their lips to chance-met passers to and fro, but joy (Matth. xxviii. 8) opened them freely enough to the Apostles.

[3] The question of the *number* of the angels present at the sepulchre possibly admits of some sort of explanation similar to those already adopted in not unlike cases (p. 189, note 2; p. 274, note 2), and founded on the assumption that *one* was the chief speaker, and that to him attention was particularly directed. It is, however, perhaps more probable

to them that the Lord is risen, and bid them with all speed[a] convey the tidings to the Apostles, and tell them that the risen Shepherd goeth before His flock[1] to Galilee[b], even as He had solemnly promised three days before, on the eve of His passion[c]. The message we know was speedily[d] delivered; the weeping[e] and desolate Apostles[2] were sought out and told the cheering tidings, but their sorrow clouded their faith; the words of the excited messengers seemed foolishness unto them, and they believed them not[f]. Saddened perhaps and grieved that they could not persuade those to whom they were sent, yet strong in a faith that was soon to receive its exceeding great reward, the women appear to have turned backward again[3] toward the one spot in the world on which their thoughts now were fixed,—their Master's tomb.

LECT. VIII.
[a] Matt. xxviii. 7
[b] ver. 7 Mark xvi. 7
[c] Matt. xxvi. 32 xxviii. 8
[e] Mark xvi. 10
[f] Luke xxiv. 11

that in the present case the difference is to be referred to the special excitement of the time, and the perturbed state of the observers (Luke xxiv. 5); comp. Stier, *Disc. of Our Lord*, Vol. VIII. p. 53 (Clark).

[1] The term προάγει (Matth. xxviii. 7, Mark xvi. 7) is rightly explained by Stier and others as indicating, not a mere precedence in reference to the time of going, but as marking the attitude of the risen Lord to His now partly-scattered flock: observe the connexion in Matth. xxvi. 31 sq. and Mark xiv. 27 sq.

[2] The graphic comment on the state of the Apostles when Mary Magdalene brought her message ἀπήγγειλεν τοῖς μετ' αὐτοῦ γενομένοις, πενθοῦσιν καὶ κλαίουσιν (Mark xvi. 10), seems justly to outweigh all the petty exceptions that have been taken by Meyer and others to some expressions in this verse (ἐκείνη, used without emphasis; πορευθεῖσα, τοῖς μετ' αὐτοῦ γενομένοις, instead of τοῖς μαθηταῖς αὐτοῦ) which are urged as foreign to St Mark's style. If the hypothesis already advanced (p. 26, note 1) be accepted, viz. that St Mark added this portion at a later period, we only here meet exactly with what we might have expected,—identity in leading characteristics, change in details of language.

[3] It seems reasonable to suppose that the women would return to the sepulchre. They left it in great precipitation (ἔφυγον, Mark xvi. 8), and would naturally go back again, if not for the lower purpose of fetching what they might have left there, yet for the higher one of gaining some further knowledge of a mystery which even Apostles refused to believe. Compare, thus far, Wieseler, *Chron. Synops.* p. 425 sq.

LECT. VIII.

The two Apostles at the tomb.

ᵃ Joh. xx. 5
ᵇ ver. 5.
ᶜ ver. 6
ᵈ ver. 7

Let us, however, turn back for a moment to Mary Magdalene and the two Apostles. They were now all three at the tomb. St John had reached it first, but with the feelings of a holy awe had not presumed to enter His Master's tombᵃ, though he had seen enoughᵇ to feel half convinced that Mary's tidings were true. St Peter follows, and with characteristic promptness enters the tombᶜ, and steadily surveys[1] its state, and the position of the grave-clothes. What his exact feelings then were we know not, though we know those of his brother Apostle who now entered into the tomb. He too saw the position of the grave-clothes, the swathing bands by themselves in one part of the tomb, the folded napkin in the otherᵈ, every sign of order and none of confusion[2], and he who had perhaps before believed that the tomb was empty, now believes what a true knowledge of the Scriptures might have taught him at first,—that the

---

[1] The verb θεωρεῖν, though frequently used by St John (above 20 times), seems in the present case (θεωρεῖ τὰ ὀθόνια κείμενα, κ.τ.λ. ch. xx. 6), as indeed commonly elsewhere, to mark the steady *contemplation* ('ipsius animi intentionem denotat quâ quis intuetur quidquam.' Tittm.) with which anything is regarded by an interested observer; ἅπαντα κατώπτευσεν ἀκριβῶς, Chrys.: see the good comments on this word in Tittmann, *Synon. Nov. Test.* p. 120 sq. The remark of Stier is perhaps not *wholly* fanciful, that the visibility of angels is dependent upon the existing wakefulness, or susceptibility of the beholding eye, and that thus the investigating Apostles did not see them, while to the rapt and longing Mary they become apparent: see *Disc. of Our Lord*, Vol. VIII. p. 58, and compare the somewhat similar, but over-confidently expressed 'canon' of Lücke, *Comment. üb. Joh.* Vol. II. p. 781 (ed. 3).

[2] The position of the grave-clothes is specially noticed as showing clearly that there had been no violation of the tomb: 'inde patebat, illum qui statum sepulchri mutaverat, quicunque tandem fuerit, nihil festinanter egisse...sed studio et cum certo consilio lintea corpori detraxisse, et concinno ordine in diversis locis reposuisse.' Lampe *in loc.* cited by Luthardt, p. 436. On the further deductions from this passage (ὅτι οὐκ ἦν σπευδόντων οὐδὲ θορυβουμένων τὸ πρᾶγμα, Chrys.), see above, p. 379, note 2.

The Forty Days.

Lord is risen[1]. Consoled, and elevated in thought and hope the two Apostles turn backward to their own home[2].

LECT. VIII.

Meanwhile Mary Magdalene had now returned to the tomb, though, as we must conclude from the context, without having again met the two Apostles, who would otherwise have cheered her with the hopes they themselves were feeling, and imparted to her some share of their own convictions. But she was now standing weeping by the tomb[a], unconsoled and inconsolable; her Lord was borne away and she knew not where He was laid; was not that cause sufficient for those bitter tears? Yet she will gaze at least into that quiet resting-place that once had contained her Lord and Saviour; she will gaze in, though she fears to enter. The fourth Evangelist has told us what she saw,— two angels[b] as in attitude of still watching over

The Lord's appearance to Mary Magdalene.

[a] Jo. xx. 11

[b] xx. 12

---

[1] The exact meaning of ἐπίστευσεν (John xx. 8) is somewhat doubtful. Are we to understand by it merely that the Apostles believed in Mary's report (' quod dixerat mulier, eum de monumento esse sublatum,' August. *in Joann.* Tractat. cxix.), or, in accordance with the usual and deeper meaning of the word, that he believed in the religious truth, viz. of the resurrection (τῇ ἀναστάσει ἐπίστευσαν, Chrys.)? Certainly, as it would seem, the latter. The ground of the belief was the position of the grave-clothes, which was inconsistent with the supposition of a removal of the body by enemies; ἀπὸ τῆς τῶν ὀθονίων συλλογῆς ἐννοοῦσι τὴν ἀνάστασιν, Cyril Alex. *in Joann.* Vol. IV. p. 1078 (ed. Aubert.). The supposed difficulty in the γὰρ of the succeeding member seems removed by the gloss adopted above in the text. St John *saw* and believed (εἶδεν καὶ ἐπίστευσεν): but had he known the Scripture he would not have required the evidence by which he had now become convinced; compare Robinson, *Biblioth.Sacr.*Vol. II. p. 174.

[2] The expression ἀπῆλθον πρὸς αὑτοὺς (John xx. 10) seems rightly paraphrased by Euthymius, ἀπῆλθον, —πρὸς τὴν ἑαυτῶν καταγωγήν; so, similarly, Luke xxiv. 12. The two disciples returned to the places or perhaps rather place (see above, p. 381, note 2) where they were abiding, to meditate upon the amazing miracle (compare Luke xxiv. 12): very soon afterwards, as we must infer from Luke xxiv. 24, they communicated it to the rest of the Apostles and the other brethren.

LECT. VIII.

ᵃ Jo. xx. 13

ᵇ ver. 13

ᶜ ver. 14

ᵈ ver. 14

Him who had but so lately lain there[1]. They ask her why she weepsᵃ. She has but one answer, the same artless words she uttered to the two Apostles, varied only by a slight change of personᵇ, that seems to tell of an utter grief and perplexity with which she feels herself now left to struggle unsustained and alone[2]. Yea, she turns awayᶜ, as it would seem, even from angelic sympathy. But she turns to see, perhaps now standing in some position in which immediate recognition was less easy[3], One whom she knew notᵈ, nay, whose very voice either she did not or could not recognize, until her slumbering consciousness is awakened by

---

[1] There seems something more than arbitrary fancy (Meyer) in the idea alluded to in the text. The attitude of the angels, thus specially mentioned by the Apostle, was so explained by some of the best early commentators (σημαίνοντες ὡς οὐκ ἂν ἠδίκησέ τις τὸ ἅγιον σῶμα, Cyril Alex. *in loc.*), and has been rightly so understood by some of the better modern interpreters: see Luthardt, *das Johann. Evang.* Part II. p. 438, Stier, *Disc. of Our Lord*, Vol. VIII. p. 58 (Clark).

[2] As has been already observed (p. 382, note 1) the present οἶδα (John xx. 13) of the solitary mourner is not to be regarded as simply synonymous with οἴδαμεν (ver. 2). Here, as the context shows, the woman is standing alone by the tomb; the Apostles have gone away; she feels herself unsupported in her grief, and she thus naturally expresses it: comp. ver. 15 where the first person is similarly continued.

[3] It is not at first sight easy to understand why Mary did not at once recognize our Lord, as we have no reason for thinking from the context that her eyes were specially holden (contrast Luke xxiv. 16), and every reason for rejecting the idea of some interpreters that the Lord's recent sufferings had left His features unrecognisable. The natural explanation would seem to be this,—that she was so absorbed in her sorrow, and so utterly without hope or expectancy of such a blessing, that she speaks to, and perhaps even generally looks at the supposed stranger without recognizing Him; compare the illustrative anecdote in Sherlock's able tract, *The Trial of Witnesses*, Vol. v. p. 195 (ed. Hughes). It may be also further remarked that if any knowledge of the exact locality had been vouchsafed to us, further explanation would probably be found in the ἐστράφη εἰς τὰ ὀπίσω, ver. 14. Into the question of clothing (comp. Stier, *Disc.* Vol. VIII. p. 63, note) it is idle and indeed presumptuous to enter. Whatsoever garb our Lord's wisdom thought fit, that did His power assume.

hearing her own name uttered, and that as we may presume to think, in accents that in a moment revealed all[1]. Amazement, hope, belief, conviction, all in their fullest measures burst, as it were, upon her soul. With the one word Rabboni[a], and, as the context leads us to think, with some gesture of overwhelming and bewildered joy, she turns round as if to satisfy herself not only by the eye and ear, but by the touch of the clasping hand, that it was indeed He Himself[2], no mere heaven-sent form, but her Teacher and Deliverer, whose feet she had been permitted to follow over the hills of Galilee[b], whose power had rescued her, and whose redeeming blood she had seen falling on the very ground nigh to which she then was standing. Yea, her outstretched hand shall assure her that it is her Lord. But it must not be: relations now are solemnly changed. That holy body is the resurrection-body of the ascending Lord; the eager touch of a mere earthly love is now more than

[a] Jo. xx. 16
[b] Luke viii. 1, 2

---

[1] It seems natural to think that besides the mere utterance of her name there was something also in the intonation that so vividly recalled the holy privileges of past intercourse and past teaching, that Mary not only at once recognizes her Lord, but by the very title with which she addresses Him shows how fully she reverts to previous relations and, as yet, to nothing higher; contrast John xx. 28, and compare Luthardt, das Johann. Evang. Part II. p. 439. The single word 'Rabboni,' if properly weighed, will be found to throw considerable light on the next verse: compare Hacket, Serm. viii. on Resurr. p. 619.

[2] The supposition of Lamy and, more recently, of Meyer that Mary Magdalene sought to convince herself of the reality of the Divine Form that stood before her is apparently reasonable and natural, but when pushed further as the sole explanation of the γὰρ of the following clause ('you need not convince yourself by touch, I am not yet a glorified spirit;' comp. Kinkel in Biblioth. Sacra, Vol. I. p. 168) seems utterly lacking and unsatisfactory. A desire to satisfy herself was probably in the mind of the speaker, but there were other feelings, half-disclosed in the Rabboni, to which the Lord's words were more especially intended to refer; compare Andrewes, Serm. xv. Vol. III. p. 30 (A.-C. L.).

LECT. VIII.

ever unbecoming and unmeet. With mysterious words full of holy dignity and majesty, yet at the same time of most tenderly implied consolation[1], the Lord bids her refrain. The time indeed will come when, under higher relations, love eager and demonstrative as that now shown to the risen, may hereafter unforbiddenly direct itself to the ascended Lord. But that time is not now...Still love devoted and true as that displayed by Mary of Magdala shall not be left unblessed[2]. To her is vouchsafed the privilege of being the first mortal preacher of the risen Lord. From her lips is it that even Apostles are to learn, not only that the resurrection is past but that the ascension is begun[a], and that

a Jo. xx. 17

---

[1] In the very difficult words, Μή μου ἅπτου· κ.τ.λ. (John xx. 17) two things seem clearly *implied:* (1) a solemn declaration of changed relations of intercourse with the risen Lord, expressed in the prohibitory μή μου ἅπτου; (2) a consolatory assurance that what is prohibited now shall (in another form) be vouchsafed hereafter. The Greek expositors are thus perfectly right when they recognize in the words the holy dignity of the risen Lord (ἀνάγει αὐτῆς τὴν διάνοιαν, ὥστε αἰδεσιμώτερον αὐτῷ προσέχειν, Chrys.), which, to use the words of Stier, 'withdraws sublimely from a too human touch,' but they fail, for the most part, in the second member, and either miss or neglect the full force of the γάρ. This must certainly be preserved, as involving a *consolatory* reason for the present prohibition (Photius), and as giving the necessary Divine fulness to these first words of the risen Saviour. The whole meaning then may be briefly expressed in the following paraphrase,—'Touch me not (with this touch of the past), for I have not yet entered into those relations in which I may truly be touched, though it will be with the equally loving but necessarily more reverent and spiritual touch of the future.' For further details, see especially the excellent and exhaustive sermon of Andrewes, *Serm.* xv. Vol. III. p. 23 sq. (A.-C.L.), Meyer, *Komment. üb. Joh.* p. 499 sq., Lücke, *ib.* Vol. II. p. 783 sq., Stier, *Disc. of Our Lord,* Vol. VIII. p. 67 sq., and Moberly, *Great Forty Days,* Disc. II. p. 81 sq.

[2] It seems right to recognize in the ἀναβαίνω (ver. 17) a reference to the ἀναβέβηκα of the preceding member, and in the δέ that sort of latent opposition (Klotz, *Devar.* Vol. II. p. 362) which seems to imply that the member it introduces involves contrasts to what precedes;—'I have not yet ascended, *but* delay not, go thy way and deliver the message, that My resurrection has really practically commenced;' see above, p. 377, note 1, and comp. Andrewes, *Serm.* Vol. III. p. 46.

He who 'is not ashamed to call them¹ brethren[a],' is now ascending to His Father and to their Father, and to His God and their God.

Probable effect produced on the Apostles by Mary's tidings.

What exact effect was produced on the minds of the Apostles by a message thus clear and circumstantial we cannot fully tell. From the second Evangelist it would certainly seem clear that no credence was given to Mary's declaration that the Lord was alive again and that her own eyes had seen Him[b]. This at any rate they did not and could not believe. They had but lately, as it would seem, heard strange tidings from the women, and they might possibly have come to the belief that a part at least of these tidings was true². But the Lord Himself no eye had seen³; nay the very

LECT. VIII.

[a] Heb. ii. 11

[b] Mk. xvi. 11

---

¹ Most commentators have rightly called attention to our Lord's present use of the term 'brethren' (John xx. 17) in reference to the Apostles, though they differ in their estimate of the exact sentiment it seems intended to convey. The most natural view seems that of Euthymius, that it was indirectly to assure the disciples that the Lord was still truly man, and still stood, in this respect, on the same relations with them as before; 'He named them brethren, as being himself a man, and their kinsman according to man's nature.' *In Joann.* xx. 17, Vol. III. p. 635 (ed. Matth.).

² The exact amount of information of what had taken place which the Apostles had up to this time received, and their present state of feeling, can only be generally surmised. All we know certainly is that they had received the first tidings of the women and regarded them as 'idle tales' (Luke xxiv. 11).

It is indeed possible that previous to the arrival of Mary Magdalene some of them might have learnt from St Peter and St John or from those to whom those Apostles might have mentioned it, 'that the body was not in the sepulchre' (comp. Luke xxiv. 23); the probable shortness of time, however, between the departure of the two Apostles and the second departure of Mary, and the improbability of the supposition that the disciples were already all assembled together (see above, p. 381, note 2), render it natural to think that not much more could be generally known than had been communicated by the first women.

³ Even if we adopt the supposition alluded to in the preceding note, and conceive the results of the visit of St Peter and St John to have been now known to the rest of the Apostles, it still seems clear that any account of an actual visible appearance of our Lord would have

LECT. VIII.

removal of the body, which might have been admitted and believed in, served perhaps only to confirm the vague feeling that now all trace was for ever lost, that the angels of which the women had spoken, had borne away the holy body to some sepulchre unknown as that of Moses[a]; and that the dream of any earthly union was more than ever impossible and unimaginable. The vision of angels[b] they perhaps had now begun partially to believe in[1], but that their Lord had been seen by the excited woman that now stood before them, that He had spoken with her, and made her the bearer of a message, was a dream and an hallucination too wild to deserve even a moment's attention.

[a] Deut. xxxiv. 6
[b] Comp. Luke xxiv. 23

The Lord's appearance to the other ministering women.

But they were soon to receive yet further and fuller testimony. Hitherto those that had come to them could speak only from the seeing of the eye; others were now to come who could plead the evidence of another sense, and could tell not only of what their eyes had seen but their 'hands handled.' Very shortly perhaps after Mary Magdalene had left the Apostles[2], the other ministering women,

---

been regarded little less incredible than before. The two travellers to Emmaus, though probably starting at a time (see below) when more would have been known, speak of the confirmation which the report of the women had received, but add the melancholy conviction of the disciples generally,— αὐτὸν δὲ οὐκ εἶδον, Luke xxiv. 24.

[1] After the intelligence brought by Mary Magdalene the Apostles might have been led to believe that the tomb really was empty, and further that marvellous things had been seen (compare Luke xxiv. 23), but more than this it seems certain was not believed by any except by St John. On the slowness of the Apostles to believe, see Stier, *Disc. of Our Lord*, Vol. VIII. p. 96. The reasons why women were the first bearers of the tidings of the Resurrection are alluded to by Augustine, *Serm.* XLV. Vol. V. p. 266, *Serm.* CCXXXII. ib. p. 1108 (ed. Migne).

[2] It would seem probable that the women returned with the account of having seen the Lord, not long after Mary Magdalene had left the Apostles. We have, however, no data for fixing, even roughly, the

who had brought the first tidings to the Apostles, are permitted to meet their Lord face to face, yea and to clasp the holy feet[a] before which they had at once fallen in trembling and believing adoration. They saw, they believed, they touched, and they worshipped[1]. More we know not; where they were or under what circumstances they thus beheld the Lord must remain only a matter of the merest conjecture[2]. If we adopt the Received Text we may seem to have some grounds for thinking that this appearance was vouchsafed to the women soon after leaving the sepulchre, but as

LECT. VIII.

[a] Matt. xxviii. 9

probable time, the very fact of such a return being in itself in some degree debateable; see below, p. 392, note 1. It may indeed be urged, that if the disciples had received thus early this double testimony the travellers to Emmaus would have alluded to such an appearance (comp. Luke xxiv. 22); but to this it may be replied that throughout the tidings brought by the *women* seem to have been viewed with distrust; the speakers rather appeal to what the Apostles had seen and *verified*, and to them the Lord had certainly not yet appeared.

[1] The conduct of the women when our Lord thus vouchsafed to appear to them is noticeable and instructive. It is specially recorded by St Matthew (ch. xxviii. 9) that they 'held Him by the feet,' and 'worshipped Him' (προσεκύνησαν αὐτόν). They at once recognize Him with holy awe (ver. 9) not merely as their Teacher (contrast John xx. 16) but as their risen Lord, and instinctively pay Him an adoration, which, as Bengel has rightly observed, was but rarely evinced towards our Lord by His immediate followers previous to His Passion: 'Jesum ante passionem alii potius alieniores adorarunt quam discipuli.' *In Matth.* xxviii. 9. The exact feeling which led to their embracing the Lord's feet has been differently estimated; the act *may* have been from a desire to convince themselves that it was He (Chrysost. *in loc.*), or from joy at again beholding Him they had thought lost to them (De Wette), but from the context (comp. ver. 10) seems more naturally to have been from a reverential love (ἐκ πόθου καὶ τιμῆς, Euthym.) that evinced itself in *supplicating* adoration; compare Bp Hacket, *Serm. viii. on Resurr.* p. 618 (Lond. 1675).

[2] We have nothing from which to infer where or when our Lord appeared to the women. If we adopt what seems the true reading in ver. 9 (see the following note), there seems nothing unreasonable in the conjecture that, after the delivery of the first tidings to the Apostles, they directed their steps back again to the sepulchre (see above, p. 383, note 3), and that it was on their way there that the Lord vouchsafed to appear to them.

LECT. VIII.

the text which favours such an opinion has been justly regarded extremely doubtful¹, and as such a supposition scarcely admits of any reasonable reconciliation with the distinct statement of the second Evangelist that Mary Magdalene was the first mortal to whom the risen Lord vouchsafed to show Himself ᵃ, we shall perhaps be right in conceiving that the appearance was subsequent to the first communication which the women made to the Apostles, and most undoubtedly subsequent to the appearance to Mary Magdalene². It might thus seem designed not only to add confirmation to the statements which had been made by Mary, but again to convey a special and singular command relative to the Lord's appearance in Galilee³

ᵃ Mark xvi. 9

---

¹ If we adopt the Received Text in Matth. xxviii. 9, ὡς δὲ ἐπορεύοντο ἀπαγγεῖλαι τοῖς μαθηταῖς αὐτοῦ, we have no alternative but to suppose that the appearance of our Lord took place when the women were *first* on their way to the Apostles. As, however, the above words are rejected by Lachmann, Tischendorf and Tregelles on what seems sufficient evidence (see Tisch. *in loc.* Vol. I. p. 164), and have strongly the appearance of an explanatory gloss, we are in no way necessitated by the context to refer the incident to the first journey. No valid objection to this can be urged from the πορευομένων δὲ αὐτῶν of ver. 11; the Apostle having related *all* connected with the women, reverts to the terrified guard (ver. 4) and to the further circumstances connected with them; to this fresh paragraph he suitably prefixes a note of time.

² Independently of the very distinct statement of Mark xvi. 9, ἐφάνη πρῶτον Μαρίᾳ τῇ Μαγδαληνῇ (opp. to Robinson, *Bibl. Sacra*, Vol. II. p. 178), it seems impossible, on sound principles of interpretation, to maintain with Wieseler (*Chron. Synops.* p. 426) and others, that the appearance recorded in John xx. 14 sq. is identical with that to the other women: every circumstance is not only different but contrasted; see Stier, *Disc. of Our Lord*, Vol. VIII. p. 91 (Clark), and comp. Andrewes, *Serm.* IV. Vol. II. p. 238 (A.-C. L.), Hacket, *Serm. viii. on Resurr.* p. 616 (Lond. 1675), both of whom rightly consider the appearance to Mary distinct from that to the women.

³ The repetition from our Lord's own lips of the direction which had so recently been given by the angels (Matth. xxviii. 7, Mark xvi. 7) that the disciples were to depart into Galilee, accompanied with the reiterated promise that there they should see Him (Matth. xxviii. 10), seems clearly to invest the appearance specified by St Matthew (ver. 16 sq.) as having taken place in that country with

which had been first alluded to by the angels, and appears to have been directed, and indeed understood[a] to have been directed to all the company of believers then abiding in Jerusalem.

[a] Luke xxiv. 9

But the Apostles were to receive yet a third and more convincing testimony that their Lord had risen, and had been seen, yea and spoken with by those who had known him in the flesh. Meet indeed was it that the holy Eleven should now learn to believe. Were they to be the last to welcome back their risen Saviour? Were their hearts to be duller even than that of the Lord's worst and most cruel enemies? Already we know that these things had reached the ears of the Sanhedrin[b], and that the tidings brought by the terrified soldiers had caused them deliberately to fabricate a lie for these bribed watchers to repeat[1], lest the fact of the supernatural disappearance of the body should be publicly known, and the multitude should believe what their very lie showed they themselves were in a great measure forced to

The appearance of our Lord to the two disciples journeying to Emmaus.

[b] Matt. xxviii. 11

---

great importance and significance. The very distinct and consoling κἀκεῖ με ὄψονται (ver. 10), when coupled with the remembrance that it is simply certain that on the present day (John xx. 19) our Lord appeared to the Eleven and those with them in Jerusalem, seems clearly to predispose us to believe that the appearance in Galilee was to the Church at large, and thus was identical with the appearance specified, 1 Cor. xv. 6. See, however, the further remarks, p. 411, note 1.

[1] The studious way in which this lie was propagated is alluded to by Justin Martyr (*Trypho*, cap. 108, comp. capp. 17, 117), who taxes the Jewish rulers with having sent out 'chosen men over the whole world' for this special purpose; compare also Tertullian, *adv. Marc.* III. 23. The missionary efforts of the Jews against the Christians are mentioned by Eusebius (*in Jes.* xviii. 1) in a valuable passage cited both by Thirlby and Otto in their notes on Just. M. *Trypho*, cap. 17; compare Tertull. *ad Nat.* I. 14, *adv. Judæos*, cap. 13. Some good comments on the incident of the bribery of the guards, and on the fact that it is especially related by St Matthew, will be found in Sherlock, *Trial of Witnesses*, Vol. v. p. 182, and in *Sequel of Trial*, ib. p. 274.

LECT. VIII.

admit. Were Romans to testify, and Jews to accept, and Christians still to doubt? Friends, it seemed, required fuller confirmation than enemies, and fuller confirmation was it mercifully appointed that they were yet to receive. Ere the day closed two of the Lord's followers, but neither, as it would seem, of the number of the Eleven[1], were to be the bearers of the third testimony to the still perplexed and doubting Apostles[a]......On the particulars of that interesting journey to Emmaus[2] it will not be necessary to dwell, as all is so clear and simple, and so completely free from those difficulties of adjustment with which we have

[a] Comp. Mk. xvi. 13

---

[1] Who the two disciples were has been much debated. The popular view that Cleopas was identical with Clopas or Alphæus (comp. p. 98, note), and the further not unnatural supposition that his companion was James his son are open to this etymological objection that Κλεόπας appears *not* to be identical with Κλωπᾶς, but to be a shortened form of Κλεόπατρος, like 'Αντίπας (Rev. ii. 13) aud similar forms; see Winer, *Gr.* § 16. 4. 1, p. 93. If this be so, the slight probability that the second of the two was James is proportionately weakened, and the appeal to 1 Cor. xv. 7 less plausible. We are thus thrown wholly upon conjecture. This, in its most ancient form, appears to regard the unnamed disciple as Simon (Origen, *Comment. in Joann.* 1. 7, Vol. IV. p. 8, ed. Bened.), and both as of the number of the seventy disciples; 'And you must know that these two belonged to the number of the seventy, and that Cleopas's companion was Simon,—not Peter, nor he of Cana,—but another of the seventy.' Cyril Alex. *Comment on St Luke*, Part II. p. 726 (Transl.).

[2] The site of Emmaus is somewhat doubtful. In ancient times it appears to have been identified with Nicopolis on the border of the plain of Philistia, but erroneously, as the distance of this latter place from Jerusalem (about 22 Roman miles) cannot possibly be reconciled with the distance specified by the Evangelist; see next note. In later times it has been identified with the village of el-Kubeibeh about 2½ hours N. W. of Jerusalem (Van de Velde, *Memoir to Map*, p. 309), but for this there appears no reasonable grounds of any kind. Either then with Porter (Smith, *Dict.* s. v. Vol. I. p. 548) we must consider the site yet to be identified, or we must accept the tradition of the Greek church which places it at Kuriet el-'Enab (Abu Gûsh). In defence of this latter opinion, see some good remarks of Williams, *Journal of Philology*, Vol. IV. p. 262 sq. Emmaus has more recently been identified with Kolonieh, a place 60 stades W.S.W. of Jerusalem; see esp. Caspari, *Chron.-Geogr. Einleit.* § 191, p. 207.

hitherto had to contend. We may, however, pause to remark that the *time* when the incident took place is generally defined by St Luke as having formed part of the same day^a on which our Lord rose from the grave. As we know that it was not yet evening^b when the two disciples turned backward to Jerusalem, and as we are also specially informed by the Evangelist of the distance¹ of Emmaus from the city^c, we may perhaps reasonably suppose that they started some little time before mid-day, and so very probably might have heard of the later announcements made to the Apostles by Mary Magdalene and the other ministering women. 'Him they saw not^d' seems however to be the pathetic burden of their discourse and their communings², and forms as it were the sad summary of that want of faith which the Lord was pleased so mercifully and so effectually to rebuke by the deliberate statement and exposition³

^a Mk. xxiv. 13

^b ver. 29; comp. ver. 33

^c ver. 13

^d ver. 24

---

¹ A few manuscripts (I¹ K¹ N; 5 cursive MSS.) and a few versions read ἑκατὸν ἑξήκοντα for ἑξήκοντα in Luke xxiv. 13, making the distance of Emmaus 160 instead of 60 stadia from Jerusalem. This reading has been supported by Robinson (*Palestine*, Vol. III. p. 150, ed. 2) as tending to favour his identification of Emmaus with 'Amwas (the ancient Nicopolis), but is rightly rejected by all modern editors. The statement of Josephus (*Bell. Jud.* VII. 6. 6) that there was a place of this name 60 stadia (so all the best MSS.) from Jerusalem, and the other arguments urged by Reland against the identification with Nicopolis have justly been considered satisfactory and final. See *Palæstina*, p. 426 sq.

² It is doubtful how much information the two travellers to Emmaus had received in reference to our Lord's resurrection. It might possibly be concluded from Luke xxiv. 23, 24, that they had not heard of the tidings brought by Mary Magdalene and the women relative to the Lord's appearances, but this, owing to the time at which they appear to have started, is not likely. It has been observed by a kind correspondent (Sir J. Coleridge) that the αὐτὸν δὲ οὐκ εἶδον really seems to imply a knowledge on the part of the disciples that the *women* had affirmed that they *had* seen Him; see p. 390, note 2.

³ There is some little difficulty in the explanation of the words καὶ ἀρξάμενος ἀπὸ Μωϋσέως κ.τ.λ. Luke xxiv. 27. The simplest interpreta-

LECT. VIII.

^a Luke xxiv. 27

Inability of the disciples to recognize our Lord.

^b ver. 32

^c ver. 16

of all the passages of the prophetic Scriptures that related to Himself[a] and had foretold His approaching glorification.

One other remark we may make on the apparently singular fact that the two disciples were not able to recognize our Lord till the very moment of His departure,—that they not only beheld Him, and heard His words, but felt their hearts kindle as they listened to His teaching[b], and yet never surmised even who it was that spake with them. Singular indeed such a fact does seem if we are to reason merely from what we know or think we may know of that which constitutes personal identity[1],—but in no wise singular if we will dismiss our philosophy and our speculations, and accept only what is told us by one and confirmed by another Evangelist. Plainly are we told by St Luke that the eyes of the two disciples were holden[c], that by Divine interposition[2] they were prevented from recognizing their

---

tion is either to regard the καὶ ἀρξάμενος as belonging to both parts ('beginning with Moses, and with each of the prophets as he came to them,' Meyer, Alford), or, still more simply, to consider the second ἀπὸ as a continuation and echo of the first, which necessarily turns the substantive it precedes into the genitive, and involves a slight laxity in the mode of expression, the meaning really being,—'He began with Moses, and went through all the prophets;' see Winer, *Gram.* § 67. 2. p. 557 (ed. 6).

[1] Into such considerations it seems here wholly undesirable to enter, as in ordinary cases they involve much that is debateable, and in the present much that is presumptuous. All that we are concerned to know and believe may be very simply stated. On the one hand we have before us in this portion of the Gospel history the certain fact that our Lord's body was the *same* body as that which was laid in the tomb (Luke xxiv. 39, John xx. 20), and on the other the certain fact that His form sometimes appeared to be so far *different* from it (Mark xvi. 12) as not to be recognized. The reconciliation of these two statements may be difficult, owing to our ignorance of the exact nature of the Lord's resurrection-body, but the facts no less remain.

[2] The meaning of the words οἱ ὀφθαλμοὶ αὐτῶν ἐκρατοῦντο (Luke

Lord till He was pleased to reveal Himself. Plainly too is this confirmed by St Mark who, in declaring that our Lord appeared to these disciples in a 'different form^a,' intimates with all clearness that our Lord was pleased to exercise one of the powers which had in part belonged to His former body[1] and *perhaps* wholly and naturally belonged to His resurrection-body, whereby the characterizing expression of His most holy form could be weakened or withdrawn until the power of recognition on the part of the natural beholder was completely lost[2]. What the third Evangelist expresses in one form of words, the second Evangelist expresses in another, both however asserting the same simple truth,—that the Lord was pleased to

* xvi. 12

xxiv. 16) is simply, as expressed by the Authorized Version, 'their eyes were holden' ('tenebantur,' Vulg.; 'detenti erant,' Syr.),—their eyes were prevented from exerting their full power of recognition; compare Kypke, *Obs. Sacr.* Vol. I. p. 338. The agency by which this was effected is not specified, but obviously was Divine. The *seeming* discrepancy between this passage and Mark xvi. 12, is thus excellently discussed by Augustine; "Cum legitur 'tenebantur oculi eorum ne agnoscerent cum' (Luc. xxiv. 16), impedimentum quoddam agnoscendi videtur in luminibus factum esse cernentium: cum vero aperte dicitur, 'Apparuit eis in alia effigie' (Marc. xvi. 12), utique in ipso corpore cujus alia erat effigies, aliquid factum fuisse, quo impedimento tenerentur, id est moram agnoscendi paterentur oculi eorum." *Epist.* CXLIX. 31, Vol. II. p. 643 (ed. Migne).

[1] Independently of any special exercise of our Lord's Divine power, it would seem from the fact of the Transfiguration that His pure and perfect humanity admitted of revelations of concealed glory which involved positive changes of appearance (Luke ix. 29), and yet in no way interfered with the reality of His earthly body; see Augustine, *Epist.* CXLIX. 31, Vol. II. p. 643 (ed. Migne), and Müller, *Christian Doctr. of Sin*, Vol. II. p. 329 (Clark).

[2] A few comments on this subject will be found in Stier, *Disc. of Our Lord*, Vol. VIII. p. 101 sq. (Clark), comp. also Ebrard, *Kritik der Evang. Gesch.* § III. p. 588. The explanation indirectly suggested by Sherlock, *Trial of the Witnesses*, Vol. V. p. 195 (ed. Hughes), that the want of recognition on the part of the two disciples was owing partly to the persuasion they were under that their Lord was dead, and partly to their position,—walking side by side, is neither in itself plausible, nor reconcileable with the clear statement of Mark xvi. 12.

exercise a power, whether belonging to Him in respect of His Divine nature, or of His most sinless, pure, and now glorified[1] humanity, we know not, nor need we pause to inquire, but by which, whensoever it seemed good to our Lord's Divine wisdom, the holy body suddenly ceased to be seen, or appeared without those lineaments that were necessary for recognition.

Appearance to the ten Apostles.
[a] Comp. Joh. xx. 19
[b] Luke xxiv. 33
[c] Luke xxiv. 34

But let us return to the narrative. It was late evening[a] before the two disciples returned to Jerusalem and appeared before the Apostles, who now with other members[b] of the infant Church[2] were assembled together, and on whom some recent appearance of our Lord to St Peter[c] had

---

[1] The term 'now glorified' is here only used in a general and popular sense, and not to be understood as denying that there was any further glorification of the body after the Resurrection. Upon such subjects it is not either very safe or very desirable to speculate too freely; it may, however, be added that the opinion of some of the sounder expositors of recent times,—that during the mysterious period of the forty days the glorification of the Lord's holy body was progressive,— is, if not distinctly confirmed by the sacred narrative (consider however ἀναβαίνω, John xx. 17), still by no means inconsistent with it, and deserves perhaps some slight consideration; see Stier, *Disc. of Our Lord*, Vol. VIII. p. 89, Müller, *Doctr. of Sin*, Vol. II. p. 328 (Clark), and comp. below, p. 408, note 3.

[2] The language of St Luke, εὗρον ἠθροισμένους τοὺς ἕνδεκα καὶ τοὺς σὺν αὐτοῖς, ch. xxiv. 33, leads us to conclude that others besides the Apostles were present at the appearance of our Lord which we are now considering. Whether, however, all, or whether only the ten Apostles received the first-fruits of the Holy Spirit (John xx. 22) cannot positively be decided, as St John only uses the general term μαθηταί. Analogy might seem to suggest that as others beside the Apostles (consider Acts ii. 1, 4) appear to have received the miraculous gift of the Spirit on the day of Pentecost, so it might have been now; the power of binding and loosing, however, which seems to have been specially conveyed in this gift of the Spirit (see Chrysost. *in loc.*), more naturally directs our thoughts solely to the Apostles, and leads us to think that they were on this occasion the only recipients: the ἀπαρχή of the Spirit is received by the ἀπαρχή of the Church. So Andrewes, who, in his sermon on this text, defines 'the parties to whom' as the Apostles; *Serm.* IX. Vol. III. p. 263 (A.-C. L.).

made apparently so great an impression[1], that they at once greet the new comers with the joyful tidings,—that 'the Lord had risen indeed, and appeared unto Simon[a].' And now they too in their turn have a testimony to render to the assembled disciples more full and explicit than any that had yet been delivered that eventful day. They have seen the Lord, they have journeyed with Him, they have conversed with Him, they have been instructed by Him, they have sat down with Him to an evening meal[2], they have received

[a] Luke xxiv. 34

---

[1] Of the appearance of our Lord to St Peter incidentally mentioned by St Luke, and further confirmed by 1 Cor. xv. 5, we know nothing. It certainly occurred after the return from the sepulchre (Luke xxiv. 12, John xx. 10), but whether *before* the appearance to the two disciples on their way to Emmaus (Lange, *Leben Jesu*, II. 8, 3, Part III. p. 1691) or *after* it, as conjectured by Cyril Alex. (*Comment on St Luke*, Part II. p. 728, note), cannot be determined. The effect, however, produced by it was clearly very great. The words of the disciples now show plainly their conviction of the truth of the Lord's resurrection ($\dot{\eta}\gamma\acute{\epsilon}\rho\theta\eta$ ὁ Κύριος ὄντως, ver. 34), and the very construction adopted by the Evangelist implies how eager they were in expressing it,—εὗρον ἠθροισμένους τοὺς ἕνδεκα καὶ τοὺς σὺν αὐτοῖς λέγοντας κ.τ.λ. ver. 34. They gave but little credence to the accounts of the women, but in the report of one of their own number, and that one St Peter, they very naturally put the fullest confidence: see above, p. 390, note 2.

[2] It does not appear from the inspired narrative that our Lord actually shared with them their evening meal. The words, καὶ ἐγένετο ἐν τῷ κατακλιθῆναι κ.τ.λ. (ver. 30), seem rather to imply that the Lord vouchsafed to sit down with the two disciples, and took the position, gladly offered, of master of the house, but after that He had pronounced the customary blessing (*Mishna*, 'Berachoth,' VI. 6;—the citation in Lightfoot, reproduced by most expositors, 'Tres viri qui simul comedunt tenentur ad gratias indicendum' [cap. VII. 1] appears to refer to grace *after* meat), and had broken the bread and given it to the two disciples, He permitted Himself to be recognized, and then vanished from their eyes. The act by which the Lord was pleased to awaken their powers of recognition was 'the breaking of the bread' (ἐν τῇ κλάσει τοῦ ἄρτου, ver. 35; on this force of ἐν, see notes *on* 1 *Thess.* iv. 18); but how, whether by allowing them to see the wounds on His sacred hands, or (more probably) by some solemn and well-remembered gesture, we can only conjecture. The opinion of many of the early writers that

bread from His sacred hands,—and at the very moment when recognition was permitted, they have seen Him vanish from their longing eyes. To such a testimony we marvel not to find it recorded that full belief even now was not extended. Events so circumstantial and so minutely specified seemed perhaps less to confirm than to bewilder. They might at length have been led to admit the already thrice-repeated statement that the Lord had been seen, that His sacred form had passed before the eyes of Peter, that it had even been seen by Mary Magdalene, and even further that it had been touched or thought to have been touched by the other women;—this they might at length have been disposed either wholly or in part to believe, but the present narrative seemed to involve ideas of a bodily form and substance which their subsequent fears[a] and our Lord's gentle reproof[b] showed they regarded as inconceivable and incredible[1]. We have no need then to explain away the accurate statement of the second Evangelist that they believed not[c] the strange recital of the wayfarers to Emmaus[2].

[a] Luke xxiv. 37
[b] ver. 38
[c] xvi. 13

this was a celebration of the Eucharist, seems inconsistent with the specification of time (ἐν τῷ κατακλ.) and the general circumstances of the present supper.

[1] In spite of the joyful avowal of their belief that the Lord had risen, the disciples, as the inspired narrative plainly specifies, are greatly terrified (Luke xxiv. 37) when the Lord actually appears. This was not in itself wholly unnatural, but seems to have been increased by the belief that they were beholding a spirit (ἐδόκουν πνεῦμα θεωρεῖν),—a persuasion against which our Lord's subsequent words are specially directed. This in some measure prepares us for the statement in Mark xvi. 13: see the following note.

[2] There is confessedly at first sight some difficulty in reconciling the joyful greeting of the Apostles and their spontaneous announcement of the appearance to Simon (Luke xxiv. 34) with the incredulity with which St Mark (ch. xvi. 13) tells us they received the account of the two disciples from Emmaus. It is possible that the οὐδὲ ἐκείνοις ἐπίστευ-

But lo! a yet fuller testimony was now to be vouchsafed. Even while they were considering and discussing these things, and now perhaps putting questions in every form to the two latest witnesses, the Lord Himself appears among them, and with words of holy and benedictory greeting shows unto them both His hands and His side[a]. At first, as we learn from St Luke's narrative, they were above measure perturbed and terrified; they well knew that the doors were closed, and yet they plainly beheld their Lord standing before them[1]; they knew not what to think; they conceive it must be His bodiless spirit that they are now beholding, and the flesh quailed. Though partially reassured by the sight of the wounds[b], and by the condescending love which permitted them to touch the holy body that stood before them[c], they even then could not fully be-

[a] Jo. xx. 20
[b] Luke xxiv. 39
Joh. xx. 20
[c] Luke xxiv. 39

σαν (ver. 13) may refer, not to the Apostles but to some of the others (τοῖς λοιποῖς) to whom they related it (see August. *de Consens. Evang.* III. 25), but it seems more reasonable to suppose, as in the text, that the want of belief is to be accounted for by the strangely circumstantial nature of the narrative of the two disciples, the contrasts it presented to two of the other appearances and perhaps also to the third, and also further, its seeming incompatibility with what they might have conceived to be their Master's present state. He, whose feet suppliant and adoring women deemed they clasped, seemed widely different from the humble wayfarer to Emmaus.

[1] The special notice τῶν θυρῶν κεκλεισμένων (John xx. 19), repeated ver. 26, and in the latter case without any repetition of the reason, seems to point to the mode of the Lord's entry (ἄθροον ἔστη μέσος, Chrysost.) as involving something marvellous and supernatural. How this took place we are wholly unable to explain, but the conjecture may be hazarded that it was not so much specially miraculous, as due to the very nature and properties of the body of the risen Lord: compare p. 396 sq. The attempts to show that this might have been merely a natural entry (Robinson, *Bibl. Sacra*, Vol. II. p. 182, comp. Sherlock, *Trial of Witn.* Vol. v. p. 196) do not seem successful: the ἔστη εἰς τὸ μέσον of St John appears correlative to the ἄφαντος ἐγένετο of St Luke (ch. xxiv. 31); if the latter be supernatural, so certainly would seem the former.

E. H. L.

LECT. VIII.

ᵃ Luke xxiv. 41

ᵇ Mk. v. 43

ᶜ Luke xxiv. 42

ᵈ ver. 43

ᵉ Joh. xx. 22

lieveᵃ. But that lacking belief now no longer arose from a dull or faithless heart, but from a bewildering joy[1]; it was to be excused, yea, it was so far to be borne with, that a special sign which on another occasionᵇ had probably been used in a similar way to bring final conviction was yet to be vouchsafed to the overjoyed but amazed beholders. The fish and the honey-combᶜ were taken by Him who, as Augustine has well said, had 'the power though not the need of eating[2];' they were taken in the presence of allᵈ; the Lord was pleased to eat thereof, and then, as we may infer from the context, the Apostles and assembled followers believed with all the fulness of a fervent, lasting, and enduring faith. Then at length the first-fruits of the effusion of the Holy Spirit were conveyed by an outward sign and mediumᵉ, and the mysterious power of binding and loosing was conferred upon the inspired and anew accredited Apostles[3].

---

[1] See Luke xxiv. 41, ἀπιστούντων αὐτῶν ἀπὸ τῆς χαρᾶς. With this the ἐχάρησαν ἰδόντες τὸν Κύριον of St John (ch. xx. 20) seems exactly to harmonize. Joy is the pervading feeling, so great and so overwhelming, that they can hardly believe the evidence of their very eyes and ears. Both Chrysostom and Cyril of Alexandria here refer to John xvi. 22 as now notably fulfilled.

[2] This appears to have been a favourite comment of Augustine, and is as reasonable as it is pertinently expressed: 'Fecit cum discipulis quadraginta dies, intrans et exiens, manducans et bibens, *non egestate sed potestate*; manducans et bibens, non esuriendo nec sitiendo, sed docendo et monstrando.' *Serm.* CCCXLVIII. 2, Vol. V. p. 1360. See also *Serm.* CXVI. 3, Vol. V. p. 659, *in Joann.* Tractat. LXIV. 1, Vol. III. p. 1806, an interesting passage in the *Civit. Dei*, XIII. 22, Vol. VII. p. 395, and some good remarks in Cyril Alex. *Commentary on St Luke*, Part II. p. 730 (Transl.).

[3] The mysterious power now given to the Apostles was an essential adjunct to their office as the ambassadors of Christ and, more especially, as the rulers of His Church; 'potestas ista...primitus Apostolis ut ecclesiæ magistris et rectoribus demandata est.' Barrow, *de Potest. Clav.* Vol. VIII. p. 113. It had reference, as Meyer rightly observes,

But one there yet was of the number of the holy Eleven who had not beheld with his own eyes and who could not and would not believe even the overwhelming testimony of the assembled believers. Seven days was he to remain in his unbelief. While his brother Apostles were now the probably conscious recipients of the eternal Spirit[1], the unconvinced Thomas was yet seeking for outward and material evidences[a], without which he had avowed that he could not believe. And even these were vouchsafed to the now isolated Apostle. We read in the inspired narrative of the fourth Evangelist[b], how on the day which the Lord's renewed appearance thereon had now begun to stamp with a special sanctity[2], our Lord appears

LECT. VIII.

Disbelief of Thomas: our Lord's appearance to the Eleven Apostles.

[a] Joh. xx. 25

[b] ver. 26

---

not merely to the general power of receiving into the Church or the contrary, but to their disciplinary power over individual members of it, both in respect of the retaining and the absolving of sins. On the subject generally, see Andrewes, *Serm.* Vol. v. p. 82 (A.-C. Libr.), Barrow, *de Potest. Clavium*, Vol. VIII. p. 84 sq. (Oxf. 1830), Bingham, *Works*, Vol. VIII. p. 357 sq. (Lond. 1844), and comp. Marshall, *Penit. Disc.* I. 2, p. 10 sq. (A.-C. L.), Thorndike, *Princ. of Chr. Truth*, I. 9, Vol. II. p. 157 (A.-C. L.), and the excellent comments of Moberly, *Great Forty Days*, Disc. III. p. 124 sq.

[1] It seems right and reasonable to suppose that the Apostles now felt themselves endued with that gift of the Holy Ghost which they had received from their Lord, though as yet they could have had no power of exercising it. That this was a real ἀπαρχή of *the* Holy Ghost is rightly maintained by all the best expositors; the gift was not general like that at the Pentecost, but special and peculiar (ἐπήγαγεν Ὃν ἂν ἀφῆτε κ.τ.λ. δεικνὺς ποῖον εἶδος ἐνεργείας δίδωσιν, Chrysost.), yet no less veritably a gift of the Spirit. Luthardt (*Johann. Evang.* Part II. p. 449) presses the absence of the article, and urges that it was only a spirit of the new life as coming from the risen, but not ascended Lord: for such a distinction, however, there is no sound grammatical foundation (see notes on *Gal.* v. 5), and apparently no evidence deducible from the language of the N. T.

[2] It does not seem wholly improbable that we have here the very commencement, as it were, of the celebration of the Lord's-day, and the earliest indication of that observance of the first day of the week which the Lord's resurrection had naturally evoked, and to which His present appearance gave additional sanction and validity; see Cyril Alex.

LECT. VIII.

^aJoh.xx.27

^b ver. 28

Our Lord's appearance by the lake of Tiberias.

in the same supernatural manner[1]; we mark with adoring wonder how the personal test which the doubting Apostle had required, was now vouchsafed to him^a, and it is with thankful joy that we hear that outburst of inspired conviction that now recognizes in the risen Jesus, yea in Him whose very wounds the privileged Apostle was permitted to touch, not so much the humanity as the Divinity[2];—'and Thomas answered and said unto Him, My Lord, and my God^b.'

Some time afterwards, how long we know not, followed the Lord's manifestation of Himself by

---

in *Joann.* xx. 26, Vol. IV. p. 1104, and compare *Huls. Essay* for 1843, p. 74. The fair statement of the whole contested subject would seem to be as follows,—that the dedication of one day of the week to the special service of God is binding on us by His primeval law, but that the special selection of the *first* day rests on Apostolical, and, as the present case seems to suggest, indirectly Divine appointment; compare also Abp Bramhall, *Lord's Day*, Vol. V. p. 32 sq. (A. C. L.).

[1] That our Lord's appearance was supernatural, again rests on the special notice of the fact of the closed doors; see above, p. 401, note 1. The peculiar terms (here ἔρχεται καὶ ἔστη, ver. 26, comp. ver. 19), which seem designedly used by the Evangelists in describing our Lord's appearances, are noticed by Stier, *Disc. of Our Lord*, Vol. VIII. p. 99 (Clark). Where this manifestation took place is not perfectly certain. Caspari deems it to have been in Galilee (see *Chron.-Geogr. Einleit.* § 193); the language of St John seems, however, rather to point to the same place as that of the manifestation a week before.

[2] The declaration of St Thomas has often and with justice been urged by writers upon our Lord's Divinity, but the exact circumstances under which it was made, and which add so much to its force, have not always been sufficiently considered. Let it then be observed that it is at the very time when our Lord is being graciously pleased to convince His doubting follower of the reality of His sacred body, in fact of His perfect *humanity*, that the Apostle so preeminently recognizes his Lord's *Divinity*. With his hands on the sacred wounds, with evidence the most distinct that He whom he was thus permitted to touch was *man*, the convinced disciple in terms the most explicit declares Him to be *God*. Some good comments on this text will be found in Cyril Alex. *in Joann.* xx. 28, Vol. IV. p. 1108 (ed. Aubert.), and a collection of analogous passages in Waterland, *Serm.* vi. *on our Lord's Divinity* (*Moyer's Lect.*), Vol. II. p. 129.

the lake of Tiberias, of which we have so full and explicit account from the hand of the beloved Apostle^a. The promise of the great Shepherd that He would go before His flock into Galilee^b, and would there appear unto them, was now first most solemnly fulfilled. Seven Apostles[1] are the first witnesses, and under circumstances, which the distinct and emphatic language of the inspired narrator^c leads us to believe produced an impression almost more deep and enduring than any they had yet received[2]. Upon the details, where all is told with such Divine simplicity, and where there are no difficulties either in the language, or in the sequence of the narrative, it will not perhaps be necessary to dwell. We may pause, however, to notice that again the disciples did not recognize the Lord^d, though they were near enough to the beach to hear His voice[3]. On this occasion, however, there

^a Joh. xxi. 1 sq.
^b Matt. xxvi. 32 Mk. xiv. 28
^c Joh. xxi. 24
^d ver. 4

---

[1] It is not *perfectly* certain that the two not mentioned by name (ἄλλοι ἐκ τῶν μαθητῶν αὐτοῦ δύο, ver. 2) were Apostles, as the word μαθηταί has sometimes in St John a more inclusive sense. As, however, in verse 1 it seems used to specify the Apostles (with verse 1 compare John xx. 26, to which the πάλιν naturally refers the reader), the assumption that it is used in a similar sense in ver. 2 appears perfectly reasonable; see Lücke *in loc.* Vol. II. p. 806 (ed. 3).

[2] It is not wholly improbable that the emphatic declaration of the Apostle at the close of the narrative, in reference to the truth of his testimony (John xxi. 24), may have been occasioned by the feeling that this manifestation of our Lord was perhaps the most important that had yet been vouchsafed. It was indeed a *manifestation* (ἐφανέρωσεν· ἐκ τούτου δῆλον, ὅτι οὐχ ἑωρᾶτο εἰ μὴ συγκατέβη, Chrys.) alike convincing and consolatory. On the one hand, in the various acts He was pleased to perform (ver. 13), it most clearly set forth the reality of the Lord's risen body; and on the other it assured the Apostles of the continuance of those same miraculous powers which would have ever occupied so prominent a place in their retrospect of their Master's earthly ministry. On the importance of this revelation, see Augustine, *in Joann.* Tractat. CXXII., where it is suggested that the concluding verses of the preceding chapter might have been added,—'secuturæ narrationis quasi proœmium, quod ei quodammodo faceret eminentiorem locum.' Vol. III. p. 1959 (ed. Migne).

[3] The distance at which the boat

LECT. VIII.

seems no reason to suppose that the Lord's form was specially changed, or that it was not His Divine pleasure that He should at first be recognized. It was now, it must be remembered, early dawn[a]; the wearied men probably saw the figure somewhat indistinctly, and with the unobserving eye of those who expect nothing and indeed perceive nothing different to the usual homely incidents of their daily life[1], they answer the friendly call of the stranger, and supposing Him to be one who would fain buy of them, they tell Him in the simplest way they have nothing[b]. Even when told to cast in their net in a particular place[c], they still appear to have been in no way surprised by the order. It might be the suggestion of one experienced, or who had some reasons for his suggestion that they did not know, and did not pause to consider. They obey perhaps with the feeling of men who in their ill success[d] were ready to take any suggestion by whomsoever offered. The wonderful and miraculous draught[2], however, at

[a] Joh. xxi. 4
[b] ver. 5
[c] ver. 6
[d] ver. 3

was from the shore (about 100 yards, ver. 8) would certainly be sufficient to prevent them immediately recognizing One whom, at that particular place and time, they were in no way expecting to see, unless indeed we are to suppose that there was something in the Lord's form and general appearance *strikingly* different from that of other men. This, however, we have already seen, does not appear to have been the case: compare Lect. III. p. 87, note 2.

[1] It seems natural to think that the friendly voice, 'calling, after the manner of the East, children' (Stanley, *Palest.* p. 374), and inquiring if they had any προσφάγιον, was conceived by the disciples to be that of one who wished to buy of them, —ὡς μέλλων τι ὠνεῖσθαι παρ' αὐτῶν, Chrysost. *in loc.*; compare Cyril Alex. *in Joann.* Vol. IV. p. 1113. To this Dean Trench objects, supposing it to be merely the inquiry of that natural interest, 'not unmixed with curiosity,' which all feel in the uncertainty of the fisherman's toil (*Notes on Miracles*, p. 456). It should be remembered, however, that we are only considering how the Apostles understood the speech, and this probably is all that Chrysostom meant to imply.

[2] On this miracle,—the peculiarities of which are the similarity it

once arouses their attention. The sudden contrast with their weary and profitless night's fishing, the great number of large fish^a and the care requisite to bring them to the land, all bring back to their minds the never-forgotten miracle of the early part of the past year, when three at least of those now on the lake had received the Divine call to become fishers of men, and had forsook, as they then perhaps thought, for ever that calling^b to which they had now returned. Everything brings back the past; and he on whom the past had perhaps made the most permanent impression[1] is the first to recognize the blessedness of the present. The Apostle whom the Lord loved is the first to recognize; and yet, as we might have expected, another is the first to greet[2]. He who on that very lake,

LECT. VIII.

^a Joh. xxi. 11

^b Mt. iv. 22 Luke v. 11

---

preserves to the former miracle on the lake, and the apparently symbolical character of some of its incidents,—see the interesting, but perhaps too minutely allegorizing comments of Augustine, *in Joann.* Tractat. CXXII. Vol. III. p. 1962 sq., Stier, *Disc. of Our Lord,* Vol. VIII. p. 212 sq., Trench, *Notes on the Miracles,* p. 453 sq.

[1] We may justify this casual remark not only by what followed, but by a reference to the fact that though St John had probably received his call a year previously to the former miracle (John i. 37 sq.), and had accompanied our Lord as one of His special followers, the miraculous draught of fishes constituted the epoch when he deliberately and formally left his father, his home, and all the employments of his former life (comp. Matth. iv. 22, Mark i. 20, Luke v. 11) to become a fisher of men. St Peter, we know, was much moved at the time by the miracle and its results (Luke v. 9), but the impression produced on the mind of the younger Apostle, from the circumstances with which the miracle stood in connexion, would probably have been more lasting.

[2] The differences of nature and character, in the case of the two Apostles, which the incident discloses are thus clearly stated by Chrysostom *in loc.*: 'When they recognized the Lord,' says this able commentator, 'again do the disciples display the peculiarities of their individual characters. The one, for instance, was more ardent, but the other more elevated; the one more eager, but the other endued with finer perception. On which account John was the first to recognize the Lord, but Peter to come to Him.' *In Joann.* Hom. LXXXVII. Vol. VIII. p. 594 (ed. Bened. 2).

LECT. VIII.

ᵃ Luke v. 8
ᵇ Joh. xxi. 7

and under circumstances strikingly similar, had besought his holy Master to depart from one so sin-stainedᵃ, now casts himself into the waterᵇ, and is the first to kneel at the Divine feet.

Reverential awe of the Apostles.

One other point only requires a passing comment,—the reverential awe felt by the disciples, and its connexion with the circumstances of the morning-meal. These circumstances, we know, were strange and perplexing. The fire of coalsᶜ provided by the ministry of unseen agencies[1], the fish lying thereon, the breadᵈ,—whence came they? Enough there was in this mysterious provision which the Lord had just been pleased to make for the wants of His wearied disciples, to account for the awed silenceᵉ which we are told they preserved with regard to the exact state of His holy personality[2]. Enough was there in this alone, without our being obliged to suppose that there was any special alteration in the Lord's appearance. A change doubtless there was, as the early interpreters have rightly surmised[3], but

ᶜ ver. 9

ᵈ ver. 9

ᵉ ver. 12

---

[1] It is idle to speculate on the agencies which caused the fire of coals and the fish thereon to be found on the beach. The most reasonable and reverent supposition is that it was miraculous (Chrysost., Theophyl., al.); but as nothing is added from which any inference can be drawn we must be content to leave the statement as we find it. The attempt of Lange (*Leben Jesu*, II. 8. 6, Part III. p. 1713) to account for it in a natural way is certainly not satisfactory.

[2] Observe especially the comment of the Apostle, οὐδεὶς ἐτόλμα τῶν μαθητῶν ἐξετάσαι αὐτόν, Σὺ τίς εἶ, John xxi. 12. Here again the explanation of Chrysostom seems perfectly satisfactory: 'Seeing His form somewhat different to what it was before, and with much about it that caused astonishment, they were above measure amazed, and felt a desire to make some inquiry about it; but their apprehension, and their knowledge that it was not another, but Himself, restrained the inquiry.' *In Joann.* Vol. VIII. p. 594 sq.

[3] See the above note. The exact words of Chrysostom are τὴν μορφὴν ἀλλοιοτέραν ὁρῶντες, by which we may conclude he intended to imply —a partial change, something easy to recognize but not easy to specify: compare Luthardt, *Johann. Evang.*

it was a change probably rather felt than seen, a change that might have deepened their reverential awe, but in no way interfered with the warm feelings of holy love which two at least appear to have specially evinced both in their words and their actions[a]. The very last glimpse we are permitted to behold of this third blessed interview with the disciples, so rich in symbol and so deep in meaning,—this continuance as it were, after the weary night had passed away, of the Last Supper[1], is an incident that brings back the past and mingles it as it were with the blessed and glorious present. Again St Peter and St John appear before us in their wonted relations of warmest and most clinging love to their holy Master. We see the Lord gradually and perhaps mysteriously withdrawing[2]; we see the elder Apostle perhaps obey-

[a] Comp. ver. 19, 20

Part II. p. 468. If we admit the suggestion that has already been thrown out (p. 398, note 1), we may perhaps allow ourselves to imagine that the developing glorification of the Lord was now beginning to make a more distinct impression on the beholders.

[1] Compare Stier, *Disc. of Our Lord*, Vol. VIII. p. 226,—where, as in all sounder and deeper expositions of this portion of Scripture, the mystical and typical character of the early morning meal, as well as of the preceding miracle, is properly recognized. The details of many of these interpretations and the desirableness of the attempts to allegorize every particular, *e.g.* the number of fish (Jerome, Cyril Alex., Theoph., al.), may most fairly be called in question, but the general reference of the miracle to the future labours of the Apostles, its analogy to the previous miracle and, perhaps, the retrospective reference of this morning meal to the Lord's Supper can hardly be denied by any thoughtful expositor: see Luthardt, *Johann. Evang.* Part II. p. 466 sq., Trench, *Notes on the Miracles*, p. 459 sq., and a good note of Alford *in loc.* Vol. I. p. 861 (ed. 4).

[2] It seems probable that as our Lord uttered the words 'Follow Me' (ver. 19) He commenced withdrawing from the Apostles. Peter not fully understanding the meaning of the command obeys in a literal sense. While advancing he turns and looks round and sees the Beloved Apostle following also, upon which he puts the inquiry, οὗτος δὲ τί (*i.e.* probably, ἔσται), 'what shall his lot be?' (ver. 21). It may be observed that the true meaning of

LECT. VIII.

ᵃ Joh. xxi. 19
ᵇ ver. 22

ing literally the figurative command of his Lordᵃ, and behind him the true-hearted son of Zebedee, both following the steps of their receding Saviour; we hear the solemn and mysterious wordsᵇ in answer to the unbefitting question[1], and the holy, exalted, and most impressive scene fades away from our wondering eyes.

Appearance of the Lord to the brethren in Galilee.

ᶜ Matt. xxviii. 10

But this interview, full as it was of blessedness and consolation, was not to be the last. The Lord had promised, even on the morning of His resurrection, that He would meet His Church in that landᶜ in which it had formerly been established and consolidated. And there, as it would seem, all now were assembled[2], hourly expecting the complete fulfilment of a promise, of which the last-mentioned interview had been a commencement and first-fruits. Nor did they tarry long. Probably within a few days after the appearance by the lake, and on a mountain which He had appointedᵈ, perchance that of the Beatitudes[3], the Lord mani-

ᵈ ver. 16

ἀκολούθει μοι, when viewed in connexion with what precedes, would seem to be 'follow Me,—even unto that martyr's death for my name which I have but just now foretold:' comp. Augustine, *in Joann.* Tractat. CXXIV. 1, Vol. III. p. 1970 (ed. Migne).

[1] The exact meaning of the words used in reference to St John has been much discussed. The most simple and satisfactory explanation would seem to be that alluded to by Theophylact, according to which the coming of the Lord is to be understood of that form of His Advent which in His last prophecy He was pleased to connect with His final advent,—viz. the fall of Jerusalem; comp. Matth. xvi. 28. The hypo-

thetical mode of explanation (Cyril Alex., al.), and that which refers μένειν to a *natural* death, seem much less satisfactory.

[2] It seems reasonable to suppose that the great promise uttered by the angels after the resurrection (Matt. xxviii. 7, Mark xvi. 7), and especially confirmed by our Lord (Matt. xxviii. 10), was understood to apply to the whole Church, and had induced the greater part of the brethren who were then in Jerusalem to take their way to Galilee and there await its fulfilment. Some of the Apostles, we have seen, had not only returned to Galilee but even resumed their former calling (John xxi. 2).

[3] The exact scene of the solemn meeting is not further specified than

fests Himself not only to the Eleven[a], but as the terms of His promise seem fairly to imply to the five hundred brethren[1] alluded to by St Paul[b]. The interview was of the deepest solemnity, and tends to set forth the majesty of the risen Lord in a manner far more distinct than had even yet been witnessed. While a few doubt[c] the evidence of their senses[2], and cannot apparently believe that

LECT. VIII.

[a] Matt. xxviii. 16
[b] 1 Cor. xv. 6
[c] Matt. xxviii. 17

as being 'the mountain which Jesus appointed,' and in Galilee (Matth. xxviii. 16). The only two conjectures worthy of consideration are (a) that it was Tabor, which from its situation might seem not unsuitable for a place of general meeting (see Lange, *Leben Jesu*, II. 8. 7, Part III. p. 1730), and (b) that it was the mountain on which the Sermon had been delivered, which, from its proximity to the Lake of Tiberias (see p. 179, note 1) and to the populous plain of Gennesareth, might seem, topographically considered, even more suitable than Tabor, and from its connexion with the founding of the Church much more probable, considered theologically. The supposition of Hofmann (*Leben Jesu*, § 89, p. 397) that the term 'Galilee' here used by St Matthew really refers, not to the country but to the northern summit of Olivet, which appears to have been so named (though not by any early writers), is by no means natural or probable.

[1] Nearly all the best recent expositors concur in supposing, that the appearance of our Lord mentioned by St Matthew (ch. xxviii. 16) is identical with that alluded to by St Paul (1 Cor. xv. 6) as having been vouchsafed to above 500 brethren at once: comp. Wieseler, *Chron. Synops.*

p. 434, Robinson, *Bibl. Sacra*, Vol. II. p. 185. It is true that St Matthew only specifies the *Eleven* as having gone to the appointed mountain, but the solemn character of the twice-repeated promise (see p. 392, note 3) on the morning of the Resurrection combined with the fact that our Lord *had* appeared twice previously to the collected *Apostles*, renders it highly probable that the term was here not intended to be understood as exclusive.

[2] The statement that 'some doubted,' though strongly urged by Meyer and others (comp. Winer, *Gr.* § 17. 2, p. 96) as referring to the Apostles, is far more reasonably referred to others who were with them. Though it cannot perhaps positively be asserted that St Matthew *must* have used οἱ μέν—οἱ δέ if he had meant to indicate that some *few* of the Apostles doubted, yet it seems natural to suppose that some very explicit form of expression (*e. g.* τινὲς ἐξ αὐτῶν) would certainly have been selected to mark a fact in itself so unlikely (even if we confine ourselves to St Matthew's Gospel), as the doubting of some of the Eleven while the rest were sufficiently persuaded to worship. If we admit that the events specified by St John, ch. xx. 19—29, preceded, then the supposition that the doubters were

LECT. VIII.

^a Matt. xxviii. 17

they are beholding their Lord, the chosen Eleven no sooner see than they adore^a. That adoration the Lord now not only accepts but confirms by the mighty declaration that 'all power now was given to Him in heaven and in earth.' Yea, He gives it a yet deeper meaning and fuller significance, by now issuing His great evangelical commission, and by enhancing it with that promise of boundless consolation,—that with those that execute that commission He will be present unto the end, even unto the hour when His mediatorial kingdom shall be merged in the eternity of His everlasting reign[1].

The Lord's Ascension.

One further and last interview is yet to be vouchsafed, and of that a holier mountain even than that of the Beatitudes is to be the scene and the witness. Warned, it may be, by the Lord Himself, or attracted thither by the near approach of the Pentecost[2], the Apostles and those with

---

Apostles seems plainly preposterous: see Stier, *Disc. of Our Lord,* Vol. VIII. p. 280 (Clark). The assumption of Müller and others that the doubting only lasted till the Lord came nearer (προσελθών, ver. 18) is precarious, as no hint of this is contained in the words.

[1] Our own hopes of the future, as Bp Pearson has well observed, confirm our belief in our Redeemer's eternal reign : 'He hath promised to make us kings and priests, which honour we expect in heaven, believing we shall reign with Him for ever, and therefore for ever must believe Him King. "The kingdoms of this world are become the kingdoms of the [our] Lord, and of His Christ, and He shall reign for ever and ever" (Rev. xi. 15), not only to the modificated eternity of His mediatorship, so long as there shall be need of regal power to subdue the enemies of God's elect ; but also to the complete eternity of the duration of His humanity, which for the future is co-eternal to His divinity.' *Expos. of Creed,* Art. VI.; see Moberly, *Forty Days,* p. 30 sq.

[2] Some difficulties that have been felt in the change of place in reference to the earlier and later appearances of our Lord will be modified if we remember that the period we are considering was bounded by two festivals, which would of themselves involve journeyings to and from Judæa. At first the disciples are found at Jerusalem, whither they

them return to Jerusalem, their hearts full of mighty presentiments and exalted hopes. Yet again they see their Master in the neighbourhood of the Holy City[a]; yet again they hear from those Divine lips fuller and more precise instructions[1]: they are taught to gaze backward down the great vistas of the prophetic Scriptures[b], to understand and to believe[c]. Again too they hear transcendent promises, promises of gifts and blessings now exceeding nigh[d]; but even yet they partially misunderstand, and vaguely question[2]. Such inquiries, however, are solemnly silenced[e]: they are to be the Lord's witnesses; they are not to expect an earthly kingdom, but to prepare others for a

[a] Comp. Lu. xxiv. 50

[b] ver. 44

[c] ver. 45

[d] Acts i. 5

[e] ver. 7

---

had gone with their Lord to the feast of the Passover. A few days after the conclusion of the feast they leave the city, and, in obedience to their Lord's command, go to Galilee. After the solemn appearance vouchsafed to them in that country on the appointed mountain, probably towards the close of the Forty days, they naturally go up to Jerusalem to celebrate the Pentecost. In the neighbourhood of that city they see our Lord for the last time (Luke xxiv. 44 sq.), but whether unexpectedly or otherwise we cannot at all determine.

[1] It seems not only perfectly reasonable to suppose that Luke xxiv. 44 sq. is to be regarded as on the same day with Luke xxiv. 50—53, but right to deem it actually proved by the opening verses of Acts, ch. i. The command to remain in Jerusalem must, according to Acts i. 4, 5, be placed a *few days* before the Pentecost: when we meet then with the same command in Luke xxiv. 49 are we to believe that the same writer is so inconsistent with himself as to imply that it was spoken six weeks before that festival? see Wieseler, *Chron. Synops.* p. 423 sq., and the judicious comments of Caspari, *Chron.-Geogr. Einleit.* § 195, p. 210. The insinuation of Meyer (*üb. Luk.* p. 511; see also p. 514), that St Luke followed one traditionary account of the Ascension in his Gospel and another in the Acts, is a truly hopeless way of avoiding the force of a very just and very reasonable inference.

[2] For some comments on the nature of the expectations of the Jews in reference to the Messiah's reign, see Lightfoot, *Hor. Hebr. in Act.* i. 6. The supposition, however, of this able expositor that the question of the Apostles involved a kind of deprecation of the present establishment of such a kingdom ('an jam, Domine, regnum iis restitues, qui te sic tractarunt?') is neither probable nor in accordance with the context.

LECT. VIII.

ᵃ Acts i. 8

heavenly kingdomᵃ. They marvel and they follow¹......They now stand on the mountain down which the Triumphal entry had swept into the earthly Jerusalem, and from which the Triumphal entry into the heavenly Jerusalem, and the celestial realms beyond², shall be beheld by the same chosen witnesses. They follow their Lord even to the borders of the district of Bethany³, and then, even while His uplifted hands are confirming with a blessingᵇ the words of the last promise, they behold Him parting from them, rising from Olivet higher and yet higher, still rising and still blessing, until the cloud⁴ receives Him from their

ᵇ Lu. xxiv. 51

---

¹ The term ἐξήγαγεν (Luke xxiv. 50) refers to the scene of the commencement of this interview, from which our Lord conducted His disciples towards Bethany. This may have been either in the neighbourhood of the city or more probably *in* the city,—*perhaps* in the same room with its closed doors where the Lord had already appeared twice before (John xx. 19, 26).

² Compare Heb. iv. 14, διεληλυθότα τοὺς οὐρανούς, where there seems no reason to consider the plural as without its proper force, especially when compared with Eph. iv. 10, ὁ ἀναβὰς ὑπεράνω πάντων τῶν οὐρανῶν: 'Whatsoever heaven there is higher than all the rest which are called heavens; whatsoever sanctuary is holier than all which are called holies; whatsoever place is of greatest dignity in all those courts above, into that place did He ascend, where in the splendour of His deity He was before He took upon Him our humanity.' Pearson, *Expos. of Creed*, Art. VI.

Vol. II. p. 320 (ed. Burton).

³ There seems no sufficient reason for calling in question the ancient tradition that our Lord ascended from the Mount of Olives. The usual arguments founded on the ἕως εἰς Βηθανίαν of Luke xxiv. 50 (Robinson, *Palest.* Vol. I. pp. 254, 416) are not by any means conclusive, as it seems fairly probable that the words are not to be limited to the actual village, but generally referred to the brow or side of the hill where the road strikes downward to Bethany; compare Acts i. 12, and see Lightfoot, *Hor. Hebr. in Luc.* xxiv. 50, Meyer, *ib. Apostelgesch.* i. 12, Williams, *Holy City*, Vol. II. p. 440 sq.

⁴ The cloud in which our Redeemer ascended was not only, as Stier suggests, typical of that cloud in which He will visibly return (ἐν νεφέλῃ, Luke xxi. 27), but also directs the thought to the mystery of the assumption of the faithful servants of Christ who at His second coming will be caught up 'in clouds'

sight[a], and angelic voices address to them those words of mingled warning, consolation, and prophecy—'Why stand ye gazing up into heaven? This same Jesus which is taken up from you into heaven, shall so come in like manner as ye have seen Him go into heaven[b].'...Even so come, Lord Jesus, come quickly[c]. Amen.

LECT. VIII.

[a] Acts i. 9

[b] ver. 11

[c] Rev. xxii. 20

And now let us bring these meditations to their close, yet not without the expression of an earnest hope that they may have in some degree tended to remove a few of the doubts and difficulties, which even the sober and the thoughtful have sometimes felt with regard to the connexion of this portion of the Evangelical history[1]. Above

Conclusion.

($\dot{\epsilon}\nu$ $\nu\epsilon\phi\dot{\epsilon}\lambda\alpha\iota s$, 1 Thess. iv. 17) to meet their Lord in the air: compare Lect. v. p. 235, note 1. It may be remarked further that if the words $\dot{\alpha}\nu\epsilon\phi\dot{\epsilon}\rho\epsilon\tau o$ $\epsilon\dot{\iota}s$ $\tau\dot{o}\nu$ $o\dot{\nu}\rho\alpha\nu\dot{o}\nu$ (Luke xxiv. 51) be received as genuine, of which, supported as they are by external authority, there can be no reasonable doubt (*Tisch.* rejects them on most insufficient grounds), we have the gradual ascent upwards ($\dot{\alpha}\nu\epsilon\phi\dot{\epsilon}\rho\epsilon\tau o$, imperf.) vividly put before us: the Lord is parted from His disciples, and is beheld *being* borne upwards, till the cloud at length intercepts Him from the view of the watchers beneath.

[1] If the views advanced in the preceding pages be accepted, it would seem that in the Gospels we have, in all, notices of *nine* appearances of our Lord after His resurrection; (1) to Mary Magdalen; (2) to the other ministering women; (3) to the two disciples journeying to Emmaus; (4) to St Peter; (5) to the ten Apostles; (6) to the eleven Apostles; (7) to seven Apostles by the sea of Tiberias; (8) to the eleven Apostles, and probably many others, on the appointed mountain; (9) to the Apostles in or near Jerusalem, immediately previous to the Ascension. Beside these we learn from St Paul that (10) an appearance of our Lord was vouchsafed to James (1 Cor. xv. 7). This, if we conceive the passage to be written with reference to chronological order, would seem to have been shortly after the appearance to the 500 brethren. The agreement of this enumeration of St Paul with the record of the appearances to *men* as recorded in the Gospels is very striking, and has been rightly put forward by Wieseler, *Chron. Synops.* p. 419 sq.; compare Ebrard, *Kritik der Ev. Gesch.* § 113, p. 599. Some excellent critical comments on the Evangelical narrative of the Resurrection generally,—esp. the important practical remark that the Evangelists refer throughout to the Resurrection not as a revelation but as a fact,—will be found in Caspari, *Chron.-Geogr. Einleit.* § 199 sq., p. 212—218.

LECT. VIII.

all things, may it have been granted to these humble words that they may have brought home to those who have dwelt on them the living reality of the mysteries of these Forty Days, the plain and objective truth of the Lord's appearances on earth after His resurrection, and the actual, visible, and bodily nature of His Ascension[1]. On such truths rest the surest consolations of the present; on such the holiest hopes of the future[2]. May

---

[1] On this subject it is painful to feel how much half-belief prevails at the present day even among those expositors of scripture who have in other respects some claim on our attention; see for instance the remarks of Meyer, *üb. Luk.* p. 514 sq. (ed. 3). The fact itself is not questioned, nay even the exaltation of the Lord's glorified body is admitted, but the distinct statements of one Evangelist and the implied statements of a second (Mark xvi. 19) that this exaltation took place visibly, and before the eyes of appointed witnesses, is flatly denied. Why so, we ask, when so much is, as it ought to be, accepted as true? For an answer we are referred to the silence of the two Apostolical Evangelists; see Meyer, *loc. cit.* p. 515 sq. But even if we concede such a silence, which indeed we need not concede (what meaning, for instance, could St John have assigned to our Lord's words, ch. vi. 62, if he had not seen how they were fulfilled?)—conceding it, however, for the sake of our argument, what are we to say of a mode of criticism which, in a history, where three out of the four writers of it are almost avowedly selective, is prepared to reject a miracle whenever two out of four alone relate it? If it be replied that this is no common miracle, but, like the Resurrection, forms an epoch in our Lord's life of the highest importance, the rejoinder seems as final as it is true,—that the sacred writers viewed the Ascension as a necessary part and sequel of the Resurrection, and that it is only the unsound theology of later times that has sought to separate them; see above, p. 376, and for further comments, see Olshausen, *Commentary*, Vol. IV. p. 353 sq., Lange, *Leben Jesu*, II. 8. 10, Part III. p. 1760 sq., Ebrard, *Kritik der Ev. Gesch.* § 113. 4, p. 599 sq.

[2] Well and wisely has Bp Pearson dwelt upon that truth to which the ancient writers have invariably given such prominence when treating upon the Ascension, viz. that the bodily Ascension of our Lord into heaven is the strongest corroboration of our own hope of ascending thither; see *Expos. of Creed*, Art. VI. Vol. I. p. 321 (ed. Burton). That 'where the Head is gone there the members may hope to follow,' is the inference which all sound expositors have drawn, alike from the nature of our union with our Lord, and from the eternal truth that He has vouchsafed in His own person to take our glorified humanity to His Father's throne: compare Augustine, *Serm.*

The Forty Days. 417

God's Spirit, in these latter days of scepticism and incredulity, move the hearts of His ministers and His people to hold more truly and tenaciously that living truth, which alone rests for its basis on the literal truth of the Resurrection and Ascension of our Lord,—that truth which an Apostle[a] has declared to us, even that our Master has raised us with Himself and made us in spirit ascend with Himself to His Father's kingdom, and sit there the partakers of His glory and His blessedness[1]. Where the Head is, even there has He solemnly assured us the true members now are in spirit. We are already seated there *in* Him;—that is the support and consolation of the present: we shall hereafter be made to sit there *by* Him, not in spirit only, but in our glorified human nature;— that is the hope and joy of the future[2].

Present and future are alike bound up in our belief in our Master's resurrection and ascension; and dreary indeed must this present be, and gloomy and cloudy that future, if our belief in our

[a] Eph. ii. 6

CCLXIII. 3, Vol. v. p. 1210 (ed. Migne), and the good comments of Beveridge, *Serm.* LXXVI. Vol. III. p. 432 sq. (A.-C. L.).

[1] No words can be more distinct than those which the Apostle uses in the passage above referred to,—καὶ συνήγειρεν καὶ συνεκάθισεν ἐν τοῖς ἐπουρανίοις (Eph. ii. 6). Though the passage, considered in one sense, may refer to what is yet future, yet in another and a spiritual sense it is eternally true that the faithful believer in Jesus Christ has even now been raised with his Lord, and in spirit made to sit *with* Him and *in* Him in the realms of His blessedness and glory; τῆς κεφαλῆς καθεζομένης καὶ τὸ σῶμα συγκάθηται· διὸ ἐπήγαγεν ἐν Χριστῷ Ἰησοῦ. Chrysost. *in loc.*: see also *Commentary on Eph.* p. 38 (ed. 2).

[2] 'Even now, we sit there in Him, and shall sit there with Him in the end. So He promiseth in express terms that "we shall sit with Him in His throne" (Rev. iii. 21), as He doth in His Father's. And so, not in the throne will He be above us, but only that He in the midst, and we on His right hand.' Andrewes, *Serm.* VII. Vol. I. p. 115 (A.-C. L.).

E. H. L.

LECT. VIII.

risen and our ascended Lord be uncertain, partial, or precarious. We may think perchance that we are free to speculate, to poise historical credibilities, to boast the liberty of a suspended assent to what seems all too objective and material for the falsely spiritualizing tendencies of the age in which we live[1]. We may think so now; but when the end draws near, when sorrows break us, when age weakens, when darkness begins to close around us, where will all such license of thought be and what will it avail us? How shall dust and ashes hope to ascend into the heaven of heavens, if it cannot feel with all the fulness of conviction that One who was bone of our bone, and flesh of our flesh, has entered those realms before us, and has taken up our very nature, glorified and beatified, to the right hand of the everlasting Father[2]?

[1] It is alas! not only the heretics of the past (see Augustine, de Hær. cap. 59, Vol. VIII. p. 41, Theodoret, Hæret. Fab. I. 19) who have felt and expressed difficulties on the subject of our Lord's body being taken up into heaven. Modern writers, who on other points have shown themselves sound and thoughtful expositors of Scripture, have here not scrupled to use language sadly analogous to the language of the past, and have sought for imaginary places where they might assume that the 'final residuum of the corporeity' of the Lord was deposited on His ascent to the Father; see the references in Stier, Disc. of Our Lord, Vol. VIII. p. 442 (Clark), and on the subject generally, Augustine, Epist. ccv. Vol. II. p. 942 sq., to which add the wise caution, de Fide et Symb. cap. 6, Vol. VI. p. 188 (ed. Migne).

[2] To none of the great truths relating to the two natures of our Lord is it more necessary to adhere firmly in the present age than to this. A hearty belief in the literal and local ascent of our Lord's humanity into the heavens is in itself a belief in the whole mystery of the union of the Godhead and Manhood. If, as has been truly said, in His death our Lord has assured us of His humanity, and in His resurrection has demonstrated His divinity (Pearson, Creed, Vol. I. p. 313, ed. Burton), most surely in His ascension has He displayed both. There we see, as it were, in one what in other places our imperfect nature rarely enables us to contemplate otherwise than under separate relations. In that last scene we realize all,—the human, the Divine, and the most complete manifestation of their union. It is more as man that we

May then the belief in the Resurrection and in all its attendant mysteries become in the heart of every one whose eye may fall on these concluding words of an earnest, though God knoweth, poor and weak effort to set forth His truth,—ever truer and ever fresher. May it call up our thoughts and affections to His throne[a], ever teaching us to ascend heavenward in soul and spirit now, to learn the path and to know the way, that so we may ascend in body, soul, and spirit hereafter,—yea and not ascend only, but abide there with Him for evermore, redeemed, justified, sanctified, glorified, the bidden and welcome guests at the marriage-supper of the Lamb[b], the admitted inheritors of the kingdom prepared for us from the foundation of the world[c].

[a] Col. iii. 2
[b] Rev. xix. 9
[c] Matt. xxv. 34

O holy Jesus[1], who for our sakes didst suffer incomparable anguish and pains, commensurate to thy love and our miseries, which were infinite, that thou mightest purchase for us blessings upon earth and an inheritance in heaven, dispose us by love, thankfulness, humility, and obedience, to receive all the benefit of thy passion, granting unto us and thy whole Church remission of all our sins, integrity of mind, health of body, competent maintenance, peace in our days, a temperate air, fruitfulness of the earth, unity and integrity of faith, extirpation of heresies, recon-

---

see Him leading His disciples out of Jerusalem, and walking for the last time up the slopes of Olivet; it is more as God that, with the eye of faith, we behold Him taking His seat on His Father's throne: it is, however, as the God-man in its truest aspects that we gaze on Him ascending, flesh of our flesh, and yet God blessed for ever,—man in the form that rises, God in the power that bears Him to His Father's throne: 'corpus levatum est in cælum illo levante qui ascendit.' August. *de Agon. Chr.* 25, Vol. VI. p. 304.

[1] This beautiful and catholic prayer is taken from Bp Jeremy Taylor's *Life of Christ*, III. 15, Vol. I. p. 340 (Lond. 1836).

cilement of schisms, and destruction of all wicked counsels intended against us. Multiply thy blessings upon us, holy Jesus: increase in us true religion, sincere and actual devotion in our prayers, patience in troubles, and whatsoever is necessary to our soul's health, or conducing to thy glory. Amen.

INDEX.

ADULTERY, woman taken in, 253; narrative not written by St John, 253 *n.*; probable place in the Gospel history, 310; nature of the stratagem, 311; punishment of, 310 *n.*

Agony in the Garden, 329; nature of the deprecatory prayer, 329 *n.*; ministry of the angel, *ib.*

Alphæus, identical with Clopas, 98 *n.*

Angels, 46; number of, at the sepulchre, 382 *n.*; significant attitude, 386 *n.*

Anna, the prophetess, 69.

Annas, short history of, 333 *n.*; our Lord's examination before, 333.

Antonia, tower of, 303 *n.*

Apocryphal Infancies, 95.

Apostles, sending forth of, 194; duration of their circuit, 194 *n.*; slowness of to believe in Resurrection, 389.

Appearances, our Lord's to Mary Magdalene, 386; to the other ministering women, 390; to the two disciples, 393; to the ten Apostles, 398; to St Peter, 399 *n.*; to the eleven Apostles, 403; to disciples on the lake of Gennesareth, 404; to the 500 brethren, 410; last, previous to Ascension, 413.

Ascension, festival of, 376 *n.*; description of, 414; probable place of, 414 *n.*; literal and local, 415 *n.*; half-belief in the doctrine of, 416 *n.*; great importance of a right belief in, *ib.*

Atonement, its connexion with our Lord's divinity, 4 *n.*; hortatory comments on, 366.

Baptism, our Lord's, 108; probable date of, 104 *n.*; probable locality of, 106 *n.*

Barabbas, 345 *n.*; origin of custom which led to his escape, 346 *n.*

Beeroth, 90.

Bethany, date of our Lord's last arrival at, 276 *n.*; supper at, 282; position of, 283 *n.*; roads from to Jerusalem, 285 *n.*

Bethesda, pool of, 139 *n.*; etymology of, 140 *n.*

Bethabara, 106 *n.*, 262 *n.*

Bethlehem, 62 *n.*

Bethphage, probable site of, 286 *n.*

Bethsaida-Julias, 195 *n.*; two places of that name, 208 *n.*

Betrayal of our Lord, 331; circumstances which immediately followed, 332.

Binding and loosing, power of, 398 *n.*, 402 *n.*

Brethren of our Lord, 97 *n.*; importunity of and imperfect faith, 247.

Cæsarea Philippi, 225 *n.*; events which took place in its vicinity, 226.

Caiaphas, prophecy of, 269 *n.*; examination of our Lord, 337.

Cana, 117 *n.*; miracle at, 117.

Canticles in Luke i., 54; inspiration and characteristics of, 55.

Capernaum, site of, 121 *n.*; nobleman of, 134.

Circuits, our Lord's, round Galilee, 169 *n.*; length of, 185 *n.*

Civilization, theories of, 5 *n.*

Christ, early development of, 85; advance of in wisdom, 86 *n.*; supposed outward appearance of, 87; visit of to Temple when twelve years old, 88; youth of, 94; reserve hereon of the Evangelists, 97; spiritual and mental development of, 99; a reader of the heart, 126 *n.*; reception of His teaching, 146 *n.*; date of His return to Galilee, 149 *n.*; duration of ministry, 150 *n.*; visit to Jerusalem at Feast of Tabernacles, 246; deportment of before His judges, 337 *n.*; nature of last agonies, 357; last words on the cross, 358 *n.*; nature of death, 362 *n.*; burial of, 364; recognition of not always permitted after the Resurrection, 386 *n.*; how this is to be explained, 396; appearance of after Resurrection somewhat changed, 396 *n.*; bodily nature of His Ascension, 414; His eternal reign, 412 *n.*

Cleopas, 394 *n.*

Clopas, wife of, 355.

Clothes, casting down of, 287 *n.*; rending of, 338 *n.*

Cock-crowing, 335 *n.*

Coincidences, verbal, in the four Gospels, 279 *n.*

Corn, rubbing ears of, 175 *n.*

Cross, form of, 354 *n.*

Dalmanutha, site of, 224 *n.*

Darkness, supernatural, at the crucifixion, 356 *n.*

Decapolis, confederation of, 206 *n.*

Dedication, feast of, 259 *n.*

Demoniacs, healing of, how characterized, 164 *n.*; boy, healing of, 228; Gergesene, 189.

Disciples, first that joined our Lord, 116 *n.*; the two journeying to Emmaus, 394 *n.*

Discourses of our Lord, their order doubtful, 7 *n.*; delivered in the synagogue at Capernaum, 211 *n.*; our Lord's last, 327 *n.*

Doctors, Jewish, names of those alive when our Lord was 12 years old, 92.

Eastern world, expectations of, 44 *n.*

Emmaus, position of, 394 *n.*; distance of from Jerusalem, 395 *n.*

Ephraim, site of, 269 *n.*

Essene teaching, 100.

Eucharist, institution of, 326; probably not partaken of by Judas, 326 *n.*

Eusebius, on the relations of the four Gospels, 151

Fig-tree, cursing of, 293; objections urged against, 295

Fish, constellation of, 73 *n.*

Five thousand, feeding of, 196.

Flight into Egypt, date of, and duration of stay, 80 *n.*

Four thousand, feeding of, 221; site of the miracle, 222 *n.*

Gabbatha, 347 *n.*

Galilee, divisions of, 200 *n.*; Christ's appearance in, 375 *n.*; the mountain in, where probably situated, 410 *n.*

Genealogies, comments on, 96 *n.*

Gennesareth, Lake of, storms on, 188 *n.*

Gennesareth, plain of, 162 *n.*

Gergesa, probable site of, 189 *n.*

Gethsemane, 328 *n.*

Golgotha, site of, 352 *n.*; meaning of the term, *ib.*

Gospel history, mode of studying, 6 *n.*

Gospels, inspiration of, 11 *n.*; harmonies of, 15 *n.*; correct principles of a harmony of, 19; apocryphal, 281 *n.*; characteristics of contrasted and compared, 33 *n.*; discrepancies of unduly exaggerated, 38 *n.*

Grave-clothes, position of, in the sepulchre, 384 *n.*

Index. 423

Greeks, petition of, to see our Lord, 316 n.
Guards, bribery of, 393.

Harmonists, errors of, 17.
Harvest, usual time of, 106 n.
Herod the Great, death of, 75 n.; barbarities of, 78 n.
Herod Antipas, character of, 216 n.; dismissal of our Lord to, 344; wicked levity of, 344 n.; mockery of our Lord, ib.
Herodians, 178 n., 302 n.
Hillel, school of, 272 n.
Holy Ghost, blasphemy against, 187 n.; gift of to the Apostles, 398 n., 403 n.

Innocents, murder of, 77; silence hereon of Josephus, 78.
Ἰουδαῖοι, meaning of the term in St John, 115 n., 141 n.

Jacob's well, 131 n.
Jairus' daughter, healing of, 191.
Jerusalem, our Lord's address to, 264 n.; view of from Olivet, 268 n.; appearance of at Passover, 269 n.; probable numbers assembled at, ib.; our Lord's apostrophe to, 264 n., 314.
Jericho, our Lord's visit to, 274; road from to Jerusalem, 282 n.
John the Baptist, 102; date of commencement of his ministry, 102 n.; its effects, 103; deputation of Sanhedrin to, 115; number of his disciples, 127 n.; date of captivity of, 129 n.; message of inquiry to our Lord, 184; death of, when, 196 n.
John, St, Gospel of, 14; character of, 249 n., 274 n.; difference of from that of St Peter, 407 n.; visit of to the sepulchre, 384; external characteristics of, 14 n.; individuality of, 40; genuineness of chap. xxi., 375 n.
Joseph of Arimathea, 363.
Journeys, last three, of our Lord to Jerusalem, 243; their probable dates and durations, 245 n.
Juda, city of, 52.
Judas, death of, 340 n.; sin of, ib.

Lazarus, sickness of, and death, 267; raising of, 269 n.; effect produced by the miracle, 268.
Legs, breaking of, 362 n.
Levi, same as Matthew, 172 n.; feast in his house, 173 n.
Life of Christ, history of, a history of redemption, 9.
Loins, cloth bound round, at the crucifixion, 353 n.
Luke, St, Gospel of, its external characteristics, 14 n.; individuality of, 27; universality of, 29 n.; peculiarity of the portion ch. xi. 51—xviii. 14, 238 n., 241 n.
Luthardt, Essay on St John's Gospel, 31 n.

Machærus, site of, 130 n.
Magdala, site of, 224 n.
Magi, adoration of, 70; country of, 71; ground of their expectations, 72 n.; nature of their expectations, 74 n.
Mark, St, identical with John Mark, 23 n.; Gospel of, its external characteristics, 13; written under the guidance of St Peter, 13 n., 230 n.; individuality of, 23; graphic character of, 24; genuineness of concluding verses, 26 n., 383 n.
Marriage-feasts, customs at, 118 n.
Mary Magdalene, visit of, to the sepulchre, 380 n.; appearance of our Lord to, 386.
Matthew, St, Gospel of, its external characteristics, 12; individuality of, 20; originally written in

Hebrew, 156 n.; genuineness of first two chapters of, 57 n.; order of incidents not exact, 154 n., 158 n.; how this is to be accounted for, 156.
Messages, Divine, to Joseph and Mary, 56.
Miraculous conception, dignity of, 40; mystery of, 41; narrative of, 45; not noticed by St John, 40.
Ministry, our Lord's, duration of, 150 n.
Mount, sermon on the, 179; scene of, 179 n.

Nain, site of, 182 n.
Nativity, circumstances of, 61; exact locality of, 62 n.; date of, 63 n.
Nazareth, description of, 101 n.; ill repute of, 47 n.; our Lord's first preaching at, 159; second visit to, 193.
Nicodemus, history of, 125 n.; discourse of our Lord with, 125; boldness and piety of at our Lord's burial, 363.

Parable, of Sons sent into vineyard, 300 n.; of Wicked husbandmen, ib.; collection of, by St Matthew, 21 n.
Paralytic, healing of, 171.
Pilate, official character of, 301 n.; general character of, 350 n.; our Lord's first appearance before, 341; second ditto, 345; enmity with Herod, 343 n.; awe felt by, towards our Lord, 349 n.; fate of, 351 n.
Pinnacle of the Temple, 114 n.
Portents, at our Lord's death, 358.
Presentation in Temple, 65.
Precepts, reception of, 180.
Precipitation, Mount of, 161 n.
Procurators, residence of, at Jerusalem, 339 n.
Prophecies, our Lord's last, 319 n.

Protevangelium Jacobi, narrative of Nativity, 61 n.
Puberty, age of, 89 n.
Publicans, 20 n.
Purim, feast of, our Lord's visit to Jerusalem at, 137; observances at, 137 n.
Purification, time of, 66 n.
Peter, St, confession of, 213 n.; three denials of our Lord, 334 n.; visit of to sepulchre, 384; character of as compared with that of St John, 407 n.

Resurrection, Christ's a pledge of ours, 368 n.; objections to doctrine of, 371 n.; number of the accounts of, 372 n.; differences in the incidents related, 373; exact time of, 379 n.
Resurrection-body, nature of our Lord's, 370 n.; glorification of, perhaps progressive, 398 n., 408 n.
Roads, from Judæa to Galilee, 122 n.
Roofs, nature of, 171 n.

Sabbath, observance of, 141 n.; second-first, 174 n.; miracles performed on, 177 n., 258 n.
Sabbath-day's journey, 284 n.
Sadducees, errors of, 307 n.; accepted other parts of Scripture beside Pentateuch, 308 n.
Saints, resurrection of, at our Lord's death, 360 n.
Salem, site of, 128 n.
Samaria, our Lord's first journey through, 130; second journey through, 248.
Samaritan woman, our Lord's discourse with, 132.
Samaritans, faith of, 132; expectation of a Messiah, 133 n.
Sanhedrin, meeting of, called by Herod, 75 n.; first public manifestation of their designs, 251; component parts of, 299 n.; lost the

Index. 425

power of life and death, 311 *n.*; place of meeting, 335*n.*; our Lord's examination before, 335.
Scape-goat, supposed reference to, 348 *n.*
Scribes, from Jerusalem, 170 *n.*
Scripture, inspiration of, 3 *n.*
Sects, Jewish, some characteristics of, 65 *n.*
Seventy disciples, mission of, 256 *n.*
Shammai, school of, 272 *n.*
Shekel, half, annual payment of, 230 *n.*
Shepherds, announcement to, 64.
Sidon, probably visited by our Lord, 219, 233 *n.*
Siloam, well of, 252 *n.*
Simeon, 67 *n.*; prophetic address of, 68 *n.*
Simon, the Leper, 283 *n.*
Simon of Cyrene, 353 *n.*
Solomon's porch, 260 *n.*
Son of God, 119 *n.*; meaning of the title, 213 *n.*, 255 *n.*, 260 *n.*, 284 *n.*, 337 *n.*
Sosiosh, 77 *n.*
Soul, meaning of the term, 113 *n.*
Spirit, meaning of the term, 113 *n.*
Star of the East, 72; date of appearance, 73 *n.*
Stone, great, rolled against the door of the sepulchre, 364 *n.*, 378 *n.*
Storm, stilling of, 210 *n.*
Sufferings, our Lord's predictions of His own, 281 *n.*
Supper, last, celebration of, 321; a paschal supper, but not on Nisan 14, 323 *n.*; order of incidents, 324 *n.*
Sweat, bloody, nature of, 330 *n.*
Swine, destruction of, 190 *n.*
Sychar, 131 *n.*
Synagogue, service of, 159 *n.*, 164 *n.*
Syrophœnician woman, 218 *n.*

Tabiga, a suburb of Capernaum, 162 *n.*, 166 *n.*
Taxing under Quirinus, 57; Roman in origin, Jewish in form, 59.
Temple, first cleansing of, 122; second cleansing of, 293; veil of, 359 *n.*
Temptation, scene of, 109 *n.*; no vision, 110; an assault from without, 111; addressed to the three parts of our nature, 112.
Thomas, St, disbelief of, 403; testimony of to our Lord's divinity, 404 *n.*
Thorns, crown of, 348 *n.*
Tombs, nature of, 364 *n.*
Transfiguration, 226; probable scene of, 227 *n.*
Treasury, 315.
Triumphal entry, 284.
Tyre, our Lord's journey towards, 217.

Virgin Mary, probable authority for early portions of St Luke's Gospel, 46; legendary history of, 47 *n.*; relationship to Elizabeth, 50 *n.*; character of, 50; journey of, to Elizabeth, 51; later residence of, 185 *n.*

Washing of hands, Pilate's, 348 *n.*
Wieseler (K.), value of his chronological labours, 143 *n.*, 244 *n.*
Women, court of, 315 *n.*; the ministering, 372 *n.*; visit of to the sepulchr·, 377.
World, state of at our Lord's birth, 43 *n.*

Zacchæus, 275; desire of to see our Lord, 275 *n.*
Zebedee, position of at Capernaum, 163 *n.*

E. H. L.

28

PASSAGES OF SCRIPTURE
EXPLAINED OR ILLUSTRATED.

Micah v. 2	76 n.	Luke xv. 1	265 n.
Matth. ii. 2	73 n.	xxii. 70	338 n.
ii. 9	76 n.	xxiv. 44	338 n.
ii. 13	80 n.	John i. 29	116 n.
ii. 23	81 n.	i. 33	107 n.
xiii. 58	207 n.	ii. 2	118 n.
xix. 1	271 n.	ii. 3, 4	120.
xxii. 20	305 n.	ii. 15	123.
xxvi. 29	326 n.	ii. 21	124 n.
xxvi. 45	331 n.	iii. 3	125 n.
xxviii. 7	383 n.	iv. 2	127 n.
xxviii. 9	391 n.	iv. 4	134 n.
xxviii. 17	391 n.	v. 1	136.
Mark i. 34	167 n.	v. 4	139 n.
vi. 3	94 n.	vi. 50	213 n.
vii. 24	205 n.	vii. 4	246 n.
xi. 13	293 n.	x. 32	261 n.
xi. 18	296 n.	xii. 27	317 n.
ib.	297 n.	xii. 29	318 n.
xi. 25	298 n.	xiii. 5	246 n.
xvi. 4	380 n.	xvii. 4 sq.	327 n.
xvi. 7	383 n.	xviii. 3	331 n.
Luke i. 37	49.	xviii. 24	335 n.
i. 2	155 n.	xviii. 38	343 n.
i..3	242 n.	xix. 11	350 n.
ii. 8	63 n.	xix. 12	351 n.
ii. 35	68 n.	xix. 14	354 n.
ii. 43	90 n.	xx. 8	385 n.
ii. 44	91 n.	xx. 17	377 n.
ii. 48	93 n.	ib.	388 n.
ii. 49	93 n.	xxi. 19	409 n.
iii. 1	104 n.	xxi 22	410 n.
iii. 23	104 n.	Eph. ii. 6	417 n.
iv. 39	166 n.	Col. ii. 15	357 n.
ix. 51	243 n.	1 Thess. iv. 17	235 n.
xiii. 32	263	Heb. iv. 14	414 n.

THE END.

www.ingramcontent.com/pod-product-compliance
Lightning Source LLC
Chambersburg PA
CBHW022146300426
44115CB00006B/369